Interactive Cases in Organizational Behavior

Interactive Cases in Organizational Behavior

Dennis J. Moberg
Santa Clara University

with
David F. Caldwell
Santa Clara University

HarperCollinsPublishers

To Kathleen and Carl

To Helen

Copyright © 1988 Scott, Foresman and Company.
All Rights Reserved.
Printed in the United States of America.

ISBN 0-673-38040-8

6 - MVN - 92

Preface

Our goal in writing *Interactive Cases in Organizational Behavior* was to produce an enjoyable way to master the tactical choices involved in putting organizational behavior principles into practice. By tactical choices we mean the discrete, minute-by-minute decisions managers must make in evolving situations every day. These choices include whom to talk to, what to talk about, and how to communicate expectations and create environments. This is the nitty-gritty of implementation and application that is often left out of the classroom.

Organizational behavior research has not addressed all possible tactical choices. Consequently, the Interactive Case approach presented here is much more useful as a discussion vehicle than as a definitive model for implementing principles. We have thoroughly classroom-tested all the Interactive Cases with undergraduates, MBAs, and executives, and they are presently being used in the executive development programs of several firms. While the cases are fictitious, all are based on real organizations. Some reflect our consulting experiences and others are derived from interviews with informed insiders. In all instances, the names of characters have been changed.

Interactive Cases in Organizational Behavior is intended to serve as a companion to standard textbooks and readers. As a supplement, it is suitable for undergraduate and graduate introductory courses in organizational behavior and management. As explained in the Introduction, the cases can be completed with paper and pencil or on a computer, depending on available resources.

We knew our concept for teaching decision-making skills was new when we began approaching publishers, but with perseverance we found a publisher equal to the challenge. When Jim Sitlington of Scott, Foresman saw the manuscript, we found our champion. Jim had the manuscript reviewed by some very talented people, including Lyman Porter (University of California-Irvine), Peter Frost (University of British Columbia), Rick Steers (University of Oregon), Skip Szilagyi (University of Houston), and Gary Johns (Concordia University). These reviewers helped us refine our cases and develop our Instructor's Manual. Jim also assigned Diane Culhane as the Developmental Editor. Diane's good-natured professionalism was invaluable to us as we struggled to meet deadlines and pass milestones.

Finally, we would like to offer special thanks to Shelby McIntyre of Santa Clara University's Marketing Department, who single-handedly taught the first author everything he needed to know to write the program that makes the Interactive Cases work on the computer.

Dennis J. Moberg
David F. Caldwell
Santa Clara, California

Contents

Introduction   1
    Organization of the Book   1
    Using Interactive Cases   2
    Summary   7

Module 1: Motivation   9
    Rules of Thumb About Motivating People at Work   9
    Persuading Employees to Choose to Work Hard   10
    Helping Workers Get the Most from Their Efforts   13
    Implications for Managers   14
    References   15
    Interactive Case   19

Module 2: The Problem Employee   23
    Symptoms and Problem Causes   23
    The Treatment of Problem Causes   26
    The Treatment of Symptoms   28
    Formal Discipline Systems   30
    Legal Problems   30
    The Steps to Improving Employee Work Habits   31
    References   32
    Interactive Case   35

Module 3: The New Employee   37
    Stage 1--Getting In   37
    Stage 2--Breaking In   39
    Stage 3--Staying In   42
    Conclusion   43
    References   43
    Interactive Case   47

Module 4: Communication   49
    A Fundamental Choice in Communicating in Any Direction   50
    Downward Communication   51
    Horizontal Communication   53
    Upward Communication   54
    Conclusion   55
    References   55
    Interactive Case   59

Module 5: Performance Appraisal 63
    Performance Measures Used in Appraisals   63
    Rater Biases and Methods of Avoiding Them   66
    The Performance Appraisal Interview   68
    Conclusion   74
    References   74
    Interactive Case   79

Module 6: Managing Work Teams 97
    Group Cohesiveness   97
    Group Norms   99
    Classifying Groups According to Norms and
        Cohesiveness   101
    Required Interaction Patterns (RIPs)   102
    Improving Group Performance   107
    An Example   113
    Conclusion   116
    References   117
    Interactive Case   121

Module 7: Leadership 125
    A Brief Summary of Leadership Research   125
    The Maturity of Work Groups   128
    Conclusion   130
    References   131
    Interactive Case   135

Module 8: Conflict 137
    Types of Work Conflicts   137
    What Causes Work Conflicts?   137
    The Results of Work Conflicts for the
        Organization   139
    The Results of Work Conflicts for the
        People Involved   140
    Managing Conflicts Between People   142
    Conclusion   151
    References   151
    Interactive Case   155

Module 9: Organizational Politics — 157
- The Power Gap — 157
- Personal Power Resources — 158
- The Use of Personal Power Resources — 161
- The Timing of Advocacy — 165
- Conclusion — 168
- References — 168
- *Interactive Case* — 173

Module 10: Managing a Task Force — 177
- Refining the Task Force Charter — 177
- Selection of Task Force Members — 178
- The All-Important First Meeting — 178
- Guidelines for Managing Task Force Meetings — 180
- Task Force Decision-Making Techniques — 181
- Politics of Task Forces — 183
- References — 184
- *Interactive Case* — 189

Module 11: Managing Change — 191
- Resistance to Change — 191
- Implementation Patterns — 194
- Conclusion — 201
- References — 201
- *Interactive Case 1* — 205
- *Interactive Case 2* — 211

Module 12: The New Supervisor — 215
- What Incoming Managers Should Know About Their New Jobs — 215
- The New Supervisor's "Honeymoon" — 220
- References — 226
- *Interactive Case* — 231

Appendix of Decision Points — 235

INTRODUCTION

One goal of an organizational behavior or management course is to help you understand why people do what they do in organizations. This means studying theories from sociology and psychology that explain human behavior in organizations. For many students, the biggest difficulty in studying these subjects is not in mastering these theories but in seeing how they can really be used at work.

This book takes a different approach from that in most textbooks. Typically, texts summarize the major theories and research to explain the different ways the subject has been studied. Instead of providing a survey of all the important theories which might be related to a topic, we wanted to write a book that would help you learn to *apply* a few theories very well. We particularly wanted to help you explore the specific *tactics* one might use. By tactics we mean things as specific as when you raise issues, what you say to your boss, or how you present an assignment to a subordinate. *Interactive Cases in Organizational Behavior* may not be like other textbooks you have used. It will present less material for you to read and remember, but it will require you to *use* this material to a greater extent than other textbooks.

Organization of the Book

Interactive Cases in Organizational Behavior contains twelve modules, each covering a different topic in organizational behavior and management. Each module begins with a reading that explains a series of concepts and an Interactive Case that gives you the opportunity to apply these concepts to a realistic case problem. Since the Interactive Case draws on the principles presented in the Module Reading, you should complete the reading *before* starting the Interactive Case unless your instructor recommends otherwise.

Module Readings

If you are using another textbook with *Interactive Cases in Organizational Behavior*, you may find that some of the material in the readings overlaps with what is in your text. However, please do not conclude that the readings simply duplicate what is in your other text. In all instances, the Module Reading will present material not in your text.

Interactive Cases

A major part of each module is the Interactive Case. Each case places you in the role of a manager who is facing a problem situation. After reviewing the initial information, you must decide how to proceed. Your options range all the way from doing nothing, to collecting more information, to taking decisive action. After making your decision, you see the case unfold. If you choose to ask for more information, you get it. If you take an action, you see its consequences. Once you see the results of your first decision, you are asked to make another decision. This process of making decisions, observing their results, and making more decisions continues as you work your way through the entire problem.

Interactive Cases are not like other cases you may have used. First, they require you to develop both a solution to the problem and a procedure for implementing it. Second, they unfold over time. Instead of simply making a recommendation, you have to make a series of decisions to solve the problem. As in real life, once you make a decision or take an action, the situation changes. Third, Interactive Cases give you feedback about the decisions you make. You see what outcomes your actions produce and how well your actions fit the theories described in the Module Reading. Unlike real-life situations, however, if your actions are not appropriate to the situation, you can reconsider your decisions.

Using Interactive Cases

Interactive Cases in Organizational Behavior is available with or without a computer diskette. If your book came with a diskette, you can complete the Interactive Cases with an IBM PC, XT, or compatible computer. Using the computer to complete the cases gives you more feedback about your actions and lets you move more quickly through the cases. However, both the computerized and noncomputerized versions contain the same Interactive Cases and are completed in the same general way.

Using Your Book to Complete the Interactive Cases

All you need to complete the Interactive Cases is your book and a pen or pencil. Unless your instructor has told you otherwise, complete the Module Reading *before* beginning the case. As you progress through the case, try to incorporate the principles from the reading into your decision making.

Begin by removing the Flow Diagram from the book. You will use this sheet to record your decisions, and you may be asked to turn in the completed Flow Diagram to your instructor. Next, read the description of the case situation. This material assigns you a role in a fictitious organization, describes the problem you face, and introduces you to some people with whom you may have to deal in the case. At the end of this material you are asked to choose from among several alternative actions.

Each alternative is followed by a statement directing you to a different page in the book. For example, following alternative A might be the statement saying GO TO 325B, and following alternative B GO TO 449A. These numbers and letters refer to *decision points* distributed randomly throughout the appendix of decision points. The numbers after the "GO TO" statement refer to page numbers, and the letters to positions on the pages. Decision point 548A is the first decision point on page 548, and decision point 548B appears on page 548 directly below decision point 548A.

After you make your choice, write the decision point number and letter that you are referred to on your Flow Diagram. In the example above, if you decided alternative A was the best, you would write 325B in the rectangle labeled "1st Decision." If you felt alternative B was better, you would write 449A in the first rectangle.

Once you do that, turn to that page in the appendix. There you will see the results of the action you have taken and will have to decide what you will do next. Again, make your choice, write the decision point number and letter in the second rectangle on your Flow Diagram, turn to that page, and see the results of that decision. You continue to work your way through the case by making decisions, recording your movements on your Flow Diagram, and getting new information until you successfully solve the problem. You will know you are finished with the case when you are told the problem is solved; you will usually not fill all the rectangles on your Flow Diagram.

Occasionally, the decision you make will lead to bad outcomes. For example, you might take an action to solve one problem that creates another, worse problem. When this happens, you have can reconsider your decision. When your decision is incorrect, you get information about why it was not the best option. Then you are instructed to circle your present decision point on your Flow Diagram and return to your previous decision point. Once back to that decision point, you will choose another alternative, mark the decision on your form, and turn to that page. Only by keeping an accurate record of all your decisions on your Flow Diagram can you move back and forth through the case.

You should not be troubled if you make a few errors as you move through the case. Applying organizational behavior theories to a situation is not always easy, and *not every* action you take will be explained by the Module Reading. Above all, it is important to keep in mind that experts have honest disagreements over how organizational behavior principles are best applied. That means that your instructor may (and probably will) differ with us over which alternative is best in some situations. Therefore, as you progress through the case, if you find yourself unconvinced that an "incorrect" decision is really wrong, make a note of that and bring it up with your instructor.

Using a Computer to Complete the Interactive Cases

If your book came with a computer diskette, you can complete the Interactive Cases using an IBM PC, XT, or compatible computer. Completing Interactive Cases on a computer is easy. The program gives you instructions as you go along. Using a computer to complete the cases will allow you to receive a summary of your decisions, give you feedback, and create a permanent record of your decisions.

To complete the cases on a computer, you need (a) your book, (b) a DOS diskette (available with your computer or at your school's computer lab), (c) the diskette that came with your book, and (d) a diskette provided by your instructor (your diskette will not work alone). As with the textbook version of the case, you begin by reading the case situation at the end of each reading in the book. It is important that you do this before you sit down at the computer, since some facts are presented in this material that are *not* on the diskettes.

Once you have finished reading the situation, you are ready to go. Begin by booting your computer (turning it on with a copy of DOS in the A drive). After typing the date and time, place the diskette that came with your book (Student Disk) in the A drive and the diskette provided by your instructor (Instructor's Disk) in the B drive. If the computer you are using has a hard disk, you need to copy the Instructor's Disk on to the hard disk (you may want to get help with this if you are unfamiliar with the computer).

After placing the diskettes in the drives, type *action* in response to the A> prompt and press the return key. This will begin the program. The first thing you need to do is to choose the case you wish to complete from a menu. Following this, the program will give you a detailed set of instructions about how to continue and how to use the various program options. We urge you to read these instructions.

Everything you need to operate the program is in the instructions the computer provides, but you may want to look over the following summary of commands. Basically, you work the program by typing letters associated with different commands in the program. There is *no* need to press the return (enter) key after these command letters; the program does that for you. There are three groups of commands that you will use in the computer version of Interactive Cases. The first group deals with reading the information provided at each decision point and making your choices. These commands are listed on the bottom of each screen to remind you what is available. They are as follows:

Command	Description
(N)ext screen	If more than one screen of information is available at any decision point, you will need to type N (or n) to move to the next screen.
(P)revious screen	Sometimes you will want to return to an earlier screen at a given decision point to review the information there. All you need to do is type P (or p).

(R)eady to choose	On occasion, you may find yourself ready to make a choice when you are not on the screen that lists the alternatives. Simply type R (or r), and you will be shown your alternatives and asked to choose one.
Choosing an action	When the line at the bottom of a screen asks you which alternative action you want, type the letter associated with that alternative (A through I).
(Q)uit	Regardless of what screen you are on, you can terminate the case and quit to DOS by typing Q (or q).

The second group of commands concerns the customized file that the program creates for you as you complete the case. Known as your *history file*, this contains information about what decisions you have made in the case, together with feedback about whether these decisions were wise. While you are in the case, you can access this file at any time by typing S (or s) for (S)ummary of past actions. When you do this, you will first be given a very brief summary of the initial situation you faced and then a decision-by-decision recap of every action you have taken to that point in the case. Each decision summary will appear on a different screen. Once in this summary part of the program, you have a slightly different series of commands. Again, all these commands are prompted for you at the bottom of the screen. They are as follows:

Command	Description
(F)irst decision	Following the brief summary of the initial decision, you must type F (or f) to move to the screen summarizing your first decision in the case.
(N)ext decision	After you see the summary of your decisions to that point in the case, you may proceed to the next decision by typing N (or n).
(R)ecycle through the case from this decision point	One of the special features of the program allows you to start the case over from some earlier decision point. To do this, simply select the point in your summary where you want to reenter the case and type R (or r). The program will automatically take you to that decision point and restart you in the case.

Strike any letter to return to the case	After reviewing all your decisions, you will be asked to type any letter to return. Doing so will take you to precisely that point at which you originally typed S to begin reviewing your decision summary.

It is not necessary to access this history file as you progress through the case. Most students find that they don't need to know the contents of this file until they have completed the Interactive Case. There are two exceptions. First, there may be times when you are progressing through a case that you lose your bearings. For one reason or another, you may forget exactly what you have done to get you to the point where you find yourself. By inspecting your history file, you can discover all the actions that led to your present decision point. Second, you can use the history file when you mistakenly pressed the wrong alternative letter. Let's say you intended to type the letter D, but inadvertently pressed E instead. If this ever happens, you need only access your history file through the S command and work through your decisions until you come to the one where you chose the unwanted letter. At that point you can use the (R)ecycle command to get back on track.

You will find the third series of commands when you have completed an Interactive Case. At your final decision point, you have four options:

Command	Description
(R)eview summary while preparing to print	This allows you to review your completed history file decision by decision while you create it for printing.
(P)repare to print with no review	Type P (or p) to create your final history file without a decision-by-decision review on the screen.
(Q)uit	Type Q (or q) to quit to DOS without creating a history file for later printing.
(P)rint now	If you are connected to a printer, typing P (or p) will allow you to print out your complete history file.

Completing Interactive Cases on a computer is really quite easy. These commands are clearly spelled out at the bottom of each screen where they apply. Some of our students have raised a few questions while completing the cases on the computer that we would like to answer for you.

1. What do I do if I have to leave a case before I finish it? If you have to leave a case before you get to the end, you can do so by typing Q for (Q)uit. You could also just turn off the computer. In either case, you will lose your history file and will have to start over with the case when you reenter it.

Thus, before you sit down at the computer, it is wise to budget at least 45 minutes for the case. That way you will not have to exit the case and start over later.

2. What happens if I do two or more cases at the same sitting? There is one thing you should know if you plan to complete two or more cases back to back. If you want to print out your history file, you *must* do so after completing each case. As soon as you begin another case, your history file for all previous cases you have worked on is destroyed (we had to do this to save disk space).

3. If I don't use the program to print my history file, how do I print it? You may print it with the DOS print command. Make sure your Student Disk is in drive B and DOS is in drive A. At the A> prompt, type Print b:history.mss and press the return key. You can also print it using a word processor. Again, the file name is history.mss.

4. What do I do if I hit an alternative letter by mistake? Before you make another decision, type S for (S)ummary and work your way through your history file decision by decision until you get to the summary of the decision point where you hit the wrong letter. At this point type R for (R)ecycle to enter the case at that point. Then type the letter of the alternative you originally wanted. Your final history file will show that you have recycled in this way.

Summary

Interactive Cases in Organizational Behavior offers a fun way to learn about organizational behavior. Whether you complete the cases in your book or on the computer, you can make a great many decisions and get feedback from all of them. Using your book to work on the cases requires some careful bookkeeping with your Flow Diagram. With the computer version, the bookkeeping is done for you, but you need to master several rather straightforward commands.

As eager as you may be to get going in any of the Interactive Cases, remember to complete the Module Reading before you begin (unless directed otherwise). If you are using the computer, be sure to read the beginning of each case before you boot up your disks.

All these instructions may strike you as somewhat forbidding. However, our students have found that by their second case the rules have receded into the background, and they really have fun with the cases.

1 MOTIVATION
Module Reading

Beth Wilson and Joan MacKay are both clerks in the men's clothing section of a large department store. Beth is consistently rated as the highest performing clerk in the department, with sales 35 percent above average over the past two years. She is always friendly to customers and is ready to help with taking inventory or stocking tables whenever an extra pair of hands is needed. Joan's performance is just the opposite. Her sales are well below those of the other clerks, and she avoids doing extra work whenever she can. Her behavior in dealing with customers and co-workers is generally poor.

This situation is similar to those most managers face. Almost every work group has some employees who are performing at very high levels and some who are not. Often the difference is motivation. We know the unmotivated not just by their low performance, but by other things as well. Some work at levels far below their potential; others put forth effort only when someone is watching them. Still others seem motivated enough, but they just seem to get it wrong no matter what they are asked to do.

This reading describes a method that a manager might use for motivating people to peak performance. It details a step-by-step approach to converting low-performing, indifferent employees into those who work at or close to their potential.

Rules of Thumb About Motivating People at Work

There is nothing particularly mysterious about why some people perform up to his or her potential and some do not. No one can perform up to his or her potential without working hard. Poorly managed workers waste a lot of hard work. People work hard because they choose to. They make that choice for one essential reason: working hard is more personally rewarding to them than not working hard.

People Can't Perform at Peak Levels Unless They Work Hard

All of us have known people who could do great things effortlessly. However, no one performs well without a significant investment of personal energy. It may not show at the instant of accomplishment, but peak accomplishment requires effort.

Poorly Managed Workers Waste a Lot of Hard Work

Some people fail to perform well even though they put out a lot of effort. When this happens, it is usually the manager's responsibility. Either the manager has not given the person the opportunity to perform or he or she has not communicated the assignment clearly enough. Employees cannot be expected to perform well if they are not given a chance. By saddling them with inadequate resources, by allowing them insufficient time to master the task, or by giving them tasks that are neither stimulating nor challenging, managers do not offer employees the opportunity to excel. Similarly, people have to be given a clear picture of just what is expected of them. Otherwise, wasted effort is virtually guaranteed. If a manager asks someone to do something and gives unclear directions, it is almost assured that no amount of hard work will result in peak performance.

People Work Hard Because They Choose To

Hard workers are hard workers because they have decided to be hard workers. For them the hard work alternative is much more appealing than the "take it easy," "appear to be hard working while actually coasting," and "don't even try" options. This is important to remember because it undercuts the notion that there are good workers and bad workers and underlines the notion that any worker can work hard if he or she so chooses.

Employees Choose to Work Hard When Hard Work Is More Personally Rewarding Than Not Working Hard

If an employee works overtime and weekends to complete an assignment, that person most likely values completion more highly than other activities. That doesn't mean work is the first priority in the person's life or the person is a workaholic. It simply means that the person's evaluation of all the things that are likely to result from his or her efforts is more positive than the assessment of all the other options. In short, people to expend effort because doing so has more positive consequences than not doing so.

These straightforward principles of motivation enable us to zero in on the two most important parts of motivating: persuading workers to choose to work hard, and helping workers get the most from their efforts.

Persuading Employees to Choose to Work Hard

Getting workers to decide to put out effort is not the easiest sell in the world. Many people come to work with personal experiences that are often at odds with the decision to work hard. Moreover, organizations sometimes make it difficult to persuade employees that working hard is worthwhile. How can a manager convince a worker, then, that working hard is an attractive option?

Step 1--Develop a "Can Do" Attitude

Most people have sufficient self-confidence to try to perform well. If that is the case, the selling job will be a lot easier. Self-confident people are more willing to expend effort than those individuals who are not self-confident.

Unfortunately, many people lack the confidence to attempt to do any better than they are doing. They have come to believe that high levels of performance are not within their grasp. Sometimes, this is caused by a recent performance setback that they can't explain. Other times it comes from being told over and over again that they are not capable. Whatever the cause, it is difficult to motivate such people until they develop the belief that they *can* perform at peak levels.

Dealing with workers who lack a "can do" attitude can be very frustrating, and motivating those who gave up striving to perform well years ago can be a real uphill battle.

There are a number of actions that a manager can take to develop a "can do" attitude. Among them are the following:

(1) Gradually build up the worker's self-esteem by taking every opportunity to boost the person's confidence. This means giving positive feedback as well as negative.
(2) Set up a definite trial period in which the manager agrees to tolerate low performance if there is hard evidence of effort. This is best coupled with regular and direct performance feedback given in a personal, supportive way.
(3) Deal actively with disappointment. This often means interpreting failures as indicators of progress. Examples of this are statements like: "You can't learn unless you make mistakes"; "You are just having growing pains"; or "I've never known anyone who got it perfect the first time."

Not all individuals need such encouragement; however, it will be particularly valuable for those individuals with low self-confidence.

Step 2--Convince Workers That Peak Performance Will Be Rewarded

As we have indicated, peak performers choose to be peak performers. A manager can influence this choice only if it can be shown to people that performance will be rewarded handsomely. There are really two parts to this. First, it is necessary to demonstrate that peak performance does count. Second, a manager must ensure that the rewards given for high performers are the rewards people really want.

People are seldom motivated to high levels of performance unless high performers are rewarded better than those who are not peak performers. This is not nearly as easy as it sounds. Often an organization's reward policies conflict with a manager's desire to single out peak performers and come down on those who are not pulling their weight.

A manager has two options when the formal system of rewarding people results in allocations that are not consistent with performance standards: fight for greater rewards for high performers, or attempt to find creative ways to compensate outstanding people. Fighting for greater rewards is a useful but often temporary solution since bureaucratic interpretations of reward policies usually win out over time. A more realistic answer is for the manager to look for imaginative ways to reward valued performers. Specifically, consider the sorts of things most managers have to offer their people. A partial list of some of these rewards includes the following:

(1) interesting assignments, challenging tasks,
(2) favorable interpretation of the rules, exceptions from annoying regulations,
(3) opportunity to work unsupervised,
(4) praise, recognition, awards, symbols of accomplishment,
(5) access to top managers, access to outsiders.

Thus, it is important that the manager reviews how he or she reacts to high performers and to those falling short of this mark. Clearly, it is not motivating to treat everyone the same. Managers can best increase motivation by singling out and rewarding their best workers.

What a manager must also ensure is that he or she is rewarding peak performers in ways that they value. This requires sensitivity to the rewards people in the group value most highly. Some employees are responsive only to monetary rewards, while others are motivated by symbols. Some are attuned to things about the work place, and others are more geared to fringe benefits. To have a maximum effect, rewards should be tailored to the unique needs of each person.

The best way to find out about just what rewards are motivating to a person is simply by asking him or her. A manager can ask during a counseling session about career advancement possibilities, during a chat about job likes and dislikes, or during an informal discussion on what things the individual would do if he or she were in charge. Managers can also discover the sort of rewards people prefer through trial and error and observation. A disadvantage of this approach is that it often takes longer and can be expensive.

Step 3--Be Fair in Rewarding and Punishing People

If subordinates think that their manager is being unfair, it will be very difficult to motivate them with positive rewards. By exercising good judgment and following several simple rules, a manager can avoid being seen as unfair. Among these rules are the following:

(1) living up to promises that are made,
(2) not making exceptions to reward principles, that is, avoiding playing favorites or giving special exceptions unless they are truly exceptional,
(3) explaining exceptions that are made, making sure everyone else who knows about it understands the logic for these decisions,
(4) giving everyone an equal chance to be successful.

In general, a manager wants to avoid situations where subordinates feel they have been treated unjustly. Sometimes, this is impossible. Most organizations occasionally create injustices unintentionally and unavoidably. When this is the case, to continue to motivate people, a manager should try to defend the logic behind the reward/punishment decision in question. This is sometimes extraordinarily difficult. Some people simply can not be persuaded that the rewards they (and others) have received are fair.

Helping Workers Get the Most From Their Efforts

As we saw earlier, not everyone who works hard performs at peak levels. Some employees fall short of peak performance even though they are putting out maximum effort. When this is the case, the manager should try to discover why this is happening. There are two common causes: impediments to good performance and lack of clarity. To address these problems, effective managers often take the following actions.

Step 1--Make Certain That There Are No Impediments to Peak Performance

When employees are putting out effort but are not performing well, this is often due to performance obstacles outside of the employees' control. Common among these impediments are poor equipment, inadequate budgetary resources, and poor training.

There are also some situations in which no matter how hard a worker tries, nothing seems to happen in the way of performance. For an otherwise highly motivated worker, this is very frustrating. Managers often do not learn about the presence of performance impediments until subordinates begin expressing signs of frustration. Some of the typical signs include

(1) aggressiveness--worker deals with others in a combative fashion,
(2) displacement--worker shows anger in dealing with inanimate objects,
(3) fixation--worker repeats unsuccessful actions,
(4) daydreaming--worker is inattentive,
(5) pessimism--worker is unrealistically negative,
(6) resignation--worker seems to have given up.

Performance impediments should be removed as soon as possible. Workers whose performance is blocked for a long time are quite difficult to motivate.

Step 2--Make Clear What You Expect From Your People

All too often workers have an insufficient understanding of just what they are supposed to be doing. Obviously, this can result in people performing poorly even though they are highly motivated. In order to avoid this situation, a manager must be careful that subordinates are getting clear and direct information about (a) what is expected of them in terms of objectives, schedules, etc., and (b) how they are expected to accomplish them (procedures, guidelines, etc.). Not infrequently, people get mixed or unclear signals, and a manager must be ready to clarify expectations and clear up misunderstandings that arise about specific job requirements.

Individuals whose performance is faltering are especially in need of direction. The most effective vehicle for clarifying expectations with poor performers is the *action plan*. This is a written statement that summarizes precisely what is expected from problem performers in the future. To have a maximum impact, action plans should have three important characteristics:

(1) They should be as specific and concrete as possible (general admonitions to "do the best you can" are less successful than specific ones.
(2) They should deal first and foremost with performance, not just effort.
(3) They should be developed in conjunction with the problem employee and not imposed unilaterally by the manager.

Implications for Managers

Applying these guidelines can sometimes be difficult. The most important observation a manager can make is whether the worker is putting out sufficient effort. If he or she is, then the manager needs to do those things to elicit more effort. A manager can do this by removing performance obstacles and by making performance expectations more clear. If the employee is not expending adequate effort, then different actions are required. The best way to motivate people not presently putting out peak effort is by developing a "can do" attitude, by convincing the worker that peak performance will be rewarded, and by being fair in reward decisions. These points are summarized in Figure 1 on page 15.

Figure 1

Questions to Ask About Motivating Employees

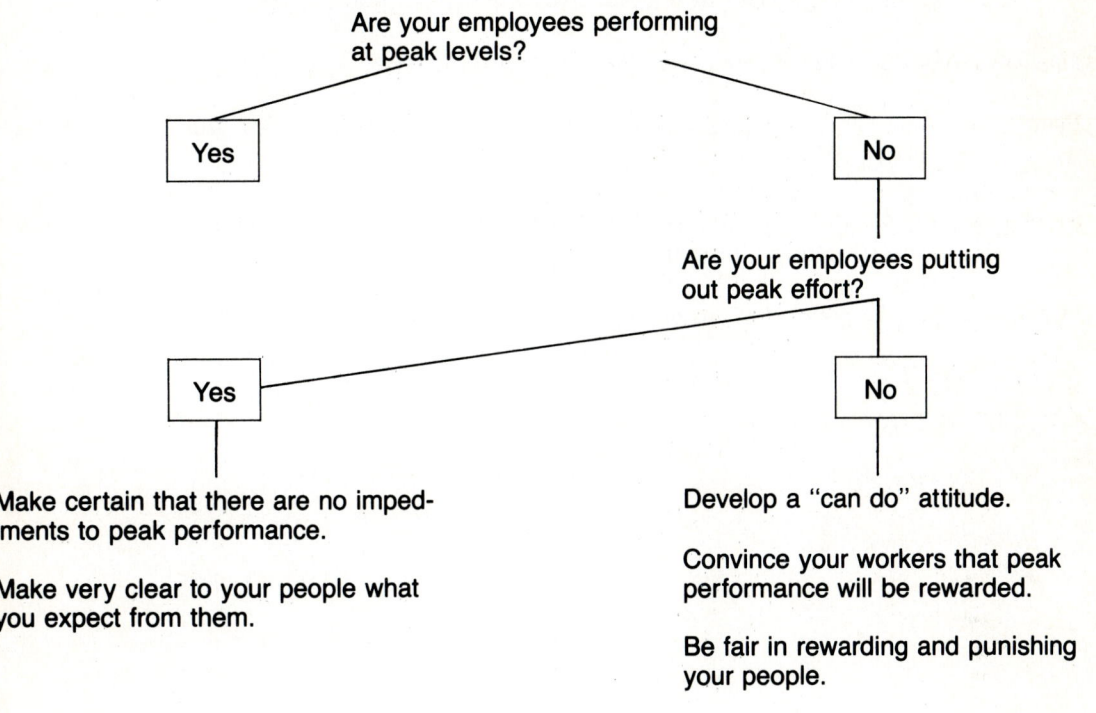

References

Adams, J. Stacy. "Toward an Understanding of Inequity." *Journal of Applied Psychology* 67 (1963): 422-436.

Alderfer, Clayton. *Existence, Relatedness, and Growth.* New York: Free Press, 1972.

Deci, Edward. *Intrinsic Motivation.* New York: Plenum Press, 1975.

Dowling, William, Jr., and Leonard Sayles. *How Managers Motivate.* New York: McGraw-Hill Book Company, 1971.

Hackman, J. Richard, and Lyman Porter. "Expectancy Theory Predictions of Work Effectiveness." *Organizational Behavior and Human Performance* 3 (1968): 417-426.

Luthans, Fred, and Robert Kreitner. *Organizational Behavior Modification and Beyond*. Glenview, Ill.: Scott, Foresman and Company, 1985.

Maslow, Abraham H. *Motivation and Personality*. New York: Harper & Row, 1970.

Porter, Lyman, and Edward Lawler III. *Managerial Attitudes and Performance*. Homewood, Illinois: Irwin-Dorsey, 1968.

Steers, Richard, and Lyman Porter. *Motivation and Work Behavior*. New York: McGraw-Hill Book Company, 1975.

Vroom, Victor. *Work and Motivation*. New York: John Wiley & Sons, 1964.

Interactive Case

You are the regional sales manager of the obstetrics division of Omega Pharmaceutical Corporation, a medium-size firm specializing in obstetric, gynecologic, and pediatric prescription drugs. You have 12 sales representatives who report to you. Each of them is responsible for a different region in the Middle Atlantic states; that is, they operate independently of one another. Sales reps call on physicians "detailing" the advantages of the firm's product line and use their personal influence to encourage them to prescribe the company's products. In addition, reps are responsible for calling on pharmaceutical wholesalers to encourage them to stock the company's products so there will be adequate supplies when retail druggists place their orders. Experience shows that if wholesaler inventories drop below 50 days in a territory, retailer stock-outs will occur in the region. As a result, retailers will be unable to fill prescriptions with Omega's product and will substitute a competitor's product.

In reviewing the recent quarterly sales volume figures below, note that five of your reps are not performing up to standard. Your boss also took notice of these five in your quarterly review with him. As he said, "You have six of the finest salespeople we have in the country. You also have the five worst. Next quarter, why don't you light a fire underneath them?"

Quarterly Sales Report

Sales Rep.	This Quarter Sales Volume	This Quarter Volume Rank	Last Quarter Volume Rank	This Qtr. Last Yr. Volume Rank	Standard Vol./Birth-rate in Region	This Quarter % M.D.s Contacted	This Quarter Days Wholesaler Supply
M. Roth	550	1	2	1	8.71	100	61
R. Smith	545	2	1	2	8.53	100	63
S. Brown	520	3	3	-	10.92	91	51
M. Sanchez	515	4	5	5	9.01	97	53
A. Bishop	510	5	4	4	8.47	89	73
S. Chapel	500	6	9	8	9.13	100	57
L. Andrews	420	7	8	10	7.88	79	60
==========	======	====	====	====	======	====	====
L. Dolan	360	8	-	-	6.71	100	50
J. Crosby	330	9	6	6	13.39	61	55
J. Clemmons	320	10	7	7	8.18	73	47
W. Thomas	310	11	11	9	6.62	77	38
W. Spaulding	280	12	12	11	9.34	70	42
Standard	400					90	50

Sales representatives are paid a straight salary plus a commission tied directly to their sales volume. The salary constitutes half of an average rep's earnings, so most reps are especially attentive to their volume figures. Promotions to sales management are infrequent, but such decisions are based on sales performance.

Turnover among reps at Omega is common. Last year 18.3 percent of Omega's reps throughout the U.S. left the firm. Presently, this is considered an acceptable turnover level. Candidates hired as reps usually have college degrees in the biological sciences and receive thorough training on the technical features of the company's total product line and on sales techniques before making their first sales call.

Several important developments have occurred in recent months. Nationwide, Omega's sales have been strong, but long-range forecasts indicate a gradual decline in the rate of growth in the obstetric line. The reason is the downturn in the birthrate coupled with the movement toward "natural childbirth." More important to your region are the economic conditions. The "softness" of the economy has forced pharmaceutical wholesalers to cut back on their inventories. Reps have had to redouble their efforts at persuading wholesalers to stock the company's products. One other development is a change in the territorial boundaries in your region. This was done to accommodate the arrival of a new rep, Lisa Dolan, to your group. Territorial boundaries are determined to allow each rep to complete a sales goal of 400 units per quarter. Factors like the birthrate, population density, and the concentration of wholesale outlets all go into the determination of territories. At the end of each quarter, you receive a computer printout that describes your reps' quarterly sales figures like the one on the preceding page.

You decide to try to motivate your five lowest performing reps in descending order starting with Lisa Dolan. Lisa is a new rep who just joined Omega five months ago. She completed her B.S. in biology from State University and was very impressive in her interviews (you personally hired her). In school, she succeeded at everything she tried. She was elected senior class vice president, had a minor in marketing, and carried a fine grade point average. She worked her way through school selling hypoallergenic cosmetics through contacts supplied to her from dermatologists (her husband is in medical school specializing in dermatology). This background gave her excellent advantages over other new sales reps. Before she began work, she completed the company three-week sales training program.

How would you open your conversation with her?

A. Ask her how well she thought she had done during the last quarter. (GO TO 528B)

B. Ask her if there is anything that has happened in her job that she was unprepared for. (GO TO 561B)

C. Point out the importance of building up wholesale inventory levels in her region. (GO TO 576C)

D. Offer to help her in any way you can to build up her sales. (GO TO 530C)

E. Ask her if she is satisfied with her present levels of sales and wholesale inventory levels. (GO TO 537A)

2 THE PROBLEM EMPLOYEE
Module Reading

At one time or another all managers have to deal with the performance problem of one of their people. These are often the most aggravating challenges a manager must face. There are several reasons why this is so frustrating. First, correcting performance problems usually takes up a lot of time. Many supervisors find that the way they allocate their time among their subordinates follows the 80/20 rule: 80 percent of their time is spent supervising 20 percent of their people. Surely ineffective performance falls into this category. Second, handling problem employees is frustrating because the poor performance of one employee often affects the performance of others. Employees who are chronically tardy, for example, slow down co-workers who need their inputs. Third, problem employees often create political problems for a manager. The way the performance problem is dealt with is often quite visible no matter how privately the situation is handled. Typically the grapevine thrives on rumors about what was said and done. Such informal scrutiny is understandable, but it places the manager in a situation where he or she may be misquoted or second-guessed. This visibility is also a problem since upper-level management may attribute performance problems to poor supervision. In effect a manager can easily suffer politically from both below and above in the chain of command. Finally, problem individuals are exasperating because there are so many written and unwritten rules that govern what actions a manager can take. Fellow employees expect that the problem employee will be dealt with fairly and equitably. Top managers are concerned about any precedents that might be created. There are legal constraints that affect what the manager can and cannot do. Navigating through these various written and unwritten rules is indeed troublesome. It is small wonder that correcting performance problems is one of the least enjoyable aspects of most managers' jobs.

Yet, there are actions that can be taken. Some problem employees are turned around. Some managers develop a knack for avoiding the pitfalls of dealing with problem employees. What they do is not particularly mysterious. They usually follow a number of relatively simple principles.

Symptoms and Problem Causes

The way an effective manager deals with an employee with poor work habits may be likened to a physician's manner with a patient. Supervisors and doctors initially have little more to go on than a group of indicators or symptoms that something is wrong. Physicians may see elevated temperature, a complaint of a headache, and nasal congestion. The symptoms a supervisor may observe include

(1) low quantity of performance (e.g., deadlines missed, quotas not met, clients not served),
(2) low quality of performance (e.g., high rework rate, incorrect paperwork, computation errors, dissatisfied customers),
(3) poor attendance (e.g., tardiness, repeated absenteeism),
(4) unsatisfactory attitude (e.g., uncooperativeness, defensiveness, argumentativeness, resistance to change, disloyalty),
(5) disruptive behavior (e.g., illegal acts, insubordination, unwillingness to work overtime, dirty office politics, threats, sabotage).

Doctors are trained to diagnose organic problem causes from specific patterns of symptoms. Certain patterns of symptoms may be indicative of a bacterial infection, a broken bone, or heart disease. In medicine, the organic causes-- not the symptoms--are the preferred target of treatment. Similarly, supervisors are best advised to first diagnose the cause or causes that account for the symptoms that are observed, and then focus the treatment on these causes. But just what are the things that cause performance problems? One research study (by Miner and Brewer) throws some light on the answer to that question. The researchers analyzed the causes of a large number of performance problems and developed a list of common causes of poor performance in the order of how frequently each cause was observed, including

(1) company policy and management decisions (e.g., placement errors, management permissiveness or neglect, poor coordination mechanisms, unintended incentives on nonperformance),
(2) employee's motivation (e.g., poor work habits, low ambition, personal motives inappropriate to the job, low effort),
(3) emotional problems of the employee (e.g., mid-life crisis, emotional immaturity, inability to cope with job stress),
(4) problems the employee is having with his/her work group relationships (e.g., inability work with co-workers, misunderstanding of group norms, inability to deal with conflicting expectations of co-workers),
(5) difficulties in the physical work setting (e.g., excessive danger, overcrowding, isolation of work station, stressful commuting),
(6) inadequate technical skills (e.g., deficiency in job ability, defects in judgment, insufficient understanding of the job requirements),
(7) problem with the employee's personal relationships (e.g., family crises, lack of family support, divorce, death),
(8) adjustment problems due to being socialized to values inappropriate to the job (e.g., culture shock, inappropriate work values, inability to cope with contemporary life),
(9) employee's physical problems (e.g., deficiency in physical skill required by the job, physical illness or handicap, cleanliness standards of the individual).

Unfortunately, not as much is known about the relation between symptoms and causes in supervising as in medicine. While physicians have models that help them narrow down the possible organic causes of some set of symptoms, managers have yet to progress to that level of sophistication. Often supervisors have little more than logic to rely on. And in using logic, the manager should keep several things in mind:

(1) Problem causes aren't necessarily simple; they can involve more than one of the factors listed above.
(2) Different causes can result in the same symptom; a symptom of poor attendance may be due to a family problem, a motivational problem, etc.
(3) The same cause can result in different symptoms; an emotional problem may show itself in symptoms of low work quality, a poor work attitude, etc.

Even with these realities in mind, it is still possible for a manager to commit several logical errors when attempting to figure out what is causing an employee's failing performance. First, there is *a tendency to act on unverified reports of symptoms*. Often the first evidence of performance deficiency is not directly observed. A great deal of care must be taken in acting on second-hand reports. More than one supervisor has acted too quickly in treating a performance problem only to discover later that the first report of the problem was greatly exaggerated. Second, there is *a tendency to ignore the distinction between acute symptoms and chronic symptoms*. Acute symptoms are those that appear suddenly and without warning. Chronic symptoms are those that are gradually worsening. The difference between acute and chronic absenteeism is that the chronic symptom shows as a steady decline in attendance whereas the acute symptom appears as a more sudden drop in attendance. The usefulness of the acute-chronic distinction is that the appearance of acute symptoms generally follows a problem-causing event (e.g., a family feud that has flared up). In contrast, the timing of a problem cause is much more difficult to identify with a chronic symptom. A third logical pitfall that managers occasionally fall into is *the tendency to confuse reasons with problem causes*. Reasons are excuses or justifications offered by poor performers themselves to explain their own behavior. Generally, reasons are self-serving, but that does not imply that they are incorrect; in some cases they may be. Fourth, there is *a tendency to attribute poor performance symptoms to causes that are outside our sphere of influence*. Occasionally managers fall into self-serving interpretations of what is causing an employee's problem performance. Thus, in inferring a problem cause, a manager may tend to ignore those causes that are really the responsibility of the manager, such as a failure to clearly communicate performance expectations. This may result in blaming the problem performer for something for which he or she is not responsible.

The Treatment of Problem Causes

In most circumstances it is generally better to treat problem causes than symptoms. Just as physicians treat symptoms only when they cannot determine the cause of an illness (or are faced with a cause that is not amenable to treatment), managers are also best advised to correct causes rather than symptoms.

The analogy of an iceberg is helpful in making this point. Symptoms are similar to the tip of the iceberg (see Figure 1). They indicate the presence of the problem (the entire iceberg) but are insufficient at defining its size and scope. Problem causes lurk under the surface, hidden from view. Treating symptoms is like sawing off the top of an iceberg at sea level. Those symptoms disappear, but the untreated causes show up in some other form--the iceberg buoys up to reveal other symptoms. Consequently, treating symptoms alone almost guarantees an ongoing battle of shearing off iceberg tips until the problem causes have dissipated naturally.

Figure 1
The Iceberg Analogy

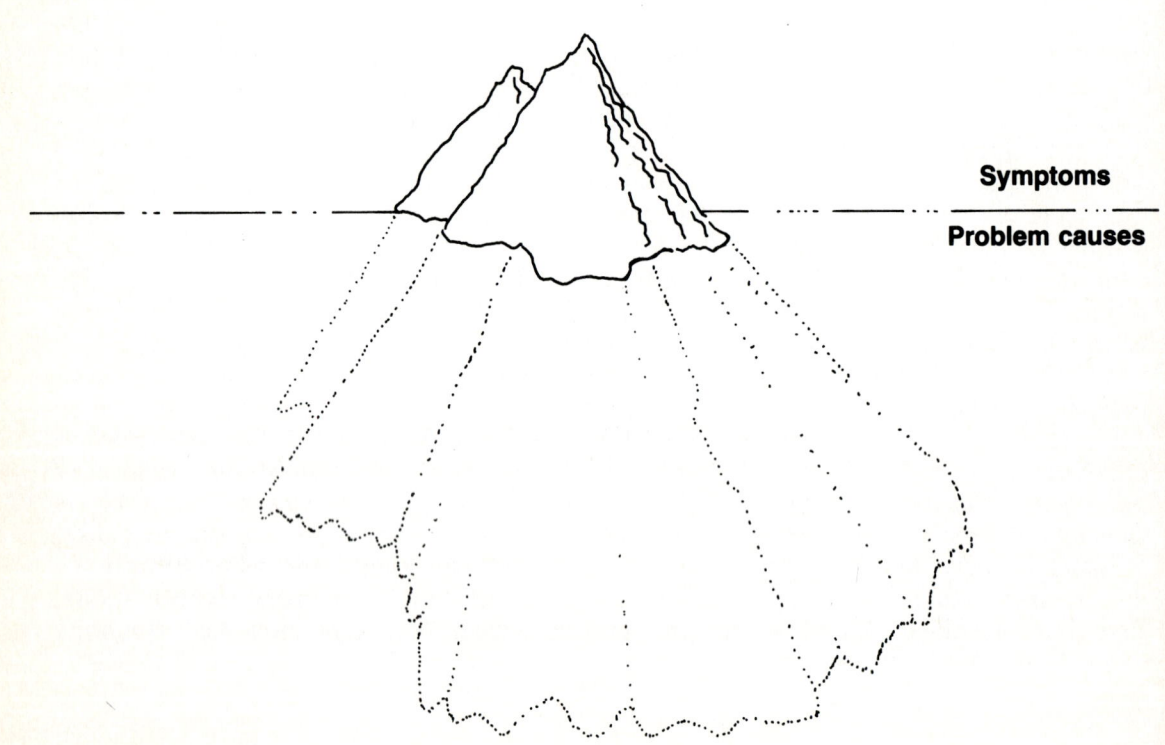

Consider this example. The supervisor of a group of 12 design engineers in a large aerospace firm noticed that the output of his people had declined since they were given a new missile system to work on. In addition, the length of time his employees were taking during morning and afternoon breaks was increasing steadily since the new assignment began. Perplexed, the supervisor called his staff together and asked for suggestions. When none were forthcoming, he asked everyone to restrict their breaks to the time allotted. While the time taken on breaks returned to acceptable levels, the output of the group deteriorated even more seriously than before. The supervisor had treated one symptom (the long breaks), but the problem cause remained untreated. In this case, the cause lay in the inability of his people to handle some of the technical problems in their designs. Each felt he or she alone was having problems. Their uneasiness about admitting this made them reluctant to tell the supervisor or bring it up in the meeting. They had been using the breaks to try to work out these problems with the help of their colleagues. So, by treating a symptom (long breaks), the supervisor was actually accentuating the problem cause.

Although treating problem causes is generally superior to treating symptoms, problem causes are certainly not easy to identify. In most all situations, it is vital to talk to the problem employee before feeling content with the diagnosis. There are several reasons for this. First, even though problem employees often give self-serving reasons for their deficient performance, if the problem cause lies in the personal life of the employee, there may be no other way to obtain this information. Sometimes merely talking to the employee may be sufficient to correct the problem cause. In many cases the cause of poor performance involves a misunderstanding of instructions or expectations which the manager can easily clear up.

Listening skills are particularly important in trying to identify the problem causes during a meeting with a problem performer. In particular, when the problem employee seems reluctant to disclose his or her views on the problem, a technique called *active listening* can be quite helpful. Briefly, active listening is based on the premise that people are much more prone to share private matters with their supervisor if they perceive that he or she is trustworthy; that is, they will not suffer punishment or be harshly judged for what they say.

The technique itself is relatively straightforward. When the employee makes a partially disclosing statement, the manager simply rephrases what the speaker has said. This allows the manager to test whether or not the employee's comments were heard accurately and makes it clear to the employee that he or she was actually listened to. Phrases such as "It sounds like you are saying . . . ," or "As I understand it, what you're saying is . . . ," can be used by the manager to test understandings. This may be coupled with an attempt to reflect the underlying feelings behind what the employee says. Phrases useful here include "I suppose that must have made you feel good . . . ," or "I guess that hurt a lot." Active listening is by no means a panacea. However, its use may help a manager uncover problems that employees are reluctant to reveal. Successful active listening requires understanding, empathy, and nonjudgmental acceptance. Without these, it is doubtful that anyone can use the techniques most effectively.

Many managers are uncomfortable using this technique. Much of the reason for this, is a desire to avoid probing into personal or private aspects of an employee's life. Some managers avoid obtaining this kind of information because they believe it is not relevant to the job; others avoid obtaining it because they feel it would bias them. It is important to note that there is no research evidence that proves that supervisors who use active listening with problem employees do better than those who do not. Basically, it has to be considered a matter of preference. Users of active listening believe that active listening is a way to support a problem employee and that support at work is often just what the problem employee needs to turn his/her performance around. Moreover, users say that they have a legitimate interest in anything that causes performance problems at work.

The Treatment of Symptoms

Whether or not active listening is used, a manager is not always able to specifically identify what is causing a particular employee to perform poorly. This leaves no recourse but to treat the symptoms of the problem. The prognosis for this treatment is actually not as bleak as the iceberg analogy described earlier would lead us to believe. In many instances the treatment of symptoms motivates the employee to take responsibility for the problem.

Our most effective tool for treating symptoms is the *action plan*. An action plan is a document that outlines the problem employee's commitments to change the symptom or symptoms and the supervisor's commitments to help the problem employee in that effort. For action plans to be effective, they must have two attributes: they must be as *specific* as possible, and they must be *arrived at in a collaborative fashion*.

Research indicates that vague action plans such as "Do the best you can to improve" are much less effective than specific ones. Vague action plans lead the employee with poor work habits to test the manager. In addition, when vague action plans are used, it increases the chances that any further disciplinary decisions will come as a complete surprise to the problem employee. For an action plan to be specific, it should

(1) identify as precisely as possible the dimensions of the symptoms. The problem employee should be given specific examples of what is considered symptomatic of poor performance.
(2) specify how reduction of the symptoms will be gauged. Measurable standards should be established if possible.

(3) articulate clearly what constitutes acceptable improvement and what does not.
(4) indicate exactly what will be done to support the problem employee's efforts to improve on these symptoms.
(5) describe what actions will be taken if there is improvement and if there is not.

A manager often can get clarity of this kind in a few words. A rather terse yet very clear action plan for a retail salesclerk is the following:

> The quality of Bill Jones' work has declined in the last three months. He has been responsible for 18 cash register errors in this period totalling $83.23. His sales area was rated unsatisfactory in cleanliness and orderliness in the independent audit during two of the last three months. Mr. Jones has agreed to be more careful in ringing up sales on the cash register and in maintaining a cleaner, more orderly work area. To satisfactorily improve, he is expected to make a maximum of three cash register errors totalling at most $25.00 during the month of June. He is also expected to be rated satisfactory or better on the June independent audit. In this respect, he should keep the floor around his work station free of boxes and debris and the shelves of merchandise neatly stacked and displayed. I will make weekly random inspections of his work area during June to give him specific feedback on cleanliness and orderliness. The June independent audit is scheduled for sometime during the last week in June. By June 30, if Mr. Jones does not meet both the expectations listed above, I will give him a written warning on his performance and have it placed in his personnel file.

A second attribute of effective action plans is that a manager should not impose a plan on the employee, but develop it with him or her. Research is clear that action plans developed by the supervisor unilaterally are usually not as effective as those developed jointly. For the plan to be motivating, the employee must feel that he/she has participated in its development. Imposed action plans often fail because the employee is not truly committed to their contents. Additionally, action plans developed without employee input often result in legalistic behavior in which the employee follows the letter of the plan but not the spirit. This undermines even the most specific action plan.

Putting together an action plan collaboratively need not result in a weak or permissive document. A manager can be as forceful as the situation merits while working out the plan with the employee. One useful test to see if the employee feels he or she has had some input is to ask if the employee thinks the final document is different than it would have been without the meeting.

In summary, a manager can treat symptoms effectively but only by developing an action plan. To be truly effective, action plans should be both specific and collaboratively reached.

Formal Discipline Systems

Most organizations have some sort of formal discipline system that might be used as a tool for managing an employee with poor work habits. Generally, formal discipline systems are termed "progressive" in the sense that they (a) link the severity of penalties to the severity of the employee's infractions and (b) specify a series of increasingly severe penalties for repetitions of relatively minor infractions. The rather mild infraction of tardiness might call for a written warning after the third infraction in one month, a one-day suspension for the fourth, a five-day suspension for the fifth, and discharge after the sixth. In contrast, drinking intoxicants on the job might require an immediate one-day suspension followed by discharge if repeated within a year.

If a formal discipline system is in effect, the manager should use it if the symptom is covered in the system. Otherwise he or she runs the risk of rendering the entire system ineffective. However, disciplinary procedures generally allow some flexibility, especially for less severe forms of nonperformance. Typically companies allow their supervisors to judge whether an instance of absenteeism should be excused or not.

In some organizations the formal discipline system is used only in cases where individuals are indeed chronic nonperformers who exhibit a host of troublesome symptoms. In these situations, putting employees who display acute and rather mild symptoms on the same track to severe punishment may be highly demoralizing.

Legal Problems

There are a host of federal, state, and local statutes that apply to the case of a supervisor disciplining a problem employee. In general these laws cover three broad considerations: wrongful discharge, employment discrimination, and unfair labor practices. While detailing all of these statutes is clearly outside the scope of this chapter, several broad guidelines are listed below. In general, a manager should

(1) document in writing all symptoms, meetings, and subsequent actions taken in the case of a problem employee,
(2) never refuse to talk with or counsel a problem employee about his/her unsatisfactory performance,

(3) act only on work-related problem causes and verifiable symptoms of poor performance,
(4) consult with professionals in personnel law before taking any action on protected-class employees,
(5) follow carefully formal discipline systems if in place,
(6) insure that the discipline action is work related,
(7) act consistently over time and persons,
(8) be certain that all actions and documents are in the spirit that the employee wants to improve.

The Steps to Improving Employee Work Habits

The following steps are offered to summarize this discussion. First, the problem should be stated clearly and specifically. As soon as a symptom of faulty work habits appears, it should be carefully verified. Facts should be obtained from appropriate sources in a way that does not invade anyone's privacy or convey the impression to others that the manager is "out to get" someone. Once gathered, the information and symptoms should be analyzed to identify probable problem causes.

Second, it is important to talk with the problem employee as soon as feasible. This meeting should be private and in a place free from interruptions. During this interview the supervisor should try to create a climate of problem solving and openness. The supervisor should give specific examples of the symptoms observed and be willing to discuss whether any supervisory actions have contributed to the problem.

Third, the manager should ask the employee for a solution and try to discover the cause of the problem employee's poor performance. If the employee is reluctant to discuss the cause, the supervisor should consider using active listening.

Fourth, the supervisor and employee should agree on an action plan that is formulated on symptoms and, if possible, problem causes. This plan should be specific and collaboratively reached. To be most useful, this plan should be written and specify

(1) what the symptoms are,
(2) how changes in the symptoms will be measured in the future,
(3) what constitutes acceptable improvement,
(4) what the supervisor will do to support the employee's efforts to improve,
(5) the consequences if no satisfactory improvement is forthcoming.

Fifth, the manager should ensure that he or she has received a commitment from the employee to try and fulfill the action plan and should arrange for specific follow-up meetings.

References

Kepner, C. H., and B. B. Tregoe. *The Rational Manager*. New York: McGraw-Hill, 1985.

Locke, E. A., and G. P. Latham. *Goal Setting: A Motivational Technique that Works*. Englewood Cliffs, N.J.: Prentice-Hall, 1984.

Locke, E. A., K. N. Shaw, L. M. Saari, and G. P. Latham. "Goal Setting and Task Performance: 1969-1980." *Psychological Bulletin* 90 (1981): 125-152.

McAfee, B., and W. Poffenberger. *Productivity Strategies: Enhancing Job Performance*. Englewood Cliffs, N.J.: Prentice-Hall, 1982.

McGregor, D. "Hot Stove Rules of Discipline." In G. Strauss and L. Sayles, eds., *Personnel: The Human Problems of Management*. Englewood Cliffs, N.J.: Prentice-Hall, 1957.

Miner, J. B., and J. F. Brewer. "The Management of Ineffective Performance." In M. D. Dunnette, ed., *Handbook of Industrial and Organizational Psychology*. Chicago: Rand McNally, 1976.

Rogers, C. R., and F. J. Roethlisberger. "Barriers and Gateways to Communication." *Harvard Business Review* 30 (1952): 46-52.

Interactive Case

You are a first-line engineering supervisor. You have a team of 12 engineering aides and draftspersons who draw up or codify schematic diagrams based on instructions from engineers. Your group is close-knit and has generally been productive.

Frank Wilson is one of your subordinates. He has been with you for three and one-half months and with the company for over three years. Frank has been well accepted by the rest of the group, and on occasion has been outspoken in complaining about things that he thinks make it difficult for your group to complete its tasks. Frank is absent today (Monday). You know he has been absent quite a bit, but when you enter today's absence in your log, you are surprised to see that he has been absent three Mondays out of the last four.

Lately your group's productivity has been falling. The group has fallen behind schedule, and you have had to use overtime to try to catch up. You know that this displeases your boss. You know that your boss wants you to do something quickly to boost productivity.

You believe that part of the reason productivity is falling is excessive absenteeism. You are particularly concerned about Frank's absences and feel that some action must be taken. Which of the following actions would you take first?

A. Talk to some of Frank's co-workers to see if they have any ideas about what might be causing Frank's absences. (GO TO 336B)

B. Check with Frank's previous supervisor to see what his past attendance record was like. (GO TO 378B)

C. Do nothing. Wait until Frank returns and then have a talk with him. (GO TO 388B)

D. Discuss the matter with your manager in order to get her advice in handling this matter. (GO TO 329A)

E. Call the Personnel Department to see what disciplinary options are open to you. (GO TO 322B)

F. Call the Personnel Department to see if there are other departments in the company that need people with Frank's qualifications so you can transfer him there. (GO TO 342B)

3 THE NEW EMPLOYEE
Module Reading

Companies spend literally thousands of dollars for each new employee they recruit, train, and indoctrinate. Yet many new recruits, too many, leave their firms before they have become worthwhile investments. Also, some of those who stay on feel needlessly passive, isolated, and rejected during their first few months of employment. The cause of these unfortunate situations often is an ill conceived, poorly implemented orientation process.

It is easy for an experienced manager to forget the stresses of being a new employee. In a number of weeks or months, one is expected to be transformed from being a total outsider into an effective contributor to the organization. For the new employee, this often means new work skills, new friends, new values, and new behavior patterns. This can be intimidating, and many new employees have some difficulties in making these adjustments.

Research by Daniel Feldman suggests that new employees pass through three predictable stages as part of the process of moving from newcomer to veteran. Stage 1 is *Getting in*. This involves the entire recruitment process culminating with the end of the first day of work. Stage 2 is *Breaking in*, the period required to become a technically able contributor *and* a socially accepted team member. Stage 3 is *Settling in*, the final, and more tranquil period in which newcomers "feel" like team members but continue to suffer some "growing pains." These "pains" include problems with people outside their immediate work group and problems adapting their work life with the nonwork responsibilities they have. The development of a successful new-employee orientation program involves tailoring the program to each of these socialization stages. Each stage creates different problems for the newcomer and each requires its own management action to contend with these problems.

Stage 1--Getting In

Orientation begins with the recruitment process. Recruiting practices set the stage for the entire orientation process. Every impression the recruit gets about the firm from applying for a job to interviewing for it affects the orientation process. If a candidate for a clerical position is told that he will have his own computer terminal when he is hired, then this establishes an expectation that, if not met, can negatively affect even the best orientation effort.

Realistic Job Previews

Experts agree that job candidates should be given realistic previews of their future positions. Overly positive or negative previews lead to unrealistic expectations that increase the likelihood of early turnover. Typically the new recruit is seeking accurate information about a number of factors in the job. Some of the important ones are the following:

(1) exactly what will be expected in terms of effort and commitment (e.g., Are 50-hour weeks common? If so, under what conditions?),
(2) what to expect from fellow team members when it comes to meetings and other occasions for group behavior (e.g., What do I have to do to prove myself to be a contributing member?),
(3) the promotional/transfer possibilities in the organization (e.g., Will I be given a chance to transfer if I don't work out in this job?),
(4) who are the other people that have a rightful demand on their time and resources (e.g., Can people from accounting tell me that I have to get a report to them?),
(5) the common supervisory posture used in their part of the organization (e.g., Will my supervisor allow me a voice in the future goals of the department?).

It is actually difficult to get all this information across. Often many people are involved in the recruiting process, and occasionally the applicant receives conflicting impressions about the job. Employees involved in the interviewing process often need be reminded how important it is to paint an accurate picture of the job the candidate is seeking.

The New Employee's First Day

Several things happen on the first day that are critical to the success of the orientation effort. First, someone has to be the initial contact person who sets the tone for the entire day. For example, consider the first-day recruiting program that was developed in one division of Texas Instruments. The initiate is told that he/she

(1) has an excellent chance for success,
(2) should take initiative in communication,
(3) ought to disregard hall talk/rumors,
(4) must take initiative in getting to know her/his supervisor.

This is more than a series of platitudes. New employees are quite impressionable on the first day, and if they take this advice, they will be saved from much of the frustration that could otherwise follow.

The second important activity on that first day is introductions. New people should have the chance to meet as many of their co-workers as possible. It is often better if they have an opportunity for an informal visit with each one.

The Initial Assignment

Research indicates that the first assignment does much to influence whether or not the new employee stays in the organization or leaves. A number of characteristics seem to distinguish those initial assignments which lead to new employees' long-term success. First, the task assigned should be technically challenging. It should give the new person the feeling that the abilities for which he/she was hired are being used. Second, the task should not involve the person in work conflicts or political problems. New people are seldom well prepared to face these sorts of challenges. Finally, if possible, new recruits should be assigned tasks that place them in work groups that get along well and have good morale.

Stage 2--Breaking In

Stage 2 is a truly critical period. During this time, new employees sufficiently master the technical features of their jobs so that by the end of this stage, they are making a positive contribution. Moreover, this is the time when new people gain acceptance among their peers, finding a role to fill within their immediate work group. The amount of time required for this stage depends on the nature of the job. Figure 1 shows the length of Stage 2 for a number of different jobs.

The Assignment of a Mentor

New employees who successfully negotiate Stage 2 often have mentors. A mentor is simply an experienced person who looks after and advises the new worker. Because mentors are so helpful, some organizations formally appoint someone to handle this assignment. Commonly the new person's supervisor acts in this capacity. However, some organizations appoint one of the new person's co-workers to be in charge of breaking him in. At a few companies, new employees are assigned an individual who is on the same level as the person's supervisor.

If a mentor is assigned, that person should be chosen carefully. Mentors should be both technically able and socially skilled. They should know the new employee's job intimately, be familiar with the new person's work group, and be given sufficient time and other resources to do the mentoring. Most important, the mentor should be a good model for the new person.

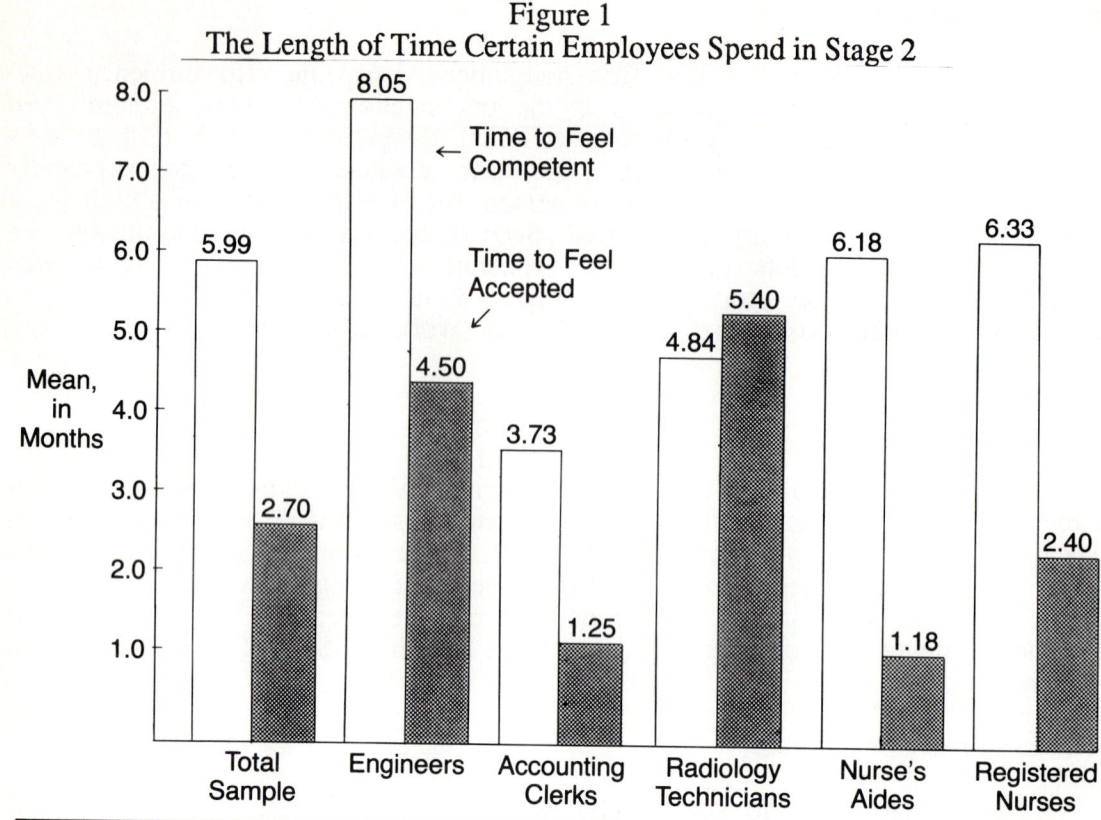

Figure 1
The Length of Time Certain Employees Spend in Stage 2

[Bar chart showing Mean in Months for Time to Feel Competent (white bars) and Time to Feel Accepted (shaded bars):
- Total Sample: 5.99 / 2.70
- Engineers: 8.05 / 4.50
- Accounting Clerks: 3.73 / 1.25
- Radiology Technicians: 4.84 / 5.40
- Nurse's Aides: 6.18 / 1.18
- Registered Nurses: 6.33 / 2.40]

Reprinted, by permission of the publisher, from "Research: A Practical Program for Employee Socialization" by Daniel Feldman in *Organizational Dynamics*, Autumn 1976, p. 78. Copyright © 1976 by American Management Association, New York. All rights reserved.

The Technical Adjustment

New employees rarely enter a position with all the knowledge and skills necessary for making an immediate contribution. Often they are given training, which may range in form from highly formalized programs to extremely informal on-the-job training. Regardless of the type or quality of the training, new people still need to adjust to the technical demands the job places on them. They have to master procedures and other bureaucratic requirements. They may have to reckon with tools and equipment that they have not used before. And they have to learn the logic and rationale behind various organizational practices.

Mentors can be very helpful assisting new employees with this transition. They can define performance standards and help the initiate develop an appropriate sense of priorities. They can offer feedback and encouragement. Perhaps most importantly, a mentor can serve as an interpreter in making sense of otherwise confusing signals and messages.

While mentors can be extremely helpful to new employees, they should avoid being too directive, or the new person will not develop a sense of identification with his or her job. In this sense, mentors should not insist on too much conformity with organizational procedures or interfere with the newcomer's creation of an individual approach to the job. Within limits, the new employee should be permitted to develop his or her own task priorities.

The Social Adjustment

In the beginning, the relationship between a new employee and the immediate work group can be very tenuous. While new recruits generally want acceptance, groups tend to be wary of new members. New employees want to be accepted because their group offers them (a) a source of information about performance standards, (b) a defense against oppressive forces, (c) a source of emotional support, and (d) a storehouse of solutions to job-related problems. In spite of this eagerness, new people are often viewed as a potential threat to their group's comfortable social equilibrium. Groups have unwritten rules that new people don't initially know, and even after they do, it takes a while for them to prove themselves willing to live according to these rules. Some groups even haze new people, subjecting them to ego-deflating experiences as a means of testing their willingness to become a group member.

As a result of these two conflicting perspectives, earning acceptance as a functioning member of the organization can be as difficult as the job itself. One sales representative with a consumer goods firm told us that he felt alone and unattached from his co-workers and clients, and an employee with the phone company told us she found the need to travel to her parents' home to get support from family and friends about her problems with new co-workers.

New employees have a great deal to learn before they are accepted. They must learn to relax in the presence of their co-workers. They must establish a role for themselves in the group. They have to figure out what is expected of them as a group member, and how to behave in social interactions.

Clearly the mentor can play a vital role in all this. Not only can a mentor give the recruit information and advice about group members in advance and feedback along the way, but the mentor can also intervene on the novice's behalf. For example, some mentors ask group members to suspend hazing and coax co-workers into being more cooperative. Mentors also need to be conscious about the importance of first impressions. For example, new people who are introduced as "brilliant," or "the best we have hired in ages" may find themselves excluded from the group or severely tested for reasons that are beyond their control.

At the completion of Stage 2, new employees no longer feel new. They seldom feel self-conscious about their technical skills, and they have earned acceptance onto their work team. Yet there is more ahead. Pressures outside their work group and with their adaptation to working life loom large as adjustment challenges.

Stage 3--Staying In

There is more to adapting to a new position than mastering the technical and social aspects of the job. Most jobs require some interaction with employees outside the immediate work group, and many jobs place demands on people's private lives that are difficult to accommodate. These are the issues that challenge new employees during Stage 3.

Becoming Effective With Outside Employees

New employees have a lot to learn when it comes to dealing effectively with employees outside their immediate work group. Seasoned workers know the subterranean organization: the structure that establishes that some departments are more powerful than others and that certain key people are much more powerful than their position would suggest. These "political realities" are not at all discernable to novices, and even graduating from Stage 2 does not qualify employees for savvy of this sort.

It is difficult, even for an experienced employee, to spell out all the "informal" knowledge necessary to make the bureaucracy function to help one accomplish his or her job, but certainly the newly hired have to learn about the individual personalities that are behind the impersonal public forms of communications one has to deal with. Equally important are the historical events that mark the relationships one must work within. Finally, one must somehow assimilate the confidential realities that exist in every organization, i.e., the "juiciest" facts that no one is told unless and until one has truly "paid the dues."

Mentors are especially critical during this part of Stage 3, for most of the knowledge that needs to be passed on is not available in print. This knowledge may be the "wisdom" of the organization, and few things can substitute for learning it directly from an experienced mentor. Dramatic events need to be demystified. Seemingly insignificant nuances need to be elevated in importance. Bland facts need to be colored. There is actually no substitute for experience at this stage.

Balancing Work Demands With Demands on One's Private Life

An often ignored aspect of orientation is that employees typically have problems adjusting to the conditions surrounding their employment. Balancing home and work demands is a challenge to everyone, but it is especially so for certain type of employees. For example, single parents, people new in the area, people with special commuting problems, and people without a well-developed social support system, often face very real difficulties that remain hidden.

Mentors can help with these sorts of problems, but only if they are truly sensitive to the situation. Unfortunately, lifestyle differences between the mentor and the new employee may make this difficult. For example, single people may not understand the problems and needs of new parents. Similarly, employees who live close to their work are often ignorant of the plight of the commuter. Mentors need to be careful about giving their proteges advice. Instead, they may be more helpful by introducing them to people who have successfully coped with their special problem. In addition, a mentor may put the new employee in touch with the resources that are available in the company to help with these problems.

Conclusion

Once a manager knows the principles, effective orientation requires little more than planning and good communication. Yet its returns can be great. Effectively oriented employees are likely to begin quickly to make a contribution. They are also committed and loyal.

References

Feldman, Daniel. "A Practical Program for Employee Socialization." *Organizational Dynamics* 5 (1976): 64-80.

Feldman, Daniel. "A Socialization Process That Helps New Recruits Succeed." *Personnel* 57 (1980): 11-23.

Feldman, Daniel. "The Multiple Socialization of Organization Members." *Academy of Management Review* 6 (1981): 309-318.

Gomersall, E. R., and M. Scott Myers "Breakthrough in On-the-Job Training." *Harvard Business Review* 44 (1966): 62-72.

Hall, Douglas T. *Careers in Organization*. Pacific Palisades, Calif.: Goodyear, 1976.

Schein, Edgar. "Organizational Socialization and the Profession of Management." *Industrial Management Review* 9 (1968): 1-16.

Van Maanen, John. "Breaking In: Socialization to Work." In Robert Dubin, ed., *Handbook of Work, Organization, and Society*. Chicago: Rand McNally, 1976.

Wanous, John P. "Effects of Realistic Job Preview on Job Acceptance, Job Attitudes and Job Survival." *Journal of Applied Psychology* 58 (1973): 327-332.

Course:_____ Name:_____

Instructor:_____ Date:_____

Flow Diagram for The New Employee Interactive Case

Detach this page from your book before you begin the Interactive Case. As you make each decision, write the decision point number *and* letter following the GO TO statement in the appropriate rectangle *before* you turn to that page. If you are referred to a previous decision point, circle the decision point number and letter you last wrote and proceed to the first uncircled rectangle above that one in your flow diagram. Do not erase the numbers and letters once you have written them. You will not necessarily fill all the rectangles.

Start		6th Decision		12th Decision	
1st Decision		7th Decision		13th Decision	
2nd Decision		8th Decision		14th Decision	
3rd Decision		9th Decision		15th Decision	
4th Decision		10th Decision		16th Decision	
5th Decision		11th Decision		17th Decision	

→ turn over

18th Decision	27th Decision	36th Decision
19th Decision	28th Decision	37th Decision
20th Decision	29th Decision	38th Decision
21st Decision	30th Decision	39th Decision
22nd Decision	31st Decision	40th Decision
23rd Decision	32nd Decision	41st Decision
24th Decision	33rd Decision	42nd Decision
25th Decision	34th Decision	43rd Decision
26th Decision	35th Decision	44th Decision

Interactive Case

You are the Manager of the System Test Group of Venus Missile and Space Corporation, a large aerospace firm. You have 15 years of experience, six with Venus. You have nine subordinates (avg. age = 36) responsible for trouble-shooting missile system prototypes. Each of your subordinates is given a temporary project assignment (duration 1-24 months), but you maintain direct supervision and control (i.e., they are not accountable to a project manager except through you). You are proud of the reputation for technical excellence your team has earned.

Bill Smythe has just joined your group. Fresh out of a major engineering school (B.S.E.E. with high honors), Bill is a welcome addition to the team. He earned an A- average in college, was a member of the honor society, and was active in campus activities. He is older (26) and more mature than most new employees. He is married with two school-aged children. He was a highly sought-after college recruit, receiving offers from virtually every company he interviewed with. During his plant visit, he struck you as bright, eager to learn, and articulate. Bill was given a very competitive salary offer by Venus, but he indicated to you that it was not the highest he had received.

He has been given a standard orientation to the company by people in the Personnel Department, and you have introduced him to the others in the group (he spent an hour with each). You also instructed him to take initiative in contacting you whenever he runs into problems no matter how slight or trivial they seem to be.

You need to decide which of four possible assignments to give him. These four possibilities are described below. In the descriptions, you note: (a) the likelihood (in percentage terms) that Bill will be able to make a meaningful contribution to the team he is assigned to, and (b) the value of Bill's development if he is personally successful (on a scale from 0 = low to 100 = high).

Assignment 1. Junior Control Engineer, Dart Project. Join a team of four members to test a ballistics control system for a Dart missile. The team is headed by Bob Blair. The Dart missile is like other systems developed previously, except that the new control system requires several new standards never required before. Smythe's senior thesis in school dealt with ballistics control systems. Estimated probability of making a net contribution to the team = 60 percent. Value to Bill's development if he is personally successful = 40 points out of 100.

Assignment 2. Junior Control Engineer, Solaris Project. Join a team of three members to test the propulsion control system for a Solaris booster. The team is headed by K. C. Wong, who is very enthusiastic about Bill joining the team (K. C. graduated from the same engineering school as Bill). The Solaris project will require a unique control system that has never been implemented before. The project is presently behind schedule because of the novelty of its design. It would offer a fantastic learning opportunity for any junior engineer. Estimated probability of making a net contribution to the team = 30 percent. Value to Bill's development if he is personally successful = 80 points out of 100.

Assignment 3. Junior Control Engineer, Systems Test Group. Act as your administrative assistant. Perform several studies regarding planning and scheduling in preparation for upcoming budget negotiations. While this assignment has only a modest technical component, it is a great way for Bill to learn the inner workings of your department and may allow him to find his own technical place in the group. Estimated probability of making a net contribution to the group = 100 percent. Value to Bill's development if he is personally successful = 20 points out of 100.

Assignment 4. Junior Control Engineer, Systems Test Group and Member, Micascope Divisional Task Force. Join a task force of seven members conducting a manufacturing feasibility study of Micascope, a laser-refracting targeting system. The task force is chaired by the assistant to the divisional manager. This assignment would give Bill a chance to work with some of the most dynamic members of the division. The feasibility study proposed is somewhat controversial, with some task force members committed to manufacturing and some dead set against it. The division manager is said to favor manufacturing, but he has agreed to "let the chips fall where they may." While he handpicked the members of the task force from other departments, his confidence in you permitted him to ask you to appoint the department member of your choice. Since all of the other members of your group are busy with project work, Bill seems like a natural. Estimated probability of making a net contribution to the task force = 50 percent. Value to Bill's development if he is personally successful = 80 points out of 100.

At this point, what would you do?

  A. Ask Bill which assignment he would prefer. (GO TO 364A)

  B. Assign him to one of the four assignments without asking for his preferences. (GO TO 335A)

4 COMMUNICATION
Module Reading

Managers and supervisors spend nearly 80 percent of every day communicating. It is no small wonder that so many of the problems any manager faces are communication problems. Yet many of these problems are avoidable. It is not just a matter of trying harder or even being more "sensitive." One secret of more effective communication lies in understanding the differences between the types of relationships a manager must deal with and communicating accordingly. Managers must communicate upward, downward, and horizontally, and each of these directions requires a different set of techniques. It is the failure to act upon these differences that causes so many communication difficulties.

Figure 1 shows how frequently managers communicate upward, downward, and horizontally. Downward communication is most common, and upward and horizontal communication are less frequent. However, each horizontal and upward message is likely to be consequential. A failure to communicate with a manager's boss or a key peer can spell disaster.

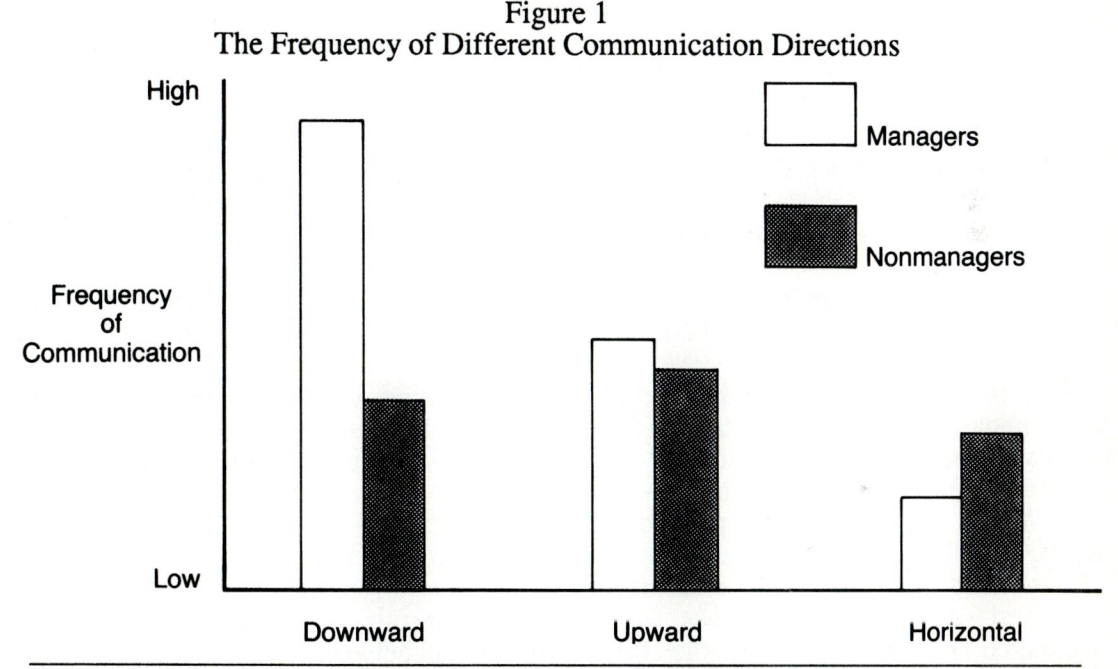

Figure 1
The Frequency of Different Communication Directions

From "Communication in Administrative Bureaucracies" by Samuel B. Bacharach and Michael Aiken in *Academy of Management Journal*, Vol. 20, No. 3, 1977. Copyright © 1977 by the Academy of Management. Reprinted by permission of the Academy of Management and Samuel B. Bacharach.

A Fundamental Choice in Communicating in Any Direction

When a manager has a message to convey, the most fundamental decision is whether to communicate it orally or in written form. In general, some situations dictate communication in writing, some orally, and some both. A few general rules governing when to use each follow:

Oral communication by itself is best when a manager

(1) has to reprimand an employee,
(2) wants to communicate in confidence or "off the record,"
(3) is settling a dispute between subordinates,
(4) is involved in a minor violation of a policy in order to solve a problem or get something done,
(5) wants to communicate something but does not want to establish a precedent.

Written communication by itself is best when a manager

(1) wants to brief a large audience about nonurgent information,
(2) wants to get a reaction from someone who is hesitant to respond orally,
(3) wants to give someone information requiring future action.

Written communication followed by oral communication is best when a manager

(1) wants to prepare someone for future group interaction (e.g., a meeting),
(2) wants to communicate with a majority, recognizing that the minority will require some oral communication.

It is also important to keep the receiver in mind when deciding whether to communicate orally or in writing. Some people are naturally listeners and others readers. Clearly, messages should be sent orally to listeners even though the situation would otherwise demand a written form.

When in doubt it is probably better to send a message orally than in writing. Talking to someone allows more immediate feedback than a written message. At the same time, a manager should not fall into the trap of believing that oral communication does not require careful planning. Listeners are challenged by the fact that the time differential between the rate of thought (400 to 500 words/min.) and the rate of speech (100 to 150 words/min.) is significant. In other words, it takes planning to assure that listeners exercise the patience to listen.

Downward Communication

The most frequent of all managerial communication is downward. The most common messages flowing in this direction are the following:

(1) job instructions,
(2) rationale for tasks in relation to the organization's goals,
(3) organizational policies and practices,
(4) feedback about performance,
(5) indoctrination of goals.

When there are problems in downward communication, they are typically due to the fact that (a) the message is unclear, (b) the message communicates expectations that are at odds with the expectations of others (other supervisors, other employees, policies, etc.), and (c) the message is too restrictive in relation to the task. A number of things can be done to address these problems.

In this section, we will describe two common scenarios: giving instructions and providing counseling. Both of these forms of downward communication suffer from being ambiguous, conflicting, or restrictive.

Communicating Assignments

When a manager gives an assignment to one of his or her employees, communication can be improved if the manager does certain things. These include

(1) using language that the subordinate understands,
(2) being certain (with feedback) that the employee understands the logic and requirements of the assignment,
(3) being very direct about the ends that are expected,
(4) scheduling a time for reporting back the results of the assignment,
(5) trying, if possible, to ascertain whether the employee has the time and resources to complete the assignment,
(6) being open to the means the employee uses to meet the expected ends.

The most controversial point is the last one, but it is well-documented that employees feel most motivated by assignments in which they themselves can determine the *method*. In general, it is helpful if the manager asks subordinates if they have ideas about how to complete the assignment. Not only is this potentially motivating, but many times employees come up with far better methods for completing the assignment than the manager originally envisioned.

Counseling Employees

Managers counsel anytime they offer advice to an employee. Counseling, however, can be rather "touchy." Not everyone welcomes advice; even fewer appreciate advice that is poorly communicated. Accordingly, it is important to keep several principles in mind when a manager counsels an employee.

Many useful ideas about effective employee counseling can be drawn from the well-known psychologist Carl Rogers. He asserts that people communicate openly to the extent that they perceive their counterparts are trustworthy and authentic. When a person perceives another as incongruent (dishonest or unauthentic), he or she will "close down" and become dishonest and unauthentic. When counseling, a manager should try to be as open and truthful as possible. It is also helpful to try to respond to the totality of what is being communicated. This includes nonverbal as well as verbal messages, and the feelings behind messages as well as the messages themselves. Rogers suggests that counselors take the following steps:

(1) listen for the content of messages,
(2) listen for the feelings behind the messages,
(3) note all cues, verbal and nonverbal,
(4) reflect back to the other person, in the counselor's own words, what is being heard.

Should a manager communicate with an employee in a less than congruent way in a counseling situation, the employee will most likely detect that and the session will be seriously jeopardized. In addition, the nonverbal signals a manager sends in the session may convey unexpressed feelings that can disrupt the session.

These are some of the more important nonverbal cues a manager might watch for in communications with employees:

(1) the physical space between the manager and subordinate (close conveys intimacy, distance conveys perceived status differences),
(2) the orientation of body positions (face-to-face conveys competition, side-to-side conveys cooperation),
(3) the employee's posture (stiffness conveys formality, looseness conveys relaxation),
(4) facial expressions,
(5) gestures,
(6) eye contact.

Engaging employees in counseling can expose the manager to occasionally risky interpersonal situations. Once in a while employees will say (or otherwise communicate) hurtful messages. These occur occasionally during counseling, and a manager should be prepared for them. A good formula for responding to threatening comments is to state, "When you X, it makes me feel Y, and I'd like to suggest Z." The alternative of denying one's feelings is generally less effective since it is generally coupled with nonverbal messages that contradict the verbal messages.

Horizontal Communication

Less frequent but potentially more important communications are those directed horizontally to peers and people who provide services. The most common messages flowing in this direction are

(1) coordination of activities,
(2) exercise of influence to acquire necessary resources and support,
(3) information about colleagues' work attitudes.

The most common problems in lateral communication are that (a) historically little information flows in this direction; (b) different units have entirely different ways of approaching organizational problems; and (c) different units often have conflicting stakes (i.e., the incentives do not always favor cooperation).

Horizontal relationships are characterized by a power gap. When supervisors or managers turn to their peers for support and cooperation, they find themselves with less power and influence than they need. Authority differences exist between organizational levels, but when individuals at the same level communicate, they generally do so as equals. And when peers require cooperation from others, they must rely on the good faith of their colleagues.

In the absence of authority, managers have to rely on informal means of influence. Among these are

(1) persuasion based on organizational logic, (i.e., what you think is in the best interest of the organization),
(2) the exercise of pressure,
(3) personal favors,
(4) persuasion based on the interests of one's counterpart.

Take the case of a supervisor who is trying to get an employee-relations staff person to approve a merit raise larger than that allowed under existing policies for one of his key subordinates. The supervisor can argue convincingly that such a raise is in the best interests of the organization (persuasion based on organizational logic). She can exert pressure on the staff person that unless the raise is granted, the matter will be reported to an upper-level manager known to favor the policy exception (pressure). She can ask for the raise to be approved as a personal favor. Or she can search for "benefits" that approving the policy exception would give the employee-relations person. For example, if the person is known to be promoting a new training program, the supervisor can promise support for that program in return for a favorable decision (counterpart's interests).

In general, personal favors and benefit selling (informal means 3 and 4 above) are the most successful. The use of persuasion based on organizational logic and the use of pressure are frequently less effective. This implies that managers who try to exercise influence in horizontal communication should begin with an understanding of their counterpart's needs, wants, and points of view. It is simply good business to use good salesmanship in horizontal communication.

Upward Communication

For most managers, the most important person they must communicate with is their boss. The messages conveyed upward include

(1) information on achievement, progress, and future plans,
(2) information about work problems that require assistance from higher up in the organization,
(3) ideas for improvement,
(4) information on subordinate attitudes about work issues.

One of the most fundamental principles governing upward communication is known as *management by exception*. This states that only exceptional deviations from orders, plans, and policies should be communicated upward. This implies that individuals should not report every little thing to their bosses but should restrict their upward communication to truly important issues. Yet ask bosses what they insist upon among their people and they typically say, "*No surprises!*" Thus, on the one hand subordinates are told to restrict their upward communication and on the other, they are expected to keep their bosses informed. There are remedies to this apparent contradiction, but each requires a great deal from the subordinate. First, they must find a way to learn their boss's objectives and communication style. Only by understanding the boss can a person figure out just what he or she considers a top priority. Another thing frequently ignored by subordinates is that most bosses have preferred modes of communication. Some bosses are listeners and others are readers. Some bosses are more open to upward communication in the morning and others in the afternoon. Some bosses are much more receptive just after a business trip and some before. Effective subordinates will attempt to find ways to discover these idiosyncrasies.

One important fact that many subordinates fail to recognize is that their boss often experiences data overload. Most managers are exposed to much more data than they can possibly process and act upon. Data overload is often the reason bosses seem to be poor listeners, forget appointments, and seem distracted. Managing a boss who is experiencing data overload is difficult; however, there are some techniques that help in these situations. Individuals with such a boss should use their boss's time very selectively. They should plan every conversation with their boss, eliminating superfluous data and getting down to the bare essentials. One technique is to precede an encounter with the words "I need five minutes of your time, during which I'd like to discuss topic X and after which I would like a decision on Y."

In summary, several principles can be used to improve communicating with a boss:

(1) State the objective of the communication concisely in terms of the needs and interests of the boss.
(2) Detail the objective of the communication and support it with facts.
(3) Ask for and/or respond to questions.
(4) Probe for agreement.
(5) Summarize and confirm conclusion.

Conclusion

Most managerial problems are at some level communication problems. Effective managers solve these problems by being sensitive to the particular demands of the direction of the communication. It is not just a matter of being more clear. Giving assignments to subordinates demands a different approach from asking peers for help. Similarly, keeping bosses informed requires an approach much different from counseling a troubled employee.

References

Argyle, Michael. "Nonverbal Communication in Human Social Interaction." In R. Hinde, ed., *Nonverbal Communication.* New York: Cambridge, 1972.

Bacharach, S. B., and Michael Aiken. "Communication in Administrative Bureaucracies." *Academy of Management Journal* 18 (1977): 365-377.

Ekman, P., and W. V. Friesen. "Nonverbal Leadage and Clues to Deception." *Psychiatry* 32 (1971): 88-105.

Harper, R. G., A. N. Wiens, and J. D. Matarzzo. *Nonverbal Communication.* New York: John Wiley & Sons, 1978.

Hawkins, Brian, and Paul Preston. *Managerial Communication.* Santa Monica, Calif.: Goodyear, 1981.

Kotter, John. *Power and Influence in Organizations*. New York: Free Press, 1985.

Level, Dale Jr. "Communication Effectiveness: Method and Situation." *Journal of Business Communication* 10 (1972): 19-25.

Mintzberg, Henry. *The Nature of Managerial Work*. New York: Harper & Row, 1973.

Rue, Leslie, and Lloyd Byars. *Communication in Organizations*. Homewood, Ill.: Richard D. Irwin, 1980.

Simpson, R. "Vertical and Horizontal Communication in Formal Organizations." *Administrative Science Quarterly* 4 (1959): 188-196.

Course:_____   Name:_____

Instructor:_____   Date:_____

Flow Diagram for Communication Interactive Case

Detach this page from your book before you begin the Interactive Case. As you make each decision, write the decision point number *and* letter following the GO TO statement in the appropriate rectangle *before* you turn to that page. If you are referred to a previous decision point, circle the decision point number and letter you last wrote and proceed to the first uncircled rectangle above that one in your flow diagram. Do not erase the numbers and letters once you have written them. You will not necessarily fill all the rectangles.

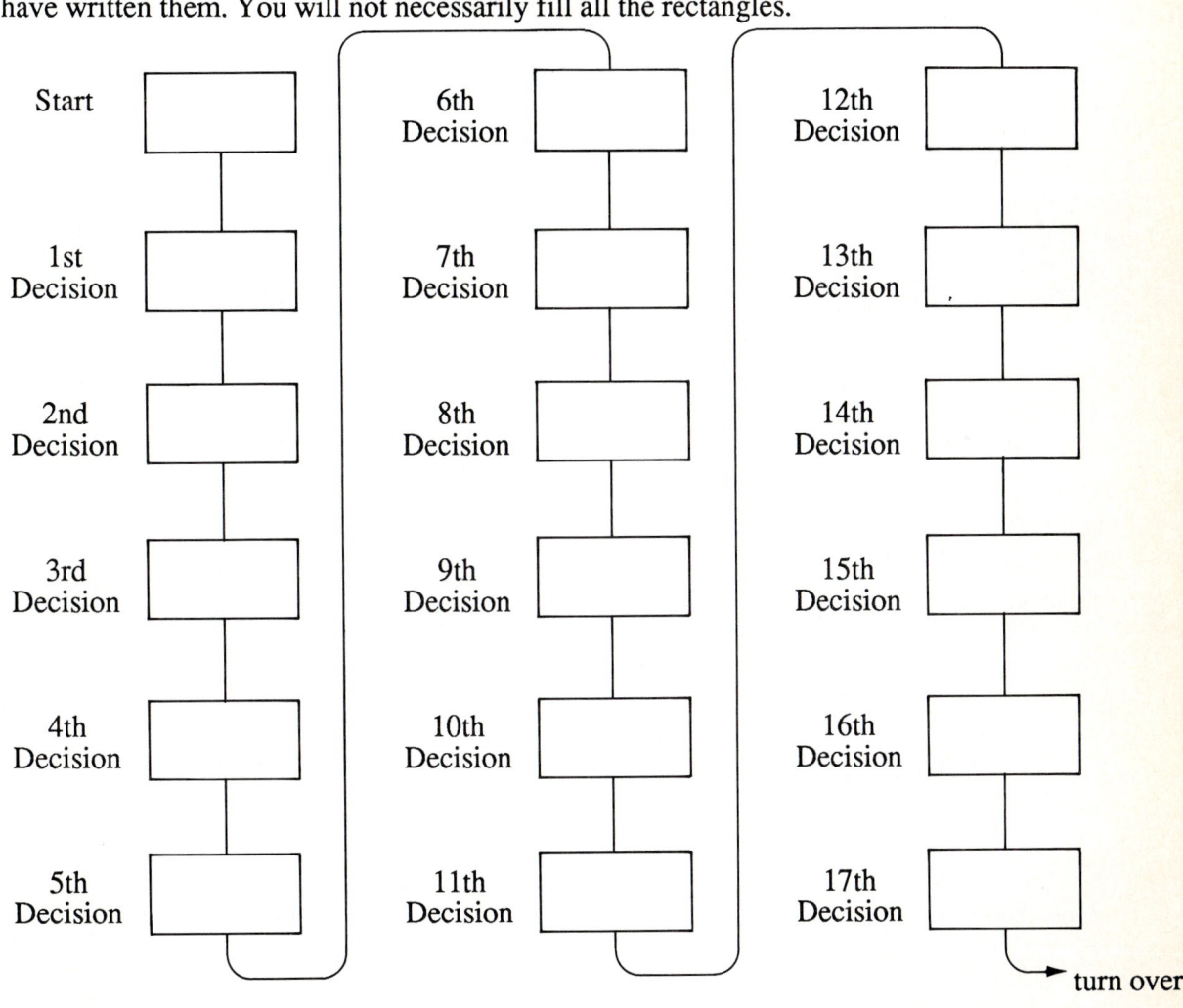

Start		6th Decision		12th Decision	
1st Decision		7th Decision		13th Decision	
2nd Decision		8th Decision		14th Decision	
3rd Decision		9th Decision		15th Decision	
4th Decision		10th Decision		16th Decision	
5th Decision		11th Decision		17th Decision	

→ turn over

18th Decision

19th Decision

20th Decision

21st Decision

22nd Decision

23rd Decision

24th Decision

25th Decision

26th Decision

27th Decision

28th Decision

29th Decision

30th Decision

31st Decision

32nd Decision

33rd Decision

34th Decision

35th Decision

36th Decision

37th Decision

38th Decision

39th Decision

40th Decision

41st Decision

42nd Decision

43rd Decision

44th Decision

Interactive Case

You work for Gamage-Nash, Inc., an eight-store chain of department stores located in Colorado. You are one of nine department managers at the store in the Academy Mall in Colorado Springs. You report to Marion Scott, the Softlines Division Manager at the store. An organization chart appears below.

Colorado Springs Gamage-Nash Store

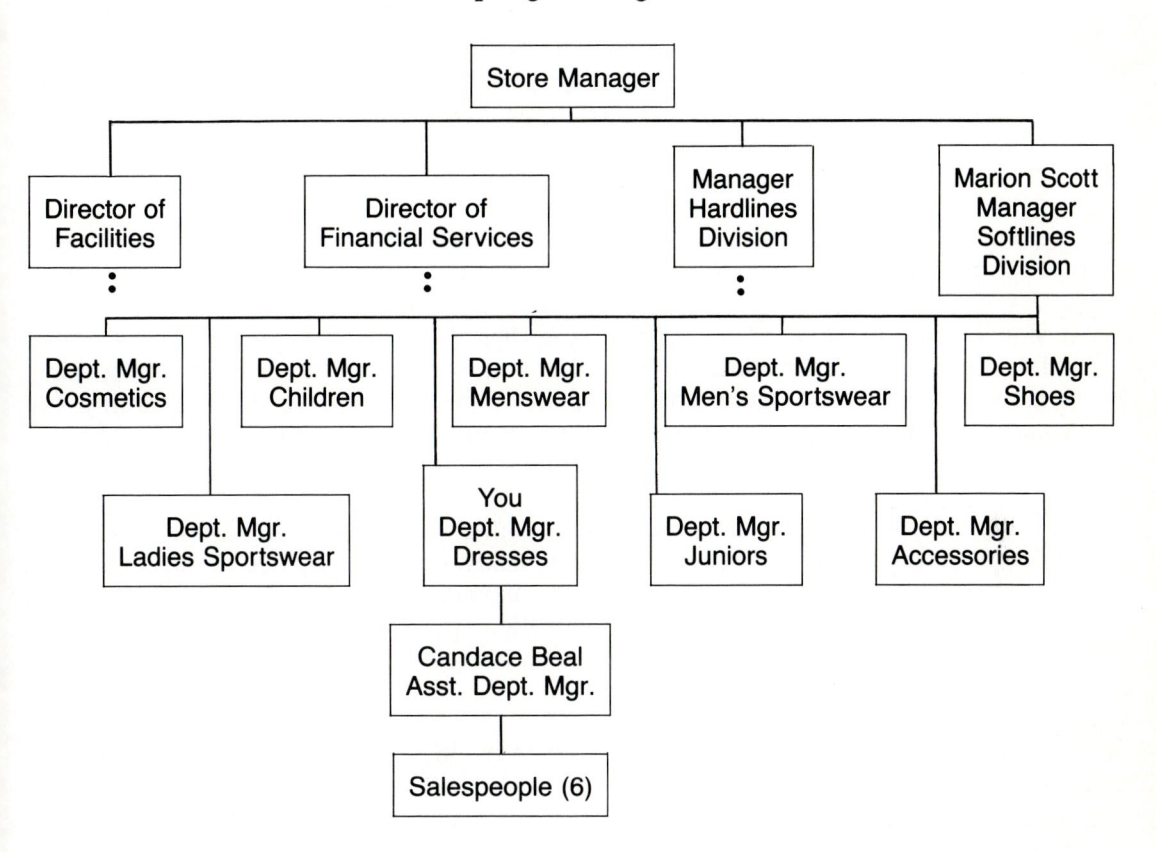

```
                          Store Manager
        ┌──────────────┬──────────────┬──────────────┐
   Director of    Director of      Manager       Marion Scott
   Facilities    Financial        Hardlines       Manager
                 Services         Division        Softlines
                                                  Division
        ⋮              ⋮              ⋮
   Dept. Mgr.    Dept. Mgr.    Dept. Mgr.    Dept. Mgr.    Dept. Mgr.
   Cosmetics     Children      Menswear      Men's         Shoes
                                             Sportswear
   Dept. Mgr.                  You           Dept. Mgr.    Dept. Mgr.
   Ladies                      Dept. Mgr.    Juniors       Accessories
   Sportswear                  Dresses
                                │
                          Candace Beal
                          Asst. Dept. Mgr.
                                │
                          Salespeople (6)
```

You carry four product lines in your department: coats and furs, contemporary dresses, traditionals and petites, and better dresses and suits. Accordingly, you interact frequently with the buyer for each of these lines, who is responsible for the merchandising of that line throughout Gamage-Nash. These buyers report along a completely different chain of command from the one shown above, and they divide their time among all eight stores.

Within this case, you will have occasion to communicate with four different persons: Marion Scott, your boss and the Manager of the Softlines Division;

Candace Beal, your Assistant Department Manager; Becky Stark, one of your salespeople; and Jean Volk, the buyer for one of your lines, contemporary dresses. Each of these four individuals is described below.

Marion Scott (Manager of Softlines)--32, ten years experience. Has only been in this position for a year, and feels a bit overwhelmed. Is very well thought of by her boss and other company people, but has not yet found her self-confidence in this job. You like her very much; and it appears to be mutual, since you received a nice merit raise last year and a spot bonus two months ago. Not an avid reader, Marion dislikes paperwork. Unfortunately, she is so busy, so much on the go, that it's hard to tell if what you tell her really gets through. In fact, there have been a couple of instances when she has either forgotten what you told her or never even heard it. Sometimes you wonder what you could do to make yourself more credible with her so she would pay more attention to what you tell her.

Candace Beal (Assistant Manager, Dresses Department)--43, four years experience. You originally hired Candace as a salesperson. It was a bit of a risk since she was just getting over a divorce from a wealthy professional, and at that point didn't have her feet on the ground. It was her first job in retailing, and for a while you had to do a lot of hand holding. However, she really took to it, and now she is eager to make retailing her career. Recently you have decided to delegate more and more of your job to her to prepare her to be your replacement.

Becky Stark (Salesperson)--20, nine months experience. Becky is a delight. A modeling school graduate, Becky shows extremely good taste in the clothes she wears, and she dresses mannequins superbly. She works 20 hours a week for you. She is enrolled at a local college majoring in retailing. You plan to use her this summer and are hopeful that she will join Gamage-Nash upon graduating.

Jean Volk (Buyer, Contemporary Dresses)--38, 10 years experience. By and large you have a good relationship with Jean, even though there are tensions in working with any buyer. Buyers are responsible for acquiring the merchandise you sell, and there are often differences between the assortment you get from the buyer and the assortment you know will sell. For example, you have a good understanding of the modern dresses sold at other outlets on the Academy Mall, and customers often request particular styles and brands. Normally Jean takes your inputs into account, but occasionally she doesn't and really misses the mark. Last fall, for example, you had to mark down the entire line from a particular vendor because a specialty store on the mall offered the same item at nearly one-third the price. That miscalculation cost Jean considerably from a political standpoint. Rumor is that her immediate superior (Divisional Merchandise Manager, Dresses and Cosmetics), a man known for his no-nonsense approach and his vigilance to volume figures, is monitoring her performance closely and that her job may be in jeopardy. It seems clear that right now Jean needs nothing to draw adverse attention to herself.

It is early March, and you have just completed your winter clearance sales to make room for the spring lines. Things are generally going pretty well, and you are optimistic about prospects of the new season. One development that you want to take advantage of is that because last winter was so mild, a furrier in the mall has recently gone out of business. This leaves what you feel is a significant residual demand for your coats and furs section. In order to take advantage of this development, you hope to be able to increase the square footage of space allocated to this product group. This will require you to cut back on the space devoted to the better dresses and suits line, a move sure to be opposed by the buyer of that line.

Changes in the allotment of floor space are decisions made by your boss and her counterpart in the merchandising area (Divisional Merchandise Manager, Dresses and Cosmetics). For you to make this happen, you will have to persuade your boss that this reallocation makes sense. In communicating this message, what would you do?

A. Write her a thorough memo, specifying in some detail the basis of your thinking and the rationale of your proposal. (GO TO 506B)

B. Send her a note indicating you desire to meet with her on "a matter of importance." Then, follow up in a day or two. (GO TO 513B)

C. Before her weekly staff meeting, tell her that you want to speak with her about a reallocation of square footage. Ask her when it would be convenient to get together. (GO TO 493B)

D. See her the first thing in the morning to discuss the matter. (GO TO 504B)

E. Ask Marion's secretary for advice on when would be a good time to discuss this matter. (GO TO 494A)

F. Since your boss is so busy, talk with the Divisional Merchandise Manager, Dresses and Cosmetics, informally to see if this issue--the change in square footage--is one that she might be concerned about. This would save you even having to bother your boss with this issue. (GO TO 495B)

5 PERFORMANCE APPRAISAL
Module Reading

There is probably no area where there are so many differences between theory and practice than in performance appraisal. Management experts regularly point out the shortcomings of existing appraisal practices. Yet, their suggestions are seldom taken to heart. This is unfortunate. A great deal of research has been devoted to the subject of performance appraisal in work organizations, much of it both practical and useful. In this chapter we review some of that research about how to evaluate employee performance. First, we introduce the concept of performance measures, so that we can discuss what sorts of measures are most effective. Second, we cover the topic of rater bias and how it may be avoided. Third, we discuss at length some principles of how to conduct a performance appraisal interview.

Recent estimates are that about 90 percent of business organizations have formal appraisal systems for their supervisors, middle managers, and professional/technical employees; 80 percent have appraisal systems for their office and sales people; and 59 percent reported having formal appraisal systems for production workers. Thus, there seems little question that performance appraisal is a common process in most organizations.

Performance Measures Used in Appraisals

By measures we mean the dimensions of the employee's performance that make up the appraisal. Common measures include the quantity of output and the quality of output. In most instances, combinations of specific measures are used. Generally three types of measures are used in performance appraisals: (a) objective data; (b) personnel data; and (c) judgmental data. Objective data include all those pieces of information about the actual level and quality of output attributable to the person. Personnel data include such things as the person's attendance record, their completion of training courses, and their rate of advancement in the organization. Judgmental data include any observation made by someone in the organization about the person's performance.

Many of us trust the objective measures over the judgmental ones. However, one must be very careful when using all types of performance measures. In many instances, objective data do not accurately reflect an individual's complete performance. For example, the number of traffic citations that police officers write up during a month may not be a good reflection of their overall performance. While it is true that judgmental measures are more subject to bias than objective ones, even objective data must be scrutinized carefully before one assumes that they are truly useful. Essentially, unless objective data are used with "judgment," overall performance measures composed of them are not only sterile, but may be inappropriate.

Behavior Versus Feelings/Attitudes

As a general rule, measures chosen as indices of performance should reflect actual work behavior rather than feelings and attitudes. Assessing the dispositions of workers invites biases of all kinds. Feelings and attitudes are subject to interpretation and inference. Although we may want to include some measure of employee loyalty in our performance measures, this is highly suspect. Unless supervisors are careful to relate loyalty to specific behaviors (tendency to follow procedures without questioning, tendency to enforce rules in the absence of the supervisor, etc.), loyalty measures are open to bias.

Specific Behavior Versus Global Behavior

It is also important to keep measures specific. General measures like "promotability" or "aptitude" should be more specific to be useful. Moreover, giving problem people general feedback will not result in improvement. Imagine if someone told you that you were not "performing up to your potential." How would you know exactly what to do to improve?

Using traits as performance measures is also troublesome. A trait is an attribute of the individual appraised rather than a measure of that person's job performance. The two may be related, of course, but using traits for evaluation purposes not only invites subjectivity but also tends not to be job relevant. Take the trait of intelligence. Managers should *not* engage in judgments here, but should instead focus on whether the employee demonstrates the sort of analytical thinking required by specific aspects of his or her job. This is a subtle distinction, but feedback that takes the form "Bill is X" is not as useful as feedback in the form "Bill may be expected to Y."

Influenceable Measures Versus Noninfluenceable Measures

Influenceable measures are superior to noninfluenceable measures. A measure is influenceable if employees can actually do something about their performance levels. For example, if the performance of a machine operator was measured by the number of units produced per day, the manager should ensure that the operator is really in control of the output of his machine. It may be that the output of his machine is more influenced by raw material quality or atmospheric conditions than by anything that the operator might do while tending it.

Using noninfluenceable measures creates severe motivational problems. Employees do not understand how to improve performance levels. For example, if a manager holds a retail sales clerk accountable for his sales of baby clothes, and the birth rate in the community has decreased, what can he do to improve his sales figures?

Outcome Measures Versus Activity Measures

Managers also need to be careful to select measures that reflect the outcomes of the employee's efforts as well as the activities he or she performs along the way. For example, a retail sales clerk may attain a large sales volume (outcome), but actually keep a messy work station (activity). Presuming that orderliness is important for safety and sanitation, measuring performance only in terms of outcomes or activities in this instance distorts the value of the measure. Performance measures should ideally be as inclusive as possible; i.e., they must capture as much of what actual constitutes performance from the organization's standpoint as possible. Measuring performance only in terms of outcomes or activities fails in this regard.

Unilaterally Determined Versus Participatively Determined

There is also the question how performance measures are arrived at. Ideally, performance measures should be selected as the result of a participative discussion between the manager and the individual being appraised. This not only assures higher motivation, but it also allows the performance appraisal process to be more satisfying to the employee.

Yet it is here that we see great differences between theory and practice. By far the most common measures used in performance appraisal are those embedded in rating scales given to the manager and worker to use in the performance assessment. Table 1 reports the results of a study that shows that participatively developed measures are quite uncommon.

Figure 1 on page 68 represents a common rating form. Managers asked to use such forms have little choice but to use the measures contained in them. Yet there is still some room for discretion. For example, some organizations allow managers to use "development plans" of their own creation as a means of following up on the appraisals on the standard forms. Such plans may involve mutual goal setting and the participative development of performance measures.

Rater Biases and Methods of Avoiding Them

Since judgment plays such a central role in performance appraisal, a manager must be careful to avoid biases. Common biases include leniency errors, halo errors, and central tendency errors. Leniency errors occur when particular managers are unusually harsh or lenient in their appraisals. Halo errors involve the tendency to allow one or two general impressions to affect one's entire evaluation. And central tendency errors occur when managers avoid assigning extreme rating values to any employee. While a manager may not be aware that he or she is biasing appraisals in these ways, the problem is usually apparent to those who assemble performance appraisal statistics or make salary decisions based upon them. As a means of controlling for them, such officials often create specific policies that govern what distribution of appraisal ratings are permitted. Some organizations require appraisers to rank order their subordinates. Others insist on a specific distribution of ratings. These policies do not do away with halo errors, but they do tend to address leniency and central tendency problems.

Table 1
Appraisal Techniques Used in Business

Technique	Small Organizations (Percent)	Large Organizations (Percent)	All (n=216) Organizations (Percent)
Rating Scale	59.5	54.2	56.7
Essay	25.8	24.2	24.9
MBO	8.5	16.6	12.7
Others	6.2	5.0	5.7

From "Performance Appraisal--A Survey of Current Practices" by Alan H. Locher and Kenneth S. Teel in *Personnel Journal*, May 1977. Copyright © 1977 by Personnel Journal. Reprinted by permission of Personnel Journal, Inc. All rights reserved.

Another approach to minimizing the effects of rating errors is to use multiple ratings of performance. In many instances, especially in jobs involving multiple managers (e.g., a secretary shared between several managers), it is helpful to gather ratings from these different managers. In other situations clients may be asked to offer their inputs. Universities and other service organizations regularly gather appraisal information of this kind. The logic behind such practices is that by using several different raters, the effects of certain errors tend to cancel each other out. Ideally one would want a high degree of agreement between appraisers, but failing that, different perspectives may in certain instances be valuable in and of themselves.

A special case is when peers are asked to do appraisals. Clearly one's co-workers may have a unique and valuable perspective into the performance of an individual. However, peer evaluations should not be used when salary levels are at stake or when rewards of various kinds are distributed competitively.

Some managers ask their subordinates to do a self-appraisal. Some even ask their people to complete a rating form on themselves before the appraisal interview. Although such ratings are frequently higher than the manager's, this is an attractive one from a developmental perspective. By examining the similarities between appraisals, both the manager and subordinate may learn a great deal about the other's view of the subordinate's job.

The Performance Appraisal Interview

One of the most troublesome aspects of performance appraisal for any manager is facing the individual to discuss his or her performance. No matter how much work and preparation a manager has done, the appraisal interview is potentially stressful for both parties. Again, however, there are some firm principles that managers can use to defuse this potentially explosive situation.

Planning for the Encounter

It probably goes without saying that the performance appraisal interview should be carefully planned. It is critical for the manager to set aside a period of time when the appraisal will not be interrupted. While the choice of a location to conduct the interview may not seem especially important, it is conventional wisdom to conduct the interview in a neutral place. By "neutral" we mean one where the trappings of the manager's position are not displayed. Managers who conduct appraisal interviews in their offices run the risk of stifling a genuine interchange. It is generally preferable to choose locations where both people can be comfortable and at ease.

Identifying the Performance Data to Feed Back

Prior to the interview, the manager should decide what information about the person's performance to cover during the interview. The manager should be mindful that appraisal interviews are not ideal communication environments. Frequently subordinates find the information they receive to be overwhelming. They may be incapable of taking in as much information as the manager might be prone to include. This is especially true for negative feedback. Subordinate defensiveness increases with each piece of negative feedback they receive. Moreover, there is probably a limit to the number of pieces of any type of feedback an individual can digest at any point in time. A handy general principle is to give no more than five pieces of feedback in an appraisal interview, three positive and two negative. It is also helpful to "sandwich" the negative feedback with the positive. In selecting the measures to focus on in the interview, a manager should be aware of potentially biasing tendencies. He or she should also select information to feedback that is reliable (ideally the manager should have more than one observation on which the assessment is

Exhibit 1
A Common Rating Scale Used in Performance Appraisal

Employee Performance Appraisal
(Salary Grade 3-6)

Employee:_____   Department:_____
Appraiser:_____   Date:_____

Check the space that indicates how typical each statement is of the <u>employee's behavior on the job.</u>

	Very Typical	Somewhat Typical	Not at all Typical
1. Does a high quality job	_____	_____	_____
2. Produces a large volume of work	_____	_____	_____
3. Cooperates and gets along with fellow employees	_____	_____	_____
4. Asks questions when uncertain	_____	_____	_____
5. Does *not* engage in disruptive or unproductive behaviors such as complaining, carrying on long personal conversations or wandering around	_____	_____	_____
6. Knows the procedures involved in the job and organization	_____	_____	_____
7. Willingly carries out unusual or unpleasant duties when necessary	_____	_____	_____
8. Catches the mistakes of others and takes notice of important details	_____	_____	_____
9. Looks for better ways to do the job	_____	_____	_____
10. Is well versed in technical terminology	_____	_____	_____
11. Uses accurate grammar and spelling	_____	_____	_____
12. Is rarely avsent or tardy without reason	_____	_____	_____
13. Understands how the department relates to other departments	_____	_____	_____
14. Handles multiple demands on time fairly and effectively	_____	_____	_____
15. Handles pressure well; meets deadlines	_____	_____	_____
16. Is courteous in dealings with clients and others outside the department	_____	_____	_____
17. Cares for and maintains equipment	_____	_____	_____
18. Keeps confidences and respects the secrecy of competitive information	_____	_____	_____
19. "Catches on" quickly	_____	_____	_____
20. Organizes information well; is good at analyzing things	_____	_____	_____

Briefly describe any critical incidents that you think illustrate important descriptors.

Overall Rating:
Outstanding:_____ Excellent:_____ Good:_____ Fair:_____ Poor:_____

manager should have more than one observation on which the assessment is based). In addition, the manager should make sure that he or she is prepared to give at least one specific example for each piece of feedback.

Choosing an Interview Format

There are countless possibilities when it comes to the format for an appraisal interview. One way of classifying the alternatives is shown in Table 2.

Tell and Sell. In this format, the manager simply (a) lets the employee know how he or she is doing; (b) gains the employee's acceptance of the evaluation; and (c) has the employee agree to follow a plan for improvement. As straightforward as this sounds, a tell and sell approach is only of limited usefulness. The major problem seems to hinge on the limited role given to the employee. As a general rule, it is preferable to keep appraisal interviews highly participative, with the manager actually doing little of the talking. Subordinate participation in the interview has been found to result in both greater satisfaction and a higher motivation to improve. All this is not to say, however, that a tell and sell approach is incorrect in all circumstances. New or inexperienced employees are likely to respond much more favorably to tell and sell than other, more participative approaches. Moreover, if a particular employee has received little day-to-day feedback from the manager or senses on the basis of prior contact that he or she will be criticized during the appraisal, tell and sell may offer the best alternative.

Tell and Listen. This approach requires the manager to use effective listening techniques in the interview. Listening sounds simple, but actually, most managers find it difficult to truly listen during appraisal interviews. Part of this, no doubt, comes from the perception of most managers that they are paid to give directions and to lead. To sit back and be inactive runs counter to their view of what a good manager should do. Listening skills are critical, however, to the tell and listen method.

Actually, there are some principles for giving feedback, as shown in Table 3, that are useful in Tell and Listen. For example, it is often better to approach giving feedback in a way that describes behavior rather than evaluates it. Similarly, it is better to convey the impression that the interview is spontaneous rather than carefully planned or contrived.

Using other specific listening skills is also desirable if one is to use a tell and listen approach. First, it may be helpful for a manager to practice paraphrasing and repeating employee inputs followed by a pause so the employee may react. Second, a manager should try to reflect back the underlying feelings and attitudes that the manager perceives the employee to have as a means of conveying the impression that the employee was understood. Finally, a manager should use his or her skills at summarizing discussions in order to acknowledge progress and the active role the employee has played during the session. These general principles seem easy, but are actually difficult to put into practice.

Table 2
Three Methods of Conducting Performance Appraisal Interviews

Method	Tell and Sell	Tell and Listen	Problem Solving
Objectives	To communicate evaluation; to persuade employee to improve	To communicate evaluation; to release defensive feelings	To stimulate growth and development of employee
Role of Interviewer	Judge	Judge	Helper
Perspective of Interviewer	People profit from criticism and appreciate help	One can respect the feelings of others if one understands them	Discussion develops new ideas and mutual interests
Skills of Interviewer	Salesmanship; patience	Listening; summarizing	Listening; summarizing; questioning
Reactions of Employee	Suppresses defensive behavior; attempts to cover hostility	Expresses defensive behavior; feels accepted	Problem-solving
Possible Gains	Success most probable when employee respects interviewer	Employee develops favorable attitude toward interviewer	Almost assured of improvement in some respect
Risks of Interviewer	Loss of loyalty; inhibition of independent judgment; face-saving problems	Need for change may not be developed	Employee may lack ideas; change may be other than what the manager wants
Probable Outcomes	Perpetuates existing practices and values	Permits interviewer to change views in light of employee's response	Both learn, because experience is pooled; change is facilitated

Adaptation of Norman R. F. Maier, *The Appraisal Interview: Three Basic Approaches*, San Diego, CA: University Associates, Inc., 1976. Used with permission.

Problem-Solving. In the problem-solving interview, the manager is actually less passive than in the tell and listen approach. However, he or she will have to apply all the listening techniques of tell and listen. The difference is that the manager acknowledges that the employee's inputs are vital to the evaluation. Moreover, to use problem solving, the manager must recognize that critical impediments in the way of employee performance can only be removed if both the manager and employee work in close cooperation with each other. Put another way, the manager must be convinced that higher performance may result only from a mutual give and take with the subordinate.

Table 3
Communication Climates in Appraisal Interviews

Communication Climate That Produces Defensiveness	General Principle	Communication Climate That Produces Supportiveness
Evaluation	Messages that judge the subordinate increase defensiveness	Description
Control	Messages that accuse and control increase defensiveness	Problem Orientation
Strategy	Messages suggesting manipulation and hidden agendas increase defensiveness	Spontaneity
Neutrality	Messages conveying a lack of concern increase defensiveness	Empathy
Superiority	Messages that are condescending increase defensiveness	Equality
Certainty	Messages suggesting dogmatism increase defensiveness	Provisionalism

From "Defensive Communication" by Jack Gibb in *Journal of Communication*, Vol. 11, No. 3, 1961. Copyright © 1961 by the International Communication Association. Reprinted by permission.

Problem solving is a technique that is appropriate only when there is a real climate of trust between superior and subordinate. The power differences between them should be modest; i.e., both should view each other more as colleagues than unequals. However, the gains in using problem-solving can be remarkable. This approach combines all the advantages of the tell and listen approach with the extra bonus of total cooperation as opposed to happy compliance.

Discussing Wage and Salary Issues During the Interview

Whether one chooses tell and sell, tell and listen, or problem-solving, there remain several other areas of concern in conducting appraisal interviews. For one, there is the question of whether to discuss salary issues during the interview. One important purpose of performance appraisal is to assure that merit pay adjustments reflect performance levels. So it is only natural for a manager to discuss the relation between an employee's performance rating and the additional wages he or she might expect for the following year. However, this practice has been shown to be inconsistent with both the tell and listen approach and the problem-solving approach. Bringing up salary issues tends to arouse a great deal of anxiety, so much so that two-way communication is thwarted. Accordingly, salary discussions are appropriate only if the format chosen is tell and sell.

Discussing Career Issues During the Interview

Another issue concerns discussing the career interests and motivations of the individual being appraised. Many managers feel that the performance appraisal session is a good opportunity to do career counseling. The individual's performance may be examined in the context of the person's career plans and aspirations. Is he or she on track, are there other positions that the employee wants to move into next, and does the employee want to expand his or her skills in some way? Typically, such discussions thrive in a climate of openness and mutual trust. Accordingly, it may be more appropriate to engage in career discussions in a tell and listen or problem-solving format than in tell and sell.

Discussing the Impediments to Higher Employee Performance

Any time an employee's performance is below potential, it is generally helpful to explore the reasons for this. Ideally this should be done on a regular basis and not reserved strictly for the appraisal interview. Nonetheless, many managers prefer to spend time during the interview trying to figure out why the person is not doing better, if that is the case. The tone of this part of the interview varies with the format chosen. In tell and sell, the manager is not as likely to rely on employee inputs in determining just what the impediments to higher performance might be. In tell and listen and problem solving, more employee input is solicited.

Whatever format is used, effective managers realize that there are some instances when they are the performance impediment. For example, a manager may have given incorrect directions, misinterpreted a policy, or provided inadequate training. Of course managers are not to blame for all performance problems, but standards of fairness dictate that when poor performance results wholly or in part because of incomplete or incorrect supervision, the employee should not have to suffer inequitable ratings. Accordingly, some attention should always be focused on the obstacles to higher performance.

Action Planning

In cases where present levels of performance need improvement, a manager should negotiate some sort of an action plan with the subordinate regarding what will be done about that performance deficiency in the future. This usually comes at the later stages of the appraisal interview, often after the summary evaluation has been given. Experts suggest that in order to have the best impact, action plans need to be (a) specific rather than vague, (b) written rather than oral, and (c) developed participatively rather than imposed by the manager.

Action plans are the result of "contract counseling." The employee agrees to practice a certain desired behavior, and the manager agrees to provide assistance. The specific steps involved are as follows:

(1) The two parties agree to an assessment that some specific aspect of work behavior or outcomes needs improvement.
(2) A plan is developed participatively for correcting the problem that involves specific things the manager will do and specific things the employee will do.
(3) This plan is documented in writing and signed by both parties.
(4) The progress on the plan is monitored by both parties to it.

Since action plans are ideally participative enterprises, it is much easier to engage in action planning following a tell and listen or problem-solving appraisal session than a tell and sell approach. Tell and sell interviews involve one-way communication, so few subordinates will be in the mood for participation following them. Therefore, we recommend that action planning not be conducted as part of a tell and sell session. Rather, at the close of a tell and sell interview, a manager should schedule a second meeting no more than a day or two later, when action planning is on the agenda. This way the employee will have had time to digest the evaluation he or she has received and to be better prepared for the participation that is really crucial to the development of an effective action plan.

Opening and Closing the Interview

The two remaining issues deal more with the specific details of appraisal interviews than with their planning: how to open the interview and how to close it. Opening an appraisal interview may seem to be a rather trivial consideration, but it is not. It is vital for a manager to begin on a note that communicates expectations for the encounter in such a way that the person interviewed is put at ease. We have already mentioned how important the interview setting is, but it is also important to say the right thing at the outset. While we are reluctant to provide a specific script, several general guidelines might be helpful. First, it is better to frame the meeting as a help session rather than an evaluation setting. Second, it is preferable to make clear just what amount of participation and involvement the manager wants from the subordinate in the session. And third, it is usually helpful to acknowledge the tension likely to be felt by both participants.

The close of the interview is equally important. An effort should be made to summarize the proceedings and to thank the employee for whatever contribution he or she has made. Most critically, the manager should make very clear what follow-up actions can be expected both on the part of the manager and the employee. For example, if the level of output is a problem, the manager should be explicit how he or she intends to monitor this measure in the future and what level of output is going to be viewed as satisfactory.

Conclusion

Performance appraisal is by no means a simple undertaking. There are a number of choices a manager has to make, many of them consequential. Managers must be careful to use measures that correctly reflect performance. They need to plan the appraisal interview carefully, from its place and time all the way to the selection of the sort of feedback to provide. Once in the interview, other choices have to be made. Managers need to define some level of involvement on the part of the employee and must be very sensitive about communicating feedback correctly.

References

Bassett, G. A., and H. H. Meyer. "Performance Appraisal--A Survey of Current Practices." *Personnel Journal* 56 (1977): 2-14.

Burke, R. J., and D. S. Wilcox. "Characteristics of Effective Employee Performance Review and Development Interviews." *Personnel Psychology* 22 (1969): 291-305.

Cummings, L. L., and D. P. Schwab. *Performance in Organizations: Determinants and Appraisal*. Glenview, Ill.: Scott, Foresman and Company, 1973.

Cummings, L. L., and D. P. Schwab. "Designing Appraisal Systems for Information Yield." *California Management Review* 20 (1978): 18-25.

Greller, M. M. "Performance Appraisal: Dilemmas and Possibilities." *Organizational Dynamics* 5 (1981): 29-39.

Guion, R. M. *Personnel Testing*. New York: McGraw-Hill, 1965.

Holley, W. H., and H. S. Field. "Performance Appraisal and the Law." *Labor Law Journal* 29 (1976): 278-286.

Keeley, M. A. "A Contingency Framework for Performance Evaluation." *Academy of Management Review* 3 (1978): 428-438.

McGregor, D. "An Uneasy Look at Performance Appraisal." *Harvard Business Review* 35 (1957): 89-94.

Meyer, H. H., E. Kay, and J. R. P. French, Jr. "Split Roles in Performance Appraisal." *Harvard Business Review* 54 (1965): 123-129.

Oberg, W. "Making Performance Appraisal Relevant." *Harvard Business Review* 50 (1972): 61-67.

Odiorne, G. S. *Management by Objectives*. New York: Pittman, 1965.

Sperry, L., and L. R. Hess. *Contract Counseling*. Reading, Mass.: Addison-Wesley, 1974.

Interactive Case

You work for Epsilon, Inc., a wholly owned subsidiary of a Fortune 500 conglomerate. Epsilon produces minicomputers for industrial and commercial applications. Last year 80 percent of Epsilon's sales were from a fully integrated product line, and 20 percent of its sales were from customized equipment. You work in the Industrial Products Division of Epsilon, a division composed entirely of customized applications.

Your title is Manager, Ajax Project. You supervise the efforts of 17 people working on a project that is to deliver a series of minicomputers to a governmental contractor. The project began two years ago and is not expected to scale down for at least three more years. At that time, the contracts will either be renewed or the project personnel will be reassigned to other projects or divisions. Since Epsilon is presently growing at a rapid rate, there is no fear among project personnel that the ending of Ajax will affect their security with the firm.

Each year you are expected to formally appraise the five exempt people who report directly to you. You have completed the appraisals of all your people except your administrative assistant, Ms. Betty Young. This action case regards your appraisal of Ms. Young.

Performance appraisals at Epsilon serve several important purposes. First, they are to be truly "developmental opportunities." Managers are expected to devote a considerable amount of time and effort to the development of each of their people, and the appraisal is seen as an important part of the developmental process. Part of the appraisal interview is expected to focus on specifying the directions for employee development, and a form is to be filled out indicating mutually agreed-upon developmental goals for the upcoming year.

A second purpose of performance appraisal at Epsilon is to recognize and reward high performers. In that spirit, the appraisal form filled out by the supervisor includes five summary categories: outstanding, excellent, good, fair, and poor. Next year these summary categories will relate to merit pay adjustments are shown in Table 1.

Since you have already completed your initial assessment of Betty's performance including a tentative summary evaluation of "excellent," your immediate task is to determine a list of three strong points and two weak points to feed back to her during the appraisal interview. This requirement of three positive points and two negative points may strike you as a bit arbitrary. However, evidence indicates that that is the maximum number of different pieces of information a person in a situation like this is likely to act upon. In essence, then, your assignment is to distill the performance data you have about Betty into information you and she will be able to act upon during your performance appraisal interview with her. As part of her job, Betty does typing, clerical, and administrative work for the professionals in the Ajax Project. Accordingly, it is your practice to ask that each of these people fills out a performance appraisal document on Betty. In addition, since your development plan last year called for Betty to receive guidance from Alice Wilson, an administrative assistant in another project, you also asked her to fill one out.

Table 1
Relation Between Evaluation and Merit Pay

Summary Evaluation	Merit Pay Over and Above Cost of Living Adjustment
Outstanding*	4%
Excellent	2.5%
Good	1%
Fair	0%
Poor	N/A

*Only two "outstanding" ratings may be given to administrative assistants per division. Therefore, this rating can not be given without the approval of Mike Wagner, your boss.

In total, then, you have a rather large data bank of performance information on Betty (provided on the next few pages). A table of contents for this data bank is provided below:

p. 81 - An organization chart,
p. 82 - A brief description of the people involved,
p. 83 - Your evaluation of Betty's performance filled out one year ago,
p. 84 - The developmental plan you and Betty agreed to one year ago,
p. 85 - A job description of Betty's position,
p. 86 - Your evaluation of Betty's present performance,
p. 87 - Additional critical incidents and outcomes of developmental efforts,
p. 89 - An appraisal form on Betty filled out by John Jensen,
p. 90 - An appraisal form on Betty filled out by Homer Ashe,
p. 91 - An appraisal form on Betty filled out by Milt Strong,
p. 92 - An appraisal form on Betty filled out by Barbara Mann,
p. 93 - An appraisal form on Betty filled out by Alice Wilson,
p. 94 - A memo from the Systems Analysis Group on the word processing problem.

Please inspect these documents before you go on with this case.

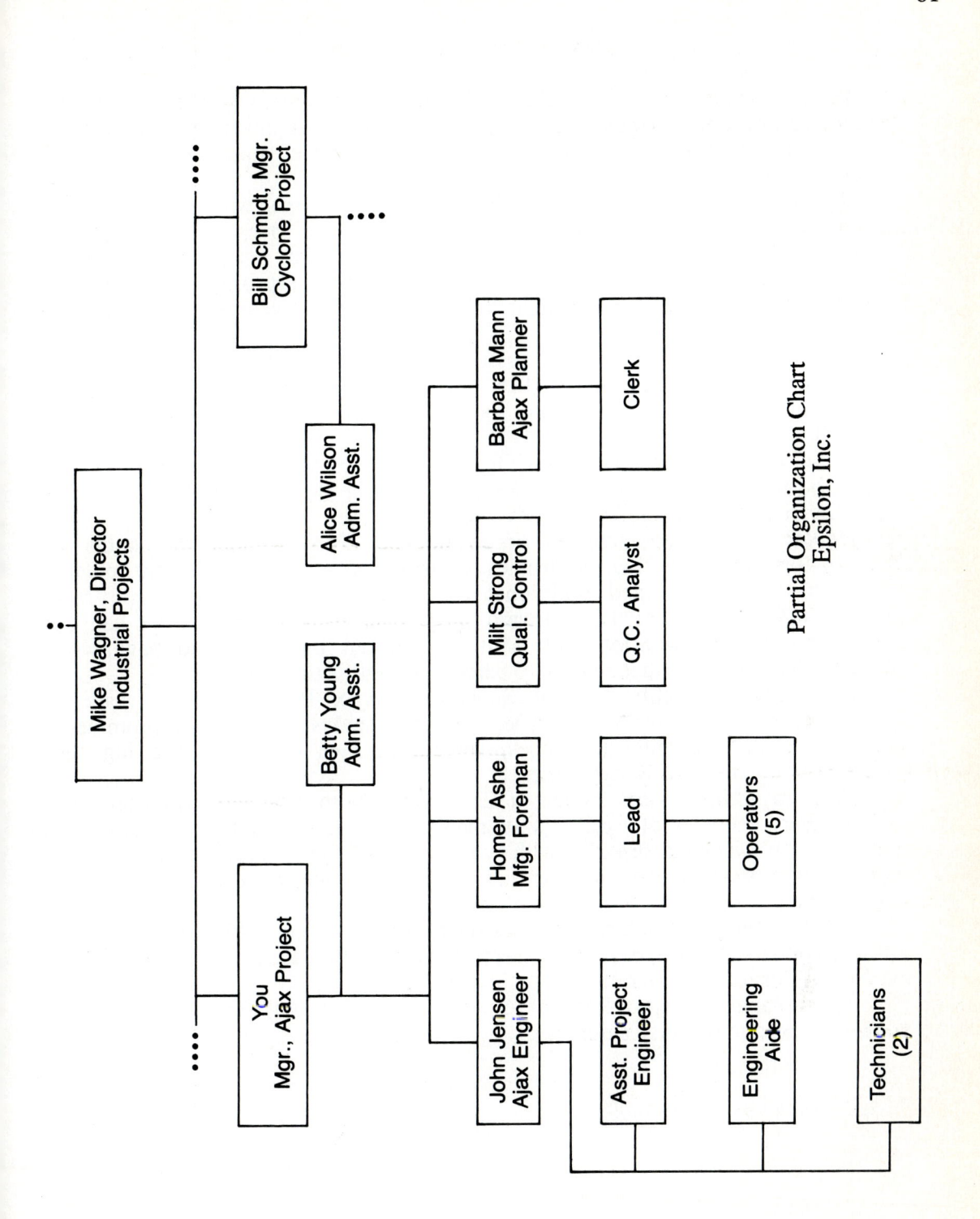

Partial Organization Chart
Epsilon, Inc.

- **Mike Wagner, Director Industrial Projects**
  - **Bill Schmidt, Mgr. Cyclone Project**
    - Alice Wilson, Adm. Asst.
  - **You, Mgr., Ajax Project**
    - Betty Young, Adm. Asst.
    - **John Jensen, Ajax Engineer**
      - Asst. Project Engineer
      - Engineering Aide
      - Technicians (2)
    - **Homer Ashe, Mfg. Foreman**
      - Lead
      - Operators (5)
    - **Milt Strong, Qual. Control**
      - Q.C. Analyst
    - **Barbara Mann, Ajax Planner**
      - Clerk

81

Description of the Characters

Mike Wagner, Director, Industrial Projects Division (49, 8 years with Epsilon)--competent, evenhanded, highly respected administrator. Most agree that he will be promoted in the next year or so. He supervises six different projects including Ajax and Cyclone.

Bill Schmidt, Manager, Cyclone Project (57, 11 years with Epsilon)--absent-minded professor type, has PhD from Cal Tech, and he loves ideas; he agreed to manage Cyclone on the condition that he could handpick his people, and he has assembled a group of oddball characters who work surprisingly well together. Mike Wagner has taken over client relations on the Cyclone Project to allow Bill to "tend the zoo," as Bill puts it.

Alice Wilson, Administrative Assistant, Cyclone Project (50, 4 years with Epsilon)--unflappable, cool under fire, diplomatic, slick, a bit distant; the real manager of Cyclone. She may be too indispensible at Epsilon to satisfy her ambitions.

John Jensen, Engineer, Ajax Project (39, 5 years with Epsilon)--solid, logical, businesslike, thinks a lot like you do. The log shows that he uses 20 percent of Betty's time.

Homer Ashe, Manufacturing Foreman, Ajax Project (52, 10 months with Epsilon)--formerly with the electronics division of a farm implement manufacturer. Very methodical and traditional as a supervisor, but his people respect him. He tends to be defensive toward people outside the project; he had some difficulties early on working with Milt Strong, but that seems to have worked itself out. The log shows that he uses 10 percent of Betty's time.

Milt Strong, Quality Control Supervisor, Ajax Project (31, 5 years with Epsilon)--ambitious, eager-beaver type, excellent analyst whom you promoted 15 months ago. Still learning the ropes, sometimes tries too hard. The log shows that he uses 35 percent of Betty's time.

Barbara Mann, Ajax Planner (32, 2 years with Epsilon)--competent, good with numbers, member of Epsilon's Women's Club; you want her to develop more confidence in working directly with your client. Highly promotable if she has another good year. Since she has her own clerk, she only uses 5 percent of Betty's time.

Betty Young, Administrative Assistant, Ajax Project (49, 21 months with Epsilon)--previously worked as a secretary with the local phone company; a member of Epsilon's Women's Club.

You, Manager, Ajax Project (6 years with Epsilon)--The log shows that you use 30 percent of Betty's time.

83

Employee Performance Appraisal
(Salary Grade 3-6)

Employee: _Betty Young_   Department: _Ajax_
Appraiser: _You_   Date: _5/16/ last year_

Check the space that indicates how typical each statement is of the employee's behavior on the job.	Very Typical	Somewhat Typical	Not at all Typical
1. Does a high quality job	✓		
2. Produces a large volume of work	✓		
3. Cooperates and gets along with fellow employees	✓		
4. Asks questions when uncertain	✓		
5. Does *not* engage in disruptive or unproductive behaviors such as complaining, carrying on long personal conversations or wandering around	✓		
6. Knows the procedures involved in the job and organization		✓	
7. Willingly carries out unusual or unpleasant duties when necessary	✓		
8. Catches the mistakes of others and takes notice of important details			✓
9. Looks for better ways to do the job	✓		
10. Is well versed in technical terminology	✓		
11. Uses accurate grammar and spelling	✓		
12. Is rarely avsent or tardy without reason	✓		
13. Understands how the department relates to other departments		✓	
14. Handles multiple demands on time fairly and effectively	✓		
15. Handles pressure well; meets deadlines	✓		
16. Is courteous in dealings with clients and others outside the department	✓		
17. Cares for and maintains equipment	✓		
18. Keeps confidences and respects the secrecy of competitive information	✓		
19. "Catches on" quickly	✓		
20. Organizes information well; is good at analyzing things	✓		

Briefly describe any critical incidents that you think illustrate important descriptors.

Very high output (see log). Missed important error on quality control document.

Overall Rating:
Outstanding: _____ Excellent: _✓_ Good: _____ Fair: _____ Poor: _____

Employee Development Plan

Instructions: Epsilon is committed to the development of every employee. Each year every employee is asked to meet with his or her immediate supervisor to agree on a plan that will guide the development of important job-related skills. Working together, the employee and supervisor should meet annually to identify those aspects of the employee's performance that deserve attention and to work out a method for improvement. Generally this should involve mutual commitments. The employee should commit to improve on *at least two elements* of job-related behaviors (as specified on the Employee Performance Appraisal Form). The supervisor should commit to *help* the employee *in whatever way feasible* to assure that a reasonable and reliable effort on the employee's part will result in performance improvements.

Actions the Employee Agrees to Take to Improve Performance Components (should be keyed to the Appraisal Form):

#6 - I agree to study the procedures manual to become better aware of the procedures of the Company as they relate to my job.

#8 - I agree to proof read every document I type and to be more vigilant to errors in the originals I am given.

#13 - I agree to devote at least 3 hours a month to becoming more familiar with the operations of other departments in the Company as they relate to the Ajax Project.

Actions the Supervisor Agrees to Take to Facilitate Employee Development Efforts:

#6 - I will personally contact the Personnel Department and ask that Betty receives their help in getting all the necessary procedures manuals and sample forms. I will go over departmental policies with her sometime this month.

#8 - I will ask members of the Ajax Project to be more careful to submit errorfree originals for typing.

#13 - I will introduce Betty to at least two other project managers and ask them to familiarize her with the operations of their departments.

Employee Signature: *Betty Young*   Date: 5/16

Supervisor Signature: *You*   Date: 5/16

Job Description

Administrative Assistant, Industrial Products Division

Job Title: Administrative Assistant
Classification: Full-time, exempt
Salary Grade: 4E

Job Duties:

1. Provides secretarial support to the project manager and team members such as, but not exclusive to,
    a) typing documents and reports including technical and statistical documents;
    b) maintaining filing systems as required by the project.

2. Provides administrative support to the project manager(s) such as, but not exclusive to,
    a) requisitioning and distributing supplies;
    b) maintaining project scheduling records and time budgets;
    c) maintaining records for any parttime or temporary employees;
    d) coordinating project efforts with other group as required.

Requirements:

1. A high school diploma or equivalent.
2. Two years progressively responsible secretarial or clerical experience.
3. Typing skill of 60 words per minute.

Employee Performance Appraisal
(Salary Grade 3-6)

Employee: *Betty Young*   Department: *Ajax*
Appraiser: *You*   Date: *5/19/ this year*

Check the space that indicates how typical each statement is of the employee's behavior on the job.

	Very Typical	Somewhat Typical	Not at all Typical
1. Does a high quality job	✓		
2. Produces a large volume of work	✓		
③ Cooperates and gets along with fellow employees		✓	
4. Asks questions when uncertain	✓		
⑤ Does *not* engage in disruptive or unproductive behaviors such as complaining, carrying on long personal conversations or wandering around		✓	
6. Knows the procedures involved in the job and organization	✓		
7. Willingly carries out unusual or unpleasant duties when necessary	✓		
8. Catches the mistakes of others and takes notice of important details	✓		
9. Looks for better ways to do the job	✓		
10. Is well versed in technical terminology	✓		
11. Uses accurate grammar and spelling	✓		
12. Is rarely avsent or tardy without reason	✓		
13. Understands how the department relates to other departments	✓		
⑭ Handles multiple demands on time fairly and effectively		✓	
15. Handles pressure well; meets deadlines	✓		
⑯ Is courteous in dealings with clients and others outside the department			✓
17. Cares for and maintains equipment	✓		
18. Keeps confidences and respects the secrecy of competitive information	✓		
19. "Catches on" quickly	✓		
20. Organizes information well; is good at analyzing things	✓		

Briefly describe any critical incidents that you think illustrate important descriptors.

None yet

Overall Rating:
Outstanding: _____ Excellent: ✓ *(?)* Good: _____ Fair: _____ Poor: _____

Additional Critical Incidents
and Outcomes of Developmental Efforts

1. *Betty's Reactions to Last Year's Appraisal*

When you gave Betty her performance appraisal interview last year, she was surprised and alarmed. Since she had only been with the company for slightly less than a year, she knew she still had some procedures to learn, but the feedback about missing details and not catching others' mistakes really threw her. At first she blamed others in the department for giving her sloppy work to type, things to file without proper codes, and phone messages to return without adequate instructions. But when you showed her two concrete examples of how errors and details she missed caused difficulties (especially for Milt Strong), she agreed to do better. Your evaluation of her lack of knowledge about procedures and the relationship between Ajax and other departments was admittedly harsh. You firmly believe, however, that Ajax is simply too dependent on the goodwill it has in other parts of the organization to have it jeopardized by an administrative assistant who doesn't follow procedures or who isn't very diplomatic. In this regard, you wanted Betty to get to know Alice Wilson in the Cyclone Project. Cyclone is staffed by a group of oddballs and mavericks who are constantly in trouble with the company bureaucracy. Alice handles such problems brilliantly.

2. *The Ongoing Word Processing Problem*

Four months ago, the Systems Analysis Group announced that all departmental administrative assistants should interface into the company-wide word processing system. This really excited Betty, who was eager to streamline her typing of technical reports, production schedules, forecasts, and control documents. She followed through by attending half-day seminars, taking system documentation home to study, and practicing at the new office terminal. The "bugs" in the system continue to make it unworkable for the most part. In spite of what appears to you to be effort "above and beyond the call of duty" on Betty's part, documents have been lost, reports have been misfiled in system storage, and a statistical analysis was formatted so unprofessionally that it was criticized by corporate-level quality control people.

Although you are reluctant to blame these problems on Betty, she is obviously not handling the frustrations caused by these systems problems. Two weeks ago she raised her voice to a contract auditor who interrupted her while she was trying unsuccessfully to retrieve a document from systems storage. On another occasion, you heard through the grapevine that she had gone "over the head" of a systems analyst to complain about the lack of service she was receiving. Finally, Barbara Mann told you last week that Betty had been spending a lot of time complaining about the word processing system. Her clerk also complained to you that Betty was taking up a lot of her time "harping" about the computer system.

3. *Productivity*

The people in Ajax have always considered Betty a very fast worker. You were concerned that she did not cut her speed this year in an attempt to be more careful about picking up details or the mistakes of others. You have been pleased to note that after comparing last year's log to this year's, she has turned out just as many documents this year as last year. Moreover, you have noted on two occasions that she has caught mistakes you made. In one case you went to a meeting with the wrong file folder, and she brought you the correct one just before you were to make an important presentation to a client. The second case involved a proposal you had planned to send to your boss appealing for a budget adjustment. She apparently had discovered data from her interviews with Alice Wilson that had benefited your case more than you had at the time.

4. *Complaint from Milt Strong*

Milt Strong complained a year and a half ago about Betty's performance. Apparently she missed an obvious decimal point error in a technical report that caused some equipment to be reworked after it had actually passed inspection. Milt Strong has not talked to Betty for a month following this error, and to date has still not gotten over the problem. Now that a quality control report was criticized by corporate people due to a word processing problem, Milt is still angry.

Employee Performance Appraisal
(Salary Grade 3-6)

Employee: **Betty** Department: **Ajax**
Appraiser: **John Jensen** Date: **5/13/this year**

Check the space that indicates how typical each statement is of the employee's behavior on the job.

Statement	Very Typical	Somewhat Typical	Not at all Typical
①. Does a high quality job		X	
2. Produces a large volume of work	X		
③. Cooperates and gets along with fellow employees		X	
4. Asks questions when uncertain	X		
⑤. Does *not* engage in disruptive or unproductive behaviors such as complaining, carrying on long personal conversations or wandering around		X	
6. Knows the procedures involved in the job and organization	X		
7. Willingly carries out unusual or unpleasant duties when necessary	X		
⑧. Catches the mistakes of others and takes notice of important details		X	
9. Looks for better ways to do the job	X		
10. Is well versed in technical terminology	X		
11. Uses accurate grammar and spelling	X		
12. Is rarely avsent or tardy without reason	X		
13. Understands how the department relates to other departments	X		
14. Handles multiple demands on time fairly and effectively	X		
15. Handles pressure well; meets deadlines	X		
⑯. Is courteous in dealings with clients and others outside the department		X	
17. Cares for and maintains equipment	X		
18. Keeps confidences and respects the secrecy of competitive information	X		
19. "Catches on" quickly	X		
20. Organizes information well; is good at analyzing things	X		

Briefly describe any critical incidents that you think illustrate important descriptors.

Betty has made great progress this year. She knows the company well now. Her leg work on getting us new office furniture and fixtures for our P.C.'s was extraordinarily helpful. The bureaucracy around here astounds me! JJ

Overall Rating:
Outstanding:_____ Excellent: **X** Good:_____ Fair:_____ Poor:_____

Employee Performance Appraisal
(Salary Grade 3-6)

Employee: _Betty_ Department: _Acc_
Appraiser: _Homer Ashe_ Date: _May 20_

Check the space that indicates how typical each statement is of the employee's behavior on the job.	Very Typical	Somewhat Typical	Not at all Typical
1. Does a high quality job	✓		
2. Produces a large volume of work	✓		
3. Cooperates and gets along with fellow employees	✓		
4. Asks questions when uncertain	✓		
5. Does *not* engage in disruptive or unproductive behaviors such as complaining, carrying on long personal conversations or wandering around	✓		
6. Knows the procedures involved in the job and organization	✓		
7. Willingly carries out unusual or unpleasant duties when necessary	✓		
8. Catches the mistakes of others and takes notice of important details	✓		
9. Looks for better ways to do the job	✓		
10. Is well versed in technical terminology	✓		
11. Uses accurate grammar and spelling	✓		
12. Is rarely avsent or tardy without reason	✓		
13. Understands how the department relates to other departments	✓		
14. Handles multiple demands on time fairly and effectively	✓		
15. Handles pressure well; meets deadlines	✓		
16. Is courteous in dealings with clients and others outside the department	✓		
17. Cares for and maintains equipment	✓		
18. Keeps confidences and respects the secrecy of competitive information	✓		
19. "Catches on" quickly	✓		
20. Organizes information well; is good at analyzing things	✓		

Briefly describe any critical incidents that you think illustrate important descriptors.

She sticks up for the project! Very loyal!

Overall Rating:
Outstanding: ✓   Excellent: ___   Good: ___   Fair: ___   Poor: ___

Employee Performance Appraisal
(Salary Grade 3-6)

Employee: _Mrs Young_   Department: _Ajax_
Appraiser: _Milt Strong_   Date: _11 May_

Check the space that indicates how typical each statement is of the employee's behavior on the job.	Very Typical	Somewhat Typical	Not at all Typical
1. Does a high quality job			✓
2. Produces a large volume of work		✓	
3. Cooperates and gets along with fellow employees		✓	
4. Asks questions when uncertain			✓
5. Does *not* engage in disruptive or unproductive behaviors such as complaining, carrying on long personal conversations or wandering around		✓	
6. Knows the procedures involved in the job and organization		✓	
7. Willingly carries out unusual or unpleasant duties when necessary		✓	
8. Catches the mistakes of others and takes notice of important details			✓!
9. Looks for better ways to do the job		✓	
10. Is well versed in technical terminology		✓	
11. Uses accurate grammar and spelling		✓	
12. Is rarely avsent or tardy without reason		✓	
13. Understands how the department relates to other departments		✓	
14. Handles multiple demands on time fairly and effectively		✓	
15. Handles pressure well; meets deadlines		✓	
16. Is courteous in dealings with clients and others outside the department		✓	
17. Cares for and maintains equipment		✓	
18. Keeps confidences and respects the secrecy of competitive information		✓	
19. "Catches on" quickly			✓
20. Organizes information well; is good at analyzing things		✓	

Briefly describe any critical incidents that you think illustrate important descriptors.

Mrs. Young's errors continue to cause problems for me. The incorrect formatting on the report was appalling and unforgiveable!

Overall Rating:
Outstanding: ____   Excellent: ____   Good: ____   Fair: ✓   Poor: ____

Employee Performance Appraisal
(Salary Grade 3-6)

Employee: __BETTY YOUNG__   Department: __AJAX__
Appraiser: __BARBARA MANN__   Date: __MAY 13__

Check the space that indicates how typical each statement is of the employee's behavior on the job.

	Very Typical	Somewhat Typical	Not at all Typical
1. Does a high quality job	YES		
2. Produces a large volume of work	YES		
3. Cooperates and gets along with fellow employees		YES	
4. Asks questions when uncertain	YES		
5. Does *not* engage in disruptive or unproductive behaviors such as complaining, carrying on long personal conversations or wandering around		YES	
6. Knows the procedures involved in the job and organization	YES		
7. Willingly carries out unusual or unpleasant duties when necessary	YES		
8. Catches the mistakes of others and takes notice of important details	YES		
9. Looks for better ways to do the job	YES		
10. Is well versed in technical terminology	YES		
11. Uses accurate grammar and spelling	YES		
12. Is rarely avsent or tardy without reason	YES		
13. Understands how the department relates to other departments	YES		
14. Handles multiple demands on time fairly and effectively	YES		
15. Handles pressure well; meets deadlines	YES		
16. Is courteous in dealings with clients and others outside the department		YES	
17. Cares for and maintains equipment	YES		
18. Keeps confidences and respects the secrecy of competitive information	YES		
19. "Catches on" quickly	YES		
20. Organizes information well; is good at analyzing things	YES		

Briefly describe any critical incidents that you think illustrate important descriptors.

WHEN FRUSTRATED, BETTY LIKES TO COMPLAIN TO MY ASSISTANT. SHE'S BEEN VERY FRUSTRATED BY THE COMPUTER BUT HER COMPLAINING HAS BECOME DISRUPTIVE

Overall Rating:
Outstanding:_____ Excellent: __YES__ Good:_____ Fair:_____ Poor:_____

Employee Performance Appraisal
(Salary Grade 3-6)

Employee: _Mrs. Young_   Department: _Ajax_
Appraiser: _Mrs. Wilson_   Date: _May 10_

Check the space that indicates how typical each statement is of the employee's behavior on the job.	Very Typical	Somewhat Typical	Not at all Typical
1. Does a high quality job		✓	
2. Produces a large volume of work		✓	
3. Cooperates and gets along with fellow employees		✓	
4. Asks questions when uncertain		✓	
5. Does *not* engage in disruptive or unproductive behaviors such as complaining, carrying on long personal conversations or wandering around		✓	
6. Knows the procedures involved in the job and organization			✓
7. Willingly carries out unusual or unpleasant duties when necessary		✓	
8. Catches the mistakes of others and takes notice of important details		✓	
9. Looks for better ways to do the job		✓	
10. Is well versed in technical terminology			✓
11. Uses accurate grammar and spelling		✓	
12. Is rarely avsent or tardy without reason		✓	
13. Understands how the department relates to other departments			✓
14. Handles multiple demands on time fairly and effectively		✓	
15. Handles pressure well; meets deadlines		✓	
16. Is courteous in dealings with clients and others outside the department		✓	
17. Cares for and maintains equipment		✓	
18. Keeps confidences and respects the secrecy of competitive information		✓	
19. "Catches on" quickly			✓
20. Organizes information well; is good at analyzing things		✓	

Briefly describe any critical incidents that you think illustrate important descriptors.

I would rate Mrs. Young as below average in intelligence. I question whether Epsilon should hire people "below average."

Overall Rating:
Outstanding: ____ Excellent: ____ Good: _✓_ Fair: ____ Poor: ____

MEMORANDUM

TO: You
FR: Larry Famingdale, Manager, Systems Analysis Group
RE: Word Processing Problem

Three months ago last Thursday we sent out a memo inviting administrative assistants in the Industrial Products Division to interface with our new Software Package. This package has proved to be a significant tool for enhancing the productivity of secretarial/clerical people in the Instruments Division, and we wanted to offer the service to your division.

Unfortunately, a number of problems arose in the implementation of the package that we did not anticipate. Most notably, the administrative assistants in your division lacked word processing experience. Thus, we were faced with the necessity of training beyond our capacity to train. In a memo dated 12 days ago, we thus advised all assistants to cease and desist using the system except for experimental purposes. This later memo was necessitated by a complaint arising from corporate level regarding a quality control document that was incorrectly formatted. After investigating this incident, it is our conclusion that the software package, as presently constituted, is not amenable to this type of use, and we have thus changed the existing documentation.

We hope the problems we have had in getting the software package in line with the Industrial Products Division have not inconvenienced you. You may rest assured that we intend for these problems to be ironed out in the future.

95

Now that you have completed the review, which of the following are negative elements of Betty's performance that you should provide for her during the appraisal interview?

A. Betty is apparently careless. (GO TO 379B)

B. Betty often complains to others instead of problem solving with you. (GO TO 324B)

C. Betty doesn't use adequate diplomacy when dealing with clients. (GO TO 416A)

D. Betty is insensitive to the impact she has on others. (GO TO 356A)

E. Betty lacks attentiveness to details. (GO TO 378A)

F. Betty makes too many mistakes. (GO TO 414C)

G. Betty isn't smart enough to catch on quickly. (GO TO 393A)

H. Betty went over the head of a systems analyst to complain about the service she was getting--a violation of protocol. (GO TO 421C)

6 MANAGING WORK TEAMS
Module Reading

Most of us have very mixed feelings when we have to work on committees, task forces, and other teams. Sometimes they are a total waste of time; other times, incredibly effective. These conflicting experiences with groups are even reflected in recognizable sayings. We all know that "two heads are better than one." But we all have seen instances where "too many cooks spoil the broth."

These mixed feelings carry over into the decisions managers make about dealing with subordinates. At various times all managers have had teams that were highly productive. As well, most have been responsible for teams that found it difficult to accomplish even the simplest tasks. The purpose of this chapter is to lay out a set of actions a manager can take to improve the *performance* of a team of subordinates. We have little to say about the personalities of individual team members. Rather, we will consider the subordinates *as a group*. The actions we will describe are based on some very sound principles about work teams and begin with a diagnosis of the group in question.

Group Cohesiveness

The diagnosis begins with the manager attempting to gauge the cohesiveness of the group. Cohesiveness refers to how much group members like each other and how much they value their group membership. In highly cohesive groups there is an intangible sense of goodwill and team spirit. Some call it "esprit de corps." Members of these groups enjoy one another's company and consider the chance to work with their co-workers an important source of personal satisfaction. In less cohesive groups, this attraction is missing, and group members don't seem to value their membership on the team as highly. Instead of viewing other team members as friends or colleagues, they are seen as "people they *have to* work with." In extreme cases, individuals lack respect for their co-workers and may even be outwardly hostile toward them. Yet, overtly conflict-ridden groups are fairly rare; when we talk about groups with low cohesiveness, we generally mean those made up of persons who are outwardly indifferent rather than hostile toward one another.

Characteristics of Groups with High and Low Cohesiveness

Highly cohesive work groups have the following characteristics:

(1) Group members have a strong, positive regard for one another.
(2) Much of each employee's loyalty to the organization is due to group loyalty. A sense of team pride is apparent.

(3) There is very little apparent conflict on the team.
(4) Group members cooperate with each other voluntarily (the manager does not have to provide any special incentives to get team members to pull together).
(5) The way members of the group interact does not change much over time (the influence of informal leaders is quite stable).

A quite different set of characteristics is seen in work groups that have low levels of cohesiveness:

(1) Team members of the group feel either indifferently or negatively toward one another.
(2) Little of each employee's loyalty to the organization is the result of group loyalty (there is very little sense of team pride).
(3) The group has relatively high levels of conflict (even if this conflict is not openly expressed, members are likely to feel it).
(4) Cooperation between group members occurs only when the manager insists on it or when incentives require it.
(5) The way members interact varies greatly over time (informal relations shift; no one holds the respect of his fellows very long).

Is Cohesiveness Desirable?

Not surprisingly, members of highly cohesive groups are happier at work and have higher morale than people in work groups with low cohesiveness. So if given the choice, employees would certainly prefer working in a cohesive work group. For the organization, though, the effects of cohesiveness are not as positive. As surprising as it might seem at this point, work groups with high cohesiveness perform no better on average than those with low levels of cohesiveness. It is true that people in cohesive groups are more cooperative, but they simply can't be counted upon to cooperate in ways that are truly beneficial to the organization.

This is not to say that cohesiveness has no effect on performance whatsoever. Actually it does, but its effect is primarily on the *range* of individual performance in a group, not the overall performance of the group itself. Individuals in highly cohesive groups are more likely to perform at about the same level, be it high or low, than are individuals in less cohesive groups. In contrast, people in groups with low cohesiveness perform at different levels; some perform much higher than their fellow group members and some much lower. There is one major reason for this. In a group where workers like and respect one another, they are much more likely to agree with one another about what constitutes a "fair day's work." This leads group members to strive for and enforce that agreed upon level of performance. In groups without these close social ties, members are less likely to talk about what each person "should be contributing," and even if they do, they are likely to disagree on what an acceptable level is.

In summary, cohesiveness is an attribute of a group. Some groups are highly cohesive and some are not. A group with high cohesiveness has strong ties between members, so much so that the group becomes an important source of work satisfaction for its members. Highly cohesive groups are virtually conflict-free; differences are settled informally through mutual adjustments. Most employees prefer to work in a highly cohesive work group. However, cohesiveness has a greater effect on the range of individual performance in a group than it does on the level of performance of the group as a whole.

Group Norms

Norms are the informal rules that develop and are enforced within a group about how group members should behave. In a sense, norms describe the "right" and "wrong" way for individuals to act as members of a group. An example of the types of norms groups develop include whether or not to talk about one's private life, whether or not to "tattle," whether or not to knock on office doors before one enters, and whether or not to "cheat" on expense accounts. Clearly not all norms a group develops are important to us as managers. The significant ones are those that have something to do with group performance.

Some groups develop norms that are consistent with how a manager wants workers to behave, and some do not. For example, if in a sales office the salespeople pressure each other for higher sales volume, this is a sign that group norms are aligned with performance. On the other hand, if the group has the norm that they should not excel for fear of making co-workers look bad, then this is a clear indication that norms are antagonistic to performance.

It is not hard to see the impact of norms on individuals in organizations. We have all been in work groups where it is "okay" to knock off work a little early or where group members expect one another to use sick leaves to take off "mental health" days. Similarly we have been members of work teams where people seem to be driven, where group members expect each other to put out maximum effort, and where team members help each other to perform well. The contrasts between these groups are due primarily to differences in group norms.

Characteristics of Groups with Norms Aligned with Performance and with Norms Antagonistic to Performance

Work groups with norms that are aligned with performance have the following characteristics:

(1) Group members informally enforce high standards of performance on one another (if one member is not performing satisfactorily, other

group members will confront the poor performer and pressure him or her to improve).
(2) The best performing members of the group are given the most respect by their co-workers.
(3) When the group needs a spokesperson, it will choose the team's manager to represent its interests.
(4) Group effort and performance do not decline in the temporary absence of the manager.

When the norms of the work group are antagonistic to performance, groups have a different set of characteristics:

(1) Group members restrict performance by punishing or ridiculing workers who are top performers.
(2) The most respected members of the group are those who get away with low levels of individual performance or who are known by their rebelliousness or indifference to authority.
(3) The groups's manager is viewed as an outsider who does not represent the views of the work group.
(4) The group requires careful monitoring to insure that the methods and goals prescribed by the supervisor are followed.

No one knows precisely how work group norms come into being. However, it is clear that managers usually have some impact over their development. Unclear, contradictory, or unfair management actions often set the stage for the development of antagonistic performance norms. Conversely, nothing contributes more to norms aligned with performance than effective managerial leadership.

Is Having Norms Aligned with Performance Desirable?

In a word, yes. Groups with norms aligned with performance consistently outperform those with antagonistic norms. In such groups, the members themselves are committed to meeting organization goals and are even willing to help each another achieve these goals. When norms are not aligned with performance, members do not work as hard to achieve organization goals, nor are they prone to help each other do anything more than fool around. To summarize, groups all develop some set of informal standards of behavior to which group members are held. Violate them and group members risk exclusion from the group or worse. Norms heavily influence the performance of a work group. If a group has norms that are aligned with performance, then the group will perform well. In contrast, groups with norms that are at odds with performance typically do only well enough to get by.

Classifying Groups According to Norms and Cohesiveness

Earlier, we indicated that the first step in developing a more effective work groups is diagnosing its social attributes. Figure 1 shows how the two social dimensions of groups, cohesiveness and norms, combine.

Figure 1
The P-1 Model

		Cohesiveness of the Work Group	
		Low	High
Norms of the Group	Aligned with Performance	P-2	P-1
	Antagonistic with Performance	P-3	P-4

A P-1 group is one that is both cohesive and has norms aligned with performance. A P-2 is a noncohesive group with aligned norms, and so on. In this scheme, the numbers 1, 2, 3, 4, are more than just identifiers. As well they indicate the level of group performance that we would predict for any combination of norms and cohesiveness. The highest performing group is a P-1 group (high cohesiveness, aligned norms). This is followed by a group that has aligned norms but is not cohesive (P-2). A group with low cohesiveness and antagonistic norms (P-3) is third ranked in terms of predicted performance. And the group that we would expect to perform the worst is one that has antagonistic norms and is very cohesive.

If one thinks about it, this order of performance makes sense. The reason P-1s are predicted to be the best performers is not just that they have norms that are pro-performance. This is also the case with P-2. P-1 has higher predicted performance because individuals in P-1 groups are socially bound to each other; they care what their colleagues think of them. This makes it much more likely that the group will effectively *enforce* its norms. P-2 and P-3 groups lack this kind of cohesiveness. Accordingly, the norms the group develops have less performance impact. Since group membership is not as important to members of these groups, it doesn't matter whether the group as a whole stands for performance or not. The same reasoning leads us to the conclusion that P-4 is the lowest performing group. As with P-1, P-4 groups are able to enforce its norms, and its norms in this case are antagonistic to performance.

To summarize the effect of cohesiveness and norms on work group performance:

P-1 groups have the highest level of performance because the positive norms are shared among its members and the group does not tolerate poor performers.

P-2 groups have the second highest level of performance. Although its norms are positive, the group is not very likely to enforce these norms. Many members of the group perform well, but there is a wide range of individual performance.

P-3 groups have the third highest level of performance. The group is generally not supportive of good performance, but because cohesiveness is low, these norms are not very influential on individual group members.

P-4 groups have the lowest level of performance. The norms of the group are antagonistic to high performance. Since the group is very attractive to its members, each member exerts little effort and restricts his performance to low levels.

Required Interaction Patterns (RIPs)

One other thing that is important to know in analyzing a group is its required interaction patterns, or RIPs for short. Basically, RIPs deal with the sort of interactions between team members required by the work assigned them. If the assignments allow each team member to work alone without any appreciable interaction with colleagues, then we would say that the group has *simple RIPs*. For example, if a manager supervises a team of tax accountants, that group would have a simple RIP because the people work alone; they interact with their peers only at infrequent staff meetings, training sessions, and technical briefings.

At the other end of the RIP scale, we have teams in which members have to interact frequently and in complicated ways in order to complete their work. Such groups have *complex RIPs*. Take the case of a team of three mechanics who modify stock automobiles for off-road racing. Interaction between them must be extensive, and a high level of cooperation is required.

There are four types of required interaction patterns from simple to complex. As we progress from simple RIPs to complicated ones, each level involves more extensive communication and coordination between team members in order to complete the task. The more complex the RIP, the more challenging the required relationship is for the team members. The four different levels of RIPs are described below.

Solo-work

The simplest level of required interaction patterns is *solo-work*. Group members do not need to communicate or share anything with one another in order to complete their assignments. They are linked only by a common supervisor, a common set of resources, or common work inputs. Each member of the team works almost independently of the others. An example of a job that requires solo-work is a supermarket checker. Each checker works separately from the others, and the speed or quality of one worker does not directly affect the others. Other jobs that fall into this category are newspaper reporters, shoe salespeople, clinical psychologists, teachers, potters, telephone operators, and taxicab drivers. Figure 2 depicts solo-work as a RIP.

Figure 2
Solo-Work RIP

Group members do not need to communicate or share anything with one another to complete their assignments. They are linked only by a common supervisor, a common set of resources, or common work inputs. Each member of the team works almost independently of the others.

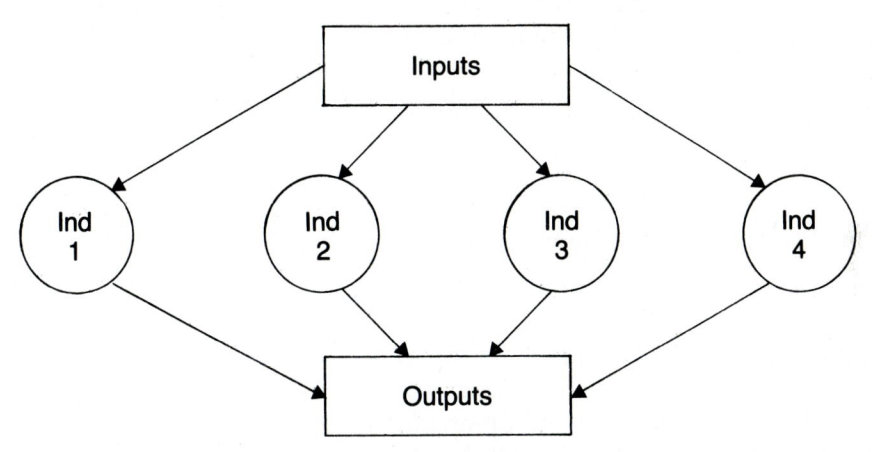

Supermarket Checkers, Teachers, Newspaper Reporters

One-way Workflow

Groups with *one-way workflow* RIPs have to have more interaction and coordination. This RIP level exists when one worker's output becomes the "raw material" for the next worker. One example of this is an assembly line. The work follows a defined series of steps, passing from one worker to another, with each modifying or adding to the product of the last. This is a more complicated RIP than solo-work. Some communication is necessary especially between workers directly connected by the flow. If conflicts are not worked out, one worker's poor performance can have a negative effect on the next worker in line. Other jobs with a one-way workflow include workers in fast-food restaurants, steel workers, lumberjacks, cannery workers, and civil servants in motor vehicle registration activities. Figure 3 shows a one-way workflow RIP.

Figure 3
One-Way Workflow RIP

One worker's output becomes the "raw material" for the next worker. Some communication and sharing is necessary especially between workers directly connected by the flow. If conflicts are not worked out, one worker's poor performance can have a negative effect on the next worker in line.

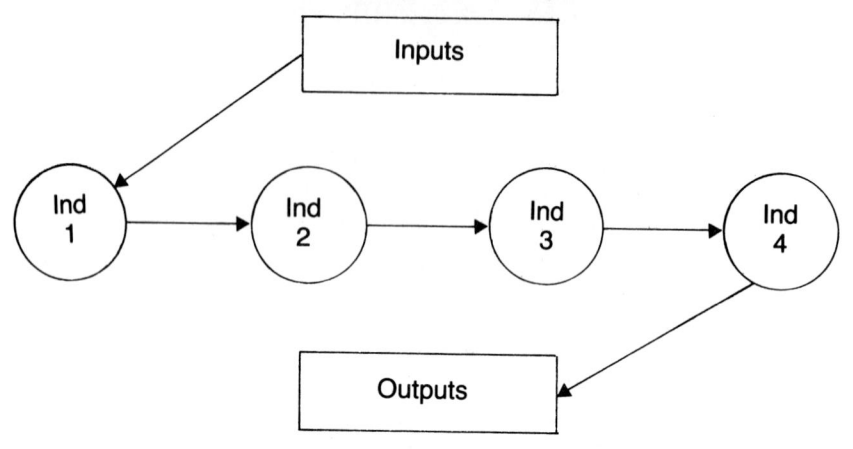

Assemblyline Workers, Materials Handlers, Small Restaurants

Two-way Workflow

When the flow of work in a group moves in two directions instead of just one, the RIP is best described as *two-way workflow*. Here the work may get passed back and forth between group members before it is completed. This is a more complex RIP than both solo-work and one-way workflow because the communication and coordination among workers has to be much more extensive than if the group can count on the workflow traveling in one direction or if it can be completed independently. An example of a work group that requires two-way RIP is a team of health care professionals in a neonatal ward. In such a group information needs to be sent back and forth between doctors, nurses, technicians, orderlies, etc. The information received by one member of the group needs to be conveyed to others and feedback is vital. Examples of other types of groups that are linked by a two-way workflow include: carpenters, highway construction workers, upholsterers, refinery workers, and commercial fishermen. Figure 4 represents two-way workflow.

Figure 4
Two-Way Workflow RIP

The flow of work in the group moves in two directions instead of just one. The work gets passed back and forth between group members before it is completed. Communication and coordination are more essential than if the RIP is solo-work or one-way workflow.

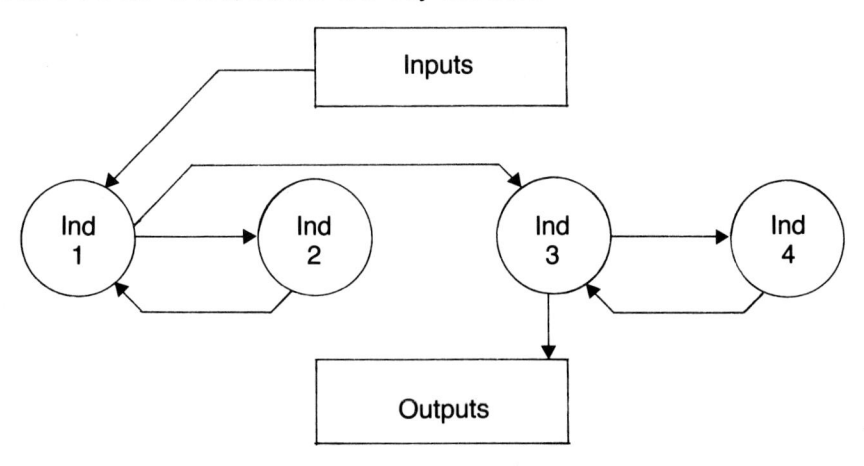

```
                    ┌─────────┐
                    │ Inputs  │
                    └─────────┘
        ┌──────┐  ┌──────┐  ┌──────┐  ┌──────┐
        │ Ind  │→ │ Ind  │→ │ Ind  │→ │ Ind  │
        │  1   │  │  2   │  │  3   │  │  4   │
        └──────┘  └──────┘  └──────┘  └──────┘
                    ┌─────────┐
                    │ Outputs │
                    └─────────┘
```

R & D Labs, Quality Rework, System Test Troubleshooting

Teamwork

The most complex required interaction pattern exists when an assignment cannot be divided into individual portions but must be completed by a face-to-face group effort. An example of this might be found in a standing committee or in a task force. Here the workflow does not follow directional patterns, as in one-way workflow or two-way workflow, but grows out of an interaction of the entire group. Communication and coordination are extremely complicated, and any single team member can have a dramatic impact on team output. *Teamwork RIP* can be found in groups of professional athletes (of team sports), mortgage brokers (they make major decisions in committees), news film crews, surgical teams, disaster relief volunteers, and musicians in an orchestra. A diagram of teamwork RIP appears in Figure 5.

Are More Complex Required Interaction Patterns Desirable?

Would a manager want a group with complex RIPs or simple ones? For most of us, the answer is probably "simple." Certainly, groups with more complex RIPs are more difficult to supervise and more stressful for the members in

Figure 5
Teamwork RIP

The work is not divided into individual portions, but is completed by a face-to-face group effort. Communication and coordination are vital in this, the most complex RIP.

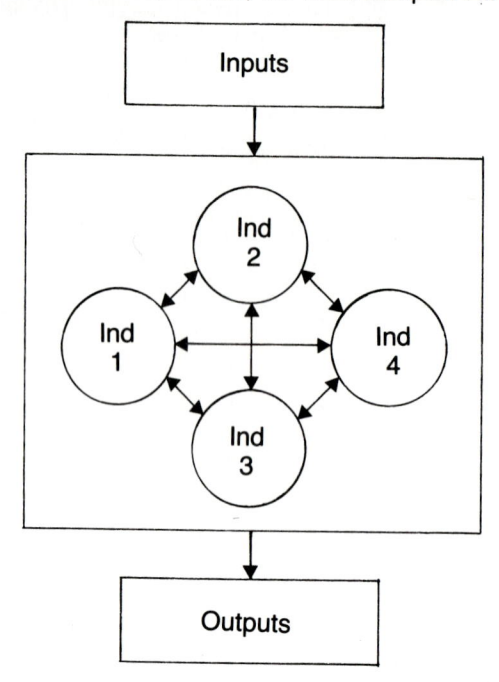

Task Forces, New Product Development Teams, Standing Committees

them. But there are some advantages to having complex RIPs that are often ignored. First, people involved in complex RIP assignments are stimulated and challenged. Building more required interaction patterns into a job is remedy for boredom and work monotony. Even more important, organizations are able to tap much more of the potential of their work force if they have jobs with complex RIPs. Working independently, employees can produce only up to their individual limits, but an effectively managed, complex RIP team may experience *synergy*, a condition where the group output is greater than the sum of the individual contributions to it. Synergy is not possible when people are given solo-work assignments. It only occurs when there is complex RIP.

Synergy is not only restricted to a particular type of RIP, but also a particular type of work group. Not all groups are capable of synergy. Some groups consume much more than they produce when linked in complicated ways. Generally, synergy is only possible when the team is a P-1 or P-2 group. The reason should be clear. P-3 and P-4 groups use the additional interaction in a complex RIP setting to enforce their negative norms, to discourage each other from putting forth more effort. P-1 and P-2 groups, in contrast, thrive on complex required interaction patterns. As they interact more, they spur each other on to higher and higher levels of performance, and synergy is the result.

In a nutshell, we are saying that if a team is presently P-3 or P-4, a manager should try to structure assignments toward simple RIPs. With a P-1 or P-2 group, complex RIPs are ideal. Figure 6 summarizes these rules.

Figure 6
The P-1 Model with RIPs Shown

	Cohesiveness of the Work Group	
	Low	High
Norms of the Group — Aligned with Performance	P-2 Complex RIP is best.	P-1 Complex RIP is best.
Antagonistic with Performance	P-3 Simple RIP is best.	P-4 Simple RIP is best.

Improving Group Performance

Once a manager has concluded whether his or her group is P-1, P-2, P-3, or P-4 and identified the nature of the group's workflow, it is possible to develop a plan for increasing the probability that it will perform better.

Depending upon the diagnosis made, there are a number of things a manager can do to boost performance. We call these things *action levers*. They are simply the actions a manager can take to get leverage on performance. There are five action levers a manager can use to improve the performance of a team:

(1) increase cohesiveness,
(2) decrease cohesiveness,
(3) align norms with performance,

(4) simplify RIPs,
(5) complicate RIPs.

Action Lever 1--Increase Cohesiveness

It makes sense to increase cohesiveness when a group is in a P-2 condition (i.e., low cohesiveness, norms aligned to performance). If the manager is successful, the group will become a P-1 group, and we would expect a P-1 group to outperform a P-2 group. Below are some specific ways to increase cohesiveness.

Assign tasks according to the preferences of group members. Try to give everyone the task that he or she most likes to do. If this is not possible, distribute the most desirable work in a way that enables everyone to be able to do it. Spread the less desirable work equitably as well. The reason is clear; a major source of conflict in a group is a feeling that some group members are better off than others. By distributing tasks according to preferences, one can remove this source of jealousy and envy.

Emphasize what the members of the team have in common. Take every opportunity to point out common backgrounds, ways of thinking about things, or concerns about shared problems. Also, discourage subgroups based on similarities not shared by all team members. For example, if the team begins to divide into subgroups based on educational background, the manager should make sure these subgroups do not promote in-group/out-group thinking.

Give the team the experience of shared success. Few things bring a group together better than a success experience. Shared success can lower the barriers that would otherwise keep individuals from being friends. Shared success allows celebrations that create a real sense of fellowship. Basically there are two ways a manager can give the group the experience of shared success. One is by looking for ways to acknowledge or celebrate occasions when the team is successful. Another is to orchestrate the situation so a success is almost guaranteed. For example, when facing an assignment that will take a long time to complete, clever managers identify early interim milestones that are easy to attain so that the "automatic" success that results can be celebrated with great fanfare.

Identify a common threat or enemy that cannot be escaped without the group cooperating and pulling together. It has long been known that common threats can unify a group. Using this principle, though, can be risky. If the manager identifies someone or something as a common enemy that proves not to be so, his or her credibility will be seriously and perhaps irreparably damaged. Similarly, if a manager identifies someone inside the organization as a common

enemy (e.g., a tough-minded top manager, a competing division, o*
department that is difficult to work with), this tactic can easily ba
then can one successfully use a common threat? Generally, it is usually
the manager to select a threat *outside* the organization. In addition, the threat
selected should constitute a real threat and one that can be shown to be neutralized by cooperative effort. For example, the director of a family planning agency was plagued with a work force that was constantly bickering and squabbling. In order to create more cohesiveness, she announced that a community group was actively lobbying for a reduction in funding for the agency and that only by pulling together to mount a campaign on behalf of the agency could they be sure that their budget would not be seriously cut. This appeal worked, and for a while the internal disputes subsided.

Action Lever 2--Decrease Cohesiveness

If the team is in a P-4 condition, then decreasing cohesiveness makes sense. P-4 groups have negative performance norms and high levels of cohesiveness. This combination is likely to lead to low levels of performance and a lot of gray hair for the manager. Since it is very difficult to move a group directly from P-4 to P-1 by changing norms, decreasing cohesiveness is often the only answer. It is generally better to have a group divided when its values are contrary to performance than it is to have a group unified against the manager. This may seem to be a negative course of action. It is, but it is often a necessary first step to break up a group that is in a P-4 state. Once the breakup is complete, other, more positive actions can be taken. Until the group is moved out of P-4, though, positive actions rarely work.

Assign tasks in a divisive way. P-4 groups can be moved to P-3 by giving team members assignments that turn group members on one another. For example, if one member likes to do a particular task, a manager may move that person into a position where he cannot perform that task. Similarly, a manager might give the most desired tasks to workers who have the lowest status in the group.

Emphasize the differences between team members. A manager can also divide a group by constantly pointing out the differences between individuals and subgroups.

Single out individuals when the group has been successful. Instead of rewarding and praising the group, the manager might pick out one or two individuals and give them all the praise. Not surprisingly, this is likely to create conflict in the team.

Create subgroups and make them compete. A manager can decrease cohesiveness by using competition. If a manager finds ways to set up contests between individuals or subgroups, the unity within the group is likely to be reduced.

These techniques may seem unnecessarily cruel and disruptive. Clearly a manager should not use them without careful consideration; however, left on their own, P-4 groups are likely to be cruel and disruptive to the organization itself.

Action Lever 3--Align Norms with Performance

A third action lever that a manager can use to get more performance from a group is to align norms with performance. Aligning norms is a time-consuming process. Norms develop slowly, and a great deal of patience is required unless the manager is starting with a brand new group. This action lever is for groups in a P-3 position. It is not advisable for P-4s since norms are not easily changed unless cohesiveness is low.

Use incentive plans based on performance. There is probably no better way to align norms with performance than to make performance worthwhile for the entire group. Anything that can make good performance positively consequential and poor performance negatively consequential does the trick. Some managers use performance bonuses, awards, or symbols, but the incentives likely to work best are those that are valuable to the group. In addition, incentives have the best effect when they are group incentives, i.e., things that are awarded to the entire group for group achievement. Examples include a free dinner for making a monthly production quota, a traveling trophy for the best quality record, and a ring for each member of a Super Bowl team.

Give a compelling pep talk. Some managers can also align norms with performance by giving a really effective speech on the mission and meaning of the group task. Not every manager can do this well, but if done well, it can be very effective.

Be a model of high performance. Nothing undermines the development of aligned norms more than a manager whose own behavior is in conflict with the performance norms he or she espouses. Accordingly, it is important for the manager to be sensitive to the sort of messages his or her actions are sending out. It seems obvious that if a manager wants to convince people to work long hours, the manager should not go home early.

Identify a common threat or enemy that cannot be escaped without the group working up to high performance standards. Earlier we discussed identifying common threats as a way to increase group cohesiveness. With some fine tuning, this tactic also helps align norms with performance. The modification is that the threat has to be relevant to performance, i.e., if the group performs well, the threat will subside or the enemy will be defeated. Again, the manager has to be very careful to use a common threat that is actually a credible threat. In addition, if the manager uses an enemy, it should be someone or something outside the company.

A construction foreman used this action lever effectively when faced with a new interpretation of codes used by building inspectors. Apparently this change was brought about because builders had not supported the mayor in a recent election. The foreman called his workers together and pointed out to them that they would (unjustly) be subjected to standards far in excess of what was reasonable. He further challenged them to rise to the occasion in order to blunt the weapon of a dishonest city government. The tactic worked, and the inspectors soon abandoned their tough practices with no apparent damage to the foreman's firm.

Action Lever 4--Simplify Required Interaction Patterns

In our initial discussion of RIPs, we asserted that given a combination of norms and cohesiveness, some RIPs are better than others. Namely, for P-1 and P-2 groups the more complex the RIPs the better (teamwork is best followed by two-way workflow, one-way workflow, and solo-work). For P-3 and P-4 groups the situation is just reversed: the simpler the RIP the better (solo-work is best followed by one-way workflow, two-way workflow, and teamwork).

While under certain circumstances some RIPs are better than others, the interaction patterns required in a team may not be changeable. For example, the manager of a radio station would be hard-pressed to change the two-way RIP of his or her employees to one-way, solo-work, or teamwork. The interaction pattern is virtually fixed. Yet this is not always the case. Sometimes a manager *can* change the required interaction patterns that link people. For example, by simply requiring that a greater number of problems are brought up, discussed, and solved during staff meetings, a manager is increasing the level of RIP in the group. Similarly, by allocating the work such that there is more feedback between team members who would otherwise pass work on in a one-directional manner, the RIP level is increased. Situations sometimes allow the simplification of RIPs. Managers can disallow talking or isolate individual workers. They can position themselves in feedback loops so all information about performance comes from them rather than others. Meetings can be eliminated. Even when it appears that the RIP is fixed, there are generally certain small things that can done to simplify them or make them more complicated. Action Lever 4 deals with simplifying RIPs. As such, it is appropriate if a manager has a P-3 or a P-4 group.

Keep the face-to-face interaction between employees at a bare minimum. This means scheduling meetings infrequently, using little employee participation or group problem solving in decision making, and restricting informal contact between co-workers. Simplifying RIPs can also be accomplished by separating employees so that face-to-face encounters are difficult. Group members can be architecturally separated, allowed to interact only through forms or computer terminals, or restricted by a no-talking rule. Of course, we are not proposing that all P-3 and P-4 groups are placed in a sort of solitary confinement until they shape up and adopt the proper norms. We are only saying that groups in these conditions do not use complex interactions for the good of the organization, so there is often little to be gained by encouraging such complicated encounters.

Divide the work so that individual employees work alone and do not need to coordinate their efforts with their co-workers. While not always possible, some jobs lend themselves to this sort of division. Team teaching should be discouraged, telephone line-workers should not be assigned in pairs (unless safety requires it), shift workers should not have to use the same tools as workers on earlier or later shifts, and chefs should be given total responsibility for one food item (salad chef, sauce chef, pastry chef, etc.). By assigning overlapping sales territories for industrial salespeople, requiring carpenters to share one pneumatic nail gun, or allowing two teamsters to travel together on a coast-to-coast run, a manager is *not* simplifying the RIP.

Break down group performance measures into individual components. Make sure that each and every individual in the group has his or her own performance index separate and distinct from everyone else's. This enables team members to work on their own performance independent of their co-workers, and it gives the illusion of independence even where there is a more complex RIP.

Eliminate feedback from one worker to another or funnel it through one channel. Feedback is a major RIP factor. The more feedback one receives from one's fellows, the more complex the RIP. The larger the number of co-workers sending feedback to any one worker, the more complex the RIP. A supervisor of a group of artisans working on the restoration of a historical building learned the hard way about the importance of feedback in simplifying RIP. Three of his people were constantly bickering about how to texture the walls of an 18th-century mansion. Each would criticize the work of the others in spite of the fact that they each worked on separate rooms. Combined with the poor work norms these artisans had, the unrequested and unnecessary collegial feedback virtually paralyzed the job until the supervisor intervened and disallowed it.

Action Lever 5--Complicate Required Interaction Patterns

Complicating RIPs makes sense when a team is in a P-1 or P-2 condition. Here the potential for synergy (whole is greater than the sum of the parts) is at its peak. More interaction generally results in higher performance. While the RIP may not be infinitely variable, some complication is probably possible. Consider the following actions.

Encourage face-to-face interaction between team members. Just as a manager may want to eliminate personal encounters to simplify RIPs, he or she will want to encourage them to complicate RIPs. Meetings should be frequent. Problems should be solved as a team and decision making should be participative whenever possible. Barriers to interaction should be eliminated. Technologies should be used that enhance rather than eliminate personal contact. Settings should be created that encourage social contact during work breaks and after hours. Cafeterias and lounges ought to be attractive and set up with an eye to facilitate conversation and interaction.

Divide the work among subgroups rather than individuals. Avoid giving individuals assignments. Instead, a manager might try to team people up if only in twos and even better in threes or fours. Such divisions build more RIPs into the work and have the potential for higher levels of performance.

Calculate performance figures based only on group data. If a manager considers the performance of the group rather than of individuals, then the manager is, in effect, increasing the complexity of their RIPs. Each worker *has to* think about the group as a whole and must better gauge his own work in the context of the others'. While this might depress individual initiative in the short run, it may better harness this energy on behalf of the entire group.

Set up multiple feedback channels and encourage workers to help each other by giving suggestions, through peer training, and even with peer performance appraisals. In a P-1 or a P-2 group, feedback is generally correct, i.e., workers manage each other the same way the manager does. As such, a manager may want to encourage peer feedback of all kinds.

The list of actions represents many different alternatives for improving a group's performance. Managers must "fit" their actions to the situation of the group. Figure 7 summarizes these actions.

An Example

In order to demonstrate how this approach can be used in a real situation, put yourself in the following situation. You are the manager of six software engineers who create programs for missile defense systems. Initially, one senior software engineer works out a flow diagram and is then joined by a junior engineer who with him completes the initial programming. The completed initial program then is assigned to another senior engineer who tests and debugs the program. A fourth engineer then evaluates the program against system requirements. This involves cycling back to the original group for further modification if needed. Due to the complexity of the programs and system requirements, cycling of this sort is quite common.

Figure 7
P-1 Model with Action Levers for Each Quadrant

		Cohesiveness of the Work Group	
		Low	High
Norms of the Group	Aligned with Performance	P-2 Complicate RIPs. Increase cohesiveness.	P-1 Complicate RIPs.
	Antagonistic with Performance	P-3 Simplify RIPs. Align norms with performance.	P-4 Simplify RIPs. Decrease cohesiveness.

The group is composed of highly mobile young engineers. It has experienced high turnover in recent months as competing firms have lured group members away from your firm with promises of lucrative contracts and plush working conditions. As such, the group seems to have developed the view that your firm is but a stepping stone to better jobs. This translates into several attitudes that are of great concern to you. First, group members often prefer to be assigned programs that have commercial applications so they can build their "resumes." The problem is that few programs your group is assigned have commercial applicability. Second, group members cooperate with one another only when it does not conflict with their efforts to secure desirable assignments for themselves.

How would you approach this situation? The first step is to diagnose the norms and cohesiveness of your team and to determine what sort of RIP is presently being used.

Norms of Your Group

There are several things that indicate that your team has norms that are *not* aligned with performance. First, the attitude that your company is only a stepping stone in their careers is a sign that your people do not identify with the firm or care about performance unless there is something in it for them. Second, the members of your team only cooperate with you and with one another when they are given certain types of assignments. This is certainly not indicative of a group that enforces high performance standards on one another. Conclusion--norms are not aligned with performance.

Level of Cohesiveness in Your Group

As you may recall, cohesiveness refers to the level of interpersonal harmony in the group. On this score, your team cannot be rated very highly. With turnover being as high as it is, it would be very rare to have high cohesiveness. In addition, the fact that group members compete with one another for programs with commercial applicability further supports the conclusion that the group has low cohesiveness. Conclusion--low cohesiveness.

Required Interaction Patterns in Your Group

Evidence suggests that your team uses a two-way workflow RIP. Each program begins with the work of a senior engineer. It is then passed through the hands of a number of other engineers, each of whom adds to it. The important point is that there is considerable cycling and feedback. This is typical of a two-way workflow RIP. Conclusion--two-way workflow RIP.

You have a P-3 group with a two-way workflow. If we put this diagnosis into our P-1 model, we get a look at what this means in terms of our action levers. As you can see from Figure 8, there are two strategies for getting leverage on the performance of your group. You can simplify the RIP to one-way workflow or solo-work. And you can try to align the norms of the group with performance.

To be precise about how you might deal with this group, take the action lever of simplifying the RIP of the group. The following are some of the specific actions that would increase performance:

(1) Assign the entire sequence of activities that go into each program to one software engineer. If this is infeasible, have all co-worker feedback flow through you.
(2) Minimize group meetings, committees, and task forces.
(3) Define performance standards for each engineer separate and independent of the accomplishments of the team.

If this was your group, it would also make sense to work on aligning norms with performance:

(1) Since programs with commercial applicability are so desirable, distribute them on the basis of who is the best performer. Think about other ways to make high performance consequential to your people.
(2) Give a compelling pep talk on the value of the group's work to our national defense. Perhaps bring in military strategists for a briefing on the importance of the missile systems your team is working on to our policy of deterrence.
(3) Personally model the sort of high effort/high performance you expect of your people.
(4) Point out how the development of the missile systems your team is working on is a vital response to the threat of nuclear annihilation, military dominance by our country's enemies, or the efforts of another aerospace firm to win future contracts. Emphasize the importance of high performance as a means of responding to these threats.

Figure 8
The Results of Our Diagnosis

Cohesiveness of the Work Group

		Low	High
Norms of the Group	Aligned with Performance	P-2 Complicate RIPs. Increase cohesiveness.	P-1 Complicate RIPs.
	Antagonistic with Performance	P-3 Simplify RIPs. Align norms with performance.	P-4 Simplify RIPs. Decrease cohesiveness.

Conclusion

For many managers, this is an entirely new way of thinking about work groups, but we think it is a valuable one. It begins with a careful diagnosis of the social circumstances in the work group, and it ends with a list of action items that are likely to lead to higher levels of group performance.

References

Aronson, E. *The Social Animal*. San Francisco: W. H. Freeman, 1976.

Feldman, D. C. "The Development and Enforcement of Group Norms." *Academy of Management Review* 4 (1984): 47-53.

Hackman, J. R. "Group Influences on Individuals." In M. D. Dunnette, ed., *Handbook of Industrial and Organizational Psychology*. Chicago: Rand McNally, 1976.

Herold, D. M. "The Effectiveness of Work Groups." In S. Kerr, ed., *Organizational Behavior*. Columbus, Ohio: Grid, 1979.

Janis, I. L. *Victims of Groupthink*. New York: Houghton Mifflin, 1972.

Lott, A. J., and B. E. Lott. "Group Cohesiveness as Interpersonal Attraction." *Psychological Bulletin* 64 (1965): 259-309.

Porter, L. W., E. E. Lawler, III, and J. R. Hackman. *Behavior in Organizations*. New York: McGraw-Hill, 1975.

Seashore, S. *Group Cohesiveness in the Industrial Work Group*. Ann Arbor, Mich.: Institute for Social Research, University of Michigan, 1954.

Slocum J., and H. Sims. "A Typology for Integrating Technology, Organization Design and Job Design." *Human Relations* 33 (1980): 193-212.

Interactive Case

You are the new Director of Employee Relations of a medium size sheet metal fabricating firm. You were hired to replace Doc Stevens, an experienced person who was very popular with your new work group. Stevens was known as a "progressive" personnel professional whose ideas and proposals were consistently opposed by top management because they were thought to be ill-suited to the special problems of the industry. Apparently you were hired because you were thought to have a more practical perspective on the nature of the Employee Relations function at the company. An organization chart appears below.

Employee Relations Department

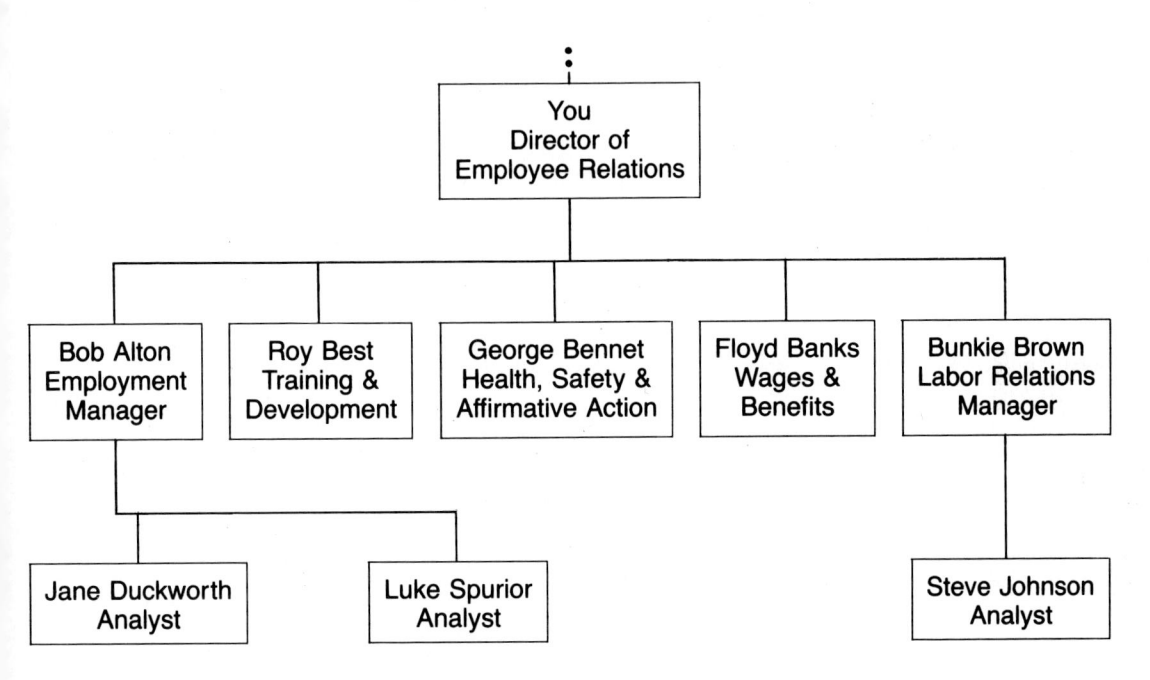

```
                    You
             Director of
         Employee Relations
    ┌──────────┬──────────┼──────────┬──────────┐
 Bob Alton  Roy Best   George Bennet  Floyd Banks  Bunkie Brown
Employment  Training & Health, Safety & Wages &   Labor Relations
 Manager   Development Affirmative Action Benefits    Manager
    │                                                   │
 ┌──┴──┐                                                │
Jane Duckworth  Luke Spurior                       Steve Johnson
  Analyst        Analyst                              Analyst
```

Eight personnel specialists report directly to you:

Bob Alton (Employment Manager) - 34, 5 years' experience. Very popular with the members of the department. Excellent performance reviews but was passed over for your job because he was outspoken on behalf of personnel policies far too progressive for the rather conservative, manufacturing-dominated group of top executives.

Jane Duckworth (Employment Analyst) - 29, 3 years' experience. Former executive assistant to the factory superintendent. Applied for and was granted a significant promotion under a job posting system. Known to be very loyal to Bob Alton and very progressive in her opinions about the role of employee relations vis-a-vis manufacturing.

Luke Spurior (Employment Analyst) - 27, 3 years' experience. Supported Alton's promotion to your position since he thought that it would allow him to move up into Alton's position. Competent and promotable. A college classmate of George Bennet's.

Roy Best (Training and Development Specialist) - 41, 4 years' experience. Very effective trainer of blue collar operators, but he has had difficulty getting an executive development program approved by top management. Very active in his professional association and thought to be actively pursuing other employment opportunities.

George Bennet (Health, Safety, and Affirmative Action Specialist) - 26, 5 years' experience. Part-time law student. Competent but often the bearer of bad news to the organization and its noncompliance with the law. Good friend of Luke Spurior's.

Floyd Banks (Wage and Benefits Specialist) - 57, 21 years' experience. Good performer, but a low-key individual. Content in his position ("a lifer") but miffed by his less-than-average merit pay increase given in spite of your predecessor's recommendation to the Executive Salary Committee.

Bunkie Brown (Labor Relations Manager) - 41, 7 years' experience. Gadfly friend of a number of people in modest places throughout the organization. His ability to get his job done is due more to his contacts and allies than his technical ability.

Steve Johnson (Labor Relations Analyst) - 28, 1 year's experience. An individual brought into the organization six months before you. Experienced for his age but still tentative.

You have three immediate objectives to accomplish that call for differing levels of cooperation among your new staff. Since your new team must accomplish these assignments in addition to their present work loads, you estimate that each of these will take you and your people one month to complete. In spite of your newness to the organization, you are very confident that these are quite conservative estimates (it would take an average group far less time to complete each).

Assignment 1 -- Preparation for Labor Negotiations. In five months your department begins negotiations with the Sheetmetal Workers Union for the first time in two years. Since the contract will affect each department member's specialty, inputs from everyone will be solicited. Bunkie Brown will draw up a list of probable union demands and these will be sent simultaneously to every other department member for an assessment of economic and administrative impact. You will then aggregate these assessments into an integrated impact report.

Assignment 2 -- Development of an Integrated Personnel Policy. Top management has asked you to submit a document outlining a reassessment of existing departmental policies and procedures, together with proposals for changes. It is due in five months. Preparing this document will involve intensive meetings of all department members.

Assignment 3 -- Creation of an Annual Staffing Plan. In five months all manpower planning for the next fiscal year is due. This is a serial process beginning with Roy Best who estimates promotions and transfers. This then goes to Bob Alton's group (Alton, Duckworth, and Spurior), which calculates new staffing needs, and then on to George Bennet, who justifies these figures into the affirmative action plan. Finally, Floyd Banks transposes these estimates into a budget form.

In considering the department as a whole, a number of things disturb you about the informal relationships on the team. First, Alton appears to be the informal leader. He is very popular, but you are concerned that he may subvert your efforts to bring the department back into line with the thinking of top management. Second, the group is very close knit. They stick up and watch out for one another, and it is clear that they derive much of their job satisfaction from working with one another. Third, influenced largely by Doc Stevens, the group has adopted and enforces very professional work norms. Every member of the department (with the possible exception of Banks) is an active member of their respective professional associations, and many times proposals for changes are put forth that are more professionally appropriate than relevant to the realities of the organization.

It is now the beginning of the first month. What would you do?

A. Give your team Assignment 1 now. (GO TO 455B)

B. Give your team Assignment 2 now. (GO TO 458B)

C. Give your team Assignment 3 now. (GO TO 433A)

D. Hold off for a month and then decide about an assignment. (GO TO 473A)

7 LEADERSHIP
Module Reading

The subject of leadership has long intrigued historians and social scientists. Volumes have been written, scholarly conferences held, and biographies devoted in an effort to solve the mystery of what makes ordinary people effective leaders. Unfortunately, all this work has not resulted in one grand theory of executive leadership. Instead, this work has resulted in several theories and important findings, some rather simple and some extraordinarily complicated, some overly abstract and some exceptionally usable.

In this chapter, we detail a model of leadership that is one of the most practical and straightforward of all those available today. It suggests the types of behaviors effective leaders frequently display and indicates the circumstances under which the various types of behaviors are most appropriate.

A Brief Summary of Leadership Research

Simply defined, leadership is the ability to get things done through other people. Most people who have studied leadership have taken one of the following approaches: the trait approach, the leadership style approach, or the situational approach.

The Trait Approach

One group of researchers has tried to discover what common traits good leaders have. One example of this is the fact that those candidates elected President of the United States have been physically taller than their opponents almost without exception. Some of the personal traits that have been linked to successful leaders include

(1) supervisory ability,
(2) need for occupational achievement,
(3) intelligence,
(4) decisiveness,
(5) self-assurance,
(6) assertiveness.

As interesting as these results are, they may not be of much help to someone preparing to assume a leadership role because these traits may be very difficult to develop if they are not part of the individual's personality and background.

The Leadership Style Approach

Other researchers have been much more interested in what leaders do than in what traits they have. Beginning in the 1940s, studies were devoted to finding out what leaders do to get results from their groups. These early studies identified two major leadership styles: a task-oriented leadership style and a people-oriented leadership style. Some of the specific leader behaviors that fall into these two categories are described in Table 1.

Table 1
Task-Oriented and People-Oriented Leader Behaviors

Lets work unit members know what is expected of them.	Is friendly and approachable.
Encourages the use of uniform procedures.	Does little things to make it pleasant to be a member of the work unit member.
Tries out his/her ideas in the work unit.	Puts suggestions made by the work unit into operation.
Makes his/her attitudes clear to the work unit.	Treats all work unit members as his/her equals.
Decides what should be done and how it should be done.	Gives advance notice of change.
Assigns work unit members to particular tasks.	Does not keep to himself/herself.
Makes sure that his/her part in the work unit is understood by the work unit members.	Looks out for the personal welfare of work unit members.
Schedules the work to be done.	Is willing to make changes.
Maintains definite standards of performance.	Explains his/her actions.
Asks that work unit members follow standard rules and regulations.	Consults the work unit before acting.

Adapted with permission of The Free Press, a division of Macmillan, Inc., from *Stogdill's Handbook of Leadership,* revised edition, by Bernard M. Bass. Copyright © 1974, 1981 by The Free Press.

Some experts note that these two categories are not mutually exclusive. It is indeed possible to be both task-oriented *and* people-oriented, and it is possible to be neither. The four possibilities are shown in Figure 1.

More recently, an effort was made to classify leadership styles in terms of the degree to which leaders use worker inputs in making decisions. The four most common categories are

1) Direction--the manager makes the decision with no solicitation of inputs from his/her subordinates; equivalent to high-task, low-people leadership style;

2) Consultation--the manager asks members of the group for their inputs and considers these inputs in making the decision; equivalent to high-task, high-people leadership style;

3) Participation--the manager conducts a group decision-making process, guiding the group to a consensus decision; equivalent to low-task, high-people leadership style;

4) Delegation--the manager gives the group the authority to make the decision and takes no role in guiding the group to a solution; equivalent to low-task, low-people leadership style.

Figure 1
The Four Leadership Styles

People-Oriented

	Low Task	High Task
High	High-People, Low-Task Orientation (participation)	High-People, High-Task Orientation (consultation)
Low	Low-People, Low-Task Orientation (delegation)	Low-People, High-Task Orientation (direction)

Task-Oriented

From *Management of Organizational Behavior: Utilizing Human Resources*, 4th ed., by Paul Hersey and Ken Blanchard, p. 96. Copyright © 1982 by Prentice-Hall, Inc. Adapted by permission of Prentice-Hall, Inc., Englewood Cliffs, New Jersey.

Once these sets of leader behaviors had been identified, researchers then attempted to discover whether any of these actions were related to successful group performance. In general, none of these behaviors (or styles) proved to be effective in all situations. Leaders with a task-oriented style were effective in some situations but not in others. Similarly, consultation served some managers well as a leadership style, but it did not work as well for managers in different situations. These findings gave birth to the situational approach to leadership.

The Situational Approach to Leadership

During the 1960s, scholars turned their attention to the situational elements that made some leadership styles more effective than others. Thus far this has proved to be the most productive approach to the study of leadership. It has resulted in a number of theories that were subsequently tested by practitioners for their applicability.

To many practicing managers, the most useful of these situational theories is the *Group Maturity Theory of Leadership*. Originally developed by Paul Hersey and Kenneth Blanchard, it is this theory that is the cornerstone of this chapter. As in all practical theories, this theory has certain assumptions. First, it assumes that the manager has enough time to think through the elements of the theory and design a leadership approach that fits the situation. Obviously this is not always the case. Emergencies, "fire drills," and crises may not allow the sort of deliberate analysis that any situational theory would require. Similarly, it assumes that the manager has sufficient position power to carry out the actions prescribed by the theory. New managers or those engaged in political problems that make their power questionable may find this theory somewhat more difficult to use than those managers who have a stronger power base.

The Maturity of the Work Group

Mature work groups require different leadership styles than immature groups. Maturity in this sense refers to the willingness and ability of the group to perform well. Specifically, mature groups

(1) want to reach high but attainable goals,
(2) express a willingness and ability to accept responsibility,
(3) have high levels of relevant skills and experience.

Table 2 provides examples of behavior that a leader can expect from very mature and very immature groups.

Table 2
Contrast Between Very Mature and Very Immature Work Groups

Maturity Factor	Very Mature Groups	Very Immature Groups
Desire to attain high but attainable goals	Respond effectively to a challenge or problem Are problem solvers Are willing to work overtime Enforce high performance standards on one another	Are complacent with mediocrity Are problem finders Are unwilling to work overtime Punish members who strive for excellence
Willingness and ability to accept responsibility	Work hard even in manager's absence Follow directives and policies even if they contain objectionable elements Demonstrate initiative rather than asking permission	Seldom volunteer for tasks that need to be performed Object to directives and policies that they find unacceptable Are overly compliant and dependent on getting permission and approval
Relevant education and experience	Have stable group composition (low turnover) Are composed of highly trained and experienced employees Are aided by policies and procedures that guide action	Have variable group composition (high turnover) Are composed of poorly trained and inexperienced employees Are not aided by policies and procedures that guide action

From *Management of Organizational Behavior: Utilizing Human Resources*, 4th ed., by Paul Hersey and Ken Blanchard, p. 157. Copyright © 1982 by Prentice-Hall, Inc. Adapted by permission of Prentice-Hall, Inc., Englewood Cliffs, New Jersey.

Between these two extremes are two other important categories: *moderately mature* and *moderately immature* groups. Moderately mature groups possess some but not all of the attributes of a very mature group, and similarly, moderately immature groups have mostly but not completely immature characteristics.

The distinction between these different levels of maturity is important, for it determines the type of leadership most effective for a work group. Figure 2 shows how maturity is theoretically related to leadership effectiveness.

Very immature groups require a healthy dose of task orientation and no people orientation. They must be led directively. Key elements in the best leadership style include enforcing procedures and high standards of performance, being clear in making assignments, and scheduling and planning the work with minimal involvement of the group.

With moderately immature groups, the appropriate leadership style changes somewhat. The leader still needs to continue with a high task orientation, but should also add high people orientation. This means being more approachable and responsive to group members as individuals, and it means defending the group when they are wrongfully challenged by others in the organization. Moreover, when it comes to decision making, the leader should use a consultation approach, i.e., ask the group for its inputs before exercising judgment.

Moderately mature groups require still another leadership style. Here the leader wants to emphasize a people orientation and not a task orientation. Moderately mature groups are able to direct themselves to a large measure, and they look to their leaders primarily for support and encouragement. The level of involvement in decision making best for the group is participation. When the leader has a problem the group is qualified to handle, the best advice may be to call them together and help them in arriving at a consensus decision.

Very mature groups may be the easiest to lead. A low-task, low-people approach is optimal. In other words, a very low profile is called for. This is because it is unnecessary for the leader to offer direction or support. Instead, effective performance can be obtained by simply pointing the group in the appropriate directions, and offering help only if the group requests it. The leader can delegate most decisions to the group, and they will readily take responsibility for them.

Conclusion

Unless a leader faces very serious time constraints or has little influence over his or her group, the leadership style that works best depends on the maturity level of the group being managed. Mature groups set high goals, willingly accept responsibility, and are highly skilled to perform the work. They work best under leaders who are low on both task and people orientation and who delegate decisions to the group. Moderately mature groups thrive under conditions of low-task and high-people styles and do best when they are invited to participate in decisions. Moderately immature groups require leaders who have a high-people/high-task oriented combination and are in the habit of consulting their employees before making important decisions. Finally, there are very immature groups. These perform well when led by managers who emphasize the task to be done and who reserve decision-making authority to themselves.

Figure 2
Relation Between Group Maturity and Leadership Effectiveness

	Low Task-Oriented	High Task-Oriented
People-Oriented High	Moderately Mature Groups (participation)	Moderately Immature Groups (consultation)
People-Oriented Low	Very Mature Groups (delegation)	Very Immature Groups (direction)

From *Management of Organizational Behavior: Utilizing Human Resources*, 4th ed., by Paul Hersey and Ken Blanchard, p. 154. Copyright © 1982 by Prentice-Hall, Inc. Adapted by permission of Prentice-Hall, Inc., Englewood Cliffs, New Jersey.

References

Argyris, Chris. *Personality and Organization.* New York: Harper & Row, 1957.

Blake, Robert R., and Jane S. Mouton. *The Managerial Grid.* Houston: Gulf, 1964.

Fiedler, Fred E. *A Theory of Leadership Effectiveness.* New York: McGraw-Hill, 1967.

Hersey, Paul, and Kenneth H. Blanchard. *Management of Organizational Behavior.* Englewood Cliffs, N.J.: Prentice-Hall, 1982.

Likert, Rensis. *The Human Organization.* New York: McGraw-Hill, 1967.

McGregor, Douglas. *The Human Side of Enterprise.* New York: McGraw-Hill, 1960.

Stodgill, Ralph M. *Manual for Leader Behavior Description Questionnaire--Form XII*. Columbus, Ohio: Ohio State University, 1963.

Stodgill, Ralph M. *Handbook of Leadership*. New York: Free Press, 1974.

Tannenbaum, Robert, and Warren Schmidt. "How to Choose a Leadership Pattern," *Harvard Business Review* 36 (1958): 95-102.

Vroom, Victor H., and Philip Yetton. *Leadership and Decision Making*. Pittsburgh, Penn.: University of Pittsburgh Press, 1973.

Interactive Case

You are the Assistant Manager of the Miami Beach branch of Caraway's Home Gallery. Caraway's is a chain of 19 furniture and home furnishings stores located in the Southeast. Sales for your store were over $6.5 million last year.

Your store employs 42 people who fall into four separate groups: home furniture salespeople, home furnishings clerks, warehouse and delivery people, and the accounting and office staff. You have direct responsibility for the latter three groups. Paul Thielman, your boss, assumes responsibility for the home furniture salespeople. An organization chart appears below.

Miami Branch of Caraway's Home Gallery

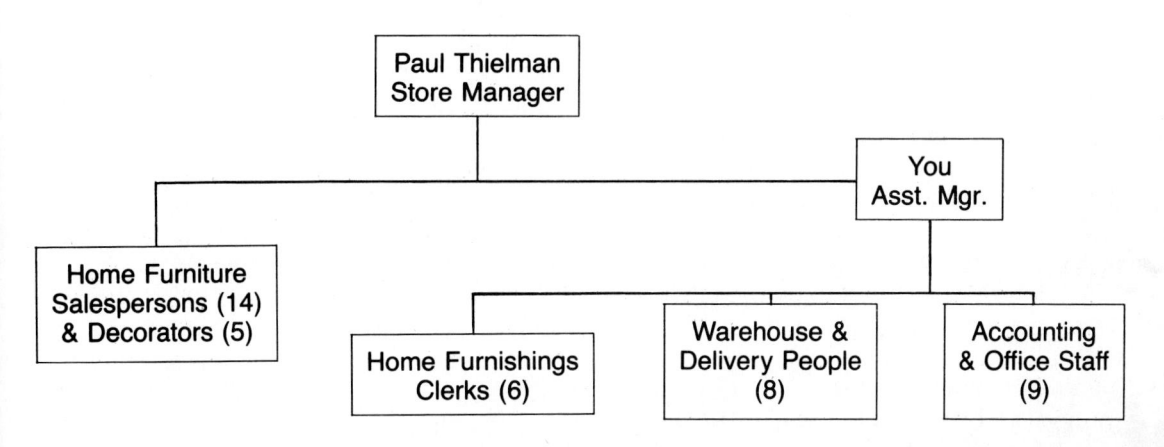

```
                    Paul Thielman
                    Store Manager
         ┌───────────────┼───────────────┐
         │                               │
         │                          You
         │                          Asst. Mgr.
         │              ┌────────────────┼────────────────┐
  Home Furniture        │                │                │
  Salespersons (14)  Home Furnishings  Warehouse &    Accounting
  & Decorators (5)   Clerks (6)        Delivery People  & Office Staff
                                       (8)              (9)
```

The home furniture salespersons sell furniture and carpets. They are all paid on commission and most had substantial sales experience before they were hired. Many of these people have been with Caraway's for over 10 years. Most earn upwards of $50,000 per year. The decorators are a subset of this group. They work directly in customers' homes giving advice about colors and decors. Like the furniture salespeople, the decorators are paid on a commission basis, but they have little physical presence in the store since they come in only once or twice a week. The members of this group all report directly to Paul Thielman, your boss. You interact with them only when Paul is out of the store or in the rare case when conflicts arise between them and your people.

The home furnishings clerks look to you for day-to-day supervision. These people sell towels, sheets, and other relatively inexpensive decorative items (e.g., artificial flowers, decorative pillows, and accent pieces). They are paid on an hourly basis totaling less than $17,000 annually. They are relatively inexperienced, and all are female.

The eight warehouse and delivery personnel are mostly (seven) male and are responsible for handling the uncrating and display of new items, maintaining inventory, and making deliveries to customers' homes. These employees range from one to over 15 years of experience at Caraway's. They are paid on an hourly rate, and most gross between $15,000 and $26,000 a year. The most highly paid and senior member of this group is the dispatcher, who acts as an informal "lead" of this group. Formally the group members all report to you, and you have learned not to rely on the dispatcher too much for the day-to-day supervision of these people.

The remaining nine people work in the office. They are composed of clerks, bookkeepers, secretaries, credit specialists, and a switchboard operator/receptionist. All of these people report directly to you, and your office location enables you to pay very close attention to them if necessary.

This morning you arrived at work and discovered that Al Thorn, the informal lead of your group of warehousemen, has given you a week's notice that he will be leaving to take a better-paying job with another firm. This is not a particularly surprising development. The morale of this group is not especially high, and group members have long complained that the pay and fringe benefit packages offered by Caraway are not competitive. They may be correct, for you have lost three warehousemen in the last year. Yet when you raised that issue with the personnel people at the home office of the company, you were told that warehouse groups always have a high turnover rate regardless of the pay.

With Al Thorn leaving, this makes it necessary for you to take a much more active leadership role in the group until you can find a replacement. This will add significantly to your work load, but you see it more as a challenge than a problem. The procedures the members of this group follow are pretty sound, and members generally have few difficulties getting the work out on schedule. In spite of the high turnover rate, all seven of the remaining workers seem to have a grasp of what's involved in the work.

At the suggestion of Caraway's personnel staff at the home office, your first step is to ask the seven remaining warehouse employees if any of them wants to be considered for Thorn's position. To your surprise, no one volunteers, even though you take the time to talk with two of the most senior people. Both echo the concern that the position doesn't pay sufficiently for the additional responsibility. When you report this to central personnel, they advise you that it will take at least three months to find a suitable replacement from the outside. Your first decision is to diagnose the maturity of the warehouse group. Which category do you think they fall into?

A. Very Immature. (GO TO 554A)
B. Moderately Immature. (GO TO 527A)
C. Moderately Mature. (GO TO 560A)
D. Very Mature. (GO TO 550A)

8 CONFLICT
Module Reading

One of the biggest challenges that a supervisor has to face is dealing with conflicts between employees. Although many of these disagreements are minor, some can be quite disruptive. If mishandled, these major ones can result in strained relations between people who *have to* work together to get the job done. Even the little disputes can snowball into serious feuds involving a host of people who were not even involved in the first place.

If a work group experiences conflict, a manager does not need to be overly concerned. Work conflicts are very common. One estimate is that supervisors spend almost one-fifth of their day dealing in some way with conflicts among their people. In spite of this, the evidence is that few managers feel they do a good job handling employee conflicts. This is unfortunate since there are some very helpful principles of bargaining and conflict resolution that have been successfully used to reduce some of the negative consequences of such conflicts. In the remainder of this chapter we will present and describe these principles.

Types of Work Conflicts

The list of issues over which employees can disagree is endless. One study dealt with the types of conflicts that lead employees to ask their supervisors for help. These are detailed in Table 1. Clearly some of these conflicts can be dealt with quite easily. Few supervisors would have trouble settling an argument over the way a policy should be interpreted. On the other hand, some of these conflicts are very difficult to handle. Accusations of discrimination, dishonesty, or breach of contract are very complicated indeed.

What Causes Work Conflicts?

Supervisors often blame work conflicts on the people involved. All of us have known people who are just disagreeable and argumentative. Yet it is better to think about the causes of conflict being difficult *situations* rather than difficult *people*. Some jobs and departments have high levels of conflict built into them. Even the most cooperative team player could not serve in these jobs and departments without experiencing conflicts with co-workers. This is important to keep in mind for two reasons. First, it is easier to change the work situation than the workers. A manager is usually given his or her employees and often has little authority to hire and fire unilaterally. Second, the manager is likely to be viewed as unfair if he or she labels certain employees as "problem people" just because they are in positions that open them up to conflicts with their fellow workers.

Table 1
Types of Conflicts Referred to Supervisors

Type of Conflict Between Employees	Frequency of Occurrence in Interviews	Percent
One employee complains about the job performance of another employee	41	25
Two workers disagree over a company policy	17	10
A worker complains that a co-worker has placed excessive demands upon him/her	12	7
One employee alleges discrimination	11	7
Disagreement between workers over pay	11	7
A worker accuses another of involvement in his/her duties	10	6
Result of an infringement on the property or rights of an employee	9	6
Disagreement concerning a breach of contract	9	6
One worker accusing the other of a dishonest act	9	6
Other types	32	20

From "Managers as Inquisitors" by Blair H. Sheppard in *Negotiating in Organizations*, edited by Max H. Bazerman and Roy J. Lewicki, p. 195. Copyright © 1983 by Sage Publications, Inc. Reprinted by permission of Sage Publications, Inc., and Blair H. Sheppard.

A number of things can make some jobs especially prone to co-worker conflict. Among them are the following:

Cause 1--Employees Must Deal with Co-workers Whose Duties Are Much Different from Their Own.

Workers in jobs that require them to interact with a diversity of people have a more conflict-ridden experience. Compare, for instance, a high school French teacher and a high school custodian. Each day a French teacher must interact with two or three co-workers. In contrast, the custodian has to interact with a large array of different co-workers. What makes this diversity so potentially conflict ridden is that different jobs generally create different ways of looking at situations. For the high school custodian, a science teacher creates one set of demands and expectations and a drama coach quite another. If employees are required to deal with a wide array of different individuals, then chances are the supervisor will have to contend with worker conflicts no matter how good the supervisor is or how good the employees are at staying out of trouble.

Cause 2--Subordinates Need to Share Limited Resources.

Work conflicts are also caused by workers having to share such things as work space, funds, raw materials, tools, and equipment. Sharing of one kind or another is common to every organization, but when resources are particularly tight, the potential for co-worker conflict is greatly enhanced. This is the reason that there are often problems between people who work at the same work station on different shifts. It is also the reason that budget cutbacks often cause conflicts between co-workers. Co-worker conflicts are almost inevitable during financial adversity.

Cause 3--Subordinates Must Work with Other People in Complicated Ways.

One of the most important causes of conflict is work interdependence. This refers to the situation where subordinates are required to work together in ways requiring complicated interactions or cooperation. Such complications arise when subordinates have to (a) rely on others for their inputs, (b) rely on others for feedback on how well they have done their work, or (c) interact with others face to face to complete their work. If the work of subordinates is interdependent, each has to rely on what the other does. Such mutual dependence is a chief factor in causing conflict between masons building the same brick wall, between a chemist and a lab assistant working on an experiment, and between a nurse and a surgeon in an operating room. Since the work between these individuals is highly intertwined or interdependent, it has a greater conflict potential.

Together, these three things--co-worker job diversity, shared resources, and complicated work relationships--create conflict between co-workers. In managing people who interact with a diversity of other people in complicated ways and under adverse circumstances, a manager is likely to have co-worker conflicts whether or not the employees are good at dealing with conflicts. So if a manager has subordinates in these types of jobs, the most effective way to reduce conflict may be to reduce the situational causes of the conflict. This is not always possible, of course, but it is worth looking at.

The Results of Work Conflicts for the Organization

While no supervisor enjoys working with people who are constantly bickering, arguing, and fighting, many experts believe that some conflict is healthy and that supervisors should not discourage conflict in all instances. In fact, mild conflicts like friendly competitions, good-natured rivalries, and minor differences of opinion can be quite positive. It is the serious conflicts that are the problem. The distinction is that serious conflicts involve two things that mild conflicts lack: blocking activities and unfair tactics. Blocking activities occur when one party keeps the other from getting all the information or resources he or she needs to do his work. Unfair tactics include labeling someone's work incorrectly, blaming others unjustly, or escalating differences to personal attacks.

Negative Results of Serious Work Conflicts

Serious conflicts can result in a host of negative things: loss of attention to work, feelings of frustration and stress, energy used in blocking opponents rather than working, poor communication, name calling, and other hurtful forms of ridicule. Besides being generally unpleasant for the parties involved, these results can be unpleasant for anyone who observes them, including uninvolved co-workers and, worst of all, clients and vendors.

Positive Results of Mild Work Conflicts

From time to time it may be wise for supervisors to stimulate arguments, surface disagreements, challenge authority, orchestrate occasions for competition, pick a fight to give emphasis to a problem, or create contests to reward victors. The following five commonly accepted principles below explain how mild conflict can help an organization:

(1) Individuals or groups in need of change require tension in order to change.
(2) Unexpressed conflicts allowed to persist for some time may have
negative long-range effects on the person's ability to work with others.
(3) Competition, disagreements, and games (if free of blocking or unfair tactics)
can stimulate higher performance without necessarily jeopardizing
future goodwill.
(4) Insincere conformity does not allow needed information to be used in making
decisions.
(5) Creating conflicts is sometimes the only way to get the attention of others
in the organization.

In general, then, both too much and too little conflict can be bad for the organization. However, most managers spend much more of their time trying to *reduce* conflict than trying to stimulate it. One reason for this is that most managers have experienced the problems created by conflicts more than they have the problems caused by the absence of conflict.

The Results of Work Conflicts for the People Involved

It is also important to think about work conflicts from the viewpoint of employees. People generally sense the work conflicts they are involved in as win-lose situations, which means that they feel they cannot get what they want unless the other person gives in. However, not all conflicts result in winners and losers. Sometimes there are no winners, and less commonly there are multiple winners. The following are the different outcomes of conflict.

Win-Lose Results

Some work conflicts can be resolved in no other way than win-lose. Conflicts over facts, for instance, usually result in at best *one* winner. Similarly, when one indivisible prize is sought by both parties (a promotion, for example) any outcome other than win-lose is rare.

One very important reason managers dislike employee conflicts is that most conflicts initially appear to be win-lose situations, and this means that the manager has to (a) choose sides and (b) deal with losers' frustrations. Few managers relish choosing between subordinates and dealing with the disappointment of the losing side. For these reasons, some managers avoid even dealing with conflicts in the first place, and instead smooth them over or force the parties to work it out themselves. Some supervisors even punish those who bring them conflicts by making sure no one ever wins. There is another option, and it involves trying to convert win-lose situations into win-win outcomes.

Win-Win Results

Win-win means, of course, that both parties in a conflict feel that they got what they wanted. In other words, a way is found to allow both persons to achieve their desired goals. As we have said, win-win outcomes are elusive; few conflicts ever appear in a win-win way at first. An example may clarify this. Sam and Bill are both material handlers in a wholesale nursery. In June both apply to take their annual vacations in August, the peak harvesting month. Able to allow only one of his people to take his vacation at that time, Sam and Bill's supervisor has a problem. Choose one and the manager runs the risk of creating frustrations and perhaps losing the respect of other members of his team. Instead of choosing one or the other, a manager might begin by talking with both employees. In this case, after discussing the issue with both Sam and Bill, the manager discovered that while Sam wanted an August vacation for its own sake, Bill did not. Bill applied for August because that was the only time he could get reduced-fare flights to Phoenix to visit his parents. After making some inquiries with the company's internal travel officer, the supervisor learned that with company discounts, Bill could purchase tickets to Phoenix during November at the August equivalent. Given this careful work, the supervisor found out that the conflict could be resolved with both Sam and Bill winning. It is not possible to resolve all work conflicts in this way, but win-win results are certainly worth shooting for. Not only are both parties more satisfied, but also their settlement is more stable and their relationship better.

Lose-Lose Results

Conflicting subordinates can both lose as a result of a conflict. This occurs when settlements satisfy the total desires of neither party. For example, in the situation above the supervisor could have simply disallowed *both* August vacations on the grounds that if both could not take off in August, neither could. A similar lose-lose option in the example would have been if the manager had allowed both to take only half their vacation time in August.

As the name implies, lose-lose situations are not good for anyone, yet lose-lose results are not as uncommon as many people think. In order to avoid having to make potentially unpopular or incorrect choices, managers are occasionally tempted to smooth over a conflict situation or ask the parties to resolve the situation without help. In many of these cases, though, the result of these practices is a lose-lose outcome.

Managing Conflicts Between People

There *are* proven ways to manage work conflicts that have positive results both for employees and for the organization. However, much depends on the particular circumstances involved. For this reason, it is critical that the manager know both the people who work for him or her and the culture of the organization. This is vital for several reasons. First, knowing subordinates allows a manager to understand something about the history of the relationship between the parties. Conflicts are often the result of unresolved problems in the past or merely a form of some long-standing issue in the relationship. It is also important for the manager to know the people in order to tell whether individuals in the situation are speaking for themselves or representing others. Sometimes people speak for others in conflicts, either by fighting another person's battles or by joining the side of a popular co-worker.

It is also important that a manager appreciate how the culture of an organization affects expectations about conflict. Some organizations have cultures that suppress the expression of disagreement. Other organizational cultures are more uninhibited. Some companies have unwritten rules against going to higher authorities with unresolved conflicts and some do not. If a supervisor is not aware of these unwritten rules about conflict, it is easy to misjudge the importance of a particular conflict or to handle it in a fashion that others are not used to.

Step 1--Meeting with Each Employee Separately to Define the Conflict and Create the Proper Atmosphere

Once a manager knows that there is a conflict and has decided that it is serious enough to act on, the first step should be to find out how the conflicting parties see the issue. The best way to do this is to talk with the individuals separately and privately. During this meeting, the supervisor should keep several things in mind.

During the interview the manager should try to separate information and emotion. The initial interview is often emotionally charged. People sometimes say things that under other circumstances they would not say. Clearly, overheated situations like this require cool heads, and the supervisor must take the lead. First of all, it is important for the supervisor to be an attentive, nonevaluative listener. One technique is for the manager to respond to emotionally charged statements by restating them in a form that strips away the strong feelings. This both allows a ventilation of anger and makes it clear that the issue has an acceptable, nonemotional version. Second, it is important for the manager to appear initially neutral, to avoid taking sides. The conflicting parties will often try to coax the manager into making some sort of statement about how the situation will be resolved, but he or she should remain neutral. Third, the manager should begin to depersonalize the issue. Statements made against the personal character of one's "opponent" should immediately be ruled out of bounds.

During the interview the manager should try to change the way the parties are viewing the conflict. Research shows that if people view the conflict in certain ways, they will be more likely to find acceptable settlements. Table 2 details the perspectives that are favorable for settlement and those that are not.

The initial meeting is an ideal time to begin to work on these perspectives. If an employee expresses the opinion that losing is inevitable, the manager should immediately challenge that opinion. If a person believes that he will *never* have to work with a co-worker after the conflict is settled, again the manager should make it clear that they will be expected to work together in the future. Essentially, then, the manager should not just listen during this first meeting but should try to shape the way the issue is seen.

During the interview the manager should begin to distinguish between the demands of the parties and their interests. People in a conflict state their demands clearly and forcefully. By demands we mean what they say they really want, not what they wish they could get. Employees generally do not state the interests they have that underlie their demands. Research has shown that interests are much easier to reconcile than demands. Demands define one way to satisfy interests, but there are often other pathways to resolution. Consider the case of two librarians arguing over whether a window should be open or closed.

Table 2
Views of Conflict That Make Resolution Easier and Harder

Resolution is *Easier* if the person perceives the conflict this way	Resolution is *Harder* if the person perceives the conflict this way
I appreciate the other person's point of view.	My viewpoint is the only correct and and valid one.
I know why the other person has taken his/her position.	I don't understand why the other person has taken his/her position
It's a problem between the two of us.	A lot of people are involved in this dispute.
The issue can be defined in simple, concrete terms.	The issue is complicated by symbols, words, and matters of principle.
I have hope that this conflict can be worked out.	I have little hope that this conflict can ever be resolved.
I don't represent anyone else in this dispute.	I represent a lot of people. I don't want to let them down.

The demands were clear but not the interests of the parties. The head librarian overheard the argument and interviewed each of the individuals. She asked one party *why* she wanted the window open, and was told, "to get some fresh air." She asked the other *why*, and was told, "to avoid a draft." At that point, a solution was obvious--a window was opened in the next room.

Discovering interests is actually much more difficult than this example suggests. One reason is that people seldom respond honestly to "why" questions when they are involved in a conflict. Typically one has to probe more than once to find out all the interests that underlie a position, and unlike our example above, there is often more than one interest involved. Adding further to this difficulty is that interests are often organized into hierarchical trees with more basic interests underpinning the surface ones. So it is useful to go deeper than the interests first mentioned if these interests do not suggest a solution. In analyzing conflict situations it is helpful to look for complementary interests.

During the interview the manager should make it clear how he or she plans to deal with the conflict as the third party. This is the last thing to do during the initial interview. Basically there are three options depending on the amount of control the manager wants to maintain. Only one of these approaches is effective in most instances. Table 3 illustrates how these approaches vary.

One approach is called "arbitration." This is where the manager assumes the role of "judge" in the conflict. An example of this approach follows: The supervisor of a group of stock brokers was told by one of his subordinates that another broker had "stolen" one of her customers. The supervisor then went to the "thief" and asked if he knew that the customer was the other broker's.

Table 3
Options of Third Party Involvement

		Process Control	
		High	Low
Outcome Control	High	Arbitration	Arbitration
	Low	Mediation	Delegation

From "Managers as Inquisitors" by Blair H. Sheppard in *Negotiating in Organizations*, edited by Max H. Bazerman and Roy J. Lewicki, p. 199. Copyright © 1983 by Sage Publications, Inc. Reprinted by permission of Sage Publications, Inc., and Blair H. Sheppard.

When he answered positively, the supervisor told him never to do that again and asked the customer either to use the original broker or to take her business elsewhere. Arbitration is a fast, definitive process, and it is most effective when one of the conflicting parties has obviously violated a rule or policy. In most other situations, though, it is not very effective. Unless a manager is particularly good at finding win-win outcomes, he or she will probably not arrive at as good a settlement as the employees themselves might. Moreover, the parties to the conflict seldom are as committed to a settlement imposed upon them as one they have fashioned themselves. Consequently, some repetition of the conflict is very likely.

A second way of handling conflicts is called "delegation." Here the manager tells the two parties that they must solve the conflict themselves. Delegation is a popular approach among supervisors who would rather smooth over conflicts than deal with them. However, like arbitration, it is often not effective. Left on their own, conflicting parties are often unable to work through conflicts because they lack the skills, information, or impartiality to do so.

Generally the best approach for a manager to take in dealing with conflicts between people is "mediation." For this reason the rest of this chapter deals with the principles of mediation. When a supervisor mediates, he or she gives up some control over just what the agreement will be but exerts considerable influence over the resolution process. In effect, the supervisor guides the two parties to discover the solution to *their* problem. Although mediation is preferred by managers and subordinates alike, it is actually used less frequently than arbitration. For that reason, supervisors who declare their intention to mediate a conflict are sometimes not believed. Moreover, because most employees have little experience with mediation, they are often unsure how to respond to a supervisor who tries to guide the process without making a final decision.

Step 2--Getting the Parties Together for an Initial Meeting

Sometime very soon after the first separate meetings the manager should get the parties together. This first meeting will most likely be quite tense. At this point the parties are unsure what the final outcome will be, and they will probably not know what will be coming next. During this first meeting the manager should be guided by one fundamental principle--keep communication open. This should be reinforced in everything done in the meeting starting with the location of the meeting. The meeting should be conducted in a "neutral" setting. The seating positions of the parties should symbolically convey the impression that the conflict is a problem the two parties have to solve. One way to accomplish this is for the manager to sit across from (not between) the two individuals and close to a chalkboard or easel. This will reinforce the notion that the session is devoted to solving the problem rather than conflict with one another.

It is useful for the manager to begin this meeting by asking each party to state their positions. Active listening, where the other party must repeat back his opponent's position, is often helpful at this point. As well, the manager must be ready to try to eliminate personal comments or aggressiveness.

Once the parties have stated their demands, the manager should try to see whether the parties are willing to talk to one another about the interests that underlie their demands. By this time the manager will probably have some sort of idea what these interests are from the separate meetings. However, if the parties talk about their interests, it may improve the chances of arriving at a mutually acceptable solution.

This process can be summarized as follows:

(1) ask each employee to state the problem,
(2) ask each employee to state other's view of the problem,
(3) ask each to confirm accuracy of other's repetition.

Step 3--Asking Each to Suggest Solutions

Once positions have been laid out and understood, it is then possible to generate alternative solutions. Here it may be useful for the manager to use brainstorming. The rules of brainstorming are simple:

(1) The object is quantity of ideas not quality.
(2) Freewheeling is encouraged, the wilder the idea the better.
(3) Piggybacking (building on the ideas of others) is welcomed.
(4) Above all, no evaluation or judging of ideas is permitted.

During brainstorming, the manager should be mindful that the session will probably start slowly and may seem to end at several points as the parties struggle to come up with another idea. It is important that the manager continue through these apparently unproductive intervals. The best ideas often follow directly after quiet periods. While there are no accepted rules of thumb, if one is facing an important conflict, at least a half-hour should be invested in the brainstorming phase.

Step 4--Using Recesses Strategically

One of the most powerful tools a supervisor has in dealing with conflicts is the recess. Called at the proper time, the recess can mean the difference between a lasting settlement and one that is violated before the ink is dry. Recesses can do several things.

Recesses can be used to cool off emotionally charged episodes. Initial meetings between the parties can get quite heated, and a short recess can allow the parties to collect themselves. If a recess is called for this purpose, it is important that the manager make clear that this is the reason. In addition, the parties should be encouraged to spend this time alone considering whether they are doing everything they can to solve the problem.

Recesses can be called to conduct further private inquiries about interests. This essentially is "shuttle diplomacy." A manager can use the recess to explore interests or to test tentative settlements. Earlier we distinguished between interests and demands and indicated that supervisors should conduct separate meetings in order to explore interests before getting the parties together. We also stated that eliciting interests from the party to a conflict is very difficult; people are not used to talking directly about their needs. If a manager does not have a clear picture about the interests of the parties, a recess may be helpful before the brainstorming session is conducted. For example, after the parties have stated their demands at their first mediation session together, a manager could say, "Okay, I think we are now more clear about just what each of us wants. Let's take an hour to reflect on what we have just heard and to see if we can begin to come up with some viable solutions." During this hour the manager could then shuttle between the parties, further probing them for their interests and testing ideas about how the matter might be settled.

Recesses can be used to de-escalate the conflict. The threat of escalation is always present during joint meetings. Conflicts escalate when the parties become heavily committed to their viewpoints and argue relentlessly for their demands. Calling recesses allows the manager to break the cycle of strong statements and to refocus energy from the parties to the problem.

Step 5--Focusing on Objective Facts, Areas of Mutual Need, or Mutual Goals

Excellent win-win settlements sometimes are illuminated during brainstorming sessions or are otherwise proposed by one of the parties, but the manager must be prepared to develop win-win options if they do not come from the parties. Win-win alternatives come in many forms, but the most common are listed below:

Expanding the pie. Many work conflicts hinge on a shortage of such resources as time, money, space, or machines. When this is the case, win-win agreements can be devised by expanding the resources available. For example, if two product managers are arguing over which product is given priority in manufacturing, the vice president can expand production capacity through overtime to satisfy both parties. Similarly, a conflict due to the necessity of sharing a machine can be solved by buying duplicate equipment.

Expanding the pie seems an obvious solution to many work conflicts, yet there are occasions when the way to expand is not at all clear. For example, there were severe conflicts between teams of loading dock workers until it was discovered that the dock could be widened. Similarly, word processing specialists quarreled over not being able to get things done fast enough due to an over-used printer until a flexible work schedule was introduced that enabled the company to spread the use of the printer over fourteen hours per regular working day.

Nonspecific compensation. The manager should also be watchful for options in which one party can offer the other compensation for "giving in" in some sort of unrelated "coin." For example, if two assistant football coaches believe that different players should be cut from the squad to get down to the legal team size, one could offer the other a "utility" player from his own group if that coach went along with the particular coach's preference. Or a chef could offer the headwaiter a prized recipe for agreeing to hire an unwanted relative as an assistant.

Logrolling. In some conflict situations the interests of both parties can be ranked from the most important to the least important. In this case, one party might discover that by conceding his least important interest, the most important interest of his opponent would be served. Consider the case of two regional sales managers who disagreed over the form of a new incentive pay scheme for their salespeople. The interests the two had that underlay their demands fit the following priorities:

	Regional Manager 1	Regional Manager 2
High Priority	Minimize expense accounts	Provide incentives on developing new accounts
	Reward top performers	Reward top performers
Low Priority	Reward servicing major customers	Minimize paperwork

When it was realized that if each regional manager gave in on his or her least important concern, the other's most important interest could be served, a new pay plan was quickly developed that satisfied both managers' most important interests.

Bridging. In bridging neither party gets what was originally asked for, but an option is invented that satisfies the most important interests of the parties involved. Take the example of two childcare workers who had been in constant disagreement over work methods until a new supervisor arrived. One worker wanted to allow the children to watch television while the other was dead-set against it as a matter of principle. When the new supervisor interviewed the two workers, he discovered that the workers had different but potentially complementary interests. The one who opposed television was most concerned about maximizing the exposure the children received to verbal rather than audiovisual stimulation and was suspicious about the quality of verbally oriented educational television. The one who wanted to use television was most concerned that the children be exposed to a multitude of media (records, films, television, etc.). Thus the new supervisor was able to help the two people settle their differences by having the person against television prescreen programs the other suggested before allowing the children to see them. Notice that this solution was found because one party's strongest interest was content and the other's was form.

Structural solutions. Unfortunately, not all conflicts have win-win resolutions. Accordingly, it makes little sense to explore the situation endlessly until one is found. Before settling on a win-lose alternative, however, a manager should consider the feasibility of resolving the conflict in a structural way. Basically, structural options act on the causes of work conflicts: job diversity, resource sharing, and interdependent activities. If a win-win settlement does not seem possible, one of the structural options listed below may be suitable:

(1) Moving employees between jobs to develop an appreciation of each other's point of view (job rotation can be used to develop empathy for an opponent's position).
(2) Using rules to regularize resource sharing (when a valued resource must be shared, a rule could require that it be distributed according to seniority or turn-taking or some such thing).
(3) Separating the parties to the conflict and reducing the complexity of their required work interactions (some work conflicts can be settled by simply separating the parties from one another).

Step 6--Bring Both to Agreement of Specific Steps to Resolve Conflict

When win-win options are uncovered, the rest of the process is quite simple. All that needs to be done is to work out the implementation plan and agree on some sort of follow-through. When none of the alternatives are truly win-win, the process is a bit more tricky.

Using the criteria of quality and acceptability. One way to aid in implementation is for the manager to ensure that the final settlement is the best both technically and politically. A technically sound settlement may be doomed if it lacks the acceptance of the parties. And a popular settlement that lacks technical feasibility is equally poor.

Being alert to the importance of intangibles. As the parties talk about their favored solutions, it is important for the manager to be alert to unstated preferences for intangibles. Some important intangibles include appearing tough to co-workers, having the settlement implemented quietly or in a piece-by-piece fashion, and guaranteeing that the present settlement will not serve as a precedent in the future. Intangibles are often a stumbling block because the parties are reluctant to admit how important they really are. For that reason effective mediators are very careful not to require parties to justify their personal preferences. This is a particularly difficult thing for managers to avoid when they are acting as mediators. Unfortunately, many managers are in the habit of evaluating interests.

Using tentativeness as a tool. An important consideration that every mediator must master is that commitments should be considered flexible until the very end of any negotiations. Strong, seemingly irreversible statements by the parties should be respected as limiting, but not binding. Prior to the last step in the process, virtually everything is negotiable. Therefore, the manager should be very careful to respect firm statements but to view them as flexible. It is appropriate to write down (commit to permanence) only final agreements. Statements made prior to the final step should not be referred to except in the most general terms.

Making clear the responsibilities for follow-through. The final step in mediation is to let the parties know just who else will be responsible for the enforcement of the agreement. If a written statement is filed, it is appropriate to make clear that the document will be preserved as part of the record.

Conclusion

Work conflicts are a natural result of many forces in today's organizations. Although they are potentially quite disruptive, work conflicts are not universally negative. In fact, there are instances where a little more conflict increases effectiveness. This chapter focuses on a manager's responsibility to settle conflicts between subordinates. As in every problem situation, the first task is information gathering. Initially it is best to interview each of the conflicting parties to obtain data and begin to create a conducive climate for the negotiations. Following that, the manager should strive to keep communications between the parties open and to facilitate mutual problem solving. At the heart of the process is the search for the interests that underlie the demands of the parties in order to discover win-win options for the settlement.

References

Bazerman, Max H., and Margaret A. Neale. "Heuristics in Negotiation." In M. Bazerman and R. J. Lewicki, eds., *Negotiating in Organizations*. Beverly Hills, Calif.: Sage, 1983.

Blake, R. R., H. A. Shepard, and J. S. Mouton. *Managing Intergroup Conflict in Industry*. Houston: Gulf, 1964.

Deutsch, Morton. *The Resolution of Conflict*. New Haven: Yale University Press, 1973.

Filey, Alan C. *Interpersonal Conflict Resolution*. Glenview, Ill.: Scott, Foresman and Company, 1975.

Fisher, Roger, and William Ury. *Getting to Yes*. Boston: Houghton-Mifflin, 1981.

Lewicki, Roy J., and Joseph A. Litterer. *Negotiation*. Homewood, Ill.: Irwin, 1985.

Mintzberg, Henry. "The Manager's Job: Forklore and Fact." *Harvard Business Review* 53 (1975): 49-61.

Pruitt, Dean G. *Negotiation Behavior*. New York: Academic Press, 1981.

Pruitt, Dean G. "Achieving Integrative Agreements." In M. Bazerman and R. J. Lewicki eds., *Negotiating in Organizations*. Beverly Hills, Calif.: Sage, 1983.

Schmidt, S., and T. Kochan. "Conflict: Toward Conceptual Clarity." *Administrative Science Quarterly* 17 (1972): 359-370.

Schmidt, Warren H., and Robert Tannenbaum. "Management of Differences." *Harvard Business Review* 39 (1960): 107-115.

Shea, G. F. *Creative Negotiating*. Boston: CBI Publishing, 1975.

Sheppard. Blair H. "Managers as Inquisitors." In M. Bazerman and R. J. Lewicki eds., *Negotiating in Organizations*. Beverly Hills, Calif.: Sage, 1983.

Thomas, Kenneth W., and Louis R. Pondy. "Toward an 'Intent' Model of Conflict Management Among Principal-Parties." *Human Relations* 30 (1977): 1089-1102.

Thomas, Kenneth W., and Warren H. Schmidt. "A Survey of Managerial Interests with Respect to Conflict." *Academy of Management Journal* 19 (1976): 315-318.

Tushman, Michael L. "A Political Approach to Organizations." *Academy of Management Review* 2 (1977): 206-216.

Walton, R. E. *Interpersonal Peacemaking*. Reading, Mass.: Addison-Wesley, 1969.

Interactive Case

You are the general manager for a factory that produces brushes for a large health products firm. The plant is located in the southern part of the United States, is nonunionized, and has 109 full-time employees on its payroll. Your primary responsibility is to meet a weekly production quota supplied by the corporate headquarters. In your two and one-half years in your present position, you have been able to do so 63 percent of the time, a record that, although average by corporate numerical standards, is actually quite good given the fluctuating availability of your raw materials (notably plastics) and the rather antiquated equipment you have to work with. Your boss understands these constraints, but little can be done because the brush market is considered a "loss-leader" in the corporate strategic plan. All in all, you are satisfied with your operation, and you enjoy the respect and admiration your employees have for you.

Today you have one pressing problem to solve. It deals with a work conflict between your internal auditor (Phyllis Smart) and one of your production foremen (Virgil Stonehill). You decide to deal with this situation right away because it seems to have a direct and important impact on the overall effectiveness of the plant.

Phyllis Smart is the internal auditor of your plant. Her job is to break down weekly quota figures into discrete schedules and monitor progress against these standards. She is young and somewhat inexperienced, but you think she has made fine progress in her first 22 months with the organization. She has a degree in industrial administration from the local state university, and after having been hired through a corporate recruitment effort, she was trained at headquarters before being assigned to your plant. She is an excellent analyst and a loyal subordinate.

Virgil Stonehill is the foreman of your dental brush line. He supervises 18 people and has worked at the plant for 13 years. He worked his way up to his present position from machine operator to maintenance specialist to foreman. He is 53 years old and a retired Navy machinist. His crew all refer to him as "Double" because he currently draws a Navy pension.

Virgil is not one of your best foremen. While he has a very good relationship with his crew, his line has had the worst quality record in the plant. Although this may be due in part to the equipment he has been assigned, you are not convinced that he is adequately quality conscious. Three months ago a very serious quality problem occurred. Twenty thousand toothbrushes were produced that failed quality standards. This caused your plant to be rated the second lowest in performance within the corporation during that quarter. Following that incident, you conducted a full-scale investigation which discovered that Virgil had miscalculated the setup time necessary to meet weekly quotas. Although his line's machinery is admittedly old, he apparently didn't account for these limitations and pressed his crew for a level of output that the machines couldn't bear. You learned of the conflict between Phyllis and Virgil through the following memo:

Memorandum

TO: You
FR: Phyllis Smart, Internal Auditor
RE: Production Reports

Mr. Virgil Stonehill has decided to obstruct my efforts to maximize the efficiency of the plant. I expressly informed him that his weekly production figures had to be submitted to me each Monday by noon. For the past two weeks he did not do so until Thursday morning. This caused serious problems in the procurement of dyes. This resulted in an overstock of clear brushes (now at 31 percent over the standard of 60 days). Please instruct Mr. Stonehill to comply with my information requirements.

What would you do now?

A. Call Phyllis into your office to clarify her memo. (GO TO 507A)

B. Call Virgil in to get his side of the story. (GO TO 507C)

C. Call both parties into your office to settle this issue face to face. (GO TO 488B)

D. Instruct Virgil to get his information to Phyllis by noon Mondays. (GO TO 495C).

E. Ask some of the other foremen if they have difficulty complying with Phyllis' requirements to have their weekly figures in by Monday noon. (GO TO 516A)

9 ORGANIZATIONAL POLITICS
Module Reading

Mention the term "office politics" and many of us see red. One reason is that most of us have been victimized by politics at work, and that has given us very negative feelings toward the things we associate with politics: favoritism, selfish interests, and dirty tricks. Yet office politics in the broadest sense are not necessarily dirty or even unjust. They simply are a way to get things done outside the normal chain of command. In fact, managers cannot accomplish much without using politics. It is not only useful, it is essential. This does not excuse the excesses, of course, but it is important to consider office politics a tool as well as a problem.

The Power Gap

Playing politics is essential because managers are often not given enough authority to do their jobs. If a manager has an employee who is not performing and whose performance cannot be improved, can the manager fire the employee? Similarly, is the manager given full rein when he or she needs support from a staff person who is reluctant to help? How about policies that are put in force that are silly, even counterproductive? Can a manager really oppose them without jeopardizing his or her job? Most managers know that they do not have all the authority they would like to have. We call this difference between the power a manager needs to do a good job and the amount of authority he or she is given *the power gap*.

Power gaps differ from job to job, of course, but most managers know that they have a power gap in their work. It is one of the frustrating aspects of being a manager. Faced with a power gap, one successful remedy is to become political. This may not set well with some people, but it is a fact of organizational life.

We now examine some of the typical situations that require a manager to act politically. These situations fall into three groups: relations with superiors, relations with subordinates, and lateral relations.

Relations with Superiors

Most directives that come from people above a manager in the chain of command help rather than hurt getting the job done. Yet there are occasions when senior people make decisions that create real problems for the manager. When this happens, it is difficult to know just what to do. Senior people are privy to information that those lower in the organization do not have, making it difficult to question decisions from above. At the same time, the individual manager is the expert when it comes to his or her own area of responsibility, so when decisions are made, an individual manager has a right to question whether the directive is suitable to the local problems of the group. Clearly a manager faces a significant power gap whenever he or she experiences conflicts with people above him or her in the hierarchy. To have any impact, it is sometimes necessary for the manager to exercise a considerable amount of informal influence.

Relations with Subordinates

Managers also experience a power gap in dealing with their own people. In certain circumstances, some subordinates may even have more power than their managers. Consider the following types of employees:

(1) experts in a particular part of the work,
(2) employees who are so popular with others that if they were disciplined, it would have serious repercussions,
(3) individuals who are almost impossible to replace,
(4) key people in the workflow.

Such individuals as these may be difficult to confront without some political maneuvering.

Lateral Relations

Most managers have a host of people in other work groups on whom they rely. Other groups provide them with the raw materials or support they need in order to perform well. If these other groups do not cooperate, managers cannot order them to do so. The manager may have no recourse but to use politics. Consider purchasing people, for example. If a manager needs a new piece of capital equipment, he or she will need their help even if there is a budget for it. Other managers in the department are also important. They can make the situation very difficult if relationships are poor.

Personal Power Resources

Power is the ability to influence others. Every position in an organization carries some power with it, but people can supplement this formal power with personal power resources. There are four types of personal power: information power, expert power, reward/punishment power, and relationship power.

Information Power

Power accrues to those who have inside information about how the organization really works. Often there is more to understanding the organization than just the organization chart and policy manuals. Some policies are ignored; certain people are more or less influential than their position in the chart would suggest. Information about the following can be a source of power:

(1) the history of the organization,
(2) who the key people are,
(3) how certain people will react to particular situations,
(4) which policies are important and which are not,
(5) other employees' needs, interests, and ambitions,
(6) what a particular decision means for the future,
(7) the nature of the relationships among key people,
(8) the jargon of the organization,
(9) what the critical tasks and departments are,
(10) how committed others are to various positions on an issue.

Not surprisingly, information power is often related to seniority. The longer one has been with an organization, the more he or she knows about it. However, people do not get information power by just being around for a long time. It is cultivated by asking questions, by watching carefully as events unfold, and by testing ideas in order to learn more.

Managers with information power can reduce their power gap tremendously. If a manager knows his or her boss's background, friends, and ambitions, it gives an edge in upwards relations. Similarly, if a manager knows that a staff person he or she has to work with is not thought highly of and will soon be transferred, it enables action to be taken accordingly. In short, information power allows making the best use of the other personal power resources the manager possesses.

Expert Power

A second source of personal power comes from expertise. If a manager has knowledge or skills that are both critical to the work and difficult to replace, then he or she can parlay that expertise into influence. All of us have seen many situations where people thought to be experts can persuade others.

One does not necessarily have to be an expert in order to have expert power. It is what other people think the individual knows or can do that really matters. Expert power is helpful in reducing the power gap. A boss is much more apt to defer to a subordinate who is seen as knowledgeable. Subordinates respect their manager more if they think he or she is technically able. And expert power is probably the most commonly used resource in lateral relationships.

Reward/Punishment Power

The ability to reward and punish is another power resource. All managers have some influence over merit pay and promotional decisions but often neglect the other ways they can reward others. For example, managers reward others every time they

(1) give interesting or "visible" assignments,
(2) provide recognition in front of one's peers,
(3) excuse someone from an undesired requirement,
(4) write a congratulatory letter,
(5) introduce someone to a high official,
(6) interpret a policy so that it favors an individual.

Similarly, managers do not generally recognize all the ways they can punish others. For example, managers punish when they

(1) ignore someone's call for help,
(2) supervise too closely,
(3) give unpopular assignments,
(4) allow someone to make a mistake they know about in advance,
(5) call attention to someone's failures,
(6) criticize someone's work.

Just as managers sometimes forget the various ways they reward or punish subordinates, they seldom think about the ways they do so in lateral or upward relations. Think, for example, how a manager might reward or punish the boss. Think also about what sorts of rewards or punishments might be used in dealing with others at the same level.

Most managers underestimate their abilities to reward and punish people other than their direct subordinates; however, there are often opportunities to do so. Take the case of a staff person with whom a manager has to work. Assume that the manager is not getting the sort of service from that person that is necessary. From an authority standpoint the manager has little recourse; the staff person does not report to him or her. It is easy to conclude that the manager is powerless in this situation, but if you consider what resources the manager has and what problems and needs the staff person has, it can open up possibilities. The staff member may be experiencing a lack of visibility, and the manager could help him or her meet certain key people in the organization. The staff person may be having difficulties obtaining some software, and the manager could lend him some. The staff member may be having a problem getting the budget he or she needs, and the manager could lobby for his or her case or support the staff person's efforts with discretely placed testimonials. A manager can reward people (or punish them) even when he or she does not have authority over them. It simply requires a careful analysis of needs and resources.

Relationship Power

No personal power resource is better known than relationship power. We often hear of "old boy networks" or the saying, "It's not so much what you know as who you know." Such comments reflect an important political reality. It is easier (and more rewarding) to work with people who are liked, respected, and admired than those who are not liked or known. Additionally, most managers find that work conflicts are much easier to work through with friends than within the context of formal relationships.

Who a manager knows, and more importantly who he or she can work with harmoniously *is* important. Many successful managers could not get anything done if they did not have co-workers, bosses, and subordinates with whom they had solid relationships.

There are two dimensions to relationship power. One is goal compatibility and the other is interpersonal trust. Goal compatibility refers to the mutuality of interests and objectives. For example, two co-workers may develop a relationship based on their mutual interest in seeing a particular product succeed or in a shared vision for the organization. Interpersonal trust grows out of a relationship such that each party comes to count on the other even when the other may have incentives not to help or assist. For example, if a manager risks not completing an assignment to help a friend in need, then that is a demonstration of interpersonal trust. Similarly, a manager demonstrates trust when he or she "saves" a colleague from making a mistake, even when that mistake would make the manager look good personally.

The Use of Personal Power Resources

How does a manager influence someone over whom he or she has no authority? There are several means to choose between, some with a high likelihood of success and some with a low likelihood of success. We will start with those uses of political tactics that are seldom effective.

Ineffective Political Tactics

Certain political tactics have a relatively low likelihood of success. They either create ill feelings in their wake, thus promising at best short-term gains. Or, they are likely to fail to result in successful influence even in the short run.

Tactic 1--The Use of Powerless Persuasion. Probably the most common influence attempt is the persuasive appeal. It may be directed upward to one's boss to get him or her to change priorities. It may be focused laterally at peers to build support for a pet project. And it may be targeted downward to attempt to elicit a higher commitment to objectives.

Persuasion is so common because it is a familiar tool of authority. Most authoritative communication is of a persuasive nature. The difference in using persuasion as a political tool is that there are not the sanctions attached to it that there are with authority. When your boss "persuades" you that a task needs to be completed by a certain date, there is the implied message that if you do so, you will gain approval and with it other rewards. In contrast, political persuasion has no such implicit sanction.

It is this lack of sanctioning with powerless political persuasion that accounts for its ineffectiveness. Unless a manager can mobilize power in support of the persuasive appeal, it will fall on deaf ears.

Tactic 2--The Use of Powerless Pressure. The frequency with which pressure is used as a political tactic varies from organization to organization, but in most cases, it is relatively rare. The reason is that the use of threats and pressure seldom yields good long-term results.

The use of pressure generally results in bad feelings. No one likes to be pressured into doing things, and even if there is short-term compliance, there will likely be hard feelings that will have to be dealt with at some point. Moreover, the use of pressure is often seen as a sign of weakness rather than a sign of strength. People who use pressure frequently often take on the undesirable reputation of being insecure and unstable.

Powerless pressure even fails to result in short-term results. Without being able to back up a threat with some sort of power, it will often be ignored, and the manager will suffer all the negative aftereffects with no gains whatsoever.

To summarize, pressure is generally not a very effective method of political influence. It promises at best positive, short-term results. Even these are in jeopardy if the individual does not use other power resources to back up the threat.

Tactic 3--The Use of Manipulation. Of all the forms of political influence none arouses more concern and derision than manipulation. Basically manipulation involves concealing the attempt to influence. This takes two forms: the manipulation of situations and information.

The object of situational manipulation is to create the conditions that influence the target to some predetermined point of view. For example, a situational manipulator could orchestrate a staff meeting such that the people who agree with him are given more time to argue their case. Or a situation could be created that penalizes those who oppose a particular position.

The use of information to manipulate others is unfortunately quite common. Information can be distorted, released at the proper time, or withheld indefinitely as a means of manipulation. Similarly, manipulators can disguise themselves as impartial advisors but actually give slanted advice.

Manipulation suffers from one very important flaw--it is deceitful. If discovered, the manipulator becomes an outcast trusted by no one, his or her credibility forever lost. Candidly, there are probably many more attempts at manipulation than are ever discovered. The risks of discovery are high, though, and many people choose not to engage in manipulation because it is seen as sleazy.

Tactic 4--The Use of Escalation. Escalation is taking an issue to a higher authority for resolution. There are several reasons that it is generally ineffective. First, escalation is generally seen as a sign of failure. One does not typically escalate unless all other political tactics have been used. Second, one can never be sure of the outcome when one escalates. Even assurances stated before the fact don't guarantee the outcome. Third, escalation is organizational high drama. Other people soon discover what has happened, and the escalator seldom emerges with an unblemished reputation. Finally, escalation smacks of a despicable childhood behavior--tattling.

Effective Political Tactics

There are many tactics that hold much more promise. In general, they involve the intelligent use of personal power.

Tactic 1--The Powerful Use of Persuasion. As we have seen, powerless persuasion is ineffective. If a manager persuades from a relatively strong power base, he or she holds much more potential to influence others. Some of the ways that persuasion can be strengthened with personal power include

(1) Framing the appeal as appropriate within some compelling version of organizational realities. Assume that a manager is trying to convince an office manager that he or she needs more word processing support. The manager could frame the appeal in terms of a rumor that the office is currently under scrutiny by senior management. This use of information power can add to the likelihood of success.
(2) Framing the appeal to take advantage of the manager's relative expertise. Expert power can increase the effectiveness of the appeal unless others who are equally expert, oppose the manager.
(3) Framing the appeal to the target's needs, interests, and problems rather than to the manager's. This essentially adds a personal reward or punishment element to the manager's request. By doing this, the manager is attaching a direct and attractive benefit to compliance.

(4) Framing the appeal as an investment in an ongoing relationship. Relationships carry with them the norm of reciprocity. People do favors for their colleagues either to compensate them for past favors received or in the anticipation of future favors in return.

Powerful persuasion is by no means the answer to every political situation. It requires that the target listens to what the manager has to say and respects the power put behind the appeal.

Tactic 2--The Powerful Use of Pressure. Although pressure seldom reaps positive, long-term results, one should never exercise pressure without the support of an adequate personal power base. Otherwise the attempt at pressure will be seen as an idle threat. Some of the ways that one can strengthen pressure include the following:

(1) Framing the threat as appropriate within some compelling vision of organizational realities. For example, the manager could warn that he or she has inside information that certain bad things will happen if the target person does not comply.
(2) Framing the threat to take advantage of one's own relative expertise. Assume that a manager is knowledgeable about the market conditions relative to a new product, and wants to exert pressure against its release. In this case the manager could begin with a demonstration of his or her expertise and proceed to give an assessment of the reasons that the release will result in failure.
(3) Framing the threat to the target's needs, interests, and problems rather than one's own. This makes the threat more personally vital. For example, if a manager wants to stop a careless employee who is financially dependent on overtime wages from continuing to use unsafe methods, the manager could threaten to withhold his overtime unless he complies. Similarly, if the target values a relationship that the manager has some control over, the manager could frame the threat in terms of the actions that could be taken to undermine that relationship.
(4) Framing the threat as a personal assault. By demonstrating that the undesired behavior is jeopardizing a relationship, a manager adds clout to the threat if the relationship is valued by the target.

Tactic 3--The Use of Coalitions. Alliances, interest groups, and coalitions are important factors in the political reality of any organization. People get together to support or oppose things, and effective politicians realize that they must form alliances when issues require more power than they themselves possess.

Tactic 4--Use Alternative Relationships. Most political situations arise because a manager is dependent on someone either above, below, or at the same organizational level. So far we have described the political methods of managing those dependencies. However, a manager can also deal with dependencies by avoiding them altogether. For example, assume that a manager is not getting adequate support from a centralized computer center. One way of dealing with this problem is purchasing a microcomputer for the office or subcontracting the service "on the outside."

Most managers can think of ways to use alternative relationships in lateral relations and relations with subordinates, but it is sometimes harder to conceive of how this tactic can be used with superiors. Actually, the use of alternative relationships is not uncommon with bosses. Many managers build relations with senior managers who are not directly above them in the chain of command. Known alternatively as sponsors or mentors, these senior people act as counselors, advisors, and protectors much in the same way as one's own manager otherwise would.

Having a sponsor poses special problems. First, the manager must realize that the bond between mentor and protege carries with it certain expectations. The person being mentored is expected to act upon advice given, support the mentor in dealing with his or her peers and superiors, and use the sponsor's time selectively. Second, care must be taken not to alienate either one's own manager or the sponsor. This can be tricky if one receives conflicting directions. Finally, the choice of a sponsor is a critical decision. More than one manager has erred by "hitching his wagon to a falling star."

The Timing of Advocacy

Conflicts abound in every organization. New policies, reorganizations, changes in strategic direction, and personnel decisions are seldom popular with everyone. Yet to be an effective politician, a manager must be careful about just when, if ever, to take sides. Clearly one of the most difficult and elusive challenges one faces in playing politics is exercising good timing. Many of us have a serious tendency of acting impulsively and not being sufficiently patient. As we have seen, political tactics enacted without an adequate reservoir of personal power are doomed to failure, and that often means waiting until power has been mobilized before acting.

Timing Considerations Before Contentious Decisions Have Been Made

Issues of consequence tend to polarize organizations. During the debate on these issues, some people line up in favor of or in opposition to the alternatives under debate, and others remain uncommitted to any alternative. It is at just such times that a manager should be especially vigilant to who is on what side. Considering the power each person brings to the debate often allows a sensitive manager to predict what decision will be made.

It is critical to remember that debates create coalitions. Individuals who share a side are unified by those commitments, and each finds such support rewarding. Similarly, people on opposite sides often resent each other and find their opponents' positions punitive. This implies that one's position on issues of conflict has political consequences far broader than whether or not one was on the winning side.

Assume, for example, that a manager wants a particular product introduced. His or her view is shared by a number of people, but the boss is opposed. In this sort of situation, pushing hard for introduction may solidify the manager's relationship with those who share his or her view but only at the risk of alienating the boss.

Because the risks of alienating key people during such debates are so high, some individuals prefer to remain uncommitted even though they favor a particular position. The strength of any commitment is a function of how clearly, irrevocably, and publicly the declaration is made. Consequently, a manager can remain uncommitted by *not* making clear, public, and irrevocable statements on the issue. This gives the manager flexibility to make a stand at some later time when the situation and the risks are more clear. In summary, then, declaring support or opposition to an issue under discussion is politically risky. It may earn you friends whose future support may be helpful, but it may also earn you enemies that you neither want nor need. Accordingly, it is generally prudent to time the stands a manager makes during debates to minimize these risks. Remaining uncommitted often gives an opportunity to test alternative political stands and reduce the risks of making the wrong choices.

Timing Considerations After Unwanted Decisions Have Been Announced

The politics associated with a debate do not end when the decision is announced and formalized. Those who originally supported the chosen option are filled with energy to make it a success, but others seldom share the enthusiasm. Those who were early opponents are expected to "climb on board" and make the decision successful, but they typically need encouragement to do so. And those who did not feel that their voice was heard during the debate are especially annoyed, requiring even higher levels of encouragement to support the final decision.

The most important thing for a manager to realize about this post-decision period is that the winning coalition is strengthened politically by having been victorious. Those originally uncommitted have swung to the winning side and can counter any opposition by declaring that the debate has ended.

A manager must move very cautiously in opposition to a decision that has weathered a debate, but he or she does have two options. The manager can quietly build power that can be drawn upon in an attempt to mobilize opposition to the decision. Or the manager can build a case supporting a modification of the original decision. We will discuss each of these tactics.

Tactic 1--Build Power. As we have discussed, the victors in any debate generally enjoy a considerable amount of power. However, there are three groups of employees who remain potential allies behind anyone who wants to attempt a reversal: those who originally opposed the decision; those who did not feel represented in the decision process; and those who are dismayed to discover that the decision did not result in what it promised. To mobilize opposition, these are the groups a manager could turn to.

A manager should be prepared to move very quietly in building power in opposition to a decision of this kind. Immediately after the decision is announced, the victorious coalition is commonly poised to deal sternly with opposition, and the substantial power they possess at this point makes it unwise to be branded as "uncooperative." An unobtrusive posture is certainly warranted.

Tactic 2--Build a Rational Case for a Modification. Few major decisions are ever totally reversed. Total reversals make the original decision illegitimate and are entirely too great a threat to the face of the original proponents. The best a manager can usually hope for is something that can appear to be a modification, even if it is essentially a reversal. To accomplish these reduced goals, it is critical to mobilize a rational argument that makes the modification superior to the original decision.

The three most common rational arguments in favor of modification are as follows:

(1) the conditions are different than those considered in the original decision,
(2) the decision as it stands conflicts with important organizational norms or practices in ways that were not originally foreseen,
(3) the implementation of the decision needs to be fine-tuned to local conditions.

Whichever of these arguments a manager chooses to use, it should be framed in such a way that the original advocates are excused for any oversight. In addition, a manager should avoid using arguments that were used in the initial debate.

Clearly, turning around an unwanted decision is one of the most challenging of all political problems. Like any political move, it requires personal power. However, it also puts a premium on quiet coalition building and persuasion skills. Timing is vital at each point, for the opponents of modification are both strong and initially resistant to opposition.

Conclusion

Organizational politics can provide a manager with some of his or her greatest challenges. Everyone experiences a power gap, and the only recourse is to supplement authority with power. This can be a slow process, but the normal methods of influence without power are ineffectual without it. In any event, some tactics have little to recommend them. And others have a great deal more potential. Debates over alternative policies and organizational directions are heated politically. During such debates, managers should be careful about making stands that will jeopardize their political standing. After decisions have been made, new challenges arise.

References

Allen, Robert W., Dan L. Madison, Lyman W. Porter, Patricia A. Renwick, and Bronston T. Mayes. "Organizational Politics: Tactics and Characteristics of Its Actors." *California Management Review* 22 (1979): 77-83.

Cavanagh, Gerald F., Dennis J. Moberg, and Manuel Velasquez. "The Ethics of Organizational Politics." *Academy of Management Review* 6 (1981): 363-374.

Gandz, Jeffrey, and Victor V. Murray. "The Experience of Workplace Politics." *Academy of Management Journal* 23 (1980): 237-251.

Kipnis, David. *The Powerholders*. Chicago: University of Chicago Press, 1976.

Kipnis, David, Stuart M. Schmidt, and Ian Wilkinson. "Intraorganizational Influence Tactics: Explorations in Getting One's Way." *Journal of Applied Psychology* 65 (1980): 440-452.

Kotter, John P. "Power, Dependence and Effective Management." *Harvard Business Review* 55 (1977): 125-136.

Kotter, John P. *Power and Influence*. New York: Free Press, 1985.

Mechanic, David. "Source of Power of Lower Participants in Complex Organizations." *Administrative Science Quarterly* 7 (1962): 32-48.

Pfeffer, Jeffrey. *Power in Organizations*. New York: Pittman, 1981.

Porter, Lyman W., Robert Allen, and Harold L. Angle. "The Politics of Upward Influence." In L. L. Cummings and Barry M. Staw, eds., *Research in Organizational Behavior*, Vol. 3. New York: JAI Press, 1981.

Strauss, George. "Tactics of Lateral Relationship: The Purchasing Agent." *Administrative Science Quarterly* 7 (1962): 134-156.

Course:_____   Name:_____

Instructor:_____   Date:_____

Flow Diagram for Organizational Politics Interactive Case

Detach this page from your book before you begin the Interactive Case. As you make each decision, write the decision point number *and* letter following the GO TO statement in the appropriate rectangle *before* you turn to that page. If you are referred to a previous decision point, circle the decision point number and letter you last wrote and proceed to the first uncircled rectangle above that one in your flow diagram. Do not erase the numbers and letters once you have written them. You will not necessarily fill all the rectangles.

Start	☐	6th Decision	☐	12th Decision	☐
1st Decision	☐	7th Decision	☐	13th Decision	☐
2nd Decision	☐	8th Decision	☐	14th Decision	☐
3rd Decision	☐	9th Decision	☐	15th Decision	☐
4th Decision	☐	10th Decision	☐	16th Decision	☐
5th Decision	☐	11th Decision	☐	17th Decision	☐

➤ turn over

18th Decision
19th Decision
20th Decision
21st Decision
22nd Decision
23rd Decision
24th Decision
25th Decision
26th Decision

27th Decision
28th Decision
29th Decision
30th Decision
31st Decision
32nd Decision
33rd Decision
34th Decision
35th Decision

36th Decision
37th Decision
38th Decision
39th Decision
40th Decision
41st Decision
42nd Decision
43rd Decision
44th Decision

Interactive Case

You are the Sales Manager of the Automation Systems Group of the Fluid Products Division of the Blake-Emerson Corporation, a Fortune 500 conglomerate. The Fluid Products Division manufactures and sells pumps, valves, cylinders, and compressors for industrial use. Together the division commands a 6 percent market share, the industry's fifth largest. Emerson Billingsworth is the Director of the Fluid Products Division, and Bill Banquet, your boss, reports to him as Marketing Manager (an organization chart appears below).

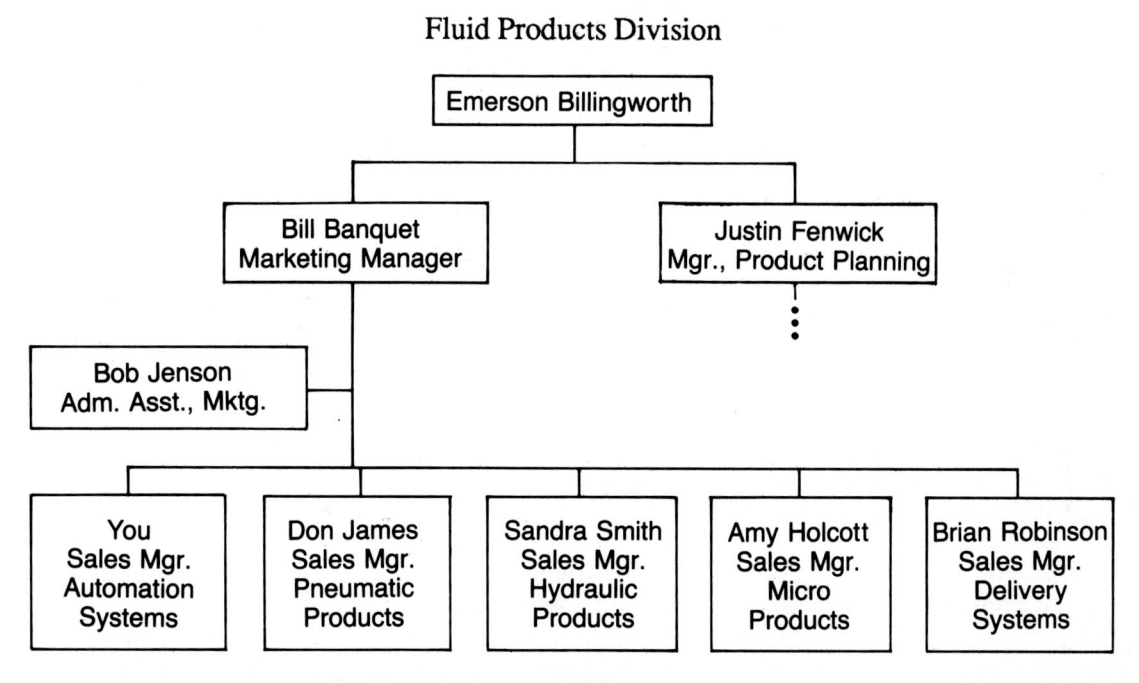

Fluid Products Division

```
                    Emerson Billingworth
                            |
            ┌───────────────┴───────────────┐
    Bill Banquet                    Justin Fenwick
  Marketing Manager              Mgr., Product Planning
            |
  Bob Jenson
  Adm. Asst., Mktg.
            |
  ┌─────────┬─────────┬─────────┬─────────┐
  You    Don James  Sandra    Amy      Brian
 Sales    Sales     Smith    Holcott   Robinson
  Mgr.     Mgr.    Sales Mgr. Sales Mgr. Sales Mgr.
Automation Pneumatic Hydraulic  Micro    Delivery
 Systems  Products  Products  Products  Systems
```

Banquet has five subordinates including you. Each of the others is responsible for a different product line: pneumatics, hydraulics, microproducts (miniature valves and cylinders), and delivery systems (pumps, tubing, storage vessels, etc.). Your product line is the most diverse, for you sell automation systems (i.e., integrated clusters of valves and cylinders used in conjunction with tools in automated machinery). Such systems are used in packaging, customized fabrication, and robotics.

You have eight sales engineers reporting to you. Each is responsible for different sets of industrial applications, and each travels 50 percent of the time. They are a close-knit group, and your relationship with them is extraordinarily good considering that you have been with the corporation and in your position for only eight months. Your predecessor left the firm in what some describe as a messy situation arising from a difference of opinion with Bill Banquet's predecessor. Banquet himself has only been Marketing Manager for two months, having formerly served as Sales Manager of the Delivery Systems Group.

Your relationship with Banquet seems fine, although he lacks the sense of humor on which you pride yourself. He is very bright and is clearly cautious about making waves until he has established himself in his position.

The performance of the Fluid Products Division has been very poor for the last 18 months. This has resulted in cutbacks in personnel in most parts of the division, notably in those parts of the organization dealing with hydraulic and pneumatic products. The staff organization was somewhat surprisingly spared these cuts. In the case of Product Planning, for example, no cuts in personnel have as yet been made. In fact, due to the role of the Product Planning Department in cost control, the influence of that department was on the rise during these hard times. This unit was known to be a favorite of top division management, which has a strong manufacturing orientation.

Fortunately, your sales force was relatively unscathed by the cuts. Only one sales engineer had to be laid off, and that was a year before you became Sales Manager. The reason your unit fared so well is that the demand for automation systems maintained acceptable levels throughout the downturn.

Two days ago, a bombshell memo appeared in your morning mail. A copy appears below.

Memorandum

TO: Sales Managers, Fluid Products Division
FR: Emerson Billingsworth, Director
RE: New Policy

As you know, the economic performance of our division has suffered at the hands of the worst recession that has hit our industry in recent memory. A central factor that has contributed to our poor performance is our lack of control of inventory costs. At the recommendation of Justin Fenwick, and after consultation with several managers, I have decided to put in place a new policy. Add the following to your policy manual:

"To facilitate production planning and to get inventory costs under control, all sales engineers must specify their monthly expected sales in all product categories. Any actual sales over the expected figure by 20 percent or more will have to be back-ordered if a stockout is experienced. Any sales under the expected figure by 20 percent will necessitate a negative adjustment against the unit's reported sales volume goals in direct proportion to the additional carrying costs that accrue."

I ask your cooperation in complying with this new policy. Mr. Fenwick's people have developed forms that should facilitate reporting your monthly sales estimates. Those for next month should be submitted by the 15th to his office.

You are very concerned about the effects of this new policy on your sales group. The product line you are responsible for is the most diverse among all those in the division, and sales are the most uneven; it is the nature of the business. Thus, the policy essentially places extraordinary pressure on your subordinates to plan in the face of almost incalculable uncertainties. You know with certainty that if your sales engineers are held to this policy, there will be many instances of overages and underages, and that it will all but squash any incentives to develop new accounts unless they have product needs that are easy to estimate.

In general, how would you approach this situation?

A. Diplomatically oppose the new policy as it applies to your unique circumstances. Petition for an exemption. (GO TO 239A)

B. Gather information about what this policy means to your peers, your boss, and the staff unit involved (Product Planning). (GO TO 281A)

C. Instruct your subordinates what to do about this new policy. (GO TO 242B)

10 MANAGING A TASK FORCE
Module Reading

Task forces are simply groups of people who are put together to tackle problems that require diverse talent for decision making and/or implementation. Several things make task forces tricky to manage. First, since they are composed of people with different backgrounds and affiliations, task forces are often conflict-ridden. Second, task forces are highly visible. They are typically composed of well-known and respected employees, and they are generally given significant assignments. This visibility creates special problems for the task force manager because the stakes are so great and because task force members are frequently subjected to attempts from colleagues not on the task force to influence them. Third, task forces are most often required to complete their assignments under very strict time demands. Yet its members have other work responsibilities, so the time pressures they experience are often enormous. Finally, task forces require the use of techniques of group decision making that some if not all of its members are unfamiliar with.

In this chapter, we lay out guidelines for use in managing a task force. We specify some of the things managers should do in refining their charter. We detail the number and type of people to include on a task force. We offer several suggestions about how to manage the all-important first task force meeting. And we acquaint you with some group decision-making techniques that you may not be familiar with.

Refining the Task Force Charter

The most common reasons task forces are created are to look into problems and suggest solutions, to implement changes, and to coordinate cross-departmental issues. Sometimes a task force is given a charter that includes all three of these assignments. For example, a task force may be asked to make recommendations about a problem, work on the implementation of its decision, and work through the coordination details.

Whatever the scope of the charter managers are given, they should try to get as specific a set of directions as possible. Unfortunately, there is a real tendency to leave certain parts of the initial assignment vague, and more than one task force has failed because of this. Managers should take initiative in clarifying the following:

(1) the expected output of the task force in terms of deliverables and milestones,
(2) the authority of the group in terms of its access to information, its budget, and its independence in considering options without approval

and in terms of requiring bosses to free task force members from other assignments,
(3) their boss's desire for involvement in the task force (as a final decision maker, as an evaluator at certain milestones, or as a reviewer of every task force decision),
(4) any other decision or commitment that has been made that affects the task force (promises made by those in authority, customs regarding task forces in the organization, commitments made to include certain individuals on the task force).

Selection of Task Force Members

A great deal of research has gone into the question of the proper size for a task force. Generally this indicates the superiority of odd-sized groups over even ones, with five as an optimal number and seven as second best. Groups much larger than that suffer from little participation and social loafing.

The choice as to who to include on a task force is an important one. As we have indicated, task forces are generally staffed with employees with a lot of visibility. This is the way it should be. Individually, task force members should possess the following attributes:

(1) organizational credibility,
(2) sufficient experience to be able to represent their constituency,
(3) an intrinsic interest in the task force issue,
(4) able to devote sufficient time and attention to the task force.

Collectively, it is also important to look for certain combinations. First, it is best to avoid groups that have personality conflicts. Building a task force with no work-related conflict is almost impossible, but combinations should be avoided that have conflicts of a personal nature. Second, managers should compose the task force so that there is a balance between the various constituencies that they want represented. The credibility of the entire task force usually hinges on the extent to which it represents groups that have a legitimate interest in its outcome. Third, managers should seek combinations of task force members that represent a balance between task-oriented members and people-oriented members. Task forces need task-oriented members to keep them focused on the job at hand and to give them a sense of urgency and direction. People-oriented members offer support and concern for such necessary social functions as reinforcement, encouragement, and humor.

The All-Important First Meeting

The first task force meeting is the most important. In the way they manage this meeting, managers set a tone that continues throughout the entire process. Therefore, it is important to plan this first meeting carefully. Above all, they should avoid *paralyzing* controversy. By that we mean any conflict that will polarize the committee prematurely. If managers suspect that there is a difference between task force members, they should check these out by talking with prospective members before the first meeting. They should be prepared to exclude members who refuse to work with other members because of personality conflicts or who are unwilling to negotiate key points.

After having thoroughly checked out members for their sensitivities, managers now must get their task force members together for the first time. As we have said, this meeting is critical to the success of the total effort, and good managers are careful to make no mistakes. Since the task force members may not know each other very well, it is important to do something to get members acquainted. There are two parts to this. First, managers should create an agenda that will help members get to know each other, and second, they should introduce members at the first meeting in the best way possible. According to George Huber, there are three ways to design an agenda for the first meeting:

(1) Send members of the task force biographical sketches of their fellow task force members.
(2) Schedule an early break to facilitate socialization.
(3) Before the first meeting, schedule a coffee hour or meal.

Whatever the agenda, members will have to be introduced at the first meeting. The two options are either to let members introduce themselves or to have the task force leader introduce them. Generally it is preferable for the manager to do the introductions. The reason is that some members are more likely to be modest than others, and sometimes dominant members take advantage of the floor to try to establish themselves. By doing the introductions, the manager starts everyone out on an even footing.

Once task force members know each other, the manager should tell them their charter. Here it is critical that managers give them as *complete* a picture as possible. Even if certain elements of the charter are controversial, they should withhold nothing.

This done, managers should then try to shape norms that the task force should follow. Norms are simply standards of behavior that the group accepts and enforces upon one another. Managers can help shape these norms in the first meeting by getting members to agree that they are needed for the group to be successful. Effective task forces have norms that regulate three areas of behavior: attendance, conflict, and representation. Accordingly, managers should get the task force to agree on the importance of each member's attendance at every meeting and on the importance of being on time. They also should try to get task force members to agree that work-related conflicts are a natural part of what will happen during meetings and that they are actually desirable. Many task forces fail because conflicts are smoothed over or avoided altogether.

Finally, they should try to deal with the issue of representation in a direct and forthright way. Task forces are teamed by individuals drawn from different parts of the organization in order to represent certain skills and points of view. This creates a dual allegiance. Task force members are unsure whether they should be loyal to the task force or loyal to their constituency. This problem is compounded if task force members are subjected to pressures from their host departments during the process. Therefore, it is often helpful to get members to agree to keep their deliberations confidential. This minimizes pressures from the outside and allows members to develop some loyalty to the task force itself.

Guidelines for Managing Task Force Meetings

Most task forces require several meetings to complete their assignment. At each meeting, the task force leader should be prepared to manage the process with three things in mind: helping the group stay on track, assuring equitable participation, and using consensus as a way of settling differences.

Helping the Group Stay on Track

No one is more important than the task force leader in keeping the group pointed toward its objectives. While this involves bringing discussions that wander off the subject back to the issue at hand, the best time to intervene is at the beginning and end of each meeting. Consider the following four guidelines offered by Huber:

(1) At the beginning of each meeting, review the progress that has been made to date and define the task of the meeting.
(2) At the beginning of each meeting, or as early as possible, get a report from each member with a preassigned task.
(3) At the end of each meeting, summarize what was accomplished, where this puts the task force on its schedule, and what the group's task will be at the next meeting.
(4) At the end of each meeting, make public and clear which members have which assignments to complete by the next meeting. Ask these members to publicly acknowledge their assignments.

If followed, these guidelines establish a very purposive, businesslike climate for the task force, where the focus is on objectives and where each meeting is seen as another step forward.

Assuring Equitable Participation

While one never has equal participation at every meeting, it is important that those who have a contribution to make do so and that the discussion is not dominated by a minority. All of us have been to meetings where one or two people do all the talking, and it is tough to get a word in edgewise. Managers don't want that to happen in a task force that they are responsible for, so they need to guide the process.

Although it is tempting to confront a domineering member, the best approach is to invoke the standard of fairness. If Bill is talking too much, a manager should simply say, "Bill, I think all of us understand your points, but in all fairness, I think we want to give others the chance to be heard." If this fails, try it again. If they are still unable to wrestle the floor from him, speak with him after the meeting and again use the word "fair" as the basis for an appeal to his sensitivities.

Overly quiet or reserved members need guidance to increase their participation. They could say something like, "Bob, we haven't heard your thinking on this matter." However, forcing people to participate like this may cause them to withdraw even further. Accordingly, it is better to say something like, "I hope that before this discussion ends, we hear from everyone who has a contribution to make."

Using Consensus to Settle Differences

It is inevitable that differences of opinion will arise on the task force. On these occasions, managers have several options. Some task forces settle differences through voting, allowing the majority or plurality to prevail. However, voting is actually a rather ineffective way of resolving differences on a task force, and it typically creates a minority that is uncommitted to the resolution. Using the consensus method is superior. A consensus decision is reached when

(1) no member is opposed to the resolution,
(2) all members can live with the resolution,
(3) all members understand and appreciate the logic behind the resolution reached.

Notice that this is not the same as unanimity. It is not a resolution all members agree upon, only one they do not disagree with or can live with. As part of the consensus-finding process, it is crucial that managers make sure that everyone understands and accepts the logic behind the resolution of differences. That way, if anyone outside the task force asks, the logic behind the resolution can be correctly represented.

Task Force Decision-Making Techniques

There are four decision-making techniques that can be used in a task force. It pays to be familiar with all of them.

Ordinary Group Discussion

The most frequently used decision-making technique is a familiar one--an ordinary group discussion led by the manager that results in a consensus decision. The main advantage of this approach is its familiarity. Task force members have no doubt participated in groups of this sort, so they don't have to learn new behaviors. The disadvantage of ordinary group discussions, though, is that they are often quite open to biases. For one, they seldom result in the exhaustive search for alternatives. In addition, they tend to be dominated by the most powerful subgroup. Finally, they are often subject to premature solutions followed by bolstering.

Managers who use the ordinary group discussion method should utilize the following guidelines:

(1) Begin with an examination of the assumptions that bear on the decision to be made. For example, if you are implementing a change, ask whether the change has to be implemented all at once or whether it can be implemented in parts.
(2) Simplify complex decision problems. For example, some problems are entirely too complex to be handled all at once but can be divided into parts.
(3) Discuss the positive features of alternatives before you discuss the negatives. There is a tendency for negative attributes to be more salient than they should be.
(4) Separate the search for alternatives from their evaluation. First, articulate all the alternatives you can. After you are content that you have a complete list, evaluate them.

Use of Subgroups

A second decision technique is to divide the problem into parts and assign them to subgroups. This technique works well in very complex problems divisible into independent parts. When subgroups are used, however, it does create potential coordination problems that the task force leader is ultimately responsible for. Managers can either provide the coordination themselves, perhaps by attending all subgroup meetings and keeping them focused in complementary directions, or they can use complete task force meetings as the coordination vehicle.

Brainstorming

When managers believe the final decision relies heavily on the quality of the alternatives considered, they should consider using brainstorming. Here the task force is given a problem and is asked to develop alternative solutions. It is not used for choosing among alternatives, only for developing alternatives. The rules of brainstorming are as follows:

(1) Criticism is ruled out; judgment or evaluation of ideas must be withheld until a later time.
(2) Freewheeling is welcomed; the wilder or more radical the idea, the better.
(3) Quantity of ideas is wanted; the more alternative topics the better.
(4) Combination and improvement are desirable; task force members should suggest how the ideas of others can be turned into new ideas.

Managers who use this method must take an active role in enforcing these rules. In particular, they should stop any task force member who makes evaluative comments.

Nominal Group Technique

The Nominal Group Technique (N.G.T.) is helpful in both alternative generation and evaluation. It is useful in any complex decision-making situation where the quality of the output depends on the development of many unique alternatives and their consensual evaluation. The best way to describe the technique is as a series of steps:

(1) Team members work alone and in silence, writing down all the alternatives they can think of.
(2) Members share their ideas using a round-robin procedure during which members are encouraged to add items to their list of topic ideas.
(3) Participants discuss each recorded idea in order to clarify its meaning and intent and to provide initial evaluation.
(4) Task force members use rank-voting to indicate their feelings concerning the importance of the ideas. Group output is then determined by summing the ranked votes.
(5) Members discuss the results of the initial voting and take a final vote.

Each of these group decision-making techniques has its own strengths, and each suffers from unique problems. Table 1 summarizes these techniques.

Politics of Task Forces

Managers need to be sensitive to the political aspects of managing a task force. Above all, it is important to appreciate that whenever a task force is established, it is a formal recognition that there is a problem with which the formal organization cannot cope. As such, there is almost always opposition to

Table 1
Comparison of Task Force Decision Techniques

Criteria	Ordinary	Subgroup	Brainstorming	N.G.T.
Number of ideas	Low	Low	Moderate	High
Quality of ideas	Low	Low	Moderate	High
Social Pressures	High	Moderate	Low	Moderate
Cost	Moderate	Low	Low	Low
Task Orientation	Low	Moderate	High	High
Potential for Conflict	High	Moderate	Low	Moderate
Feelings of Accomplishment	Varies	Varies	Low	Moderate
Commitment to Decision	High	High	Not Applicable	Moderate
Development of a "We" Feeling	High	High	High	Moderate

Adapted, by permission of the publisher, from "Group Decision Making: What Strategy to Use?" by Keith Murningham in *Management Review* 70, 1981, p. 61. Copyright © 1981 by American Management Association, New York. All rights reserved.

the formation of a task force, and this often means pockets of opposition to what the task force is trying to accomplish. Cautious task force managers realize this and try to identify the parties that oppose them so that they may be alert to sabotage efforts. A second political reality is that the task force is a springboard to individual politicking. As we said earlier, task forces are very visible, and they are often magnets to those who seek career gains from membership. It is wise to be careful to exclude those who want their involvement on the task force to be a springboard to their own career advancement.

Finally, it is important to note that members may be subjected to a great deal of outside influence during the entire process. They may be pressured by their bosses to take one position or another. Or they may be subjected to other interest groups with some interest they want represented. On occasion this results in members saying and doing things that are at cross-purposes with the task force itself. In any case, be very careful. As a manager of a task force, you don't want to alienate a task force member if that member's political activities are not "in the way."

References

Berkowitz, L. "Sharing Leadership in Small Decision Making Groups." *Journal of Abnormal and Social Psychology* 48 (1953): 231-238.

Delbecq, Andre L., Andrew H. Van de Ven, and Donald H. Gustafson. *Group Techniques for Program Planning*. Glenview, Ill.: Scott, Foresman and Company, 1975.

Filey, Alan. "Committee Management: Guidelines from Social Science Research." *California Management Review*, 13 (1970): 13-21.

Gibb, Jack R. "The Effects of Group Size and of Threat Reduction Upon Creativity in a Problem Solving Situation." *American Psychologist* 6 (1950): 322-328.

Hall, J., and H. W. Watson. "The Effects of a Normative Intervention on Group Decision Making Performance." *Human Relations* 23 (1970): 229-317.

Hogarth, Robin. *Judgement and Choice*. New York: John Wiley & Sons, 1980.

Huber, George P. *Managerial Decision Making*. Glenview, Ill.: Scott, Foresman and Company, 1980.

Janis, Irving L., and L. Mann. *Decision Making*. New York: Free Press, 1977.

Maier, Norman R. F. *Problem Solving Discussions and Conferences*. New York: McGraw-Hill, 1963.

Murninghan, Keith. "Group Decision Making: What Strategy to Use?" *Management Review* 70 (1981): 55-61.

Course:_____   Name:_____

Instructor:_____   Date:_____

Flow Diagram for Task Force Interactive Case

Detach this page from your book before you begin the Interactive Case. As you make each decision, write the decision point number *and* letter following the GO TO statement in the appropriate rectangle *before* you turn to that page. If you are referred to a previous decision point, circle the decision point number and letter you last wrote and proceed to the first uncircled rectangle above that one in your flow diagram. Do not erase the numbers and letters once you have written them. You will not necessarily fill all the rectangles.

Start	6th Decision	12th Decision
1st Decision	7th Decision	13th Decision
2nd Decision	8th Decision	14th Decision
3rd Decision	9th Decision	15th Decision
4th Decision	10th Decision	16th Decision
5th Decision	11th Decision	17th Decision

→ turn over

18th Decision

19th Decision

20th Decision

21st Decision

22nd Decision

23rd Decision

24th Decision

25th Decision

26th Decision

27th Decision

28th Decision

29th Decision

30th Decision

31st Decision

32nd Decision

33rd Decision

34th Decision

35th Decision

36th Decision

37th Decision

38th Decision

39th Decision

40th Decision

41st Decision

42nd Decision

43rd Decision

44th Decision

Interactive Case

You are the Assistant to the Publisher of the *Madison Register*, a daily newspaper in a growing southwestern city. Presently the *Register* enjoys a circulation of 150,000 subscribers and runs advertisements from over 3,500 businesses. An organization chart appears below.

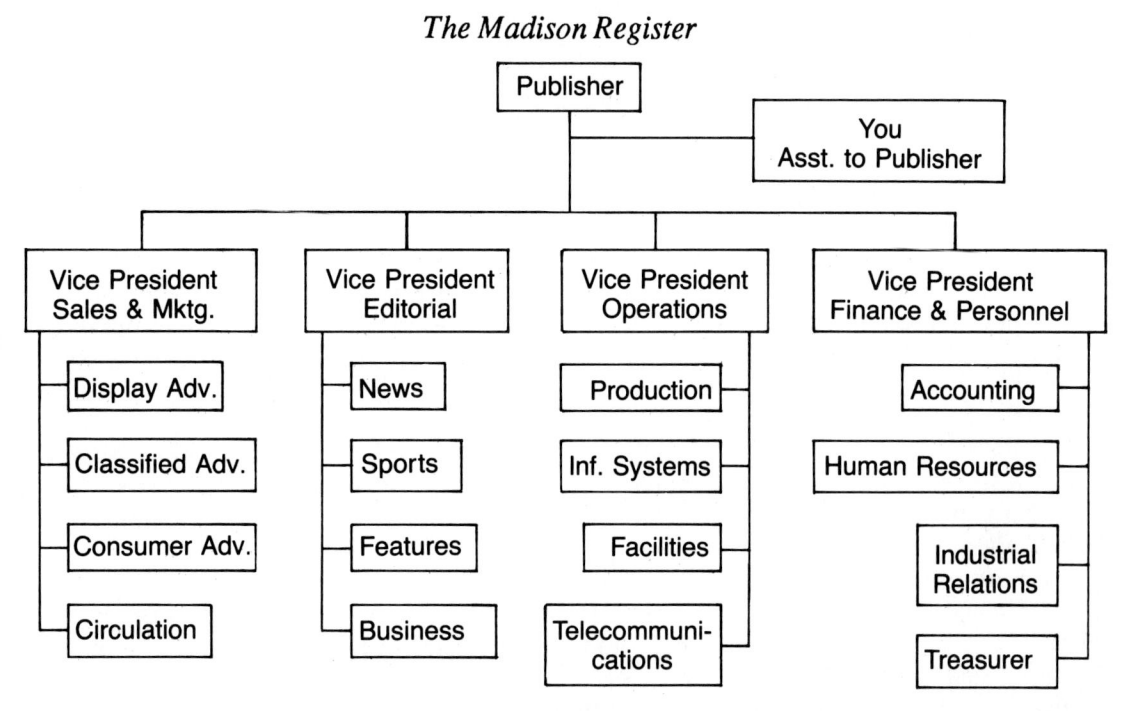

The Madison Register

```
                          Publisher
                             |
                             |────────── You
                             |           Asst. to Publisher
        ┌────────────────┬───┴────────────┬────────────────┐
   Vice President    Vice President   Vice President   Vice President
   Sales & Mktg.       Editorial        Operations    Finance & Personnel
        |                   |                |                |
   ├ Display Adv.      ├ News            ├ Production     ├ Accounting
   ├ Classified Adv.   ├ Sports          ├ Inf. Systems   ├ Human Resources
   ├ Consumer Adv.     ├ Features        ├ Facilities     ├ Industrial Relations
   └ Circulation       └ Business        └ Telecommuni-   └ Treasurer
                                           cations
```

Each season you have the responsibility of mobilizing a task force that decides on the topic and works out the coordination details for the special seasonal edition. This is an important assignment. Eighteen months ago, your newspaper won a Pulitzer Prize for its special edition on the artificial heart. Last season the special edition topic was drugs and minor league baseball. While it was critically acclaimed, it had less effect on circulation and advertising revenues than your boss had hoped. Thus, you suspect that your boss will ask you to frame a topic this season that has more "bottom-line potential."

By tradition you have drawn your task force from among the *Register's* 16 directors (those managers who report to the vice presidents). The size of the task force has varied from four to 11, but your boss has always insisted that you include two representatives from the Editorial Department (by far the most influential group in the *Register*).

You enter the walnut-paneled office of your boss (the Publisher) to receive your final instructions. He is a gentle man, more humble than his credentials attest. He is the "dean" of the press in the Southwest, and has pulled the *Register* out of oblivion to real stature within the region. He directs you to an overstuffed chair in front of a coffee table on which 11 of the nation's greatest newspapers are fanned out before you. He clears his throat and begins, "I want our next seasonal issue to be special, very special. Since our Pulitzer, I think our people in Editorial have become a bit complacent and self-important. Our last special issue was amateurish from an editorial viewpoint, and I really think we should chart some new territory. Above all,"

You lean forward, anticipating that he will then give you your charter.

"I want this issue to sell newspapers. Mark [Vice President of Sales and Marketing] has been working real hard, but the results have been disappointing. We need something really dynamite to break the market open. Our competition is vulnerable right now [last week one of their most popular columnists defected to the *Register*].

"One more thing. You know all the problems we had last summer with Operations? [The layout of the last special edition required the use of three color photographic prints on interior pages that the pressmen had a great deal of difficulty with.] Well, let's keep them better informed. After all the problems with the last special [edition], I promised Tony [Vice President of Operations] that he will get all the background pieces 36 hours in advance of press time. I know that puts you in a bind, but a promise is a promise, and frankly, that line from Editorial that anything more than 12 hours is an affront to their professionalism is so much !#%*..." He goes on to recite a story you have heard before about his experiences as a cub reporter with a Milwaukee paper.

Your meeting comes to a close with the following surprise:

"So you don't question my sincerity in wanting you to do something really extraordinary, I intend to put my money where my mouth is. There is no need to broadcast this outside of the task force, but I have told Finance to free up a line budget of $28,000 for this edition [this *is* extraordinary; it is fully 50 percent more than he gave you for the previous special issue]. So, you see, I want a top-flight effort, and I don't want to hear from Operations or anyone else that there are any problems with coordination."

He then asks you if you have any questions. How would you respond?

A. "No. Do you have any other instructions?" (GO TO 435B)

B. "What involvement do you personally want on this project?" (GO TO 465B)

C. "Do you want me to continue the practice of having two representatives from the Editorial Department on the task force?" (GO TO 438A)

11 MANAGING CHANGE
Module Reading

No skill is any more vital to a manager than the ability to successfully implement change. The pace of change is accelerating in most organizations, and managers who do not possess change management skills will surely be left behind. There are basically three types of organizational changes: administrative changes, technical changes, and changes in the goods and services the organization produces. Administrative changes include reorganizations, personnel moves, and changes in policies and procedures. Technical changes emerge from advancements in what is known about how to do the work. This includes such current developments as the introduction of computers, the automation of the production facility, and the improvement of the techniques of dealing with clients. The introduction of new products and services also requires careful supervision. Some organizations face this type of change on almost a monthly basis.

In this chapter, we outline a number of principles that are extremely useful in implementing all of these types of organizational changes. We first describe the common reasons employees resist organizational changes. Resistance arises for many different reasons, and it is critical that managers respond carefully to the resisters according to the reasons for their resistance. Next we describe the most important single decision a manager has to make about implementing a change--whether it should be implemented through delegation or through a top-down process in which the manager makes most of the implementation decisions. Finally, we detail some of the specific steps that should be used in each of these types of implementation patterns.

Resistance to Change

Every experienced manager realizes that most organizational changes will be greeted by some resistance. However, too few managers plan systematically for resistance or respond to it effectively. Instead they tend to view resistance as a sign of misguided loyalty, selfishness, or failure on the part of the resisters to see the "big picture." This viewpoint can cause the manager serious problems. The reasons for resistance extend far beyond these factors, and the manager who does not devote careful thought to them is likely to be in serious trouble. The four most common reasons employees resist change are

   (1) a fear that the change will require them to lose things they value personally,
   (2) a perceived threat to one's organizational vested interests,
   (3) a misunderstanding of the implications of the change,

(4) an honest belief that the change does not make sense for the organization.

Fear of a Personal Loss

Most changes threaten some people personally. Technical changes like the automation of the assembly line, the introduction of a computerized information system, or the use of a new chemical in the production process may arouse real personal fears. Administrative changes and new product introductions have a similar impact.

The first question that many employees ask about a coming organizational change is probably, "Will the change eliminate my job?" Even if assurances are given, doubts and concerns will likely persist until late in the implementation process. Some employees have personal experience with job loss precipitated by an organizational change or have heard stories that keep the fears alive.

There is no easy way to contend with resistance motivated by a fear of a loss of position and income. People want a guarantee of their job security, but a manager cannot always do that with total honesty. Changes always involve some uncertainties; in some cases, a manager may not even be sure of the precise directions the change will take. This makes absolute guarantees difficult and may damage credibility if the manager must later terminate someone whose job is made obsolete by the change.

As a general rule, when honesty and giving guarantees conflict, a manager should opt for honesty. If possible, though, a carefully planned and worded statement may be provided that offers some assurance without going further than what possibly can be delivered. For example, a manager can offer to do everything in his or her power to protect jobs or can give guarantees conditional on employee cooperation with the change.

A related type of fear that employees experience when faced with a change is due to a disruption in the social equilibrium. Most employees settle into comfortable social situations at work. They adjust to what others expect of them and find stable roles within their immediate work groups. Many changes disrupt this social stability. They require employees to work with new people, they break up cohesive work groups, and they force employees to have to make entirely new social adjustments.

What makes social disequilibrium so difficult to deal with is that employees rarely see it as the cause of their discomfort. Most employees consider themselves self-reliant and may not be aware of the satisfaction they get from their immediate work group. Cut off from their old social bonds at work, they may feel disoriented and may take out their frustrations on the change itself.

The best way to manage this cause of resistance is to plan for it. A manager can provide time and support for new co-workers to adjust, facilitate communication with previous contacts, and encourage new friendships to form.

Threat to Organizational Vested Interests

Employees may also resist changes that threaten the advantages their jobs offer them under the present system. Every position offers certain vested interests. A particular employee may not have to work especially hard, may be provided with an excess of resources, may be the beneficiary of certain favors, or may be in a position of considerable influence. Changes often threaten these benefits.

This type of resistance arises more frequently with administrative changes than technical or new product changes. Reorganizations and changes in administrative procedures almost always alter which jobs are most influential and may lead to a reallocation of privileges and benefits.

Again, this cause of resistance is best dealt with by careful planning. Those whose vested interests are threatened can be pinpointed, and their losses can potentially be lessened. In some cases a manager could even negotiate the particulars of new assignments to soften the blow of a change. For example, those who lose influence because of a change could be offered larger offices or more clerical support in order to "buy" their support for the change. Clearly such accommodations are not always feasible. In such cases, those adversely affected should be monitored carefully so they do not engage in disruptive political activity in an effort to sabotage the change.

Misunderstandings of the Implications of the Change

Employees also resist change when they do not understand how the change will impact them and the organization. Commonly this is due to a lack of trust in the initiators of change. To such employees the initiators lack the credibility to paint a believable picture either of the need for the change or of the organization after the change.

In many ways, this is the easiest cause of resistance to deal with. Two strategies are common. Individuals with credibility can be sold on the change individually and asked to speak out on behalf of the change effort. Alternatively, a manager can use scaled-down demonstrations to show precisely what form the change will take on a larger scale.

An Honest Belief That the Change Does Not Make Sense for the Organization

Loyal, honest employees often resist change for what are very good reasons from their perspective. Explanations about the need for or directions of the change simply do not persuade them that the change is in the organization's best interest. When confronted with resistance of this sort, managers are often tempted to provide more information about the change and its intended effects. Interestingly, this sometimes does not work. Individuals opposing change because they do not believe it to be in the organization's interest often have their own information that is sometimes more credible than that offered.

A more effective way of dealing with this form of resistance is to include those who express reservations about the change in the planning of the change. Other factors (to be described in the next section) permitting, this is the best way of dealing with employees who have potentially helpful perspectives on the change. With such participation the change program may actually improve.

Implementation Patterns

Certain changes require that the specifics of the implementation plan be delegated to the people who will implement it, and other changes call for a top-down approach where the manager spells out the implementation plan. The conditions that are best for each appear in Table 1.

Table 1
Contingency Factors in Implementing Change

Factor	Favorable for Top-Down Implementation	Favorable for Delegation Implementation
Time available for change	Change must be achieved immediately	No definite time limits for implementation
Degree to which the problem is	Crisis is recognized by everyone	Problem not generally recognized
Location of knowledge about the change	The manager is more knowledgeable than anyone	Knowledge is dispersed throughout the organization
Employee expectations	Employees expect authoritative change	Employees are used to being consulted
Power of manager	Great	Small

From *Managing Organizational Behavior* by Cyrus F. Gibson. Copyright © 1986 by Richard D. Irwin, Inc. Reprinted by permission of the author.

The time available for implementing the change is one factor that should be considered in choosing the implementation strategy. If time is limited, then it is better for the manager to implement the change rather than to involve subordinates directly in the implementation plan. The extent to which employees appreciate the need for change is a second factor. If the problem the change addresses is not widely sensed, then using delegation is the best approach. The location of the technical knowledge regarding the change is factor number three. If the manager is expert in the problem solution and the subordinates have little knowledge about the change, then a top-down implementation is called for. Alternatively, if subordinates have knowledge that may be necessary for the change to be successful, delegation is the preferred approach. The fourth contingency factor is the expectations employees have about being included in decisions. If employees have a history of being included in decision making, then it may be unwise to break with this practice when a change must be implemented. Lastly, a manager should be sensitive to his or her own power to implement the change without the involvement of others. Top-down implementation requires that the manager possess a great deal of power. If the manager does not have that power, then it is probably better to delegate the change effort.

When these six factors are all aligned, the preferred approach to change is clear. However, many situations are mixed. When mixed, a manager must use discretion. For example, if time is particularly pressing or if a manager totally lacks confidence in the technical abilities of subordinates to offer valuable technical inputs, then a top-down approach may be appropriate even though the manager lacks substantial power or suspects that the need for change is not widely appreciated.

Top-Down Implementation

A manager should attempt to follow four steps in a top-down implementation of a change:

(1) detail the coming change and explain the reasons for it,
(2) let employees ask questions, express opinions and concerns,
(3) respond to employee questions and concerns,
(4) get commitment and set up review.

There are certain principles that apply in each of these steps.

Step 1--Detail the coming change and explain the reasons for it. When the decision is made to implement a change in a top-down fashion, substantial effort toward planning the change is necessary before the implementation process can begin. At the end of this planning period, the manager must address employees in a careful fashion. What is said (or not said) during this introduction can have a dramatic impact on the success of the change effort.

Several elements are usually included in effective announcements of the change. First, the manager should be very clear about the reasons for the change. This has two facets. It should be pointed out what is wrong with the present situation and what advantages will be offered by the new system. For example, if a new organization structure is being put into place, the manager should be ready to point out both how the present structure is causing problems and how the new structure promises the best solution to those problems. As obvious as this sounds, many managers do not do this. Often they have spent so much time planning the change that they do not realize their people are unaware of both the need for change and the advantages of the proposed approach. As a consequence, their employees react to their announcement with statements like, "If it ain't broke, don't fix it!" or, "I'm not convinced that the proposed change will deliver what is expected!"

As the manager makes the case for change, the following factors should be considered:

   (a) The most persuasive reasons for change include both external factors and internal factors. If possible, it should be pointed out how the change will improve internal operations and external relations (i.e., with customers, suppliers, or others outside the immediate work group).
   (b) Sometimes the best way to demonstrate the superiority of the new system is by using outsiders who are known experts in the new system. Some managers use outside consultants for this purpose. Others have outsiders experienced with the sort of change they are implementing come in and describe their positive experiences with the new system.
   (c) People tend to identify best with changes that are described in clear, understandable ways. Hence, it is advisable to avoid overly complex or detailed explanations of the new system. Too many technological innovations fail because a manager engages in unnecessarily technical descriptions of the change.
   (d) The use of banners, mottos, slogans, and acronyms often gives the change program both importance and meaning. Such symbols allow for a shorthand way of referring to the change and create a way of referring to the program more frequently. Repetition signals that the change is important. In addition, if the symbols are cleverly coined, it gives the program more visibility with others. For example, one change effort to selectively alter course load for professors was called CLAP (course load adjustment program). And the motto pinned on a safety program in a small community symphony was "See Sharp or Be Flat."
   (e) The explanation of the change will be most effective if it shapes expectations about when the positive results will be experienced. For example, if a manager is responsible for putting in a new telecommunications system, it is vital to let people know that they can

expect the new system to have minor "bugs" for six months to a year.

Step 2--Let employees ask questions, express opinions and concerns. Directly after the change is introduced, a manager must be prepared to address employee questions, opinions, and concerns. If the change was anticipated, one could expect many more questions than if it came as a surprise. In any event, it should be expected that questions will arise over the entire course of implementation. Hence a manager will want to keep channels of communication as open as possible. It is vital to recognize that as the change process unfolds, the manager will become more and more dependent on the efforts of those who have to accommodate the change. This implies that the manager can be much more directive and forceful early in the process, but will have to be more prepared for negotiation and accommodation later. This makes it especially important that expressions of resistance be encouraged early in the change process, when more response alternatives are available.

Step 3--Respond to employee questions and concerns. As questions, opinions, and concerns arise, it is important for the manager to pay attention to the possible causes for resistance that underlie them. As we have mentioned, each cause for resistance requires a slightly different response pattern. Sometimes the manager's response will not be sufficient. In those cases one strategy is to ask others to testify about the change: what it involves and what it promises.

Although using others to support the change is sometimes required, it is not without risks. By not being available at critical times, a manager can inadvertently signal a lack of interest in the problems experienced by those who must shoulder the weight of the change.

Step 4--Get commitment and set up review. One of the most powerful tools in eliciting commitment to a change is to implement it in phases. By implementing the change in stages, employees often find it easier to support the change. There are two reasons for this. First, phasing allows the involvement of those most committed to the change early and delays the commitments of those who are initially more reluctant. Second, it allows those initially less committed to observe directly what the change means before they have to put themselves irretrievably behind the effort.

Obviously phasing requires careful orchestration. It is important to select as the first phase that part of the total change program with the highest likelihood for success. Once the first phase is successfully completed, it is useful to celebrate the early successes and publicly acknowledge all those responsible for the success of the initial stages.

In expanding the change from its initial success, it is important for the manager to be sensitive to fine-tuning the implementation to local conditions and unexpected problems as they arise. Few changes are ever implemented completely according to the initial plan. Slight modifications are almost always necessary as factors that were not anticipated are discovered.

At the same time, successful top-down implementation requires the manager to be bold with those individuals who drag their feet as the final stages proceed. Effective managers continue to be sensitive to the various causes for resistance, but are not shy in their responses. They often use the argument that fairness requires at least trying the change and refuse to tolerate any resistance that jeopardizes the entire program. Moreover, they frequently use every occasion of voluntary turnover (top-down changes frequently result in people quitting or transferring) as an opportunity to bring in people more committed to the change.

Delegation Implementation

As we have described, using delegation to implement a change is warranted (a) when time is available, (b) when the problem the change addresses is not generally recognized, (c) when employees have valuable insights about the direction of the change, (d) when the manager lacks the power to implement the change alone, and (e) when employees have traditionally been included in change decisions in the past.

In spite of its clear advantages in certain situations, implementation by delegation is foreign to many managers and absolutely unknown in some organizations. For that reason it is important that the manager have a clear charter for managing the change process. Obtaining such a charter is often painstaking. Some bosses are reluctant to give the manager and particularly his or her group the discretion and authority that they need to work out all the implementation details. Often supervisors have proceeded with delegation with a vague "go-ahead" from the boss only to discover that the group had made a series of decisions that the boss found unacceptable. Thus, even before beginning the delegation process, it is essential that the manager elicit a clear charter from the boss which clearly specifies both the authority to delegate and the parameters of the decision.

This is particularly true when the change has far-reaching implications. If the change is a minor one or in cases where delegation is commonplace, it is not necessary to clear intentions with the boss. However, if the change is major or the use of delegation is unique, then getting a clear charter is necessary.

With this charter in place, the following steps should be taken:

(1) explain the need for delegation,
(2) use delegation of the task to motivate,
(3) explain the task and ask employee's view,

(4) specify responsibility and authority,
(5) confirm employee's understanding and set up review.

There are certain principles that apply in each of these steps.

Step 1--Explain the need for delegation. Just as in top-down implementation, it is vital that the manager begin by offering the group a clear and complete description of the situation that creates the need for change. In doing so, it is important not to minimize the need for change. If the change is necessitated by a problem that jeopardizes the survival of the organization, employees are likely to be more motivated to change if they know that. Providing such information may be valuable even if the manager suspects that the group may not need to know. The reason for the complete openness about the need for change is that groups are seldom motivated to change without a real threat. The status quo is often too comfortable for a group to be motivated to change unless there is the necessary impetus. Moreover, it is very possible that the group will learn of all the elements that constitute the need for change as they progress, and it is better for them to hear it from the manager than to learn it themselves.

Step 2--Use delegation of the task to motivate. Delegation can be a tremendous motivator and a source of frustration at the same time. It motivates best when

   (a) employees trust the intentions of the delegator,
   (b) they are given sufficient time, information, and resources to work on
         the implementation plan,
   (c) they can see their plan put into action.

Delegation is frustrating when

   (a) employees are suspicious about the intentions of the delegator,
   (b) they are given insufficient time, information, and resources to work on
         the implementation plan,
   (c) they are told they will have a voice in the implementation only to be
         told later their recommendations were unacceptable.

Accordingly, a manager should avoid sending mixed messages about intentions to delegate and make certain that sufficient time, information, and resources are provided to the group. Finally, the manager must be prepared to pave the way for the group's decisions to be put into action. Most employees have had experience with counterfeit delegation that fails on one or more of these counts, so if a manager is to be successful, he or she must be prepared to meet these challenges directly and forthrightly.

Step 3--Explain the task and ask the employee's view. When it is time to explain the task, it is generally helpful for the manager to develop a specific time line to give the group particular milestones. This makes the manager's expectations about performance very clear along the way to the group's ultimate product.

Many groups also need assistance with their group decision process. Here an effective manager should be prepared to intervene in order to assure that the conflict between the individuals of the group is at the correct level. In general a moderate degree of conflict is desirable, for it stimulates innovative solutions. It is not advisable for the group to be either too content with the first alternative it considers or too torn by disagreements about favored choices.

One technique in guiding the group's decision process is to require a consensus decision rule. Consensus is a decision tool in which the group agrees to seek those alternatives that everyone can at least "live with." Alternatively, it is a decision rule that requires every individual to understand and accept the logic behind the favored option. Not all employees are familiar with consensus, so often a manager must explain this decision rule to the group and be prepared to intervene when they have problems with it.

"Groupthink" is a related problem. Groupthink arises when the group is too ready to accept an alternative that is thought to be popular. Essentially its presence signals that there is insufficient conflict in the group's deliberations. When the group appears to be too quick to settle, effective managers often intervene. One useful technique is to appoint a devil's advocate (someone assigned the role of taking a contrary position) or to directly challenge the group's decision. This may ensure that delegation results in the best product.

Step 4--Specify responsibility and authority. Few managers are entirely comfortable turning over decision-making authority to others. In delegating decision making, it is important that the manager understand his or her reservations and monitor the process closely, but *at a distance*, to assure that the group is staying on track. This will require the manager to be alert to a tendency to take back decision authority from the group.

One reason managers are so gun-shy about delegating a change to their people is that they suspect their boss will second-guess their group's decision. Much of this concern will be allayed if the supervisor has received a clear charter from his or her boss before beginning the change effort. Even having done this, it is wise for the manager to provide the boss with ongoing reports as the group progresses with its deliberations. This not only serves to remind the boss of the original charter, but also tends to surface concerns which can be dealt with before exposing the group decision to a veto from someone high in the organization.

Step 5--Confirm the employee's understanding and set up a review. After having explained expectations about both the process and outcomes of the group's activities during delegation, a manager can expect questions. Some of them may even be heated and emotionally laden. It is important to understand that when delegation is used, the approach to resistance to change is fundamentally different than it is when a change is implemented in a top-down fashion. While top-down implementation deals with resistance by understanding and responding to it as it unfolds, delegation strives to eliminate it by involving people directly in the implementation decisions.

Conclusion

Supervising change is one of a manager's most challenging assignments. Implementing change is a problem-filled endeavor. But with the principles we have outlined in this chapter, implementing change can potentially proceed smoothly and with less difficulty.

References

Allen, Stephen A. "Organizational Choice and General Influence Networks for Diversified Companies." *Academy of Management Journal* 34 (1978): 339-352.

Biggart, Nicole W. "The Creative-Destructive Process of Organizational Change." *Administrative Science Quarterly* 22 (1977): 412-431.

Gibson, Cyrus F. *Managing Organizational Behavior.* Homewood, Ill.: Irwin, 1980.

Greiner, L. E. "Patterns of Organizational Change." *Harvard Business Review* 45 (1967): 119-130.

Hedberg, Bo L. T., Paul Nystrom, and William Starbuck. "Camping on Seesaws: Prescriptions for a Self-Designing Organization." *Administrative Science Quarterly* 26 (1976): 66-80.

Kotter, John P., and Leonard A. Schlesinger. "Choosing Strategies for Change." *Harvard Business Review* 57 (1979): 109-127.

Lawrence, Paul R. "How to Deal with Resistance to Change." *Harvard Business Review* 30 (1954): 49-58.

Leavitt, Harold J. "Applied Organizational Change in Industry." In James G. March, ed., *Handbook of Organizations.* Chicago: Rand McNally, 1965.

Lewin, Kurt. "Group Decision and Social Change." In G. E. Swanson, T. M. Newcomb, and E. L. Hartley, eds., *Readings in Social Psychology*. New York: Holt, Rinehart & Winston, 1952.

Zaltman, Gerald, and Robert Duncan. *Strategies for Planned Change*. New York: John Wiley & Sons, 1979.

Course:_____   Name:_____

Instructor:_____   Date:_____

Flow Diagram for Managing Change Interactive Case 1

Detach this page from your book before you begin the Interactive Case. As you make each decision, write the decision point number *and* letter following the GO TO statement in the appropriate rectangle *before* you turn to that page. If you are referred to a previous decision point, circle the decision point number and letter you last wrote and proceed to the first uncircled rectangle above that one in your flow diagram. Do not erase the numbers and letters once you have written them. You will not necessarily fill all the rectangles.

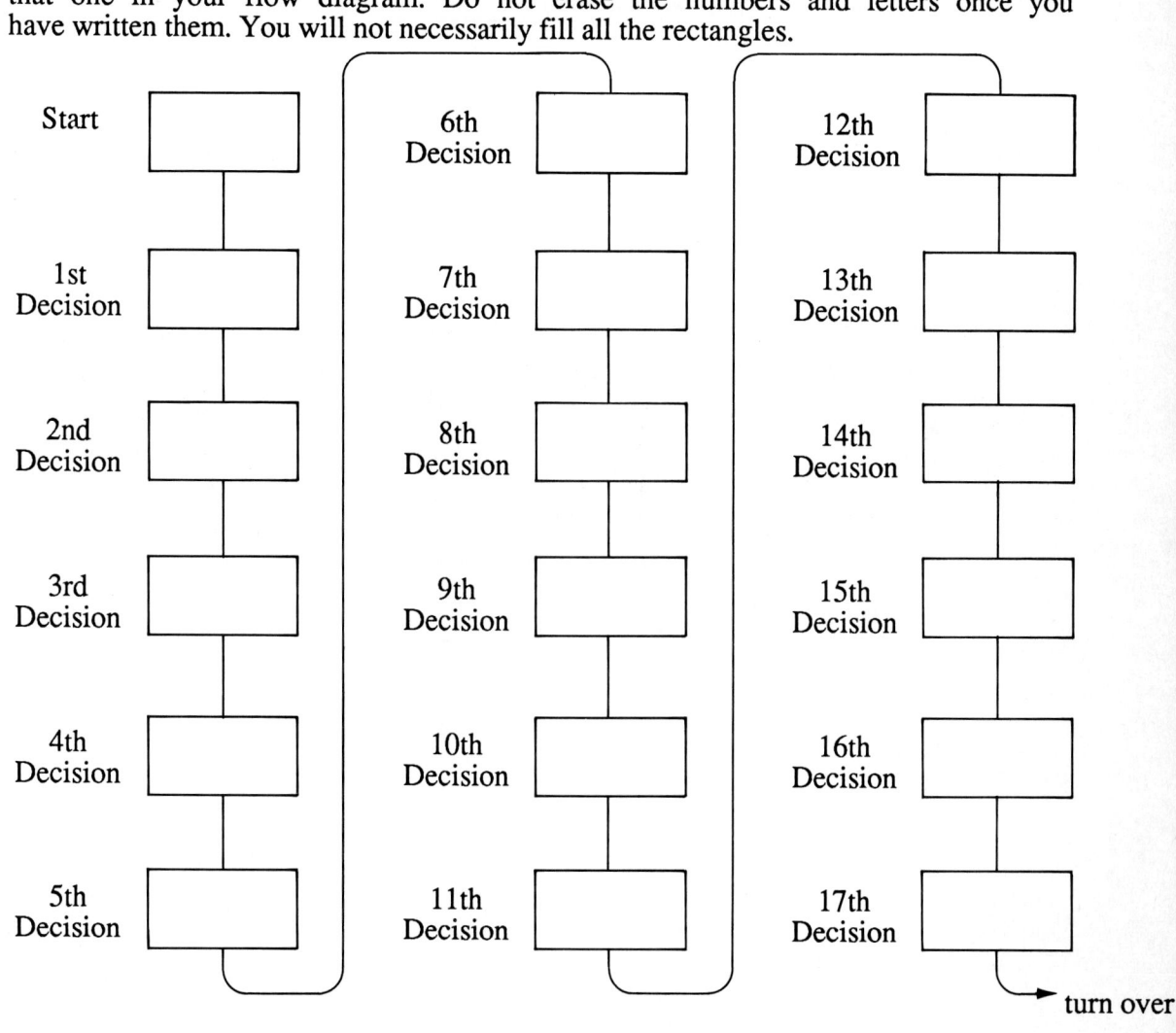

Start

1st Decision

2nd Decision

3rd Decision

4th Decision

5th Decision

6th Decision

7th Decision

8th Decision

9th Decision

10th Decision

11th Decision

12th Decision

13th Decision

14th Decision

15th Decision

16th Decision

17th Decision

→ turn over

18th Decision	27th Decision	36th Decision
19th Decision	28th Decision	37th Decision
20th Decision	29th Decision	38th Decision
21st Decision	30th Decision	39th Decision
22nd Decision	31st Decision	40th Decision
23rd Decision	32nd Decision	41st Decision
24th Decision	33rd Decision	42nd Decision
25th Decision	34th Decision	43rd Decision
26th Decision	35th Decision	44th Decision

Interactive Case 1

You are the newly appointed Head Librarian of the Lake County Library District (LCLD). LCLD has three branches and employs 25 full-time people including 10 professional librarians. An organization chart appears on page 206.

The LCLD has a fine reputation for community service. This is due more than anything to your predecessor, Ms. Alma Brickhouse. Ms. B (as she was known throughout the county) prided herself on the fact that there were more library cards issued per capita in Lake County than in any other county in the state.

Assisted by her husband who served as Community Service Director and who retired with her a month ago, Ms. B was a highly visible figure in every community in the county. In her frequent speeches to the Kiwanis Club and other service groups, she consistently summarized the mission of the LCLD with the motto, "The county is served when we make the time to listen." So common was this saying that it appeared on all LCLD stationary and on library cards given to patrons.

While Ms. B had a commanding presence (she was six feet tall), she was more than a caricature. She knew every person who worked for LCLD by name, and she commanded respect from most of them, especially the older ones whom she had hired and indoctrinated with her community service ideals. Ms. B's approach to management was traditional. She reserved most decisions to herself, and rarely delegated or involved others in policy-making.

If there was any shortsightedness in her approach, it was professionalism. Her emphasis on local concerns alienated most every professionally oriented librarian she hired. At the end of her tenure, she left a staff more devoted to her as a matriarch of the county than to the ideals of modern librarianship as touted in professional schools. Tangible evidence of this emphasis was State University's action against LCLD. Last year, State University dropped LCLD from the approved list of library systems for its graduate interns. In other library systems, interns are used as an important source of inexpensive labor and as a force for improvement and revitalization. However, at LCLD they were viewed as troublemakers and problem-finders.

The rather antiprofessional posture of Ms. B had one other negative effect on LCLD: the state library accreditation commission recently put LCLD on probation. This means that the district will only qualify for increases in its state grants if it "takes immediate action to restore a level of professionalism commensurate with a system of its size." Among the professional standards used by the accreditation agency is "the level of use of computer technology in cataloging, the maintenance of reference sources, the linkage with other resource centers, and the tracking of lended materials." Presently no use is being made of computers at LCLD.

Lake County Library District

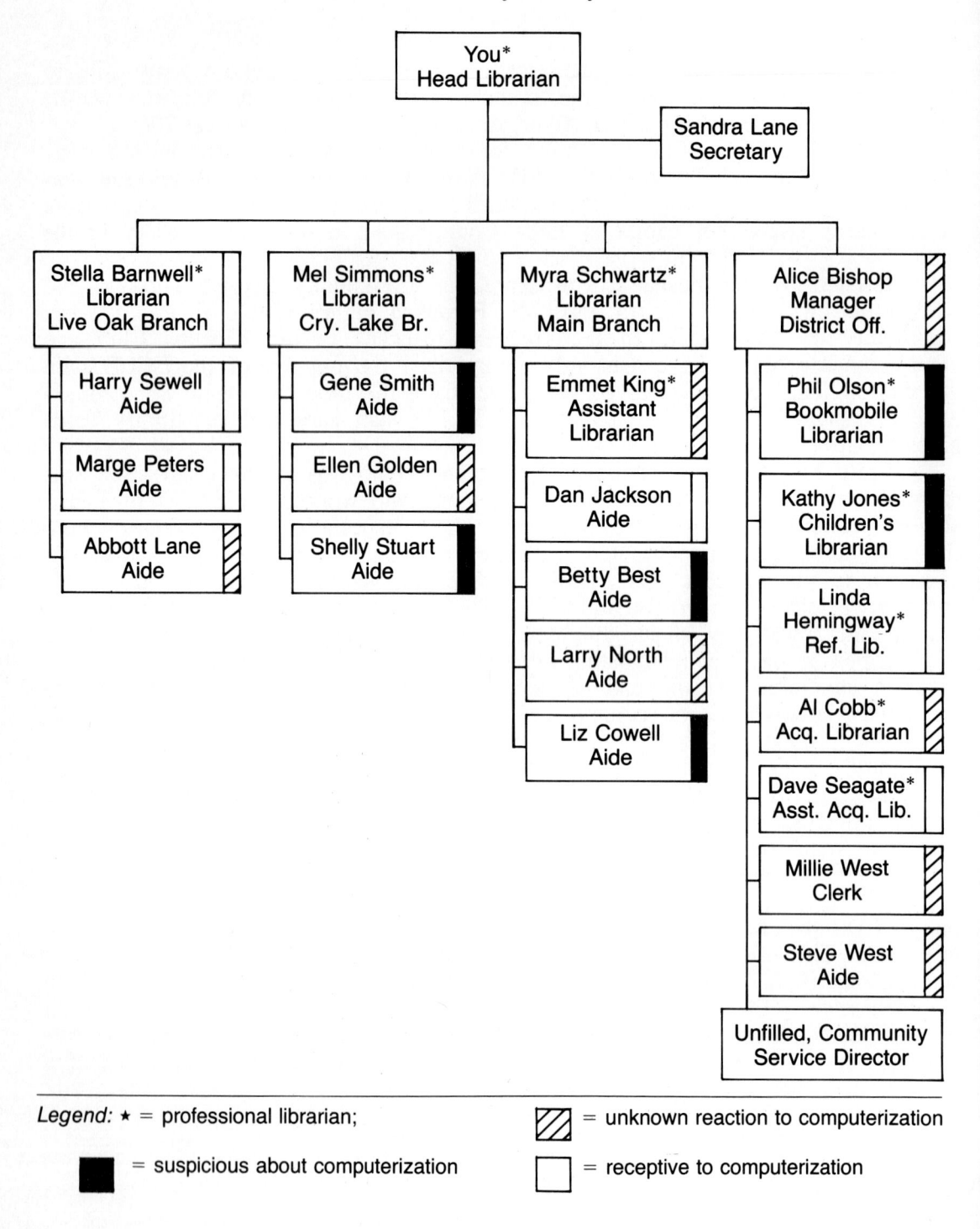

```
                    ┌──────────────────┐
                    │ You*             │
                    │ Head Librarian   │──────┬──────────────────┐
                    └──────────────────┘      │ Sandra Lane      │
                              │               │ Secretary        │
                              │               └──────────────────┘
```

- **You*** — Head Librarian
  - **Sandra Lane** — Secretary

- **Stella Barnwell*** — Librarian, Live Oak Branch
  - Harry Sewell — Aide
  - Marge Peters — Aide
  - Abbott Lane — Aide (unknown reaction)

- **Mel Simmons*** — Librarian, Cry. Lake Br. (suspicious)
  - Gene Smith — Aide
  - Ellen Golden — Aide (unknown reaction)
  - Shelly Stuart — Aide (unknown reaction)

- **Myra Schwartz*** — Librarian, Main Branch
  - Emmet King* — Assistant Librarian (unknown reaction)
  - Dan Jackson — Aide
  - Betty Best — Aide (suspicious)
  - Larry North — Aide (unknown reaction)
  - Liz Cowell — Aide (suspicious)

- **Alice Bishop** — Manager, District Off. (unknown reaction)
  - Phil Olson* — Bookmobile Librarian (suspicious)
  - Kathy Jones* — Children's Librarian (suspicious)
  - Linda Hemingway* — Ref. Lib.
  - Al Cobb* — Acq. Librarian (unknown reaction)
  - Dave Seagate* — Asst. Acq. Lib.
  - Millie West — Clerk (unknown reaction)
  - Steve West — Aide (unknown reaction)
  - Unfilled, Community Service Director

Legend: ★ = professional librarian; ▨ = unknown reaction to computerization; ■ = suspicious about computerization; ☐ = receptive to computerization

Your appointment as Head Librarian was testament to the county government's concern about LCLD's questionable accreditation record. You were selected over several other applicants for the job because you had experience with computerized library systems. You have been given the resources to implement a computer system and the objective to have the system "up and operational" in one year. However, it is clear that your operations budget will not be increased in the next few years. Directly after your appointment, you had a chance to talk with each of your people. Each was aware of your charter. After your interviews you noted three classes of openness toward computerization: one group openly receptive, one group uncommitted, and one group openly suspicious. The organization chart on page 206 shows how these three groups are distributed over the organization.

Those who are suspicious about implementation feel computers (1) may be used as an excuse to "weed out unneeded personnel," (2) will require people to learn extensive programming skills they have neither the aptitude for nor the interest in, and (3) will dilute efforts at delivering personal service. These concerns are not entirely unfounded. First, LCLD is currently overstaffed. If two interns are hired per year at minimum wage, two positions that presently call for professional librarians (King's and Seagate's) could be scaled down to senior clerical positions. While your employees are covered by civil service protection, you are confident that the commission will rule on behalf of a change in job classification. Second, all personnel will have to become literate in *BIBLIOTEK*, the software program to be used, by the end of the year if the milestone is to be met. Third, implementing the system *will* necessitate a temporary reduction in personal service to patrons. While this should only last a year, it is clear that the total cooperation of the staff is needed to assure that the fine image of the LCLD in the county is maintained. You are contemplating the best way to bring about this change.

Considering all these facts, what would you do?

A. Implement the change in a top-down fashion by prescribing the necessary direction of change and enforcing it accordingly. (GO TO 294A)

B. Implement the change by involving all employees in decisions about *how* to put the system in place. (GO TO 262A)

C. Implement the change by involving all employees in decisions about *whether* or not to implement the computer system. (GO TO 278A)

D. Implement the change by involving a select group of employees in decisions about *how* to put the system in place. (GO TO 237A)

Course:_____   Name:_____

Instructor:_____   Date:_____

Flow Diagram for Managing Change Interactive Case 2

Detach this page from your book before you begin the Interactive Case. As you make each decision, write the decision point number *and* letter following the GO TO statement in the appropriate rectangle *before* you turn to that page. If you are referred to a previous decision point, circle the decision point number and letter you last wrote and proceed to the first uncircled rectangle above that one in your flow diagram. Do not erase the numbers and letters once you have written them. You will not necessarily fill all the rectangles.

Start		6th Decision		12th Decision	
1st Decision		7th Decision		13th Decision	
2nd Decision		8th Decision		14th Decision	
3rd Decision		9th Decision		15th Decision	
4th Decision		10th Decision		16th Decision	
5th Decision		11th Decision		17th Decision	

→ turn over

18th Decision	27th Decision	36th Decision
19th Decision	28th Decision	37th Decision
20th Decision	29th Decision	38th Decision
21st Decision	30th Decision	39th Decision
22nd Decision	31st Decision	40th Decision
23rd Decision	32nd Decision	41st Decision
24th Decision	33rd Decision	42nd Decision
25th Decision	34th Decision	43rd Decision
26th Decision	35th Decision	44th Decision

Interactive Case 2

You are the Manufacturing Manager for Arion Systems, a company that produces and sells telecommunications equipment. Most of Arion's business comes from a few lines of relatively standard PBX systems. Arion competes in the PBX market primarily on price. This price advantage comes from efficiencies that you and your colleagues have introduced into the manufacturing process.

You have a team of three talented professionals working for you. In the one year you all have been together, production has improved substantially. It seems that your group has been able to pull together and solve most every problem that has come up. The members of your team are as follows:

Larry Beeson (Assembly Supervisor)--Larry is responsible for 207 assemblers who are organized into assembly teams. He has been at Arion for two years and has eight years of industry experience. He is a particularly competent manager who "runs a very tight ship."

Robin Broderick (Test Supervisor)--Robin is responsible for 43 technicians who test incoming parts and completed systems. They also rework defective systems and perform warranty repairs. Robin was promoted into this position from within the test group about three years ago.

Marilyn Wilson (Material Supervisor)--Marilyn has been with Arion for one year. Previously she worked for a large aerospace firm. She is responsible for scheduling and procuring component parts. She supervises five scheduling specialists and 16 parts clerks.

An organization chart of Arion appears on page 212.

After a weekly staff meeting this morning, Eugene Marshall, Arion's President, cornered you to discuss something that was entirely new to you. It regarded custom production. Presently only a small part of Arion's business comes from systems designed after the unique needs of a particular customer. This custom production is located in the Engineering Department. Each custom system is designed by the engineering staff and is built by small groups of technicians assigned to various engineering teams. In your conversation, Eugene tells you that he expects custom work to become a larger and larger part of the business in the next five to 10 years. Moreover, Eugene has decided that in order to enjoy more efficiency he wants to begin to incorporate the custom production into your department. Eugene further mentions that he has talked to some friends at another company who use "flexible assembly" to handle custom jobs. He described this as the development of assembly groups that have the manpower and equipment to do long production runs *and* custom items simultan-

Manufacturing Department, Arion Systems

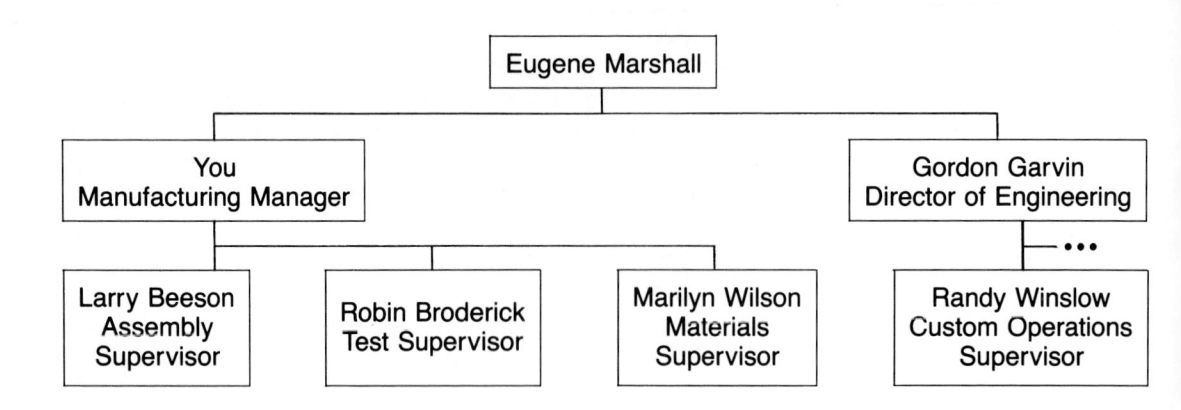

```
                        Eugene Marshall
                              |
        ┌─────────────────────┴─────────────────────┐
        You                                   Gordon Garvin
  Manufacturing Manager                   Director of Engineering
        |                                          |
  ┌─────┼─────────┬──────────┐                    ├─ • • •
Larry Beeson  Robin Broderick  Marilyn Wilson   Randy Winslow
 Assembly     Test Supervisor    Materials     Custom Operations
 Supervisor                     Supervisor        Supervisor
```

eously. He ends the conversation by saying, "Let's try that approach if it makes sense for us."

After this brief encounter, you return to your office and start thinking about what needs to be done. You don't know much about how custom production is done in the Engineering Department, but you do know that 18 technicians are involved in the process. Further, these technicians are assigned in groups of between two and four to various engineers. The technicians are highly skilled and view themselves as "associate" engineers. The engineers and technicians work closely together on projects and often spend hours talking about the engineering problems involved in particular systems. The person responsible for the technicians is an engineer by the name of Randy Winslow. At the staff meeting this morning, it was announced that Winslow would be leaving in two weeks to visit the Birmingham, England, plant of Arion on a six-month troubleshooting assignment. It is common knowledge that Winslow will probably be permanently assigned to the British affiliate of Arion, and that may have been a contributing factor in Eugene's decision to give you Winslow's unit.

As you begin to think about how to absorb custom production into your department, you know you have many options. After some study, you identify three main alternatives:

> *The "Superteam" approach*--Under this plan the engineering technicians would develop their own independent assembly group with specially assigned test workers and scheduling people. This group would handle custom and short production run items.

The "Flexible Assembly" approach--This option divides the technicians among your Assembly group (headed by Larry Beeson) so that each group would be capable of both standard and custom production. This is the approach that Eugene Marshall mentioned.

The "Contracting" approach--This would assign the technicians to your Test group (headed by Robin Broderick). There they would handle all single-item orders. As some of these became market successes, they would be assigned to Assembly for longer production runs.

All of these approaches have advantages and disadvantages, and your team may even have other options worth considering.

At this point, what would you do?

A. Schedule a meeting with Eugene to clarify the assignment he has given to you. (GO TO 286A)

B. Decide yourself which of the above approaches you should choose as a method of bringing custom production into your group. (GO TO 280A)

C. Call a meeting of the members of your group to consider which of the alternatives should be implemented. (GO TO 310B)

12 THE NEW SUPERVISOR
Module Reading

Becoming a manager or supervisor can be one of the most rewarding of all occupations. A manager can have influence over many people's working lives, can contribute to the value of the goods and services produced by the organization, and can do more to link the interests of senior management with those of the lower level employees than anyone else in the organization. Being a manager can also be loaded with frustrations. Often the manager becomes the person in the middle of a host of expectations by others. Accordingly one classic view of the first level manager is as "a master and victim of doubletalk."

In this module reading we will present principles that will help a new supervisor make an immediate positive contribution in the first few weeks on the job and at the same time avoid some of the pitfalls and pratfalls that give every new supervisor problems. We begin by laying out what new supervisors should know about their new jobs. Next we specify the ways to deal with the challenges a new manager will be likely to face during the early weeks and months of the job.

What Incoming Managers Should Know About Their New Jobs

No one is ever totally prepared to begin managing a group. New managers find themselves having to master an entirely new set of skills very quickly. They have to respond to the expectations of many people both above and below them in the organization and have to quickly develop a correct sense of what is and what is not possible to accomplish.

New Skills

Often the supervisor will have a better technical understanding of his or her subordinates' work than anyone else in the chain of command and therefore will be viewed by those above him or her as having the "final word" on the technical aspects of employees' jobs. This means that the supervisor should be at least familiar with the tools and techniques subordinates use and should have mastery of the associated formal procedures.

A new supervisor must also have a broader perspective than the people supervised including a working understanding of how the various parts of the organization fit together into a meaningful whole. This perspective many be very different from that of subordinates who frequently have not developed an overall perspective of the organization and of how their group contributes to it.

When one is promoted into a supervisory or management position, one must quickly develop a set of new skills, often without much practice or preparation. Among these are such skills as exercising leadership in assigning tasks, giving directions, dealing with work conflicts, and implementing and managing changes in the group.

New Time Allocations

As individual contributors, workers spend virtually all of their time doing their own work. Supervisors, on the other hand, find their days filled mostly with leadership activities. One breakdown of a typical supervisor's day is shown in Table 1. Leading includes orienting and training subordinates, motivating and directing them, and guiding them to high standards of performance. In essence, the supervisor must substitute coaching for doing.

Table 1
How Supervisors Spend Their Time

Activity	Time Spent
Leading	55%
Controlling	20%
Planning	10%
Organizing	10%
Implementing Changes	5%

Source: Henry Mintzberg. *The Nature of Managerial Work.* New York: Harper & Row, 1973.

While this may seem to offer the supervisor a great deal of latitude, in fact there are frequently so many demands and constraints on the supervisor, particularly early in the job, that there is actually little discretion that can be exercised. Some of these constraints may take the form of limited resources or low skill level of subordinates. Demands often take the form of difficult performance objectives, tightly defined operating procedures and standards, and reporting responsibilities, including meetings and written reports and memos. As Figure 1 indicates, the resulting area of choice or discretion between the constraints and demands placed on a supervisor is rather small.

The Expectations of Subordinates

Subordinates rarely appreciate just how limited are the choices a manager can make. Typically they underestimate the narrow range of discretion defined

Figure 1
The Differences in Demands, Constraints
and Choices for Two Jobs

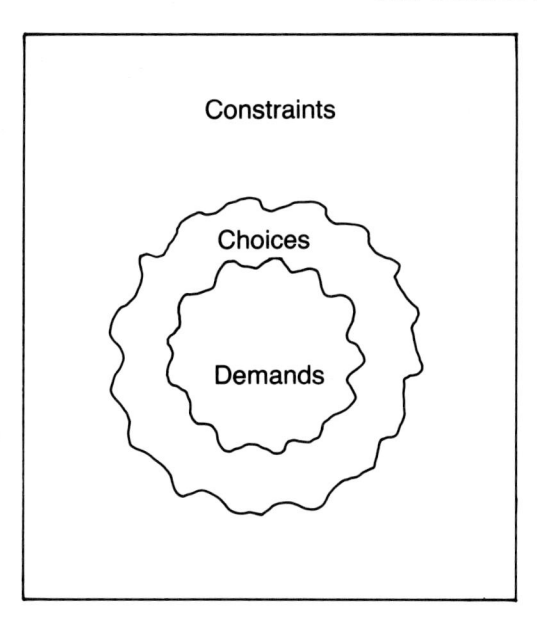

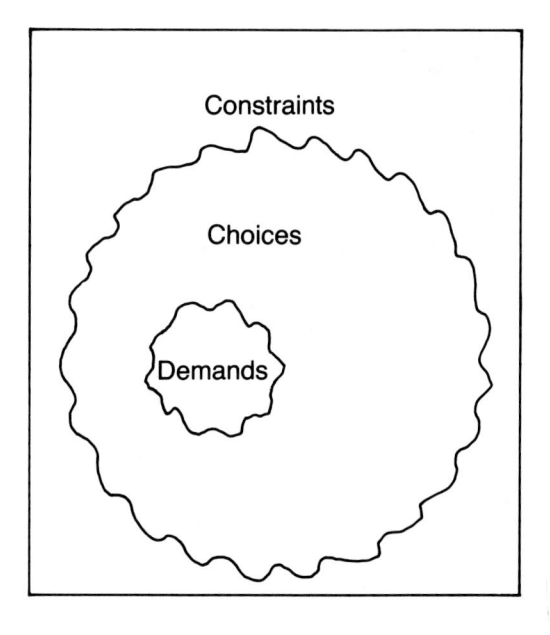

Typical for a first-level supervisor

Typical for a company president

From *Choices for a Manager* by Rosemary Stewart, p. 7, copyright © 1982. Reprinted by permission of Prentice-Hall, Inc., Englewood Cliffs, New Jersey.

by the constraints and demands on the manager. This often results in unrealistic expectations.

Realistic or not, subordinates have three types of expectations as to how a manager will handle situations. First, they expect the manager to be the definitive word on the formal policies and procedures governing their work and how these impact on how they do their jobs. For example, if two subordinates differ over how the vacation policy applies to their particular situation, they will turn to the manager for the correct interpretation. Second, they expect the manager to be the guarantor of justice in the workplace. Third, subordinates expect their manager to represent their interests in dealing with other groups and higher authorities.

Subordinate expectations are often behind much of the testing that every new supervisor experiences. Often subordinates will feel uneasy until they know how a new manager is going to handle certain situations. It is difficult to generalize about how a new manager should respond to these tests except to say that a manager should expect them, understand that they are efforts at uncertainty reduction not trickery, and be aware that the response to them may powerfully shape future expectations of subordinates.

The Expectations of Peers

The supervisors of other work groups also have definite expectations that every new supervisor should appreciate. Peers are potential competitors for resources and for their boss's attention. Accordingly, one expectation that experienced supervisors generally have of a new supervisor is that he or she will compete fairly. This rules out name-calling, currying favors with the boss in a devious way, and shifting blame. A second expectation that supervisors have of new peers is that they respect confidences. Peers have to believe that what is said "off the record" will not be related to others. Similarly, they expect that when they are quoted or their points of view represented, the new supervisor will do so accurately. Finally, other supervisors expect that the new supervisor will be no more permissive with their subordinates than they are. Permissive supervisors create tremendous pressures on their peers. For example, if a new supervisor is not as tough on tardiness as others are, it makes the experienced supervisors look unreasonable and overly strict.

The Expectations of the Boss

A new supervisor's boss also has important expectations. Probably the most important of these can be summed up in two words: "no surprises." Few things will upset a manager more than learning things from others that their subordinates should have told them earlier. Unfortunately, however, managers are not always precise in just what matters they want to be kept informed about. Consequently, a new supervisor will often find him- or herself in the position of having to guess about what should and should not be reported. Yet since the consequences violating the "no surprises" rule are so negative, it is often necessary to clarify just what things a boss wants to be kept informed of and what matters are unimportant to him or her.

A related expectation that bosses have is that a new supervisor respects their time. Virtually every manager experiences severe time pressures, and they expect that their subordinate supervisors (a) will not initiate contact unless it is really necessary, (b) will plan the encounter carefully to assure that it is efficient, and (c) will choose occasions in which the boss can devote the necessary attention to the subject at hand. Again, managers are not always clear about their preferences in these regards. Some bosses want all upward communication documented in writing, and some are more casual about it. Some want their subordinates to "get down to business" in an encounter without a lengthy exchange of pleasantries, while some seem to relish a "warm-up period." Finally, some managers are prepared to discuss any matter at any time, and others have daily rituals that make some times better than others. A new supervisor must be prepared to adapt to these individual differences.

Third, a boss expects support from those supervisors reporting to him or her. While this has many meanings, it typically implies doing nothing that will make a boss look bad. It also means accepting the boss's sense of priorities. This requires that the new supervisor have a good feel for the boss's problems and objectives. As we will discuss in a later section, this is one of the first things a new supervisor should attempt to find out.

Performance Uncertainties

As we have seen, new supervisors face many kinds of uncertainties as they begin their jobs. Over time many of these uncertainties will be reduced, but one sort of uncertainty is likely to remain. With few exceptions, a supervisor will never have a total understanding of how his or her boss's performance is rated by higher officials, nor will the new supervisor understand the motivations of subordinates, at least initially. Table 2 describes this state of affairs. Notice that a supervisor is likely to have a much better understanding of the motivation of his or her boss than of his or her employees. Moreover, the supervisor is likely to have a better grasp of subordinates' performance than the boss's. Although this is somewhat intuitive, realizing it saves the new supervisor from being unnecessarily frustrated by these uncertainties.

Table 2
Performance Uncertainties of Supervisors

	Boss Observing Subordinate's Behavior	Subordinate Observing Boss's Behavior
Evaluating Performance	Has much information	Has little information
Explaining Motives	Has little information	Has much information

From *How to Run Any Organization: A Manual of Practical Sociology* by Theodore Caplow. Copyright © 1976 by Theodore Caplow. Reprinted by permission of Holt, Rinehart and Winston, Inc.

The New Supervisor's "Honeymoon"

Typically, new supervisors are granted a grace period, known as a "honeymoon," in which their minor mistakes are excused and expectations are not demanding. The length of this honeymoon differs from position to position, but typically it is at least a month and no more than six months. Its end is usually heralded by a conflict with the boss or someone else outside the supervisor's area of direct responsibility.

During this honeymoon period, one of the most important things the new supervisor can do is to attempt to understand the history of the projects that are assigned and the backgrounds of each of the people with whom he or she must work. The reason for this is that it allows the new supervisor to better understand the job requirements. Further, if the new supervisor knows the background of a situation, he or she may be in a better position to figure out what is coming in the future.

Adapting to the Technical Challenges of the Job

For the typical new supervisor, the earliest challenges are technical. As we have seen, supervisors are expected to possess a more thorough technical understanding of the work than any other manager. If the supervisor has been promoted from the group, this is not likely to be problematic. The supervisor will already have a working knowledge of the technical elements of the jobs to be supervised. However, when the new supervisor comes from outside, he or she may need to be more tentative and receptive to those who can provide technical education. Three sources of technical information for the new supervisor are the boss, peers, and subordinates.

Learning the Ropes from the Boss. No one is in a better position than the boss to assist the new supervisor in initially adapting to the technical requirements of the job. The manager should have an excellent sense of priorities and be able to coach the new supervisor on how to meet the technical challenges of the new position. The manager is likely to offer initial assignments that have a broader charter than the new supervisor might desire. Often managers do not provide the sort of detail that they need to new supervisors. This may require the new supervisor to ask for the level of detail that he or she feels is necessary. At the very least, it is important that the new supervisor leave these initial meetings with a sense of what the boss considers to be a definition of acceptable performance.

When the new supervisor receives a directive, he or she should be prepared to clarify just how the boss expects to be included in the assignment. This may require clarifying the following:

(1) Should the supervisor give facts and information to the manager?
(2) Should the supervisor generate alternatives for the manager?
(3) Should the supervisor recommend a course of action?
(4) Should the supervisor select an alternative, inform the manager, and wait for approval?
(5) Should the supervisor take action and only inform the manager if there are problems?

The new supervisor will be lucky if he or she gets this sort of detail. However, if at all possible, it is important to get as much clarity about the charter as possible.

Learning the Ropes from Peers. A new supervisor's peers can be a very good source of guidance during the honeymoon period, but they must be consulted carefully. Generally they have a better sense of the boss's priorities and motivation than anyone else, but as potential competitors they may not be as straightforward as they appear.

The best way to deal with this potential for bias is to use the age-old standards of journalism. Specifically, the new supervisor should question peers carefully and not accept information as credible without confirming it with another source.

Learning the Ropes from Subordinates. A new supervisor can also learn a great deal of helpful information from subordinates. They are the closest to the work itself, and this often puts them in a superior position to recommend changes and improvements. At no time is this edge in technical understanding greater than during the honeymoon period. This creates a real dilemma for the new supervisor. Should the subordinates' superior technical understanding be acknowledged and relied on or should the supervisor defer action until he or she has more information even though this runs the risk of not acting in a timely fashion?

Two factors bear on this dilemma: prudence and succession. If the new supervisor is prudent about following the advice of subordinates, there is little reason to worry. The major risk of bowing to the relative expertise of subordinates is that it may be too narrow. It may be blind to the "big picture," or it may result in unfair advantages to some people at the expense of others. By talking with people, analyzing suggestions skeptically, and checking situations out firsthand, the new supervisor can reduce this risk.

Succession is the second factor. Whether the new supervisor follows a strong or weak predecessor and whether he or she has risen to the new position from within or outside the organization should affect how the supervisor acts on subordinates' suggestions early on. Consider Table 3. If the new supervisor has been promoted from within the firm *and* follows a strong predecessor, he or she is in a poor position to introduce immediate changes. Consequently, new supervisors in this situation probably should avoid any hasty changes that are recommended by subordinates. On the other hand, if the predecessor was weak, the new supervisor shouldn't lose the opportunity to make necessary changes.

Table 3
Initiating Changes During the Honeymoon

	Strong Predecessor	**Weak Predecessor**
Inside Successor	Lie low	New broom
Outside Successor	New broom	Lie low

From *How to Run Any Organization: A Manual of Practical Sociology* by Theodore Caplow. Copyright © 1976 by Theodore Caplow. Reprinted by permission of Holt, Rinehart and Winston, Inc.

When the new supervisor comes from the outside, the situation is exactly reversed. Following a weak predecessor in this instance means that the new supervisor probably lacks an understanding of just what made the predecessor weak and is not likely to have the sort of resources (complete records, high performing subordinates, effective precedents, etc.) that strong predecessors tend to leave. For these reasons, lying low is advised until the supervisor has a better technical understanding of the work. Outside successors should act early when their predecessor was a strong performer. Replacing strong people with individuals from the outside shows that the predecessor was not inclined to subordinate development. Otherwise the predecessor would have had someone inside ready to take over when he or she left. In such a case, unless the new supervisor can demonstrate a readiness to involve people more than the predecessor did, he or she will likely continue the tradition of being overly compliant and dependent.

It is not always easy to ascertain whether a predecessor was strong or weak. Commonly a new supervisor's boss will avoid labeling predecessors as weak even if they were. As well, the new supervisor's perception may not be accurate. For these reasons, the new supervisor should be deliberate during the honeymoon period in all but the clearest cases.

Adapting to the Social Challenges of a New Job

Becoming a supervisor alters social contacts at work. A new supervisor needs to make new friends and change the nature of old relationships. However, he or she typically has more time to do this than to master the technical features of the new job. There are three parts to this social adaptation: sensing the existing social realities of the group, creating an interpersonal climate with subordinates, and learning about subordinates as individuals.

Sensing the Existing Social Realities of the Group. Even if a supervisor has been promoted from within the work group, he or she will have a slightly different social identity which has to be integrated into the social system. In establishing this new identity, it is important to keep in mind four features of the existing social reality of the new group: the group's norms, the group's status system, the friendship relations in the group, and the group's informal communication grapevine. Every work team has a group of unstated rules which regulate the social affairs of the group. Team members enforce these rules (or norms) on fellow group members. Individuals who are unwilling to respect these norms are treated as deviants, and may be excluded from certain social support given those who comply. For example, a group may have the norm that no one should tattle to the supervisor. Any workers who do are excluded from lunch conversations, parties, and other celebrations, or are even ignored when asking others in the group for help in doing his or her work. A supervisor can try to shape the norms of his or her new team. However, it is prudent to do so only after having developed a good sense for what the norms are, which individuals are most active in policing them, and who has been excluded as a result of their enforcement.

A second factor in the existing social reality of the group is the team's informal status system. Every group has a pecking order from the most popular team members to the least popular. When new supervisors take disciplinary action against members with high status, they may in effect take on the entire group. Sometimes this discipline is necessary, but undertaking it too early, before the new supervisor has built some credibility, is not without risks. The informal status system may also influence how employees compare the new supervisor to the previous one. This suggests that the new supervisor must be careful how the previous supervisor is described. For example, the predecessor may have occupied a very high status position in the group's pecking order, even if he or she was viewed as weak or ineffectual. For that reason, it is usually recommended that new supervisors not criticize their predecessors publicly.

Third, it is important for the new supervisor to try to gauge the friendship relations among the team members. Often work teams are made up of cliques or informal subgroups that tend to share perceptions and work attitudes. Commonly there are individuals in the group who do not get along well together. If the new supervisor is ignorant of likes and antipathies, he or she can easily blunder in making assignments, moving workstations, or expecting spontaneous cooperation.

Finally, the new supervisor needs to learn the structure of his or her group's informal communication network. Every group has a grapevine. If the new supervisor knows who is linked into it, this can be a tremendous source of information. In fact, one may be able to learn more about the social realities of the group by listening to the grapevine than in any other way. If the grapevine can be tapped, the new supervisor will quickly discern the positions of individuals in the status system, what the norms are, and even who likes and dislikes whom. Moreover, once one senses how to gain access to the grapevine, it may be that a well-placed rumor fed into the grapevine will be the quickest way of communicating certain things to people without making them public.

Creating an Interpersonal Climate with Subordinates. A second element in a new supervisor's adaptation to the social situation at work is to shape the relationship with new subordinates. One question is, "How close a relationship should the new supervisor have with his or her people?" Some new supervisors want to be quite intimate, others value a more distant and professional relationship, and still others fall somewhere between these two extremes. Whatever the choice, it is important to remember that more than anything, subordinates expect their supervisor to be fair. So for most supervisors the question is, "Can I be fair *and* intimate?" If the answer to this question is "No," some distancing is most likely called for.

Learning About Subordinates as Individuals. The final aspect of a new supervisor's social adaptation is in getting to know subordinates as individuals. Depending on how close the supervisors wants to be to the new subordinates, this may include finding out about their personal goals and ambitions, their strong and weak points as workers, their needs and values, and perhaps even something about their personal lives. As this information is gathered, it is vital to be wary of first impressions. Psychologists tell us that first impressions have a tremendous impact on our evaluations of others. Yet a new supervisor is in a terrible position to form accurate first impressions during his or her first few days and weeks on the job. There are two reasons for this. First, when new to a job, one is in a state of real information overload. One has to learn a great deal very fast, and many of the initial judgments may be inaccurate. Second, most subordinates try to make a positive first impression. Their initial posture is likely to be ingratiating. They may flatter, express common opinions, and offer favors in an attempt to manage the new supervisor's first impressions of them. Some subordinates are undeniably excellent at this game, so it is critical that initial judgments be suspended.

Adapting to the Political Challenges of the New Job

The end of the new supervisor's honeymoon often occurs when he or she has the first political problem either with the boss, a peer, or senior official. Consequently, to be most effective, the new supervisor will want to develop an understanding of the politics of the organization. Although the term "politics" has a negative connotation, politics exist in every organization, and any supervisor who ignores politics is destined for problems in getting work done.

Developing an Understanding of the Politics of the Organization. Essentially, politics include all those uses of power that are outside the formal chain of command. Thus, to understand the politics of an organization, the new supervisor has to figure out who has the power. For example, some vice presidents are more powerful than others because they are known to have the CEO's ear, some engineers are more powerful than others because they are considered technical "gurus," and some staff officials are powerful because they have access to information no one else has. In assessing the politics of an organization, the new supervisor should consider that the people with power have one or more of the following attributes:

(1) They have a visible track record of performance.
(2) They are considered experts in a technical area critical to the success of the organization.
(3) They have close associations with high officials.
(4) They are "wired" into the organization's information network.
(5) They have control over the purse strings and other resources others want and need.
(6) They are personally attractive people who command a lot of attention and admiration among others.

Thus, by observing who seems to have power, a new supervisor should be able to produce a "political" organizational structure that might be different from the formal one.

Another important feature of the politics of any organization is the sponsorship of products, policies, projects, and reorganizations. Every policy has an author, every product a champion, every project a sponsor. By recognizing who is behind these things, one can learn a lot about how the organization works politically. One new supervisor learned the hard way about the importance of knowing sponsorship. His first assignment was to evaluate a training program that the company was offering. He did so and became convinced that it was ill conceived and a waste of resources. When he bluntly reported his findings to his manager, he was embarrassed to learn that his boss had personally designed the program and was convinced that it was an excellent one. The question was not that he should have withheld his honest opinion; it was that if he had known something about sponsorship, he would have been much more tactful.

Building Political Bridges. As soon as possible, a new supervisor should build political bridges so that when the honeymoon ends, he or she is equipped to cope politically in the organization. Adroit politicians know that developing professional relationships with others is a sound way to develop power. This may mean getting to know as many people as possible, inquiring about their organizational problems and objectives, and being willing to aid them if the situation arises. Investing in relationships works for two reasons: (a) people develop confidence in others only over time and do not include unknowns in their own political activities, and (b) much of what happens politically happens because of the norm of reciprocity (you scratch my back and I'll scratch yours). Therefore, it makes good sense for the new supervisor to invest effort in developing solid professional relationships, based on getting to know people and on developing mutual understandings.

A second element of bridge building deals with unwritten supervisory norms. Just as a team of subordinates has norms that govern its members, so too does a group of supervisory peers. If the new supervisor expects the support of his or her co-workers, it may be necessary to comply with these norms. Recall that often these norms call for the new supervisor to (a) compete fairly, (b) respect confidences, and (c) be no more permissive with his or her subordinates than others are. By respecting these norms, the new supervisor may avoid being excluded by peers from important sources of information and support.

Third, the new supervisor should be prepared to defend the interests of his or her group when it is threatened by unreasonable demands from others. Of course, one should be selective in this defense. Digging in one's heels when the loss is sure is seldom advised. However, when the group is threatened by unreasonable demands, the new supervisor should carefully analyze the situation. If the situation is in fact unreasonable, the new supervisor should be willing to defend his or her group. The resulting conflict may end the honeymoon, but the consequence of inaction, particularly if the case is clear, may be loss of respect among subordinates.

References

Baskin, Otis, and Craig E. Aronoff. *Interpersonal Communication in Organizations*. Santa Monica, California: Goodyear, 1980.

Berlew, D. E., and Douglas T. Hall. "The Socialization of Managers." *Administrative Science Quarterly* 11 (1966): 207-223.

Black, James M. *Executive on the Move*. New York: American Management Association, 1964.

Caplow, Theodore. *How to Run Any Organization*. New York: Holt, Rinehart & Winston, 1976.

Katz, Daniel, and Robert Kahn. *The Social Psychology of Organization*. Second edition. New York: John Wiley & Sons, 1978.

Katz, Robert L. "Skills of an Effective Administrator." *Harvard Business Review* 52 (1974): 90-102.

Kotter, John. *Power and Influence in Organizations*. New York: Free Press, 1986.

McMurry, Robert N. "Power and the Ambitious Executive." *Harvard Business Review* 51 (1973): 132-151.

Mintzberg, Henry. *The Nature of Managerial Work*. New York: Harper & Row, 1973.

Roethlisberger, Fritz J. "The Foreman: Master and Victim of Double-talk." *Harvard Business Review* 23 (1945): 283-298.

Stewart, Rosemary. *Choices for the Manager*. Englewood Cliffs, New Jersey: Prentice-Hall, 1982.

Weber, Ross A. *Management*. Homewood, Ill.: Richard D. Irwin, 1975.

Course:_____   Name:_____

Instructor:_____   Date:_____

Flow Diagram for New Supervisor Interactive Case

Detach this page from your book before you begin the Interactive Case. As you make each decision, write the decision point number *and* letter following the GO TO statement in the appropriate rectangle *before* you turn to that page. If you are referred to a previous decision point, circle the decision point number and letter you last wrote and proceed to the first uncircled rectangle above that one in your flow diagram. Do not erase the numbers and letters once you have written them. You will not necessarily fill all the rectangles.

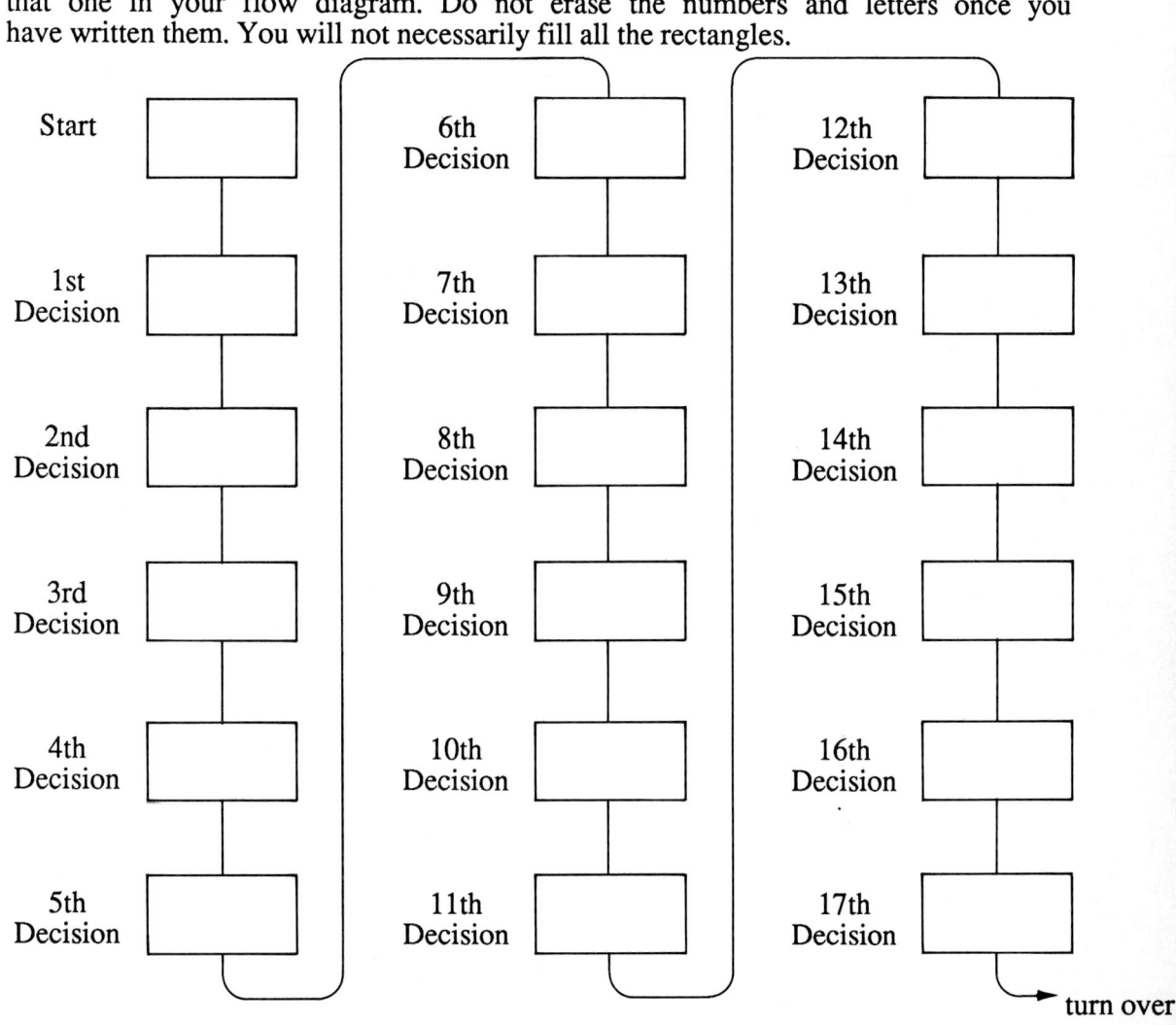

Start	6th Decision	12th Decision
1st Decision	7th Decision	13th Decision
2nd Decision	8th Decision	14th Decision
3rd Decision	9th Decision	15th Decision
4th Decision	10th Decision	16th Decision
5th Decision	11th Decision	17th Decision

→ turn over

18th Decision	27th Decision	36th Decision
19th Decision	28th Decision	37th Decision
20th Decision	29th Decision	38th Decision
21st Decision	30th Decision	39th Decision
22nd Decision	31st Decision	40th Decision
23rd Decision	32nd Decision	41st Decision
24th Decision	33rd Decision	42nd Decision
25th Decision	34th Decision	43rd Decision
26th Decision	35th Decision	44th Decision

Interactive Case

Yesterday you received word that you have been promoted to the position of Supervisor of Group A in the Demand Deposit Accounting Department of the First Springfield Bank. Last night you took your spouse out to your favorite restaurant to celebrate. This is a promotion you had looked forward to for three years. You had worked your way up to the Lead of Unit 2 in Group A and had hoped that you would be the Lead chosen to replace Donald Scott, your predecessor. Scott is 58 and has been transferred to a staff position at the corporate level to make way for your promotion.

Scott was anything but an effective supervisor. He had been a supervisor for 23 years and seemed more interested in his retirement than in mobilizing an effective organization. It is generally known that Scott was moved out of the department to allow a younger person like yourself to move up. Personally, you suspect that had Scott not had 40 years of service with the bank, he would have been terminated.

Looking back, you feel quite confident that you were a good Lead. You commanded the respect of the other 11 members of your immediate work group. Moreover, you consider yourself well liked by your six former peers (your new subordinates), although you had few occasions to work with them directly. You are only vaguely familiar with your three new peers.

In your new position you report directly to Karen Stryker, Manager of the Demand Deposit Accounting Department. An organization chart is on page 232.

The Demand Deposit Accounting Department is responsible for the entire flow of paper and electronic transactions involving all sorts of demand deposits (checks, interbank transfers, drafts, etc.). The department is divided into four groups: Group A, responsible for encoding documents into the computer; Group B, responsible for maintaining the computer system; Group C, responsible for preparing monthly customer reports; and Group D, responsible for special accounts and transfers.

Your group (A) is comprised of 51 people and six leads who are responsible for encoding checks into the computer and taking action on the following:

(a) overdrafts--signaling appropriate bank officials which customers had overdrawn their checking account that day;
(b) stop payments--posting holds on checks when customers authorize stop payment;
(c) charge backs--posting credits on accounts on checks that previously bounced;
(d) voids--returning checks that are voided by failure to include date, signature, etc.;
(e) holds--holds placed on accounts in order for out-of-region deposits to clear.

Demand Deposit Accounting Department

```
                    William Spencer
                    Dir. Operations
                           |
                    Karen Stryker
              Mgr., Demand Dep. Acctg. Dept.
                           |
      ┌──────────────┬─────────────┬──────────────┐
     You          Brian Curtin   Joyce Evanston  Leo Leiter
  Supervisor     Supervisor     Supervisor     Supervisor
   Group A        Group B        Group C        Group D
      |              |              |              |
   Lucy           Leroy          Daryl          Fern           James          Terrence
   Morris         Jackson        Peters         Kaufman        Hopkins        Post
   Lead, Unit 1   Lead, Unit 2   Lead, Unit 3   Lead, Unit 4   Lead, Unit 5   Lead, Unit 6
```

The volume of work is extraordinary. Each day your group processes 40,000 checks at a value of $8 million.

Each of your six groups does the same work with the exception of one (under Lead Terrence Post) which handles checks of Springfield's select clients, i.e., commercial accounts that the bank considers of prime strategic value. Post was considered the favorite for your position and was noticeably peeved when he was not selected.

Today is your first day as supervisor, and you have scheduled meetings all day, first with your boss and then with your new peers. As you enter your boss's office, she welcomes you and moves around from her desk to sit across from you in a matching easychair. She openly confesses that you were her first choice for the supervisor's position, and she expresses enthusiasm about working with you. As she talks, you think to yourself that this is too good to be true. Since you did not work with Karen very often in the past (your predecessor did not permit any direct interaction), you are surprised by her praise for your potential. Still, this is an optimistic occasion, and you feel in the limelight.

She tells you that she is pleased that you were the one promoted because she feels you have the ability to improve the quality of your group's performance. For your group, quality means timeliness and accuracy. Since your group processes so many transactions involving so much money, even a small percentage of error is very costly. In addition, if your group does not process each day's demand deposits and has to hold some transactions to the following day, it means that the bank has to carry that "holdover" as a zero-return investment. Presently your group has an error rate of .06 percent (six errors per 10,000 transactions) and a holdover rate of 2 percent per day (on an average day, 2 percent of the dollar transactions are not processed until the next day).

Your boss tells you that you should do your best to bring those figures down without adding to the size of your staff. Specifically, she tells you that you can expect to hear from Corporate Employee Relations people soon about a program they are launching called *NET* (No Error Transactions). You have heard about this program before, and the members of your old work group reacted very cynically and negatively to what they heard about it. It involves the use of consultants from the local university for whom you have absolutely no respect, but Karen then tells you that the program sounds very good to her.

At the end of your conversation with Karen Stryker, how would you respond?

A. So she won't be surprised, inform her that the *NET* program will be greeted with a great deal of resistance. (GO TO 382B)

B. Ask your boss for the background on the *NET* program. (GO TO 396B)

C. Diplomatically probe for what problems and ambitions your boss has. (GO TO 326A)

D. Clarify just what your boss means by "do the best you can" to improve quality. (GO TO 418B)

E. Try to persuade Karen that *NET* is a bad idea. (GO TO 421B)

F. Ask you boss for her assessment of your predecessor. (GO TO 390B)

APPENDIX OF DECISION POINTS

Decision Point 236A

Sam Blakestone was manager of the Automation Systems Group for five years, and he was with the division for seven. Now with a competing firm, Sam jumps at the chance to express his opinion when you phone him.

"It sounds like Fenwick finally got his way. He's been trying to get the monkey off his back for years. He's no professional, I'll tell you that! He's probably been getting heat for inventory costs, so he invents a policy to put the heat elsewhere. Typical, real typical. You guys are just lucky he's 64 and one year away from retirement!"

What would you do now?

A. Speak with Bill Banquet (your boss) about his "reading" of the new policy. (GO TO 316B)

B. Phone a friend of yours who works as a financial analyst at the corporate level (Blake-Emerson, the parent company) for his perspective on how to respond to this policy change. (GO TO 308A)

C. Bring this issue up at a weekly staff meeting of the sales managers (chaired by Bill Banquet). (GO TO 295A)

D. Diplomatically oppose the new policy as it applies to your unique circumstances. Petition for an exemption. (GO TO 252A)

E. Instruct your subordinates what to do about the new policy. (GO TO 320A)

Decision Point 236B

You delegate the implementation of the change to your team. They work well together and come up with a solution you had not even considered. The team devotes a great deal of time to working out the details of its plan, and you sense that the group is truly excited about it. When the group presents their plan to you, you suspect that there may be some difficulty in getting Eugene Marshall and Gordon Garvin to accept the recommendations. Your suspicions are correct. Eugene, on Gordon's advice, rejects the plan out of hand. Your group is very angry and is not likely now to be very helpful in further efforts at integrating the techs.

Re-evaluate your last decision. Circle the #236B you just wrote in your flow diagram. Then move to the first uncircled step above this one in your flow diagram.

Decision Point 237A

You appoint an implementation committee made up of professional librarians and aides known to be at least indifferent to the computerization effort. You chair the committee to make sure that it stays "on target." However, from the beginning you have problems working out the details of the plan with the group. Although you "stacked" the committee, the meetings become endless discussions of details that stimulate petty disagreements. In addition, committee members become targets of blunt comments from their colleagues not on the committee. Two members become so disillusioned with the seeming pointlessness of the meetings and the snipes they receive from their colleagues that they ask to leave the committee.

Using participation in this instance was inadvisable for several reasons: (1) Expertise as to how to implement computerization is not dispersed in the workforce. You were the one most qualified to determine the implementation plan. (2) LCLD employees are not used to participation. Ms. B's maternalistic approach made them unfamiliar with participative management. (3) Time is of the essence in this change. (4) The problem the change addresses is readily apparent once stated, i.e., it is unambiguous and incontrovertible.

Re-evaluate your last decision. Circle the #237A you just wrote in your flow diagram. Then move to the first uncircled step above this one in your flow diagram.

Decision Point 237B

Your opening question to Bill Banquet results in the following answer: "When I first heard of the new policy, I really tried putting the damper on it. But Fenwick had a lot of influence with Billingsworth, and with the upcoming cuts in Product Control, he had no choice. Somebody had to take on the planning responsibility Product Control used to have, and I sure didn't want manufacturing to call the shots. Now we're under a microscope. If we can show that we can plan well, we'll be able to keep production schedules responsive to the market. My concern is that if we resist this thing, or water it down, the pressure on inventory costs will mean more stockouts when we really need product."

At this point what would you do?

A. Deliver your proposal as planned. (GO TO 311B)

B. Center the discussion on the alternatives of shorter planning periods and training for the sales engineers. (GO TO 272B)

C. Abandon your campaign to find relief from the problems with the policy and instruct your subordinates to comply after explaining to them what Banquet has just told you. (GO TO 304A)

Decision Point 238A

You feel that there are still some issues that need to be resolved with Robin. When you meet him, which approach would you take?

A. Stress to Robin the importance of everyone working together on this project. Point out that everyone in the group had input and now is the time to move on to implementation. (GO TO 257B)

B. Probe Robin to see why he raised the objections he did. (GO TO 268B)

Decision Point 238B

You had an opportunity to chat with three of your peers (Amy Holcott is out of town). All of them expressed irritability with the new policy, but none seemed put out enough to fight it. Don James' (Sales Manager--Pneumatic Products) opinion was typical: "I don't know if my people are good enough planners for us to make our estimates within the 20 percent window. I suspect that they are, but there's no telling. Right now, with the market so sour, most of our business is repeat business. My hunch is that simply keeping our estimates to the high side of historical figures should suffice; at least that's what I am telling my people to do. They're sure not going to like the extra paperwork, that I can assure you. But most of my sales engineers are still jittery about being laid off, so it shouldn't be too bad."

What would you do now?

A. Speak with Bill Banquet (your boss) about his "reading" of the new policy. (GO TO 279B)

B. Phone a friend of yours who works as a financial analyst at the corporate level (Blake-Emerson, the parent company) for his perspective on how to respond to this policy change. (GO TO 248B)

C. Call your predecessor (now with another firm) for his perspective on how to handle this situation. (GO TO 236A)

D. Bring this issue up at a weekly staff meeting of the sales managers (chaired by Bill Banquet). (GO TO 295A)

E. Diplomatically oppose the new policy as it applies to your unique circumstances. Petition for an exemption. (GO TO 252A)

F. Instruct your subordinates what to do about the new policy. (GO TO 320A)

Decision Point 239A

No matter how diplomatic you are, this course of action is entirely too premature. You work for a person who has been in his job for a short time, and you have found him to be cautious. Declaring yourself opposed to this policy change now would lead at best to uncertain results. You need more information before committing yourself (even if it is to comply).

When policies like this are declared, especially policies that require 100 percent compliance to be effective and that weren't arrived at participatively, those responsible are likely to be in a defensive posture. That is, those who have publicly committed themselves are unlikely to reverse their position even when the force of logic is compelling.

Clearly you should gather additional information before deciding how best to respond to what appears to be a policy requirement that will adversely affect your unit's ability to do its work.

Re-evaluate your last decision. Circle the #239A you just wrote in your flow diagram. Then move to the first uncircled step above this one in your flow diagram.

Decision Point 239B

At the next meeting of your team, you sit in. The meeting seems to lack any direction. The discussion shifts back and forth over the same ground, and you are not sure what direction the group wants to take. Shortly before the meeting is scheduled to break up, you mention that the "flexible assembly" approach was suggested by Eugene. Directly after this, Marilyn says that the flexible assembly idea seems pretty good. Larry immediately agrees with her and Robin adds support as well. Quickly everyone seems to agree that this approach ought to be pursued. As the meeting breaks up, you are a bit unsure about your next step. While you are happy with the group's decision, you are not certain that your group is truly committed to it or that everyone thinks that it is the best choice. What would you do?

A. Before the meeting breaks up, poll the team members to see if "flexible assembly" is really their choice. (GO TO 267B)

B. Accept the group's recommendation and tell them that you will develop a set of plans for implementing flexible assembly. (GO TO 281B)

C. Accept the group's recommendation and ask them to develop a set of implementation recommendations. (GO TO 272A)

D. Schedule another meeting for the group to discuss their recommendation. (GO TO 283C)

Decision Point 240A

You return to your team with Eugene's specific concerns. The members react very negatively. You settle them down, but Robin is particularly upset. Even though some of Eugene's concerns appear legitimate to you, Robin openly ridicules them. You adjourn the meeting with no real progress made.

At the next meeting the group continues to be immobilized by its frustrations over Eugene's actions. You decide to go back to Eugene to explore the basis for his opposition. When you enter his office, he says, "How are things going with the super-team plan?" You answer that that's what you are there to talk about. He interrupts, "Gordon Garvin thinks your plan is terrific. He says the timing couldn't be better from his viewpoint. What did you want to talk to me about?"

Apparently Eugene has changed his position 180 degrees. "Good news," you think to yourself. Yet when you return to your group, it takes the news very sullenly. The rumor has spread that Garvin saved the plan, not you, and the group has lost respect for your leadership. Its future actions lack real enthusiasm.

Re-evaluate your last decision. Circle the #240A you just wrote in your flow diagram. Then move to the first uncircled step above this one in your flow diagram.

Decision Point 240B

Sterling Cartwright is a man of about 40 who has been with the company for only three weeks. You ask him about Banquet's opinion of the way the new policy is working. He responds: "Bill is concerned. He really is. He doesn't like the way it puts the burden on you. Just the other day he met with Mr. Billingsworth about it."

You ask him what Banquet is doing about this situation. He says, "Bill has a plan, and I'm sure it will work in time, but with the cuts in product planning, things are a bit uncertain. I'm sure something will happen in a few months."

What would you do now? (Bill Banquet is out of town.)

A. Go see Mildred Barnes of the Product Control Department. (GO TO 290A)

B. Meet privately with Brian Robinson to work out a strategy for addressing this policy problem. (GO TO 269A)

C. Phone William Barstow, your friend at the corporate headquarters. (GO TO 273A)

D. Instruct your subordinates about what to do now. (GO TO 304A)

Decision Point 241A

Now that you have decided to hire Sloan Kilgore, you must decide precisely what to say to your staff during your public announcement. You have already decided that you will order the implementation on a phased basis. You also will include in your remarks word of the change in the Director of Community Service position and the appointment of Sloan Kilgore.

In light of the fact that your staff may not appreciate the need for change, how would you discuss this issue during your announcement?

- A. Emphasize that the change is necessary largely for external reasons. Indicate that the LCLD will suffer greatly without accreditation. (GO TO 246A)

- B. Emphasize that the change is necessary largely for internal reasons. Assert that computerization is bound to bring about more efficiency in the district and better service for patrons in the long run. (GO TO 271A)

- C. Emphasize both the internal and external need for change. (GO TO 260B)

Decision Point 241B

You decide to include Randy Winslow in your plans. This backfires. In the period before he leaves for England, he is particularly prone to defending the interests of his group of engineering technicians. Immediately after your conversation with him, he informs both the leader of his techs and his boss, Gordon Garvin (Director of Engineering), that you are trying to take over Engineering. As a result, your change program suffers an enormous political setback. Eugene is pressured from several sides to call you off, and finally when he senses growing opposition, he does so.

Re-evaluate your last decision. Circle the #241B you just wrote in your flow diagram. Then move to the first uncircled step above this one in your flow diagram.

Decision Point 241C

By pressing Bill Banquet for a decision, you are implicitly sacrificing your own discretion in helping to orchestrate some sort of response to your concerns. You have informed him of the rationale for an exemption, but he has signaled you indirectly that he is unprepared for anything as bold as you have proposed at this point (an exemption).

Re-evaluate your last decision. Circle the #241C you just wrote in your flow diagram. Then move to the first uncircled step above this one in your flow diagram.

Decision Point 242A

You and Eugene spend five hours assessing the three alternatives under consideration. Early on, "flexible assembly" seems to be the most viable plan. At the end of that time, you are clear on the steps that need to be taken to implement the change. You realize that each member of your group has an important role to play if the process is to be successful. Marilyn will have to have much more flexible scheduling procedures. She will also have to shift from handling large quantities of relatively few parts to handling smaller quantities of a larger number of parts. Larry will have to reorganize his assembly lines, train his lead supervisors in the new process, and integrate most of the engineering techs into his group. Robin will absorb a number of the new techs and will also have to decide how to handle increased parts testing and more specialized warranty work.

When you give each person his or her assignment, there is a bit of grumbling. You remind the team that this project is important. Two weeks later when you check back with your team, there is little progress and the group seems to be generally resistant to your direction.

At this point in time you are faced with few options, none of which is very attractive. By embarking upon a change without involving your team in important decisions about it, you have forced a top-down implementation pattern on a situation more appropriate to shared responsibility: (1) the change does not require immediate action; (2) the problem the change addresses is not commonly recognized throughout the organization; (3) knowledge relevant to the change is dispersed throughout the organization; and (4) your team has been successful when you have offered them a voice in decisions in the past.

Re-evaluate your last decision. Circle the #242A you just wrote in your flow diagram. Then move to the first uncircled step above this one in your flow diagram.

Decision Point 242B

How do you know if compliance to this policy is necessary? Obviously it affects your unit in a negative way. Yet you have not gauged the reactions to it. Deciding to comply blindly presumes that no one but Emerson Billingsworth has any influence over policy. Further, if you plan to instruct your subordinates to do anything less than fully comply with this policy, how do you know that this action will be effective without first gauging how others react to it?

Clearly you should first gather more information before deciding what to do. Blind obedience or precipitous reaction is rarely as effective as an informed, deliberate move.

Re-evaluate your last decision. Circle the #242B you just wrote in your flow diagram. Then move to the first uncircled step above this one in your flow diagram.

Decision Point 243A

The first time you send Fenwick a memo detailing expected deviations, he sends you back the following memo:

Memorandum

TO: You
FR: Justin Fenwick
RE: Product Planning

I received your recent memo detailing expected deviations from this month's product plan. I hope you appreciate that production planning is a highly complex endeavor. With our shrinking staff, we simply cannot integrate these deviations into this month's plan. Accordingly there is no need for you to send us these data. Presumably they will be useful for your own internal purposes. I certainly hope you did not send us these unrequested figures as a sign of unwillingness to fully cooperate with the new policy. As you no doubt appreciate, Mr. Billingsworth expects total cooperation with the policy. Anything short of that and we cannot guarantee product availability. I know I can count on you to make this new system a success.

cc: E. Billingsworth; B. Banquet

As well intentioned as your action might have been, it certainly backfired. Re-evaluate your last decision. Circle the #243A you just wrote in your flow diagram. Then move to the first uncircled step above this one in your flow diagram.

Decision Point 243B

Maintaining the position of Director of Community Service has two flaws. First, it leaves the responsibility for the technical aspects of the change fully on your shoulders. This is troublesome in that there are many other responsibilities built into your position. Leaving community service options to someone else creates an advocate for these efforts at just the time when it has to be moved down the priority list to accommodate the computerization program. Second, it is symbolic of continuity when what you are really after is discontinuous change.

Re-evaluate your last decision. Circle the #243B you just wrote in your flow diagram. Then move to the first uncircled step above this one in your flow diagram.

Decision Point 244A

Linda Hemingway tells you that she heard a rumor that the computerization effort would result in the closing of the Crystal Lake Branch. You have no plans to close the Branch, nor does anyone else that you know of. You ask Linda to trace the rumor for you, but because she is initially reluctant to do so, you don't press the issue.

How would you react to this situation?

A. Ask Linda to tell all the people in the Crystal Lake Branch that there are absolutely no plans to close the Branch in the foreseeable future. (GO TO 308B)

B. Take time to try and find out the source of the rumor before proceeding further. (GO TO 309C)

C. Attend a weekly meeting of all Crystal Lake personnel (scheduled the next day) and clarify this matter. (GO TO 304B)

Decision Point 244B

Your second meeting with Eugene is short and to the point. He authorizes the funds necessary for the change and tells you he will take care of Gordon Garvin (Director of Engineering). He then informs you that it is true that Randy Winslow (the manager of the technicians currently doing the custom work in Engineering) will be moving to England, and that that was one of the reasons he wants you to begin thinking about the change now. When you follow up with a question about his time preference, Eugene tells you that he expects the market to take an important turn (toward customization) in two years, so you ought to have completed the change within 18 months. Thus, Eugene isn't thinking about this change in crisis proportions.

As you leave Eugene's office, you are comfortable now with the charter he has given you. Clearly this is an important matter that has far-reaching effects. You look over the three alternatives once again and begin to sketch out some of the issues that will have to be addressed before implementation can proceed. The more you think about the issue, the more appealing the "flexible assembly" option seems. What would you do now?

A. Go back to Eugene and together decide which alternative (flexible assembly, super-teams, contracting) should be implemented. (GO TO 242A)

B. Call a meeting with the members of your team (Larry Beeson, Robin Broderick, and Marilyn Wilson) in order to study the issue of how to incorporate custom production into your department. (GO TO 289B)

Decision Point 245A

Your decision to change the position and fill it with a computer system specialist is a correct one. It brings in another specialist to assist in the introduction and maintenance of the system. It reduces your dependence on a person (Alice Bishop) who has told you she has some questions about the practicality of the system during your initial interviews with her. It also reinforces the high visibility necessary for effectively implementing a major change in a top-down fashion.

You interview three outside candidates. Which one is best qualified?

A. Bob Bramsen--Professional librarian; ambitious; upwardly mobile though somewhat abrasive person formerly in a university library; experienced in implementing computerization in an urban library system. (GO TO 296B)

B. Marcia Gamble--Master's degree in computer science; bachelor's in English; very personable and sociable; wrote her master's thesis on merging library files using *BIBLIOTEK*. (GO TO 272C)

C. Sloan Kilgore--Professional librarian; was a consultant to the firm that originally developed *BIBLIOTEK*; very diplomatic and socially skilled. (GO TO 241A)

Decision Point 245B

It *is* a good idea to phase the implementation rather than doing it all at once. However, you have chosen a sequence that is not advisable.

Starting with the Main Branch has two major problems. First, one could infer from the organization chart that the Main Branch is the largest and its operations the most complex. It is not necessary to confront such a comparatively difficult situation right from the start. Second, it is prudent to orchestrate the phasing such that you can be relatively certain of successes in the early phases. You will note that the Main Branch (while headed by someone in favor of computerization) is staffed with some of the most prominent detractors of the plan. The Live Oak Branch would be a more logical choice for this first test.

Re-evaluate your last decision. Circle the #245B you just wrote in your flow diagram. Then move to the first uncircled step above this one in your flow diagram.

Decision Point 246A

Research indicates that successful change managers emphasize both the external *and* internal conditions that create the need for change. Re-evaluate your last decision. Circle the #246A you just wrote in your flow diagram and move to the first uncircled step above this one in your flow diagram.

Decision Point 246B

When you meet next with your group, you spell out the general problems of how to integrate the engineering techs into your work group. You mention that this may be difficult because you must maintain current production as well as develop the ability to shift to heavier use of single item production within the next couple of years. At this point Marilyn mentions that it seems to her that flexible assembly may be a good long-run solution to a change in the market, but not a very good approach over the short run because it will disrupt all the assembly teams.

As the meeting draws to a close, you feel you have a good sense of where your team stands. They all see the need for the change and realize that over the long run it will radically change the way production is carried out. As well, you are aware that they are concerned about the potential disruptiveness of the flexible assembly approach.

The group agrees that the problem is much as you describe it. After a short discussion, Larry suggests that since it will be two years before the complete implementation of "flexible assembly" is necessary, one intermediate step might be to implement the "super-team" approach initially. Larry suggests that this will isolate the techs and give you an opportunity to phase in the changes. Marilyn and Robin both speak up to support his idea. As the group discusses this idea, you become more and more convinced of its reasonableness. As well, you sense genuine excitement on your team. You accept the recommendation and agree to take it to Eugene for his approval. Eugene's first reaction is negative. He expresses concern that you seem to be acting too conservatively and that he's never heard of a "super-team" before. How would you react?

A. Gently try to persuade Eugene that your team's recommendation makes a great deal of sense. Provide detail that makes the case compelling. (GO TO 303A)

B. Defend your team's decision. Indicate that the idea of a "super-team" is only an interim move. Tell Eugene that your team's analysis was thorough. (GO TO 262B)

C. Ask Eugene what his specific concerns are with the idea so that you can return to discuss them with your team. (GO TO 240A)

Decision Point 247A

Mildred Barnes and you have established a pleasant relationship during the past month. Through mutual and harmless teasing, you have built a rapport that both of you relish. She tells you, "You know why the policy was put in place, don't you? Well, Billingsworth was facing significant pressure from corporate to cut staff personnel. Justin (Fenwick) had been successful in protecting us until then, but when the axe fell, it was obvious that we could not continue to do all the product planning for manufacturing. As you know, we had been analyzing sales trends and setting manufacturing requirements. The new policy was followed by a 22 percent cut in our staff. Jack Collins was the last to be cut. I was lucky to survive this purge, believe me.

"Your group and Robinson's are the most hard-hit. When we were doing the product forecasting, your two units were always the hardest to predict. Don't quote me, but you are getting screwed in all this.

"If you ask me, product scheduling is going toward shorter time frames. Now we are asking for projections one month ahead, but in the next few months with the computer models we are playing with, we should be able to shorten that to two weeks."

Later in the conversation she says, "If your people are having a rough time, there is one thing I could do--training. I've been teaching planning methods at a junior college, and I'd be more than willing to work with your salespeople to give them tools to use in figuring their product requirements."

As you are leaving Mildred's office, her secretary slips you a note that William Barstow, your friend in the corporate office, is trying to reach you by phone. You ask to use a phone in a deserted office and phone him. William tells you, "Well, by now you've heard about the personnel cuts in Product Control in your division. Personnel cuts are now a thing of past. This quarter's earnings are up, and it now appears that we are about as lean as we can be. I've checked with some of my contacts, and it's clear that your policy problem is not without precedent in the corporation. Two other divisions in Atlanta and Trenton have their salespeople estimate product demand as part of the planning effort. Marketing managers there gave their salespeople extensive training in statistical estimation procedures, and each has access to a computer terminal so they can report deviations from the plan in real time."

What would you do now?

A. Since Bill Banquet is out of town, talk with Sterling Cartwright (his new administrative assistant). (GO TO 304C)

B. Meet privately with Brian Robinson to work out a strategy for addressing this policy problem. (GO TO 309B)

C. Instruct your subordinates about what to do now. (GO TO 304A)

Decision Point 248A

You call a meeting of your team to consider the three options you have come up with. Your group jumps at the chance to take on this problem, but there is a subtle uneasiness on two counts: (a) Marilyn and Robin remain unconvinced that change is really called for; and (b) it is unclear how the group's recommendations are going to be used in decision making. After considerable discussion, your team decides to deal with this issue as a hypothetical question. This is not really a satisfactory posture, but it is the only one you can exercise leadership around. Apparently you brought a charge to your team without a very clear charter from your boss. This resulted in your group having to take on an academic frame of reference.

Re-evaluate your last decision. Circle the #248A you just wrote in your flow diagram. Then move to the first uncircled step above this one in your flow diagram.

Decision Point 248B

You have known William Barstow for years. You attended the same university together, and while he is two years older than you, you and he have fond memories of your experiences as members of the debate team. When you tell him of the policy directive, he gives you some interesting information:

"I haven't heard anything about the policy, but I can tell you that the Fluid Products Division is getting a lot of heat to get its costs under control. The word is that Billingsworth's argument that his division has strong profit potential is no longer credible until he can produce the numbers. The division is now under considerable pressure not to cut its line personnel, but rather its staff. The view from these lofty heights is that the axe is due to fall soon on just about every staff unit in the division."

If true, this would mean that Justin Fenwick's group is in for some cuts, but your group should not be affected.

What would you do now?

A. Speak with Bill Banquet (your boss) about his "reading" of the new policy. (GO TO 274B)
B. Call your predecessor (now with another firm) for his perspective on how to handle this situation. (GO TO 283B)
C. Bring this issue up at a weekly staff meeting of the sales managers (chaired by Bill Banquet). (GO TO 295A)
D. Diplomatically oppose the new policy as it applies to your unique circumstances. Petition for an exemption. (GO TO 252A)
E. Instruct your subordinates what to do about the new policy. (GO TO 320A)

Decision Point 249A

Will Barstow has much to say: "Well, by now you've heard about the personnel cuts in Product Control in your division. My hunch that personnel cuts are now a thing of the past is a conviction. This quarter's earnings are up, and it now appears that we are about as lean as we can be.

"I've checked with some of my contacts, and it's clear that your policy problem is not without precedent in the corporation. Two other divisions in Atlanta and Trenton have their salespeople estimate product demand as part of the planning effort. Marketing managers there gave their salespeople extensive training in statistical estimation procedures, and each has access to a computer terminal so they can report deviations from the plan in real time."

As you hang up the phone, Mildred Barnes of the Product Control Department appears in the doorway of your office. Mildred Barnes and you have established a pleasant relationship during the past month. Through mutual and harmless teasing, you have built a rapport that both of you relish. When you have an opportunity to sit down and have a serious discussion with her, she gives you a unique perspective: "You know why the policy was put in place, don't you? Well, Billingsworth was facing significant pressure from corporate to cut staff personnel. Justin (Fenwick) had been successful in protecting us until then, but when the axe fell it was obvious that we could not continue to do all the product planning for manufacturing. You know we had been analyzing sales trends and setting manufacturing requirements accordingly. Well, the new policy was followed by a 22 percent cut in our staff. Jack Collins was the last of these cuts, and he left just last week. I was really lucky to survive this purge, believe me.

"Your group and Robinson's are the most hard-hit. But that's not really surprising. When we were doing the product forecasting, your two units were always the hardest to predict. Don't quote me, but you guys are getting screwed in all this.

"If you ask me, product scheduling is going toward shorter time frames. Now we are asking for projections one month ahead, but in the next few months with the computer models we are playing with, we should be able to shorten that to two weeks." Later in the conversation she says, "If your people are having a rough time, there is one thing I could do--training. I've been teaching planning methods at a junior college where I live, and I'd be more than willing to work with your salespeople to give them tools to use in figuring their product requirements."

What would you do now?

A. Talk to your peers about their experiences with the new policy. (GO TO 311A)

B. Instruct your subordinates about what to do now. (GO TO 304A)

Decision Point 250A

If the issue of insecurity is not addressed, the change is likely to arouse fears that it will threaten the employment status of some of the work force. Even though the members of LCLD are protected by their civil service status, they are still prone to feelings of insecurity that should be anticipated and acknowledged.

Re-evaluate your last decision. Circle the #250A you just wrote in your flow diagram. Then move to the first uncircled step above this one in your flow diagram.

Decision Point 250B

You begin the next meeting with your team by providing a detailed summary of your initial conversation with Eugene and a report of what Tom told you. You try to make clear to the group the necessity of the change and the importance it holds for the Production group. After you provide your summary, you get a number of questions from Larry and Robin which seem to indicate that they don't feel it is particularly necessary to integrate the technicians doing custom work into the Production Department. You reiterate the importance of the change and offer to arrange for your group to receive a firsthand report of the shift in the PBX market. As you continue to talk, you begin to notice that the group is becoming less resistant to the ideas you are presenting. Larry and Marilyn make comments that suggest that they are quite concerned about how to cope with the new market conditions. Even Robin admits that the scenario you describe could be a real threat if Arion does not respond to it.

At this point you feel that your team is motivated to respond to the situation you outlined. You know that you now need to spell out what your team will need to do to develop the capability to increase custom production.

What would you do now?

A. Give members a progress report on the analysis you have done so far and tell them that you will continue analyzing alternatives and report back to them. (GO TO 285B)

B. Lay out the "flexible assembly" plan and ask the group to develop procedures for implementing it. (GO TO 260A)

C. Provide the group with the information you have collected about the three alternatives and tell the group to provide you with a set of recommendations. (GO TO 270B)

D. Give members the information you have assembled, and tell them to develop a workable plan and implement it. (GO TO 236B)

Decision Point 251A

You encourage the group members and remind them of the importance of the project. They agree to increase their effort. Four days later, you check with Robin. He tells you that no one seems to be getting anywhere in developing recommendations.

At this point what would you do?

A. Have Randy Winslow (the head of the engineering technicians) join the group to stimulate things. (GO TO 285A)

B. Arrange to meet with your group at its next meeting. (GO TO 239B)

Decision Point 251B

Computerization will force fundamental changes in the organizational culture of LCLD. Ms. B's emphasis on service over professionalism did more than shape expectations; it created habits and entire patterns of thinking. Apparently there are individuals ready to move on to other missions and tasks for LCLD, but it is unlikely that a meek approach will get the sort of attention within LCLD that is needed. Remember, these are civil service employees who have a high degree of employment security and are probably aware of their power to resist change in this instance. A dramatic point of departure is called for here, and an announcement with significant visibility does just that. In addition, high visibility demonstrates your resolve to "go the distance." A more low-key posture, and your people may be tempted to test just how committed you truly are.

Re-evaluate your last decision. Circle the #251B you just wrote in your flow diagram. Then move to the first uncircled step above this one in your flow diagram.

Decision Point 251C

You have decided to provide a sketchy outline of the importance of this project for Arion's future. The outcome of this is to increase the "nervousness" of your team. Unfortunately, this anxiety is not channeled into constructive effort. Rather, it comes out as a general mistrust of you and the organization.

Two weeks later the group has not made any progress on the assignment. The only outcome seems to be that you have heard rumors that Marilyn is looking for a new job because she doesn't think there is much of a future at Arion.

Re-evaluate your last decision. Circle the #251C you just wrote in your flow diagram. Then move to the first uncircled step above this one in your flow diagram.

Decision Point 252A

In deciding to act before consulting your boss, you are running the risk of implementing a policy that he may want to oppose or to implement in a way that is beneficial to the goals of the sales force. Accordingly your last decision was not correct. To remedy this situation, assume you had the discussion with Bill Banquet shown below, and then decide what you are going to do.

Your meeting with Bill Banquet was unexpectedly short. Bill confessed being distracted by the resignation that morning of Bob Jenson, his administrative assistant. Jenson was known to be looking for another position, but the timing of his decision seemed to have taken Banquet by surprise.

Bill responded curtly to your open-ended probe, "Did you see the memo about the new product planning policy?"

Bill: "Yes, I've seen it. I wasn't consulted on it in advance, but I was told that it was coming. I know the salespeople are not going to like it."

You: "Not only that, but I doubt if my people can be expected to estimate their product needs within the 20 percent window. You know that our situation is different than the other groups."

Bill: "I know, I know. Listen, I've got to go. I've got to get over to Employee Relations to sign the forms for authorization to replace Jenson before my flight to Toledo. Look, do the best you can with the policy. I'll see you in a week."

What would you do now?

A. If you haven't done so yet, phone a friend of yours who works as a financial analyst at the corporate level (Blake-Emerson--the parent company) for his perspective on how to respond to this policy change. (GO TO 254A)

B. If you haven't done so yet, call your predecessor (now with another firm) for his perspective on how to handle this situation. (GO TO 315A)

C. Wait and bring this issue up at a weekly staff meeting of the sales managers (chaired by Bill Banquet). (GO TO 295A)

D. Diplomatically oppose the new policy as it applies to your unique circumstances. Petition for an exemption. (GO TO 253B)

E. Instruct your subordinates what to do about the new policy. (GO TO 291B)

Decision Point 253A

It is now three months after your announcement, and the personnel changes you made in the wake of Simmons' resignation are working well. You are optimistic that Hemingway will be a much better catalyst for change in the Crystal Lake Branch than an unknown quantity (the outsider). After all, she has been in on the early stages of the change, and she indicated her support for the change during your initial interview with her. While the personnel change seems to be working well, the Live Oak implementation hits a serious snag. An unforeseen software problem delays progress for two weeks.

More seriously, you are approached by two aides from the Crystal Lake Branch, who complain about the temporary cutbacks in the "Children's Story Hour" program necessitated by the computerization effort. You assure them that this cutback will only be temporary, but they counter that they are worried that the loss of patrons may severely affect their monthly withdrawals (Crystal Lake is the smallest branch).

What would you do?

A. Reiterate your statement and ask their patience. (GO TO 268C)

B. Call Linda Hemingway (Crystal Lake librarian) and ask her to keep you posted on the attitude of her aides. (GO TO 310A)

C. Call Linda Hemingway and ask her if there are other reasons for her aides' concerns. (GO TO 244A)

Decision Point 253B

There are several ways for you to oppose diplomatically this new policy. Which option would you choose?

A. Ask Bill Banquet to use his influence to earn an exemption from this policy requirement for your group in light of its special circumstances. (GO TO 306A)

B. Go directly to Justin Fenwick and petition him for an exemption from this policy requirement. (GO TO 313C)

C. Send a memo to Emerson Billingsworth (the announcement came from him so it is proper) detailing in explicit form your case for an exemption from this new policy. (GO TO 315C)

Decision Point 254A

You have known William Barstow for years. You attended the same university together, and while he is two years older than you, you and he have fond memories of your experiences as members of the debate team. When you tell him of the policy directive, he gives you some interesting information:

"I haven't heard anything about the policy, but I can tell you that the Fluid Products Division is getting a lot of heat to get its costs under control. The word is that Billingsworth's argument that his division has strong profit potential is no longer credible until he can produce the numbers. The division is now under considerable pressure not to cut its line personnel, but rather its staff. The view from these lofty heights is that the axe is due to fall soon on just about every staff unit in the division."

If true, this would mean that Justin Fenwick's group is in for some cuts, but your group should not be affected.

What would you do now?

A. Call your predecessor (now with another firm) for his perspective on how to handle this situation. (GO TO 299A)

B. Bring this issue up at a weekly staff meeting of the sales managers (chaired by Bill Banquet). (GO TO 295A)

C. Diplomatically oppose the new policy as it applies to your unique circumstances. Petition for an exemption. (GO TO 253B)

D. Instruct your subordinates what to do about the new policy. (GO TO 291B)

Decision Point 254B

Each member of the team gives a very general statement about the need to respond to the changing market. However, you continue to wonder about the strength of the group's commitment.

At this point what would you do?

A. Lay out an implementation plan for flexible assembly. (GO TO 276B)

B. Conclude that you are probably worrying over nothing. Instruct the group to develop procedures for implementing "flexible assembly." (GO TO 277A)

C. Assign one team member to develop and present an argument for flexible assembly and another member to play "devil's advocate" and present counterarguments. Once those arguments are all out, lead a general discussion. (GO TO 288B)

Decision Point 255A

You had an opportunity to chat with three of your peers (Amy Holcott is out of town). All of them expressed irritability with the new policy, but none seemed put out enough to fight it. Don James' (Sales Manager--Pneumatic Products) opinion was typical:

"I don't know if my people are good enough planners for us to make our estimates within the 20 percent window. I suspect that they are, but there's no telling. Right now, with the market so sour, most of our business is repeat business. My hunch is that simply keeping our estimates to the high side of historical figures should suffice; at least that's what I am telling my people to do. They're sure not going to like the extra paperwork, that I can assure you. But most of my sales engineers are still jittery about being laid off, so it shouldn't be too bad."

What would you do now?

A. Call your predecessor (now with another firm) for his perspective on how to handle this situation. (GO TO 299A)

B. Bring this issue up at a weekly staff meeting of the sales managers (chaired by Bill Banquet). (GO TO 295A)

C. Diplomatically oppose the new policy as it applies to your unique circumstances. Petition for an exemption. (GO TO 253B)

D. Instruct your subordinates what to do about the new policy. (GO TO 291B)

Decision Point 255B

Your choice of a new motto is not the best option. Banners and mottos can be powerful symbols in a top-down change. Effectively constructed, they are compelling and superordinate. Compelling means that they are attractive and energizing. Superordinate means that they are appreciated by groups that might differ on other issues.

"Where Service Is Always Professional" is neither compelling nor superordinate. It is not compelling because it implies cold, impersonal interactions between patrons and library staff. It is not superordinate because the history of LCLD was characterized by periodic conflict between professionally oriented staff and community-service-oriented staff. Thus, rather than healing these old schisms, your new motto seems to declare one winner in an old contest.

Re-evaluate your last decision. Circle the #255B you just wrote in your flow diagram. Then move to the first uncircled step above this one in your flow diagram.

Decision Point 256A

You have decided to meet with Eugene and discuss the major political, cost, and timetable factors surrounding his decision to bring the technicians into your department. You have identified three specific points that you want to cover:

1. You are concerned about how Randy Winslow's boss, Gordon Garvin (Director of Engineering), will react to this change. You and Gordon have occasionally had difficulty cooperating in the past, and you want Eugene to coordinate the transition with Gordon.
2. You estimate that it will take about one week to redesign the manufacturing process and move equipment, no matter what approach is chosen. As well, you think that it will be another two weeks to get the performance of the assembly group back to current levels.
3. The direct costs of the reorganization, including new equipment and overtime, are likely to be between $60,000 and $87,500. You are not sure where that money will come from.

After you lay out these points, Eugene quickly shifts the discussion. He says that the market is changing, moving away from the standard PBX system you have been manufacturing toward more customized systems. He expresses confidence in your ability to meet the challenge brought about by this market change. At that point he ends the meeting by saying that he has another very important appointment, but that he could see you later that afternoon if you felt it was *really* necessary.

What would you do now?

A. Schedule a meeting with Eugene for later that afternoon. (GO TO 244B)

B. Take Eugene's comments as a signal that he is unprepared to deal with the points that you have raised until you have made more progress. Arrange to meet with your group soon to begin the process of analyzing which alternative (flexible assembly, super-teams, contracting) to choose. (GO TO 248A)

C. Do nothing. Clearly Eugene does not consider this a priority, so wait until he brings it up again. (GO TO 264A)

Decision Point 257A

Bill Banquet is out of town. This gives you time to gather other information. The following information sources are available to you. Which would you choose first?

A. Your peers. (GO TO 265A)

B. Mildred Barnes of the Product Control Department. (GO TO 319A)

C. Since Bill Banquet is out of town, Sterling Cartwright (his new administrative assistant). (GO TO 275B)

D. William Barstow, your friend at the corporate headquarters. (GO TO 318A)

Decision Point 257B

You instruct your team to begin to develop an implementation plan for "flexible assembly." The group works hard and develops a detailed set of procedures. All seems to be going well until the techs are actually moved into their new quarters. Although Larry has few initial problems, the situation in Robin's "shop" is dreadful. Two of the tech's assigned to him quit, and Gordon Garvin begins taking "pot shots" at your plan. Apparently you didn't do enough to assure yourself that Robin was on board before you moved the team to implementation questions.

Re-evaluate your last decision. Circle the #257B you just wrote in your flow diagram. Then move to the first uncircled step above this one in your flow diagram.

Decision Point 257C

You decide to hire someone from the outside to replace Mel Simmons. The results are unfortunate. While familiar with *BIBLIOTEK*, she is unfamiliar with the operations of LCLD. Accordingly when it comes time for the Crystal Lake Branch to come "on line," she makes a number of judgment errors that jeopardize the entire change effort. Moreover, since her subordinates are not wholly supportive of the change, she decides to take a tough posture in order to earn their respect. The overall effect is that you have created a new set of problems for yourself.

Re-evaluate your last decision. Circle the #257C you just wrote in your flow diagram. Then move to the first uncircled step above this one in your flow diagram.

Decision Point 258A

It is now two weeks after your speech. You have completed your public relations campaign emphasizing the benefits of a computerized library information system. It has generated a great deal of community interest, but you notice that some of your people in the district office seem to be slow to respond to learning *BIBLIOTEK* whenever they have community service chores to do. When confronted, these people assert that you said in your speech that Ms. B's service philosophy should be maintained. Apparently you have not adequately differentiated your overriding philosophy from Ms. B's.

What would you do now?

A. Make it clear that top priority should be given to the computerization program even if service activities have to suffer a bit in the short run. (GO TO 313B)

B. Contact Ms. B to earn her endorsement for the computerization effort. Encourage her to speak out on the benefits of computerization on service to the community in the long run. (GO TO 295B)

C. Announce a new motto that differentiates your philosophy from Ms. B's. (GO TO 314A)

Decision Point 258B

Sterling Cartwright is a man of about 40 who has been with the company for only three weeks. You ask him about Banquet's opinion of the way the new policy is working. He responds: "Bill is concerned. He really is. He doesn't like the way it puts the burden on you. Just the other day he met with Mr. Billingsworth about it."

You ask him what Banquet is doing about this situation. He says, "Bill has a plan, and I'm sure it will work in time, but with the cuts in product planning, things are a bit uncertain. I'm sure you can expect something in the next few months."

What would you do now? (Bill Banquet is out of town.)

A. Meet with your peers to determine their experience with the new policy. (GO TO 311A)

B. Instruct your subordinates about what to do now. (GO TO 304A)

Decision Point 259A

Sam Blakestone was manager of the Automation Systems Group for five years and was with the division for seven. Now with a competing firm, Sam jumps at the chance to express his opinion when you phone him:

"It sounds like Fenwick finally got his way. He's been trying to get the monkey off his back for years. He's no professional, I'll tell you that! He's probably been getting heat for inventory costs, so he invents a policy to put the heat elsewhere. Typical, real typical. You guys are just lucky he's 64 and one year away from retirement!" What would you do now?

- A. Talk with your peers (the other sales managers who report to Bill Banquet) to gauge their reaction to the new policy. (GO TO 282B)

- B. Bring this issue up at a weekly staff meeting of the sales managers (chaired by Bill Banquet). (GO TO 295A)

- C. Diplomatically oppose the new policy as it applies to your unique circumstances. Petition for an exemption. (GO TO 298A)

- D. Instruct your subordinates what to do about the new policy. (GO TO 314B)

Decision Point 259B

You are correct in planning a "phased" effort. This will enable you to demonstrate a small victory, which will add to the momentum of the change effort. Choosing the Live Oak Branch as your test site is also correct, for the personnel there seem least resistant to it at the outset.

Your second challenge is to determine how to announce the change. It occurs to you that you could introduce it with different levels of visibility and fanfare. Which of the following would you choose?

- A. *High visibility*--Call a meeting of all personnel and announce your plan for the implementation of the computer system. Simultaneously send out a press release to county newspapers that details the plan and promises better service after the system is operational. Solicit invitations to speak to community service groups (e.g., Lions Club, Rotary, etc.) about the change. (GO TO 266A)

- B. *Moderate visibility*--Call a meeting of all personnel and announce your plan for the implementation of the computer system. (GO TO 251B)

- C. *Low visibility*--Tell the professional librarians your plans and ask them to communicate this information to their aides and assistants. (GO TO 297A)

Decision Point 260A

You instruct your team to begin to plan the implementation of the flexible assembly option. The group works hard and develops a detailed set of plans. Marilyn develops a plan for more flexible scheduling procedures. As well, she prepares for shifting inventory from large counts of a relatively few parts to small counts of more parts. Larry completes a plan for reorganizing his assembly lines and training his lead supervisors. Robin completes a set of plans for dealing with changing warranty repairs.

When the techs are moved into the Production group, the changes are much more complicated than anyone anticipated. The techs still think of themselves as engineers and have a difficult time fitting into assembly functions. Worse, the presence of the techs disrupts your assembly workers and interferes with your group's ability to complete its normal production runs.

Overall, there are many more problems than you anticipated. Costs are higher than you forecast, and it is clear that you will not be able to bring them under control. In short, this change was more than the group could take. Just this morning Robin expressed his intention to quit Arion as a result of this situation.

Re-evaluate your last decision. Circle the #260A you just wrote in your flow diagram. Then move to the first uncircled step above this one in your flow diagram.

Decision Point 260B

In your speech, what would you say to ease the feelings of employment insecurity that are likely to be stimulated by your announcement?

A. Nothing. There is no reason to deal with this issue in advance. (GO TO 250A)

B. Indicate that specific staffing cuts are not foreseen but that no guarantees can be made. (GO TO 268A)

C. State that you realize the hard work that everyone will have to do to make computerization a success. Indicate that you will do everything you can to ensure that the job of everyone who cooperates is safe. (GO TO 270A)

D. Promise that no one will lose his or her job because of computerization. (GO TO 315B)

E. Acknowledge that the LCLD is currently overstaffed but say that you plan to deal with this problem through natural attrition. (GO TO 316A)

Decision Point 261A

You lay out the advantages and disadvantages of each of the three alternatives with Eugene. After a lengthy discussion, the two of you decide that "flexible assembly" offers the greatest net advantages. You then arrange for the implementation of this alternative. Immediately you run into resistance. The members of your team are miffed by not being included in the process, and Larry Beeson tells you that he has had considerable experience with "flexible assembly" at another firm--experience that would have led Arion in another direction.

Re-evaluate your last decision. Circle the #261A you just wrote in your flow diagram. Then move to the first uncircled step above this one in your flow diagram.

Decision Point 261B

You had an opportunity to chat with three of your peers (Amy Holcott is out of town). All of them expressed irritability with the new policy, but no one seemed put out enough to fight it. Don James' (Sales Manager--Pneumatic Products) opinion was typical:

"I don't know if my people are good enough planners for us to make our estimates within the 20 percent window. I suspect that they are, but there's no telling. Right now, with the market so sour, most of our business is repeat business. My hunch is that simply keeping our estimates to the high side of historical figures should suffice; at least that's what I am telling my people to do. They're sure not going to like the extra paperwork, that I can assure you. But most of my sales engineers are still jittery about being laid off, so it shouldn't be too bad."

What would you do now?

A. Speak with Bill Banquet (your boss) about his "reading" of the new policy. (GO TO 274B)

B. Call your predecessor (now with another firm) for his perspective on how to handle this situation. (GO TO 283B)

C. Bring this issue up at a weekly staff meeting of the sales managers (chaired by Bill Banquet). (GO TO 295A)

D. Diplomatically oppose the new policy as it applies to your unique circumstances. Petition for an exemption. (GO TO 252A)

E. Instruct your subordinates what to do about the new policy. (GO TO 320A)

Decision Point 262A

You decide to implement the change through participation. You call all employees together in a town hall fashion. You point out the need for computerization in your opening remarks and throw the subject open for suggestions as to how to implement the change. The suggestions from the floor cover every option from delaying the change to implementing it on far too optimistic a schedule. By the end of the proceedings, you realize that opening the topic up to full and open dialogue has splintered support for feasible alternatives into committed coalitions unwilling to negotiate or compromise. As a means of keeping the enthusiasm of the meeting alive, you appoint a panel of the most active participants to serve as the implementation committee. Sharply divided, the committee is unable to agree on a plan until after important deadlines have passed.

Using participation in this instance is inadvisable for several reasons: (1) Expertise as to how to implement computerization is not dispersed in the work force. You were the one most qualified to determine the implementation plan. (2) LCLD employees are not used to participation. Ms. B's maternalistic approach made them unfamiliar with participative management. (3) Time is of the essence in this change. (4) The problem the change addresses is readily apparent once stated, i.e., it is unambiguous and incontrovertible.

Re-evaluate your last decision. Circle the #262A you just wrote in your flow diagram. Then move to the first uncircled step above this one in your flow diagram.

Decision Point 262B

Your rather "direct" approach with Eugene works well. He gives you the green light for implementation. He agrees to clear things with Gordon Garvin and gives you a budget number for the funds you need for implementation. He also compliments you and your group for its careful work and creative solution.

It is now about two months later. The "super-team" is up and running well. The only difficulty is that the "engineering values" of the techs still create a bit of conflict with the manufacturing people. This level of conflict convinces you that you made a good decision in not throwing everyone together at once.

You are convinced that when you phase in "flexible assembly," the process will be smooth. Larry, Robin, and Marilyn have begun to develop ways of phasing in the changes necessary. You are sure that your team is working more effectively now than ever!

You have mobilized your team to implement a difficult change. **Congratulations!**

Decision Point 263A

You have a chance to "buttonhole" several of the other sales managers. Their comments follow:

Sandra Smith (Sales Mgr., Hydraulic Products): "I'll tell you one thing. My sales engineers certainly don't like the extra paperwork, but we've been able to do pretty well making the 20 percent window. In fact (she winks), it feels good moving from #4 to #2! All kidding aside, I think it's good that we now require our salespeople to plan their product needs. After all, the Personnel people are always harping that we should prepare them for moving into the managerial ranks."

Brian Robinson (Sales Mgr., Delivery Systems): "All that sounds fine and good, but the fact remains that the policy penalizes those of us who have uncertain demand or complex lines. No, this thing is stupid. The strategic plan for this year identifies my line as vitally important, and then they turn around and discourage our development of new accounts because one can never plan them systematically. I've talked to Banquet about this and he agrees, but he hasn't done anything about it!"

Don James (Sales Mgr., Pneumatic Products): "My sales engineers have had a helluva time getting their numbers right. Even with our standard lines, they consistently overestimated their needs. I suspect that they will get better and that the product will be available. It's creating hell with our volume, I'll tell you."

What would you do now? (Bill Banquet is out of town.)

A. Since Bill Banquet is out of town, talk with Sterling Cartwright (his new administrative assistant). (GO TO 304C)

B. Meet privately with Brian Robinson to work out a strategy for addressing this policy problem. (GO TO 309B)

C. Instruct your subordinates about what to do now. (GO TO 304A)

Decision Point 264A

You go on with your normal duties, in effect ignoring Eugene's concern about "flexible assembly." Three weeks pass and nothing else happens. Then you happen to see one of Eugene's friends in the hallway near your office. She greets you with the following comments, "Oh, Eugene has been telling me how well you are doing in planning the move Arion is making toward more customization. He's really counting on you, you know. My, he had such good things to say about you."

Clearly Eugene has expectations for your efforts that you did not accurately sense. Now that you know this is a high priority with him, what would you do?

A. Schedule a meeting with Eugene for later that afternoon. (GO TO 244B)

B. Take Eugene's earlier comments as a signal that he is unprepared to deal with the points that you have raised until you have made more progress. Arrange to meet with your group soon to begin the process of analyzing which alternative (flexible assembly, super-teams, contracting) to choose. (GO TO 248A)

Decision Point 264B

The last issue you should decide on before your speech is what to do about a motto or theme for the "new LCLD." Ms. B consistently articulated the theme "The County Is Served When We Make the Time to Listen."

In your speech, how would your address the issue of symbols?

A. Postpone developing a new motto for the time being. Instead demonstrate how the computerization effort is simply a logical extension of Ms. B's motto, such as "Computers will give us more time to listen and more services to render." (GO TO 306B).

B. Announce a new motto: "Where Service Is Always Professional." Arrange to have all stationery and library cards embossed with that new motto. (GO TO 255B)

C. Announce a new motto: "Looking for Better Ways to Serve You Best." Arrange to have all stationery and library cards embossed with that new motto. (GO TO 291A)

Decision Point 265A

You have a chance to "buttonhole" several of the other sales managers. Their comments follow:

Sandra Smith (Sales Mgr., Hydraulic Products): "I'll tell you one thing. My sales engineers certainly don't like the extra paperwork, but we've been able to do pretty well making the 20 percent window. In fact (she winks), it feels good moving from #4 to #2! All kidding aside, I think it's good that we now require our salespeople to plan their product needs. After all, the Personnel people are always harping that we should prepare them for moving into the managerial ranks."

Brian Robinson (Sales Mgr., Delivery Systems): "All that sounds fine and good, but the fact remains that the policy penalizes those of us who have uncertain demand or complex lines. No, this thing is stupid. The strategic plan for this year identifies my line as vitally important, and then they turn around and discourage our development of new accounts because one can never plan them systematically. I've talked to Banquet about this and he agrees, but he hasn't done anything about it!"

Don James (Sales Mgr., Pneumatic Products): "My sales engineers have had a helluva time getting their numbers right. Even with our standard lines, they consistently overestimated their needs. I suspect that they will get better and that the product will be available. It's creating hell with our volume, I'll tell you."

What would you do now? (Bill Banquet is out of town.)

A. Go see Mildred Barnes of the Product Control Department. (GO TO 247A)

B. Since Bill Banquet is out of town, talk with Sterling Cartwright (his new administrative assistant). (GO TO 240B)

C. Phone William Barstow, your friend at the corporate headquarters. (GO TO 312A)

D. Meet privately with Brian Robinson to work out a strategy for addressing this policy problem. (GO TO 269A)

E. Instruct your subordinates about what to do now. (GO TO 304A)

Decision Point 266A

A highly visible campaign of announcing your intentions leaves little doubt as to your resolve for getting the system up and operational in a year. Anything less than this, and Personnel may be apt to test your resolve or underestimate it. You chose correctly.

Your third challenge is to decide what to do about the position of Community Service Director vacated by Ms. B's husband when the two of them retired. Your options include filling the position with a person who will continue to serve as the primary liaison between LCLD and the community and who will spearhead such efforts as the Joy of Reading Program and the Children's Story Hour Program. This individual would also be responsible for arranging new cooperative ventures between LCLD and other libraries in the county (computerization will ultimately allow computer linkages among all libraries in the county thus establishing an integrative information resource system). In contrast, you could change the nature of the position to Director of Library Information Systems. This will necessitate a change in classification through the civil service system, but you have good reason to believe that this could be done without delay or opposition. The implications of these two options are as follows:

Option 1: Replace Ms. B's husband with a new Director of Community Relations. You will need to ask Alice Bishop to serve as the primary detail person regarding computer implementation. She is familiar with the operational details of the *BIBLIOTEK* system, so she possesses the necessary technical skills to act in this capacity. However, you will have to be very involved with the change to the point of having to delegate almost all responsibility for community service to the new director. This option will enable the LCLD to maintain a high profile in its concern for community service.

Option 2: Change the position to Director of Library Information Systems and fill it with a professional. This will enable you to bring in an expert on the library computer system. He or she will be prepared to handle the details of the change and the linkages to other library systems. This will free you to be more visible in the community and to deal with your responsibilities in a more flexible fashion.

Which option would you choose?

A. Option 1. (GO TO 243B)

B. Option 2. (GO TO 245A)

Decision Point 267A

You tell your people to ignore the policy. Two days after the reports are due, you hear from Justin Fenwick's secretary that unless the reports are submitted, you will not get adequate supplies of product to meet sales. You are now left with no choice. You have been identified as uncooperative and resistant to change, and this label reduces your ability to mount a campaign on behalf of an exemption.

Re-evaluate your last decision. Circle the #267A you just wrote in your flow diagram. Then move to the first uncircled step above this one in your flow diagram.

Decision Point 267B

Since you are not sure that the group is really convinced of its decision, you decide to poll each member individually. As you go around your team, everyone gives what you see as "lukewarm" support of flexible assembly.

At this point what would you do?

A. Accept the group's recommendation and tell it that you will develop a set of plans for implementing flexible assembly. (GO TO 281B)

B. Accept the group's recommendation and ask it to develop a set of implementation recommendations. (GO TO 272A)

C. Schedule another meeting for the group to discuss its recommendation. (GO TO 283C)

Decision Point 267C

The group members respond very negatively to the new policy. They grouse at having to process more paperwork and express pessimism at trying to forecast their needs with the required accuracy. Their first month's estimates are very uneven. Some of your people spend a great deal of effort on their plans and some approach it in entirely too cavalier a fashion. The estimates are accordingly among the least accurate in the Marketing Department. While you expected miscalculations, you certainly did not expect this.

Re-evaluate your last decision. Circle the #267C you just wrote in your flow diagram. Then move to the first uncircled step above this one in your flow diagram.

Decision Point 268A

You plan to indicate that specific staffing cuts are not foreseen but that no guarantees can be made. While it is good that you plan to say something about the effect of the change on personnel decisions, your statement will do little to allay fears. Those who are concerned realize that you cannot make uncategorical guarantees, but they would like to have stronger assurances that you don't have specific people targeted to be cut.

Re-evaluate your last decision. Circle the #268A you just wrote in your flow diagram. Then move to the first uncircled step about this one in your flow diagram.

Decision Point 268B

As you begin to talk with Robin, you start to think about why people might resist change. You know that people will resist a change if the new procedures will threaten their jobs or adversely affect their economic situation. But as Robin begins to talk, his resistance seems to center on the problems of dealing with the engineering techs. He tells you that he thinks it will be hard to convince the new techs to focus on production issues rather than engineering problems. He ends by saying that he fears that the new techs will subvert all the hard work he spent turning his techs around. Robin finally says that he knows that within a couple of years the nature of the production will have to change, but that just mixing the engineering techs into the group may be more disruptive than necessary. You thank him for his frankness. Now what?

A. Meet with your entire group and share this general problem. (GO TO 246B)

B. Have your group develop procedures for implementing flexible assembly. (GO TO 260A)

C. Go to Eugene Marshall with the group's recommendation and ask for his approval. (GO TO 282A)

Decision Point 268C

Mild resistance to change like these complaints should be taken as a signal that firmer resistance will develop if their concerns are not addressed. In addition, there may be a basis for their concerns that is not being stated directly here. The appropriate action is to delve into the real concerns versus the stated concerns. Otherwise the resistance will probably snowball.

Re-evaluate your last decision. Circle the #268C you just wrote in your flow diagram. Then move to the first uncircled step about this one in your flow diagram.

Decision Point 269A

You meet with Brian to discuss how to deal with this together. You agree that you should first gather data. Robinson talks with Sterling Cartwright and you contact Mildred Barnes. She and you have created a good relationship in the past month. She tells you: "You know why the policy was put in place, don't you? Billingsworth was facing a lot of heat from corporate to cut staff personnel. Justin (Fenwick) had been successful in protecting us until then, but when the axe fell, it was clear that we could not continue to do all the product planning for manufacturing. We had been analyzing sales trends and setting manufacturing goals. Well, the new policy was followed by a 22 percent cut in our staff.

"Your group and Robinson's are the most hard-hit. But that's not really surprising. When we were doing the product forecasting, your two units were always the hardest to predict. If you ask me, product scheduling is going toward shorter time frames. Now we are projecting one month ahead, but soon we should be able to shorten that to two weeks."

Later in the conversation she says, "If your people are having a rough time, there is one thing I could do--training. I've been teaching planning methods at a junior college, and I'd be more than willing to work with your salespeople to teach them new planning tools."

You next contact William Barstow. He says: "Well, by now you've heard about the personnel cuts in Product Control in your division. My strong belief is that those are the last of the personnel cuts we shall see. This quarter's earnings are up, and it now appears that we are about as lean as we can be. I've checked with some of my contacts, and your policy problem is not without precedent in the corporation. Two other divisions have their salespeople estimate product demand as part of the planning effort. Marketing managers there give their salespeople training in planning methods, and each has a computer terminal so they can report deviations from the plan in real time."

You see Brian again, and he tells you he learned nothing from Cartwright. It seems that the two of you have three major alternatives: (1) lobby for an exemption for those units of strategic importance (your unit like Robinson's has been identified as being strategically important to the firm; (2) lobby for a reduction in the planning period from one month to one or two weeks; (3) lobby for training for your sales engineers. You both agree that (1) is the best alternative, (2) is the second best, and (3) is the worst.

How would you approach Bill?

A. Approach Bill Banquet (once he returns from his trip) and propose alternative (1), while being prepared to settle for alternative (2) or (3) if he doesn't think (1) feasible. (GO TO 311B)
B. Same as A above except begin by asking Banquet his assessment of how well the policy is working. (GO TO 237B)

Decision Point 270A

Your plan to deal with the employment insecurity issue is excellent. While you make no promises of outcomes, you indicate that you will fight for their security because you realize you are asking them to fight to make computerization work. That's a nice *quid pro quo*: "I'm asking you to scratch my back, so I'll scratch yours in return." Such understandings of reciprocation do much to allay fears of insecurity.

You now must decide what you will say in your speech about the specifics of the implementation plan. What would you do?

A. Outline a specific timetable for the change specifying training objectives and implementation targets. Arrange time targets for early stages that are rather pessimistic to "guarantee" early perceived successes. (GO TO 264B)

B. Outline a specific timetable for the change specifying training objectives and implementation targets. Arrange time targets for all stages based on "most likely" outcomes. (GO TO 279A)

C. Stay clear of specifying a timetable so you can keep your options open. (GO TO 300A)

Decision Point 270B

You spend the rest of the meeting providing the group with the data you collected relating to the "super-team," "flexible assembly," and "contracting" alternatives. Also, you tell the group that there are probably lots of other good alternatives that you haven't considered. After answering questions and having a general discussion about the change, you tell the group to get back to you within two weeks with a recommendation for you to consider.

A week later, at a regularly scheduled staff meeting, you ask your people for a progress report. Larry says that progress is "real slow" and that they seem to be stalled. Both Marilyn and Robin echo these concerns. When you check with your team about why this is occurring, your staff indicates that it has been meeting but just can't seem to make much headway.

At this point what would you do?

A. Have Randy Winslow (the head of the engineering technicians) join the group to stimulate things (he is in town for two weeks). (GO TO 285A)

B. Encourage the group and remind members of the importance of the task. (GO TO 251A)

C. Arrange to join your team at its next meeting. (GO TO 239B)

Decision Point 271A

Research indicates that successful change managers emphasize both the external *and* internal conditions that create the need for change.

Re-evaluate your last decision. Circle the #271A you just wrote in your flow diagram. Then move to the first uncircled step about this one in your flow diagram.

Decision Point 271B

You have a chance to "buttonhole" several of the other sales managers. Their comments follow:

Sandra Smith (Sales Mgr., Hydraulic Products): "I'll tell you one thing. My sales engineers certainly don't like the extra paperwork, but we've been able to do pretty well making the 20 percent window. In fact (she winks), it feels good moving from #4 to #2! All kidding aside, I think it's good that we now require our salespeople to plan their product needs. After all, the Personnel people are always harping that we should prepare them for moving into the managerial ranks."

Brian Robinson (Sales Mgr., Delivery Systems): "All that sounds fine and good, but the fact remains that the policy penalizes those of us who have uncertain demand or complex lines. No, this thing is stupid. The strategic plan for this year identifies my line as vitally important, and then they turn around and discourage our development of new accounts because one can never plan them systematically. I've talked to Banquet about this and he agrees, but he hasn't done anything about it!"

Don James (Sales Mgr., Pneumatic Products): "My sales engineers have had a helluva time getting their numbers right. Even with our standard lines, they consistently overestimated their needs. I suspect that they will get better and that the product will be available. It's creating hell with our volume, I'll tell you."

What would you do now? (Bill Banquet is out of town.)

A. Go see Mildred Barnes of the Product Control Department. (GO TO 290A)
B. Phone William Barstow, your friend at the corporate headquarters. (GO TO 273A)
C. Meet privately with Brian Robinson to work out a strategy for addressing this policy problem. (GO TO 269A)
D. Instruct your subordinates about what to do now. (GO TO 304A)

Decision Point 272A

You instruct the group to develop procedures for implementing "flexible assembly." The group accepts this assignment somewhat grudgingly but begins work on procedures. Two weeks later you expect a report from the group that will present procedures for implementation. At the end of that period your group presents you with a report that can only be described as sloppy and incomplete.

At this point what would you do?

A. Schedule a meeting to re-evaluate "flexible assembly." (GO TO 283C)

B. Develop the implementation procedures yourself. (GO TO 281B)

C. Give the report back to the group with specific instructions as to how to make it more useful. (GO TO 277A)

Decision Point 272B

You present your proposal and it goes well. Banquet agrees to lobby with Fenwick and Billingsworth to explore the possibility of shorter time frames for certain products, especially those of strategic importance. This proposal is appealing to both parties because (1) it is a practice used in other divisions of the corporation, and (2) it permits Fenwick to argue effectively for restoring some of his staff cuts. Banquet also agrees to free up $2,500 from his discretionary budget for training to cover the time it requires to take your case to Billingsworth and Fenwick.

Both actions bear fruit. Two months later the policy is modified to suit your unit's needs, and all but one product plan fall within the 20 percent window. No customers are lost due to the inventory underage contingency. **Congratulations!** You have just completed the Organizational Politics Interactive Case.

Decision Point 272C

Marcia Gamble is not the best candidate. Change agents ideally have both high social/diplomatic skills and technical credibility. Marcia lacks technical credibility. In a professional organization, technical credibility begins with a professional degree, e.g., M.D., J.D., Ph.D., R.N., etc. Marcia's master's degree just doesn't measure up because it's not a M.L.S. (master's of library science, the "union card" for librarians).

Re-evaluate your last decision. Circle the #272C you just wrote in your flow diagram. Then move to the first uncircled step about this one in your flow diagram.

Decision Point 273A

Will Barstow has much to say: "Well, by now you've heard about the personnel cuts in Product Control in your division. My hunch that personnel cuts are now a thing of the past is a conviction. This quarter's earnings are up, and it now appears that we are about as lean as we can be.

"I've checked with some of my contacts, and it's clear that your policy problem is not without precedent in the corporation. Two other divisions in Atlanta and Trenton have their salespeople estimate product demand as part of the planning effort. Marketing managers there gave their salespeople extensive training in statistical estimation procedures, and each has access to a computer terminal so they can report deviations from the plan in real time."

As you hang up the phone, Mildred Barnes of the Product Control Department appears in the doorway of your office. Mildred Barnes and you have established a pleasant relationship during the past month. Through mutual and harmless teasing, you have built a rapport that both of you relish. When you have an opportunity to sit down and have a serious discussion with her, she gives you a unique perspective: "You know why the policy was put in place, don't you? Well, Billingsworth was facing significant pressure from corporate to cut staff personnel. Justin (Fenwick) had been successful in protecting us until then, but when the axe fell, it was obvious that we could not continue to do all the product planning for manufacturing. You know we had been analyzing sales trends and setting manufacturing requirements accordingly. Well, the new policy was followed by a 22 percent cut in our staff. Jack Collins was the last of these cuts, and he left just last week. I was really lucky to survive this purge, believe me.

"Your group and Robinson's are the most hard-hit. But that's not really surprising. When we were doing the product forecasting, your two units were always the hardest to predict.

"If you ask me, product scheduling is going toward shorter time frames. Now we are asking for projections one month ahead, but in the next few months, we should be able to shorten that to two weeks."

Later in the conversation she says, "If your people are having a rough time, there is one thing I could do--training. I've been teaching planning methods at a junior college where I live, and I'd be more than willing to work with your salespeople to give them tools to use in figuring their product requirements."

What would you do now?

A. Meet privately with Brian Robinson to work out a strategy for addressing this policy problem. (GO TO 309B)

B. Instruct your subordinates about what to do now. (GO TO 304A)

Decision Point 274A

While your situation certainly calls for significant action, you don't need to jeopardize the security of someone who has been working hard for you by bringing in an outsider at this point. Remember, too, that it will take you considerable time to find, orient, and train a person from the outside.

Re-evaluate your last decision. Circle the #274A you just wrote in your flow diagram. Then move to the first uncircled step about this one in your flow diagram.

Decision Point 274B

Your meeting with Bill Banquet was unexpectedly short. Bill confessed being distracted by the resignation that morning of Bob Jenson, his administrative assistant. Jenson was known to be looking for another position, but the timing of his decision seemed to have taken Banquet by surprise. Bill responded curtly to your open-ended probe, "Did you see the memo about the new product planning policy?"

Bill: "Yes, I've seen it. I wasn't consulted on it in advance, but I was told that it was coming. I know the salespeople are not going to like it."

You: "Not only that, but I doubt if my people can be expected to estimate their product needs within the 20 percent window. You know that our situation is different than the other groups."

Bill: "I know, I know. Listen, I've got to go. I've got to get over to Employee Relations to sign the forms for authorization to replace Jenson before my flight to Toledo. Look, do the best you can with the policy. I'll see you in a week."

What would you do now?

A. Call your predecessor (now with another firm) for his perspective on how to handle this situation. (GO TO 299A)

B. Wait and bring this issue up at a weekly staff meeting of the sales managers (chaired by Bill Banquet). (GO TO 295A)

C. Diplomatically oppose the new policy as it applies to your unique circumstances. Petition for an exemption. (GO TO 253B)

D. Instruct your subordinates what to do about the new policy. (GO TO 291B)

Decision Point 275A

It is now nine months since the implementation effort began. The system is up and operational in the Live Oak Branch and 75 percent operational in the Main Branch. Crystal Lake is ahead of its implementation schedule.

But just as you are feeling really content with the way things are unfolding, a bombshell is dropped--Emmet King, the assistant librarian of the Main Branch, resigns! Initially somewhat skeptical of computerization, Emmet was the person primarily responsible for the success of the computerization effort at the Main Branch, and he really seemed to be enthusiastic. His timing could not be worse! The progress of the entire implementation at Main Branch is presently at a very delicate stage and one that is unique to Main Branch.

What would you do about the vacancy left by King's exit?

A. Fill it with an intern "from the outside." (GO TO 298B)

B. Fill it with a professional from the outside (this will risk having to let someone from the full-time staff go at the end of the year unless some other professional voluntarily leaves in the next three months). (GO TO 274A)

C. Fill it with the intern you hired into the district office seven months ago. Replace this intern with another intern from the "outside." (GO TO 292B)

Decision Point 275B

Sterling Cartwright is a man of about 40 who has been with the company for only three weeks. You ask him about Banquet's opinion of the way the new policy is working. He responds: "Bill is concerned. He really is. He doesn't like the way it puts the burden on you. Just the other day he met with Mr. Billingsworth about it."

You ask him what Banquet is doing about this situation. He responds: "Bill has a plan, and I'm sure it will work in time, but with the cuts in product planning, things are a bit uncertain. I'm sure you can expect something in the next few months."

What would you do now? (Bill Banquet is out of town.)

A. Talk to your peers about their experience with the new policy. (GO TO 271B)
B. Go see Mildred Barnes of the Product Control Department. (GO TO 301A)
C. Phone William Barstow, your friend at the corporate headquarters. (GO TO 249A)
D. Instruct your subordinates about what to do now. (GO TO 304A)

Decision Point 276A

You have an opportunity to chat with three of your peers (Amy Holcott is out of town). All of them expressed irritability with the new policy, but none seemed put out enough to fight it. Don James' (Sales Manager--Pneumatic Products) opinion was typical: "I don't know if my people are good enough planners for us to make our estimates within the 20 percent window. I suspect that they are, but there's no telling. Right now, with the market so sour, most of our business is repeat business. My hunch is that simply keeping our estimates to the high side of historical figures should suffice; at least that's what I am telling my people to do. They're sure not going to like the extra paperwork, that I can assure you. But most of my sales engineers are still jittery about being laid off, so it shouldn't be too bad."

What would you do now?

A. Speak with Bill Banquet (your boss) about his "reading" of the new policy. (GO TO 316B)

B. Phone a friend of yours who works as a financial analyst at the corporate level (Blake-Emerson--the parent company) for his perspective on how to respond to this policy change. (GO TO 308A)

C. Bring this issue up at a weekly staff meeting of the sales managers (chaired by Bill Banquet). (GO TO 295A)

D. Diplomatically oppose the new policy as it applies to your unique circumstances. Petition for an exemption. (GO TO 252A)

E. Instruct your subordinates what to do about the new policy. (GO TO 320A)

Decision Point 276B

You have given your group the assignment to implement a decision to which it is not really committed. As the group continues working on the assignment, you find yourself being forced to spend more and more time working on implementation. Under these circumstances, the long-run success of the change program is remote. Essentially your team is suffering from group-think. Little in the way of real incisive analysis is going on, and the group is looking for a way to make an easy decision.

Re-evaluate your last decision. Circle the #276B you just wrote in your flow diagram. Then move to the first uncircled step above this one in your flow diagram.

Decision Point 277A

The group comes back with a set of procedures that you think are satisfactory. However, when it is time to try out the new procedures, things don't seem to work out. Your people just seem to be "going through the motions." When the engineering techs are introduced into the system, confusion results. Integrating the techs is going to be difficult and you are now not optimistic about the chances for success.

Re-evaluate your last decision. Circle the #277A you just wrote in your flow diagram. Then move to the first uncircled step above this one in your flow diagram.

Decision Point 277B

You have known William Barstow for years. You attended the same university together, and while he is two years older than you, you and he have fond memories of your experiences as members of the debate team. When you tell him of the policy directive, he gives you some interesting information:

"I haven't heard anything about the policy, but I can tell you that the Fluid Products Division is getting a lot of heat to get its costs under control. The word is that Billingsworth's argument that his division has strong profit potential is no longer credible until he can produce the numbers. The division is now under considerable pressure not to cut its line personnel, but rather its staff. The view from these lofty heights is that the axe is due to fall soon on just about every staff unit in the division."

If true, this would mean that Justin Fenwick's group is in for some cuts, but your group should not be affected.

What would you do now?

A. Talk with your peers (the other sales managers who report to Bill Banquet) to gauge their reaction to the new policy. (GO TO 255A)

B. Call your predecessor (now with another firm) for his perspective on how to handle this situation. (GO TO 259A)

C. Bring this issue up at a weekly staff meeting of the sales managers (chaired by Bill Banquet). (GO TO 295A)

D. Diplomatically oppose the new policy as it applies to your unique circumstances. Petition for an exemption. (GO TO 298A)

E. Instruct your subordinates what to do about the new policy. (GO TO 314B)

Decision Point 278A

You decide to open up the issue of whether to implement computerization to the entire group. The outcome of this effort parallels your interviews: some are in favor and some against. Opening up this issue to public debate, however, has hardened positions and polarized the work force.

Using participation in this instance is inadvisable for several reasons: (1) Expertise as to how to implement computerization is not dispersed in the work force. You were the one most qualified to determine the implementation plan. (2) LCLD employees are not used to participation. Ms. B's matriarchical approach made them unfamiliar with participative management. (3) Time is of the essence in this change. (4) The problem the change addresses is readily apparent once stated, i.e., it is unambiguous and incontrovertible.

Re-evaluate your last decision. Circle the #278A you just wrote in your flow diagram. Then move to the first uncircled step above this one in your flow diagram.

Decision Point 278B

Sam Blakestone was manager of the Automation Systems Group for five years and was with the division for seven. Now with a competing firm, Sam jumps at the chance to express his opinion when you phone him:

"It sounds like Fenwick finally got his way. He's been trying to get the monkey off his back for years. He's no professional, I'll tell you that! He's probably been getting heat for inventory costs, so he invents a policy to put the heat elsewhere. Typical, real typical. You guys are just lucky he's 64 and one year away from retirement!"

What would you do now?

A. Talk with your peers (the other sales managers who report to Bill Banquet) to gauge their reaction to the new policy. (GO TO 276A)
B. Speak with Bill Banquet (your boss) about his "reading" of the new policy. (GO TO 300B)
C. Phone a friend of yours who works as a financial analyst at the corporate level (Blake-Emerson, the parent company) for his perspective on how to respond to this policy change. (GO TO 303B)
D. Bring this issue up at a weekly staff meeting of the sales managers (chaired by Bill Banquet). (GO TO 295A)
E. Diplomatically oppose the new policy as it applies to your unique circumstances. Petition for an exemption. (GO TO 284A)
F. Instruct your subordinates what to do about the new policy. (GO TO 321A)

Decision Point 279A

It is important to orchestrate the phasing of the change so that you have an early success. Using "most likely time estimates" is going to guarantee only a 50 percent success rate. You want a higher rate than that to make sure you have a success to celebrate.

Re-evaluate your last decision. Circle the #279A you just wrote in your flow diagram. Then move to the first uncircled step about this one in your flow diagram.

Decision Point 279B

Your meeting with Bill Banquet was unexpectedly short. Bill confessed being distracted by the resignation that morning of Bob Jenson, his administrative assistant. Jenson was known to be looking for another position, but the timing of his decision seemed to have taken Banquet by surprise.

Bill responded curtly to your open-ended probe, "Did you see the memo about the new product planning policy?"

Bill: "Yes, I've seen it. I wasn't consulted on it in advance, but I was told that it was coming. I know the salespeople are not going to like it."
You: "Not only that, but I doubt if my people can be expected to estimate their product needs within the 20 percent window. You know that our situation is different than the other groups."
Bill: "I know, I know. Listen, I've got to go. I've got to get over to Employee Relations to sign the forms for authorization to replace Jenson before my flight to Toledo. Look, do the best you can with the policy. I'll see you in a week."
What would you do now?

A. Phone a friend of yours who works as a financial analyst at the corporate level (Blake-Emerson, the parent company) for his perspective on how to respond to this policy change. (GO TO 254A)

B. Call your predecessor (now with another firm) for his perspective on how to handle this situation. (GO TO 315A)

C. Wait and bring this issue up at a weekly staff meeting of the sales managers (chaired by Bill Banquet). (GO TO 295A)

D. Diplomatically oppose the new policy as it applies to your unique circumstances. Petition for an exemption. (GO TO 253B)

E. Instruct your subordinates what to do about the new policy. (GO TO 291B)

Decision Point 280A

You have decided to make decisions yourself about this situation before refining your charter from your boss. This is unwise. He gave you a very cryptic assignment in an informal encounter, and the assignment has far-reaching consequences for the entire company. Certainly you want to clarify what he is asking you to do and what problem or opportunity he is responding to.

Re-evaluate your last decision. Circle the #280A you just wrote in your flow diagram. Then move to the first uncircled step above this one in your flow diagram.

Decision Point 280B

You have a chance to "buttonhole" several of the other sales managers. Their comments follow:

Sandra Smith (Sales Mgr., Hydraulic Products): "I'll tell you one thing. My sales engineers certainly don't like the extra paperwork, but we've been able to do pretty well making the 20 percent window. In fact (she winks), it feels good moving from #4 to #2! All kidding aside, I think it's good that we now require our salespeople to plan their product needs. After all, the Personnel people are always harping that we should prepare them for moving into the managerial ranks."

Brian Robinson (Sales Mgr., Delivery Systems): "All that sounds fine and good, but the fact remains that the policy penalizes those of us who have uncertain demand or complex lines. No, this thing is stupid. The strategic plan for this year identifies my line as vitally important, and then they turn around and discourage our development of new accounts because one can never plan them systematically. I've talked to Banquet about this and he agrees, but he hasn't done anything about it!"

Don James (Sales Mgr., Pneumatic Products): "My sales engineers have had a helluva time getting their numbers right. Even with our standard lines, they consistently overestimated their needs. I suspect that they will get better and that the product will be available. It's creating hell with our volume, I'll tell you."

What would you do now? (Bill Banquet is out of town.)

A. Since Bill Banquet is out of town, talk with Sterling Cartwright (his new administrative assistant). (GO TO 304C)

B. Meet privately with Brian Robinson to work out a strategy for addressing this policy problem. (GO TO 309B)

C. Instruct your subordinates about what to do now. (GO TO 304A)

Decision Point 281A

The following information sources are available to you. Which would you choose first?

A. Talk with your peers (the other sales managers who report to Bill Banquet) to gauge their reaction to the new policy. (GO TO 238B)

B. Speak with Bill Banquet (your boss) about his "reading" of the new policy. (GO TO 302B)

C. Phone a friend of yours who works as a financial analyst at the corporate level (Blake-Emerson, the parent company) for his perspective on how to respond to this policy change. (GO TO 305B)

D. Call your predecessor (now with another firm) for his perspective on how to handle this situation. (GO TO 278B)

E. Bring the issue up at a weekly staff meeting of the sales managers (chaired by Bill Banquet). (GO TO 295A)

Decision Point 281B

Based on the group's recommendation, you begin to develop a way of implementing the plan. You spend five days diagramming the revised assembly lines, determining personnel assignments, and planning new equipment. Each member of the team has an important role to carry out if the process is to be successful. Marilyn will have to have much more flexible scheduling procedures. She also will have to shift from handling large quantities of relatively few parts to handling smaller quantities of a larger number of parts. Larry has to reorganize his assembly lines, train his lead supervisors in the new process, and integrate most of the engineering techs into his group. Robin will absorb a number of new techs and will also have to make plans as to how to handle increased parts testing and more specialized warranty work.

As your team starts to make these changes, things seem to take much longer than you estimated. When you are finally ready to test the new procedures, things don't work as well as anticipated. In addition, you don't sense that your team is really motivated to make things work. By involving the group in making the decision but not really getting their commitment, you lost some of the advantages of participation. Also, by not having the group aid in implementation planning, you did not take advantage of its expertise.

Re-evaluate your last decision. Circle the #281B you just wrote in your flow diagram. Then move to the first uncircled step above this one in your flow diagram.

Decision Point 282A

You begin your meeting with Eugene by describing the process your group went through to arrive at the "flexible assembly" recommendation. Eugene surprises you by saying, "I don't know where you came up with the idea of flexible assembly. It sounds like it might work, but what I'm concerned with is that you implement a system that can get the job done. The way you have described it leads me to believe that Robin would really have a hard time with it, but you must know best."

Like so many harried executives, Eugene seems to have fallen victim to a very poor memory. He was the person who introduced you to the idea of flexible assembly in the first place. Clearly his initial enthusiasm for flexible assembly was not the result of thorough analysis.

With the green light from Eugene, how would you proceed?

A. Have your group develop procedures for implementing "flexible assembly." (GO TO 257B)

B. Go back to Robin to probe more deeply into the reasons for his concern about flexible assembly. (GO TO 309A)

Decision Point 282B

You had an opportunity to chat with three of your peers (Amy Holcott is out of town). All of them expressed irritability with the new policy, but none seemed put out enough to fight it. Don James' (Sales Manager--Pneumatic Products) opinion was typical:

"I don't know if my people are good enough planners for us to make our estimates within the 20 percent window. I suspect that they are, but there's no telling. Right now, with the market so sour, most of our business is repeat business. My hunch is that simply keeping our estimates to the high side of historical figures should suffice; at least that's what I am telling my people to do. They're sure not going to like the extra paperwork, that I can assure you. But most of my sales engineers are still jittery about being laid off, so it shouldn't be too bad."

What would you do now?

A. Bring this issue up at a weekly staff meeting of the sales managers (chaired by Bill Banquet). (GO TO 295A)

B. Diplomatically oppose the new policy as it applies to your unique circumstances. Petition for an exemption. (GO TO 253B)

C. Instruct your subordinates what to do about the new policy. (GO TO 291B)

Decision Point 283A

You decide to begin implementing flexible assembly. Immediately you run into resistance. The members of your team are miffed about not being included in the process, and Larry Beeson tells you that he has had considerable experience with "flexible assembly" at another firm--experience that would have led Arion in another direction.

Re-evaluate your last decision. Circle the #283A you just wrote in your flow diagram. Then move to the first uncircled step above this one in your flow diagram.

Decision Point 283B

Sam Blakestone was manager of the Automation Systems Group for five years. Now with a competing firm, Sam is openly critical of Fenwick:

"It sounds like Fenwick finally got his way. He's been trying to get the monkey off his back for years. He's no professional, I'll tell you that! He's probably been getting heat for inventory costs, so he invents a policy to put the heat elsewhere. Typical, real typical. You guys are just lucky he's 64 and one year away from retirement!"

What would you do now?

A. Speak with Bill Banquet (your boss) about his "reading" of the new policy. (GO TO 296A)
B. Bring this issue up at a weekly staff meeting of the sales managers (chaired by Bill Banquet). (GO TO 295A)
C. Diplomatically oppose the new policy as it applies to your unique circumstances. Petition for an exemption. (GO TO 252A)
D. Instruct your subordinates what to do about the new policy. (GO TO 320A)

Decision Point 283C

What would you do at this meeting?

A. Lay out an implementation plan for flexible assembly. (GO TO 276B)
B. Continue the discussion by having members explain why they support the "flexible assembly" approach. (GO TO 254B)
C. Assign one team member to develop and present an argument for flexible assembly and another member to play "devil's advocate" and present counterarguments. Once those arguments are all out, lead a general discussion. (GO TO 288B)

Decision Point 284A

You decided to act before consulting either your boss or your peers. This was incorrect. By not consulting your peers, you now lack adequate information about the potential force that might be mobilized in opposition to this policy. You have an opportunity to chat with three of your peers (Amy Holcott is out of town). All of them expressed irritability with the new policy, but none seemed put out enough to fight it.

Don James' (Sales Manager--Pneumatic Products) opinion was typical: "I don't know if my people are good enough planners for us to make our estimates within the 20 percent window. I suspect that they are, but there's no telling. Right now, with the market so sour, most of our business is repeat business. My hunch is that simply keeping our estimates to the high side of historical figures should suffice; at least that's what I am telling my people to do. They're sure not going to like the extra paperwork, that I can assure you. But most of my sales engineers are still jittery about being laid off, so it shouldn't be too bad."

Your second error was choosing to act before consulting your boss. In doing so, you were running the risk of implementing a policy that he might actually want to oppose. Your discussion with him went like this.

You: "Bill, did you see the memo about the new product planning policy?"
Bill: "Yes, I've seen it. I wasn't consulted on it in advance, but I was told that it was coming. I know the salespeople are not going to like it."
You: "Not only that, but I doubt if my people can be expected to estimate their product needs within the 20 percent window. You know that our situation is different than the other groups."
Bill: "I know, I know. Listen, I've got to go. I've got to get over to Employee Relations to sign the forms for authorization to replace Jenson before my flight to Toledo. Look, do the best you can with the policy. I'll see you in a week."

What would you do now?

A. If you haven't done so yet, phone a friend of yours who works as a financial analyst at the corporate level (Blake-Emerson, the parent company) for his perspective on how to respond to this policy change. (GO TO 254A)
B. If you haven't done so yet, call your predecessor (now with another firm) for his perspective on how to handle this situation. (GO TO 315A)
C. Wait and bring this issue up at a weekly staff meeting of the sales managers (chaired by Bill Banquet). (GO TO 295A)
D. Diplomatically oppose the new policy as it applies to your unique circumstances. Petition for an exemption. (GO TO 253B)
E. Instruct your subordinates what to do about the new policy. (GO TO 291B)

Decision Point 285A

Inviting Randy to join the group does not work well. At the meeting he begins by announcing that Arion's success will be due to "good engineering" and that moving the techs to production will make "good engineering" much harder. This attitude does not set well with your team members, and they respond defensively. The meeting continues with sniping between your group and Randy.

The next day you get a call from Gordon Garvin suggesting that the two of you get together with Eugene Marshall to see if this change is really necessary. Although Eugene had committed to clearing things with Gordon Garvin, bringing Randy into the group so soon forced Eugene to deal with Gordon under adverse circumstances. Also, having Randy join the group has not increased its progress; in fact, it has solidified positions.

Re-evaluate your last decision. Circle the #285A you just wrote in your flow diagram. Then move to the first uncircled step above this one in your flow diagram.

Decision Point 285B

You decided to implement the "flexible assembly" plan. You spend five days diagramming the modified assembly lines, determining personnel assignments, and planning new equipment. At the end of that time you understand what steps need to be taken to implement the change. You realize that each member of your group has an important role to play if the process is to be successful. Marilyn will have to have much more flexible scheduling procedures. She will also have to shift from handling large quantities of relatively few parts to handling smaller quantities of a larger number of parts. Larry will have to reorganize his assembly lines, train his lead supervisors in the new process, and integrate most of the engineering techs into his group. Robin will absorb a number of the new techs and will also have to decide how to handle increased parts testing and more specialized warranty work. When you give the members their assignments, there is a bit of grumbling. You remind them that this project is important. Two weeks later, when you check back, little progress has been made, and the group seems to be generally resistant to your direction.

You are now faced with few options, none of which is very attractive. By implementing the change without involving your team, you have forced a top-down implementation pattern on a situation that called for shared responsibility: (1) the change does not require immediate action; (2) the problem the change addresses is not commonly recognized; (3) knowledge relevant to the change is dispersed throughout the organization; and (4) your team was successful when you have offered it a voice in decisions in the past.

Re-evaluate your last decision. Circle the #285B you just wrote in your flow diagram. Then move to the first uncircled step above this one in your flow diagram.

Decision Point 286A

You call Eugene's office and set up a meeting for next Tuesday. At that meeting, which of the following would you do?

A. Lay out the advantages and disadvantages of each of the three alternatives you have and, with Eugene, select an alternative to pursue. (GO TO 261A)

B. Accept "flexible assembly" as a *fait accompli* (i.e., accomplished fact) and get Eugene's okay to proceed with the implementation. (GO TO 283A)

C. Before the meeting give Randy Winslow a call before he leaves for England with the idea of informally "checking out" his opinions on the different alternatives. (GO TO 241B)

D. Discuss with Eugene the major issues in the change process and be prepared to negotiate a series of cost, timetable, and political issues. (GO TO 256A)

Decision Point 286B

You have known William Barstow for years. You attended the same university together. When you tell him of the policy directive, he gives you some interesting information:

"I haven't heard anything about the policy, but I can tell you that the Fluid Products Division is getting a lot of heat to get its costs under control. The word is that Billingsworth's argument that his division has strong profit potential is no longer credible until he can produce the numbers. The division is now under considerable pressure not to cut its line personnel, but rather its staff. The view from these lofty heights is that the axe is due to fall soon on just about every staff unit in the division."

If true, this would mean that Justin Fenwick's group is in for some cuts, but your group should not be affected. What would you do now?

A. Talk with your peers (the other sales managers who report to Bill Banquet) to gauge their reaction to the new policy. (GO TO 282B)

B. Bring this issue up at a weekly staff meeting of the sales managers (chaired by Bill Banquet). (GO TO 295A)

C. Diplomatically oppose the new policy as it applies to your unique circumstances. Petition for an exemption. (GO TO 298A)

D. Instruct your subordinates what to do about the new policy. (GO TO 314B)

Decision Point 287A

You have an opportunity to chat with three of your peers (Amy Holcott is out of town). All of them expressed irritability with the new policy, but none seemed put out enough to fight it. Don James' (Sales Manager--Pneumatic Products) opinion was typical: "I don't know if my people are good enough planners for us to make our estimates within the 20 percent window. I suspect that they are, but there's no telling. Right now, with the market so sour, most of our business is repeat business. My hunch is that simply keeping our estimates to the high side of historical figures should suffice; at least that's what I am telling my people to do. They're sure not going to like the extra paperwork, that I can assure you. But most of my sales engineers are still jittery about being laid off, so it shouldn't be too bad."

What would you do now?

A. Speak with Bill Banquet (your boss) about his "reading" of the new policy. (GO TO 296A)

B. Bring this issue up at a weekly staff meeting of the sales managers (chaired by Bill Banquet). (GO TO 295A)

C. Diplomatically oppose the new policy as it applies to your unique circumstances. Petition for an exemption. (GO TO 252A)

D. Instruct your subordinates what to do about the new policy. (GO TO 320A)

Decision Point 287B

You have decided not to share the information about the importance of the change with your group. When you call your group together and describe plans for bringing the engineering techs into Production, none of your people displays any enthusiasm for the ideas you have presented. You know that if you were to give them a general assignment to work on, it is unlikely that much would be accomplished. However, you realize that if you were to spell out specific steps for each person to take in implementing the change, each person would comply and you could monitor and control the group's progress.

Faced with the group's lack of motivation, what would you do?

A. Spell out all you have heard including the importance of the change and the risks involved. (GO TO 250B)

B. Provide members of your group with detailed instructions as to what they are to do to bring about the change in Production to implement "flexible assembly." (GO TO 285B)

Decision Point 288A

Your answer is unresponsive to a latent issue that is likely to be the basis of the question: control. In general, administrative changes are more resisted than technical changes simply because they realign control and power relationships. As a change, computerization has an administrative component, so this question is probably based on a concern about a loss of power and control. Specifically, computerization often scares professionals because they fear that it will result in more restrictions to their autonomy and less influence in the organization.

Re-evaluate your last decision. Circle the #288A you just wrote in your flow diagram. Then move to the first uncircled step above this one in your flow diagram.

Decision Point 288B

Your approach works well. You assign Marilyn to present the case for "flexible assembly" and Robin to present counterarguments. The discussion that follows is quite lively, and a number of new ideas about the advantages and disadvantages of flexible assembly get voiced. The most positive support for flexible assembly comes from Larry. He argues that, over the long term, Arion will have to develop strong capabilities in custom production, and that flexible assembly is the technique that will disperse those skills throughout Production without diluting them.

Your team generally agrees with Larry's thinking. A number of concerns about flexible assembly come up as well. Robin expresses the strongest argument against it. He says that it won't work well because people will be confused about what they are supposed to do and that supervising mixed teams will be nearly impossible. As you press him, he is unable to come up with examples of what he means or real evidence to support his position. He finally says that he doesn't really think any change in the way things are done is necessary. You decide to poll the group. Although Marilyn and Larry are fairly supportive of flexible assembly, Robin is noncommittal but says that he will go along with whatever you decide. It is clear that the group has completed its original charge.

At this point what would you do?

A. Instruct the group to begin studying how to implement the flexible assembly approach. (GO TO 257B)

B. Schedule another meeting. Arrange to meet with Robin privately in the meantime. (GO TO 238A)

Decision Point 289A

It is not a good idea to implement a change all at once if it can be phased. Phasing facilitates the implementation of change for two reasons. First, it allows a demonstration effect that shows the benefits of the change on a small scale. Second, it galvanizes opinion in favor of the change, since observers now have evidence of its efficacy.

Re-evaluate your last decision. Circle the #289A you just wrote in your flow diagram. Then move to the first uncircled step above this one in your flow diagram.

Decision Point 289B

Larry, Robin, and Marilyn are all experienced production people who believe in their abilities to "mass produce" almost any system. You schedule your meeting with them two days from now.

As you are preparing to go home for the day, you run into Tom Meyers, the Director of Marketing. You begin to chat about business in general, and Tom brings up the issue of customization. He tells you that his market research indicates that within two to three years foreign producers will dominate the standard PBX market on the basis of price (Arion's present niche). However, there will remain plenty of money to be made in custom systems since foreign competitors lack that capability.

In effect, Tom Meyers has echoed Eugene Marshall's point of view. Surely bringing custom production into your department is vital, but not terribly urgent. Unlike so many other things, it looks like you finally have enough lead time to approach this deliberately.

As you plan your meeting with Larry, Robin, and Marilyn, you are not sure what the agenda of the meeting should be. Specifically, you are not sure how much of your conversations with Eugene and Tom you want to relate to your team. Foreign competition is a natural anxiety producer, and the notion that existing markets could disappear is rather unnerving.

Which of the following would you do?

A. Do not relate the information you heard from Tom and Eugene in order to avoid raising their anxiety level. (GO TO 287B)

B. Provide a sketchy outline of what you have heard from others. (GO TO 251C)

C. Spell out all you have heard including the importance of the change and the risks involved. (GO TO 250B)

Decision Point 290A

Mildred Barnes and you have established a pleasant relationship during the past month. Through mutual and harmless teasing, you have built a rapport that both of you relish. When you have an opportunity to sit down and have a serious discussion with her, she gives you a unique perspective: "You know why the policy was put in place, don't you? Well, Billingsworth was facing significant pressure from corporate to cut staff personnel. Justin (Fenwick) had been successful in protecting us until then, but when the axe fell it was obvious that we could not continue to do all the product planning for manufacturing. You know we had been analyzing sales trends and setting manufacturing requirements accordingly. Well, the new policy was followed by a 22 percent cut in our staff. I was really lucky to survive this purge, believe me.

"Your group and Robinson's are the most hard-hit. But that's not really surprising. When we were doing the product forecasting, your two units were always the hardest to predict. Don't quote me, but you guys are getting screwed in all this. If you ask me, product scheduling is going toward shorter time frames. Now we are asking for projections one month ahead, but in the next few months with the computer models we are playing with, we should be able to shorten that to two weeks."

Later in the conversation she says, "If your people are having a rough time, there is one thing I could do--training. I've been teaching planning methods at a junior college where I live, and I'd be more than willing to work with your salespeople to give them tools to use in figuring their product requirements."

As you are leaving Mildred's office, her secretary slips you a note that William Barstow, your friend in the corporate office, is trying to reach you by phone. You ask to use a phone in a deserted office and phone him. He says: "Well, by now you've heard about the personnel cuts in Product Control in your division. I'm now sure we have seen the last of personnel cuts. This quarter's earnings are up, and we are now about as lean as we can be.

"I've checked with some of my contacts, and it's clear that your policy problem is not without precedent in the corporation. Two other divisions in Atlanta and Trenton have their salespeople estimate product demand as part of the planning effort. Marketing managers there gave their salespeople extensive training in statistical estimation procedures, and each has access to a computer terminal so they can report deviations from the plan in real time."

What would you do now?

A. Meet privately with Brian Robinson to work out a strategy for addressing this policy problem. (GO TO 309B)

B. Instruct your subordinates about what to do now. (GO TO 304A)

Decision Point 291A

Your speech goes well. In the question-and-answer session that follows, only one question emerges from the floor: "Does computerization mean that I will have to follow regulations on fines, returns, and maximum withdrawal levels that I have been waiving for some of my elderly patrons?" How would you respond?

A. "Computerization means increased service not more restrictive controls on professionals. All of us make judgments about the administration of rules on our patrons. While a more thorough record of these will be available to us in the District Office with computerization, increased controls will only be brought to bear if practices are excessive." (GO TO 299B)

B. "The new system will better serve patrons like this. They will automatically be informed by mail of their overdue withdrawals, and that should itself save you from having to waive the rules." (GO TO 288A)

C. "If the rules at LCLD are outdated, then we should have a look at them." (GO TO 305A)

Decision Point 291B

There are several ways for you to instruct your subordinates to respond to this new policy. Which option would you choose?

A. Tell your subordinates to ignore the policy directive and the product planning forms for the time being until you have a chance to appeal for an exemption. (GO TO 267A)

B. Instruct your subordinates to comply with the new policy. When they resist, be prepared to defend the need for better product planning but assure them that you are working to bring the new policy into line with your group's special circumstances. (GO TO 267C)

C. Ask for your group's advice as to how to implement this new policy requirement. Be prepared to justify the logic behind the policy, should the group advocate resistance. (GO TO 307A)

D. Instruct your subordinates to comply with the new policy but to report to you any significant deviations from the monthly product plan as they arise. By reporting these deviations to Justin Fenwick as addenda to each plan, you will have grounds to argue against penalties imposed against your group for inaccurate estimates. (GO TO 243A)

Decision Point 292A

Your meeting with Bill Banquet was unexpectedly short. Bill confessed being distracted by the resignation that morning of Bob Jenson, his administrative assistant. Jenson was known to be looking for another position, but the timing of his decision seemed to have taken Banquet by surprise. Bill responded curtly to your open-ended probe, "Did you see the memo about the new product planning policy?"

Bill: "Yes, I've seen it. I wasn't consulted on it in advance, but I was told that it was coming. I know the salespeople are not going to like it."
You: "Not only that, but I doubt if my people can be expected to estimate their product needs within the 20 percent window. You know that our situation is different than the other groups."
Bill: "I know, I know. Listen, I've got to go. I've got to get over to Employee Relations to sign the forms for authorization to replace Jenson before my flight to Toledo. Look, do the best you can with the policy. I'll see you in a week."

What would you do now?

A. Talk with your peers (the other sales managers who report to Bill Banquet) to gauge their reactions to the new policy. (GO TO 255A)

B. Call your predecessor (now with another firm) for his perspective on how to handle this situation. (GO TO 259A)

C. Wait and bring this issue up at a weekly staff meeting of the sales managers (chaired by Bill Banquet). (GO TO 295A)

D. Diplomatically oppose the new policy as it applies to your unique circumstances. Petition for an exemption. (GO TO 298A)

E. Instruct your subordinates what to do about the new policy. (GO TO 314B)

Decision Point 292B

The intern works out extremely well. He knows the inner workings of the LCLD and is able to start immediately. Excellent choice.

It is now 342 days after your introductory speech. You have done well. All three branches have their systems up and operational, and your effort has been recognized in the county, the profession, and with the accreditation agency.

Congratulations! You have successfully completed the first Managing Change Interactive Case.

Decision Point 293A

Sam Blakestone was manager of the Automation Systems Group for five years and was with the division for seven. Now with a competing firm, Sam jumps at the chance to express his opinion when you phone him: "It sounds like Fenwick finally got his way. He's been trying to get the monkey off his back for years. He's no professional, I'll tell you that! He's probably been getting heat for inventory costs, so he invents a policy to put the heat elsewhere. Typical, real typical. You guys are just lucky he's 64 and one year away from retirement!" What would you do now?

A. Talk with your peers (the other sales managers who report to Bill Banquet) to gauge their reaction to the new policy. (GO TO 294B)

B. Phone a friend of yours who works as a financial analyst at the corporate level (Blake-Emerson, the parent company) for his perspective on how to respond to this policy change. (GO TO 286B)

C. Wait and bring this issue up at a weekly staff meeting of the sales managers (chaired by Bill Banquet). (GO TO 295A)

D. Diplomatically oppose the new policy as it applies to your unique circumstances. Petition for an exemption. (GO TO 298A)

E. Instruct your subordinates what to do about the new policy. (GO TO 314B)

Decision Point 293B

It is now two months later. The change is going very well. Together you and Sloan Kilgore have successfully brought the system nearly up at the Live Oak Branch. At this point it appears that you will be able to beat the timetable by one month (as you predicted). All the news is not good, however. Mel Simmons, Head Librarian at the Crystal Lake Branch, has just resigned. Thus, you face the problem of replacing the head of a branch where the resistance to computerization is the strongest. What would you do now?

A. Hire someone from the outside who has experience with *BIBLIOTEK* to replace Simmons. (GO TO 257C)

B. Replace Simmons with Linda Hemingway, promote Dave Seagate to Hemingway's old position (reference librarian), and replace Seagate with an intern. This option will free funds that can be used in acquiring new hardware and streamlined software. It will also make Seagate's position more secure. (GO TO 253A)

Decision Point 294A

You have correctly decided to implement this change in a top-down fashion. You now have several decisions to make about how to carry forth this effort. Your first challenge is to plan how to phase in the change. Three options occur to you. Which would you choose?

A. Implement the change so that it is operational in the Live Oak Branch first and then in the Main Branch and finally in the Crystal Lake Branch. (GO TO 259B)

B. Implement the change so that it is operational in all the branches simultaneously. (GO TO 289A)

C. Implement the change so that it is operational in the Main Branch first and then in the Live Oak Branch and finally in the Crystal Lake Branch. (GO TO 245B)

Decision Point 294B

You had an opportunity to chat with three of your peers (Amy Holcott is out of town). All of them expressed irritability with the new policy, but none seemed put out enough to fight it. Don James' (Sales Manager--Pneumatic Products) opinion was typical: "I don't know if my people are good enough planners for us to make our estimates within the 20 percent window. I suspect that they are, but there's no telling. Right now, with the market so sour, most of our business is repeat business. My hunch is that simply keeping our estimates to the high side of historical figures should suffice; at least that's what I am telling my people to do. They're sure not going to like the extra paperwork, that I can assure you. But most of my sales engineers are still jittery about being laid off, so it shouldn't be too bad."

What would you do now?

A. Phone a friend of yours who works as a financial analyst at the corporate level (Blake-Emerson--the parent company) for his perspective on how to respond to this policy change. (GO TO 310C)

B. Wait and bring this issue up at a weekly staff meeting of the sales managers (chaired by Bill Banquet). (GO TO 295A)

C. Diplomatically oppose the new policy as it applies to your unique circumstances. Petition for an exemption. (GO TO 253B)

D. Instruct your subordinates what to do about the new policy. (GO TO 291B)

Decision Point 295A

Bill Banquet returns from Toledo and promptly calls a regular staff meeting. You bring up the policy at the meeting, and this opens up a gripe session that causes Bill Banquet to wince. Forced to make a public declaration, he throws his weight behind the policy indicating that managers should try the new system for a while to see if it will bring down inventory costs without jeopardizing sales. When pressed for how long this trial period would be, Banquet says, "Three months."

The problem with this action is that you have chosen a forum for information gathering that (1) is outside your control and (2) forces your boss into making commitments he may not be prepared to make. The results speak for themselves. Bill Banquet's hand was forced, and now you face the certainty of three months of compliance, whereas you might have been able to do better for your unit. You have also created a situation where your boss has had to appear weak in the face of this edict.

Re-evaluate your last decision. Circle the #295A you just wrote in your flow diagram. Then move to the first uncircled step above this one in your flow diagram.

Decision Point 295B

Flattered by the statements in the press that you made about her outstanding contribution and pleased that you had not altered her overriding philosophy, Ms. B graciously accepts your invitation to speak out on behalf of computerization. You seize this initiative to again reinforce the notion that short-term deficits in service will be more than made up in the future.

Time passes. It is now two months later. The change is going very well. Together you and Sloan Kilgore have successfully brought the system nearly up at the Live Oak Branch. At this point it appears that you will be able to beat the timetable by one month (as you predicted).

All the news is not good, however. Mel Simmons, Head Librarian at the Crystal Lake Branch, resigns. Now you face the problem of replacing the head of a branch where the resistance to computerization is the strongest.

What would you do?

A. Hire someone from the outside who has experience with *BIBLIOTEK* to replace Simmons. (GO TO 257C)

B. Replace Simmons with Linda Hemingway, promote Dave Seagate to Hemingway's old position (reference librarian), and replace Seagate with an intern. This option will free funds that can be used in acquiring new hardware and streamlined software. It will also make Seagate's position more secure. (GO TO 253A)

Decision Point 296A

Your meeting with Bill Banquet was unexpectedly short. Bill confessed to being distracted by the resignation that morning of Bob Jenson, his administrative assistant. Jenson was known to be looking for another position, but the timing of his decision seemed to have taken Banquet by surprise.

You: "Did you see the memo about the new product planning policy?"
Bill: "Yes, I've seen it. I wasn't consulted on it in advance, but I was told that it was coming. I know the salespeople are not going to like it."
You: "Not only that, but I doubt if my people can be expected to estimate their product needs within the 20 percent window. You know that our situation is different than the other groups."
Bill: "I know, I know. Listen, I've got to go. I've got to get over to Employee Relations to sign the forms for authorization to replace Jenson before my flight to Toledo. Look, do the best you can with the policy. I'll see you in a week."

What would you do now?

A. Wait and bring this issue up at a weekly staff meeting of the sales managers (chaired by Bill Banquet). (GO TO 295A)

B. Diplomatically oppose the new policy as it applies to your unique circumstances. Petition for an exemption. (GO TO 253B)

C. Instruct your subordinates what to do about the new policy. (GO TO 291B)

Decision Point 296B

Bob Bramsen is not the best candidate. Change agents ideally have both high social/diplomatic skills and technical credibility. While he has the technical credentials necessary to do well, his social skills are questionable. Specifically, he is going to have to elicit the cooperation of others in order to be successful. Ambitious and upwardly mobile Bramsen may be a bit too abrasive for this assignment.

Re-evaluate your last decision. Circle the #296B you just wrote in your flow diagram. Then move to the first uncircled step above this one in your flow diagram.

Decision Point 297A

Computerization will force fundamental changes in the organizational culture of LCLD. Ms. B's emphasis on service over professionalism did more than shape expectations; it created habits and entire patterns of thinking. Apparently there are individuals ready to move on to other missions and tasks for LCLD, but it is unlikely that a meek approach will get the attention that is needed. Remember, these are civil servants who have more than a modicum of employment security, and who are probably aware of their power to resist change in this situation. A dramatic point of departure is called for here. Your action does not do enough to dramatize this effort. Anything less than total commitment on your part may be seen as half-hearted. It invites others to test your resolve and attempt to discover just how tough-minded you are.

Re-evaluate your last decision. Circle the #297A you just wrote in your flow diagram. Then move to the first uncircled step above this one in your flow diagram.

Decision Point 297B

You had an opportunity to chat with three of your peers (Amy Holcott is out of town). All of them expressed irritability with the new policy, but none seemed put out enough to fight it. Don James' (Sales Manager--Pneumatic Products) opinion was typical: "I don't know if my people are good enough planners for us to make our estimates within the 20 percent window. I suspect that they are, but there's no telling. Right now, with the market so sour, most of our business is repeat business. My hunch is that simply keeping our estimates to the high side of historical figures should suffice; at least that's what I am telling my people to do. They're sure not going to like the extra paperwork, that I can assure you. But most of my sales engineers are still jittery about being laid off, so it shouldn't be too bad."

What would you do now?

A. Phone a friend of yours who works as a financial analyst at the corporate level (Blake-Emerson--the parent company) for his perspective on how to respond to this policy change. (GO TO 254A)
B. Call your predecessor (now with another firm) for his perspective on how to handle this situation. (GO TO 315A)
C. Wait and bring this issue up at a weekly staff meeting of the sales managers (chaired by Bill Banquet). (GO TO 295A)
D. Diplomatically oppose the new policy as it applies to your unique circumstances. Petition for an exemption. (GO TO 253B)
E. Instruct your subordinates what to do about the new policy. (GO TO 291B)

Decision Point 298A

In deciding to act before consulting your peers, you now lack adequate information about the potential force that might be mobilized in opposition to this policy. Accordingly, your last decision was not correct. To remedy this situation, assume that you now have an opportunity to chat with three of your peers (Amy Holcott is out of town). All of them expressed irritability with the new policy, but none seemed put out enough to fight it. Don James' (Sales Manager--Pneumatic Products) opinion was typical: "I don't know if my people are good enough planners for us to make our estimates within the 20 percent window. I suspect that they are, but there's no telling. Right now, with the market so sour, most of our business is repeat business. My hunch is that simply keeping our estimates to the high side of historical figures should suffice; at least that's what I am telling my people to do. They're sure not going to like the extra paper-work, that I can assure you. But most of my sales engineers are still jittery about being laid off, so it shouldn't be too bad."

What would you do now?

A. If you haven't done so yet, phone a friend of yours who works as a financial analyst at the corporate level (Blake-Emerson--the parent company) for his perspective on how to respond to this policy change. (GO TO 254A)

B. If you haven't done so yet, call your predecessor (now with another firm) for his perspective on how to handle this situation. (GO TO 315A)

C. Wait and bring this issue up at a weekly staff meeting of the sales managers (chaired by Bill Banquet). (GO TO 295A)

D. Diplomatically oppose the new policy as it applies to your unique circumstances. Petition for an exemption. (GO TO 253B)

E. Instruct your subordinates what to do about the new policy. (GO TO 291B)

Decision Point 298B

Now that your change is at a very sensitive stage, you do not want to risk bringing in an unknown quantity. Using a *new* intern will allow you to be honest to your pledge of not jeopardizing the security of your full-time people. However, it will take you a considerable amount of time to find, orient, and train anyone *new* for this position. There is a better way.

Re-evaluate your last decision. Circle the #298B you just wrote in your flow diagram. Then move to the first uncircled step above this one in your flow diagram.

Decision Point 299A

Sam Blakestone was manager of the Automation Systems Group for five years and was with the division for seven. Now with a competing firm, Sam jumps at the chance to express his opinion when you phone him:

"It sounds like Fenwick finally got his way. He's been trying to get the monkey off his back for years. He's no professional, I'll tell you that! He's probably been getting heat for inventory costs, so he invents a policy to put the heat elsewhere. Typical, real typical. You guys are just lucky he's 64 and one year away from retirement!"

What would you do now?

A. Wait and bring this issue up at a weekly staff meeting of the sales managers (chaired by Bill Banquet). (GO TO 295A)

B. Diplomatically oppose the new policy as it applies to your unique circumstances. Petition for an exemption. (GO TO 253B)

C. Instruct your subordinates what to do about the new policy. (GO TO 291B)

Decision Point 299B

It is two weeks after your speech. You have completed your public relations campaign announcing computerization through the media and via speeches to community groups. On each occasion you repeated the new motto for the LCLD, "Looking for Better Ways to Serve You Best."

This new motto seems to have been greeted well by everyone except Ms. B. Miffed by your apparent effort to discredit her administration, she is cold to your computerization plan. This is not much of a problem except that she still has many friends in LCLD. Noteworthy among these is Mel Simmons, the head librarian at the Crystal Lake Branch. He becomes increasingly resistant to the *BIBLIOTEK* training, even going so far as to refuse to send some of his aides to certain training sessions conducted by Sloan Kilgore at the District Office. His claim is that the scheduling of these sessions interferes with branch work schedules.

What action would you take?

A. Ask Mel Simmons for his cooperation with the computerization effort. (GO TO 307B)

B. Tell Mel Simmons to do whatever it takes get his aides to take the training so that his branch will be on schedule. Tell him that otherwise you will close the branch to patrons when required training is scheduled. (GO TO 293B)

Decision Point 300A

Now is *not* the time to maintain flexibility. It may be perceived as a sign of a lack of your commitment, and it may translate into ambiguous performance standards for your subordinates. It is important to be explicit about the schedule.

Re-evaluate your last decision. Circle the #300A you just wrote in your flow diagram. Then move to the first uncircled step above this one in your flow diagram.

Decision Point 300B

Your meeting with Bill Banquet was unexpectedly short. Bill confessed being distracted by the resignation that morning of Bob Jenson, his administrative assistant. Jenson was known to be looking for another position, but the timing of his decision seemed to have taken Banquet by surprise.

You: "Did you see the memo about the new product planning policy?"
Bill: "Yes, I've seen it. I wasn't consulted on it in advance, but I was told that it was coming. I know the salespeople are not going to like it."
You: "Not only that, but I doubt if my people can be expected to estimate their product needs within the 20 percent window. You know that our situation is different than the other groups."
Bill: "I know, I know. Listen, I've got to go. I've got to get over to Employee Relations to sign the forms for authorization to replace Jenson before my flight to Toledo. Look, do the best you can with the policy. I'll see you in a week."
What would you do now?

A. Talk with your peers (the other sales managers who report to Bill Banquet) to gauge their reactions to the new policy. (GO TO 294B)

B. Phone a friend of yours who works as a financial analyst at the corporate level (Blake-Emerson, the parent company) for his perspective on how to respond to this policy change. (GO TO 286B)

C. Wait and bring this issue up at a weekly staff meeting of the sales managers (chaired by Bill Banquet). (GO TO 295A)

D. Diplomatically oppose the new policy as it applies to your unique circumstances. Petition for an exemption. (GO TO 298A)

E. Instruct your subordinates what to do about the new policy. (GO TO 314B)

Decision Point 301A

Mildred Barnes and you have established a pleasant relationship during the past month. Through mutual and harmless teasing, you have built a rapport that both of you relish. When you have an opportunity to sit down and have a serious discussion with her, she gives you a unique perspective, "You know why the policy was put in place, don't you? Well, Billingsworth was facing significant pressure from corporate to cut staff personnel. Justin (Fenwick) had been successful in protecting us until then, but when the axe fell, it was obvious that we could not continue to do all the product planning for manufacturing. You know we had been analyzing sales trends and setting manufacturing requirements accordingly. Well, the new policy was followed by a 22 percent cut in our staff. Jack Collins was the last of these cuts, and he left just last week. I was really lucky to survive this purge, believe me.

"Your group and Robinson's are the most hard-hit. But that's not really surprising. When we were doing the product forecasting, your two units were always the hardest to predict. Don't quote me, but you guys are getting screwed in all this. If you ask me, product scheduling is going toward shorter time frames. Now we are asking for projections one month ahead, but soon we should be able to shorten that to two weeks."

Later in the conversation she says, "If your people are having a rough time, there is one thing I could do--training. I've been teaching planning methods at a junior college, and I'd be more than willing to work with your salespeople to give them tools to use in figuring their product requirements."

As you are leaving Mildred's office, her secretary slips you a note that William Barstow, your friend in the corporate office, is trying to reach you by phone. You ask to use a phone in a deserted office and phone him. He tells you: "Well, by now you've heard about the personnel cuts in Product Control in your division. My hunch that personnel cuts are now a thing of the past is a conviction. This quarter's earnings are up, and it now appears that we are about as lean as we can be. I've checked with some of my contacts, and it's clear that your policy problem is not without precedent in the corporation. Two other divisions in Atlanta and Trenton have their salespeople estimate product demand as part of the planning effort. Marketing managers there gave their salespeople extensive training in statistical estimation procedures, and each has access to a computer terminal so they can report deviations from the plan in real time."

What would you do now?

A. Talk to your peers about their experiences with the new policy. (GO TO 311A)

B. Instruct your subordinates about what to do now. (GO TO 304A)

Decision Point 302A

This accomplishment calls for fanfare not only to reinforce those who made a contribution, but also to dramatize progress in order to generate support for the total effort. Your approach lacks gusto. Re-evaluate your last decision. Circle the #302A you just wrote in your flow diagram. Then move to the first uncircled step above this one in your flow diagram.

Decision Point 302B

Your meeting with Bill Banquet was unexpectedly short. Bill confessed being distracted by the resignation that morning of Bob Jenson, his administrative assistant. Jenson was known to be looking for another position, but the timing of his decision seemed to have taken Banquet by surprise.

You: "Did you see the memo about the new product planning policy?"
Bill: "Yes, I've seen it. I wasn't consulted on it in advance, but I was told that it was coming. I know the salespeople are not going to like it."
You: "Not only that, but I doubt if my people can be expected to estimate their product needs within the 20 percent window. You know that our situation is different than the other groups."
Bill: "I know, I know. Listen, I've got to go. I've got to get over to Employee Relations to sign the authorization to replace Jenson before my flight to Toledo. Look, do the best you can with the policy. I'll see you in a week."

What would you do now?

A. Talk with your peers (the other sales managers who report to Bill Banquet) to gauge their reactions to the new policy. (GO TO 297B)

B. Phone a friend of yours who works as a financial analyst at the corporate level (Blake-Emerson, the parent company) for his perspective on how to respond to this policy change. (GO TO 277B)

C. Call your predecessor (now with another firm) for his perspective on how to handle this situation. (GO TO 293A)

D. Wait and bring this issue up at a weekly staff meeting of the sales managers (chaired by Bill Banquet). (GO TO 295A)

E. Diplomatically oppose the new policy as it applies to your unique circumstances. Petition for an exemption. (GO TO 298A)

F. Instruct your subordinates what to do about the new policy. (GO TO 314B)

Decision Point 303A

You decide to persuade Eugene that your team's recommendation makes a great deal of sense. The more you say, though, the more Eugene resists the idea. At one point he even criticizes your people as being prone to "superficial analysis." The discussion is not going well, to say the least. Your conversation is interrupted by a phone call. Sitting there in his large office and waiting for him to finish the call, you have to decide what you are going to do next.

A. Defend your team's decision. Indicate that the idea of a "super-team" is only an interim move. Tell Eugene that your team's analysis was thorough. (GO TO 262B)

B. Ask Eugene what his specific concerns are with the idea so that you can return to discuss them with your team. (GO TO 240A)

Decision Point 303B

You have known William Barstow for years. You attended the same university together. When you tell him of the policy directive, he gives you some interesting information:

"I haven't heard anything about the policy, but I can tell you that the Fluid Products Division is getting a lot of heat for getting its costs under control. The word is that Billingsworth's argument that his division has strong profit potential is no longer credible until he can produce the numbers. The division is now under considerable pressure not to cut its line personnel, but rather its staff. The view from these lofty heights is that the axe is due to fall soon on just about every staff unit in the division."

If true, this would mean that Justin Fenwick's group is in for some cuts, but your group should not be affected. What would you do now?

A. Talk with your peers (the other sales managers who report to Bill Banquet) to gauge their reaction to the new policy. (GO TO 287A)

B. Speak with Bill Banquet (your boss) about his "reading" of the new policy. (GO TO 317B)

C. Wait and bring this issue up at a weekly staff meeting of the sales managers (chaired by Bill Banquet). (GO TO 295A)

D. Diplomatically oppose the new policy as it applies to your unique circumstances. Petition for an exemption. (GO TO 284A)

E. Instruct your subordinates what to do about the new policy. (GO TO 321A)

Decision Point 304A

It is premature for you to give your subordinates directions as to how to proceed. You simply don't know at this point whether some sort of modification more favorable to your unit can be worked out.

Re-evaluate your last decision. Circle the #304A you just wrote in your flow diagram. Then move to the first uncircled step above this one in your flow diagram.

Decision Point 304B

You attend the meeting and take the opportunity to correct the false rumor that computerization will lead to the closing of the branch. Further, you indicate that, if anything, computerization will ensure the viability of the Crystal Lake Branch. Once computerization is implemented, it will mean that every Crystal Lake patron will have access to the entire LCLD collection, and therefore better service. It is now six months since your announcement, and the Live Oak Branch computer system is now up and operational two weeks before the deadline. You now have to decide how to acknowledge this achievement.

A. Send a memo to all employees congratulating the Live Oak staff for its achievement. (GO TO 302A)

B. Hold an open-house "celebration" at the Live Oak Branch so other employees can see the system in action. Publicly congratulate members of the branch. Arrange for press coverage of the event. (GO TO 275A)

Decision Point 304C

Sterling Cartwright is a man of about 40 who has been with the company for only three weeks. You ask him about Banquet's opinion of the way the new policy is working. He responds: "Bill is concerned. He really is. He doesn't like the way it puts the burden on you. Just the other day he met with Mr. Billingsworth about it."

You ask him what Banquet is doing about this situation. He tells you, "Bill has a plan, and I'm sure it will work in time, but with the cuts in product planning, things are a bit uncertain. I'm sure you can expect something in the next few months."

What would you do now? (Bill Banquet is out of town.)

A. Meet privately with Brian Robinson to work out a strategy for addressing this policy problem. (GO TO 309B)

B. Instruct your subordinates about what to do now. (GO TO 304A)

Decision Point 305A

Your answer is unresponsive to a latent issue that is likely to be the basis of the question: control. In general, administrative changes are more resisted than technical changes simply because they realign control and power relationships. As a change, computerization has an administrative component, so this question is probably based on a concern about a loss of power and control. Computerization often scares professionals because they fear that it will result in more restrictions to their autonomy and less influence in the organization.

Re-evaluate your last decision. Circle the #305A you just wrote in your flow diagram. Then move to the first uncircled step above this one in your flow diagram.

Decision Point 305B

You have known William Barstow for years. You attended the same university together. When you tell him of the policy directive, he gives you some interesting information:

"I haven't heard anything about the policy, but I can tell you that the Fluid Products Division is getting a lot of heat to get its costs under control. The word is that Billingsworth's argument that his division has strong profit potential is no longer credible until he can produce the numbers. The division is now under considerable pressure not to cut its line personnel, but rather its staff. The view from these lofty heights is that the axe is due to fall soon on just about every staff unit in the division."

If true, this would mean that Justin Fenwick's group is in for some cuts, but your group should not be affected. What would you do now?

A. Talk with your peers (the other sales managers who report to Bill Banquet) to gauge their reaction to the new policy. (GO TO 261B)

B. Speak with Bill Banquet (your boss) about his "reading" of the new policy. (GO TO 292A)

C. Call your predecessor (now with another firm) for his perspective on how to handle this situation. (GO TO 313A)

D. Wait and bring this issue up at a weekly staff meeting of the sales managers (chaired by Bill Banquet). (GO TO 295A)

E. Diplomatically oppose the new policy as it applies to your unique circumstances. Petition for an exemption. (GO TO 284A)

F. Instruct your subordinates what to do about the new policy. (GO TO 321A)

Decision Point 306A

You ask Bill Banquet to use his influence to earn an exemption for your unit. He responds as follows: "I understand that you may have difficulties abiding by this policy. However, it's not at all clear to me that you can't make it work."

You respond by demonstrating with factual information that your sales group uses a more complex array of products and experiences a more uncertain demand than the other units Banquet is responsible for. Further, you indicate the morale problems that will be created if your unit is adversely penalized because of the unique nature of the business it does. He then asks you for your recommendation, and you propose an exemption. He reacts: "Well, we'll have to see about that. I understand your concerns, but we have to be very sure before we propose anything that far-reaching."

How would you respond to this?

A. Indicate that you will direct your subordinates to comply with the policy for the time being, and that you will keep him up to date on how successful your people are at estimating their product requirements. (GO TO 291B)

B. Ask Bill what exactly it is that he wants you to do. (GO TO 241C)

C. Go to Emerson Billingsworth and petition your case there. (GO TO 315C)

Decision Point 306B

Your speech goes well. In the question-and-answer session that follows, only one question emerges from the floor: "Does computerization mean that I will have to follow regulations on fines, returns, and withdrawal levels that I have been waiving for some of my elderly patrons?" How would you respond?

A. "Computerization means increased service not more restrictive controls on professionals. All of us make judgments about the administration of rules on our patrons. While a more thorough record of these will be available to us in the District Office with computerization, increased controls will only be brought to bear if practices are excessive." (GO TO 258A)

B. "The new system will better serve patrons like this. They will automatically be informed by mail of their overdue withdrawals, and that should itself save you from having to waive the rules." (GO TO 288A)

C. "If the rules at LCLD are outdated, then we should have a look at them." (GO TO 305A)

Decision Point 307A

You have decided to direct your subordinates to comply with the new policy for the time being, but asked them to participate in the decisions as to how to implement the policy. The resulting discussion is rocky, but it does develop the group sentiment that they are in it together and they should make the best of it.

Two months later the effects of the new policy had an opportunity to be felt, and felt they were. Your unit failed to make the 20 percent planning window on 30 percent of the products sold. As a result, four orders are delayed, two of which are cancelled by customers due to the delay. Additionally, 15 parts are over-ordered, leading to a decrease by 17 percent in the reported sales volume credited to your unit. This results in your unit falling from the number two position in sales volume in the department to the number three position.

Your sales engineers complain bitterly about the new policy, especially when their estimates over- or undershoot actual product requirements. Accounting for penalties, all but one of your sales engineers failed to meet their volume goals, and all expressed concern that their merit pay would be adversely affected.

Because of your heavy travel schedule during the month, you have had little opportunity to interact with your boss, your peers, or with others outside your immediate sphere of responsibility. The sole exception is Mildred Barnes, an analyst in the Product Control Department. Barnes reports directly to Justin Fenwick and is the analyst responsible for translating your unit's product plans into production schedules.

At this point what would you do?

A. Go to your boss and tell him of your concerns and the concerns of your subordinates, with the intention of moderating the negative effects of this policy. (GO TO 257A)
B. Gather information about how others in the organization view this policy now that it has been in place for two months. (GO TO 317A)
C. Instruct your subordinates about what to do now. (GO TO 304A)

Decision Point 307B

Your approach does little to neutralize the resistance of Mel Simmons. His skepticism, fueled by Ms. B's ego involvement, persists in spite of your efforts, and it seriously interferes with your change program. Swift, forceful action is called for.

Re-evaluate your last decision. Circle the #307B you just wrote in your flow diagram. Then move to the first uncircled step above this one in your flow diagram.

Decision Point 308A

You have known William Barstow for years. You attended the same university together. When you tell him of the policy directive, he gives you some interesting information:

"I haven't heard anything about the policy, but I can tell you that the Fluid Products Division is getting a lot of heat to get its costs under control. The word is that Billingsworth's argument that his division has strong profit potential is no longer credible until he can produce the numbers. The division is now under considerable pressure not to cut its line personnel, but rather its staff. The view from these lofty heights is that the axe is due to fall soon on just about every staff unit in the division."

If true, this would mean that Justin Fenwick's group is in for some cuts, but your group should not be affected.

What would you do now?

A. Speak with Bill Banquet (your boss) about his "reading" on the new policy. (GO TO 296A)
B. Wait and bring this issue up at a weekly staff meeting of the sales managers (chaired by Bill Banquet). (GO TO 295A)
C. Diplomatically oppose the new policy as it applies to your unique circumstances. Petition for an exemption. (GO TO 252A)
D. Instruct your subordinates what to do about the new policy. (GO TO 320A)

Decision Point 308B

You decided to ask Linda to carry your message back to her people that there are no plans to close the Crystal Lake Branch. This settles things down for a while, but Linda reports to you that there are still a lot of insecurities about the future of the branch.

You should really have gone out and clarified the situation in person. This would have had two main advantages. First, since there was no basis in fact for the rumor, it gave you a chance to demonstrate your credibility with these people. You could tell them no closure was planned, and you would be proven correct over time. Second, appearing in person would give you the chance to explain how computerization helps rather than hinders the longevity of the branch. As it was, you opened yourself up to communication distortion by sending your message through Linda. While she would not have meant to misquote you, this is too important an issue to risk the possibility of missed signals.

Re-evaluate your last decision. Circle the #308B you just wrote in your flow diagram. Then move to the first uncircled step above this one in your flow diagram.

Decision Point 309A

Your conversation with Robin is not very fruitful. He continues to be vague about his feelings toward "flexible assembly." He tells you that he would prefer to gradually introduce it rather than be forced to deal both with the disruption it will cause and the problems the new work will pose for his group.

What would you do now?

A. Meet with your entire group and share this general problem. (GO TO 246B)

B. Have your group develop procedures for implementing flexible assembly. (GO TO 260A)

Decision Point 309B

After discussing strategy with Robinson in some detail, you consider three major alternative actions: (1) lobby for an exemption for those units of strategic importance (your unit, like Robinson's, has been identified as strategically important to the corporation); (2) lobby for a reduction in the planning period from one month to one or two weeks; and (3) lobby for training for your sales engineers.

You both agree that (1) is the most preferred alternative, (2) is the second best, and (3) is the worst. You now have to decide how to go forward with your proposals for policy modifications. Which would you do?

A. Approach Bill Banquet (once he gets back from his trip) and present a carefully-thought-out proposal for alternative (1), being prepared to settle for alternative (2) or (3) if he doesn't think it feasible. (GO TO 311B)

B. Same as A above except begin by asking Banquet his assessment of how well the policy is working. (GO TO 237B)

Decision Point 309C

You decided to take time to try to find out the source of the rumor before taking any other action. This was incorrect. Rumor control during the implementation of change is a crucial activity. False rumors must be corrected immediately, regardless of the source. That way the accurate information will itself serve to discredit the person who started the rumor.

Re-evaluate your last decision. Circle the #309C you just wrote in your flow diagram. Then move to the first uncircled step above this one in your flow diagram.

Decision Point 310A

Mild resistance to change, such as these complaints illustrate, should be taken as a signal that firmer resistance will develop if the concerns are not addressed. In addition, there may be a basis for the concerns that is not being stated directly here. The appropriate action is to delve into the real concerns versus the stated concerns. Otherwise the resistance will probably snowball.

Re-evaluate your last decision. Circle the #310A you just wrote in your flow diagram. Then move to the first uncircled step above this one in your flow diagram.

Decision Point 310B

You have decided to give your group the assignment that Eugene gave you. This is unwise. He gave you a very cryptic assignment in an informal encounter, and the assignment has far-reaching consequences for the entire company. Certainly you want to clarify what he is asking you to do and what problem or opportunity he is responding to before involving your group in this matter.

Re-evaluate your last decision. Circle the #310B you just wrote in your flow diagram. Then move to the first uncircled step above this one in your flow diagram.

Decision Point 310C

You have known William Barstow for years. You attended the same university together, and while he is two years older than you, you and he have fond memories of your experiences as members of the debate team. When you tell him of the policy directive, he gives you some interesting information:

"I haven't heard anything about the policy, but I can tell you that the Fluid Products Division is getting a lot of heat to get its costs under control. The word is that Billingsworth's argument that his division has strong profit potential is no longer credible until he can produce the numbers. The division is now under considerable pressure not to cut its line personnel, but rather its staff. The view from these lofty heights is that the axe is due to fall soon on just about every staff unit in the division."

If true, this would mean that Justin Fenwick's group is in for some cuts, but your group should not be affected.

What would you do now?

A. Wait and bring this issue up at a weekly staff meeting of the sales managers (chaired by Bill Banquet). (GO TO 295A)
B. Diplomatically oppose the new policy as it applies to your unique circumstances. Petition for an exemption. (GO TO 253B)
C. Instruct your subordinates what to do about the new policy. (GO TO 291B)

Decision Point 311A

You have a chance to "buttonhole" several of the other sales managers. Their comments follow:

Sandra Smith (Sales Mgr., Hydraulic Products): "I'll tell you one thing. My sales engineers certainly don't like the extra paperwork, but we've been able to do pretty well making the 20 percent window. In fact (she winks), it feels good moving from #4 to #2! All kidding aside, I think it's good that we now require our salespeople to plan their product needs. After all, the Personnel people are always harping that we should prepare them for moving into the managerial ranks."

Brian Robinson (Sales Mgr., Delivery Systems): "All that sounds fine and good, but the fact remains that the policy penalizes those of us who have uncertain demand or complex lines. No, this thing is stupid. The strategic plan for this year identifies my line as vitally important, and then they turn around and discourage our development of new accounts because one can never plan them systematically. I've talked to Banquet about this and he agrees, but he hasn't done anything about it!"

Don James (Sales Mgr., Pneumatic Products): "My sales engineers have had a helluva time getting their numbers right. Even with our standard lines, they consistently overestimated their needs. I suspect that they will get better and that the product will be available. It's creating hell with our volume, I'll tell you."

What would you do now? (Bill Banquet is out of town.)

A. Meet privately with Brian Robinson to work out a strategy for addressing this policy problem. (GO TO 309B)

B. Instruct your subordinates about what to do now. (GO TO 304A)

Decision Point 311B

Banquet listens carefully to your proposal but reacts negatively to your first alternative (an exemption). When you try to emphasize the other alternatives as a fallback position, he keeps reintroducing the infeasibility of an exemption. Even when you agree that an exemption would be out of the question, Banquet seems to hold onto the view that the other alternatives would be perceived by "the powers that be" as a sign that the original policy was ill conceived. Your negotiation posture has caused your alternatives to be seen as versions of the same overall action--resistance. Clearly you need a different negotiation strategy with Bill Banquet.

Re-evaluate your last decision. Circle the #311B you just wrote in your flow diagram. Then move to the first uncircled step above this one in your flow diagram.

Decision Point 312A

Will Barstow has much to say: "Well, by now you've heard about the personnel cuts in Product Control in your division. Personnel cuts are now a thing of the past. This quarter's earnings are up, and it now appears that we are about as lean as we can be. I've checked with some of my contacts, and it's clear that your policy problem is not without precedent in the corporation. Two other divisions in Atlanta and Trenton have their salespeople estimate product demand as part of the planning effort. Marketing managers there gave their salespeople training in statistical estimation procedures, and each has a computer terminal so they can report deviations from the plan in real time."

As you hang up the phone, Mildred Barnes of the Product Control Department appears in the doorway of your office. Mildred Barnes and you have established a pleasant relationship during the past month. Mildred tells you, "You know why the policy was put in place, don't you? Well, Billingsworth was facing significant pressure from corporate to cut staff personnel. Justin (Fenwick) had been successful in protecting us until then, but when the axe fell, it was obvious that we could not continue to do all the product planning for manufacturing. You know we had been analyzing sales trends and setting manufacturing requirements accordingly. Well, the new policy was followed by a 22 percent cut in our staff. I was really lucky to survive this purge, believe me.

"Your group and Robinson's are the most hard-hit. But that's not really surprising. When we were doing the product forecasting, your two units were always the hardest to predict. Don't quote me, but you guys are getting screwed in all this.

"If you ask me, product scheduling is going toward shorter time frames. Now we are asking for projections one month ahead, but in the next few months with the computer models we are playing with, we should be able to shorten that to two weeks."

Later in the conversation she says, "If your people are having a rough time, there is one thing I could do--training. I've been teaching planning methods at a junior college where I live, and I'd be more than willing to work with your salespeople to give them tools to use in figuring their product requirements."

What would you do now?

A. Since Bill Banquet is out of town, talk with Sterling Cartwright (his new administrative assistant). (GO TO 304C)

B. Meet privately with Brian Robinson to work out a strategy for how to address this policy problem. (GO TO 309B)

C. Instruct your subordinates about what to do now. (GO TO 304A)

Decision Point 313A

Sam Blakestone was manager of the Automation Systems Group for five years and was with the division for seven. Now with a competing firm, Sam jumps at the chance to express his opinion when you phone him, "It sounds like Fenwick finally got his way. He's been trying to get the monkey off his back for years. He's no professional, I'll tell you that! He's probably been getting heat for inventory costs, so he invents a policy to put the heat elsewhere. Typical, real typical. You guys are just lucky he's 64 and one year away from retirement!" What would you do now?

A. Talk with your peers (the other sales managers who report to Bill Banquet) to gauge their reaction to the new policy. (GO TO 287A)

B. Speak with Bill Banquet (your boss) about his "reading" of the new policy. (GO TO 317B)

C. Wait and bring this issue up at a weekly staff meeting of the sales managers (chaired by Bill Banquet). (GO TO 295A)

D. Diplomatically oppose the new policy as it applies to your unique circumstances. Petition for an exemption. (GO TO 284A)

E. Instruct your subordinates what to do about the new policy. (GO TO 321A)

Decision Point 313B

At this point you need either to differentiate your philosophy from Ms. B's or to get her support for computerization in order to give your people adequate direction.

Re-evaluate your last decision. Circle the #313B you just wrote in your flow diagram. Then move to the first uncircled step above this one in your flow diagram.

Decision Point 313C

Your meeting with Justin Fenwick is strained, and Fenwick responds to your petition defensively, re-explaining the logic of the policy and attempting to persuade you to go along. He is unyielding even when you outline your reservations. Several days after your meeting, you hear through the grapevine that as far as the Product Planning Group is concerned, you are a troublemaker.

Re-evaluate your last decision. Circle the #313C you just wrote in your flow diagram. Then move to the first uncircled step above this one in your flow diagram.

Decision Point 314A

Announcing a new philosophy at this point is likely to demonstrate a lack of leadership. You are essentially contradicting yourself. Your credibility may not recover.

Re-evaluate your last decision. Circle the #314A you just wrote in your flow diagram. Then move to the first uncircled step above this one in your flow diagram.

Decision Point 314B

In deciding to act before consulting your peers, you now lack adequate information about the potential force that might be mobilized in opposition to this policy. Accordingly, your last decision was not correct. To remedy this situation, read the results of a discussion with your peers shown below, and then decide what to do.

You have an opportunity to chat with three of your peers (Amy Holcott is out of town). All of them expressed irritability with the new policy, but none seemed put out enough to fight it. Don James' (Sales Manager--Pneumatic Products) opinion was typical:

"I don't know if my people are good enough planners for us to make our estimates within the 20 percent window. I suspect that they are, but there's no telling. Right now, with the market so sour, most of our business is repeat business. My hunch is that simply keeping our estimates to the high side of historical figures should suffice; at least that's what I am telling my people to do. They're sure not going to like the extra paperwork, that I can assure you. But most of my sales engineers are still jittery about being laid off, so it shouldn't be too bad."

What would you do now?

A. If you haven't done so yet, phone a friend of yours who works as a financial analyst at the corporate level (Blake-Emerson--the parent company) for his perspective on how to respond to this policy change. (GO TO 254A)

B. If you haven't done so yet, call your predecessor (now with another firm) for his perspective on how to handle this situation. (GO TO 315A)

C. Wait and bring this issue up at a weekly staff meeting of the sales managers (chaired by Bill Banquet). (GO TO 295A)

D. Diplomatically oppose the new policy as it applies to your unique circumstances. Petition for an exemption. (GO TO 253B)

E. Instruct your subordinates what to do about the new policy. (GO TO 291B)

Decision Point 315A

Sam Blakestone was manager of the Automation Systems Group for five years and was with the division for seven. Now with a competing firm, Sam jumps at the chance to express his opinion when you phone him:
"It sounds like Fenwick finally got his way. He's been trying to get the monkey off his back for years. He's no professional, I'll tell you that! He's probably been getting heat for inventory costs, so he invents a policy to put the heat elsewhere. Typical, real typical. You guys are just lucky he's 64 and one year away from retirement!"
What would you do now?

A. Phone a friend of yours who works as a financial analyst at the corporate level (Blake-Emerson, the parent company) for his perspective on how to respond to this policy change. (GO TO 310C)

B. Wait and bring this issue up at a weekly staff meeting of the sales managers (chaired by Bill Banquet). (GO TO 295A)

C. Diplomatically oppose the new policy as it applies to your unique circumstances. Petition for an exemption. (GO TO 253B)

D. Instruct your subordinates what to do about the new policy. (GO TO 291B)

Decision Point 315B

You plan to promise that no one will lose his or her job because of computerization. This is an unnecessarily broad commitment. You don't want to give unconditional guarantees like this one, or you will be in the position of severely losing credibility if and when you have to terminate a person for cause.
Re-evaluate your last decision. Circle the #315B you just wrote in your flow diagram. Then move to the first uncircled step above this one in your flow diagram.

Decision Point 315C

Approaching Emerson Billingsworth at this point produces disastrous consequences. He informs your boss of your action and takes no action to relieve your unit of responsibility to complete the product planning task.
Re-evaluate your last decision. Circle the #315C you just wrote in your flow diagram. Then move to the first uncircled step above this one in your flow diagram.

Decision Point 316A

You plan to deal with feelings of insecurity about the change by acknowledging that LCLD is overstaffed, but you will deal with that through natural attrition. This is not going to be very comforting. First of all, it is likely that not everyone knew LCLD was overstaffed. Second, it is unclear how many people have to voluntarily leave (retire, quit, etc.) before other jobs are absolutely safe. Simply speaking, while you have been honest, you have to be more straightforward if you really want to defuse feelings of insecurity at the outset.

Re-evaluate your last decision. Circle the #316A you just wrote in your flow diagram. Then move to the first uncircled step above this one in your flow diagram.

Decision Point 316B

Your meeting with Bill Banquet was unexpectedly short. Bill confessed being distracted by the resignation that morning of Bob Jenson, his administrative assistant. Jenson was known to be looking for another position, but the timing of his decision seemed to have taken Banquet by surprise.

You: "Bill, did you see the memo about the new product planning policy?"
Bill: "Yes, I've seen it. I wasn't consulted on it in advance, but I was told that it was coming. I know the salespeople are not going to like it."
You: "Not only that, but I doubt if my people can be expected to estimate their product needs within the 20 percent window. You know that our situation is different than the other groups."
Bill: "I know, I know. Listen, I've got to go. I've got to get over to Employee Relations to sign the forms for authorization to replace Jenson before my flight to Toledo. Look, do the best you can with the policy. I'll see you in a week."
What would you do now?

A. Phone a friend of yours who works as a financial analyst at the corporate level (Blake-Emerson, the parent company) for his perspective on how to respond to this policy change. (GO TO 310C)

B. Wait and bring this issue up at a weekly staff meeting of the sales managers (chaired by Bill Banquet). (GO TO 295A)

C. Diplomatically oppose the new policy as it applies to your unique circumstances. Petition for an exemption. (GO TO 253B)

D. Instruct your subordinates what to do about the new policy. (GO TO 291B)

Decision Point 317A

The following information sources are available to you. Which would you choose?

A. Your peers. (GO TO 265A)

B. Mildred Barnes of the Product Control Department. (GO TO 319A)

C. Since Bill Banquet is out of town, Sterling Cartwright (his new administrative assistant). (GO TO 275B)

D. William Barstow, your friend at the corporate headquarters. (GO TO 318A)

Decision Point 317B

Your meeting with Bill Banquet was unexpectedly short. Bill confessed being distracted by the resignation that morning of Bob Jenson, his administrative assistant. Jenson was known to be looking for another position, but the timing of his decision seemed to have taken Banquet by surprise.

You: "Did you see the memo about the new product planning policy?"
Bill: "Yes, I've seen it. I wasn't consulted on it in advance, but I was told that it was coming. I know the salespeople are not going to like it."
You: "Not only that, but I doubt if my people can be expected to estimate their product needs within the 20 percent window. You know that our situation is different than the other groups."
Bill: "I know, I know. Listen, I've got to go. I've got to get over to Employee Relations to sign the forms for authorization to replace Jenson before my flight to Toledo. Look, do the best you can with the policy. I'll see you in a week."
What would you do now?

A. Talk with your peers (the other sales managers who report to Bill Banquet) to gauge their reactions to the new policy. (GO TO 282B)

B. Wait and bring this issue up at a weekly staff meeting of the sales managers (chaired by Bill Banquet). (GO TO 295A)

C. Diplomatically oppose the new policy as it applies to your unique circumstances. Petition for an exemption. (GO TO 298A)

D. Instruct your subordinates what to do about the new policy. (GO TO 314B)

Decision Point 318A

Will Barstow has much to say: "Well, by now you've heard about the personnel cuts in Product Control in your division. Personnel cuts are now a thing of the past. This quarter's earnings are up, and it now appears that we are about as lean as we can be.

"I've checked with some of my contacts, and it's clear that your policy problem is not without precedent in the corporation. Two other divisions in Atlanta and Trenton have their salespeople estimate product demand as part of the planning effort. Marketing managers there gave their salespeople training in statistical estimation procedures, and each has a computer terminal so they can report deviations from the plan in real time."

As you hang up the phone, Mildred Barnes of the Product Control Department appears in the doorway of your office. Mildred Barnes and you have established a pleasant relationship during the past month. Mildred tells you: "You know why the policy was put in place, don't you? Well, Billingsworth was facing significant pressure from corporate to cut staff personnel. Justin (Fenwick) had been successful in protecting us until then, but when the axe fell, it was obvious that we could not continue to do all the product planning for manufacturing. You know we had been analyzing sales trends and setting manufacturing requirements accordingly. Well, the new policy was followed by a 22 percent cut in our staff. Jack Collins was the last of these cuts, and he left just last week. I was really lucky to survive this purge, believe me.

"Your group and Robinson's are the most hard-hit. But that's not really surprising. When we were doing the product forecasting, your two units were always the hardest to predict.

"If you ask me, product scheduling is going toward shorter time frames. Now we are asking for projections one month ahead, but soon with our computer models, we should be able to shorten that to two weeks."

Later in the conversation she says, "If your people are having a rough time, there is one thing I could do--training. I've been teaching planning methods at a junior college where I live, and I'd be more than willing to work with your salespeople to give them tools to use in figuring their product requirements."

What would you do now?

A. Talk to your peers about their experience with the new policy. (GO TO 263A)

B. Since Bill Banquet is out of town, talk with Sterling Cartwright (his new administrative assistant). (GO TO 258B)

C. Instruct your subordinates about what to do now. (GO TO 304A)

Decision Point 319A

Mildred Barnes and you have established a pleasant relationship during the past month. Mildred tells you: "You know why the policy was put in place, don't you? Billingsworth was facing heavy pressure from corporate to cut staff personnel. Justin (Fenwick) had been successful in protecting us until then, but when the axe fell, it was obvious that we could not continue to do all the product planning for manufacturing. You know we had been analyzing sales trends and setting manufacturing requirements accordingly. Well, the new policy was followed by a 22 percent cut in our staff. I was really lucky to survive this purge, believe me.

"Your group and Robinson's are the most hard-hit. But that's not really surprising. When we were doing the product forecasting, your two units were always the hardest to predict. Don't quote me, but you guys are getting screwed in all this. If you ask me, product scheduling is going toward shorter time frames. Now we are asking for projections one month ahead, but in the next few months with the computer models we are playing with, we should be able to shorten that to two weeks."

Later in the conversation she says, "If your people are having a rough time, there is one thing I could do--training. I've been teaching planning methods at a junior college, and I'd be more than willing to work with your salespeople to give them tools to use in figuring their product requirements."

As you are leaving Mildred's office, her secretary slips you a note that William Barstow, your friend in the corporate office, is trying to reach you by phone. You ask to use a phone in a deserted office and phone him. William begins: "Well, by now you've heard about the personnel cuts in Product Control in your division. I am certain that there will be no more personnel cuts. This quarter's earnings are up, and it now appears that we are about as lean as we can be. I've checked with some of my contacts, and it's clear that your policy problem is not without precedent in the corporation. Two other divisions in Atlanta and Trenton have their salespeople estimate product demand as part of the planning effort. Marketing managers there gave their salespeople extensive training in statistical estimation procedures, and each has access to a computer terminal so they can report deviations from the plan in real time."

What would you do now?

A. Since Bill Banquet is out of town, talk with Sterling Cartwright (his new administrative assistant). (GO TO 258B)

B. Talk with your peers about their experience with the new policy. (GO TO 280B)

C. Instruct your subordinates about what to do now. (GO TO 304A)

Decision Point 320A

In deciding to act before consulting your boss, you are running the risk of implementing a policy that he may want to oppose or to implement in a way that is beneficial to the goals of the sales force. Accordingly, your last decision was not correct. To remedy this situation, assume you met with Bill Banquet.

Your meeting with Bill Banquet was unexpectedly short. Bill confessed being distracted by the resignation that morning of Bob Jenson, his administrative assistant. Jenson was known to be looking for another position, but the timing of his decision seemed to have taken Banquet by surprise.

You: "Did you see the memo about the new product planning policy?"
Bill: "Yes, I've seen it. I wasn't consulted on it in advance, but I was told that it was coming. I know the salespeople are not going to like it."
You: "Not only that, but I doubt if my people can be expected to estimate their product needs within the 20 percent window. You know that our situation is different than the other groups."
Bill: "I know, I know. Listen, I've got to go. I've got to get over to Employee Relations to sign the forms for authorization to replace Jenson before my flight to Toledo. Look, do the best you can with the policy. I'll see you in a week."

What would you do now?

A. If you haven't done so yet, phone a friend of yours who works as a financial analyst at the corporate level (Blake-Emerson--the parent company) for his perspective on how to respond to this policy change. (GO TO 254A)

B. If you haven't done so yet, call your predecessor (now with another firm) for his perspective on how to handle this situation. (GO TO 315A)

C. Wait and bring this issue up at a weekly staff meeting of the sales managers (chaired by Bill Banquet). (GO TO 295A)

D. Diplomatically oppose the new policy as it applies to your unique circumstances. Petition for an exemption. (GO TO 253B)

E. Instruct your subordinates what to do about the new policy. (GO TO 291B)

Decision Point 321A

You decided to act before consulting either your boss or your peers. This was incorrect. Your peers would have given you information about how much power can be mobilized against the policy. Let's assume you talked with them, and start over from that point. All of them expressed irritability with the new policy, but none seemed put out enough to fight it. Don James' (Sales Manager--Pneumatic Products) opinion was typical: "I don't know if my people are good enough planners for us to make our estimates within the 20 percent window. I suspect that they are, but there's no telling. Right now, with the market so sour, most of our business is repeat business. My hunch is that simply keeping our estimates to the high side of historical figures should suffice; at least that's what I am telling my people to do. They're sure not going to like the extra paperwork, that I can assure you. But most of my sales engineers are still jittery about being laid off, so it shouldn't be too bad."

In choosing to act before consulting your boss, you were running the risk of implementing a policy that he may want to oppose. Let's also assume you met with Bill Banquet. Your meeting with Bill Banquet was unexpectedly short. Bill was distracted by the resignation that morning of Bob Jenson, his administrative assistant.

You: "Bill, did you see the memo about the new product planning policy?"
Bill: "Yes, I've seen it. I wasn't consulted on it in advance, but I was told that it was coming. I know the salespeople are not going to like it."
You: "Not only that, but I doubt if my people can be expected to estimate their product needs within the 20 percent window. You know that our situation is different than the other groups."
Bill: "I know, I know. Listen, I've got to go. I've got to get over to Employee Relations to sign the forms for authorization to replace Jenson before my flight to Toledo. Look, do the best you can with the policy. I'll see you in a week."

What would you do now?

A. If you haven't done so yet, phone a friend of yours who works as a financial analyst at the corporate level (Blake-Emerson, the parent company) for his perspective on how to respond to this policy change. (GO TO 254A)
B. If you haven't done so yet, call your predecessor (now with another firm) for his perspective on how to handle this situation. (GO TO 315A)
C. Wait and bring this issue up at a weekly staff meeting of the sales managers (chaired by Bill Banquet). (GO TO 295A)
D. Diplomatically oppose the new policy as it applies to your unique circumstances. Petition for an exemption. (GO TO 253B)
E. Instruct your subordinates what to do about the new policy. (GO TO 291B)

Decision Point 322A

You decide to transfer the problem employee and consult your boss on how to proceed further. You put through the paperwork and have the employee transferred to Lucy Morris's group. All goes well with the transfer, although Lucy tells you later that the employee in question expressed surprise at the transfer. Your boss is somewhat surprised when you tell her of your decision. She lets you know that her involvement in the issue is unnecessary.

Later Post and Hopkins approach you separately with other requests for your involvement in personnel problems. Clearly your decisive action has convinced them that if they "delegate upward," you will do their work for them.

Re-evaluate your last decision. Circle the #322A you just wrote in your flow diagram. Then move to the first uncircled step above this one in your flow diagram.

Decision Point 322B

You decided to call Personnel to find out what disciplinary options are available to you. You are told that the disciplinary sequence runs as follows:
   1st offense--written warning (filed with Personnel)
   2nd offense--second written warning (filed with Personnel and carrying an automatic one-day suspension without pay)
   3rd offense--termination
Personnel also informs you that chronic absenteeism is a relevant offense.
   What would you do?

A. Write Frank up for chronic absenteeism and leave a copy of the warning in an envelope on his desk for him to see when he comes in. (GO TO 332C)

B. Ask Personnel if there are other departments that need people with Frank's qualifications so you can transfer him there. (GO TO 342B)

C. Talk to some of Frank's co-workers to see if they have any idea what might be causing Frank's absences. (GO TO 336B)

D. Check with Frank's previous supervisor to see what his past attendance record was like. (GO TO 378B)

E. Do nothing. Wait until Frank returns and have a talk with him. (GO TO 388B)

F. Discuss the matter with your manager in order to get her advice and input in handling the matter. (GO TO 329A)

Decision Point 323A

You decided to include two additional pieces of information in your discussion with Betty:

   8. her self-rating on the performance appraisal form,
  10. the specific assessments others have made of her.

This is partially correct. It is perfectly acceptable to ask Betty to prepare a form on herself. However, it is inappropriate to share with her the specific assessments others have made of her performance. Not only does this violate confidences, but it simply emphasizes the multiple-boss situation she is working in. Now that you have decided what to cover (and what not to cover), you now must decide how to conduct the appraisal interview. The following strategies are common.
Which would you use?

A. Approach 1. (GO TO 398B)
 --Ask her to complete her own appraisal form before the meeting.
 --Put her at ease.
 --Examine the similarities and differences between your filled-out form and hers together.
 --Cover the five specific points you have identified previously, starting with a positive point, then a negative, etc.
 --Ascertain your role in her deficient performance.
 --Give her your summary rating and invite her reactions/inputs.
 --Review last year's development plan and jointly develop next year's plan.

B. Approach 2. (GO TO 355C)
 --Put her at ease.
 --Tell her the five strong and weak points of her performance (one positive, one negative, one positive, etc.), inviting her explanation.
 --Announce your summary rating.
 --Indicate elements you want in her next year's development plan after reviewing last year's plan.
 --Complete next year's development plan.

C. Approach 3. (GO TO 365A)
 --Put her at ease.
 --Tell her the five strong and weak points of her performance (one positive, one negative, one positive, etc.), inviting her reactions on each.
 --Try to ascertain how she thinks you might have supported her better given her weaknesses.
 --Give her your summary evaluation and solicit her reactions.
 --Review last year's development plan together.
 --Work together developing next year's development plan.

Decision Point 324A

Bill and this other person really hit it off. They become very close friends, but Bill continues to be rejected by his fellow group members. His co-workers now seem to feel that he lacks real interest in them, and they begin to give him the "cold shoulder."

Three weeks later, Bill sends you a memo indicating that he would like to transfer to the division where his new friend works. You are convinced that granting the transfer would hurt you, Bill, and ultimately the entire organization.

What would you do now?

A. Grant his request for the transfer because you don't think Bill can possibly earn the approval of his group under these circumstances. (GO TO 416B)

B. Discourage Bill from taking the transfer and urge him to withdraw his request. (GO TO 349A)

Decision Point 324B

You identified the following statement as a negative element of Betty's performance: "Betty often complains to others instead of problem solving with you." This is correct. First of all, it is a specific behavior rather than a trait. Second, you have reliable evidence on which to base this assessment. Barbara Mann and her clerk have both mentioned this tendency.

What other negative element of Betty's performance do you wish to feed back to her?

A. Betty is apparently careless. (GO TO 379B)

B. Betty doesn't use adequate diplomacy when dealing with clients. (GO TO 388A)

C. Betty is insensitive to the impact she has on others. (GO TO 356A)

D. Betty lacks attentiveness to details. (GO TO 378A)

E. Betty makes too many mistakes. (GO TO 414C)

F. Betty isn't smart enough to catch on quickly. (GO TO 393A)

G. Betty went over the head of a systems analyst to complain about the service she was getting--a violation of protocol. (GO TO 421C)

Decision Point 325A

In answer to your Spencer's question about nominating your boss for Manager of the Year, you respond, "No, I don't, but please don't ask me why."

He then says, "What do you mean? I have to ask you why you don't think your boss is qualified. In fact, I order you to tell me."

Now you are in a real bind. You detail the situation with your predecessor, and Spencer thanks you for your candor. The two of you finish lunch in almost complete silence and return to work. Two days later your boss calls you into her office. She tells you that she has heard of your encounter with Spencer and that as long as she works for the bank she will personally see to it that you receive the minimum in cost-of-living adjustments and no merit increases. Further, she threatens to make it very difficult for you in any way that she can.

Re-evaluate your last decision. Circle the #325A you just wrote in your flow diagram. Then move to the first uncircled step above this one in your flow diagram.

Decision Point 325B

Your daily meetings with Bill go well, but they are very time consuming. He begins bringing up even the most trivial issues, and in some cases, you even find yourself doing his work. The meetings grow in duration until one day, you cut it off and firmly suggest that Bill try to go it alone for a while. Cut loose, Bill flounders again, misses deadlines on important tasks, and completes unimportant ones with more "flair" than necessary. You conclude that Bill is not seeing the forest for the trees. What would you do now?

A. Indicate to Bill that it's probably best to stick it out. Bolster his sagging confidence and suggest that he talk to someone in the Solaris design team about a good reference book in aeronautics. (GO TO 355A)

B. Reassign Bill to one of the other assignments you had originally considered for him and replace him with another person. Bolster his sagging confidence by assuming full responsibility for his misplacement. (GO TO 339A)

C. Move another person from your department onto the Solaris team to relieve some of the pressure on Bill. Talk to K. C. Wong about the importance of pacing Bill so he can regain his confidence, but not at the expense of meeting Solaris milestones. (GO TO 391B)

D. Meet with K. C. Wong and delegate responsibility to him for a more effective breaking in of Bill. Tell K. C. that you don't want him to sacrifice the objectives of the Solaris project, but that you think Bill deserves more of his time. (GO TO 401B)

Decision Point 326A

Your boss does not respond directly. Instead she turns the conversation back to you and your new responsibilities. This rebuff makes you more nervous about *NET*.

What would you say when there is a pause in the discussion?

A. So she won't be surprised, inform her that the *NET* program will be greeted with a great deal of resistance. (GO TO 382B)

B. Ask your boss for the background on the *NET* program. (GO TO 396B)

C. Clarify just what your boss means by "do the best you can" to improve quality. (GO TO 366B)

D. Try to persuade Karen that *NET* is a bad idea. (GO TO 421B)

E. Ask you boss for her assessment of your predecessor. (GO TO 390B)

Decision Point 326B

You decided to let K. C. Wong handle this situation. K. C. feels the best thing to do is tell Bill that Sam needs practice dealing with problems like this and that Bill should stay out of it next time. Bill disagrees strongly with K. C.'s position and storms out of his office muttering something about loyalty.

Bill enters your office the next day still hot over the issue. After settling him down, what would you do?

A. Indicate how he could have better assessed the situation between Sam and the client in terms of Sam's fundamental weaknesses, K. C.'s responsibilities in this instance, and the attributes of the client involved. (GO TO 414B)

B. Inform Bill that Sam needs practice bailing himself out of situations like this, and that Bill should not get involved in Sam's development. (GO TO 332B)

C. Tell Bill that clients should be allowed to say whatever they want, even if it is uncomplimentary, and that one important role of a Venus employee is to be a flak-catcher. (GO TO 400B)

D. Tell Bill that his actions in this situation are irresponsible, and that you cannot tolerate any more difficulties of this nature. (GO TO 368B)

Decision Point 327A

Frank Wilson has a severe personal problem. He is absent on Mondays not by choice, but because of factors largely outside his control. Under these circumstances, it is not surprising that Frank is irritable in response to anything but sensitive treatment.

Had you given Frank reason to confide in you, he would have told you: "The problem is my wife. We just got together again after we had been separated for eight months. She found out that she has an incurable kidney disease, and she wanted to come back on account of Eric, that's our son. Anyway, she has dialysis treatments three times a week, Mondays, Wednesdays, and Fridays. The toughest day of the week is Sunday, since she's on her second day without dialysis, and her body chemistry is all off. She gets real irritable, and she, Eric, and I always get in a fight over one thing or another. Mostly, it's Eric. He blames me for our first breakup, and when Barbara is weak, he just piles it on. The last two Sundays he just walked out.

"Last Monday I had to bail him out of jail all the way over in Clay County. It was 9:00 a.m. before we got home. Now that he's back at home without a driver's license, Sundays are going to mighty tough. If he acts up, Barbara is going to need me more than ever, and her dialysis appointment isn't until noon Mondays. I've talked with her doctor about her Sunday mood problems, but he says he doesn't want to give her any more drugs."

If you were sitting across from Frank when he told you this, how would you react?

A. "Well, it's real helpful to know what's been troubling you. Now, then, you must realize that I am being held responsible for production, so to be fair to the company, I am going to have to give you a formal warning on your attendance. I will pull it from your file if you are able to work the next four Mondays in a row. Otherwise, I am going to have to give you a second warning, and you know what that means." (GO TO 372A)

B. "I understand. It sounds to me that you realize how important it is to improve your attendance record. I know now that you have got a tricky problem on your hands. I just want you to know that you've got my support. Do the best you can with your absences, and I'll cover for you as long as I can." (GO TO 332A)

C. "I think I understand your situation, but you know my situation as well. I am getting pressure for production, and your absences are troublesome. We need to work out a plan that will result in a level of production that is your fair share. Do you have any ideas that we might put to use?" (GO TO 368A)

D. "I know someone who is a professional family counselor. He's a neighbor of mine, and he is really good. Here's his phone number. If you need help with this thing, you should see a professional." (GO TO 389B)

Decision Point 328A

You decide to do nothing right now about the different information you have received from your peers. You invite your new Leads in one at a time to get to know them better. First, you speak with Daryl Peters, your Unit 3 Lead. Your meeting with him goes very well. You discover that he is a very cooperative guy, and you find his approach to people problems very similar to your own. You suspect that he is "buttering you up" a bit, but you sort of enjoy that treatment.

Your meeting with Lucy Morris (Unit 1) is more challenging. After an exchange of pleasantries, she asks if you will allow her to do something that your predecessor had opposed. She outlines the issue as follows:

"Is it okay if we rearrange the accounts so we balance out the customer-phone calls? The way we do it now is by account number, and that means that some of us make 50 phone calls a day and others three. That's really not fair and it causes real morale problems. Don (your predecessor) said that having each clerk responsible for a sequence of account numbers made it quicker to spot errors, but that's hogwash. It just takes a second longer to look up who's on what account. What do you say, can we make the change?"

Lucy's proposal sounds fine. It has nothing whatsoever to do with *NET*, and while you never had this sort of problem in your old unit, you can understand how an uneven distribution of customer contacts might result in real morale problems. What would you do now?

A. Ask her to be more specific about the advantages and disadvantages of the change. (GO TO 361A)

B. Since the change sounds reasonable, give her the green light. (GO TO 419B)

C. Tell her that you will consider her request and get back to her. (GO TO 373A)

D. Tell her that with *NET* coming, you would like to wait a bit before making any changes that might have an impact on quality. (GO TO 330B)

Decision Point 328B

Bill's relationship with this new person provides him with an excellent anchor for completing his integration. Through this relationship, Bill and his wife learn how to become active in the rural education district. Bill purchases a four-wheel drive vehicle at the urging of his new friend, and his commuting problems soon disappear. **Congratulations!** You have just completed the New Employee Interactive Case.

Decision Point 329A

You have decided to discuss the problem with your manager before taking any other action. She says: "No, I don't know Wilson, but I do know that we are behind on our schedule. I just got out of a staff meeting, and people were all over my case. It was embarrassing! I don't care what you do, but get some life into that team of yours, and get them back on schedule. It looks like we're going to have to use more overtime again. That is really playing hell with my budget."

What would you do now?

A. Talk to some of Frank's co-workers to see if they have any idea what might be causing Frank's absences. (GO TO 336B)
B. Check with Frank's previous supervisor to see what his past attendance record was like. (GO TO 378B)
C. Do nothing. Wait until Frank returns and have a talk with him. (GO TO 388B)
D. Call the Personnel Department to see what disciplinary options are open to you. (GO TO 322B)
E. Call the Personnel Department to see if there are other departments that need people with Frank's qualifications so you can transfer him there. (GO TO 342B)
F. Write Frank up for chronic absenteeism and leave a copy of the warning in an envelope on his desk for him to see when he comes in. (GO TO 332C)

Decision Point 329B

You have just lost a potentially valuable member of the organization because you protected him too long from more challenging assignments. As a result, Bill delivered you an ultimatum that you apparently were unwilling to accept. Bill's resignation creates significant political problems for you. K. C. Wong complains bitterly over your treatment of Bill, and you hear through the grapevine that the division manager is very displeased that you lost him. It appears that he had personally stuck his neck out to get Bill's rather high salary offer approved. Under these circumstances, you would have been better to have gracefully given in to his ultimatum (You could have made the assignment temporary to save face).

Re-evaluate your last decision. Circle the #329B you just wrote in your flow diagram. Then move to the first uncircled step above this one in your flow diagram.

Decision Point 330A

You decided to cover Betty's progress on knowing company procedures first. This is correct. The reason is that she underevaluated herself on this dimension, and covering this subject first begins the interview on a very positive note.

You tell Betty that you are very pleased that she has made so much progress in getting to know company procedures, and that you think she has been too harsh on herself on her form. She thanks you, and tells you that "it is a miracle" that her progress has been so positive given all the problems she has been having with the computer system.

At this point what would you say?

A. "Okay, let's talk about those problems." (GO TO 404A)

B. "Yes, I am generally familiar with the problems you are referring to, and we'll get to that in a minute. I just want to make sure you hear me when I tell you that your performance on this dimension is really exceptional, and I truly appreciate your progress." (GO TO 345B)

C. "I know all about your computer problems. I agree that your progress is excellent given your frustrations." (GO TO 419A)

Decision Point 330B

Lucy seems content with your assessment that waiting for *NET* makes sense. Yet the more you wait, the more your peers' comments weigh on you. Recall that they gave you information that
 (1) your boss has a very low opinion of the quality of your group's performance;
 (2) your boss may be under pressure to make *NET* work;
 (3) *NET* seems to be in for some major implementation problems.

On several occasions Leo Leiter repeated his statement that your group's quality was increasingly disappointing to your boss. Now that you have staked your reputation with your subordinates on the success of *NET*, Leiter's statements are beginning to get to you.

What would you do to deal with your feelings of increasing tension about your boss's appraisal of your group?

A. Return to Curtin and Evanston to see if they think your group is considered by your boss to have the poorest quality record. (GO TO 411A)

B. Return to your boss to see if she really does consider your group to have the poorest quality performance. (GO TO 371B)

Decision Point 331A

You invite Frank into your office, and Frank explodes into a verbal tirade: "I'm really mad about this. I've put in three years in this damn company, and I certainly deserve to be told to my face if there's a problem! Okay, okay, so I've been absent. I've got a problem at home, okay? You just get off my back, or so help me . . . " You interrupt him at this point.

What would you say in this situation?

A. "Wait a minute, Frank, who do you think you are talking to? I'm writing you up for insubordination. Now get out of here and get back to work!" (GO TO 383A)

B. "Frank, I can see that you're pretty angry, but I think you'd better settle down a little before you say something you'll regret later. I'll tell you what, why don't you sit here in my office and cool down while I give Janet some paperwork. Help yourself to some coffee, and I'll be back in about 20 minutes." (GO TO 357A)

C. "Okay, Frank, take it easy. I gave you the warning because with our production schedules, we just can't afford to support people who are absent all the time. What's this about a problem at home?" (GO TO 348B)

Decision Point 331B

Your conversation with Fern ends, and you both return to work. Fern's stories disturb you greatly, and you decide to look into the records to see whether there is any evidence of any other impropriety. You find several entries in the supervisory budget that don't add up. You are unsure of just how entries should add up, and you consult your supervisory procedures. This leads you to the conclusion that, at best, your predecessor committed errors in judgment regarding administrative procedures, and at worst, petty larceny. Three items in last year's budget indicate that $600 is unaccounted for. After Fern's comments, you tend to believe the latter.

What would you do with this information?

A. Report the matter to the budgetary authority, the Department of Administrative Services. (GO TO 363A)

B. Talk with your boss about what you have found. (GO TO 377A)

C. Speak off the record with several of your peers to find out if this sort of budget imbalance is common. (GO TO 370C)

Decision Point 332A

You have urged Frank to do the best he could to improve his attendance habits. As a result, Frank is absent for the following three Mondays, and you are left with no choice but to dismiss him. This causes severe problems because of declining production levels, co-worker dissatisfaction, and what you think may be the feeling among your people that you have been unfair. Your boss is growing less and less satisfied with your work.

Apparently, the method you chose of trying to get Frank to correct his attendance habits did not work. Re-evaluate your decision. Circle the #332A you just wrote in your flow diagram. Then go back in your flow diagram to the first uncircled number above this step.

Decision Point 332B

Bill strongly disagrees with your statement, and, in a rare show of temper, leaves your office and slams the door behind him. You call him in the next day to clear the air.

What would you say now?

A. Indicate how he could have better assessed this particular situation in terms of Sam's fundamental weaknesses, Bob Blair's responsibilities, and the particular client involved. (GO TO 414B)

B. Tell Bill that clients should be allowed to say whatever they want even if it is uncomplimentary and that one important role of a Venus employee is to be a flak-catcher. (GO TO 400B)

Decision Point 332C

The next morning, when you arrive for work, you find Frank waiting outside your office with the warning in his hand. He looks angry. He belligerently says, "What the hell is this? I really want to talk this over with you now!"

You resent the tone he is taking, and you feel that you have been careful to follow all disciplinary guidelines.

What would you do at this point?

A. Politely but firmly tell Frank that the warning covers everything that needs to be said and suggest that you both get to work. (GO TO 354C)

B. Tell Frank that since he feels so strongly about this you will talk to him now. (GO TO 331A)

C. Arrange to meet Frank later that morning. (GO TO 357A)

Decision Point 333A

Bill apologizes for being so aggressive with the client and goes back to work. Two weeks later, you overhear Bill making disparaging remarks about several design engineers who "think they know more about control systems" than his project team. Later that day, you hear that Bill engaged in verbal bantering with one of the design engineers in the cafeteria. The bantering escalated into name calling and ended when Bill called one of the designers "a jerk who should design with a crayon."

Fearing that this attitude may endanger the necessary work relationship between the team and the designers, you decide to intervene.

What would you say to Bill?

A. Indicate how he could have better handled the situation in the cafeteria in terms of necessary good relationships between the designers and his team, the responsibility he has to deal with such conflicts in a more diplomatic way, and the particular attributes of the design group involved. (GO TO 414B)

B. Tell Bill that he should let K. C. Wong deal with the designers for a while until things cool off. (GO TO 337B)

C. Verify the story of the cafeteria incident with K. C. Wong before calling Bill in. (As it is now 4:30 p.m., this will necessitate a one-day delay.) (GO TO 393B)

Decision Point 333B

In discussing Frank's absences with him, which general approach would you be most likely to take?

A. Tell him that your boss is on your back for more productivity, and ask for his help in correcting his attendance problem. (GO TO 370B)

B. Explain the necessity of good attendance if production goals are to be met and point out to him how much his attendance is adversely affecting production. Urge him to do better. (GO TO 332A)

C. Mention to him in as positive a way as you can that if he doesn't improve you will be forced to give him a written warning. (GO TO 341A)

D. Ask him what difficulty he is having. (GO TO 360B)

E. Ask him if he is feeling better today. (GO TO 362A)

Decision Point 334A

You return to Curtin and Evanston to see if they agree with Leo Leiter that Karen considers your group to be a quality problem. Both of them deny that Karen feels that way; in fact, Brian Curtin tells you that he doesn't know how your predecessor did so well on quality since he was such a "second-class" supervisor. Evanston tells you not to listen to Leiter about such things: "He likes to stir things up."

That behind you, you can now concentrate on your subordinates. Your third interview is with James Hopkins and Terrence Post (recall that Post is the Lead for an "elite" group who was disturbed that he wasn't given your promotion). Due to a conflict in schedules, you must interview them at the same time.

After some discussion, they detail a human relations problem they are having. It seems that one of the operators is receiving some harassment from a number of the others. The operator in question has recently "given up her three children" and left her husband to live with a foreign man who is in the U.S. illegally. The other employees consider this morally reprehensible and are giving her "the silent treatment" and not cooperating with her. Although the operator in question is in Post's unit, the employees involved in the harassment come from Hopkins' unit as well. Although the two Leads do not name names, they share the suspicion with you that a number of "troublemakers" may be behind the situation. They also suggest that you transfer the employee in question and report the matter to your boss.

How would you proceed?

A. Transfer the problem employee and consult your boss on how to proceed further. (GO TO 322A)

B. Talk with your boss about this matter before taking any further action. (GO TO 403B)

C. Tell your two Leads that they should handle the situation as they see fit, but that you are not in favor of the transfer except as a last resort. Let them know that you will assist them in handling the situation any way you can. (GO TO 344A)

D. Interview all the operators who are harassing the operator with the intention of modifying their behavior. (GO TO 408A)

E. Talk with the operator who is being harassed to determine her point of view. (GO TO 367B)

F. Find out if the situation is causing real performance problems. (GO TO 385A)

Decision Point 335A

You decided not to ask Bill for his assignment preference. What assignment would you give him?

A. *Assignment 1*. Junior Control Engineer, Dart Project. Join a team of four headed by Bob Blair to test a ballistics control system for a Dart missile. The Dart is like other systems developed previously, except that the new control system requires several standards never required before. Smythe's senior thesis dealt with ballistics control systems. Estimated probability of making a net contribution to the team = 60 percent. Value to Bill's development if he is personally successful = 40 points out of 100. (GO TO 402A)

B. *Assignment 2*. Junior Control Engineer, Solaris Project. Join a team of three headed by K. C. Wong to test the propulsion control system for a Solaris booster. Wong is very enthusiastic about Bill joining the team. The Solaris project will require a unique control system that has never been implemented before. The project is presently behind schedule because of the novelty of its design. It would offer a fantastic learning opportunity for any junior engineer. Estimated probability of making a net contribution to the team = 30 percent. Value to Bill's development if he is personally successful = 80 points out of 100. (GO TO 343A)

C. *Assignment 3*. Junior Control Engineer, Systems Test Group. Act as your administrative assistant. Perform several studies regarding planning and scheduling in preparation for upcoming budget negotiations. While this assignment has only a modest technical component, it is a great way for Bill to learn the inner workings of your department and may allow him to find his own technical place in the group. Estimated probability of making a net contribution to the group = 100 percent. Value to Bill's development if he is personally successful = 20 points out of 100. (GO TO 394A)

D. *Assignment 4*. Junior Control Engineer, Systems Test Group, and Member, Micascope Divisional Task Force. Join a task force of seven members conducting a feasibility study of Micascope, a laser-refracting targeting system. The task force is chaired by the assistant to the divisional manager. This assignment would give Bill a chance to work with some of the most dynamic members in the division. The proposed study is somewhat controversial, with some members committed to manufacturing and some against it. The division manager is said to favor manufacturing, but he has agreed to "let the chips fall where they may." While he handpicked the members of the task force from other departments, his confidence in you permitted him to ask you to appoint the department member of your choice. Since all of the other members of your group are busy with project work, Bill seems like a natural. Estimated probability of making a net contribution to the task force = 50 percent. Value to Bill's development if he is personally successful = 80 points out of 100. (GO TO 382C)

Decision Point 336A

Your statement is inappropriate because it conveys a climate that is entirely too informal. While you want to put Betty at ease, you don't want to give her the impression that you don't take it very seriously. In particular, your statement "rather than a chance for me to make firm statements" implies that you are not going to commit yourself during the interview.

Re-evaluate your last decision. Circle the #336A you just wrote in your flow diagram. Then go back in your flow diagram to the first uncircled number above this step.

Decision Point 336B

You decide to ask others in your group if they know what Frank's problem might be. You go to his co-workers and ask if they think they know why he is missing so much work. No one seems to be willing to discuss the matter with you. You finally ask one of your newest employees if she knows anything. She says that a friend of hers who works in data processing told her that he saw Frank and some woman in a car headed out of town that morning (Monday). Further, her friend told her that Frank looked drunk. You know that your company has a good alcoholism counseling program. What would you do now?

A. Check with Frank's previous supervisor to see what his past attendance record was like. (GO TO 378B)

B. Call Frank aside upon his return and have a talk with him. (GO TO 333B)

C. Discuss the matter with your manager in order to get her advice and input in handling the situation. (GO TO 329A)

D. Call the Personnel Department to see what disciplinary options are open to you. (GO TO 322B)

E. Call the Personnel Department to see if there are other departments that need people with Frank's qualifications so you can transfer him there. (GO TO 342B)

F. Instruct Frank to report to the company counseling center when he returns to work since you don't feel competent to cope with his drinking. (GO TO 373C)

G. Write Frank up for chronic absenteeism and leave a copy of the warning in an envelope on his desk for him to see when he comes in. (GO TO 332C)

Decision Point 337A

You confront Post and Hopkins about what you have learned. They look at one another rather sheepishly, and it is clear that this was a test of your supervisory skills. You tell them that you don't consider any further action warranted and ask them to return to work. As they are leaving, you ask Post to wait in your office for a minute. You then privately tell him that you expect no repetition of this sort of thing. This was a tricky situation, and you handled it well.

Your next appointment is with LeRoy Jackson. He is the Lead who took your old position with Unit 2. The two of you have a delightful conversation. He was one of the people you used to play cards with at lunch before your promotion. At the end of your conversation, LeRoy tells you that some of the people in your old unit have been asking why you aren't playing cards with them at lunch anymore. What would you say?

A. "Well, now that I am a supervisor, I don't think it is appropriate for me to do that anymore." (GO TO 372B)

B. "I'll be there tomorrow. I wouldn't want the old card game to go on without me." (GO TO 417B)

C. "I'll come around at lunch from time to time, don't worry." (GO TO 374A)

D. "I'll tell you what. I have to spread my lunchtime evenly among all the units now. Tell the group that should mean that they'll have to endure my presence about once a month." (GO TO 392B)

Decision Point 337B

Bill discusses the situation with his team leader, and the two of them agree that Bill should "stay out of the way" of the design group. In spite of this distance, the designers retaliate for Bill's indiscretion by taking the incident up the chain of command to a common manager. Top management sends you a pointed memo that says in effect, "Keep that kid of yours in tow, or else!"

While taking a coffee break in the cafeteria, one of the design engineers talks loudly about top management's reprimand so that Bill can overhear it. Bill flies off the handle again and threatens to punch the engineer in the nose. Bill's project leader breaks up the confrontation and takes Bill aside for a scolding. Bill resigns the next morning.

Re-evaluate your last decision. Circle the #337B you just wrote in your flow diagram. Then move to the first uncircled step above this one in your flow diagram.

Decision Point 338A

"The problem is my wife. We just got together again after she and I had been separated for eight months. She found out that she has an incurable kidney disease, and she wanted to come back on account of Eric, that's our son. Anyway, she has dialysis treatments three times a week, Mondays, Wednesdays, and Fridays. The toughest day of the week is Sunday, since she's on her second day without dialysis, and her body chemistry is all off. She gets real irritable, and she, Eric, and I always get in a fight over one thing or another. Mostly, it's Eric. He blames me for our first breakup, and when Barbara is weak, he just piles it on. The last two Sundays he just walked out.

"Last Monday I had to bail him out of jail all the way over in Clay County. It was 9:00 a.m. before we got home. Now that he's back at home without a driver's license, Sundays are going to be mighty tough. If he acts up, Barbara is going to need me more than ever, and her dialysis appointment isn't until noon Mondays. I've talked with her doctor about her Sunday mood problems, but he says he doesn't want to give her any more drugs."

At this point what would you say?

A. "Well, it's real helpful to know what's been troubling you. Now, then, you must realize that I am being held responsible for production, so to be fair to the company, I am going to have to give you a formal warning on your attendance. I will pull it from your file if you are able to work the next four Mondays in a row. Otherwise, I am going to have to give you a second warning, and you know what that means." (GO TO 372A)

B. "I understand. It sounds to me that you realize how important it is to improve your attendance record. I know now that you have got a tricky problem on your hands. I just want you to know that you've got my support. Do the best you can with your absences, and I'll cover for you as long as I can." (GO TO 332A)

C. "I think I understand your situation, but you know my situation as well. I am getting pressure for production, and your absences are troublesome. We need to work out a plan that will result in a level of production that is your fair share. Do you have any ideas that we might put to use?" (GO TO 368A)

D. "I know someone who is a professional family counselor. He's a neighbor of mine, and he is really good. Here's his phone number. If you need help with this thing, you should see a professional." (GO TO 389B)

Decision Point 339A

What assignment would you give him?

A. *Assignment 1.* Junior Control Engineer, Dart Project. Join a team of four members to test a ballistics control system for a Dart missile. The team is headed by Bob Blair. The Dart missile is like other systems developed previously, except that the new control system requires several standards never required before. Smythe's senior thesis in school dealt with ballistics control systems. Estimated probability of making a net contribution to the team = 60 percent. Value to Bill's development if he is personally successful = 40 points out of 100. (GO TO 402A)

B. *Assignment 2.* Junior Control Engineer, Systems Test Group. Act as your administrative assistant. Perform several studies regarding planning and scheduling in preparation for upcoming budget negotiations. While this assignment has only a modest technical component, it is a great way for Bill to learn the inner workings of your department and may allow him to find his own technical place in the group. Estimated probability of making a net contribution to the group = 100 percent. Value to Bill's development if he is personally successful = 20 points out of 100. (GO TO 394A)

C. *Assignment 4.* Junior Control Engineer, Systems Test Group, and Member, Micascope Divisional Task Force. Join a task force of seven members conducting a manufacturing feasibility study of Micascope, a laser-refracting targeting system. The task force is chaired by the assistant to the divisional manager. This assignment would give Bill a chance to work with some of the most dynamic members of the division. The feasibility study proposed is somewhat controversial, with some task force members committed to manufacturing, and some dead set against it. The division manager is said to favor manufacturing, but he has agreed to "let the chips fall where they may." While he handpicked the members of the task force from other departments, his confidence in you permitted him to ask you to appoint the department member of your choice. Since all of the other members of your group are busy with project work, Bill seems like a natural. Estimated probability of making a net contribution to the task force = 50 percent. Value to Bill's development if he is personally successful = 80 points out of 100. (GO TO 382C)

Decision Point 340A

You decide to confront your boss with your feelings about her dealings with your predecessor's apparent impropriety. When you tell her your concerns, she offers the following explanation:

"Well, Donald [Scott] asked me not to say anything, but I can see that you are really troubled. You mustn't tell anyone what I am about to tell you. [You nod appropriately.] Donald is dying of brain cancer. Only three other people in the company know, William Spencer, Terrence Post (the head of your Unit 6), and myself. He experiences periodic lapses of memory and doesn't recall anything about the $600 you discovered. He may have taken it, I don't know, but there is really no point in pursuing it. He is in a position now where he will do no harm to anyone since he has no budgetary authority. Post thinks that he spent the $600 on painting the offices of the Leads. You probably remember that your office was painted. Well, no one in the company can trace how he paid for that. He either paid for it with his own personal funds or with the help of the $600. The surprising thing is that the debit in facilities is for $1500, so even with the $600, we don't know where the other $900 came from."

Your boss then changes the subject to her upcoming vacation, a trip to Yellowstone Park. She will be away for three weeks. You give her your best wishes for a truly enjoyable vacation. Your doubts aside now, you draft a letter to William Spencer. It is the best prose you are capable of.

A week after she is gone, you receive a memo addressed to all supervisors from your boss dated the first of the month that reminds you of a policy that preceded you as a supervisor, but that required all your operators to audit their reports before submitting them. Your peers had informed you that this policy was unworkable and had been ignored for the past three years. It would require supervisors to spend about 14 hours per week assembling data that had never been used in the past. Moreover, such an effort on your part would raise all sorts of questions on the part of your staff that would be very difficult to answer satisfactorily. Your investigation also reveals that this policy has nothing whatsoever to do with the *NET* effort.

Since your boss is gone now, you have no way of ascertaining whether she in fact meant for the policy to be enforced for the first time. You check with your peers, and they are unanimous that someone in the office of Budget Control has simply redated an old memo. You now face the choice of either opposing a memo signed by your boss or investing 14 hours a week in an activity that you don't believe is worthwhile. What would you do?

  A. Call your boss on vacation, tracking her down in the various campgrounds in Yellowstone. (GO TO 406B)
  B. Fight the appropriate staff group of the company on the grounds that an investment of 14 hours of your time is not warranted. (GO TO 386A)
  C. Comply with the policy with the idea that if your boss returns to discover a problem, she will be very displeased. (GO TO 389A)

Decision Point 341A

You have decided that this situation is best dealt with by using the system of discipline used in the company. However, it doesn't work in this case. Frank continues his habit of Monday absences through the final warning and he ultimately is terminated. Now you face the job of recruiting a replacement and dealing with the growing dissatisfaction of your boss and your people.

It is not that formal discipline systems like this one are poorly designed, it is that they must be administered carefully. Careful administration means moving beyond enforcing the relationship between undesired behavior and punitive outcomes.

Re-evaluate your decision. Circle the #341A you just wrote in your flow diagram. Then go back in your flow diagram to the first uncircled number above this step.

Decision Point 341B

Your coaching of Bill pays off to some extent. He becomes more assertive in asking for help, and his once cluttered desk is more orderly. However, he still has apparently not grasped the sense of priorities he needs to have to manage his own work well. You even notice that he is taking more work home at times when there is a relative lull in the project.

What would you do now?

A. Take time to remind others in your group of the importance of helping Bill adapt to his job. (GO TO 399B)

B. Agree to meet daily with Bill to coach him on how to handle the specific, day-to-day problems that come up in his work. (GO TO 359B)

C. Remind Bill of his agreement that he would take initiative if he had questions or was having difficulties. Indicate that he will not succeed unless he begins to ask questions, tells Bob Blair of his problems, and takes control of his own situation. (GO TO 407A)

D. Begin to give Bill a detailed account of how to contend with the challenges and problems of his work. Agree to meet with him in three days to review his progress and advise him on new situations. (GO TO 362B)

E. Meet with Bob Blair and delegate responsibility to him for a more effective breaking in of Bill. Tell Bob that you don't want him to sacrifice the objectives of the Dart test system, but that you think Bill deserves more of his time. (GO TO 381A)

Decision Point 342A

You identified the following statement as a positive element of Betty's performance: "Betty's volume of output is large." This is correct. The only negative bit of information you have on this score is Milt Strong's evaluation form and it probably suffers from a negative halo effect. What other statement do you think reflects a positive piece of feedback?

A. Betty sticks up for the project. (GO TO 403A)

B. Betty has demonstrated initiative. (GO TO 360A)

C. Betty's knowledge of procedures has improved markedly. (GO TO 419C)

D. Betty has worked well under pressure. (GO TO 383B)

E. Betty is conscientious. (GO TO 348A)

Decision Point 342B

You have decided to ask Personnel about the possibilities of transferring Frank. Personnel tells you that there is an opening in the Research Department for someone with Frank's qualifications. Since the position offers more money, you conclude that Frank would probably welcome the change. Certainly, the pressure on productivity is not nearly as great there as it is in your department.

What would you do at this juncture?

A. Talk to Frank about the transfer when he returns. (GO TO 359A)

B. Talk with some of Frank's co-workers to see if they have any idea what might be causing Frank's absences. (GO TO 336B)

C. Check with Frank's previous supervisor to see what his past attendance was like. (GO TO 378B)

D. Call Frank aside upon his return without the intention of discussing the transfer. (GO TO 333B)

E. Discuss the matter with your manager in order to get her advice and input in handling his absenteeism. (GO TO 329A)

F. Call Personnel to see what disciplinary options are open to you. (GO TO 322B)

Decision Point 343A

It is one month later, and from what you've heard, Bill is not working out. In fact, the whole Solaris team effort has failed to live up to your expectations. Originally enthusiastic about Bill, Wong has expressed grave reservations about whether Bill was ready for this assignment. He even suggested that Bill be replaced by a more experienced person so the team can get back on track.

You review the technical reports, and this confirms your suspicion that the Solaris system is indeed a complex one, and that perhaps more tried-and-proven solutions should be attempted, rather than the novel approach that excited Wong so much in the first place. You call Bill into your office, and after an exchange of pleasantries, the following conversation takes place:

You: "Bill, what's your assessment of the problems of the Solaris project?"
Bill: "I don't know. Everything we try just seems to blow up on us. The booster is really hairy and we can't seem to figure out a way to monitor thrust parameters."
You: "And how do you feel about your contribution?"
Bill: "I've talked to K. C. about this, and I think I'm way over my head. I just wish I'd taken more course work in aeronautics, because some of the properties of this system put me in deep yoga."
You: "What do you mean?"
Bill: "The other two guys really know their stuff, and they've been real nice in giving me tests to run that are easy, but I just don't think I'm making much more of a contribution than a technical assistant. And, you know, I don't even think I'm a good technical assistant. I'm botching even the simplest runs. It's not fair to them."

What would you do now?

A. Indicate to Bill that it's probably best to stick it out. Bolster his sagging confidence and suggest that he talk to someone in the Solaris design team about a good reference book in aeronautics. (GO TO 355A)
B. Reassign Bill to one of the other assignments you had originally considered for him, and replace him with another member. Bolster his sagging confidence by assuming responsibility for the misplacement. (GO TO 339A)
C. Agree to meet daily with Bill to coach him on how to handle the specific, day-to-day problems that come up in his work. (GO TO 325B)
D. Move another person from your department onto the Solaris project team to relieve some of the pressure on Bill. Talk to K. C. Wong about the importance of pacing Bill so he can regain his confidence, but not at the expense of meeting Solaris milestones. (GO TO 391B)
E. Meet with K. C. Wong and delegate responsibility to him for a more effective breaking in of Bill. Tell K. C. that you don't want him to sacrifice the objectives of the Solaris system, but that you think Bill deserves more of his time. (GO TO 401B)

Decision Point 344A

Your next appointment is with LeRoy Jackson. He is the Lead who took your old position with Unit 2. The two of you have a delightful conversation. He was one of the people you used to play cards with at lunch before your promotion.

At the end of your conversation, LeRoy tells you that some of the people in your old unit have been asking why you aren't playing cards with them at lunch anymore. What would you say?

A. "Well, now that I am a supervisor, I don't think it is appropriate for me to do that anymore." (GO TO 372B)

B. "I'll be there tomorrow. I wouldn't want the old card game to go on without me." (GO TO 417B)

C. "I'll come around at lunch from time to time, don't worry." (GO TO 374A)

D. "I'll tell you what. I have to spread my lunchtime evenly among all the units now. Tell the group that should mean that they'll have to endure my presence about once a month." (GO TO 392B)

Decision Point 344B

She apologizes for this tendency and agrees to work on that in the future. You proceed to end the feedback portion of the interview by praising her initiative. She accepts this graciously, and you feel that you have covered everything that you wanted to. How would you end this portion of the discussion?

A. Summarize what you have said. Ask her if she wants to bring up any other aspect of her performance that she wants feedback on. Ask her if she has any further questions before you move into the development plan for next year. (GO TO 385B)

B. Reiterate the need for her to control her frustrations. Ask her if she has any further questions before you move into the development plan for next year. (GO TO 401A)

C. Give Betty her summary evaluation. Ask her if she has any other questions before you move into the development plan for next year. (GO TO 418A)

D. Ask her if she has any further questions. Answer them. Give her the summary evaluation. Move into the discussion of her development plan for next year. (GO TO 420A)

Decision Point 345A

You and Bill have a problem-solving discussion. The two of you identify several alternative responses to his commuting problem and his school problem. You give him several suggestions (carpooling; transferring the children to a suburban private school). Two months pass and Bill's performance goes down again. At his performance appraisal interview, you express concern over his declining effort, and Bill breaks down. He and his wife have separated. A "city girl," she never fully adapted to the country life-style. She apparently made few friends and suffered from "cabin fever." Apparently, your problem-solving meeting with Bill didn't go far enough to address his problems of integrating his personal life with his career.

Re-evaluate your last decision. Circle the #345A you just wrote in your flow diagram. Then move to the first uncircled step above this one in your flow diagram.

Decision Point 345B

She thanks you again for the compliment. You then open the discussion of her problems with the computer system. She speaks with both anger and passion about her problems. She tells you that she had been working real hard this past year to make up to Milt Strong for the problems she had created for him the year before last. She knows that he was very embarrassed by the incident involving the misformatted quality control document, but she only used the word processing system at his insistence. You then acknowledge how frustrating that must have been.

Now you need to give Betty a negative piece of feedback. You decide you should feed back to her the criticism that she often complains to others instead of problem solving with you.

How would you approach this topic?

A. "You know, Betty, job frustrations are common in your position, but it is important that you find outlets for expressing your frustrations that do not disrupt the work of others. Take the problems you had with the computer system. I would prefer if you came to me with these problems instead of others." (GO TO 356C)

B. "Betty, you've really got to get control of yourself on problems like the computer issue. From now on, instead of complaining to others about it, why not come to me for help?" (GO TO 396A)

C. "This brings me to an area where performance improvement is warranted. Barbara Mann tells me that you have been complaining to her about your computer problems and that that is disruptive. We just can't have that going on. If you have a problem with your work, see me, don't bother others with it." (GO TO 384B)

Decision Point 346A

You decided to include attention to Betty's career plans as part of your appraisal of her performance. This is perfectly acceptable. Now that you have decided what to cover (and what not to cover), you now must decide how to conduct the appraisal interview. The following strategies are common.
Which would you use?

   A. Approach 1. (GO TO 398B)
   ---Ask her to fill out a performance appraisal form on herself before the meeting.
   ---Put her at ease.
   ---Examine together the similarities and differences between your filled-out form and hers.
   ---Cover the five specific points you have identified previously, starting with a positive point, then a negative, etc.
   ---Ascertain your role in her deficient performance.
   ---Give her your summary rating and invite her reactions/inputs.
   ---Go over last year's development plan and jointly develop next year's plan.

   B. Approach 2. (GO TO 355C)
   ---Put her at ease.
   ---Tell her the five strong and weak points of her performance (one positive, one negative, one positive, etc.), inviting her explanation of each.
   ---Announce your summary rating.
   ---Indicate elements you want in her next year's development plan after reviewing last year's plan.
   ---Complete next year's development plan.

   C. Approach 3. (GO TO 365A)
   ---Put her at ease.
   ---Tell her the five strong and weak points of her performance (one positive, one negative, one positive, etc.), inviting her reactions on each.
   ---Try to ascertain how she thinks you might have supported her better given her weaknesses.
   ---Give her your summary evaluation and solicit her reactions.
   ---Review last year's development plan together.
   ---Work together developing next year's development plan.

Decision Point 347A

It is one month later, and there are several signs that Bill is now considered a legitimate member of the team. He is seldom excluded from group informal activities, and he has even been included in a Friday night poker party organized by one of the men who had initially been hard on him.

So completely has Bill been integrated into his team that he has begun to show defensiveness whenever an outsider or client criticizes the team or any member of it. One situation is particularly important. One of Bill's team members, Sam Scanlon, is a very capable engineer but is socially very meek and self-conscious. Unfortunately, this trait has caused him to be the least visible and most uninfluential member of your entire work group--a distinction that is some concern to you. Two days ago Sam was briefing a panel of clients on the Solaris project. Everyone on the project team was present. Sam's presentation was technically sound but lacked polish in delivery. One of the members of the panel (a person you know to be caustic in such situations) interrupted Sam in the midst of his monotone and took issue with some of his conclusions. Sam struggled for a response, but was failing miserably. His attacker pressed the matter. Sam struggled some more. K. C. Wong interrupted and clarified the logic. Seemingly satisfied, the client eased up. But later he repeated his concerns. With that Bill let loose with a pointed, almost personal attack on the client that stopped him but cast a pall over the rest of the meeting.

What would you do now?

A. Let K. C. Wong handle the matter. (GO TO 326B)

B. Indicate to Bill how he could have better assessed the situation in terms of Sam's fundamental weaknesses, K. C. Wong's responsibilities, and the particular personality of this client. (GO TO 414B)

C. Inform him that Sam needs practice bailing himself out and that he should not get involved in his development. (GO TO 372C)

D. Tell Bill that clients should be allowed to say whatever they want even if it is uncomplimentary and that one important role of a Venus employee is to be a flak-catcher. (GO TO 333A)

E. Tell Bill that his actions in this situation are irresponsible and that you cannot tolerate any more difficulties of this nature. (GO TO 368B)

Decision Point 348A

You identified the following statement as a positive element of Betty's performance: "Betty is conscientious." According to the chapter, this is incorrect. Your statement reflects a trait and not a behavior.

Re-evaluate your last decision. Circle the #348A you just wrote in your flow diagram. Then go back in your flow diagram to the first uncircled number above this step.

Decision Point 348B

You have asked Frank about his personal problem during a rather tense conversation. Under the circumstances, Frank would probably say, "My problem at home is my own business," or something like that. You have simply not given Frank any reason to trust or even respect you.

Re-evaluate your last decision. Circle the #348B you just wrote in your flow diagram. Then go back in your flow diagram to the first uncircled number above this step.

Decision Point 348C

She moves forward in her chair and responds, "That's a very good question. Why don't you get in contact with Liz Hamilton in Employee Relations and ask her for guidance. Liz is a solid person, and I trust what directions she can give you in this regard. Yes, that's a very good idea. Call her today. Let her know that I suggested that you call, but don't make a big deal out of it, you know what I mean?"

At this point what would you say?

A. Thank her for the background, express optimism at the opportunity she has helped to give you, and return to your office to prepare to meet your new peers. (GO TO 391A)

B. Ask her if she would like you to keep her posted on your meeting with Liz Hamilton before you take action. (GO TO 395A)

C. Tell her that you will contact Hamilton at once. Shift the subject diplomatically and ask her for her assessment of your predecessor. (GO TO 390B)

D. Tell her that you will contact Hamilton at once. Shift the subject diplomatically and probe for what problems and ambitions your boss has. (GO TO 352A)

Decision Point 349A

Convinced by your arguments, Bill withdraws his request for a transfer. Unfortunately, however, the rumor that Bill wants out of the group begins to spread throughout his project team. This results in Bill being given "the silent treatment" for a couple of days, and Bill comes in again with the idea of a transfer.

What would you do now?

A. Grant his request for a transfer because you don't think Bill can possibly earn the acceptance of his group under these circumstances. (GO TO 416B)

B. Give Bill a candid, accurate assessment of the social strengths and weaknesses of the other members of his work team, and advise him of specific actions he might take to gain more acceptance into the group. Monitor his social performance closely. (GO TO 358A)

C. Talk privately to other members of Bill's team and encourage each of them to serve as a mentor to Bill. (GO TO 387B)

D. Ask his team leader to allow Bill to be a spokesman for the team in an upcoming meeting with divisional management (at which all will be in attendance), so that he will have a chance to earn his team's approval. (GO TO 397B)

Decision Point 349B

You ask directly if his problem has something to do with alcohol. He says, "It most certainly does not!"

What would you say to Frank's denial?

A. "Frank, I have reason to believe that it is, and I should tell you that it is affecting your work. If it continues, it may cost you your job. Now I want to help. Why don't you go down there and talk to the people in the center. They are really equipped there to help you." (GO TO 373C)

B. "Frank, if it isn't alcohol, then what is it?" (GO TO 357A)

C. "Okay, you say it's not alcohol, but tell me honestly, Frank, have you really been sick for the last three Mondays out of four, or is it something else?" (GO TO 354A)

Decision Point 350A

You decided to conduct your interview with Betty in a nearby conference room. This was a correct decision. It is a neutral spot, and you are unlikely to be disturbed there. Now you need to do some planning about what sort of information you want to cover in your interview with Betty. Clearly, you will want to include the following (not necessarily in this order):

1. your summary evaluation (outstanding, excellent, good, fair, or poor),
2. three strong points and two weak points about her performance,
3. her inputs/reactions to 1 and 2 above,
4. her progress relative to last year's development plan,
5. inputs to next year's development plan.

Below are several other pieces of information your might also include:

6. the relationship between your summary evaluation and her merit pay increase,
7. her performance in comparison to others in the Ajax Project,
8. her self-rating on the employee performance appraisal form,
9. her career plans,
10. the specific assessments others have made of her performance.

Which of these other pieces of data (6 through 10 above) would you cover?

A. 6, 8, and 9. (GO TO 412A)

B. 6, 8, and 10. (GO TO 407B)

C. 6, 7, and 8. (GO TO 369B)

D. 7, 8, and 10. (GO TO 420C)

E. 7 and 9. (GO TO 376A)

F. 8 and 10. (GO TO 323A)

G. 9 alone. (GO TO 346A)

H. 8 alone. (GO TO 415A)

I. None of these. (GO TO 410A)

Decision Point 351A

You decided to cover Betty's demonstrated initiative first. This is not the best alternative. It is much better to compliment her first on her knowledge of procedures. The reason here is that she underevaluated herself on this dimension, and covering this subject first will begin the interview on a very positive note. You tell Betty that you are very pleased that she has made so much progress in getting to know company procedures, and that you think she has been too harsh on herself on her form. She thanks you, and tells you that "it is a miracle" that her progress has been so positive given all the problems she has been having with the computer system.

At this point what would you say?

A. "Okay, let's talk about those problems." (GO TO 404A)

B. "Yes, I am generally familiar with the problems you are referring to, and we'll get to that in a minute. I just want to make sure you hear me when I tell you that your performance on this dimension is really exceptional, and I truly appreciate your progress." (GO TO 345B)

C. "I know all about your computer problems. I agree that your progress is excellent given your frustrations." (GO TO 419A)

Decision Point 351B

Your daily meetings with Bill go well, but they are very time consuming. He begins bringing up even the most trivial issues, and in some cases you even find yourself doing his work. The meetings grow in duration until one day you suggest that Bill try to go it alone for a while. Cut loose, Bill flounders again, misses deadlines on important tasks, and completes unimportant ones with more "flair" than necessary. You conclude that Bill is not seeing the forest for the trees.

What would you do now?

A. Meet with K. C. Wong and delegate responsibility to him for a more effective breaking in of Bill. Tell K. C. that you don't want him to sacrifice the objectives of the Solaris system, but that you think Bill deserves more of his time. (GO TO 384A)
B. Begin again to give Bill a detailed account of how to contend with the challenges and problems of his work. Agree to meet with him in three days to review his progress and advise him on new situations. (GO TO 375B)
C. Talk to K. C. Wong about sharing responsibility for breaking Bill in. (GO TO 386C)

Decision Point 352A

Your boss does not respond directly. Instead she turns the conversation back to you and your new responsibilities. Apparently your boss is not ready to discuss her situation with you until she has developed more confidence in you. It was not incorrect for you to try, but you need to return to your last decision point and try another alternative.

Re-evaluate your last decision. Circle the #352A you just wrote in your flow diagram. Then move to the first uncircled step above this one in your flow diagram.

Decision Point 352B

The plan you have worked out with Frank accomplishes several objectives. Frank's attendance does improve. He does miss the next two Mondays, but he attends regularly after that time. In addition, since you have already administered the second warning by the time Frank's attendance improves, this "protects the company" from his falling back into his old habits. The cost of this protection, though, is three days of lost production (two Mondays and a one-day suspension on the second warning). There are instances where this loss is justified and instances where it is not.

You did an excellent job. **Congratulations!** This completes the Problem Employee Interactive Case.

Decision Point 352C

You identified the following statement as a positive element of Betty's performance: "Betty's volume of output is large." This is correct. The only negative bit of information you have on this score is Milt Strong's evaluation form, and it probably suffers from a negative halo effect.

What other statement do you think reflects a positive piece of feedback?

A. Betty sticks up for the project. (GO TO 403A)

B. Betty's knowledge of procedures has improved markedly. (GO TO 361B)

C. Betty has worked well under pressure. (GO TO 383B)

D. Betty is conscientious. (GO TO 348A)

Decision Point 353A

You have chosen to cover up the real reason that Spencer sought you out in the cafeteria. This was not an unacceptable choice, except that you missed an opportunity to clear the air with your boss about the missing $600. The rationale for doing so now is that your boss is apparently being contemplated for an award, and if you continue to be dissatisfied with her explanations, you should really protect the best interest of the organization and somehow pass on your information to the proper authorities.

Re-evaluate your last decision. Circle the #353A you just wrote in your flow diagram. Then move to the first uncircled step above this one in your flow diagram.

Decision Point 353B

You tell Frank that he will be written up if he doesn't report for counseling. He tells you that he doesn't need counseling, but what he does need is for you to "get off my back" and "out of my personal life." He goes on to say, "I'm not going to see some shrink, and if you don't like it, go ahead and write me up." With that, he starts to walk out the door. What would you do now?

A. Wait until Frank returns and ask him to meet with you later that day. (GO TO 357A)

B. Call Frank back and tell him that either he goes to counseling or he faces discharge. (GO TO 383A)

C. Fill out a written warning on Frank for refusal to go to the counseling center. Send one copy to Frank and one to Personnel. (GO TO 341A)

Decision Point 353C

You identified the following statement as a positive element of Betty's performance: "Betty's knowledge of procedures has improved markedly." This is correct. Your observations and Jensen's confirm this. What other statement do you think reflects a positive piece of feedback?

A. Betty's volume of output is large. (GO TO 361B)

B. Betty sticks up for the project. (GO TO 403A)

C. Betty has worked well under pressure. (GO TO 383B)

D. Betty is conscientious. (GO TO 348A)

Decision Point 354A

You asked Frank if he has really been ill. He says, "Look, I know the rules. They say that either illness or the illness of someone in your immediate family is allowable as sick leave. And it's been one of the two, I assure you!"
What would you do now?

A. Explain to Frank that his absences are causing real problems in production, and urge him to do better. (GO TO 332A)

B. Ask Frank what the difficulty is. (GO TO 357A)

C. Tell Frank that you don't like his attitude, and that if he is such an expert on the rules, then he knows that you can nail him any time you want. (GO TO 383A)

Decision Point 354B

Spencer says, "I'm so glad you think so. I am going to nominate her for Manager of the Year." This leaves you very depressed since you *know* that she has certainly committed some questionable acts as a manager. Of course every supervisor must from time to time acknowledge certain questionable practices on the part of others, but your action is consistent with a rather cynical point of view. You will gain no favor with your action.
Re-evaluate your last decision. Circle the #354B you just wrote in your flow diagram. Then move to the first uncircled step above this one in your flow diagram.

Decision Point 354C

After your comment to Frank, he doesn't say anything, but goes directly back to work. That afternoon, one of the men tells you that Frank has been telling other employees that you treated him unfairly. Later that same afternoon, as you pass Frank, you catch a glimpse of a gesture he makes behind your back. The other employees laugh. When you turn around, Frank is back at work. What would you do now?

A. Ask the employees who laughed to tell you what they saw. (GO TO 375A)

B. Warn Frank that he had better stick to work and forget about making "smart" comments toward you. (GO TO 383A)

C. Call Frank over to a more private place, and ask him what is on his mind. (GO TO 357A)

Decision Point 355A

The bad situation with Bill continues to grow. He botches a critical test given him with inadequate instructions, and the other two members of his team "jump all over him." Too embarrassed to tell you, Bill sulks for two days before signing a resignation letter. Bill never took the time to get a good reference book in aeronautics.

Re-evaluate your last decision. Circle the #355A you just wrote in your flow diagram. Then move to the first uncircled step above this one in your flow diagram.

Decision Point 355B

You have told Frank that you understood him to say that his attendance is important to him but he may not want to talk about it. In return, he says, "It's a family problem," and lowers his eyes. Now what would you say?

A. "Frank, if it's a family problem, there's really no one here at the company who can help you with it. I do know someone who is a professional family counselor. He's a neighbor of mine, and he's very good. Here's his phone number. If you need help with this, you should see a pro." (GO TO 389B)

B. "A family problem?" (GO TO 338A)

C. "Does the problem involve alcohol, Frank?" (GO TO 349B)

D. "Okay, Frank, if it's a family matter, then I don't want to butt in. I have to tell you though that I have to give you a formal warning on your attendance. I'll pull it from your file if you are able to work the next four Mondays. Otherwise, I'm afraid I'll have to give you a second warning, and you know what that means." (GO TO 372A)

Decision Point 355C

The format you chose is basically a tell-and-sell approach. This is ineffective for several reasons. First, this approach is unlikely to be very satisfying for Betty. Studies have shown that participative sessions are much more satisfying than nonparticipative ones, and tell-and-sell is not very participative. Second, this approach is unlikely to be very motivating for Betty. Again, studies indicate that people's motivation to improve hinges on their participation in the development plan.

Re-evaluate your last decision. Circle the #355C you just wrote in your flow diagram. Then go back in your flow diagram to the first uncircled number above this step.

Decision Point 356A

You identified the following statement as a negative element of Betty's performance: "Betty is insensitive to the impact she has on others." This is inappropriate, because, it is too general to be of use for feedback purposes.

Re-evaluate your last decision. Circle the #356A you just wrote in your flow diagram. Then go back in your flow diagram to the first uncircled number above this step.

Decision Point 356B

You learn that Bill has committed himself to try the suggestions given him by both the men, a commitment he cannot possibly follow. Thus, in spite of your conversation with the co-workers, and before you can talk to Bill, he is absent for three days and submits his resignation on the fourth day.

Apparently having two mentors put Bill in a box he could not get out of. With his credibility on the line, and desperate to gain the acceptance from his fellow workers, he felt no other option but to quit and join a firm that had courted him during his recruiting period.

Re-evaluate your last decision. Circle the #356B you just wrote in your flow diagram. Then move to the first uncircled step above this one in your flow diagram.

Decision Point 356C

Betty responds that you were out of town when all the problems she had with the computer system came up, and she needed guidance as to how to deal with the systems analysts. This is informative. You realize that you have never told Betty just what to do when she confronts problems like this in your absence. Therefore, you and Betty talk at some length about developing a procedure for handling these sorts of problems in the future. Following that, you give her positive feedback on her work volume. She responds well to this positive evaluation, and now you move to the topic of her dealings with clients.

How would you approach giving her this negative feedback?

A. Mention to her the specific incident where she raised her voice to a contract auditor (a client). Emphasize the need for Betty to be diplomatic when dealing with outside people. (GO TO 397A)
B. Say, "Betty, we touched on your problems in dealing with your frustration earlier. Well, there have apparently been occasions when you have not been as diplomatic as you should have been with clients." (GO TO 344B)
C. Say, "Did you raise your voice with a contract auditor when you were having a problem with the computer?" (GO TO 358B)

Decision Point 357A

Your meeting with Frank seems tense and strained. You ask Frank what difficulty he is having. He says, "Look, all I need is some support from you right now. I'm working through a very difficult personal problem right now, and you are not making it any easier for me. I know I've been absent a lot lately, but damn it, I've given this company over three years of my life, and it seems that I deserve more consideration."

What would you say now?

A. Tell him you consider his statement insubordination and you are going to write him up for it. (GO TO 383A)

B. Say, "Okay, okay, I guess I have been a little hard on you. It's just that I'm really getting heat from my boss, and I don't know why you've been absent so much. If there is something I can do that would help you with your problem so the absenteeism straightens out, I want you to know that I'll do what I can." (GO TO 370B)

C. Ask him what his personal problem is. (GO TO 348B)

D. Say, "Tell me honestly, Frank, have you really been sick for the last three Mondays out of four, or is it something else?" (GO TO 354A)

E. Ask him if his problem has something to do with alcohol. (GO TO 349B)

F. Say, "Okay, Frank, if it's personal, then I don't want to butt in. I have to tell you though that I have to give you a warning on your attendance. I'll pull it from your file if you are able to work the next four Mondays. Otherwise, I'm afraid I'll have to give you a second warning, and you know what that means!" (GO TO 341A)

Decision Point 357B

You tell Spencer everything you know about the situation between your predecessor and your boss. The two of you finish lunch in almost complete silence and return to work. Two days later your boss calls you into her office. She proceeds to tell you that she has heard of your encounter with Spencer and that as long as she works for the bank she will personally see to it that you receive the minimum in cost-of-living adjustments and no merit increases. Further, she threatens to make it difficult for you in any way that she can.

Re-evaluate your last decision. Circle the #357B you just wrote in your flow diagram. Then move to the first uncircled step above this one in your flow diagram.

Decision Point 358A

It is one month later, and there are several signs that Bill is now considered a legitimate member of the team. He is seldom excluded from group informal activities, and he has even been included in a Friday night poker party organized by one of the employees who had initially been hard on him.

So completely has Bill been integrated into his team that he has begun to show defensiveness whenever an outsider or client criticizes the team or any member of it. One situation is particularly important. One of Bill's team members, Sam Scanlon, is a very capable engineer but is socially very meek and self-conscious. Unfortunately, this trait has caused him to be the least visible and influential member of your entire work group--a distinction that is some concern to you. Two days ago Sam was briefing a panel of clients on the Dart project. Everyone on the project team was present. Sam's presentation was technically sound but lacked polish in delivery. One of the members of the panel (a person you know to be caustic in such situations) interrupted Sam in the midst of his monotone and took issue with some of his conclusions. Sam struggled for a response, but was failing miserably. His attacker pressed the matter. Sam struggled some more. Bob Blair interrupted and clarified the logic. Seemingly satisfied, the client eased up. But later he repeated his concerns. With that, Bill let loose with a pointed, almost personal attack on the client that stopped him but cast a pall over the rest of the meeting.

What would you do now?

A. Let Bob Blair handle the matter. (GO TO 392A)

B. Indicate to Bill how he could have better assessed the situation in terms of Sam's fundamental weaknesses, Bob Blair's responsibilities, and the particular personality of this client. (GO TO 414B)

C. Inform him that Sam needs practice bailing himself out and that he should not get involved in his development. (GO TO 332B)

D. Tell Bill that clients should be allowed to say whatever they want, even if it is uncomplimentary, and that one important role of a Venus employee is to be a flak-catcher. (GO TO 400B)

Decision Point 358B

This is an accusatory statement. It results in Betty becoming very defensive. In general, it is preferable to describe rather than evaluate when giving negative feedback. Re-evaluate your last decision. Circle the #358B you just wrote in your flow diagram. Then go back in your flow diagram to the first uncircled number above this step.

Decision Point 359A

You decide to talk to Frank about the transfer. He is delighted by the prospect of more money, and he impresses the Research people during his transfer interviews. By Thursday, he is no longer a member of your department.

The consequences of the decision, though, are not good. Your team's performance continues lackadaisical. Frank apparently provided a spark to teamwork, and petty squabbles now emerge among your people. Your manager continues to hound you for higher productivity. You have had real difficulty replacing Frank, more than you anticipated when you made the decision to transfer him. And, if all that isn't bad enough, you just received a call from Frank's supervisor in the Research Department asking you about Frank's attendance problem. He got pretty steamed about the fact that you sent him "a lemon," as he put it.

Clearly, transferring Frank is not the best solution to the problem under these circumstances. If you want a second chance, circle the #359A you just wrote in your flow diagram, and move back in your flow diagram to the first uncircled number above this step.

Decision Point 359B

Your daily meetings with Bill go well, but they are very time consuming. He begins bringing up even the most trivial issues, and in some cases you even find yourself doing his work. The meetings grow in duration until one day you suggest that Bill try to go it alone for a while. Cut loose, Bill flounders again, misses deadlines on important tasks, and completes unimportant ones with more "flair" than necessary. You conclude that Bill is not seeing the forest for the trees. What would you do now?

A. Meet with Bob Blair and delegate responsibility to him for a more effective breaking in of Bill. Tell Bob that you don't want him to sacrifice the objectives of the Dart system, but that you think Bill deserves more of his time. (GO TO 381A)

B. Begin again to give Bill a detailed account of how to contend with the challenges and problems of his work. Agree to meet with him in three days to review his progress and advise him on new situations. (GO TO 362B)

C. Talk to Bob Blair about sharing responsibility for breaking Bill in. (GO TO 379C)

D. Take time to remind others in your group of the importance of helping Bill adapt to his job. (GO TO 399B)

Decision Point 360A

You identified the following statement as a positive element of Betty's performance: "Betty has demonstrated initiative." This is correct. Your observations and Jensen's confirm this.

What other statement do you think reflects a positive piece of feedback?

A. Betty sticks up for the project. (GO TO 403A)

B. Betty's knowledge of procedures has improved markedly. (GO TO 361B)

C. Betty has worked well under pressure. (GO TO 383B)

D. Betty is conscientious. (GO TO 348A)

Decision Point 360B

Your meeting with Frank seems relatively relaxed. You ask Frank what problem he is having, and he says, "Well, it's rather personal, and I'm not sure I want to talk about it. I know I can't go on being absent like this."

What would you say now?

A. "I'm glad you realize how important it is that you improve your attendance record. Do the best you can to make it to work, okay?" (GO TO 332A)

B. "Tell me honestly, Frank, have you really been sick for the last three Mondays out of four, or is it something else?" (GO TO 354A)

C. "Okay, Frank, if it's personal, then I don't want to butt in. I have to tell you though that I have to give you a formal warning on your attendance. I'll pull it from your file if you are able to work the next four Mondays. Otherwise, I'm afraid I'll have to give you a second warning and you know what that means." (GO TO 372A)

D. "Frank, do you have an alcohol problem?" (GO TO 349B)

E. "If you don't want to talk about it, that's fine, but we need to work out a plan that will result in the level of production we need from you. Do you have any ideas that we might put to use?" (GO TO 379A)

F. "I see, you think it's important to improve your attendance, but you are not sure you want to talk about what is causing the attendance problem." (GO TO 355B)

Decision Point 361A

Lucy lays out the advantages and disadvantages of her proposal in some detail and you are really quite impressed with the fact that she has done her homework. At the same time, the data you got from the interviews with your peers continue to weigh on you. Recall that they gave you information that
 (1) your boss has a very low opinion of the quality of your group's performance;
 (2) your boss may be under pressure to make *NET* work;
 (3) *NET* seems to be in for some major implementation problems.

On several occasions Leo Leiter repeated his statement that your group's quality was increasingly disappointing to your boss. Now that you have staked your reputation with your subordinates on the success of *NET*, Leiter's statements are beginning to get to you.

What's your next move?

A. Forget your fears and implement Lucy's plan. (GO TO 419B)

B. Return to Curtin and Evanston to see if they think your group is considered by your boss to have the poorest quality record. (GO TO 334A)

C. Return to your boss to see if she really does consider your group to have the poorest quality performance. (GO TO 371B)

Decision Point 361B

You have successfully identified the three positive elements of Betty's performance. They are captured in the following statements:
 (1) Betty's volume of output is large.
 (2) Betty has demonstrated initiative.
 (3) Betty's knowledge of procedures has improved markedly.

It is now time to plan your appraisal interview with Betty. In preparing yourself for this discussion, where would you plan to conduct this interview?

A. In the company cafeteria after everyone has left but the clean-up crew. (GO TO 403C)

B. In your office. (GO TO 421A)

C. In Betty's office. (GO TO 382A)

D. In a nearby conference room. (GO TO 350A)

Decision Point 362A

You ask Frank if he is feeling better. Taking your question as sarcasm, he says, "I'd feel a lot better if I worked for another supervisor!"
What now?

A. Tell Frank that you consider his statement insubordination and you are going to write him up for it. (GO TO 383A)

B. Ask him what his problem is. (GO TO 357A)

C. Ask him if his problem has something to do with alcohol. (GO TO 349B)

Decision Point 362B

Bill responds well to the periodic meetings you and he set up. This closer monitoring and more frequent coaching begin to show in Bill's confidence and technical performance. Yet other problems begin to show up. You notice that he still is hesitant to initiate contact with his other team members when he is having a problem. And when he does ask for help, his requests are often misunderstood or perceived as a call for reassurance rather than as a legitimate concern. What is particularly disturbing is that Bill has yet to be accepted as a real member of the team. He is frequently excluded from lunches with the other members, and he has been given some mild hazing by one of the men.
How would you react to this?

A. Start going to lunch with him regularly. (GO TO 369A)

B. Set up an informal meeting between Bill and a new recruit from another division who has been successfully accepted as a member of his team. (GO TO 324A)

C. Give Bill a candid, accurate assessment of the social strengths and weaknesses of the other members of his work team. Advise him of specific strategies that he might use to gain acceptance into the group. Monitor his social performance closely. (GO TO 358A)

D. Talk privately to the other members of Bill's team and encourage each of them to serve as Bill's mentor. (GO TO 387B)

E. Ask his team leader to allow Bill to be the spokesman for the team in an upcoming meeting with division management (at which all department members will be present), so that he will have a better chance to earn his team's acceptance. (GO TO 397B)

Decision Point 363A

You decide to report the indiscretion of your predecessor with an administrative authority. They open a full-scale investigation. As the person who has made the complaint, you are on record as the person who is responsible for this action. A week passes with little action, but all of a sudden you receive subtle messages you should drop your complaint. At this point you decide to confront your boss with your concerns. She offers the following explanation:

"Well, Donald [Scott] asked me not to say anything, but I can see that you are really troubled. Donald is dying of brain cancer. Only three other people in the company know, Spencer, Post, and me. He experiences periodic lapses of memory and he doesn't recall anything about the $600 you discovered. He may have taken it, I don't know, but there is really no point in pursuing it. He is in a position now where he will do no harm to anyone, since he has no budgetary authority. Post thinks that he spent the $600 on painting the offices of the Leads. You probably remember that your office was painted. Well, no one in the company can trace how he paid for that. He either paid for it with his own personal funds or with the help of the $600."

Your boss then changes the subject to her upcoming vacation, a trip to Yellowstone Park. She will be away for three weeks. You give her your best wishes for a truly enjoyable vacation. Your doubts gone, you draft a letter to William Spencer. It is the best prose you are capable of.

A week after she is gone, you receive a memo addressed to all supervisors from your boss dated the first of the month that reminds you of a policy that preceded you as a supervisor, but required that all your operators audit their reports before submitting them. Your peers had informed you that this policy was unworkable and had been ignored for the past three years. It would require supervisors to spend about 14 hours per week assembling data that had never been used in the past. Moreover, such an effort would raise all sorts of questions that would be very difficult to answer satisfactorily. Your investigation also reveals that this policy has nothing whatsoever to do with the *NET* effort.

Since your boss is gone now, you have no way of ascertaining whether she in fact meant for the policy to be enforced for the first time. You check with your peers, and they are unanimous that someone in the office of Budget Control has simply redated an old memo. You now face the choice of either opposing a memo signed by your boss or investing 14 hours a week in an activity that you don't believe is worthwhile. What would you do?

A. Call your boss on vacation, tracking her down in the various campgrounds in Yellowstone. (GO TO 406B)
B. Fight the appropriate staff group of the company on the grounds that an investment of 14 hours of your time is not warranted. (GO TO 386A)
C. Comply with the policy with the idea that if your boss returns to discover a problem, she will be very displeased. (GO TO 389A)

Decision Point 364A

You asked Bill and he told you he wanted to work on the Solaris project. Which assignment would you give him?

A. *Assignment 1*. Junior Control Engineer, Dart Project. Join a team of four headed by Bob Blair to test a ballistics control system for a Dart missile. The Dart is like other systems developed previously, except that the new control system requires several standards never required before. Smythe's senior thesis dealt with ballistics control systems. Estimated probability of making a net contribution to the team = 60 percent. Value to Bill's development if he is personally successful = 40 points out of 100. (GO TO 402A)

B. *Assignment 2*. Junior Control Engineer, Solaris Project. Join a team of three headed by K. C. Wong to test the propulsion control system for a Solaris booster. Wong is very enthusiastic about Bill joining the team. The Solaris project will require a unique control system that has never been implemented before. The project is presently behind schedule because of the novelty of its design. It would offer a fantastic learning opportunity for any junior engineer. Estimated probability of making a net contribution to the team = 30 percent. Value to Bill's development if he is personally successful = 80 points out of 100. (GO TO 343A)

C. *Assignment 3*. Junior Control Engineer, Systems Test Group. Act as your administrative assistant. Perform several studies regarding planning and scheduling in preparation for upcoming budget negotiations. While this assignment has only a modest technical component, it is a great way for Bill to learn the inner workings of your department and may allow him to find his own technical place in the group. Estimated probability of making a net contribution to the group = 100 percent. Value to Bill's development if he is personally successful = 20 points out of 100. (GO TO 394A)

D. *Assignment 4*. Junior Control Engineer, Systems Test Group, and Member, Micascope Divisional Task Force. Join a task force of seven members conducting a feasibility study of Micascope, a laser-refracting targeting system. The task force is chaired by the assistant to the divisional manager. This assignment would give Bill a chance to work with some of the most dynamic members in the division. The proposed study is somewhat controversial with some members committed to manufacturing and some against it. The division manager is said to favor manufacturing, but he has agreed to "let the chips fall where they may." While he handpicked the members of the task force from other departments, his confidence in you permitted him to ask you to appoint the department member of your choice. Since all of the other members of your group are busy with project work, Bill seems like a natural. Estimated probability of making a net contribution to the task force = 50 percent. Value to Bill's development if he is personally successful = 80 points out of 100. (GO TO 382C)

Decision Point 365A

The format you chose is basically a tell-and-listen approach. You schedule your meeting with Betty. She arrives on time, and sits across from you at the conference table.
How would you open the discussion?

A. "The underlying purpose of this talk is to discuss your job, and its primary purpose is to enable me to help you. Both of us should keep this in mind throughout our talk." (GO TO 386B)

B. "I've been studying your last year's performance, and I want to give you my frank, honest evaluation of how well you've done." (GO TO 418C)

C. "I wanted to set some time aside to talk about your performance this year. Obviously this topic is one that can be uncomfortable for both you and me, but let's approach it as a guidance and feedback session rather than one full of evaluations and accusations." (GO TO 408B)

D. "I'm sure that you want to know how I see your performance last year. I'm also interested in how you see it. So let's view this session as an exchange of views rather than a chance for me to make firm statements." (GO TO 336A)

E. "I'm glad we are going to have some time together to discuss your last year's performance. I've spent a lot of time preparing for this session so that we can cover a lot of ground and still have time for questions." (GO TO 390A)

Decision Point 365B

You opt to do something "bold and decisive" to impress your boss. You decide that a reorganization of your former unit is something that would not only be popular with your former subordinates, but indicative of your new regime. It works magnificently. People moved to their new assignments and are very pleased to do so. Moreover, the performance of your former unit improves markedly. The problem is, however, that three of your unit clerks apply successfully for an upgrade in their job classifications. The resulting pay adjustments more than erase the productivity increases. Although you chose to do something within your technical expertise, you were betrayed by a lack of knowledge of some issues with which you were unfamiliar as a Lead.
Re-evaluate your last decision. Circle the #365B you just wrote in your flow diagram. Then move to the first uncircled step above this one in your flow diagram.

Decision Point 366A

Betty reluctantly agrees with your position. You now must enter the developmental portion of the interview. In general, how would you approach this part of the session?

A. Begin by asking her inputs. Offer yours. Negotiate a developmental plan. Keep it participative. (GO TO 373B)

B. List the items on which you want improvement. Ask her how you can support her efforts to improve. Keep it specific. (GO TO 417A)

C. Begin with a discussion of Betty's career goals. Integrate into your discussion action items that not only address ways that might improve her performance but also get her closer to her career ambitions. (GO TO 405C)

Decision Point 366B

You ask your boss what she means when she asks you to do the best you can with the *NET* assignment. She responds that she just wants you to support the program. You then inquire if there is anything you should be doing to prepare your group for *NET* before the program is formally announced. She moves forward in her chair and responds:

"That's a very good question. Why don't you get in contact with Liz Hamilton in Employee Relations and ask her for guidance. Liz is a solid person, and I trust what directions she can give you in this regard. Yes, that's a very good idea. Call her today. Let her know that I suggested that you call, but don't make a big deal out of it, you know what I mean?"

At this point what would you say?

A. Thank her for the background, express optimism at the opportunity she has helped to give you, and return to your office to prepare to meet your new peers. (GO TO 391A)

B. Ask her if she would like you to keep her posted on your meeting with Liz Hamilton before you take action. (GO TO 395A)

C. Tell her that you will contact Hamilton at once. Shift the subject diplomatically and ask her for her assessment of your predecessor. (GO TO 390B)

D. Tell her that you will contact Hamilton at once. Shift the subject diplomatically and probe for what problems and ambitions your boss has. (GO TO 352A)

Decision Point 367A

Bill and this other person really hit it off. They become very close friends, but Bill continues to be rejected by his fellow group members. His co-workers now seem to feel that he lacks real interest in them, and they begin to give him the "cold shoulder."

Three weeks later, Bill sends you a memo indicating that he would like to transfer to the division where his new friend works. You are convinced that granting the transfer would hurt you, Bill, and ultimately the entire organization.
What would you do now?

A. Grant his request for the transfer because you don't think Bill can possibly earn the approval of his group under these circumstances. (GO TO 416B)

B. Discourage Bill from taking the transfer and urge him to withdraw his request. (GO TO 380B)

Decision Point 367B

You decide to discuss the matter with the employee in question. When you do, you discover that the situation is clearly not as bad as it has been portrayed by your two Leads.
What would you do about this?

A. Talk to Post and Hopkins about what you have discovered. (GO TO 337A)

B. Reprimand Post and Hopkins for exaggerating the situation. (GO TO 413A)

C. Ignore the situation. Let the matter drop with no further action on your part. (GO TO 393C)

Decision Point 367C

It is unwise to show her your completed form at this time for two reasons. First, she will immediately notice the relative negativeness of it, and this will not enable you to begin on a positive note. Second, it will give the appearance that you have already made up your mind, and this might hinder discussion and participation.
Re-evaluate your last decision. Circle the #367C you just wrote in your flow diagram. Then go back in your flow diagram to the first uncircled number above this step.

Decision Point 368A

You have asked Frank to negotiate some standard of attendance that you both can live with. Frank responds that working Mondays poses a real problem because of his wife's problems. He says, though, that if he can get the next couple of Mondays off, he thinks he can straighten out things with his family situation.
How would you respond?

A. Tell him that Monday attendance is essential and that he should do the best he can to turn his attendance around. (GO TO 332A)

B. Persuade him that letting him have Mondays off would set a bad precedent for the other employees. (GO TO 381B)

C. Tell him that you are willing to let him miss the next two Mondays if he makes up the time on Saturday when the other employees are working overtime. After that, you will not be able to tolerate further Monday absences without disciplinary action. (GO TO 384C)

Decision Point 368B

You decided to take a tough stand with Bill. Apparently he is not one who responds well to straightforwardness, for he reacts very negatively to your comments, and his resignation letter appears on your desk at the end of the day.
Re-evaluate your last decision. Circle the #368B you just wrote in your flow diagram. Then move to the first uncircled step above this one in your flow diagram.

Decision Point 368C

You identified the following statement as a positive element of Betty's performance: "Betty has demonstrated initiative." This is correct. Your observations and Jensen's both confirm this.
What other statement do you think reflects a positive piece of feedback?

A. Betty's volume of output is large. (GO TO 361B)

B. Betty sticks up for the project. (GO TO 403A)

C. Betty has worked well under pressure. (GO TO 383B)

D. Betty is conscientious. (GO TO 348A)

Decision Point 369A

You have decided to go to lunch with Bill regularly. He is a pleasant lunch companion, this is a good chance to catch up on what is happening with him. After about two weeks, you notice that Bill begins to expect your lunches to continue indefinitely. He arrives every day at noon, and shows disappointment any time you have made other plans.

What's worse, Bill's lack of social acceptance by his peers is really becoming a problem. They now are apparently growing resentful of all the attention you are giving him. It is clearly time for you to break the umbilical cord with Bill.

What would you do now?

A. Set up an informal meeting between Bill and a new recruit from another division who has been accepted as a member of his team. (GO TO 324A)

B. Give Bill a candid, accurate assessment of the social strengths and weaknesses of the other members of his work team. Advise him of specific strategies that he might use to gain acceptance into the group. Monitor his social performance closely. (GO TO 358A)

C. Talk privately to the other members of Bill's team and encourage each of them to serve as Bill's mentor. (GO TO 387B)

D. Ask his team leader to allow Bill to be the spokesman for the team in an upcoming meeting with division management (at which all department members will be present), so that he will have a better chance to earn his team's acceptance. (GO TO 397B)

Decision Point 369B

You decided to include three additional pieces of information in your discussion with Betty:
  6. The relationship between your summary evaluation and her merit pay increase.
  7. Her performance in comparison to others in the Ajax Project.
  8. Her self-rating on the employee appraisal form.

According to the Module Reading, this is incorrect. Research indicates that discussions of pay and performance should be conducted separately. Moreover, it is inappropriate to discuss the evaluations of others.

Re-evaluate your last decision. Circle the #369B you just wrote in your flow diagram. Then go back in your flow diagram to the first uncircled number above this step.

Decision Point 370A

You identified the following statement as a positive element of Betty's performance: "Betty's knowledge of procedures has improved markedly." This is correct. Your observations and Jensen's confirm this.

What other statement do you think reflects a positive piece of feedback?

A. Betty's volume of output is large. (GO TO 405A)

B. Betty sticks up for the project. (GO TO 403A)

C. Betty has demonstrated initiative. (GO TO 368C)

D. Betty has worked well under pressure. (GO TO 383B)

E. Betty is conscientious. (GO TO 348A)

Decision Point 370B

You tell Frank that your boss is pressuring you for more work. Frank responds that you should make her understand that everyone in your group is doing the best he or she can. Now what would you say?

A. Explain the necessity of good attendance if production goals are to met and point out to him how much his attendance is adversely affecting production. Urge him to do better. (GO TO 332A)

B. Ask him what difficulty he is having that keeps him from producing as much as he is capable of producing. (GO TO 360B)

C. Tell Frank that his performance may be one of the reasons your boss is pressuring you. Indicate that if he doesn't improve his attendance, you will be forced to give him a written warning. (GO TO 354C)

Decision Point 370C

Your peers are full of indignation about the hypothetical case you describe. They make it clear that anyone suspected of such a budgetary imbalance would certainly be fired outright. Since this is the case, what would you do?

A. Report the matter to the budgetary authority, the Department of Administrative Services. (GO TO 363A)

B. Talk with your boss about what you have found. (GO TO 377A)

Decision Point 371A

This opening works well. Betty acknowledges her nervousness, and you respond by further putting her at ease. You ask her if she has had a chance to fill out the appraisal form on herself. She shows you her form, and it is filled with check marks in all the "very typical" columns except one, "knows the procedures involved in the job and the organization." She also checked the "outstanding" summary rating.

Would you show your completed form to Betty?

A. Yes. (GO TO 367C)

B. No. (GO TO 390C)

Decision Point 371B

You speak to your boss about the rumor that your group has a low quality record. She asks you who told you that. You tell her it was Leo Leiter. She just shakes her head and says, "My friend, you have just been hazed. Leo knows your group is not the poorest in quality. He was just making you edgy."

She then shows you the quality record that shows your group is ranked second in her department (Leo's is first). Clearly your troubling your boss about this matter has left you looking pretty silly.

Re-evaluate your last decision. Circle the #371B you just wrote in your flow diagram. Then move to the first uncircled step above this one in your flow diagram.

Decision Point 371C

Bill grows so dissatisfied with the limited technical nature of his work that he contacts a firm that heavily recruited him when he was in the job market. It again offers him a job at a higher salary than he is being paid at Venus. Job offer in hand, Bill confronts you and tells you that unless you assign him to the Solaris project, he will have to resign even though he likes Venus and you.

What would you do now?

A. Assign him to the Solaris project. (GO TO 343A)

B. Wish him well with the other firm. (GO TO 329B)

Decision Point 372A

You have decided to establish an explicit plan for Frank to follow that will correct his attendance problem. As a result, Frank's attendance does improve. Unfortunately, however, after he slips and earns his second warning, the problem shifts. Frank never misses a Monday thereafter, but on two consecutive Mondays, his performance is far below acceptable levels. On the first Monday, he receives two "emergency phone calls" from a woman who identifies herself as his wife. This keeps him from his work for a total of 45 minutes after which he is listless and unproductive. On the second Monday, he leaves work at lunchtime and returns 30 minutes late complaining that he had serious family business to attend to. Your action apparently corrected one problem but created another.

Re-evaluate your last decision. Circle the #372A you just wrote in your flow diagram, and move back in your flow diagram to the first uncircled number above this step.

Decision Point 372B

Your meeting ended, LeRoy leaves the office. Four days later you hear from the grapevine that your refusal to continue playing cards with your old unit has resulted in some very unfortunate rumors about you thinking you are "too good for them now."

Re-evaluate your last decision. Circle the #372B you just wrote in your flow diagram. Then move to the first uncircled step above this one in your flow diagram.

Decision Point 372C

Bill disagrees strongly with your statement, and in a rare show of temper, slams the door when he leaves your office. You call him in the next day to clear the air. What should you do now?

A. Indicate to Bill how he could have better assessed the incident between Sam and the client in terms of Sam's fundamental weaknesses, K. C. Wong's responsibilities in this situation, and the attributes of this particular client. (GO TO 414B)

B. Tell Bill that clients should be allowed to say whatever they want, even if it is uncomplimentary, and that one important role of a Venus employee is to be a flak-catcher. (GO TO 400B)

C. Tell Bill that it is unprofessional to show his temper to a client, his team leader, or you. Insist that he try to control himself. (GO TO 368B)

Decision Point 373A

You tell Lucy that you will consider her proposal and get back to her. This works well for a time, but two weeks later she asks again. When you put her off once more, the informal grapevine becomes loaded with rumors that you are indecisive and wishy-washy. Moreover, when the next month's performance figures come out, they indicate slipping quality in her unit.

Putting subordinates off is one of the most difficult problems for new supervisors. They want to be responsive but feel harnessed by a need to be deliberate. Rather than making ambiguous promises, it is far preferable to make specific contingencies that will raise the issue again. For example, in this instance it would have been wise to tie your decision to certain *NET* program decisions. This would have given you flexibility without seeming to put off your people.

Re-evaluate your last decision. Circle the #373A you just wrote in your flow diagram. Then move to the first uncircled step above this one in your flow diagram.

Decision Point 373B

This is an excellent approach and one that results in a development plan that is very motivating. One of the elements in the plan is that you will work on improving the relationship between Betty and Milt Strong.

Congratulations! You have just completed the Performance Appraisal Interactive Case.

Decision Point 373C

You figure that if Frank's problem is one of drinking, experts should handle it. When you tell Frank to report for counseling, he becomes angry at you and denies that he has a drinking problem. As Frank continues to talk, he becomes more emotional and more angry.

What would you do now?

A. Tell Frank that if he doesn't report for counseling, you will write him up for insubordination. (GO TO 353B)

B. Say something like, "Frank, if it isn't alcohol, then what is it?" (GO TO 357A)

C. Say, "Okay, okay, you say it's not alcohol, but tell me honestly Frank, have you really been sick for the last three Mondays out of four, or is it something else?" (GO TO 354A)

Decision Point 374A

You return to play cards several times each month with your old unit. Everything seems to go satisfactorily until you hear through the grapevine that the operators in the other units are expressing a lot of jealousy about you "favoring" one unit over the others. Now you are faced with several options, none of which are very acceptable.

Re-evaluate your last decision. Circle the #374A you just wrote in your flow diagram. Then move to the first uncircled step above this one in your flow diagram.

Decision Point 374B

You have decided to go to lunch with Bill regularly. He is a pleasant lunch companion, and you discover that this is a good chance to catch up on what is happening with him. After about two weeks, you notice that Bill begins to expect your luncheon meetings to continue indefinitely. He arrives everyday at noon, and shows disappointment any time you have made other plans.

What's worse, Bill's lack of social acceptance by his peers is really becoming a problem. They now are apparently growing resentful of all the attention you are giving him. It is clearly time for you to break the umbilical cord with Bill.

What would you do now?

A. Set up an informal meeting between Bill and a new recruit from another division who has been accepted as a member of his team. (GO TO 367A)

B. Give Bill a candid, accurate assessment of the social strengths and weaknesses of the other members of his work team. Advise him of specific strategies that he might use to gain acceptance into the group. Monitor his social performance closely. (GO TO 347A)

C. Talk privately to the other members of Bill's team and encourage each of them to serve as Bill's mentor. (GO TO 383C)

D. Ask his team leader to allow Bill to be the spokesman for the team in an upcoming meeting with division management (at which all department members will be present), so that he will have a better chance to earn his team's acceptance. (GO TO 397B)

Decision Point 375A

You asked the employees who laughed to tell you what they saw. The people were embarrassed and appeared to be nervous. Finally one of them said: "We were just laughing at a joke Frank told at lunch. It didn't have anything to do with you." What would you do now?

A. Call Frank over to a more private place and ask him what's on his mind. (GO TO 357A)

B. Warn Frank that he had better stick to work and forget about making smart comments. (GO TO 383A)

Decision Point 375B

It is one month later. Bill responds well to the periodic meetings you and he set up. This closer monitoring and more frequent coaching begin to show in Bill's confidence and technical performance. Yet, other problems begin to appear. You notice that he still is hesitant to initiate contact with his other team members when he is having a problem. And when he does ask for help, his requests are often misunderstood or perceived as a call for reassurance rather than as a legitimate concern. What is particularly disturbing is that Bill has yet to be accepted as a real member of the team. He is frequently excluded from lunches with the other members, and he has been given some mild hazing by one of the men. How would you react to this?

A. Start going to lunch with him regularly. (GO TO 374B)

B. Set up an informal meeting between Bill and a new recruit from another division who has been accepted as a member of his team. (GO TO 367A)

C. Give Bill a candid, accurate assessment of the social strengths and weaknesses of the other members of his work team. Advise him of specific strategies that he might use to gain acceptance into the group. Monitor his social performance closely. (GO TO 347A)

D. Talk privately to the other members of Bill's team and encourage each of them to serve as Bill's mentor. (GO TO 383C)

E. Ask his team leader to allow Bill to be the spokesman for the team in an upcoming meeting with division management (at which all department members will be present), so that he will have a better chance to earn his team's acceptance. (GO TO 397B)

Decision Point 376A

You decided to include two additional pieces of information in your discussion with Betty:
7. her performance in comparison to others in the Ajax Project;
9. her career plans.

This is partially correct. It is perfectly acceptable to raise questions as to an employee's career plans during an appraisal interview. However, it is inappropriate to make performance comparisons between Betty and other Ajax personnel. Now that you have decided what to cover (and what not to cover), you now must decide how to conduct the appraisal interview. The following strategies are common. Which would you use?

A. Approach 1. (GO TO 398B)
   ---Ask her to fill out her own appraisal form before the meeting.
   ---Put her at ease.
   ---Examine together the similarities and differences between your filled-out forms and hers.
   ---Cover the five specific points you have identified previously, starting with a positive point, then a negative, etc.
   ---Ascertain your role in her deficient performance.
   ---Give her your summary rating and invite her reactions/inputs.
   ---Go over last year's development plan and jointly develop next year's plan.

B. Approach 2. (GO TO 355C)
   ---Put her at ease.
   ---Tell her five strong and weak points of her performance (one positive, one negative, one positive, etc.), inviting her explanation of each.
   ---Announce your summary rating.
   ---Indicate elements you want in her next year's development plan after reviewing last year's plan.
   ---Complete next year's development plan.

C. Approach 3. (GO TO 365A)
   ---Put her at ease.
   ---Tell her the five strong and weak points of her performance (one positive, one negative, one positive, etc.), inviting her reactions on each.
   ---Try to ascertain how she thinks you might have supported her better given her weaknesses.
   ---Give her your summary evaluation and solicit her reactions.
   ---Review last year's development plan together.
   ---Work together developing next year's development plan.

Decision Point 377A

Karen asks for all the relevant documents. She tells you she will take care of it. Two months pass and *NET* implementation begins. With all the activity, you completely forget about the matter. However, one Friday after a meeting, you ask her what she did with the paperwork you gave her. To your shock, she tells you, "I looked into it, and I am sure it was an oversight. Just forget it."

You then ask her for the paperwork (you are supposed to keep some of the records you gave her in your own file). She tells you she will get them for you. At the end of the following week, you again ask her for the records. She says that she apparently lost them and, much to your surprise, adds, "Listen, I told you that as far as I am concerned the matter is closed."

This disturbs you no end. Quietly you check around and learn that a person was apparently fired on less evidence than you gave her on Scott. You now wonder if she might have been involved with Scott in this apparent misappropriation of company funds. Adding to your dilemma is that next week you face an internal audit, and your inside sources tell you that it will certainly discover that the documents you gave your boss are missing from your records. You are worried about having to explain that. This afternoon, quite unexpectedly your boss's boss, William Spencer, meets you by chance in the cafeteria.

Spencer: "Well, now that you have been a supervisor for three months, how do you like it?"

You: "Fine, Mr. Spencer, just fine. I had wanted this promotion for a long time, and I really like being responsible for such a big part of the operation." [You bite your lip at having said such a corny thing.]

Spencer: "And how is *NET* coming?"

You [truthfully]: "I'll tell you, Mr. Spencer, when I first heard about *NET*, I was worried that it would make some of my units look bad, but actually it has really helped me improve the error rate."

Spencer: "I've noticed the improvement throughout the department, and I'm sure much of that is attributable to the hard work of supervisors like you. By the way, how do you like working for Karen?"

Luckily you have just filled your mouth with chicken salad, so you don't have to answer right away. Some of the things flying through your mind are (1) your peers told you your boss was under extreme pressure to do well with *NET*, and your last three months' experience supports that observation; (2) you remain concerned that your boss has covered up the immoral action of your predecessor, and you don't know why; and (3) you have frankly lost faith that she is the best manager for her job. How will you respond to this question?

   A. "If you want to know the truth, I think Karen is a fine manager but not an excellent manager." (GO TO 420B)
   B. "I have no complaints, Mr. Spencer. Do you ask with anything specific in mind?" (GO TO 405B)
   C. "Perfect, she's really an excellent manager." (GO TO 354B)

Decision Point 378A

You identified the following statement as a negative element of Betty's performance: "Betty lacks attentiveness to details." According to the chapter, this is incorrect. There is simply no evidence that she continues to have this problem. Although Milt Strong "dinged her" on this dimension, his evaluation apparently suffers from a negative halo effect, i.e., he is letting one experience or dimension color his entire evaluation. Moreover, there is evidence that Betty was not responsible for the error that Strong holds her responsible for. In fact, Betty has made real progress on this performance dimension. Remember when you went to the meeting with the wrong file and she "saved the day."

Re-evaluate your last decision. Circle the #378A you just wrote in your flow diagram. Then go back in your flow diagram to the first uncircled number above this step.

Decision Point 378B

His previous supervisor is very informative. He says: "Frank Wilson? Why, I know Frank very well. He was one of my best workers. I was real sorry to see him take the transfer over to your shop. We got along real well. I think the only reason he took the transfer was that he and his wife got back together, and he needed the extra money. Attendance record? No, Frank never had attendance problems when he worked for me."

What would you do now?

A. Call Frank aside upon his return and have a talk with him. (GO TO 333B)

B. Discuss the matter with your manager in order to get her advice and input in handling the situation. (GO TO 329A)

C. Call the Personnel Department to see what disciplinary options are open to you. (GO TO 322B)

D. Call the Personnel Department to see if there are other departments that need people with Frank's qualifications so you can transfer him there. (GO TO 342B)

E. Talk to some of Frank's co-workers to see if they have any idea what might be causing Frank's absences. (GO TO 336B)

F. Write Frank up for chronic absenteeism and leave a copy of the warning in an envelope on his desk for him to find when he comes in. (GO TO 332C)

Decision Point 379A

You have asked Frank to negotiate some standard of attendance that you both can live with. Frank responds that working Mondays poses a real problem for him right now, but if he can get the next couple of Mondays off, he thinks he can straighten out in a month or so.
How would you react to this?

A. Tell him that you are willing to let him miss the next two Mondays if he makes up the time on Saturday when the other employees are working overtime. After that, you will not be able to tolerate further Monday absences without disciplinary action. (GO TO 384C)

B. Tell him that Monday attendance is essential and that he should do the best he can to turn his attendance habits around. (GO TO 332A)

C. Persuade him that letting him have Mondays off would set a very bad precedent for the other employees. (GO TO 381B)

Decision Point 379B

You identified the following statement as a negative element of Betty's performance: "Betty is apparently careless." According to the Module Reading, this is incorrect. This statement is a trait, not a behavior. As such, it is not a performance element you want to feed back to Betty.
Re-evaluate your last decision. Circle the #379B you just wrote in your flow diagram. Then go back in your flow diagram to the first uncircled number above this step.

Decision Point 379C

Bob Blair agrees to give him two hours a week, and you give him two hours a week as well. This works well until, without either of you knowing, Bill gets conflicting advice from you and Bob on how to deal with a sensitive issue with a client. Bob's advice reflects a superior approach because of his better knowledge of the project, but Bill follows your suggestion. As a result, Bob publicly "dresses him down" at a team meeting for not following his advice. Two days later, Bill leaves the company without even talking to you about it.
Re-evaluate your last decision. Circle the #379C you just wrote in your flow diagram. Then move to the first uncircled step above this one in your flow diagram.

Decision Point 380A

"Well, thanks for the observation," says Mr. Spencer. "You're doing a fine job, keep it up."

As he walks out of the cafeteria, you notice Karen, your boss, approaching you. She waits to see that Spencer is out of sight and then sits down in the seat he occupied.

"What did he want?" she asks.

How would you respond?

A. "Nothing. We were just talking about unimportant things." (GO TO 353A)

B. "Well, he asked me if I thought you would be a good candidate for Manager of the Year." (GO TO 387A)

C. "Nothing important. But do you have 10 minutes so we could talk about something that's been troubling me?" This will permit you to raise the question of your predecessor again. (GO TO 340A)

Decision Point 380B

Convinced by your arguments, Bill withdraws his request for a transfer. Unfortunately, however, the rumor that Bill wants out of the group begins to spread throughout his project team. This results in Bill being given the "silent treatment" for a couple of days, and Bill comes in again with the idea of a transfer.

What would you do now?

A. Grant his request for a transfer because you don't think Bill can possibly earn the acceptance of his group under these circumstances. (GO TO 416B)

B. Give Bill a candid, accurate assessment of the social strengths and weaknesses of the other members of his work team, and advise him of specific actions he might take to gain more acceptance into the group. Monitor his social performance closely. (GO TO 347A)

C. Talk privately to other members of Bill's team and encourage each of them to serve as a mentor to Bill. (GO TO 383C)

D. Ask his team leader to allow Bill to be a spokesman for the team in an upcoming meeting with divisional management (at which all will be in attendance), so that he will have a chance to earn his team's approval. (GO TO 397B)

Decision Point 381A

Bob Blair does not work out as Bill's mentor. He is entirely too busy to give Bill all the attention he deserves, and he sometimes grows impatient when Bill doesn't catch on quickly. Bill continues to show an inability to set correct priorities to his work tasks. In addition, he is beginning to show signs of a loss of confidence again. What would you do now?

A. Begin yourself to give Bill a detailed account of how to contend with the challenges and problems in his work. Agree to meet with him in three days to review his progress and advise him on new situations. (GO TO 362B)

B. Talk to Bob Blair about sharing responsibility for breaking Bill in. (GO TO 379C)

C. Remind Bill of his agreement that he would take initiative if he had questions or was having problems. Indicate that he will not succeed unless he begins to ask questions, tells Bob Blair of his problems, and begins to take control of his own situation. (GO TO 407A)

D. Take time to remind others in your group of the importance of helping Bill adapt to his job. (GO TO 399B)

Decision Point 381B

You have told Frank that letting him have Mondays off would be a bad precedent for the other employees. He answers that he doesn't know what else he can suggest. What would you say now?

A. Tell him that Monday attendance is essential and that he should do the best he can to turn his attendance around. (GO TO 332A)

B. Tell him that you want to help him, but you must protect the interests of the company as well. Offer to withhold a first warning until the next Monday he is absent, and promise you will have to give him a second warning the following Monday if he is absent again. Explain that this means that he can miss Mondays but only at the expense of getting closer and closer to being terminated. At the same time, it fits his need to have more time to work out his personal problem. (GO TO 352B)

C. Tell him that you are willing to let him miss the next two Mondays if he makes up the time on Saturday when the other employees are working overtime. After that, you will not be able to tolerate further Monday absences without disciplinary action. (GO TO 384C)

Decision Point 382A

You decided to conduct your interview with Betty in her office. This is unadvisable. You want a site that is free from distractions, and in her office you are likely to be interrupted by phone calls and people dropping in.

Re-evaluate your last decision. Circle the #382A you just wrote in your flow diagram. Then go back in your flow diagram to the first uncircled number above this step.

Decision Point 382B

You inform Karen that the *NET* program will likely meet with considerable resistance. She tells you that better not happen. Clearly she is telling you that she is totally committed to a program that you have serious doubts about.

What would you do now?

A. Ask your boss for the background on the *NET* program. (GO TO 396B)

B. Diplomatically probe for what problems and ambitions your boss has. (GO TO 326A)

C. Clarify just what your boss means by "do the best you can" to improve quality. (GO TO 418B)

D. Try to persuade Karen that *NET* is a bad idea. (GO TO 421B)

Decision Point 382C

Unaware of the underlying political nature of the feasibility study, Bill is courted by proponents and opponents of the laser-refracting targeting system. This reminds Bill of the treatment he was given by the various recruiters who tried to entice him to join their firms when he was in college. Mistaking this attention for a vote of confidence in his ability, Bill sides with the opposition group. His stand is based on publicly stated but faulty technical reasoning, and it flaws the case of the opposition group. The division manager predictably sides against Bill's group, and Bill becomes the scapegoat for those opposing the decision. Bill leaves the company two days later.

Re-evaluate your last decision. Circle the #382C you just wrote in your flow diagram. Then move to the first uncircled step above this one in your flow diagram.

Decision Point 383A

You are telling Frank that he must respect your position as his supervisor. He tells you, "While it is obvious to me that you don't respect me, at least I have enough self-respect not to put up with your being on my case. I don't have to take that crap from my family, and I don't have to take it from you. I quit!" With that he walks out the door.

This situation has gone further than you thought it would. While you have "taken care" of Frank's attendance problem and maintained discipline in your work group, you have lost a skilled employee. This may cause difficulties, particularly if you are behind schedule. You will have to find a replacement and spend valuable time training that person. Furthermore, there is a chance that the new employee will cause you more difficulty than Frank did.

Under these circumstances, we want to offer you a second chance. GO TO 327A, and you will learn Frank's problem and can start the interactive case over from that point.

Decision Point 383B

You identified the following statement as a positive element of Betty's performance: "Betty has worked well under pressure." According to the chapter, this is incorrect. You have no evidence to substantiate this observation.

Re-evaluate your last decision. Circle the #383B you just wrote in your flow diagram. Then go back in your flow diagram to the first uncircled number above this step.

Decision Point 383C

Surprisingly, this appeal really works, and two members of Bill's team begin coaching Bill, taking him under their wing. You are delighted to see that Bill is finally accepted into the group.

After two weeks, however, a problem arises. Bill and his team leader have a mild disagreement, and two of Bill's new mentors give him conflicting advice on how to handle it. Unsure how to proceed, Bill comes to you.

What would you do now?

A. Give Bill a candid assessment of the social strengths and weaknesses of the other members of his work team and advise him of specific strategies he might use to solve his problem with his boss without upsetting either of his two mentors. (GO TO 347A)

B. Talk to the two mentors independently and privately and see if you can mediate this problem for Bill. (GO TO 356B)

Decision Point 384A

K. C. Wong does not work out as Bill's mentor. He is entirely too busy to give Bill all the attention he deserves, and he sometimes grows impatient when Bill doesn't catch on quickly.

Bill continues to show an inability to set correct priorities to his work tasks. In addition, he is beginning to show signs of a loss of confidence again. What would you do now?

A. Agree to meet daily with Bill to coach him on how to handle the specific, day-to-day problems that come up in his work. (GO TO 351B)

B. Begin yourself to give Bill a detailed account of how to contend with the challenges and problems in his work. Agree to meet with him in three days to review his progress and advise him on new situations. (GO TO 375B)

C. Talk to K. C. Wong about sharing responsibility for breaking Bill in. (GO TO 386C)

Decision Point 384B

Betty reacts very defensively to your statement. The reason is that your statement "We just can't have that going on" suggests certainty rather than provisionalism. In communicating negative feedback, it is important not to create a climate in which your point of view appears rigid. An additional problem with your statement is that it attributes this criticism to Barbara Mann. This is dangerous, for it may interfere with the work relationship between Betty and Barbara.

Re-evaluate your last decision. Circle the #384B you just wrote in your flow diagram. Then go back in your flow diagram to the first uncircled number above this step.

Decision Point 384C

Frank responds well to the plan the two of you have worked out. He does miss the next two Mondays, but he makes up the work on the subsequent Saturdays, and as a bonus, he tells his colleagues that you have been more than fair with him. He even talks a fellow worker out of looking for a job with a competitor that pays more.

Congratulations! You did very well. You handled a difficult situation admirably. This completes the Problem Employee Action Case.

Decision Point 385A

You ask your Leads whether the situation is causing real performance problems, and they tell you that while performance has not seriously deteriorated yet, they are sure that if the "silent treatment" continues, the problem person's error rate will certainly rise. This is consistent with your experience since some cooperation between employees is needed for error rates to be kept down.

Now what?

A. Transfer the problem employee. (GO TO 401C)

B. Tell your two Leads that they should handle the situation as they see fit, but that you are not in favor of the transfer except as a last resort. Let them know that you will assist them in handling the situation any way you can. (GO TO 344A)

C. Interview all the operators who are harassing the operator with the intention of modifying their behavior. (GO TO 408A)

D. Talk with the operator who is being harassed to determine her point of view. (GO TO 367B)

Decision Point 385B

You don't want to give her any more than five pieces of feedback during your appraisal interview. By asking her if there is any other area where she wants feedback, you are potentially stimulating a discussion of other areas of her performance. Should she do that, you could respond generally by saying that all other areas are more than satisfactory, but you should avoid specifics. You also did not give Betty her summary evaluation. Therefore, she asks you for it.

What would you say?

A. "Betty, at the beginning of this discussion, I thought I was going to give you an 'excellent' summary rating. However, as a result of this talk, I am going to try to get you an 'outstanding.' You understand that I will have to talk to Mike (your boss) because the company only permits a limited number of 'outstandings' in any one year." (GO TO 417C)

B. "It seems to me that, on the whole, your performance this past year has been excellent." (GO TO 406A)

C. "Betty, I really don't want to say. I'll get back to you on this in a few days." (GO TO 389C)

Decision Point 386A

When your boss returns from her vacation, she tells you that she has heard of the memo and that she did not send it. Someone "at the corporate level" simply redated a two-year-old memo and sent it out. She is livid about this obvious breach of protocol.

Your resistance to the memo is vindicated. You are pleased that you guessed right. As a new supervisor, though, you are now more confident of your instincts than ever, for you have successfully completed the New Supervisor Interactive Case. **Congratulations!**

Decision Point 386B

Your opening statement puts Betty at ease. Now you must give Betty her first piece of feedback. You choose to compliment her first on her knowledge of procedures. You tell Betty that you are very pleased that she has made so much progress in getting to know company procedures, and that you think she has been too harsh on herself on her form. She thanks you, and tells you that "it is a miracle" that her progress has been so positive given all the problems she has been having with the computer system. At this point, what would you say?

A. "Okay, let's talk about those problems." (GO TO 404A)

B. "Yes, I am generally familiar with the problems you are referring to, and we'll get to that in a minute. I just want to make sure you hear me when I tell you that your performance on this dimension is really exceptional, and I truly appreciate your progress." (GO TO 345B)

C. "I know all about your computer problems. I agree that your progress is excellent given your frustrations." (GO TO 419A)

Decision Point 386C

K. C. Wong agrees to give him two hours a week, and you agree to give him two hours a week as well. This works out well until, without your knowledge, you and K. C. give him conflicting advice about how to deal with a particular problem with a client. K. C.'s advice is actually better, for it reflects a better understanding of the specific situation. However, Bill follows your suggestion. As a result, K. C. publicly "dresses him down" at a team meeting for not following his advice. Two days later, Bill leaves the company without even talking to you.

Re-evaluate your last decision. Circle the #386C you just wrote in your flow diagram. Then move to the first uncircled step above this one in your flow diagram.

Decision Point 387A

You tell your boss that she is being considered for Manager of the Year. While truthful, it betrays an implied confidence with your boss's boss that comes back to haunt you. William Spencer discovers that you have told your boss and he informs you through a third party that he is "disappointed in your indiscretion."

Re-evaluate your last decision. Circle the #387A you just wrote in your flow diagram. Then move to the first uncircled step above this one in your flow diagram.

Decision Point 387B

Surprisingly, this appeal really works, and two members of Bill's team begin coaching Bill, taking him under their wing. You are delighted to see that Bill is finally accepted into the group. After two weeks, however, a problem arises. Bill and his team leader have a mild disagreement, and two of Bill's new mentors give him conflicting advice on how to handle it. Unsure how to proceed, Bill comes to you. What would you do now?

A. Give Bill a candid assessment of the social strengths and weaknesses of the other members of his work team and advise him of specific strategies he might use to solve his problem with his boss without upsetting either of his two mentors. (GO TO 358A)

B. Talk to the two mentors independently and privately and see if you can mediate this problem for Bill. (GO TO 356B)

Decision Point 387C

You asked Frank why Mondays pose such a problem for him. He says, "It just seems as though all my problems converge on that day."
What would you say now?

A. Tell him that you are willing to let him miss the next two Mondays if he makes up the time on Saturday when the other employees are working overtime. After that, you will not be able to tolerate further Monday absences without disciplinary action. (GO TO 384C)

B. Tell him that Monday attendance is essential and that he should do the best he can to turn his attendance habits around. (GO TO 332A)

C. Persuade him that letting him have Mondays off would set a very bad precedent for the other employees. (GO TO 381B)

Decision Point 388A

You have successfully identified the two negative elements of Betty's performance. They are captured in the following two statements:
1. Betty often complains to others instead of problem-solving with you;
2. Betty doesn't use adequate diplomacy when dealing with clients.

Now it is time for you to identify three positive elements of feedback to give Betty. Which would you choose?

A. Betty's volume of output is large. (GO TO 342A)

B. Betty sticks up for the project. (GO TO 403A)

C. Betty has demonstrated initiative. (GO TO 404C)

D. Betty's knowledge of procedures has improved markedly. (GO TO 370A)

E. Betty has worked well under pressure. (GO TO 383B)

F. Betty is conscientious. (GO TO 348A)

Decision Point 388B

It is now two days later. Frank has not returned to work yet. You tried to call him at home yesterday and got no answer. What would you do now?

A. Talk with some of Frank's co-workers to see if they have any idea what might be causing Frank's absences. (GO TO 336B)

B. Check with Frank's previous supervisor to see what his past attendance record was like. (GO TO 378B)

C. Discuss the matter with your manager in order to get her advice and input in handling the matter. (GO TO 329A)

D. Call the Personnel Department to see what disciplinary options are open to you. (GO TO 322B)

E. Call the Personnel Department to find out if there are any departments that need people with Frank's qualifications so you can transfer him. (GO TO 342B)

F. Continue to wait for Frank to return so you can have a talk with him. (GO TO 333B)

Decision Point 389A

You decide to comply with the policy with the idea that if your boss returns to discover a problem, she will be very displeased. When she returns, she is displeased all right, but with you for not fighting for the department. She tells you that she did not send the memo in question. Someone "at the corporate level" simply redated a two-year-old memo and sent it out. She is livid about this obvious breach of protocol. However, now that you have shown that you can provide the requested information, it will be very difficult to turn back. She lectures you on the need to question such memos from staff people in her absence, rather than simply being "blindly obedient."

Re-evaluate your last decision. Circle the #389A you just wrote in your flow diagram. Then move to the first uncircled step above this one in your flow diagram.

Decision Point 389B

Frank thanks you for the advice and agrees to call the family counselor. He is absent the following Monday, but on the next Tuesday, you learn that he has resigned his position with the company. Two weeks later, you get a call from Personnel. Frank has filed a lawsuit on the grounds that the counselor to whom you referred him caused the breakup of his marriage. The judge agrees with the plaintiff and orders your company to pay $15,000 in punitive damages. The ruling hinged on the fact that you acted as an agent of the company in referring Frank to a counselor and thus such a referral constituted a condition of employment.

Even though you made the referral on the best of intentions, supervisors are best advised not to make specific referrals except to company counselors. Since you were not aware of this potential liability, re-evaluate your last decision. Circle the #389B you just wrote in your flow diagram. Then move to the first uncircled number above this one in your flow diagram.

Decision Point 389C

It is unadvisable to defer giving Betty her summary evaluation. Even though you might want the time to explore the possibilities of giving her an outstanding rating with your boss, Betty is going to be very uneasy with this lack of closure.

Re-evaluate your last decision. Circle the #389C you just wrote in your flow diagram. Then go back in your flow diagram to the first uncircled number above this step.

Decision Point 390A

This opening statement will do little to put Betty at ease. It conveys the impression that you have carefully planned your interview. While it is true that you have, you want to create a communication climate that is as spontaneous as possible.

Re-evaluate your last decision. Circle the #390A you just wrote in your flow diagram. Then go back in your flow diagram to the first uncircled number above this step.

Decision Point 390B

You inquire about your boss's assessment of your predecessor. She says, "Don was a fine supervisor. I was sorry to see him go. He was loyal and very eager to do a good job. I realize that he wasn't popular in your group, but I think all of us should remember that he did the best he could. What's done is done, as far as I'm concerned. Besides, he is in a job now where he can do us a lot of good."

You are surprised and disappointed by Karen's rather positive comments. You were hoping she would give you a blank check for change by criticizing your predecessor. However, you were expecting something that very rarely happens. Superiors of marginal supervisors infrequently bad-mouth them after they have left their former position.

Re-evaluate your last decision. Circle the #390B you just wrote in your flow diagram. Then move to the first uncircled step above this one in your flow diagram.

Decision Point 390C

You are correct in withholding this document at this time. This enables you to better control the discussion. You now need to begin by providing Betty with some positive feedback.

Which positive element that you identified previously would you feedback to Betty at this time?

A. Betty's volume of output is large. (GO TO 413B)

B. Betty has demonstrated initiative. (GO TO 351A)

C. Betty's knowledge of procedures has improved markedly. (GO TO 330A)

Decision Point 391A

You return to your office and prepare for your discussions with your peers. When you arrive, your phone is ringing. You pick it up and Liz Hamilton from Employee Relations (the chairman of the *NET* implementation committee) asks you to come to her office at once. In spite of the fact that you have other appointments, you know that *NET* is high priority so you cancel them and immediately go to Liz's office. She details the implementation plan, and it is much more far-reaching than you ever imagined. Your operators will have to be reassigned, and entirely new forms and documents are involved. Most disturbing is that a number of issues you had assumed to be part of your responsibilities will now be taken away.

Presuming that all these matters have been approved by your boss, you proceed with the implementation obediently. Two weeks later, before work, your boss hails you in the parking lot. She is visibly upset. She asks you why you did not tell her about the changes in operator assignments. You respond that you thought she knew. Unfortunately, you didn't receive a very clear assignment from your boss on the *NET* program, and this has caused a problem.

Re-evaluate your last decision. Circle the #391A you just wrote in your flow diagram. Then move to the first uncircled step above this one in your flow diagram.

Decision Point 391B

The progress of the Solaris project improves markedly, and Bill seems to have weathered his crisis of confidence. Even though his responsibilities have been cut, he still shows signs of time mismanagement and a poor sense of priorities.

What would you do now?

A. Agree to meet daily with Bill to coach him on how to handle the specific, day-to-day problems that come up in his work. (GO TO 351B)

B. Meet with K. C. Wong and delegate responsibility to him for a more effective breaking in of Bill. Tell K. C. that you don't want him to sacrifice the objectives of the Solaris project, but that you think Bill deserves more of his time. (GO TO 384A)

C. Begin yourself to give Bill a detailed account of how to contend with the challenges and problems in his work. Agree to meet with him in three days to review his progress and advise him on new situations. (GO TO 375B)

D. Talk to K. C. Wong about sharing responsibility for breaking Bill in. (GO TO 386C)

Decision Point 392A

You decided to let Bob Blair handle this situation. Bob feels the best thing to do is to tell Bill that Sam needs practice dealing with problems like this and that Bill should stay out of it next time.

Bill disagrees strongly with Bob's position and storms out of his office muttering something about loyalty. Bill enters your office the next day still hot over the issue. You succeed in settling him down.

What would you do now?

A. Indicate how Bill should have handled the situation with the client in light of Sam's fundamental weaknesses, Bob Blair's responsibilities, and the particular client involved. (GO TO 414B)

B. Inform him that Sam needs practice bailing himself out and that he should not get involved in Sam's development. (GO TO 332B)

C. Tell Bill that clients should be allowed to say whatever they want, even if it is uncomplimentary, and that one important part of being a Venus employee is to be a flak-catcher. (GO TO 400B)

Decision Point 392B

Your equitable arrangement works very well. Not only are you able to enjoy the company of your old unit, but you are also able to keep closer to the problems of the other units as well. The last subordinate with whom you have a discussion is Fern Kaufman of Unit 4. Fern expresses relief that your predecessor is finally gone. She details several episodes in which Don Scott blamed problems on her unit when he was actually responsible. While you remember some of the situations she mentions in a general way, you have never heard some of the details before. They are very disturbing. Scott not only was lazy and ineffectual, but he blamed others who were not in a position to fight back. "Unbelievable," you say to yourself.

At the end of the interview, Fern asks you what you thought of Scott. What should you say?

A. "I think his actions speak for themselves. I was not aware that this was going on. I think the most important thing is that we pick up the pieces and go from here. Obviously you won't have to worry about a repeat of these behaviors from me." (GO TO 331B)

B. "Scott is a scoundrel. I have never heard such stories. Good riddance, that's all I can say!" (GO TO 422A)

Decision Point 393A

You identified the following statement as a negative element of Betty's performance: "Betty isn't smart enough to catch on quickly." According to the chapter, this is incorrect. This statement is a trait, not a behavior. As such, it is not a performance element you want to feed back to Betty.

Re-evaluate your last decision. Circle the #393A you just wrote in your flow diagram. Then go back in your flow diagram to the first uncircled number above this step.

Decision Point 393B

You wait to verify the facts of the episode before taking action. Unfortunately, Bill resigns the next morning minutes before you can talk to his team leader. Apparently a more immediate response was preferable.

Re-evaluate your last decision. Circle the #393B you just wrote in your flow diagram. Then move to the first uncircled step above this one in your flow diagram.

Decision Point 393C

You decide to let the matter drop, and that is the last you hear of it until three days later. Post meets you in the hallway and asks what you plan to do about it. You tell him that you have investigated the situation, and it is your assessment that it is not serious enough to warrant a transfer. He tells you that he hopes you are correct.

Your next appointment is with LeRoy Jackson. He is the Lead who took your old position with Unit 2. The two of you have a delightful conversation. He was one of the people you used to play cards with at lunch before your promotion. At the end of your conversation, LeRoy tells you that some of the people in your old unit have been asking why you aren't playing cards with them at lunch anymore. What would you say?

- A. "Well, now that I am a supervisor, I don't think it is appropriate for me to do that anymore." (GO TO 372B)

- B. "I'll be there tomorrow. I wouldn't want the old card game to go on without me." (GO TO 417B)

- C. "I'll come around at lunch from time to time, don't worry." (GO TO 374A)

- D. "I'll tell you what. I have to spread my lunchtime evenly among all the units now. Tell the group that should mean that they'll have to endure my presence about once a month." (GO TO 392B)

Decision Point 394A

It is one month later, and you are delighted with Bill's work. While Bill was willing at first, he's begun to balk at some of the tasks that you've assigned him recently. This you attribute to a friend he's made on one of the design teams who introduced him to the concept of the half-life of his technical education. The last conversation you had with Bill included the following:

You: "When you're through with this last budget analysis, I want you to spend a week updating the PERT diagram."

Bill: "Another one?"

You: "Yup, Betty has got all kinds of typing to do, and she just can't get to it for a while."

Bill (eyes down): "I hope when I finish that there will be some engineering for me to do for a while."

You: "I know you do, Bill."

Bill: "If I don't get started pretty soon, I'm afraid I'll lose my edge. Do you know that the half-life of my educational background is 18 months? As I figure it, my technical know-how has already decreased 9 percent! That scares me. I talked to K. C. Wong about helping him on the Solaris project, and we sure think I'd be able to lend a hand."

What would you do after Bill completes the PERT diagram update?

A. Give him Assignment 1. Junior Control Engineer, Dart Project. Join a team of four members to test a ballistics control system for a Dart missile. Estimated probability of making a net contribution to the team = 60 percent. Value to Bill's development if he is personally successful = 40 points out of 100. (GO TO 402A)

B. Give him Assignment 2. Junior Control Engineer, Solaris Project. Join a team of three members to test the propulsion control system for a Solaris booster. Estimated probability of making a net contribution to the team = 30 percent. Value to Bill's development if he is personally successful = 80 points out of 100. (GO TO 343A)

C. Give him Assignment 4. Junior Control Engineer, Systems Test Group, and Member, Micascope Divisional Task Force. Join a task force of seven members conducting a manufacturing feasibility study of Micascope, a laser-refracting targeting system. The task force is chaired by the assistant to the divisional manager. Estimated probability of making a net contribution to the task force = 50 percent. Value to Bill's development if he is personally successful = 80 points out of 100. (GO TO 382C)

D. Continue him as your administrative assistant, but find him administrative tasks with an engineering component. (GO TO 371C)

Decision Point 395A

You ask your boss if you should keep her informed of your discussions with Liz Hamilton. She says, "Yes, please do. That will permit me to monitor the program more closely." You walk out of her office feeling ten feet tall. When you return to your office, your phone is ringing. You pick it up and Liz Hamilton asks you to come to her office at once. Although you have appointments, you know that *NET* is high priority, so you go to Liz's office. She details the implementation plan, and it is much more far-reaching than you ever imagined. Your operators will have to be reassigned, and some of your responsibilities will now be taken away. Concerned, you have introductory meetings with three of your new peers. The results of these meetings are summarized below:

Brian Curtin (Supervisor, Group B: Computer Systems) tells you that your boss is under extreme pressure to implement the *NET* program. He knows that her last performance review was not as high as she expected, and he suspects that *NET* is being forced on her. He tells you he is personally in favor of *NET*, but that it will take a lot longer to implement than anyone realizes.

Joyce Evanston (Supervisor, Group C: Documents) tells you that she really loves her job. She was promoted just 18 months ago and has been able to accomplish a great deal so far. She tells you that Karen really respects supervisors who are decisive and bold. Her predecessor learned that the hard way. He was very cautious; Karen criticized him no end. Joyce doesn't think Karen really likes *NET* very much but is being forced to implement it.

Leo Leiter (Supervisor, Group D: Special Accounts) tells you that your boss considers the quality of your group to be the lowest, and that you were promoted to turn the situation around. According to Leo, *NET* will certainly not help you do that. He advises you to be very careful.

Together, these interviews leave you with several troubling observations: (1) your boss has a very low opinion of the quality of your group's performance; (2) your boss may be under pressure to make *NET* work; (3) *NET* seems to be in for some major implementation problems.

What will you do now?

A. Return to Curtin and Evanston to see if they think your group is considered by your boss to have the poorest quality record. (GO TO 411A)
B. Return to your boss to see if she really does consider your group to have the poorest quality performance. (GO TO 371B)
C. Do nothing right now; speak with your subordinates. (GO TO 328A)
D. Warn your boss that your peers are not very optimistic about *NET*. (GO TO 404B)
E. Look for something "bold and decisive" to do to impress your boss. (GO TO 365B)

Decision Point 396A

Betty reacts very defensively to your statement. The reason is that it is phrased in a superior fashion. Your opening sentence, "Betty, you've really got to get control of yourself," conveys condescension. In providing negative feedback, it is important to strive to create a climate of equality, rather than superiority.

Re-evaluate your last decision. Circle the #396A you just wrote in your flow diagram. Then go back in your flow diagram to the first uncircled number above this step.

Decision Point 396B

You ask your boss for the background on the *NET* program. She informs you that the people in Corporate Employee Relations have earned an endorsement for *NET* from some very high officials in the bank. She also tells you that even if it didn't have such high-level support, she would support it on the grounds that it gives visibility to her department because *NET* will identify her department as the most error-free in the division.

You indirectly refer to the consultants for whom you have so little respect, and your boss declares them now totally out of the picture. Apparently their role was only in the development of the *NET* program, and they will play no part in the implementation. This additional background was very valuable. You are now much more optimistic about *NET* and impressed with your boss's managerial instincts. Karen stands and walks around to the other side of her desk in an apparent signal that your meeting is ending.

What would you say?

A. Thank her for the background, express optimism at the opportunity she has helped to give you, and return to your office to prepare to meet your new peers. (GO TO 391A)

B. Ask her if she wants you to do anything to prepare for *NET* before being contacted by the *NET* implementation team. (GO TO 348C)

C. Tell her that you are relieved the consultants will not be involved in the implementation since they alienated some of the members of your former work group. Be frank in telling her that there may still be some resistance to *NET* because of what they did. (GO TO 400A)

D. Ask your boss for her assessment of your predecessor. (GO TO 390B)

E. Diplomatically probe for what problems and ambitions your boss has. (GO TO 352A)

Decision Point 397A

She asks you if there had been any other specific instances where you had heard that she was undiplomatic with a client. Since you have no other such information, it weakens the effect of your negative feedback. You noticed that several members of the Project staff did mention Betty's tendency not to be diplomatic, but you do not have the specifics of the basis for their evaluations. It is better to begin with a general statement and then offer an example than to begin with an example when giving negative feedback.

Re-evaluate your last decision. Circle the #397A you just wrote in your flow diagram. Then go back in your flow diagram to the first uncircled number above this step.

Decision Point 397B

Bill fumbles and mumbles his way through the presentation much to the chagrin of the entire team. Knowing his performance was weak but hoping for approval, he asks his colleagues for their assessment of his performance. They respond with little tact, and Bill resigns a week afterward.

Re-evaluate your last decision. Circle the #397B you just wrote in your flow diagram. Then move to the first uncircled step above this one in your flow diagram.

Decision Point 397C

You ask Lucy to be more specific about the advantages and disadvantages of her proposal. She does so in great detail, and the more you hear, the more convinced you are that her idea is sound. Ordinarily, supervisors are able to make such changes without consulting with their superiors.

At this point how would you proceed?

A. Talk to your boss about the proposal because you are a new supervisor, even though you realize that if you were an experienced supervisor you would not require her endorsement. (GO TO 422C)

B. Since the change sounds reasonable, give her the green light. (GO TO 419B)

C. Tell her that you will consider her request and get back to her. (GO TO 373A)

D. Tell her that with *NET* coming, you would like to wait a bit before making any changes that might have an impact on quality. (GO TO 409A)

Decision Point 398A

You've decided to withdraw from helping Bill with his work/family problems. Two months later, Bill's commuting difficulties multiply and his attendance record worsens. This results in his project failing to meet important milestones, and now it is clear that you are going to have to take some action.

What would you do now?

A. Encourage Bill to take the initiative on this problem. Explore alternatives with him and advise him what action to take. (GO TO 345A)

B. Introduce Bill to a person in another division who, like Bill, lives in the country and has school-aged children. (GO TO 328B)

Decision Point 398B

You decided to use a problem-solving format. This is perfectly acceptable. You schedule your meeting with Betty. She arrives on time and sits across from you at the conference table.

How would you open the discussion?

A. "The underlying purpose of this talk is to discuss your job, and its primary purpose is to enable me to help you. Both of us should keep this in mind throughout our talk." (GO TO 371A)

B. "I've been studying your last year's performance, and I want to give you my frank, honest evaluation of how well you've done." (GO TO 418C)

C. "I wanted to set some time aside to talk about your performance this year. Obviously this topic is one that can be uncomfortable for both you and me, but let's approach it as a guidance and feedback session rather than one full of evaluations and accusations." (GO TO 422B)

D. "I'm sure that you want to know how I see your performance last year. I'm also interested in how you see it. So let's view this session as an exchange of views rather than a chance for me to make firm statements." (GO TO 336A)

E. "I'm glad we are going to have some time together to discuss your last year's performance. I've spent a lot of time preparing for this session so that we can cover a lot of ground and still have time for questions." (GO TO 390A)

Decision Point 399A

"Well, thanks for the observation," says Mr. Spencer. "You're doing a fine job, keep it up." As he walks out of the cafeteria, you notice Karen, your boss, approaching you. She waits to see that Spencer is out of sight and then sits down in the seat he occupied.

"What did he want?" she asks.

How would you respond?

A. "Nothing. We were just talking about unimportant things." (GO TO 353A)

B. "Well, he asked me if I thought you would be a good candidate for Manager of the Year." (GO TO 387A)

C. "Nothing important. But do you have 10 minutes so we could talk about something that's been troubling me?" This will permit you to raise the question of your predecessor again. (GO TO 340A)

Decision Point 399B

You have spoken to the others in your group about the importance of helping Bill. Unfortunately, there is no noticeable change in Bill's attitude or performance. The only outcome of this action is that one of the group members advises Bill incorrectly on how to complete a technical task.

What would you do now?

A. Coach Bill on how to be the member of a test engineering team. (GO TO 341B)

B. Agree to meet daily with Bill to coach him on how to handle the specific, day-to-day problems that come up in his work. (GO TO 359B)

C. Remind Bill of his agreement to take the initiative if he had questions or was having problems. Indicate that he will not succeed unless he begins to take control of his own situation. (GO TO 407A)

D. Begin yourself to give Bill a detailed account of how to contend with the challenges and problems in his work. Agree to meet with him in three days to review his progress and advise him on new situations. (GO TO 362B)

E. Meet with Bob Blair and delegate responsibility to him for a more effective breaking in of Bill. Tell Bob that you don't want him to sacrifice the objectives of the Dart test system, but that you think Bill deserves more of his time. (GO TO 381A)

Decision Point 400A

You inform Karen that the *NET* program will likely meet with considerable resistance. She tells you that better not happen. Clearly she is telling you that she is totally committed to a program that you have serious doubts about.

What would you say now?

A. Thank her for the background, express optimism at the opportunity she has helped to give you, and return to your office to prepare to meet your new peers. (GO TO 391A)

B. Ask her if she wants you to do anything to prepare for *NET* before being contacted by the *NET* implementation team. (GO TO 348C)

C. Ask you boss for her assessment of your predecessor. (GO TO 390B)

D. Diplomatically probe for what problems and ambitions your boss has. (GO TO 352A)

Decision Point 400B

Bill apologizes for being so aggressive with the client and goes back to work. Two weeks later, you overhear Bill making disparaging remarks about several design engineers who "think they know more about control systems" than his project team. Later that day you hear that Bill engaged in verbal bantering in the company cafeteria with one of the design engineers. The bantering escalated into name calling and ended when Bill called one of the designers "a jerk who should design with a crayon."

Fearing that this attitude may endanger the necessary work relationship between the team and the designers, you decide to intervene.

What would you say to Bill?

A. Indicate how he should have handled the situation in the cafeteria in terms of necessary good relationships between the designers and his team, the responsibility he has to deal with such conflicts in a more diplomatic way, and the particular attributes of the design group involved. (GO TO 414B)

B. Tell Bill that he should let his team leader deal with the designers for a while until things cool off. (GO TO 337B)

C. Verify the story of the cafeteria incident with his team leader before calling Bill in. (As it is now 4:30 p.m., this will necessitate a one-day delay.) (GO TO 393B)

Decision Point 401A

Your reiteration is unnecessary. It serves to create a climate of evaluation rather than description. In general, you want to avoid conveying this sort of climate when providing feedback. You also did not give Betty her summary evaluation. Therefore, she asks you for it.
What would you say?

A. "Betty, at the beginning of this discussion, I thought I was going to give you an 'excellent' summary rating. However, as a result of this talk, I am going to try to get you an 'outstanding.' You understand that I will have to talk to Mike (your boss) because the company only permits a limited number of 'outstandings' in any one year." (GO TO 417C)

B. "It seems to me that, on the whole, your performance this past year has been excellent." (GO TO 406A)

C. "Betty, I really don't want to say. I'll get back to you on this in a few days." (GO TO 389C)

Decision Point 401B

The situation with Bill continues to worsen. He botches a critical test given to him with inadequate instructions, and the other members of his team "jump all over him." Too embarrassed to tell you, Bill sulks for two days before signing his resignation letter.
Re-evaluate your last decision. Circle the #401B you just wrote in your flow diagram. Then move to the first uncircled step above this one in your flow diagram.

Decision Point 401C

You decide to transfer the problem employee and consult your boss on how to proceed further. You put through the paperwork and have the employee transferred to Lucy Morris's group. All goes well with the transfer, although Lucy tells you later that the employee in question expressed surprise at the transfer.
Later Terrence Post and James Hopkins approach you separately with other requests for your involvement in personnel problems. Clearly your decisive action has convinced them that if they "delegate upward," you will do their work for them.
Re-evaluate your last decision. Circle the #401C you just wrote in your flow diagram. Then move to the first uncircled step above this one in your flow diagram.

Decision Point 402A

It is one month later, and from what you've heard, Bill is doing okay. The test team leader, Bob Blair, has said little except that Bill is performing much as he did when he was new with the company. Bill has completed several test analyses, but his rate of output is markedly slow. According to Blair, Bill does not manage his time well. He is slow to get a sense of priorities. He spends a large amount of time on a relatively unimportant procedure, and then is entirely too superficial on a report intended for a client. The last time you talked to Blair, he apologized for not being able to spend more time with Bill. Yesterday you took time to visit Bill in his cubicle. The following discussion took place:

You: (after pleasantries) "How do you like working on the Dart?"
Bill: "Fine, just fine, I'm learning a lot."
You: "Good! Have you found your thesis work helpful?"
Bill: "Well, yes. Sort of. Professor Babcock was sure off though. I guess he never had to meet a payroll."
You: "That's pretty typical. But Bob Blair tells me that you are making a meaningful contribution."
Bill: "He did? Wow! Well, I've tried."
You: "Do you like working with Don [a Dart team member]?"
Bill: "Well, yes, I guess so. I don't see him much."
You: "You don't? I thought you two would have been working closely."
Bill: "Well, he has helped me a couple of times, but I don't see him much. I did have a problem I thought he could help me with, but I guess I was hesitant to ask."

What would you do now?

A. Take time to remind others in your group of the importance of helping Bill adapt to his job. (GO TO 399B)
B. Coach Bill on how to be the member of a test engineering team. (GO TO 341B)
C. Agree to meet daily with Bill to coach him on how to handle the specific, day-to-day problems that come up in his work. (GO TO 359B)
D. Remind Bill of his agreement to take initiative if he had questions or was having problems. Indicate that he will not succeed unless he begins to ask questions, tells Bob Blair his problems, and begins to take control of his own situation. (GO TO 407A)
E. Begin yourself to give Bill a detailed account of how to contend with the challenges and problems of his work. Agree to meet with him in three days to review his progress and advise him on new situations. (GO TO 362B)
F. Meet with Bob Blair and delegate responsibility to him for a more effective breaking in of Bill. Tell Bob that you don't want him to sacrifice the objectives of the Dart test system, but that you think Bill deserves more of his time. (GO TO 381A)

Decision Point 403A

You identified the following statement as a positive element of Betty's performance: "Betty sticks up for the project." According to the chapter, this is incorrect. This statement was on Homer Ashe's appraisal form, but you have no verification of it, nor is it very specific. In addition, you probably should not use Ashe's inputs since he has only been with the firm for a short while, and his form has the appearance of one that suffers from a positive halo effect.

Re-evaluate your last decision. Circle the #403A you just wrote in your flow diagram. Then go back in your flow diagram to the first uncircled number above this step.

Decision Point 403B

You decide to talk with your boss about the human relations problem in Post's and Hopkins' units. Your boss expresses absolutely no interest in getting involved. She tells you that situations like this do not concern her and that you should handle it yourself.

What is your next move?

A. Transfer the problem employee. (GO TO 401C)

B. Tell your two Leads that they should handle the situation as they see fit, but that you are not in favor of the transfer except as a last resort. Let them know that you will assist them in handling the situation any way you can. (GO TO 344A)

C. Interview all the operators who are harassing the operator with the intention of modifying their behavior. (GO TO 408A)

D. Talk with the operator who is being harassed to determine her point of view. (GO TO 367B)

E. Find out if the situation is causing real performance problems. (GO TO 385A)

Decision Point 403C

You decided to conduct your interview with Betty in the cafeteria. This is unadvisable. Although the choice of a "neutral" setting is proper, the cafeteria is likely to be a noisy, distracting place. You want all of Betty's attention, so a quiet setting is much more appropriate.

Re-evaluate your last decision. Circle the #403C you just wrote in your flow diagram. Then go back in your flow diagram to the first uncircled number above this step.

Decision Point 404A

By moving directly into this issue, you cannot be sure that Betty received the strength of your positive feedback about the volume of her work. It is better to repeat your feedback than to run the risk that Betty will underestimate its importance.

Re-evaluate your last decision. Circle the #404A you just wrote in your flow diagram. Then go back in your flow diagram to the first uncircled number above this step.

Decision Point 404B

You decide to warn your boss that your peers are not very optimistic about *NET*. You do so, and she tells you she is aware of the problems. When you return to your office, you are confronted by Leo Leiter who tells you he just got a phone call from your boss, who warned him that he had better support *NET*. Leo is visibly upset with you for "betraying a confidence."

He says, "Listen, what I say to you is off the record, understand? I don't want to have to look over my shoulder every time I tell you something. It's going to be a long time before I speak in confidence to you again, believe me!" In effect, your actions ruined one peer relationship with no gains for you or your boss.

Re-evaluate your last decision. Circle the #404B you just wrote in your flow diagram. Then move to the first uncircled step above this one in your flow diagram.

Decision Point 404C

You identified the following statement as a positive element of Betty's performance: "Betty has demonstrated initiative." This is correct. Your observations and Jensen's both confirm this.

What other statement do you think reflects a positive piece of feedback?

A. Betty's volume of output is large. (GO TO 352C)

B. Betty sticks up for the project. (GO TO 403A)

C. Betty's knowledge of procedures has improved markedly. (GO TO 353C)

D. Betty has worked well under pressure. (GO TO 383B)

E. Betty is conscientious.(GO TO 348A)

Decision Point 405A

You identified the following statement as a positive element of Betty's performance: "Betty's volume of output is large." This is correct. The only negative bit of information you have on this score is Milt Strong's evaluation form and it probably suffers from a negative halo effect.

What other statement do you think reflects a positive piece of feedback?

A. Betty sticks up for the project. (GO TO 403A)

B. Betty has demonstrated initiative. (GO TO 361B)

C. Betty has worked well under pressure. (GO TO 383B)

D. Betty is conscientious. (GO TO 348A)

Decision Point 405B

Spencer responds, "Well, yes, there is. I am thinking of nominating Karen for Manager of the Year at the next annual management retreat, and I felt I should make inquiries of her subordinates. The Manager of the Year Award is given to those at her level who have demonstrated high standards of excellence and integrity. Do you think Karen measures up?"

What would you say?

A. "No, I don't, but please don't ask me why." (GO TO 325A)

B. "Actually, there is something I think I should tell you about." Be prepared to tell Mr. Spencer all you know about the situation with Karen's cover-up of your predecessor's apparent indiscretion. (GO TO 357B)

C. "I think so. She has certainly played very straight with me." (GO TO 380A)

D. "You couldn't make a finer choice. I have absolutely no reservations about having her named Manager of the Year." (GO TO 399A)

Decision Point 405C

This is an excellent approach and one that results in a development plan that is very motivating. One of the elements in the plan is that you will work on improving the relationship between Betty and Milt Strong.

Congratulations! You have just completed the Performance Appraisal Interactive Case.

Decision Point 406A

She expresses frustration at your summary evaluation. She says: "'Excellent.' You gave me an 'excellent' last year. I really think I deserve an 'outstanding.' You congratulated me on the progress I've made on last year's development plan. It seems to me that I've done everything you asked me to do without any decrease in my output. The only problems you pointed out were problems due to your lack of direction. I don't understand."

How would you respond?

A. "Betty, it is true that your performance has been very strong this year. However, there is still room for improvement. My philosophy is that people should not be given outstanding ratings unless their performance is flawless." (GO TO 414A)

B. "Maybe you're right. I'll tell you what I'll do. I'll talk to Mike Wagner (your boss) about the possibilities of upgrading you to an 'outstanding.' I can't guarantee anything, mind you, but let me see if he has room for one more person at that level. You know, of course, that only two assistants per division may qualify for that rating." (GO TO 417C)

C. "There is really nothing wrong with an excellent rating. You should realize that that will qualify you for a 2.5 percent merit pay increase over and above the cost-of-living adjustment." (GO TO 416C)

D. "I understand your position, believe me. However, I still think there is room for some improvement. It seems to me that we can work out a development plan this year that is very achievable, and that if your performance on all dimensions holds constant at its present level and you accomplish the things we set out in the plan, I will be more than happy to rate you outstanding next year." (GO TO 366A)

Decision Point 406B

You decide to phone your boss on vacation. She is very angry that you have disturbed her. She tells you that she is not interested in the situation and advises you to handle it yourself.

What would you do now?

A. Fight the appropriate staff group of the company on the grounds that an investment of 14 hours of your time is not warranted. (GO TO 386A)

B. Comply with the policy with the idea that if your boss returns to discover a problem, she will be very displeased. (GO TO 389A)

Decision Point 407A

Bill continues to have difficulty on Bob Blair's team. Bob and the other members of the team are very often too busy to help him, and there are signs that they are growing increasingly irritated with his distracting questions. Through the grapevine, you learn that Bill has contacted a firm that had heavily recruited him.

What would you do now?

A. Take time to remind others in your group of the importance of helping Bill adapt to his job. (GO TO 399B)

B. Agree to meet daily with Bill to coach him on how to handle the specific, day-to-day problems that come up in his work. (GO TO 359B)

C. Begin yourself to give Bill a detailed account of how to contend with the challenges and problems in his work. Agree to meet with him in three days to review his progress and advise him on new situations. (GO TO 362B)

D. Meet with Bob Blair and delegate responsibility to him for a more effective breaking in of Bill. Tell Bob that you don't want him to sacrifice the objectives of the Dart test system, but that you think Bill deserves more of his time. (GO TO 381A)

Decision Point 407B

You decided to include three additional pieces of information in your discussion with Betty:

6. the relationship between your summary evaluation and her merit pay increase.
8. her self-rating on the employee performance appraisal form.
10. the specific assessments others have made of her.

According to the Module Reading, this is incorrect. While it is perfectly acceptable to have included 8, you do not want to discuss merit pay with Betty at this time. Research indicates that discussions of pay and performance should be conducted separately. In addition, it is not appropriate to share with Betty the specific assessments others have made of her performance. Not only might there be confidences involved, but doing so emphasizes the multiple-boss arrangement that she is in.

Re-evaluate your last decision. Circle the #407B you just wrote in your flow diagram. Then go back in your flow diagram to the first uncircled number above this step.

Decision Point 408A

You decide to interview each of the members of the two units with the idea of modifying their behavior toward the problem employee. You try to convince each of them that the personal lives of employees are really a private concern, and if the problem employee's work performance is satisfactory (you checked and it is), that is all that is important. As the interviews progress, you become convinced that two or three "troublemakers" are probably at the center of the problem. Accordingly, when employees express resentment toward the employee in question, you are firm in your statements. Your actions apparently work, because three days after your interviews, the problem employee's co-workers are much more cooperative toward the problem employee.

Two months pass and the employee who had once been the object of so much negative attention quits. During her exit interview, you learn that she was never subjected to that much harassment. Sure, a couple of the older employees gave her a little trouble, but she says you blew the situation way out of proportion. Clearly you were set up. Two of your Leads gave you a test by exaggerating a problem that they themselves should have been directed to solve. Instead, you got personally involved and, in effect, wasted a lot of time and effort. In retrospect, you now realize that the two Leads in question, Terrence Post and James Hopkins, have been bringing you the most trivial matters ever since.

Re-evaluate your last decision. Circle the #408A you just wrote in your flow diagram. Then move to the first uncircled step above this one in your flow diagram.

Decision Point 408B

Your opening statement puts Betty at ease. Now you must give Betty her first piece of feedback. You choose to compliment her first on her knowledge of procedures. You tell Betty that you are very pleased that she has made so much progress in getting to know company procedures, and that you think she has been too harsh on herself on her form. She thanks you and tells you that "it is a miracle" that her progress has been so positive given all the problems she has been having with the computer system.

At this point what would you say?

A. "Okay, let's talk about those problems." (GO TO 404A)
B. "Yes, I am generally familiar with the problems you are referring to, and we'll get to that in a minute. I just want to make sure you hear me when I tell you that your performance on this dimension is really exceptional and that I truly appreciate your progress." (GO TO 345B)
C. "I know all about your computer problems. I agree that your progress is excellent, given your frustrations." (GO TO 419A)

Decision Point 409A

Your decision seems to satisfy Lucy, and she monitors the progress of the *NET* program to see how it influences her proposal. This gives you more time and causes Lucy to be more committed to *NET* than she would otherwise be.

Your third interview with your new subordinates is with James Hopkins and Terrence Post (recall that Post is the Lead for an "elite" group who was disturbed that he wasn't given your promotion). Due to a conflict in schedules, you must interview them at the same time. After some discussion, they detail a human relations problem they are having. It seems that one of the operators is receiving some harassment from a number of the others. The operator in question has recently "given up her three children" and left her husband to live with a foreign man who is in the U.S. illegally. The other employees consider this morally reprehensible and are giving her "the silent treatment" and not cooperating with her. Although the operator in question is in Post's unit, the employees involved in the harassment come from Hopkins's unit as well.

Although the two Leads do not name names, they share the suspicion with you that a number of "troublemakers" may be behind the situation. They also suggest that you transfer the employee in question and report the matter to your boss.

How would you proceed?

A. Transfer the problem employee and consult your boss on how to proceed further. (GO TO 322A)

B. Talk with your boss about this matter before taking any further action. (GO TO 403B)

C. Tell your two Leads that they should handle the situation as they see fit, but that you are not in favor of the transfer except as a last resort. Let them know that you will assist them in handling the situation any way you can. (GO TO 597B)

D. Interview all the operators who are harassing the operator with the intention of modifying their behavior. (GO TO 408A)

E. Talk with the operator who is being harassed to determine her point of view. (GO TO 367B)

F. Find out if the situation is causing real performance problems. (GO TO 385A)

Decision Point 410A

You decided to include none of the additional information you were presented with. That is perfectly acceptable.

Now that you have decided what to cover (and what not to cover), you now must decide how to conduct the appraisal interview. The following strategies are common.

Which would you use?

A. Approach 1. (GO TO 398B)
   - Ask her to fill out a performance appraisal form on herself before the meeting.
   - Put her at ease.
   - Examine together the similarities and differences between your filled out form and hers.
   - Cover the five specific points you have identified previously, starting with a positive point, then a negative, etc.
   - Ascertain your role in her deficient performance.
   - Give her your summary rating and invite her reactions/inputs.
   - Go over last year's development plan and jointly develop next year's plan.

B. Approach 2. (GO TO 355C)
   - Put her at ease.
   - Tell her the five strong and weak points of her performance (one positive, one negative, one positive, etc.), inviting her explanation of each.
   - Announce your summary rating.
   - Indicate elements you want in her next year's development plan after reviewing last year's plan.
   - Complete next year's development plan.

C. Approach 3. (GO TO 365A)
   - Put her at ease.
   - Tell her the five strong and weak points of her performance (one positive, one negative, one positive, etc.), inviting her reactions on each.
   - Try to ascertain how she thinks you might have supported her better given her weaknesses.
   - Give her your summary evaluation and solicit her reactions.
   - Review last year's development plan together.
   - Work together developing next year's development plan.

Decision Point 411A

You return to Curtin and Evanston to see if they agree with Leo Leiter that Karen considers your group to be a quality problem. Both of them deny that Karen feels that way; in fact, Brian Curtin tells you that he doesn't know how your predecessor did so well on quality, since he was such a "second-class" supervisor. Evanston tells you not to listen to Leiter about such things: "He likes to stir things up."

You now invite your new Leads in one at a time to get to know them better. First you speak with Daryl Peters, your Unit 3 Lead. Your meeting with him goes very well. You discover that he is a very cooperative guy, and you find his approach to people problems very similar to your own. You do suspect that he is "buttering you up" a bit, but you sort of enjoy the treatment.

Your meeting with Lucy Morris (Unit 1) is more challenging. After an exchange of pleasantries, she asks if you will allow her to do something that your predecessor had opposed. She outlines the issue as follows:

"Is it okay if we rearrange the accounts so we balance out the customer phone calls? The way we do it now is by account number, and that means that some of the girls make 50 phone calls a day and others three. That's really not fair and it causes real morale problems. Don (your predecessor) said that having each clerk responsible for a sequence of account numbers made it quicker to spot errors, but that's hogwash. It just takes a second longer to look up who's on what account. What do you say, can we make the change?"

Lucy's proposal sounds fine. It has nothing whatsoever to do with *NET*, and while you never had this sort of problem in your old unit, you can understand how an uneven distribution of customer contacts might result in real morale problems.

What would you do now?

A. Ask her to be more specific about the advantages and disadvantages of the change. (GO TO 397C)

B. Since the change sounds reasonable, give her the green light. (GO TO 419B)

C. Tell her that you will consider her request and get back to her. (GO TO 373A)

D. Tell her that with *NET* coming, you would like to wait a bit before making any changes that might have an impact on quality. (GO TO 409A)

Decision Point 412A

You decided to include three additional pieces of information:
6. the relationship between your summary evaluation and her merit pay increase.
8. her self-rating on the employee performance appraisal form.
9. her career plans.

According to the Module Reading, this is incorrect. While it is perfectly acceptable to have included 8 and 9, you do not want to discuss merit pay with Betty at this time. Research clearly demonstrates that discussions of pay and performance should be conducted separately. Now that you have decided what to cover (and what not to cover), you now must decide how to conduct the appraisal interview. The following strategies are common. Which would you use?

A. Approach 1. (GO TO 398B)
   ---Ask her to fill out her own appraisal form before the meeting.
   ---Put her at ease.
   ---Examine together the similarities and differences in the forms.
   ---Cover the five specific points you have identified previously, starting with a positive point, then a negative, etc.
   ---Ascertain your role in her deficient performance.
   ---Give her your summary rating and invite her reactions/inputs.
   ---Go over last year's development plan and jointly develop next year's plan.

B. Approach 2. (GO TO 355C)
   ---Put her at ease.
   ---Tell her the five strong and weak points of her performance (one positive, one negative, one positive, etc.), inviting her explanation of each.
   ---Announce your summary rating.
   ---Indicate elements you want in her next year's development plan after reviewing last year's plan.
   ---Complete next year's development plan.

C. Approach 3. (GO TO 365A)
   ---Put her at ease.
   ---Tell her the five strong and weak points of her performance (one positive, one negative, one positive, etc.), inviting her reactions on each.
   ---Try to ascertain how she thinks you might have supported her better given her weaknesses.
   ---Give her your summary evaluation and solicit her reactions.
   ---Review last year's development plan together.
   ---Work together developing next year's development plan.

Decision Point 413A

You call Post and Hopkins and tell them what you have learned. They look at each other rather sheepishly, and it is clear that this was a test of your supervisory skills. You then deliver a strongly worded speech about the importance of reporting situations truthfully. At the end of your speech, Post offers the rather feeble excuse that the two of them had thought it was of potential importance, and with *NET* coming, they wanted to make sure that you were alerted to any potential threats to quality. Your two Leads leave the office and you return to work. Two days later you hear through the grapevine that Post and Hopkins have told everyone of your encounter and claimed you treated them unfairly.

Your reprimand was unnecessary, especially to both of them together. Post's explanation, while not persuasive to you, was persuasive to others. Early in a supervisor's tenure, he or she is often tested by subordinates. Tests are one way to resolve questions about how you will handle situations and how you will react to their suggestions. Generally it is better to meet such tests with the knowledge that they are really pretty harmless. Your heavy-handedness was an invitation to resentment.

Re-evaluate your last decision. Circle the #413A you just wrote in your flow diagram. Then move to the first uncircled step above this one in your flow diagram.

Decision Point 413B

You decided to cover Betty's volume of output first. This is not the best alternative. It is much better to compliment her first on her knowledge of procedures. The reason is that she underevaluated herself on this dimension, and covering this subject first will begin the interview on a very positive note.

You tell Betty that you are very pleased that she has made so much progress in getting to know company procedures, and that you think she has been too harsh on herself on her form. She thanks you and tells you that "it is a miracle" that her progress has been so positive, given all the problems she has been having with the computer system.

At this point what would you say?

A. "Okay, let's talk about those problems." (GO TO 404A)
B. "Yes, I am generally familiar with the problems you are referring to, and we'll get to that in a minute. I just want to make sure you hear me when I tell you that your performance on this dimension is really exceptional and that I truly appreciate your progress." (GO TO 345B)
C. "I know all about your computer problems. I agree that your progress is excellent given your frustrations." (GO TO 419A)

Decision Point 414A

Your statement does not make clear that an outstanding rating is possible. You want to make certain that Betty understands that you and she can work together toward that goal. Your use of the term "flawless" seems to convey the impression that an outstanding rating will forever be beyond reach.

Re-evaluate your last decision. Circle the #414A you just wrote in your flow diagram. Then go back in your flow diagram to the first uncircled number above this step.

Decision Point 414B

It is now two months later, and Bill has become a highly valued member of your group. His technical, social, and political integration into the organization seems complete, and you have recommended that he receive the highest performance rating available to young recruits. His accomplishments, once only known to the members of the group, are increasingly becoming visible to division management. You are really proud of him.

Recently, however, Bill has been having difficulty putting his personal life in order. Since he and his wife live in the country, his two young children are enrolled in a one-room school, and his wife has expressed concern that the school is not stimulating enough. In addition, Bill has reported having trouble with his commuting. It seems that he is occasionally unable to get to work on time because of icy roads.

In light of Bill's problem of integrating his private life with his professional life, what would you do?

A. Do nothing. You've gone far enough. Bill's personal life is up to him. (GO TO 398A)

B. Encourage him to take initiative on this problem. Explore alternatives with him and advise him what action to take. (GO TO 345A)

C. Introduce Bill to a person in another division who, like Bill, lives in the country and has school-aged children. (GO TO 328B)

Decision Point 414C

You identified the following statement as a negative element of Betty's performance: "Betty makes too many mistakes." According to the Module Reading, this is incorrect. It is too general to be useful feedback.

Re-evaluate your last decision. Circle the #414C you just wrote in your flow diagram. Then go back in your flow diagram to the first uncircled number above this step.

Decision Point 415A

You have decided to ask Betty to prepare a self-appraisal as part of the appraisal process. This is perfectly acceptable although not required.

Now that you have decided what to cover (and what not to cover), you now must decide how to conduct the appraisal interview. The following strategies are common.

Which would you use?

A. Approach 1. (GO TO 398B)
   ---Ask her to fill out a performance appraisal form on herself before the meeting.
   ---Put her at ease.
   ---Examine together the similarities and differences between your filled-out form and hers.
   ---Cover the five specific points you have identified previously starting with a positive point, then a negative, etc.
   ---Ascertain your role in her deficient performance.
   ---Give her your summary rating and invite her reactions/inputs.
   ---Go over last year's development plan and jointly develop next year's plan.

B. Approach 2. (GO TO 355C)
   ---Put her at ease.
   ---Tell her the five strong and weak points of her performance (one positive, one negative, one positive, etc.), inviting her explanation of each.
   ---Announce your summary rating.
   ---Indicate elements you want in her next year's development plan after reviewing last year's plan.
   ---Complete next year's development plan.

C. Approach 3. (GO TO 365A)
   ---Put her at ease.
   ---Tell her the five strong and weak points of her performance (one positive, one negative, one positive, etc.) inviting her reactions on each.
   ---Try to ascertain how she thinks you might have supported her better given her weaknesses.
   ---Give her your summary evaluation and solicit her reactions.
   ---Review last year's development plan together.
   ---Work together developing next year's development plan.

Decision Point 416A

You identified the following statement as a negative element of Betty's performance: "Betty does not use adequate diplomacy when dealing with clients." This is correct. First of all, it is a specific behavior rather than a trait. Second, you have reliable evidence on which to base this assessment. Several people gave her poor marks on their evaluation forms on this item.

What other negative element of Betty's performance do you wish to feed back to her?

A. Betty is apparently careless. (GO TO 379B)

B. Betty often complains to others instead of problem solving with you. (GO TO 388A)

C. Betty is insensitive to the impact she has on others. (GO TO 356A)

D. Betty lacks attentiveness to details. (GO TO 378A)

E. Betty makes too many mistakes. (GO TO 414C)

F. Betty isn't smart enough to catch on quickly. (GO TO 393A)

G. Betty went over the head of a systems analyst to complain about the service she was getting--a violation of protocol. (GO TO 421C)

Decision Point 416B

Bill is transferred and your fears are realized. He is happy to be working with his new friend; however, he runs into technical problems again. His new supervisor asks you why you sent her a "turkey," and Bill ultimately leaves the company.

Re-evaluate your last decision. Circle the #416B you just wrote in your flow diagram. Then move to the first uncircled step above this one in your flow diagram.

Decision Point 416C

It is inappropriate to discuss salary adjustments during this type of appraisal interview.

Re-evaluate your last decision. Circle the #416C you just wrote in your flow diagram. Then go back in your flow diagram to the first uncircled number above this step.

Decision Point 417A

This approach is not adequately participative. Without a hefty amount of participation, Betty's motivation to improve will not be high.

Re-evaluate your last decision. Circle the #417A you just wrote in your flow diagram. Then go back in your flow diagram to the first uncircled number above this step.

Decision Point 417B

You return to play cards several times each week with your old unit. Everything seems to go satisfactorily until you hear through the grapevine that the operators in the other units are expressing a lot of jealousy about you "favoring" one unit over the others. Now you are faced with several options, none of which are very acceptable.

Re-evaluate your last decision. Circle the #417B you just wrote in your flow diagram. Then move to the first uncircled step above this one in your flow diagram.

Decision Point 417C

You decided to advocate giving Betty an 'outstanding' rating this year. Your decision was apparently predicated on the fact that your lack of direction to her regarding what to do in your absence contributed to the problems she had this last year. Of course, by committing yourself to "fighting for her case" with your boss, you are opening yourself up to being seen as not very influential should your efforts fail to win her an outstanding rating. It is probably a wise move to be tentative about her ultimate rating. Obviously if you do not succeed with your boss, you will have to give her a plausible explanation without going into specifics. But with your communication skills, and with the healthy relationship you now have with Betty by virtue of this excellent session, you will probably be up for this challenge.

You now must enter the developmental portion of the interview. In general, how would you approach this part of the session?

A. Begin by asking for her inputs. Offer yours. Negotiate a developmental plan. Keep it participative. (GO TO 373B)

B. List the items on which you want improvement. Ask her how you can support her efforts to improve. Keep it specific. (GO TO 417A)

C. Begin with a discussion of Betty's career goals. Integrate into your discussion action items that not only address ways that might improve her performance but also get her closer to her career ambitions. (GO TO 405C)

Decision Point 418A

You don't want to barge right into your summary evaluation until you have given Betty the opportunity to ask questions. But assuming she had none, how would you tell her your summary evaluation?

A. "Betty, at the beginning of this discussion, I thought I was going to give you an 'excellent' summary rating. However, as a result of this talk, I am going to try to get you an 'outstanding.' You understand that I will have to talk to Mike (your boss) because the company only permits a limited number of 'outstandings' in any one year." (GO TO 417C)

B. "It seems to me that, on the whole, your performance this past year has been excellent." (GO TO 406A)

C. "Betty, I really don't want to say. I'll get back to you on this in a few days." (GO TO 389C)

Decision Point 418B

You ask your boss what she means when she asks you to do the best you can with the *NET* assignment. She seems a bit put out by your question. Her response is:

"Well, it's pretty obvious, isn't it? I want you to support the implementation effort. It is absolutely critical for you not to be any sort of an obstructionist about it."

This statement leaves you in somewhat of a bind. You are really not in favor of *NET*, and your boss is telling you to keep your reservations to yourself. In general, you were wise to ask for clarification of her instructions, but you really didn't have the background on *NET* to be able to appreciate her point of view.

Re-evaluate your last decision. Circle the #418B you just wrote in your flow diagram. Then move to the first uncircled step above this one in your flow diagram.

Decision Point 418C

This opening statement will do little to put Betty at ease. It conveys the impression that you have carefully planned your interview. While it is true that you have, you want to create a communication climate that is as spontaneous as possible.

Re-evaluate your last decision. Circle the #418C you just wrote in your flow diagram. Then go back in your flow diagram to the first uncircled number above this step.

Decision Point 419A

By moving directly into this issue, you cannot be sure that Betty perceived the strength of your positive feedback about the volume of her work. It is better to repeat your feedback than to run the risk that Betty underestimates its importance. Moreover, by expressing certainty about the problem, you are going to stifle any real discussion on the computer problem.

Re-evaluate your last decision. Circle the #419A you just wrote in your flow diagram. Then go back in your flow diagram to the first uncircled number above this step.

Decision Point 419B

You give the green light to Lucy to make the change she proposed. All goes well until it is discovered that the error rate goes up dramatically. This is really quite disappointing, since Lucy and you had expected an improvement. Shortly after you receive these disappointing results, you get a call from your predecessor, who had heard of your action. He tells you that he had assigned people to positions within that unit that made the most of their skills. Some were good with customers and some were good at numbers. Lucy's plan did not take the advantages of such specialization into account. New supervisors who make changes that reverse the status quo during their first few months are vulnerable to these sorts of problems. In general, it is prudent for new supervisors to wait a while before introducing changes, unless they are directed to do or unless they have a total grasp of the issues.

Re-evaluate your last decision. Circle the #419B you just wrote in your flow diagram. Then move to the first uncircled step above this one in your flow diagram.

Decision Point 419C

You identified the following statement as a positive element of Betty's performance: "Betty's knowledge of procedures has improved markedly." This is correct. Your observations and Jensen's confirm this.

What other statement do you think reflects a positive piece of feedback?

A. Betty sticks up for the project. (GO TO 403A)

B. Betty has demonstrated initiative. (GO TO 361B)

C. Betty has worked well under pressure. (GO TO 383B)

D. Betty is conscientious. (GO TO 348A)

Decision Point 420A

How would you frame your summary evaluation?

A. "Betty, at the beginning of this discussion, I thought I was going to give you an 'excellent' summary rating. However, as a result of this talk, I am going to try to get you an 'outstanding.' You understand that I will have to talk to Mike (your boss) because the company only permits a limited number of 'outstandings' in any one year." (GO TO 417C)

B. "It seems to me that, on the whole, your performance this past year has been excellent." (GO TO 406A)

C. "Betty, I really don't want to say. I'll get back to you on this in a few days." (GO TO 389C)

Decision Point 420B

You tell Spencer that you think your boss is a fine manager but not an excellent one. He looks at you expectantly. You say nothing. He says, "What in the world do you mean? I think Karen is an outstanding manager." Clearly this was not the way out of the very delicate situation you faced.

Re-evaluate your last decision. Circle the #420B you just wrote in your flow diagram. Then move to the first uncircled step above this one in your flow diagram.

Decision Point 420C

You decided to include three additional pieces of information in your discussion with Betty:

7. her performance in comparison to others in the Ajax Project.
8. her self-rating on the employee appraisal form.
10. the specific assessments others have made of her.

According to the Module Reading, this is incorrect. It is inappropriate to discuss the performance of others and to share with her the specific assessments others have made of her performance. The latter serves to emphasize the multiple-boss situation she is working in.

Re-evaluate your last decision. Circle the #420C you just wrote in your flow diagram. Then go back in your flow diagram to the first uncircled number above this step.

Decision Point 421A

You decided to conduct your interview with Betty in your office. This is not advisable for two reasons. First, with Betty away from her desk, you are likely to be disturbed with phone calls and people coming in to see you. Second, your office is your turf; conducting your interview there is likely to suppress her willingness to participate in the process.

Re-evaluate your last decision. Circle the #421A you just wrote in your flow diagram. Then go back in your flow diagram to the first uncircled number above this step.

Decision Point 421B

You attempt to persuade Karen that *NET* is a bad idea. She reacts very forcefully that *NET* is the "salvation" for your entire department. She asks how "in the world" you have the idea that *NET* is not a sound program. You respond from the evidence that you have, and she scowls disapprovingly.

She responds, "Listen, if you are going to be a supervisor, then you are going to have to learn to keep your mouth shut unless you know what you are talking about." She then briefs you on the background of *NET*. She informs you that the people in Corporate Employee Relations have earned an endorsement for *NET* from some very high officials in the bank. She also tells you that even if it didn't have such high-level support, she would support it on the grounds that it gives visibility to her department because it will identify her department as the most error-free in the division.

You indirectly refer to the consultants, for whom you have so little respect, and your boss declares them now totally out of the picture. Apparently their role was only in the development of the *NET* program, and they will play no part in the implementation.

Re-evaluate your last decision. Circle the #421B you just wrote in your flow diagram. Then move to the first uncircled step above this one in your flow diagram.

Decision Point 421C

You identified the following statement as a negative element of Betty's performance: "Betty went over the head of a systems analyst to complain about the service she was getting--a violation of protocol." According to the chapter, this is incorrect. This is an unreliable piece of information. You heard it through the grapevine. Therefore, unless you can verify that this incident occurred, it is inappropriate feedback.

Re-evaluate your last decision. Circle the #421C you just wrote in your flow diagram. Then go back in your flow diagram to the first uncircled number above this step.

Decision Point 422A

Fern agrees with your characterization, but, unfortunately, your statement gets into the informal grapevine and back to your predecessor. He then reports it to your boss, and she asks you to make no further negative comments about him.

Re-evaluate your last decision. Circle the #422A you just wrote in your flow diagram. Then move to the first uncircled step above this one in your flow diagram.

Decision Point 422B

This opening works well. Betty acknowledges her nervousness, and you respond by further putting her at ease. You ask her if she has had a chance to fill out the appraisal form on herself. She shows you her form, and it is filled with check marks in all the "very typical" columns except one, "knows the procedures involved in the job and the organization." She also checked the "outstanding" summary rating.

Would you pull out your completed form and show it to Betty?

A. Yes. (GO TO 367C)

B. No. (GO TO 390C)

Decision Point 422C

Your boss is terse in indicating that the decision is yours and she doesn't want to be involved.

Re-evaluate your last decision. Circle the #422C you just wrote in your flow diagram. Then move to the first uncircled step above this one in your flow diagram.

Decision Point 422D

You decide to tape-record the session. This has two rather negative results. First, the presence of the tape recorder has a chilling effect. Even though the members are professionals used to having their words transcribed, it does hold down especially "wild" ideas, and the proceedings take on the appearance of a much more businesslike meeting than most brainstorming sessions should. In addition, since the participants cannot see your notes, there is much less piggybacking of ideas.

Re-evaluate your last decision. Circle the #422D you just wrote in your flow diagram. Then move to the first uncircled step above this one in your flow diagram.

Decision Point 423A

You decide to conduct the first meeting with objectives as the first agenda item. Under normal circumstances this would be very smart. However, this is a potentially controversial issue, and it's probably better to talk to task force members before raising the issue as a means of gauging just how much disagreement there is.

Let's assume you have done that and resume the interactive case from that point. Your first meeting is with Lyle Seashore. True to form, he objects to any objective for the issue that "smacks" of narrow, commercial interests. Yet when you meet with Harrison Gump, you are surprised to find him willing to select a topic for the seasonal edition that will have "broad appeal." Knowing Gump as you do, you realize that that is as close to agreeing with commercial appeal as an objective as you are likely to get.

When you raise the issue with Smithers and Foy, they have no problem with the idea of an increase in circulation as a specific objective. Clearly Seashore is in the minority, but you are concerned that if you raise the issue in your first meeting, he may be able to win Gump over on a matter of principle and deadlock the task force. How would you proceed from this point?

A. Raise the issue of objectives at your first meeting and be prepared to guide the group to the resolution that you and the publisher want. (GO TO 434A)

B. Return to Lyle Seashore and explore with him what objectives he can live with. Be prepared to tell him that if he can't live with a commercial objective, you may have to ask someone else to serve on the task force. (GO TO 433B)

C. Have your boss (the publisher) talk with Seashore to persuade him of the importance of circulation. (GO TO 427A)

Decision Point 423B

Your tough stand with Duckworth, Brown, and Johnson backfires. In the following one-month period, Johnson and Duckworth both resign to join your predecessor in his consulting firm (you discover that they had standing offers from him all the time). You are now seriously understaffed to complete three one-month assignments in three months. The results are predictably bad. Your team fails to make all three deadlines, and the quality of the work reflects the understaffing.

Re-evaluate your last decision. Circle the #423B you just wrote in your flow diagram. Then go back in your flow diagram to the first uncircled number above this step.

Decision Point 424A

In making this assignment and in conducting yourself in weekly departmental meetings and at other public occasions, what would you do?

A. Indicate that it is important for the department to "play this assignment by the book" rather than to propose any increases in the Employee Relations staffing budget, as this is premature. State that you think the long-term prospects for such an increase and for the department as a whole appear good, but indicate that you think it's wise for the group to maintain a low profile with top management for a while. (GO TO 442B)

B. Publicly congratulate those specific individuals (Floyd Banks, Bunkie Brown, and Steve Johnson) who did a fine job on the assignment. (GO TO 450C)

C. Change the format of weekly departmental meetings to allow more group discussion where members have concerns. (GO TO 429B)

Decision Point 424B

You ask if you should have the publisher talk with the members' bosses about the importance of the task force, thus freeing them from other conflicting responsibilities. They indicate that that would be helpful. You do so, and everything works out satisfactorily.

Back at the meeting you next want to give a few remarks on the political sensitivities of serving on the task force. What would you say in this regard?

A. "With the quality of people on this task force, I'm very optimistic about being able to put together a superb seasonal issue. However, I am a bit concerned that we keep to ourselves. Please, let's keep our deliberations confidential, and if you are having a problem with the way anything is done on this task force, see me before you talk about it with people not in the group. Is that agreeable to everyone?" (GO TO 467B)

B. "I'm convinced that, with the people on this task force, we cannot fail. However, our assignment is a challenging one, and it is very likely that we will step on each other's toes from time to time. For that reason, I would like to ask all of you to keep whatever conflicts arise in this room in confidence." (GO TO 476A)

C. "All of you have been carefully selected to represent your constituencies on this task force. It is very imperative that you bring the points of view of your departments to our deliberations so we can be sure that the special issue is acceptable to all involved." (GO TO 475A)

Decision Point 425A

You decided on a nine-person task force. While you were correct in picking an odd number, nine is entirely too large for a task force of this kind. Instead, five is the ideal number. Let's assume you had chosen five and continue the interactive case from this point.

You now have to determine the specific makeup of your task force. Since last season's topic involved sports, you decide that your two representatives from Editorial should come from the following:

Harrison Gump (Feature Editor)--Hard-nosed, irascible, and a bit abrasive, a real no-nonsense person. Cut out of the mold of the typical crusty city editor.

Lyle Seashore (News Editor)--Pulitzer Prize-winning investigative reporter turned editor. Arrogant workaholic and defender of the Editorial Department's prerogatives when it comes to the selection of topics for the seasonal issue.

Myra Patrick (Business Editor)--The youngest business editor at any major newspaper in the U.S. and still finding her way. Known to be incredibly imaginative but very serious. Closely controls her own staff but has yet to earn the respect of her peers.

Your choice of the other candidates is very important. In the past, the representatives from Editorial have dominated the task force, and this has caused problems working out the coordination details with the other departments. The candidates for the other two positions are:

Michael Smithers (Director of Circulation)--Community activist; articulate, amusing conversationalist; unswerving promoter of the *Register* in Madison.

Elaine Fitzgerald (Director of Consumer Advertising)--Efficient, intelligent, does not respect Smithers on the grounds that she thinks he is "vacuous."

Baron Leybolt (Director of Human Resources)--Unassuming, diligent, earnest, and eager to please; doesn't yet have much credibility in the organization.

Peter Foy (Director of Information Systems)--Extremely knowledgeable of internal operations; tough-minded (perhaps even severe); persuaded only with facts.

Haley Jones (Treasurer)--Brisk, aloof, super-rational, and businesslike.

Which of the following combinations of members would you choose?

    A. Gump, Seashore, Fitzgerald, Smithers. (GO TO 446A)
    B. Gump, Seashore, Smithers, Foy. (GO TO 483B)
    C. Gump, Patrick, Leybolt, Foy. (GO TO 456C)
    D. Gump, Patrick, Fitzgerald, Jones. (GO TO 471A)
    E. Seashore, Patrick, Smithers, Leybolt. (GO TO 432A)
    F. Seashore, Patrick, Foy, Fitzgerald. (GO TO 473B)

Decision Point 426A

It is one month later, and your personal position with your team is stronger. Bob Alton responded to your rather stern warning by leaving the company, and this gave you the opportunity to promote Luke Spurior to Alton's position (Employment Manager). You also bring an individual whom you have known for years into Spurior's former position (Employment Analyst). Her name is Sandy Schaeffer, and while not accepted immediately into the group, she and Jane Duckworth seem to get along satisfactorily.

In spite of these changes, the level of team morale seems quite low. Some individuals seem to have accepted your leadership (notably Best, Bennet, and Spurior) while others continue cool toward you (Duckworth, Brown, and Johnson). Halfway through the last month, Jane Duckworth approached you and confessed feeling disturbed that the once "family feeling" in the department is no longer there. You persuaded her not to leave the company.

Since it is now three months until your three departmental assignments are due, you must now decide what assignment to complete first.

Which assignment would you give now?

A. *Assignment 1*--Preparation for Labor Negotiations. In three months your department begins negotiations with the Sheetmetal Workers Union for the first time in two years. Since the contract will affect each department member's specialty, inputs from everyone will be solicited. Bunkie Brown will draw up a list of probable union demands and these will be sent simultaneously to every other department member for an assessment of economic and administrative impact. You will then aggregate these assessments into an integrated impact report. (GO TO 431B)

B. *Assignment 2*--Development of an Integrated Personnel Policy. Top management has asked you to submit a document outlining a reassessment of existing departmental policies and procedures, together with proposals for changes. It is due in three months. Preparing this document will involve intensive meetings of all department members. (GO TO 464B)

C. *Assignment 3*--Creation of an Annual Staffing Plan. In three months all manpower planning for the next fiscal year is due. This is a serial process beginning with Roy Best who estimates promotions and transfers. This then goes to Bob Alton's group (Alton, Duckworth, and Spurior), which calculates new staffing needs, and then on to George Bennet, who justifies these figures into the affirmative action plan. Finally, Floyd Banks transposes these estimates into a budget form. (GO TO 434B)

Decision Point 427A

You ask your boss to speak with Seashore to persuade him of the importance of circulation. Your boss declines, saying that he feels you should handle the matter.
What now?

A. Raise the issue of objectives at your first meeting and be prepared to guide the group to the resolution that you and the publisher want. (GO TO 434A)

B. Return to Lyle Seashore and explore with him what objectives he can live with. Be prepared to tell him that if he can't live with a commercial objective, you may have to ask someone else to serve on the task force. (GO TO 433B)

Decision Point 427B

It is three weeks later, and in checking on the progress of the assignment, you realize that it is behind schedule. A closer examination reveals that Bunkie Brown and Steve Johnson got their assumptions to other team members one week late, Bob Alton, Jane Duckworth, and Luke Spurior have yet to begin their work, while the others are close to completion. When you confront Alton about the delay, he offers a believable excuse, but you wonder whether he is really committed to the schedule.
What would you do about this?

A. Take a tough stand with Alton. Let him know that you expect his cooperation, but you will not tolerate any trouble with him. (GO TO 460A)

B. Take the opportunity at a weekly staff meeting to deliver a "pep talk" of sorts, emphasizing your confidence in the abilities of everyone in the group and the need for everybody to work toward objectives that are both professionally worthwhile and relevant to the needs of the company. (GO TO 465A)

C. At a weekly departmental meeting, announce the charter that you were given by top management, and state your intention to bring the department back into line with the needs of the company. (GO TO 430A)

D. Mention at a weekly staff meeting that you are pleased that Brown and Johnson gave so much thought to their assumptions and that Best, Bennet, and Banks have been making excellent progress on the assignment. Say nothing about Alton, Duckworth, and Spurior. (GO TO 428B)

Decision Point 428A

You go to Gump and confess the difficulty you are having convincing your boss. While this truthful posture earns you points for being truthful, it does not make your effort easier. You could have gotten cooperation from him without this admission.

Re-evaluate your last decision. Circle the #428A you just wrote in your flow diagram. Then move to the first uncircled step above this one in your flow diagram.

Decision Point 428B

In spite of your public statement, it takes Alton, Duckworth, and Spurior one more month to finish their assignment. Along the way you receive more excuses. When you finally are able to put together the inputs from team members (it takes you a week), you look at the results. Somehow the assumptions don't seem to "add up." Yet because it took your team twice as long to complete the assignment as you originally thought, you don't consider this issue serious enough to pursue further, and you submit the report to top management.

As for departmental morale, your personal position in the group is stronger. The high level of team spirit has eroded, but some people have clearly sided with you (e.g., Best, Bennet, Banks, Brown, and Johnson). You are unsure about Duckworth and Spurior, but Alton continues quiet and sullen in public. Halfway though the last month, Luke Spurior came in to see you and confessed feeling disturbed that the "family feeling" in the Department seems to have disappeared. You persuaded him that things would get better.

Top management reacts rather negatively to the impact report you gave them. They label it "too optimistic" and "too theoretical, as usual." You challenge these labels and express confidence in your people.

At this point what would you do?

A. Indicate at a departmental meeting that top management has challenged the report, and ask everyone to go over their assumptions. Be prepared to revise the report accordingly. (GO TO 445C)

B. Check the figures and assumptions yourself. Speak privately with Bunkie Brown to assure yourself that they are based on reasoning that you understand and accept. Take the revised report to top management and challenge them if they criticize it again. (GO TO 476B)

C. Agree with top management that the report may be too optimistic and theoretical. Ask them for more time to "whip your team into shape." (GO TO 475B)

Decision Point 429A

Foy and Smithers say very little in the ensuing discussion. However, Foy seems to be becoming convinced by the diatribes of Gump and Seashore. Finally, when you intervene, it appears too late. Foy expresses a "deep reservation" about whether the task force can proceed without more independence from "management."

Re-evaluate your last decision. Circle the #429A you just wrote in your flow diagram. Then move to the first uncircled step above this one in your flow diagram.

Decision Point 429B

Your decision to open meetings up to group discussion seriously bogs the group down. You have given the group an assignment that is already quite taxing in terms of workflow. By opening up the meetings, you are essentially making the workflow even more complicated. Since your group is not yet in a P-1 condition, this is premature.

Re-evaluate your last decision. Circle the #429B you just wrote in your flow diagram. Then go back in your flow diagram to the first uncircled number above this step.

Decision Point 429C

You decide to use brainstorming. You tell the group the ground rules:

(1) Criticism is ruled out. Judgment or evaluation of ideas must be withheld until a later time.
(2) Freewheeling is welcomed. The wilder or more radical the idea, the better.
(3) Quantity of ideas is wanted. The more alternative topics, the better.
(4) Combination and improvement is desirable. Task force members should suggest how the ideas of others can be turned into other ideas.

How would you keep track of the ideas generated?

A. Ask the group if it has any objections if you ask your personal assistant to keep track of the ideas. Position him at the flip chart. (GO TO 445B)

B. Take notes yourself on a note pad. (GO TO 455A)

C. Use a flip chart to write down the ideas yourself. (GO TO 476C)

D. Tape record the session. (GO TO 422D)

Decision Point 430A

Your statement solves a problem your people have been having with your leadership--they weren't sure whether your allegiance was to them or the opposition (top management). By announcing your charter, you place yourself clearly in top management's corner. The results are predictable. You are shut off from upward communication and treated as a "lackey." Surely you cannot remedy this negative impression for some time.

Re-evaluate your last decision. Circle the #430A you just wrote in your flow diagram. Then go back in your flow diagram to the first uncircled number above this step.

Decision Point 430B

You ask the group if anyone has any more ideas. This question elicits no further ideas, so you are left with no option but closing this part of the meeting. This is unfortunate. Typically periods of silence do emerge in every brainstorming session, and often the most imaginative and useful ideas come up right after these periods. Therefore, it is generally useful to wait out at least a few silent periods during brainstorming. Let's assume you had done that and rejoin the interactive case from that point.

You wait out the silence, and the first few ideas that emerge are truly fabulous. This stimulates a second burst of ideas from the group that lasts almost five minutes. A second silence overcomes the group, and you wait through that one as you did the first. However, few ideas of any merit arise.

With the task force becoming rather tired and the scheduled end of the meeting approaching, you decide to call an end to this session. A total of 52 different topic ideas have been generated. You instruct your assistant to duplicate and distribute the results of the brainstorming meeting to the participants.

What instructions would you give the members?

A. Ask them to look over the list of prospective topics that came out of this meeting and put them into categories that make sense to them. (GO TO 459A)

B. Tell them that the meeting was very productive, and you will follow up with the discussion at the next meeting. (GO TO 442A)

C. Ask each member to rank order the ideas that have been derived on the basis of 1 = best and 52 = worst. (GO TO 484B)

Decision Point 431A

You decide to say nothing about the arrangement your boss has with the Vice President of Operations. As a result, this subgroup makes no special plans to get copy to Operations early. This has disastrous consequences. The Vice President of Operations complains to your boss, and he gives you a verbal tongue-lashing.

Re-evaluate your last decision. Circle the #431A you just wrote in your flow diagram. Then move to the first uncircled step above this one in your flow diagram.

Decision Point 431B

In making this assignment and in conducting yourself in weekly departmental meetings and at public occasions, what would you do?

A. Indicate that these labor negotiations are a real opportunity for the department to regain its credibility with top management. Note that it will take a coordinated effort to overcome what will surely be a tough bargaining stand by the union. (GO TO 467A)

B. Change the format at weekly departmental meetings to allow more group discussion where members have concerns. (GO TO 477A)

C. Take every chance to reinforce and publicly acknowledge any efforts in line with top management's concern that Employee Relations become more relevant to the realities of the firm. (GO TO 469B)

D. Take a tough stand with Duckworth, Brown, and Johnson in order to neutralize their opposition to your leadership. (GO TO 423B)

Decision Point 431C

Your upbeat closing remarks fall short of the mark. Generally, at the end of each meeting, you should reiterate who is expected to do what before the next meeting and get an explicit commitment from those involved.

Re-evaluate your last decision. Circle the #431C you just wrote in your flow diagram. Then move to the first uncircled step above this one in your flow diagram.

Decision Point 432A

You chose the combination of Seashore, Patrick, Smithers, and Leybolt. This is not the best composition for your task force. Leybolt lacks the sort of credibility that would enable him to hold his own with the two representatives from the Editorial Department.

Re-evaluate your last decision. Circle the #432A you just wrote in your flow diagram. Then move to the first uncircled step above this one in your flow diagram.

Decision Point 432B

Your "pep talk" is greeted with almost no reaction. Later during the same day, however, you learn "through the grapevine" that several group members expressed cynicism about what you said. Although you are not sure, you suspect that this negativity comes from Bob Alton.

What would you do now?

A. Take a tough stand with Bob Alton. Let him know that you expect him to cooperate and that you expect no trouble from him. (GO TO 482A)

B. Let others in the group know privately that you know that Alton is disappointed about being passed over for your job. Indicate to group members that you are looking forward to working with him, but that you are willing to use your authority to support those who work for the department and to oppose those who work against it. (GO TO 449A)

C. Meet with each team member individually to discuss his or her career goals and aspirations. Express your support for these goals if there is evidence of a commitment for departmental goals and performance. Begin to single out individual efforts in line with your plans. (GO TO 435A)

D. At a weekly departmental meeting, announce the charter you were given by top management and state your resolve to bring the department back in line with the needs of the organization. (GO TO 461A)

Decision Point 432C

You have decided to use an ordinary group discussion to develop alternative topics for the seasonal issue. Unfortunately, there are many better methods for meeting this objective than the typical group format.

Re-evaluate your last decision. Circle the #432C you just wrote in your flow diagram. Then move to the first uncircled step above this one in your flow diagram.

Decision Point 433A

You have decided to give your team an assignment. The results are not good. Not only is the staffing plan finished late, but it contained assumptions that top management found unacceptably naive. Apparently you expected too much too soon from a group that accepts neither you as leader nor the new directions in which you were hired to lead the department.

Your assessment of the social conditions in your work group should have concluded that they are presently in a P-4 condition: high cohesiveness, negative work norms. As such, it was not a good idea to give them an assignment. Each of the assignments increased the extent to which your team members had to work together over and above their regular tasks. Although the assignment you chose involved the lowest level of required interaction, it would have been better to wait a month before considering an assignment. That way you would have had a chance to move the group toward a more favorable set of social conditions.

Re-evaluate your last decision. Circle the #433A you just wrote in your flow diagram. Then go back in your flow diagram to the first uncircled number above this step.

Decision Point 433B

You return to Lyle Seashore to discuss the matter of the objectives further. During this meeting, you discover that he has several ideas for the issue that would have a very powerful positive impact on circulation. You conclude that he will be positively inclined toward topics that will be popular, but negatively inclined toward going on record that that is the objective. You thus decide not to force the issue and leave the objectives implicit.

You decide to call the first meeting. You know that the members of your task force do not know each other very well (with the exception of Gump and Seashore). What would you do to "break the ice"?

A. Send each member a brief one-page biography (available through the Human Resource office) on each member before the meeting, and ask the task force members to introduce themselves at the beginning of the meeting. (GO TO 444C)

B. Invite the members to have breakfast together before the first meeting to facilitate socializing. (GO TO 448A)

C. At the first meeting, introduce the members yourself, highlighting those elements of their personal histories that have common elements, and then have coffee brought in to facilitate conversations during an unscheduled break. (GO TO 451A)

Decision Point 434A

You decide to raise the issue of objectives at your first meeting. This results in a very heated discussion that seriously polarizes the task force. Seashore delivers a very passionate speech on the importance of editorial independence, and you are left with few alternatives, none of them particularly appealing.

Re-evaluate your last decision. Circle the #434A you just wrote in your flow diagram, and then move to the first uncircled step above this one in your flow diagram.

Decision Point 434B

You have decided to give your work team an assignment that requires a moderate level of required interaction. The results are not good. A serious bottleneck occurs when the staffing plan moves from Roy Best to Duckworth, Spurior, and Schaeffer. Due to Spurior's inexperience and Schaeffer's newness to the team, they simply cannot agree on a set of assumptions that you consider feasible. Desperate, you intervene and press the issue. Jane Duckworth resigns over the "interference." The assignment is completed three weeks later and is rejected by top management as unrealistic. Since you now have to go back and trace the difficulties, you are forced to delay other assignments. The results are disastrous for building the credibility of the department.

Your previous action of holding off making an assignment until absolutely necessary was correct. It gave you the opportunity to work on the social fabric of the team. The results were encouraging. Your actions have moved a group that was firmly in a P-4 condition to one that is now P-3. However, your choice of a particular assignment was incorrect. The Annual Staffing Plan assignment requires more complex interaction among team members than one of the alternatives.

Re-evaluate your last decision. Circle the #434B you just wrote in your flow diagram. Then go back in your flow diagram to the first uncircled number above this step.

Decision Point 434C

You try to control Seashore by asking, "Am I the only one who disagrees with Lyle on this point?" This backfires. No one expresses a contrary position. In trying to get equitable participation in a discussion, it is preferable to invoke the norm of fairness.

Re-evaluate your last decision. Circle the #434C you just wrote in your flow diagram. Then move to the first uncircled step above this one in your flow diagram.

Decision Point 435A

It is one month later, and it is clear that your team is getting used to your style of management. On several occasions, you have congratulated those who have done well and have pointed to a need for improvement. Although your team still is uncertain about you, you notice that there seems to be much less talk about the company putting down a professional approach to Employee Relations. Alton's popularity is declining. While Duckworth and Spurior remain loyal to him, Brown and Johnson are less so. One thing that bothers you is that you have heard that Alton secretly criticizes some of your actions and comments.

There are now four months left until your team's three assignments are due. What would you do now?

A. *Assignment 1*--Preparation for Labor Negotiations. In four months your department begins negotiations with the Sheetmetal Workers Union for the first time in two years. Since the contract will affect each department member's specialty, inputs from everyone will be solicited. Bunkie Brown will draw up a list of probable union demands and these will be sent simultaneously to every other department member for an assessment of economic and administrative impact. You will then aggregate these assessments into an integrated impact report. (GO TO 447A)
B. *Assignment 2*--Development of an Integrated Personnel Policy. Top management has asked you to submit a document outlining a reassessment of existing departmental policies and procedures, together with proposals for changes. It is due in four months. Preparing this document will involve intensive meetings of all department members. (GO TO 457B)
C. *Assignment 3*--Creation of an Annual Staffing Plan. In four months all manpower planning for the next fiscal year is due. This is a serial process beginning with Roy Best who estimates promotions and transfers. This then goes to Bob Alton's group (Alton, Duckworth, and Spurior), which calculates new staffing needs, and then on to George Bennet, who justifies these figures into the affirmative action plan. Finally, Floyd Banks transposes these estimates into a budget form. (GO TO 471B)
D. Hold off making an assignment for one more month. (GO TO 444B)

Decision Point 435B

By not further clarifying your charter, you risk proceeding without a thorough understanding of what your boss wants.

Re-evaluate your last decision. Circle the #435B you just wrote in your flow diagram. Then move to the first uncircled step above this one in your flow diagram.

Decision Point 436A

This part of the session proceeds efficiently, although you have to remind your assistant to use the precise words given by each member in his abbreviated listing. When each member of the task force has exhausted his individual list, a total of 52 ideas have been generated.

You then distribute 3 X 5 cards and ask task force members to vote for their favorites using whatever criteria they want, giving a "1" to their favorite, a "2" to their next favorite, etc., through "7." You then tally these votes and come up with the following:

(1) regional development problems (the highest rated),
(2) police inadequacies in dealing with minor theft,
(3) disillusionment of the middle-class and alternative life-styles,
(4) justice for the underclass--farm workers, the homeless and indigent,
(5) organized crime and real estate scams,
(6) child abuse and alcoholism,
(7) overcrowding at the county prison.

This initial voting concluded, the meeting ends. You ask each member to reflect on these results and return prepared to discuss them further and come up with the final decision.

Three days later at the next scheduled meeting, you realize that you must now confront the issue of evaluative criteria. Before the first task force meeting, you had decided to delay the issue of decision criteria because of the publisher's rather controversial concern that the topic have circulation potential. You can delay no longer, so you open the issue of criteria.

The discussion is tense at first, with the two people from Editorial sparring with the others on the matter of journalistic independence and circulation potential without mentioning either.

At that point Lyle Seashore begins dominating the discussion. He makes his point with story after story that support the notion that circulation should not serve as the guiding force in editorial decisions.

What would you say to Seashore to regain control over this meeting?

A. "Lyle, I think all of us understand your point of view. In all fairness, we should now give someone else a chance to be heard on the matter." (GO TO 450B)

B. "Lyle, that's enough. You are beginning to repeat yourself." (GO TO 444A)

C. "Am I the only one who disagrees with Lyle on this point?" (GO TO 434C)

Decision Point 437A

You decide to ask the publisher to attend the first meeting to announce that one of the objectives of the seasonal edition is to increase circulation. He declines this invitation, preferring you to handle the situation yourself.
Now what?

A. Meet with members of the task force individually before the first meeting to "feel them out" on objectives. (GO TO 460B)

B. Conduct the first meeting with objectives as the first agenda item. (GO TO 423A)

Decision Point 437B

The group struggles with this assignment. It seems that you were too optimistic about the level of commitment in the group. In spite of the success with the last assignment, there is still ill-feeling about top management. The group is also still uncertain toward you. Given this, opening up the sensitive topic of personnel policies is ill advised. The team labors long and hard on the subject, but conflicts arise between those committed to your leadership and those who have little confidence in you. The result is that the document you take to management lacks the direction you wanted. It also takes two months to complete. This lateness compounds your problem with top management and clouds your future ability to forge a team spirit.

You have worked hard to move the group from its original P-4 condition to its present P-2 state. Of the two assignments you were offered, you have chosen the one with the highest degree of workflow complexity.

Re-evaluate your last decision. Circle the #437B you just wrote in your flow diagram. Then go back in your flow diagram to the first uncircled number above this step.

Decision Point 437C

Your decision to say nothing about the fact that your boss intends to approve the topic has very negative consequences. Gump and Seashore "get wind" that your boss has made that statement, and your credibility with the task force is seriously eroded when Gump asks you if what he has heard is true.

Re-evaluate your last decision. Circle the #437C you just wrote in your flow diagram, and then move to the first uncircled step above this one in your flow diagram.

Decision Point 438A

He tells you that he is still committed to having at least two representatives on the task force from Editorial. He warns you, though, that you will have to "control their creative juices."

Your conversation is then interrupted by his intercom, and his secretary informs him that the mayor is waiting to see him. He stands up and points you to a side door. What would you do?

A. Leave his office and get to work with your task force. (GO TO 464A)

B. Ask him, "What involvement do you personally want on this project?" (GO TO 465B)

C. Ask him, "Are there any further instructions you want to give me?" (GO TO 479B)

Decision Point 438B

It is three weeks later, and in checking the progress of the assignment, you realize that it is behind schedule. A closer examination reveals that while Brown and Johnson got their assumptions to other team members only one week late, Alton, Duckworth, and Spurior have yet to begin their work on the assignment. The other team members are ready for the inputs of Alton's group, so a bottleneck has developed. When you confront Alton about the delay, he offers a somewhat believable excuse, but you are skeptical about whether his motives are honorable. What would you do about this?

A. Take a tough stand with Alton. Let him know that you expect his cooperation, and you will not tolerate any trouble from him. (GO TO 460A)

B. Take the opportunity at a weekly departmental meeting to deliver a "pep talk" of sorts emphasizing your confidence in the abilities of the people on the team. Talk about the need for everyone to work toward goals that are both professionally credible and organizationally relevant. (GO TO 465A)

C. At a weekly departmental meeting, announce the charter you were given by top management, and state your resolve to bring the department back in line with the needs of the organization. (GO TO 430A)

D. Mention at a weekly departmental meeting that you are pleased that Brown and Johnson gave so much thought to their assumptions and that Best, Bennet, and Banks have been making excellent progress on the assignment. Say nothing about Alton, Duckworth, and Spurior. (GO TO 428B)

Decision Point 439A

It is one month later, and it is clear that the team is getting used to your style of management. On several occasions, you have publicly recognized excellent performance and called for improvement. While the group still is unsure toward you personally, you note that there is much less talk about the firm "putting down" a professional approach to employee relations. In addition, you sense that Alton is losing his influence with the team. While Duckworth and Spurior are still loyal to him, Brown and Johnson seem more uncommitted to his leadership. One thing that troubles you, though, is that Alton is being very quiet at meetings, and you have heard that he secretly criticized some of your statements and actions.

There are now four months to go until your group's three one-month assignments are due. What would you do now?

A. *Assignment 1*--Preparation for Labor Negotiations. In four months your department begins negotiations with the Sheetmetal Workers Union for the first time in two years. Since the contract will affect each department member's specialty, inputs from everyone will be solicited. Bunkie Brown will draw up a list of probable union demands and these will be sent simultaneously to every other department member for an assessment of economic and administrative impact. You will then aggregate these assessments into an integrated impact report. (GO TO 447A)

B. *Assignment 2*--Development of an Integrated Personnel Policy. Top management has asked you to submit a document outlining a reassessment of existing departmental policies and procedures, together with proposals for changes. It is due in four months. Preparing this document will involve intensive meetings of all department members. (GO TO 457B)

C. *Assignment 3*--Creation of an Annual Staffing Plan. In four months all manpower planning for the next fiscal year is due. This is a serial process beginning with Roy Best who estimates promotions and transfers. This then goes to Bob Alton's group (Alton, Duckworth, and Spurior), which calculates new staffing needs, and then on to George Bennet, who justifies these figures into the affirmative action plan. Finally, Floyd Banks transposes these estimates into a budget form. (GO TO 471B)

D. Hold off making an assignment for one more month. (GO TO 441C)

Decision Point 440A

Your choice of eight members for your task force is incorrect. Generally, it is better to have an odd number rather than an even one, and a task force of size five is generally considered best. Let's assume that you chose five as the proper task force size and continue with the interactive case from that point. You now have to determine the specific makeup of your task force. Since last season's topic involved sports, you decide that your two representatives from Editorial should come from the following:

Harrison Gump (Feature Editor)--Hard-nosed, irascible, and a bit abrasive, a real no-nonsense person. Cut out of the mold of the typical crusty city editor.

Lyle Seashore (News Editor)--Pulitzer Prize-winning investigative reporter turned editor. Arrogant workaholic and defender of the Editorial Department's prerogatives when it comes to the selection of topics for the seasonal issue.

Myra Patrick (Business Editor)--The youngest business editor at any major newspaper in the U.S. and still finding her way. Known to be incredibly imaginative but very serious. Closely controls her own staff but has yet to earn the respect of her peers.

Your choice of the other candidates is very important. In the past, the representatives from Editorial have dominated the task force, and this has caused problems working out the coordination details with the other departments. The candidates for the other two positions are

Michael Smithers (Director of Circulation)--Community activist; articulate, amusing conversationalist; unswerving promoter of the *Register* in Madison.

Elaine Fitzgerald (Director of Consumer Advertising)--Efficient, intelligent, does not respect Smithers on the grounds that she thinks he is "vacuous."

Baron Leybolt (Director of Human Resources)--Unassuming, diligent, earnest, and eager to please; doesn't yet have much credibility in the organization.

Peter Foy (Director of Information Systems)--Extremely knowledgeable of internal operations; tough-minded (perhaps even severe); persuaded only with facts.

Haley Jones (Treasurer)--Brisk, aloof, super-rational, and businesslike.

Which of the following combinations of members would you choose?

A. Gump, Seashore, Fitzgerald, Smithers. (GO TO 446A)
B. Gump, Seashore, Smithers, Foy. (GO TO 483B)
C. Gump, Patrick, Leybolt, Foy. (GO TO 456C)
D. Gump, Patrick, Fitzgerald, Jones. (GO TO 471A)
E. Seashore, Patrick, Smithers, Leybolt. (GO TO 432A)

Decision Point 441A

This admission has the effect of personalizing an issue that your team considers vitally important from a professional viewpoint. It also casts suspicion on your motives and ambitions. The subsequent policy discussions are strained and unproductive. The policy document, finished one month behind schedule, lacks focus and direction. Your team members lack commitment to its contents.

Re-evaluate your last decision. Circle the #441A you just wrote in your flow diagram. Then go back in your flow diagram to the first uncircled number above this step.

Decision Point 441B

You tell your task force members that it is up to them to get the necessary relief from other responsibilities to devote time to the task force. This does not work very well. Three members must miss the next meeting because of other commitments, after which tardiness becomes a serious problem. You miss several milestones, and the task force flounders significantly. One of the responsibilities of a task force chairman is to assure that task force members have the necessary time to devote to it. You failed this responsibility.

Re-evaluate your last decision. Circle the #441B you just wrote in your flow diagram. Then move to the first uncircled step above this one in your flow diagram.

Decision Point 441C

During this second one-month period in which you have given your team no group assignment, what would you do?

A. Take a tough stand with Bob Alton. Let him know that you expect his cooperation, and you will not tolerate any trouble from him. (GO TO 426A)

B. Take the opportunity at a weekly departmental meeting to deliver a "pep talk" of sorts, emphasizing your confidence in the abilities of the people on the team. Indicate the importance of working toward goals that are both professionally credible and organizationally relevant. (GO TO 445A)

C. Meet with each team member individually to discuss his or her career goals and aspirations. Indicate your support for these goals if there is commitment toward departmental goals and performance. (GO TO 463B)

D. At a weekly departmental meeting, announce the charter you were given by top management and state your resolve to bring the department back in line with the needs of the organization. (GO TO 448B)

Decision Point 442A

You tell your task force members that the meeting was productive and that you will follow up at the next meeting. The problem with this action is that the product of this meeting needs simplification. People have difficulty dealing with 52 separate items without simplifying them into categories of some type.

Re-evaluate your last decision. Circle the #442A you just wrote in your flow diagram. Then move to the first uncircled step above this one in your flow diagram.

Decision Point 442B

The staffing plan is completed, but one week behind schedule. This does not cause serious problems, but it does raise a few eyebrows among top management. They are pleased, though, that for the first time in several years, no staffing increases are proposed for your department.

In tracing the delay, you find out that Luke Spurior and George Bennet had a minor dispute over an interpretation in affirmative action guidelines. It seems that Bennet wanted to integrate an interpretation of the guidelines into the report that top management would have certainly objected to, and Spurior convinced him to reinterpret them in a less objectionable way.

There are now only three weeks left to complete the most difficult assignment of all--the new personnel policies.

How would you organize the meetings to accomplish this assignment?

A. Serve as chairman of the meetings yourself and assume responsibility for setting the agenda and directing the meetings. Allow other members to volunteer for other roles (taking notes, maintaining files, making the final presentation to top management, and performing necessary research). (GO TO 446B)

B. Appoint Spurior the chairman, and work with him privately on the agenda. (GO TO 468B)

Decision Point 442C

You decide to return to the members and tell them that the publisher has rejected their topic. There is no reason to do this until you have exhausted every possible way to persuade him. Hang tough.

Re-evaluate your last decision. Circle the #442C you just wrote in your flow diagram. Then move to the first uncircled step above this one in your flow diagram.

Decision Point 443A

Much to your surprise, Seashore expresses nothing negative after hearing about the need to get background material to Operations 36 hours before press time. Instead, he and Foy work very closely during the next four weeks to see to it that everything involved in the project between Operations and Editorial runs smoothly. Operations does in fact get nearly all of the background within the agreed-on time limit.

When the special seasonal issue hits the streets, it is extremely successful. All three local television stations quote the edition in their prime-time news programs, and the next month, thanks to a two-for-one special subscription offer (timed by the external subgroup), circulation is up over 6 percent!

Congratulations! You have successfully completed the Managing a Task Force Interactive Case.

Decision Point 443B

Your statement is taken as a signal that the policy assignment is unimportant ("only words"). Several department members put forth little effort on the assignment. Most seriously, when you hand the president's secretary the completed report, she asks you if it is "just words for stodgy old management."

Re-evaluate your last decision. Circle the #443B you just wrote in your flow diagram. Then go back in your flow diagram to the first uncircled number above this step.

Decision Point 443C

You ask your the members if they would like to hear from the publisher. They all indicate that that would be helpful. However, when you approach your boss with this invitation, he declines, telling you he doesn't want to get involved.

Now what?

A. Don't intervene at this point. Let the discussion unfold a bit more to see if Foy and Smithers can counter Seashore and Gump. (GO TO 429A)

B. Break into the discussion with the statement "I don't think it's the task force's role to redefine the charter given to us by the publisher." (GO TO 469A)

C. Say, "I understand your position, Lyle, but I really believe the publisher's involvement is a function of his interests and not an intention of interfering. My sense is that if we do approach him with this, that's what he will say. Why don't we proceed with our assignment and see?" (GO TO 468A)

Decision Point 444A

You try to control a dominating member by "taking him on." This may work in smoke-filled nightclubs where one is dealing with hecklers, but it doesn't work in a task force meeting.

Re-evaluate your last decision. Circle the #444A you just wrote in your flow diagram. Then move to the first uncircled step above this one in your flow diagram.

Decision Point 444B

During this second one-month period in which you have given your department no group assignment, what would you do?

A. Take a tough stand with Bob Alton. Let him know that you expect his cooperation, and you will not tolerate any trouble from him. (GO TO 466A)

B. Let others in your group know privately that you know that Alton is disappointed about being passed over for your job, but that you look forward to working with him. Indicate that you intend to use your authority to support those who work for the department and to oppose those who do not. (GO TO 463B)

C. Take the opportunity at a weekly departmental meeting to deliver a "pep talk," emphasizing your confidence in the abilities of the members of your team. Indicate the need for everyone to work toward goals that are both professionally credible and organizationally relevant. (GO TO 445A)

D. At a weekly departmental meeting, announce the charter you were given by top management and state your resolve to bring the department back in line with the needs of the organization. (GO TO 448B)

Decision Point 444C

You send members a one-page biography of their new colleagues and ask them to introduce themselves at the beginning of the meeting. This works acceptably until the public introductions. At that point Seashore and Gump give glowing introductions of themselves and Foy and Smithers say very little. This dominance by the Editorial Department people carries over into the initial discussions, and you conclude that you should have used some other device for the initial introductions.

Re-evaluate your last decision. Circle the #444C you just wrote in your flow diagram, and then move to the first uncircled step above this one in your flow diagram.

Decision Point 445A

You have elected to give a "pep talk" to try to create an overriding goal to replace the antagonistic norms with supportive norms. The result is very disappointing. "Professional" norms die hard, and your superordinate goal is not very compelling. Consequently, you are seen as having "sold out" to a manufacturing orientation that is seen as "the enemy."

The group is not yet stable in a P-3 position. You should continue to work on the group to make sure that cohesiveness declines around its antagonistic norms.

Re-evaluate your last decision. Circle the #445A you just wrote in your flow diagram. Then go back in your flow diagram to the first uncircled number above this step.

Decision Point 445B

You invite your assistant in to man the flip chart and the group begins brainstorming. The ideas come rapidly at first, so fast that your assistant has difficulty keeping up. Then when Smithers suggests the topic of the marketing of baby formula on the local Indian reservation, Gump breaks in and says, "That's very old news. The *Tucson Gazette* had a story on that last year."

This remark violates the rules of brainstorming. Would you interrupt to remind Gump of the rules?

A. Yes. (GO TO 474A)

B. No, let it ride this time. (GO TO 456A)

Decision Point 445C

Your statement that top management has challenged the assessment report stimulates an outpouring of resentment and alienation. Brown is defensive. Duckworth expresses her anti-manufacturing attitudes, and the others reflect anger and frustration. Under these circumstances, the performance on subsequent assignments is marginal, and top management continues dissatisfied with your department's work.

You have missed a tremendous opportunity to give the group (now in a P-2 condition) an experienced group success. Instead you have created an enemy in top management. A more diplomatic approach would have yielded a much more successful outcome.

Re-evaluate your last decision. Circle the #445C you just wrote in your flow diagram. Then go back in your flow diagram to the first uncircled number above this step.

Decision Point 446A

You chose the combination of Gump, Seashore, Fitzgerald, and Smithers. There is only one thing wrong with this combination. You opted to include two members of the Sales/Marketing Department. This prevents you from representing Operations. Since the objective here is creativity and coordination, you want much more diversity on your task force. Moreover, the fact that Fitzgerald and Smithers do not get along well (from Fitzgerald's point of view) makes this particular combination not very appealing. If you had to choose between them, Smithers is probably a better choice (for his social skills and his more established reputation).

Re-evaluate your last decision. Circle the #446A you just wrote in your flow diagram. Then move to the first uncircled step above this one in your flow diagram.

Decision Point 446B

How would you give your team its assignment?

A. Review the progress of the department since you became Director, and congratulate everyone specifically for his or her contribution. Indicate that this policy statement should communicate the present vision of the department but not at the expense of longer-range concerns that are simply infeasible today and will be made impossible by a radical document. (GO TO 452A)

B. Acknowledge the sensitivity around developing an employee relations policy. Be honest in labeling top management as conservative if not stodgy, and indicate that the only way to judge the accomplishments of the department is in actions, not words. (GO TO 443B)

C. Admit your own need to have a document that will be credible and realistic. (GO TO 441A)

Decision Point 446C

You decide to say nothing at this point about your boss's desire that the topic chosen has market appeal. This is a serious mistake. Although you realize that Seashore will object, it is important to give your task force a complete assignment at the outset of its deliberations. Otherwise it is likely to select a topic that will be unacceptable to the publisher.

Re-evaluate your last decision. Circle the #446C you just wrote in your flow diagram. Then move to the first uncircled step above this one in your flow diagram.

Decision Point 447A

In making this assignment and in conducting yourself in weekly departmental meetings and at public occasions, what would you do?

A. Indicate that these labor negotiations are a real opportunity for the Department to regain its credibility with top management. State that it will take a coordinated effort to overcome what will surely be a tough bargaining stand by the union. (GO TO 427B)

B. Change the format of weekly departmental meetings to allow more group discussion where members have concerns. (GO TO 450A)

C. Take every opportunity to reinforce and publicly acknowledge any efforts in line with top management's concern that employee relations become more relevant to the realities of the firm. (GO TO 438B)

Decision Point 447B

Seashore comes rushing into the meeting and apologizes for his lateness. He seems delighted to learn that the publisher has approved the topic. You then outline the charge to the two coordination subcommittees, one made up of Smithers and Gump (for external coordination) and one composed of Seashore and Foy (for internal coordination).

You are much less concerned about the external coordination group than the internal one, since the latter involves work with Operations, and you are worried that Seashore may object to the deal the publisher made with Operations about having background copy available to Operations 36 hours in advance of press time.

How would you deal with this issue?

A. Tell Foy privately of the deal that the publisher made with his boss (the Vice President of Operations) and instruct him to advise you if it is in jeopardy as the subgroup proceeds with its activities. Say nothing to Seashore about the arrangement. (GO TO 457C)

B. Meet with Foy and Seashore together (but separate from the task force) and tell them both of the agreement the Publisher has with the Vice President of Operations. (GO TO 443A)

C. Say nothing to anyone at this point, but monitor the progress of the internal coordination subgroup closely. (GO TO 431A)

Decision Point 448A

Gump and Seashore show up late at the scheduled breakfast, giving a rather feeble excuse. This erases any effect that your plan had.

Re-evaluate your last decision. Circle the #448A you just wrote in your flow diagram, and then move to the first uncircled step above this one in your flow diagram.

Decision Point 448B

Your statement solves a problem your people have been having with your leadership--they weren't sure whether your allegiance was to them or the "opposition" (top management). By announcing your charter, you place yourself clearly in top management's corner. The results are predictable. You are cut off from upward communication and treated as a "lackey." Surely you cannot remedy this negative impression for some time.

Re-evaluate your last decision. Circle the #448B you just wrote in your flow diagram. Then go back in your flow diagram to the first uncircled number above this step.

Decision Point 448C

You wait out the silence, and the first few ideas that emerge are truly fabulous. This stimulates a second burst of ideas from the group that lasts almost five minutes. A second silence overcomes the group, and you wait through that one as you did the first. However, few ideas of any merit arise.

With the task force becoming rather tired and the scheduled end of the meeting approaching, you decide to call an end to this session. A total of 52 different topic ideas have been generated. You instruct your assistant to duplicate and distribute the results of the brainstorming meeting to the participants.

What instructions would you give the members?

A. Ask them to look over the list of prospective topics that came out of this meeting and put them into categories that make sense to them. (GO TO 459A)

B. Tell them that the meeting was very productive, and you will follow up with the discussion at the next meeting. (GO TO 442A)

C. Ask each member to rank order the ideas that have been derived on the basis of 1 = best and 52 = worst. (GO TO 484B)

Decision Point 449A

It is one month later, and it is evident that your team is getting used to your style of management. On several occasions, you have publicly recognized excellent performance and called attention to a need for improvement where it was necessary. While the group still seems uncertain toward you personally, you note that there seems to be much less talk about the firm stifling a professional approach to employee relations. In addition, you sense that Alton is losing his influence with the team. Although Duckworth and Spurior continue to be loyal to him, Brown and Johnson seem increasingly indifferent to his leadership. One thing that troubles you, though, is that Alton is being very quiet at department meetings, and you have heard that he has quietly ridiculed some of your statements and actions.

There are now four months left until your department's three assignments are due. What would you do now?

A. *Assignment 1*--Preparation for Labor Negotiations. In four months your department begins negotiations with the Sheetmetal Workers Union for the first time in two years. Since the contract will affect each department member's specialty, inputs from everyone will be solicited. Bunkie Brown will draw up a list of probable union demands and these will be sent simultaneously to every other department member for an assessment of economic and administrative impact. You will then aggregate these assessments into an integrated impact report. (GO TO 447A)

B. *Assignment 2*--Development of an Integrated Personnel Policy. Top management has asked you to submit a document outlining a reassessment of existing departmental policies and procedures, together with proposals for changes. It is due in four months. Preparing this document will involve intensive meetings of all department members. (GO TO 457B)

C. *Assignment 3*--Creation of an Annual Staffing Plan. In four months all manpower planning for the next fiscal year is due. This is a serial process beginning with Roy Best, who estimates promotions and transfers. This then goes to Bob Alton's group (Alton, Duckworth, and Spurior), which calculates new staffing needs, and then on to George Bennet, who justifies these figures into the affirmative action plan. Finally, Floyd Banks transposes these estimates into a budget form. (GO TO 471B)

D. Hold off making an assignment for one more month. (GO TO 441C)

Decision Point 450A

At the first meeting when you call for discussion of concerns, there is little response. At the next meeting, however, Jane Duckworth delivers a passionate speech that expresses her strong professional values in contrast to the "narrow thinking in manufacturing." Other team members express similar attitudes and even sorrow over the "firing" of your predecessor. At this point you intervene, but it is too late.

Essentially, by opening up weekly meetings to a discussion of concerns, you have in effect created conditions of more complex work relationships. Since your team is presently in at best a P-3 state, your action is premature. All you have done is provide a forum for expressing a sense of powerlessness that may restore the antagonistic norms that are beginning to erode.

Re-evaluate your last decision. Circle the #450A you just wrote in your flow diagram. Then go back in your flow diagram to the first uncircled number above this step.

Decision Point 450B

This works very well. Seashore recedes from the discussion a bit and Foy, Gump, and you begin discussing the issue of evaluative criteria. However, you notice that Smithers is saying nothing.

What would you say to draw him into the discussion?

A. "Smithers, we haven't heard from you for awhile. What is your position on the question of criteria?" (GO TO 462A)

B. "I hope by the time we are finished with this discussion, everyone who has something to say feels that they have had a chance to make their feelings known." (GO TO 472A)

Decision Point 450C

You publicly congratulate Floyd Banks, Bunkie Brown, and Steve Johnson on a job well done on the staffing plan. However, Roy Best and George Bennet had done good work too. As a result of this oversight, Best and Bennet take a minor role in the next assignment, and the policy document lacks direction and focus in their areas of concern. You have worked hard to move the group from its initial P-4 condition to its position in P-2 or P-3. However, by singling out some individuals and not others, you have kept the group from building cohesiveness that would have had a positive impact on performance.

Re-evaluate your last decision. Circle the #450C you just wrote in your flow diagram. Then go back in your flow diagram to the first uncircled number above this step.

Decision Point 451A

Your technique of having task force members get to know each other works very well. By emphasizing common elements in the personal backgrounds of your members in your introductions, you find that Seashore and Smithers (an unlikely pair) were graduates of the same college and that Foy and Gump share a love for hiking in wilderness parks.

The break at its end, you now face the need to give the task force its charter. You map out your experiences chairing the last six special edition task forces and express your genuine hope that this coming special edition will be truly significant. You detail two major goals of the task force: to identify a topic for the seasonal edition that will be a contribution to the community and region and to facilitate the coordination problems associated with the special edition.

You also announce that, as in the past, the task force will operate as a whole at the beginning until an acceptable topic is arrived at. After that the task force will break into two subunits--one for internal coordination and the other for external coordination. (It is your experience that one subcommittee can be responsible for coordinating between Editorial and Sales/Marketing [external coordination] and the other for coordinating between Editorial and Operations [internal coordination].) Tentatively, you plan to assign Smithers and Gump to the group that is responsible for external affairs and Foy and Seashore to the group that is concerned with internal coordination.

You have already decided to sidestep the issue of objectives, but when you give the task force its charter from your boss, what will you tell them?

A. Your boss's concern that the topic chosen has market appeal, the ample budget, and your boss's desire to approve the topic. (GO TO 453A)

B. Your boss's concern that the topic chosen has market appeal and the ample budget. Say nothing at this point of your boss's desire to approve the topic. (GO TO 437C)

C. Your boss's concern that the topic chosen has market appeal and his desire to approve the topic. Say nothing at this point about the budget he has given you. (GO TO 458A)

D. Your budget and your boss's desire to approve the topic. Say nothing at this point about your boss's concern that the topic chosen have market appeal. (GO TO 446C)

Decision Point 452A

Your team works harmoniously in hammering out a statement of personnel policies. It is approved by top management, and two months later you receive authorization for a healthy budget increase. **Congratulations!** Your actions have both forged a new team spirit and developed your credibility with a skeptical top management. This completes the Managing Work Teams Interactive Case.

Decision Point 452B

You leave your boss's office feeling a bit defeated but resolved to put together the most persuasive presentation possible at your next meeting with him. You know that Harrison Gump and his reporters are already working on the topic, and you believe that if you are to convince your boss, you need some of the facts that they are uncovering. The problem is that you don't want to let Gump know you are having problems convincing the publisher that the task force's topic is satisfactory.

How would you handle this situation?

A. Go directly to the reporters involved and get the information from them. (GO TO 455C)

B. Go to Harrison Gump directly and confess that you are having some difficulty convincing your boss and ask his help. (GO TO 428A)

C. Go to Gump and ask his help in "making the best case you can" for the topic that the task force has chosen, but say nothing about the publisher's initial resistance to the idea. (GO TO 480B)

Decision Point 452C

George Bennet reacts angrily and resigns on the spot to attend law school full time. Roy Best follows suit joining your predecessor's consulting firm. The group deteriorates rapidly, and with your department seriously understaffed, you are unable to meet any of the deadlines you were given by top management.

Apparently your approach was a bit extreme, given the rather volatile situation in the department. Although it is not inappropriate to confront an informal group leader when a team is in a P-4 condition, one must be careful not to act to create yourself as a "common enemy." Otherwise you simply intensify the resistance to your leadership. By confronting Bennet as well as Alton, you have done just that.

Re-evaluate your last decision. Circle the #452C you just wrote in your flow diagram. Then go back in your flow diagram to the first uncircled number above this step.

Decision Point 453A

You decide to tell your task force everything you know about your task force's charter, its budget, and the involvement the publisher wants. This begins a very heated discussion at this, your first meeting.

Foy: "Wow, that's a lot of money. The old man really wants to throw money at this issue."
Seashore: "My concern is that he's trying to buy us off for his involvement. I can tell you that the people in Editorial are not going to like this . . . not one bit."
Gump: "That's for sure. You can't run a newspaper without offering reporters more independence than that. I was concerned when he nixed a story on toxic waste, but I'm beginning to feel just this side of outrage."
Smithers: "Harrison, Harrison, you're going to burst an artery."
Foy: "Just because he's asking to see our topic before we proceed doesn't mean that he's going to veto it."
Seashore: "That's not the point. I don't know about you, but I don't want to have to consider how the old man will react to every topic we come up with. That's ludicrous!"
Gump (turning to Seashore): "You are the master of understatement, my friend."

You are concerned that Gump and Seashore perceive the independence of the task force to be a matter of principle and may escalate the issue to the Vice President of the Editorial Department.
What would you do at this point?

A. Don't intervene at this point. Let the discussion unfold a bit more to see if Foy and Smithers can counter Seashore and Gump. (GO TO 429A)

B. Break into the discussion with the statement, "I don't think it's the task force's role to redefine the charter given to us by the publisher." (GO TO 469A)

C. Say, "I understand your position, Lyle, but I really believe the publisher's involvement is a function of his interests and not an intention of interfering. My sense is that if we do approach him with this, that's what he will say. Why don't we proceed with our assignment and see?" (GO TO 468A)

D. "Would you like me to ask the Publisher what his intentions are?" (GO TO 443C)

Decision Point 454A

Your choice of seven members for your task force is incorrect. Generally, while a size of seven is certainly a good second choice, a task force of five is generally considered best. Let's assume that you chose five as the proper task force size and continue with the interactive case from that point.

You now have to determine the specific makeup of your task force. Since last season's topic involved sports, you decide that your two representatives from Editorial should come from the following:

Harrison Gump (Feature Editor)--Hard-nosed, irascible, and a bit abrasive, a real no-nonsense person. Cut out of the mold of the typical crusty city editor.

Lyle Seashore (News Editor)--Pulitzer Prize-winning investigative reporter turned editor. Arrogant workaholic and defender of the Editorial Department's prerogatives when it comes to the selection of topics for the seasonal issue.

Myra Patrick (Business Editor)--The youngest business editor at any major newspaper in the U.S. and still finding her way. Known to be incredibly imaginative but very serious. Closely controls her own staff but has yet to earn the respect of her peers.

Your choice of the other candidates is very important. In the past, the representatives from Editorial have dominated the task force, and this has caused problems working out the coordination details with the other departments. The candidates for the other two positions are:

Michael Smithers (Director of Circulation)--Community activist; articulate, amusing conversationalist; unswerving promoter of the *Register* in Madison.

Elaine Fitzgerald (Director of Consumer Advertising)--Efficient, intelligent, does not respect Smithers on the grounds that she thinks he is "vacuous."

Baron Leybolt (Director of Human Resources)--Unassuming, diligent, earnest, and eager to please; doesn't yet have much credibility in the organization.

Peter Foy (Director of Information Systems)--Extremely knowledgeable of internal operations; tough-minded (perhaps even severe); persuaded only with facts.

Haley Jones (Treasurer)--Brisk, aloof, super-rational, and businesslike.

Which of the following combinations of members would you choose?

A. Gump, Seashore, Fitzgerald, Smithers. (GO TO 446A)
B. Gump, Seashore, Smithers, Foy. (GO TO 483B)
C. Gump, Patrick, Leybolt, Foy. (GO TO 456C)
D. Gump, Patrick, Fitzgerald, Jones. (GO TO 471A)
E. Seashore, Patrick, Smithers, Leybolt. (GO TO 432A)
F. Seashore, Patrick, Foy, Fitzgerald. (GO TO 473B)

Decision Point 455A

You decide to takes notes yourself on a note pad. This arrangement does not work well. You find that you are so busy writing you don't have any inputs to the listing. This in effect reduces the size of the group from five to four, and the group only comes up with 31 ideas. In addition, since the participants cannot see your notes, there is much less piggybacking of ideas.

Re-evaluate your last decision. Circle the #455A you just wrote in your flow diagram, and move to the first uncircled step above this one in your diagram.

Decision Point 455B

You have decided to give the group an assignment. The results are very disappointing. Not only was the impact report finished late, but it contained assumptions that top management found unacceptably naive. Apparently you expected too much too soon from a team that accepted neither you as leader nor the new directions in which you were hired to lead the department.

Your evaluation of the social conditions in your team should have concluded that the team is presently in a P-4 condition: high cohesiveness and antagonistic work norms. As such, you were ill advised to give team members an assign- ment that required more complex work relationships than in their regular work. Instead you should have held off until you had an opportunity to begin to alter the social conditions of the group.

Re-evaluate your last decision. Circle the #455B you just wrote in your flow diagram. Then go back in your flow diagram to the first uncircled number above this step.

Decision Point 455C

You decided to go directly to the reporters involved in the topic and get the information you needed to make your appeal to your boss. This did not work very well. Harrison Gump (the reporters' boss) found out about your request, and informed the other members of the task force what you were up to. The resulting rumors got back to your boss, and he remained rigid in his rejection of the topic.

Whenever you move around a task force member, you invite this sort of reaction. The benefits are simply not worth the risks.

Re-evaluate your last decision. Circle the #455C you just wrote in your flow diagram. Then move to the first uncircled step above this one in your flow diagram.

Decision Point 456A

Gump continues to make evaluative remarks, and in time Foy also begins signaling his displeasure with body language and sighs.

Brainstorming requires compliance with its no-evaluation rule. You should have enforced that rule as soon as the first violation appeared. Let's assume you had done so and proceed with the case.

The brainstorming begins again, and sheet after sheet of flip chart paper is filled and taped to the walls of your conference room. This goes on for about 20 minutes, and then there is a prolonged lull in the group.

At this point what would you do?

A. Wait out the silence. (GO TO 448C)

B. Call off the session since it is clear that the group has exhausted its creative potential. (GO TO 482B)

C. Ask if anyone has any more ideas. (GO TO 430B)

Decision Point 456B

In making this assignment and in conducting yourself in weekly departmental meetings and other public occasions, what would you do?

A. Indicate that these labor negotiations are a real opportunity for the department to regain its credibility with top management. State that it will take a coordinated effort to overcome what will surely be a tough bargaining stand by the union. (GO TO 467A)

B. Change the format of weekly departmental meetings to allow for more group discussions on issues of concern. (GO TO 477A)

C. Take every chance to reinforce and publicly acknowledge any efforts in line with top management's concern that your department become more relevant to the realities of the firm. (GO TO 469B)

Decision Point 456C

You chose the combination of Gump, Patrick, Leybolt, and Foy. While this is a representative composition, it puts an "unassuming" person on the task force who lacks organizational credibility. There is a better combination.

Re-evaluate your last decision. Circle the #456C you just wrote in your flow diagram. Then move to the first uncircled step above this one in your flow diagram.

Decision Point 457A

You summarize the decisions made at the first meeting and ask Seashore and Gump for their report. Gump hands out a list of topics that are presently being worked on in the Editorial Department by various reporters. This done, you need to instruct the group as to what technique is appropriate for the task force to use to derive topics for the seasonal issue.

What technique would you use?

A. Nominal Group Technique. (GO TO 486A)

B. Ordinary group discussion. (GO TO 432C)

C. Expert testimony. (GO TO 463A)

D. Use of subgroups engaged in ordinary group discussion. (GO TO 464C)

E. Brainstorming. (GO TO 429C)

Decision Point 457B

You have decided to give the group an assignment requiring the highest complexity of required interaction. The results are extremely disappointing. Not only was the policy statement finished late, but it contained assumptions that top management found unacceptably naive. Apparently you expected too much too soon of a team that accepts neither you as its leader nor the new directions in which you were hired to lead the department.

During the first month you did act successfully to decrease group cohesiveness a bit, as evidenced by Alton's loss of influence. However, the group is in at best a P-3 condition. Accordingly, you acted prematurely in requiring them to perform well at such a high complexity of required interaction.

Re-evaluate your last decision. Circle the #457B you just wrote in your flow diagram. Then go back in your flow diagram to the first uncircled number above this step.

Decision Point 457C

Your tactic of telling one task force member something you have not told another backfires. Lyle Seashore hears of your "deception" and resigns from the task force. Clearly, at this point, there is no need for selectively telling task force members things.

Re-evaluate your last decision. Circle the #457C you just wrote in your flow diagram. Then move to the first uncircled step above this one in your flow diagram.

Decision Point 458A

You decide to say nothing about the budget your boss has given you. This is a mistake. It is a piece of information that your task force should have in deciding a topic and in working out coordination details.

Re-evaluate your last decision. Circle the #458A you just wrote in your flow diagram. Then move to the first uncircled step above this one in your flow diagram.

Decision Point 458B

You have decided to give your team an assignment. The results are very disappointing. Not only was the policy statement finished late, but it contained assumptions that top management found unacceptably naive. Apparently, you expected too much too soon from a team that accepted neither you as leader nor the new directions you were hired to lead the department in.

Your evaluation of the social conditions in your team should have concluded that the team is presently in a P-4 condition: high cohesiveness and antagonistic work norms. As such, you were ill advised to give team members an assignment that required more complex work relationships than in their regular work. Instead, you should have held off until you had an opportunity to begin to alter the social conditions of the group.

Re-evaluate your last decision. Circle the #458B you just wrote in your flow diagram. Then go back in your flow diagram to the first uncircled number above this step.

Decision Point 458C

Seeing you concentrated in work, Gump sits back down and continues adding to his list of prospective ideas. Time passes and Seashore returns to the room, and seeing the others working, also returns to his yellow pad.

Ten more minutes pass, and after all pencils stop moving, you move onto the next step: the sharing of ideas in a round-robin fashion.

How would you keep track of the ideas generated?

A. Ask the members if they have any objections if you ask your personal assistant to keep track of the ideas. Position him at the flip chart. (GO TO 436A)

B. Take notes yourself on a note pad. (GO TO 455A)

C. Use a flip chart to write down the ideas yourself. (GO TO 476C)

D. Tape-record the session. (GO TO 422D)

Decision Point 459A

As your third task force meeting begins, it appears that there is a new sense of togetherness in the group. Smithers, whom you wanted on the team for his social skills, is actually rather quiet in the minutes just before the meeting when all the members are present. Instead, Foy and Gump are exchanging stories and engaging in boisterous laughter.

Seashore sits alone, and you try to strike up a conversation, but to no avail. His thoughts are elsewhere, and you find yourself hoping that his pensiveness has nothing to do with the task force.

You begin the meeting by asking members to report on the categories they have been able to identify from the results of the last meeting. When all the individual reports are completed, it is clear that the alternative topics fall into the following seven categories:

(1) regional development problems,
(2) police inadequacies in dealing with minor theft,
(3) disillusionment of the middle class and alternative life-styles,
(4) justice for the underclass--farm workers, the homeless and indigent ,
(5) organized crime and real estate scams,
(6) child abuse and alcoholism,
(7) overcrowding at the county prison.

You must now decide how to evaluate each of these categories. Before the first task force meeting you had decided to delay the issue of decision criteria because of the publisher's rather controversial concern that the topic have circulation potential. You can delay no longer, so you open the issue of criteria.

The discussion is tense at first, with the two people from Editorial sparring with the others on the matter of journalistic independence and circulation potential without mentioning either.

At that point Lyle Seashore begins dominating the discussion. He makes his point with story after story that all support the notion that circulation should not serve as the guiding force in editorial decisions.

What would you say to Seashore to regain control of this meeting?

A. "Lyle, I think all of us understand your point of view. In all fairness, we should now give someone else a chance to be heard on the matter." (GO TO 450B)

B. "Lyle, that's enough. You are beginning to repeat yourself." (GO TO 444A)

C. "Am I the only one who disagrees with Lyle on this point?" (GO TO 434C)

Decision Point 460A

Your tough stand with Alton backfires. Duckworth and Spurior feel equally disciplined. Alton and Duckworth both quit to join your predecessor's consulting firm. Apparently Doc Stevens had given them standing offers to join the firm even before you were made Director. You are now seriously understaffed to complete three one-month assignments in three months. The results are dreadful. Your team fails to make all of its deadlines, and the quality of the work reflects the understaffing.

While you were correct in concluding that some action on the individuals was appropriate to further decrease cohesiveness, your tough action against Alton is unwarranted for several reasons. First, although you are skeptical, Alton's excuses are believable. Second, now that you are under way with your assignments, you should appreciate that you are now dependent on your team, i.e., if they become uncommitted, you will look bad. For these reasons, it is probably more prudent to single out individuals with praise, not "tough stands."

Re-evaluate your last decision. Circle the #460A you just wrote in your flow diagram. Then go back in your flow diagram to the first uncircled number above this step.

Decision Point 460B

You decide to meet individual members of the task force before the first meeting to feel them out on objectives. Your first meeting is with Lyle Seashore. True to form, he objects to any objective for the issue that "smacks" of narrow, commercial interests. Yet when you meet with Harrison Gump, you are surprised to find him willing to select a topic for the seasonal edition that will have "broad appeal." Knowing Gump, you realize that that is as close to agreeing with commercial appeal as an objective as you are likely to get.

When you raise the issue with Smithers and Foy, they have no problem with the idea of an increase in circulation as a specific objective. Clearly Seashore is in the minority, but you are concerned that if you raise the issue in your first meeting, he may be able to win Gump over on a matter of principle and deadlock the task force. How would you proceed from this point?

A. Raise the issue of objectives at your first meeting and be prepared to guide the group to the resolution that you and the publisher want. (GO TO 434A)
B. Return to Lyle Seashore and explore with him what objectives he can live with. Be prepared to tell him that if he can't live with a commercial objective, you may have to ask someone else to serve on the task force. (GO TO 433B)
C. Have your boss (the publisher) talk with Seashore to persuade him of the importance of circulation. (GO TO 427A)

Decision Point 461A

After you make your statement, George Bennet asks whether you don't think the department has a responsibility to lead the organization to a level of professionalism befitting "the times." You respond that it is true that top management doesn't have an enlightened view of what an employee relations department should do. However, you assert, there is no way the department can hope to lead the organization without building its credibility.

A few days later, the factory superintendent (a position at the same organizational level as yours) mentions that he heard about your aim to build credibility so your department can put in place a more activist set of policies. He informs you that such politicking will never work at the company.

You have been victimized by an end run at the hands of Bunkie Brown and Bob Alton. Your credibility with top management has suffered a severe setback. And since you have yet not established yourself as the leader of your group, the situation is virtually irretrievable.

In thinking about where you went wrong, consider that your group is presently in a P-4 social condition: high cohesiveness, antagonistic work norms. Your statement that your charter is to confront these antagonistic norms, while true, serves only to unify the group against you as a common enemy. In general it is advisable to avoid appearing to take sides publicly when one's P-4 team members oppose you. It is better to handle the group individually, making it clear that there are some behaviors you want and others you don't. Going after attitudes is premature until you have taken some action on behavior.

Re-evaluate your last decision. Circle the #461A you just wrote in your flow diagram. Then go back in your flow diagram to the first uncircled number above this step.

Decision Point 461B

How would you open the next meeting?

A. Summarize what was decided at the last meeting and ask for a report from Gump and Seashore. (GO TO 457A)

B. Tell the group that you plan to use brainstorming as a method of deriving alternative topics for the seasonal issue. (GO TO 477B)

C. Tell the group that the task force will use the Nominal Group Technique for developing alternative topics for the seasonal issue. (GO TO 485B)

Decision Point 462A

You try to draw Smithers into the discussion by calling on him. Sometimes that works, but this time it doesn't. He simply clams up all the more, and the discussion moves on without his involvement. Generally it is preferable to speak more indirectly to the entire group about the unevenness of the participation. You should have said, "I hope by the time we are finished with this discussion, everyone who has something to say feels that they have had a chance to make their feelings known." Let's assume you had made that statement and proceed with the interactive case from that point.

Finally, Smithers says, "You know, I get the feeling that Harrison and Lyle think that the rest of us want to force some second-rate topic down their throats. Personally, I want a topic that will help people. Compassion not exploitation sells newspapers." This remarks breaks the impasse. The group quickly agrees that an effective topic will have the following attributes:

(1) It should increase circulation by arousing compassion in the community;
(2) It should meet the highest standards of journalistic work; and
(3) It should play into the strengths of the Editorial Department.

These criteria identified, the group assesses each of the seven broad topic areas and the clear favorite is police inadequacies in dealing with minor crime (auto burglary, shoplifting, vandalism, etc.). Harrison Gump reports that two members of his staff have been conducting some preliminary research on the topic and discovered that 61 percent of the citizenry are touched by such minor crimes each year, and that police indifference may be due to the fact that most of the community's opinion leaders have insurance. There are many facets to the issue, and the task force is really quite enthusiastic.

As the meeting comes to a close, you ask the members to return prepared to address the coordination issues associated with this topic. Seashore then asks you if you are going to talk with the publisher about the topic. You promise to do that before the next meeting.

The meeting ends, and you enter your boss's office planning to have a pretty easy time convincing him that the topic your task force has chosen is a good one. Much to your surprise, he is very unimpressed by your committee's choice. You try to persuade him, but he remains firm that the topic will have little readership appeal. Now you are in a real jam.

What would you do?

A. Ask your boss whether his mind is really made up or if he will consider other evidence you might get for him. (GO TO 475C)

B. Ask to talk with him more about this issue at a later time. (GO TO 452B)

C. Return to your task force and tell them of the publisher's rejection of the topic it has chosen. (GO TO 442C)

Decision Point 463A

You have chosen expert testimony as a method of developing alternative topics for the seasonal issue. This is an inappropriate group decision-making method for developing alternatives since no one outside the task force possesses more expertise than the task force members themselves.

Re-evaluate your last decision. Circle the #463A you just wrote in your flow diagram. Then move to the first uncircled step above this one in your flow diagram.

Decision Point 463B

It is one month later, and your personal position in the group is stronger. Unfortunately, however, the high level of group spirit you observed when you first arrived has been seriously eroded. Some individuals have sided with you (e.g., Best, Bennet, Banks, Brown, and Johnson) and others continue to be cool toward you (Duckworth and Spurior). Alton is still quiet and sullen in public. Halfway through the month, Spurior approached you and confessed feeling troubled that the "family feeling" in the department was gone. You persuaded him that things would get better in time.

Since it is now three months until your three departmental assignments are due, you must now decide what assignment to complete first. Which would you choose?

A. *Assignment 1*--Preparation for Labor Negotiations. In three months your department begins negotiations with the Sheetmetal Workers Union for the first time in two years. Since the contract will affect each department member's specialty, inputs from everyone will be solicited. Bunkie Brown will draw up a list of probable union demands and these will be sent simultaneously to every other department member for an assessment of economic and administrative impact. You will then aggregate these assessments into an integrated impact report. (GO TO 456B)

B. *Assignment 2*--Development of an Integrated Personnel Policy. Top management has asked you to submit a document outlining a reassessment of existing departmental policies and procedures, together with proposals for changes. It is due in three months. Preparing this document will involve intensive meetings of all department members. (GO TO 464B)

C. *Assignment 3*--Creation of an Annual Staffing Plan. In three months all manpower planning for the next fiscal year is due. This is a serial process beginning with Roy Best who estimates promotions and transfers. This then goes to Bob Alton's group (Alton, Duckworth, and Spurior), which calculates new staffing needs, and then on to George Bennet, who justifies these figures into the affirmative action plan. Finally, Floyd Banks transposes these estimates into a budget form. (GO TO 480A)

Decision Point 464A

You leave your boss's office without ascertaining what involvement he wants on the topic for the seasonal edition. This is a mistake. Without this sort of clarification, you cannot be certain that your boss wants the same level of involvement you assume he does.

Re-evaluate your last decision. Circle the #464A you just wrote in your flow diagram. Then move to the first uncircled step above this one in your flow diagram.

Decision Point 464B

You have decided to give your work team a highly complex assignment that promises to result in rather heated discussions during a time that your team is anything but "together." The results are unfortunate. The discussions emphasize the differences between individual opinions, and even the existing factions disintegrate. Deadlines are missed, and the resultant document lacks focus. You watch the credibility of the department with top management go down.

Your previous action of holding off making an assignment until absolutely necessary was correct. It gave you the opportunity to work on the social conditions in the group. The results for the most part were encouraging. Your actions resulted in the team moving from an initial P-4 condition to the P-3 condition that you observed when you made your last decision. The Integrated Personnel Policy assignment requires the highest level of complexity in required interaction. Clearly you should have held off giving this assignment until much later.

Re-evaluate your last decision. Circle the #464B you just wrote in your flow diagram. Then go back in your flow diagram to the first uncircled number above this step.

Decision Point 464C

You have chosen subgroups as a method of developing alternative topics for the seasonal issue. This is an inappropriate group decision-making method for developing alternatives since there is no evidence that there would be any advantage in using subgroups. Subgroups are typically used when the responsibility given to the group at large is divisible into coherent parts and when some members have interests or abilities that reflect this division.

Re-evaluate your last decision. Circle the #464C you just wrote in your flow diagram. Then move to the first uncircled step above this one in your flow diagram.

Decision Point 465A

Your "pep talk" is greeted with almost no reaction. Later the same day, you learn through the grapevine that it actually resulted in a great deal of cynicism. While you are not sure, you suspect that this negativity comes from Bob Alton.

What would you do now?

A. Take a tough stand with Bob Alton. Let him know that you expect him to cooperate. (GO TO 460A)

B. At a weekly departmental meeting, announce the charter you were given by top management and state your resolve to bring the department back in line with the needs of the organization. (GO TO 430A)

C. Mention at a weekly departmental meeting that you are pleased that Brown and Johnson gave so much thought to their assumptions and that Best, Bennet, and Banks have made excellent progress on their part of the assignment; say nothing about Alton, Spurior, or Duckworth. (GO TO 428B)

Decision Point 465B

You asked your boss what involvement he wants in your task force. He tells you that he wants to approve the topic your task force chooses before you proceed with the coordination portion of your activity. This is a departure from tradition and one that will not be particularly popular with a number of the task force members, especially those from Editorial. However, with all the money he is throwing in your direction, his request is understandable.

Next you must decide how many directors to include on this season's task force. You have discovered that a group any larger than nine is very difficult to manage. How many members should you include on your task force?

A. Four. (GO TO 470A)

B. Five. (GO TO 481A)

C. Six. (GO TO 478A)

D. Seven. (GO TO 454A)

E. Eight. (GO TO 440A)

F. Nine. (GO TO 425A)

Decision Point 466A

Your tough stand with Alton comes as a complete shock to him and to those who continue to support his informal leadership (Duckworth and Spurior). Apparently your previous action of discussing career goals with each individual gave no indication that you planned to be so firm. After all, you had, at best, suspicions about Alton's motives, supported only by an unsubstantiated rumor.

As a result of your action, Alton quits to join your predecessor's consulting firm. To make matters worse, you hear that Duckworth has decided to see an attorney about filing suit against her former boss in manufacturing for sexual harassment.

Your actions to date have been correct in terms of holding off making an assignment, but this last action did more to solidify opposition to you as a common enemy of the team.

Re-evaluate your last decision. Circle the #466A you just wrote in your flow diagram. Then go back in your flow diagram to the first uncircled number above this step.

Decision Point 466B

This arrangement works well. You talk with the vice presidents and get their cooperation. Back at the meeting, you next want to make a few remarks on the political sensitivities of serving on the task force.

What would you say in this regard?

A. "With the quality of people on this task force, I'm very optimistic about being able to put together a superb seasonal issue. However, I am a bit concerned that we keep to ourselves. Please, let's keep our deliberations confidential, and if you are having a problem with the way anything is done on this task force, see me before you talk about with people not in the group. Is that agreeable to everyone?" (GO TO 467B)

B. "I'm convinced that, with the people on this task force, we cannot fail. However, our assignment is a challenging one, and it is very likely that we will step on each other's toes from time to time. For that reason I would like to ask all of you to keep whatever conflicts arise in this room *in this room*." (GO TO 476A)

C. "All of you have been carefully selected to represent your constituencies on this task force. It is very imperative that you bring the points of view of your departments to our deliberations so we can be sure that the special issue is acceptable to all involved." (GO TO 475A)

Decision Point 467A

It is one month later, and the team completed its assignment on schedule. You received the inputs of each team member, and you were able to formulate an impact report that you have some confidence in. You are not absolutely certain of the validity of some of the assumptions, but they appear sound to you. Upon submitting the report to top management, they indicate concerns that it is much too optimistic and too theoretical "as usual." What would you do?

A. Indicate at the next department meeting that top management has challenged the report, and ask each team member for a reassessment of their inputs. Plan to take any revised figures back to top management to challenge their statements that the report is too optimistic. (GO TO 445C)

B. Check the figures yourself. Speak privately with Bunkie Brown to assure yourself that they are based on reasoning you understand and accept. Plan to take the resultant figures back to top management to challenge their statements that the report is too optimistic. (GO TO 476B)

C. Agree with top management that the report may be too optimistic and theoretical, but indicate that you need more time to "whip the team into shape." (GO TO 475B)

Decision Point 467B

Lyle Seashore asks whether reporting the involvement of the publisher in the selection of the seasonal edition topic violates the norm of confidentiality. You respond that you think it does and indicate that the group has decided to take a wait-and-see posture. With that, all the members agree that confidentiality makes sense.

That behind you, you then address one last issue: you think the task force would benefit from knowing what long-term investigative work is under way in the Editorial Department that may have the potential of serving as the basis for the task force's choice of a topic. You ask Gump and Seashore to report to the task force at the next scheduled task force meeting on these developments. They agree to do so. How would you end the meeting?

A. "Well, we're off to a good start. Let's see, at the next meeting we will begin work on the topic. See you then." (GO TO 431C)

B. "At the next meeting, we will begin work on the topic for the special issue. You all may want to think about that in preparation for the meeting. And my understanding is that Harrison and Lyle will be bringing us some inputs. Is that correct?" (GO TO 461B)

Decision Point 468A

Your comment seems to put the issue to rest for the time being. Seashore remains disturbed, but Gump agrees that the task force ought to take a wait-and-see posture. He adds: "I'll be watching his so-called involvement very carefully. If he starts managing our efforts from a distance, you will have my resignation from this effort."

You then lay out a number of procedures similar to the ones you have used with previous task forces. You tell them you will be responsible for producing and distributing minutes as a vehicle for keeping the members posted. You give them a schedule of milestones that will have to be met.

Your schedule is greeted by a chorus of groans. Each member reacts negatively to the timing of certain milestones. All but Foy argue that their other responsibilities are going to seriously interfere with their ability to make the necessary commitment to the task force.

How would you react to this development?

A. "Gentlemen, all of us are busy, but the publisher is committed to this special issue. It is really up to you to negotiate with your respective bosses to be freed up sufficiently from your other duties to give 100 percent to this assignment." (GO TO 441B)
B. "Talk with your prospective bosses about this first. If you don't get the necessary slack from them, let me know, and I'll talk with them myself." (GO TO 466B)
C. "Would you like me to ask the publisher to talk with your bosses about freeing up your time for this?" (GO TO 424B)

Decision Point 468B

Luke Spurior tries very hard as chairman but is unable to earn the respect of the others in the group. Moreover, once you are seen as the "behind the scenes" chairman, Spurior's credibility drops considerably. As a result, the assignment takes a very long time to complete, and several members of the team resent your "manipulations."

For the first time you have direct evidence that team members are enforcing work norms on one another that support your definition of performance. Therefore, you can be pretty sure that your team is in a P-2 position (low cohesiveness; supportive norms). Your decision to make Spurior the chairman will keep the group from moving to a P-1 position because the chairmanship is not Spurior's preferred role, nor is it the preferred assignment by the group.

Re-evaluate your last decision. Circle the #468B you just wrote in your flow diagram. Then go back in your flow diagram to the first uncircled number above this step.

Decision Point 469A

You say, "I don't think it's the task force's role to redefine the charter given to us by the publisher." Gump strongly objects. He says, "The publisher is a reasonable man, and I think he will be interested in what the task force thinks." Your statement was ill advised, for it gives the impression that the charter was given in a "take it or leave it" fashion.

Re-evaluate your last decision. Circle the #469A you just wrote in your flow diagram. Then move to the first uncircled step above this one in your flow diagram.

Decision Point 469B

It is one month later, and the team completed its assignment on schedule. You received the inputs of each team member, and you were able to formulate an impact report that you have some confidence in. You are not absolutely certain of the validity of some of the assumptions, but they appear sound to you. Upon submitting the report to top management, they indicate concerns that it is much too optimistic and too theoretical "as usual."

What would you do?

A. Indicate at the next department meeting that top management has challenged the report, and ask each team member for a reassessment of his or her inputs. Plan to take any revised figures back to top management to challenge their statements that the report is too optimistic. (GO TO 445C)

B. Check the figures yourself. Speak privately with Bunkie Brown to assure yourself that they are based on reasoning you understand and accept. Plan to take the resultant figures back to top management to challenge their statements that the report is too optimistic. (GO TO 476B)

C. Agree with top management that the report may be too optimistic and theoretical, but indicate that you need more time to "whip the team into shape." (GO TO 475B)

Decision Point 469C

You decide to go ahead with the meeting without Seashore and ask Gump to brief him. This results in a serious communication problem. You should have tried to contact him before proceeding with this important meeting.

Re-evaluate your last decision. Circle the #469C you just wrote in your flow diagram. Then move to the first uncircled step above this one in your flow diagram.

Decision Point 470A

Your choice of four members for your task force is incorrect. It is better to have an odd number rather than an even one, and a task force of five is generally considered best. Let's assume that you chose five as the proper task force size and continue with the interactive case from that point.

You now have to determine the specific makeup of your task force. Since last season's topic involved sports, you decide that your two representatives from Editorial should come from the following:

Harrison Gump (Feature Editor)--Hard-nosed, irascible, and a bit abrasive, a real no-nonsense person. Cut out of the mold of the typical crusty city editor.

Lyle Seashore (News Editor)--Pulitzer Prize winning-investigative reporter turned editor. Arrogant workaholic and defender of the Editorial Department's prerogatives when it comes to the selection of topics for the seasonal issue.

Myra Patrick (Business Editor)--The youngest business editor at any major newspaper in the U.S. and still finding her way. Known to be incredibly imaginative but very serious. Closely controls her own staff but has yet to earn the respect of her peers.

Your choice of the other candidates is very important. In the past, the representatives from Editorial have dominated the task force, and this has caused problems working out the coordination details with the other departments. The candidates for the other two positions are

Michael Smithers (Director of Circulation)--Community activist; articulate, amusing conversationalist; unswerving promoter of the *Register* in Madison.

Elaine Fitzgerald (Director of Consumer Advertising)--Efficient, intelligent, does not respect Smithers on the grounds that she thinks he is "vacuous."

Baron Leybolt (Director of Human Resources)--Unassuming, diligent, earnest, and eager to please; doesn't yet have much credibility in the organization.

Peter Foy (Director of Information Systems)--Extremely knowledgeable of internal operations; tough-minded (perhaps even severe); persuaded only with facts.

Haley Jones (Treasurer)--Brisk, aloof, super-rational, and businesslike.

Which of the following combinations of members would you choose?

A. Gump, Seashore, Fitzgerald, Smithers. (GO TO 446A)
B. Gump, Seashore, Smithers, Foy. (GO TO 483B)
C. Gump, Patrick, Leybolt, Foy. (GO TO 456C)
D. Gump, Patrick, Fitzgerald, Jones. (GO TO 471A)
E. Seashore, Patrick, Smithers, Leybolt. (GO TO 432A)
F. Seashore, Patrick, Foy, Fitzgerald. (GO TO 473B)

Decision Point 471A

You chose the combination of Gump, Patrick, Fitzgerald, and Jones. This composition has two problems. First, Fitzgerald does not as yet have the stature and credibility that is required for an effective task force member. Second, when you examine the descriptions of all four of these individuals carefully, you will notice that none of them has anything but a tough, efficiency-conscious, businesslike demeanor. The problem with this is that task forces operate best with compositions that have a balance between individuals who bring a businesslike orientation and those who are more socially inclined. Of all the candidates, Michael Smithers is about the only individual who has a social orientation.

Re-evaluate your last decision. Circle the #471A you just wrote in your flow diagram. Then move to the first uncircled step above this one in your flow diagram.

Decision Point 471B

You have decided to give your team an assignment that involves a moderate level of complexity in required interaction. The results are extremely disappointing. Not only was the staffing plan finished late, but it contained figures that top management challenged. Apparently you expected too much too soon from a group that accepts neither you as a leader nor the new directions in which you were hired to lead the Department.

During the first month you did act successfully to decrease group cohesiveness a bit, as evidenced by Alton's loss of influence. However, the group is presently at best in a P-3 condition. Consequently, your assignment required more complex interactions than the group was ready for.

Re-evaluate your last decision. Circle the #471B you just wrote in your flow diagram. Then go back in your flow diagram to the first uncircled number above this step.

Decision Point 471C

You tell Harrison Gump to get to work, and leave the room to ask Seashore to return. This alienates both these task force members. In situations like this, it is far better to model the behavior you want, rather than being too heavy-handed.

Reevaluate your last decision. Circle the #471C you just wrote in your flow diagram. Then move to the first uncircled step above this one in your flow diagram.

Decision Point 472A

Finally, Smithers says, "You know, I get the feeling that Harrison and Lyle think that the rest of us want to force some second-rate topic down their throats. Personally, I want a topic that will help people. Compassion not exploitation sells newspapers."

This remarks breaks the impasse. The group quickly agrees that an effective topic will have the following attributes:

(1) It should increase circulation by arousing compassion in the community;
(2) It should meet the highest standards of journalistic work;
(3) It should play to the particular strengths of the Editorial Department.

These criteria identified, the group assesses each of the seven broad topic areas and the clear favorite is police inadequacies in dealing with minor crime (auto burglary, shop-lifting, vandalism, etc.). Harrison Gump reports that two members of his staff have been conducting some preliminary research on the topic and discovered that 61 percent of the citizenry are touched by such minor crimes each year, and that police indifference may be due to the fact that most of the community's opinion leaders have insurance. There are many facets to the issue, and the task force is really quite enthusiastic.

As the meeting comes to a close, you ask the members to return prepared to address the coordination issues associated with this topic. Seashore then asks you if you are going to talk with the publisher about the topic. You promise to do that before the next meeting.

The meeting ends, and you enter your boss's office planning to have a pretty easy time convincing him that the topic your task force has chosen is a good one. Much to your surprise, he is very unimpressed by your committee's choice. You try to persuade him, but he remains firm that the topic will have little readership appeal.

Now you are in a real jam. What would you do?

A. Ask your boss whether his mind is really made up or if he will consider other evidence you might get for him. (GO TO 475C)

B. Ask to talk with him more about this issue at a later time. (GO TO 452B)

C. Return to your task force and tell them of the publisher's rejection of the topic it has chosen. (GO TO 442C)

Decision Point 473A

During the second one-month period when you have decided to give your team no group assignment, what would you do?

A. Take a tough stand with Bob Alton. Let him know that you expect his cooperation, but that you will not tolerate any trouble from him. (GO TO 474B)

B. Let others in the group know privately that you know that Bob Alton must have been very disappointed over being passed over for your job. Indicate that you look forward to working with him. Express a willingness to use your "authority" to support those who work for the department and to oppose those who work against it. (GO TO 449A)

C. Take the opportunity at a weekly departmental meeting to deliver a "pep talk" of sorts, emphasizing your confidence in the abilities of the people on your team and the need for everyone to work together toward goals that are both professionally credible and organizationally relevant. (GO TO 432B)

D. Meet with each team member individually to discuss his or her career goals and aspirations. Indicate your support for those who appear committed to your vision of the department. Begin to single out individual efforts that are in line with your plans. (GO TO 435A)

E. At a weekly departmental meeting, announce the charter you were given by top management and state your resolve to bring the department back in line with the needs of the organization. (GO TO 461A)

Decision Point 473B

You chose the combination of Seashore, Patrick, Foy, and Fitzgerald. This is not the best composition. When you examine the descriptions of all four of these individuals carefully, you will notice that none of them has anything but a tough, efficiency-conscious, businesslike demeanor. The problem with this is that task forces operate best with compositions that have a balance between individuals who bring a businesslike orientation and those who are more socially inclined. Of all the candidates, Michael Smithers is about the only individual who has a social orientation.

Re-evaluate your last decision. Circle the #473B you just wrote in your flow diagram. Then move to the first uncircled step above this one in your flow diagram.

Decision Point 474A

Gump responds well to your intervention and does not offer judgmental remarks again.

The brainstorming begins again, and sheet after sheet of flip chart paper is filled and taped to the walls of your conference room. This goes on for about 20 minutes, and then there is a prolonged lull in the group.

At this point what would you do?

A. Wait out the silence. (GO TO 448C)

B. Call off the session since it is clear that the group has exhausted its creative potential. (GO TO 482B)

C. Ask if anyone has any more ideas. (GO TO 430B)

Decision Point 474B

Bob Alton reacts little to your tough stand, except to say that he has no intention of causing you trouble. Later in the week, however, you sense that other members of your team are growing very cool to your leadership. Your secretary informs you that Alton has been telling others that you threatened him for no reason and that you lack "professional polish." Two days later, when walking down the corridor, you overhear George Bennet referring to you in the same way while talking with Bunkie Brown.

What would you do now?

A. Take the opportunity at a weekly departmental meeting to deliver a "pep talk" of sorts, emphasizing your confidence in the abilities of the people on your team and the need for everyone to work together toward goals that are both professionally credible and organizationally relevant. (GO TO 482A)

B. Meet with each team member individually to discuss his or her career goals and aspirations. Indicate your support for those who appear committed to your vision of the department. Begin to single out individual efforts that are in line with your plans. (GO TO 439A)

C. At a weekly department meeting, announce the charter you were given by top management, and state your resolve to bring the department back in line with the needs of the organization. (GO TO 461A)

D. Confront George Bennet and take a tough stand with him (as you did with Bob Alton). (GO TO 452C)

Decision Point 475A

You emphasize the need for the members to represent their departments on the task force. This creates real problems for the task force. Discussions easily polarize, and members take time between meetings to check with their bosses and other members of their departments for approval for their inputs.

In general, it is important to keep a task force free from outside pressures. You want representatives, but not representatives subjected to a great deal of pressure to represent.

Re-evaluate your last decision. Circle the #475A you just wrote in your flow diagram. Then move to the first uncircled step above this one in your flow diagram.

Decision Point 475B

Your statement to top management works its way into the grapevine and into the department via Bunkie Brown. The "whip the group into shape" phrase passes through the department like wildfire, and you are now seen as a "lackey" of manufacturing. This unfortunate label hurts you and severely suppresses the commitment of your team to your goals.

By accepting top management's indictment of work you had "some confidence in," you missed an opportunity to quietly orchestrate an experienced group success so helpful in this P-2 condition. Some sort of upward influence is called for. Otherwise you will unify the group, once again, in opposition to top management.

Re-evaluate your last decision. Circle the #475B you just wrote in your flow diagram. Then go back in your flow diagram to the first uncircled number above this step.

Decision Point 475C

You ask the publisher whether his mind is really made up. He says it is. Now you face the rather sensitive job of taking this result back to your task force. Actually, you should have heeded the old saying, "If you don't want to hear the answer, don't ask the question." There was no reason to ask for an ironclad commitment from your boss before you had mobilized the best argument possible on behalf of the task force's position.

Re-evaluate your last decision. Circle the #475C you just wrote in your flow diagram. Then move to the first uncircled step above this one in your flow diagram.

Decision Point 476A

You emphasize the need for group harmony in your little speech. This had little positive effect. One of the attributes of the diverse task force you have mobilized is conflicting opinions. By emphasizing the need for harmony, you are contradicting yourself.

Re-evaluate your last decision. Circle the #476A you just wrote in your flow diagram. Then move to the first uncircled step above this one in your flow diagram.

Decision Point 476B

You convince top management that the impact report is based on sound thinking. Bunkie Brown hears of your defense of the team through the grapevine, and your support grows within the group. Even Jane Duckworth begins to show commitment. You remain unsure, though, if these developments are sufficient to conclude that the group is now unified behind you.

Since there are two months to go before you must complete two assignments, you must select the next assignment to give the team. Which would you choose?

A. *Assignment 2*--Development of an Integrated Personnel Policy. Top management has asked you to submit a document outlining a reassessment of existing departmental policies and procedures, together with proposals for changes. It is due in two months. Preparing this document will involve intensive meetings of all department members. (GO TO 437B)

B. *Assignment 3*--Creation of an Annual Staffing Plan. In two months all manpower planning for the next fiscal year is due. This is a serial process beginning with Roy Best who estimates promotions and transfers. This then goes to Bob Alton's group (Alton, Duckworth, and Spurior), which calculates new staffing needs, and then on to George Bennet, who justifies these figures into the affirmative action plan. Finally, Floyd Banks transposes these estimates into a budget form. (GO TO 424A)

Decision Point 476C

You stand at the flip chart and play the role of recorder yourself. This does not work very well. You find that you are so busy writing you don't have any inputs to the listing. This in effect reduces the size of the group from five to four, and the group comes up with only 31 ideas.

Re-evaluate your last decision. Circle the #476C you just wrote in your flow diagram, and move to the first uncircled step above this one in your flow diagram.

Decision Point 477A

At the first meeting when you call for an open discussion of concerns, there is little response. At the next meeting, however, Jane Duckworth delivers a passionate speech that indicates her strong preference for professional values over the "narrow thinking in manufacturing." Others join the discussion, expressing their sorrow over the dismissal of your predecessor. At this point you intervene, but it is too late.

Essentially, by opening up the team to an open discussion of shared concerns, you have created a very complex required interaction. Since your team is presently in a P-3 condition, this is entirely too premature.

Re-evaluate your last decision. Circle the #477A you just wrote in your flow diagram. Then go back in your flow diagram to the first uncircled number above this step.

Decision Point 477B

You tell the group that you plan to use brainstorming as a method of deriving alternative topics for the seasonal issue. While this method may be well suited to the first aspect of your charter, it is really premature to announce it. You should have opened the meeting by summarizing the decisions made at the first meeting and asking Gump and Seashore to report on what they have discovered from their survey of ongoing topic assignments within the Editorial Department. Let's assume you had done that and resume the interactive case at that point.

You summarize the decisions made at the first meeting and ask Seashore and Gump for their report. Gump hands out a list of topics that are presently being worked on in the Editorial Department by various reporters. This done, you need to instruct the group as to what technique is appropriate for the task force to use to derive topics for the seasonal issue.

What technique would you use?

A. Nominal Group Technique. (GO TO 486A)

B. Ordinary group discussion. (GO TO 432C)

C. Expert testimony. (GO TO 463A)

D. Use of subgroups engaged in ordinary group discussion. (GO TO 464C)

E. Brainstorming. (GO TO 429C)

Decision Point 478A

Your choice of six members for your task force is incorrect. It is better to have an odd number rather than an even one, and a task force of five is generally considered best. Let's assume that you chose five as the proper task force size and continue with the interactive case from that point.

You now have to determine the specific makeup of your task force. Since last season's topic involved sports, you decide that your two representatives from Editorial should come from the following:

Harrison Gump (Feature Editor)--Hard-nosed, irascible, and a bit abrasive, a real no-nonsense person. Cut out of the mold of the typical crusty city editor.

Lyle Seashore (News Editor)--Pulitzer Prize-winning investigative reporter turned editor. Arrogant workaholic and defender of the Editorial Department's prerogatives when it comes to the selection of topics for the seasonal issue.

Myra Patrick (Business Editor)--The youngest business editor at any major newspaper in the U.S. and still finding her way. Known to be incredibly imaginative but very serious. Closely controls her own staff but has yet to earn the respect of her peers.

Your choice of the other candidates is very important. In the past, the representatives from Editorial have dominated the task force, and this has caused problems working out the coordination details with the other departments. The candidates for the other two positions are

Michael Smithers (Director of Circulation)--Community activist; articulate, amusing conversationalist; unswerving promoter of the *Register* in Madison.

Elaine Fitzgerald (Director of Consumer Advertising)--Efficient, intelligent, does not respect Smithers on the grounds that she thinks he is "vacuous."

Baron Leybolt (Director of Human Resources)--Unassuming, diligent, earnest, and eager to please; doesn't yet have much credibility in the organization.

Peter Foy (Director of Information Systems)--Extremely knowledgeable of internal operations; tough-minded (perhaps even severe); persuaded only with facts.

Haley Jones (Treasurer)--Brisk, aloof, super-rational, and businesslike.

Which of the following combinations of members would you choose?

   A. Gump, Seashore, Fitzgerald, Smithers. (GO TO 446A)
   B. Gump, Seashore, Smithers, Foy. (GO TO 483B)
   C. Gump, Patrick, Leybolt, Foy. (GO TO 456C)
   D. Gump, Patrick, Fitzgerald, Jones. (GO TO 471A)
   E. Seashore, Patrick, Smithers, Leybolt. (GO TO 432A)
   F. Seashore, Patrick, Foy, Fitzgerald. (GO TO 473B)

Decision Point 479A

Your tough stand with Alton, Duckworth, and Spurior backfires. Alton and Duckworth both quit to join your predecessor's consulting firm. You learn that he had given them an open job offer when he left your company. You are now seriously understaffed to complete three one-month assignments in three months. The results are dreadful. Your team fails to make all three deadlines, and the quality of work reflects the understaffing.

Re-evaluate your last decision. Circle the #479A you just wrote in your flow diagram. Then go back in your flow diagram to the first uncircled number above this step.

Decision Point 479B

Your boss, distracted by the appearance of the mayor in his outer office, tells you that he has no other instructions. This results in a serious misunderstanding between you and him over the involvement he wants in the work of the task force. Had you clarified his desires regarding his involvement, this misunderstanding would not have arisen. Let's assume that you did ask him what level of involvement he wanted and resume the interactive case at that point.

He tells you that he wants to approve the topic your task force chooses before you proceed with the coordination portion of your activity. This is a departure from tradition and one that will not be particularly popular with a number of task force members, especially those from Editorial. However, with all the money he is throwing in your direction, his request is understandable.

Next you must decide how many directors to include on this season's task force. You have discovered that a group any larger than nine is very difficult to manage. How many members should you include on your task force?

A. Four. (GO TO 470A)

B. Five. (GO TO 481A)

C. Six. (GO TO 478A)

D. Seven. (GO TO 454A)

E. Eight. (GO TO 440A)

F. Nine. (GO TO 425A)

Decision Point 480A

You have decided to give your work team an assignment that requires a moderate level of required interaction. The results are not good. A serious bottleneck occurs when the staffing plan moves from Roy Best to Duckworth, Spurior, and Alton. They simply cannot agree on a set of assumptions that you consider feasible. Desperate, you intervene and press the issue. Jane Duckworth resigns over the "interference." The assignment is completed three weeks later and is rejected by top management as unrealistic. Since you now have to go back and trace the difficulties, you are forced to delay other assignments. The results are disastrous for building the credibility of the department.

Your previous action of holding off making an assignment until absolutely necessary was correct. It gave you the opportunity to work on the social fabric of the team. The results were encouraging. Your actions have moved a group that was firmly in a P-4 condition to one that is now P-3. However, your choice of a particular assignment was incorrect. The Annual Staffing Plan assignment requires more complex interaction among team members than one of the alternatives.

Re-evaluate your last decision. Circle the #480A you just wrote in your flow diagram. Then go back in your flow diagram to the first uncircled number above this step.

Decision Point 480B

Gump arms you with some very persuasive information, and you return to your boss's office. You make "the best presentation of your career," and he gives you approval conditional on your ability to do a good job with the coordination issues. You believe this "condition" was more a face-saving gesture than a real requirement, but you are concerned that everything go smoothly. You recall that he told you several weeks ago that you had to get all the background material to Operations 36 hours in advance. You understand that means that whatever you do, you should make sure that Operations is "well taken care of." Clearly this will require you to exercise some persuasion with Editorial. At the next meeting of the task force, Lyle Seashore is very late. You tell the other members that the topic has been approved as soon as they arrive, but after 15 minutes elapse and Seashore is still late, you have to decide what to do.

What would you do?

A. Ask your secretary to phone Seashore and remind him that the meeting is scheduled. (GO TO 447B)

B. Go ahead anyway, with the idea that Gump can brief Seashore on the next step. (GO TO 469C)

Decision Point 481A

Five is an ideal size for your task force. The research evidence supports an odd number, and five is generally considered superior to seven or nine. You now have to determine the specific makeup of your task force. Since last season's topic involved sports, you decide that your two representatives from Editorial should come from the following:

Harrison Gump (Feature Editor)--Hard-nosed, irascible, and a bit abrasive, a real no-nonsense person. Cut out of the mold of the typical crusty city editor.

Lyle Seashore (News Editor)--Pulitzer Prize-winning investigative reporter turned editor. Arrogant workaholic and defender of the Editorial Department's prerogatives when it comes to the selection of topics for the seasonal issue.

Myra Patrick (Business Editor)--The youngest business editor at any major newspaper in the U.S. and still finding her way. Known to be incredibly imaginative but very serious. Closely controls her own staff but has yet to earn the respect of her peers.

Your choice of the other candidates is very important. In the past, the representatives from Editorial have dominated the task force, and this has caused problems working out the coordination details with the other departments. The candidates for the other two positions are

Michael Smithers (Director of Circulation)--Community activist; articulate, amusing conversationalist; unswerving promoter of the *Register* in Madison.

Elaine Fitzgerald (Director of Consumer Advertising)--Efficient, intelligent, does not respect Smithers on the grounds that she thinks he is "vacuous." New to the *Register* (two years).

Baron Leybolt (Director of Human Resources)--Unassuming, diligent, earnest, and eager to please; doesn't yet have much credibility in the organization.

Peter Foy (Director of Information Systems)--Extremely knowledgeable of internal operations; tough-minded (perhaps even severe); persuaded only with facts.

Haley Jones (Treasurer)--Brisk, aloof, super-rational, and businesslike.

Which of the following combinations of members would you choose?

    A. Gump, Seashore, Fitzgerald, Smithers. (GO TO 446A)
    B. Gump, Seashore, Smithers, Foy. (GO TO 483B)
    C. Gump, Patrick, Leybolt, Foy. (GO TO 456C)
    D. Gump, Patrick, Fitzgerald, Jones. (GO TO 471A)
    E. Seashore, Patrick, Smithers, Leybolt. (GO TO 432A)
    F. Seashore, Patrick, Foy, Fitzgerald. (GO TO 473B)

Decision Point 482A

The team is now firmly opposed to your leadership. Your combination of giving your subordinates a pep talk and giving the informal leader a reprimand sends your team members a mixed message. Striving to create a superordinate goal through the pep talk is likely to arouse cynicism and, if anything, more cohesiveness when you should be trying to decrease cohesiveness.

Re-evaluate your last decision. Circle the #482A you just wrote in your flow diagram. Then go back in your flow diagram to the first uncircled number above this step.

Decision Point 482B

You decide to call off the session since it is clear to you that the group has exhausted its creative potential. This is unfortunate. Typically periods of silence do emerge in every brainstorming session, and often the most imaginative and useful ideas come up right after these periods. Therefore, it is generally useful to wait out at least a few silent periods during brainstorming. Let's assume you had done that and rejoin the interactive case from that point.

You wait out the silence, and the first few ideas that emerge are truly fabulous. This stimulates a second burst of ideas from the group that lasts almost five minutes. A second silence overcomes the group, and you wait through that one as you did the first. However, few ideas of any merit arise.

With the task force rather tired and the scheduled end of the meeting approaching, you decide to call an end to this session. A total of 52 different topic ideas have been generated. You instruct your assistant to duplicate and distribute the results of the brainstorming meeting to the participants.

What instructions would you give the members?

A. Ask them to look over the list of prospective topics that came out of this meeting and put them into categories that make sense. (GO TO 459A)

B. Tell them that the meeting was very productive, and you will follow up with the discussion at the next meeting. (GO TO 442A)

C. Ask each member to rank order the ideas that have been derived on the basis of 1 = best and 52 = worst. (GO TO 484B)

Decision Point 483A

Virgil is willing to work overtime for an amount of $2,000 a year. Thus, your net savings amounts to $2,157. However, since you did not try to see if the parties to this conflict had flexibility in their positions, you missed an all-important way of solving this situation without spending any money at all.

Re-evaluate your last decision. Circle the #483A you just wrote in your flow diagram. Then move to the first uncircled step above this one in your flow diagram.

Decision Point 483B

You identified an excellent combination of talent. Since your assignment requires a creative approach, you needed a task force with a heterogeneous composition. This meant that the two members who came from outside Editorial should ideally be from different departments. This ruled out combinations like Smithers/Fitzgerald and Leybolt/Jones.

Another issue worth considering was the style of each member. Ideally a task force should have some combination of task- and people-oriented members. Since any two of your Editorial people are task-oriented, you needed someone who was more socially inclined. Michael Smithers was ideal in this respect.

This left two possibilities:
B. Gump, Seashore, Smithers, Foy, or
E. Seashore, Patrick, Smithers, Leybolt.

You were correct to choose B because the combination of Leybolt and Smithers would be too easily dominated by the two Editorial members. Leybolt couldn't hold his own without some support of Smithers, and Smithers couldn't have given him that support.

Your next problem is to put an agenda together. It seems to you that you should begin with a discussion of the objectives for the issue. Personally, you hope the group identifies an increase in circulation as an objective, but you realize that will not be greeted with enthusiasm among the Editorial people who are always reluctant to "sell out" to commercial interests. However, you think it will be impossible to get anywhere unless the group agrees to this objective.

How would you deal with this problem?

A. Meet with members of the task force individually before the first meeting to "feel them out" on objectives. (GO TO 460B)

B. Have the publisher come to the first meeting and announce that one of the objectives is to increase circulation. (GO TO 437A)

C. Conduct the first meeting with objectives as the first agenda item. (GO TO 423A)

Decision Point 484A

You expressed a desire to mediate the conflict between Phyllis and Virgil but reserved the option of arbitration should initial negotiations end in a stalemate. The first part of your statement was fine; mediation is the preferred way of dealing with conflicts of this type. However, one does not want to announce one's intention to resort to arbitration. Doing so only hardens the position of those who seem not to be benefiting from mediation. Saying nothing about arbitration does not preclude a manager from resorting to it in cases of a deadlock.

Re-evaluate your last decision. Circle the #484A you just wrote in your flow diagram. Then move to the first uncircled step above this one in your flow diagram.

Decision Point 484B

You ask each member to rank order the ideas from 1 to 52. This is a very difficult assignment. It is far too complex for anyone to rank order such a large number of items without breaking them into more manageable categories first.

Re-evaluate your last decision. Circle the #484B you just wrote in your flow diagram. Then move to the first uncircled step above this one in your flow diagram.

Decision Point 484C

She leaves your office, and you ask Virgil to come in. He enters, and after exchanging pleasantries, you open the discussion of his conflict with Phyllis and invite him to comment.

He responds: "I guess I am in the doghouse again, huh? Well, okay, I'll try harder to work with "Miss Smarty-pants."

How would you respond?

A. "Yes you are in the doghouse. From what Phyllis tells me you have been pretty uncooperative." (GO TO 520B)

B. "Let's soft-pedal the name-calling, Virgil. I want your side of the story. Here's a list of situations that Phyllis has prepared. Now then, describe these situations as you see them." (GO TO 485A)

C. "You're not in the doghouse, Virgil. You are a vital member of this organization. I'm trying to get to the bottom of what is going on between the two of you. Name-calling is not going to get us anywhere." (GO TO 510B)

Decision Point 485A

You stated to Virgil, "Let's soft-pedal the name-calling, Virgil. I want your side of the story. Here's a list of situations that Phyllis has prepared. Now then, describe these situations as you see them."

While it is good that you confronted him on his use of name-calling, you did not go far enough in assuring him that you intend to approach this issue in an open-minded fashion. Specifically, Virgil opened his remarks by asking you if he was still in the doghouse, an apparent reference to his previous quality problem. Accordingly, you should have given him some assurance at that point that you intend to view this situation from a neutral posture.

Re-evaluate your last decision. Circle the #485A you just wrote in your flow diagram. Then move to the first uncircled step above this one in your flow diagram.

Decision Point 485B

You tell the group that you plan to use the Nominal Group Technique as a method of deriving alternative topics for the seasonal issue. While this method may be well suited to the first aspect of your charter, it is really premature to announce it. You should have opened the meeting by summarizing the decisions made at the first meeting and asking Gump and Seashore to report on what they have discovered from their survey of ongoing topic assignments within the Editorial Department. Let's assume you had done that and resume the interactive case at that point.

Gump hands out a list of topics that are presently being worked on in the Editorial Department by various reporters. This done, you need to instruct the group as to what technique is appropriate for the task force to use.

What technique would you use?

A. Nominal Group Technique. (GO TO 486A)

B. Ordinary group discussion. (GO TO 432C)

C. Expert testimony. (GO TO 463A)

D. Subgroups engaged in ordinary group discussion. (GO TO 464C)

E. Brainstorming. (GO TO 429C)

Decision Point 486A

You decide to use the Nominal Group Technique. You tell the group the steps involved in the process:

(1) Team members work alone and in silence, writing down all their topic ideas.
(2) Members share their ideas using a round-robin procedure, during which members are encouraged to add items to their list of topic ideas.
(3) Participants discuss each recorded idea in order to clarify its meaning and intent and to provide initial evaluation.
(4) Task force members use rank-voting to indicate their feelings concerning the importance of the ideas. Group output is then determined by summing the ranked votes.
(5) Members discuss the results of the initial voting and take a final vote.

You tell the task force that you will work through steps 1 through 4, but will reserve 5 for another meeting. You and your group begin with step 1--the individual work. While you had intended to spend at least 10 minutes on this stage, Lyle Seashore gets up and walks around to Harrison Gump, whispers something in his ear, and leaves the room. Gump begins to stand up.
What would you do?

A. Look downward and model the sort of behavior you want Gump and the other task force members to act out. (GO TO 458C)

B. Tell Gump to get to work and leave the room and ask Seashore to return. (GO TO 471C)

Decision Point 486B

You decided to tell Phyllis to work out the problem she is having with Virgil herself. You encouraged this effort by telling her that her promotability may depend on her ability to handle this situation effectively alone. This is not an uncommon managerial approach to conflict resolution. Unfortunately, however, it is not very effective in many instances. The problem with this method is twofold. First, Virgil may not have a similar level of motivation to solve the conflict. Thus, you are actually stacking the deck in his favor. Second, asking employees to work out problems themselves is only appropriate if the problem is unimportant enough for a manager to dodge it for the time being. In this situation, you simply do not know yet how important this issue is.

Re-evaluate your last decision. Circle the #486B you just wrote in your flow diagram. Then move to the first uncircled step above this one in your flow diagram.

Decision Point 487A

Becky apologizes, but your rejoinder has a chilling effect on the rest of the conversation. Your meeting ends with no resolution. Two days later you arrive at work to discover a note from Becky on your desk. It reads: "I got my Statistics test back, and it was a D-. I've talked to my Dad, and he's given me a loan so I won't have to work anymore. Although I'd like to work for you this summer, I can't give you hours until then. I hope you understand."

You call her, but she has her mind made up. You have lost a valued employee needlessly.

Re-evaluate your last decision. Circle the #487A you just wrote in your flow diagram. Then move to the first uncircled step above this one in your flow diagram.

Decision Point 487B

Virgil responds, "Okay, I understand what you are getting at. Listen, if you side with Phyllis on this issue, my crew is really going to think that I have no influence whatever in this organization. I can't afford to lose their respect, believe me. There is nothing worse than a foreman whose crew thinks he has 'lost control.'"

"Furthermore," he continues, "paperwork is a real pain in the neck for me. When I come in on Monday morning, I want to get my hands dirty; I don't want to pansy around shuffling papers!"

In effect, Virgil has just told you that he has two interests beside the risk of quality problems:
(1) he wants to appear in control with his crew, and
(2) he doesn't like doing paperwork on Mondays.
As your private meeting with Virgil ends, what would you say?

A. "While I agree with you that seeming in control is important to every manager, I don't buy your personal preferences for not doing paperwork on Mondays. Doing paperwork is part of your job, and if that's what your job is, you should do it. I don't think there is any room for personal preferences in these negotiations. When we get back together, I hope you will keep that in mind." (GO TO 517B)

B. "This meeting has been real helpful, Virgil. When we get back together, let's focus on alternatives that reflect all your interests. For example, think about finding an alternative that will not result in you losing the respect of your crew." (GO TO 514A)

Decision Point 488A

At the end of your briefing, Marion approves your increase of square footage for furs contingent on her discussing the matter with the Divisional Merchandise Manager, Dresses and Cosmetics. Four days later Marion calls you and gives you the go-ahead. You rearrange your section to increase the space for furs.

The following Tuesday afternoon, you are approached by Becky Stark who seems obviously distraught. You ask her what the problem is, and she says: "I'm in a terrible fix. I think I just flunked my Statistics midterm. I don't know, I just can't seem to get math. I've talked to the professor, but he's no help. I just don't know what to do."

What would you say?

A. "Well, have you considered getting a tutor?" (GO TO 496B)

B. "Why don't you wait until you get your exam back before you worry about it. Who knows, maybe you did fine." (GO TO 521A)

C. "Are you telling me that you want to cut back on your hours?" (GO TO 492A)

D. "I'm sure you'll work it out. Things will get better, you'll see. You're a smart person." (GO TO 519B)

E. "Sounds like a frustrating situation. Can you think of anything I might do to help?" (GO TO 505B)

Decision Point 488B

You decided to call both Phyllis and Virgil into your office to settle this issue face to face. This is really premature. While such confrontation meetings are very helpful in conflict resolution, it is unadvisable for a manager to set them up before he or she is sure precisely where each party stands. In this instance you really don't know what Virgil's position is or how Phyllis will act in his presence. It is much more prudent to interview each party to the conflict individually before you arrange a confrontation meeting. That way you have a better idea what to expect from other options open to you.

Re-evaluate your last decision. Circle the #488B you just wrote in your flow diagram. Then move to the first uncircled step above this one in your flow diagram.

Decision Point 489A

Becky bolts a bit at your reaction: "Oh, I'm sorry. It's not that I didn't appreciate your help, believe me. It's just that I'm having a heckuva time balancing school and work, and it seems that rescheduling is not the answer. I need more time to study, but I need the money, too." Her voice is quivering.

You discuss the matter further and discover that by reducing her hours slightly and compensating for this by increasing her hours dramatically during her spring and summer breaks, you hit on an arrangement that is satisfactory.

Later that afternoon your boss tells you that there is a crisis with the Easter Sale scheduled this weekend. It seems that advertisements have already appeared offering a particular outfit that lists for $79.95 for $69.95. The problem is that the buyer of that line (petites and traditionals) just revealed that the supplier is facing labor problems and is unable to ship the product. This means that someone will have to go through the stock on hand and assemble a range of sizes and styles that is a comparable value at the sale price. If a list of merchandise is completed by tomorrow at 3:00 p.m., you can look it over, calculate the revised margins, and have the salespeople begin to mark down the sale items. You know the selection will be tricky, for you do not want any item marked down more than 30 percent. The last time you faced this situation two years ago, you knocked around a lot before you discovered how to do it. At last, you asked the financial people to give you a readout on the relevant product lines according to price. This enabled you to put together the assortment quickly (in about seven hours).

You have a very busy schedule for tomorrow, so you decide to delegate this job to your assistant, Candace Beal.

How would you begin to communicate this assignment to her?

A. "I need you to do something for me that is vitally important. It will take seven or eight hours, but you'll have to start right away. Can you do it?" (GO TO 503A)

B. "I hate to ask you to do this, but would you mind arranging for an equivalent range of sizes and style for the Easter Sale. You see, the vendor for this sale is unable to deliver, so we must make do with our present assortment." (GO TO 502B)

C. "Candace, drop everything you are doing and get the financial people to give you a readout on all the lines in petites and traditionals. Our vendor for the Easter special can't deliver, so we must do with our present assortment. Once you have the printout, decide which outfits are equivalent. Then give me the list for review, and if it's okay, I'll get the clerks to start marking the price tags." (GO TO 518B)

Decision Point 490A

She tells you that replacing the merchandise will come to the attention of her boss and may cause her problems. In addition, it would involve a great amount of paperwork that she personally doesn't have the time or the resources to do.

What would you say now?

A. Offer to help her with the paperwork and agree to talk with your boss about getting the message to her boss that she is being extremely helpful and alert to local conditions. (GO TO 503B)

B. Remind her that her boss is likely to be more pleased with volume figures than with the consistency of product across the entire chain. Translate your expected volume for a fashion-versus-quality assortment into volume figures to reinforce your point. Offer to help her with the additional paperwork. (GO TO 523B)

C. Be sympathetic but offer no help. After all, the mistake was hers. (GO TO 517C)

Decision Point 490B

Your meeting with Virgil ends on a positive note, and you meet privately with Phyllis. You inquire into the interests that underlie her position, and like Virgil, you have to clarify your question several times to get her to open up a bit. Finally she tells you that she has two interests besides the economic ones:
    (1) getting Virgil's reports late means that her reports to headquarters will be late, and she is afraid that will make her look bad there; and
    (2) getting Virgil's reports late means that she has to work late hours, and she has concerns about her safety when she leaves the plant late at night.

You end your meeting with Phyllis in much the same way you ended your meeting with Virgil.

When your meeting reconvenes, you want to explore new options. In creating the proper atmosphere, how would you position the parties to this conflict physically in your office?

A. Sit at the head of the table, with Virgil and Phyllis on either side of you facing each other. (GO TO 504A)
B. Sit between Phyllis and Virgil, all facing a flip chart on which you will jot down alternatives for consideration. (GO TO 506C)
C. Stand at the flip chart and position Phyllis and Virgil in chairs next to one another facing the flip chart. (GO TO 498A)

Decision Point 491A

Virgil is delighted with this decision. You work with Phyllis and arrange to pay her a special bonus to work overtime on Virgil's reports in order to reduce their negative impact. One year later you assess the situation again and discover that the total cost of this decision in only $2,325. However, this cost was totally unnecessary. Somehow you got locked into the economics of the situation without considering how to move the positions of the parties closer together. Your decision not only cost the plant a considerable sum of money, but also established a precedent that conflicts will be settled by determining whose stated position has the more or less favorable outcome, and that stated positions are accepted as is.

Re-evaluate your last decision. Circle the #491A you just wrote in your flow diagram. Then move back to the first uncircled step above this one in your flow diagram.

Decision Point 491B

Candace follows your instructions to the letter, but it takes her 11 hours instead of the seven hours you had estimated. Although your assignment was effective in terms of clarifying your expectations about results, it did not invite participation about means. Candace may have some excellent ideas about how to proceed or she may not. You have no idea without asking how she plans to proceed or offering some general guidance.

Re-evaluate your last decision. Circle the #491B you just wrote in your flow diagram. Then move to the first uncircled step above this one in your flow diagram.

Decision Point 491C

You ask Phyllis and Virgil to brainstorm other options with you. In conducting the brainstorming process, how would you arrange the parties within your office?

A. Sit at the head of the table, with Virgil and Phyllis on either side of you facing each other. (GO TO 504A)

B. Sit between Phyllis and Virgil, all facing a flip chart on which you will jot down alternatives for consideration. (GO TO 506C)

C. Stand at the flip chart and position Phyllis and Vigil in chairs next to one another facing the flip chart. (GO TO 499B)

Decision Point 492A

She responds, "I can't cut back on my hours. That would mean having to move out of the dorm and back home. I hate to say this, but the last time I asked for your help in a situation like this, things didn't work out at all." (Four months ago you went to a lot of trouble rescheduling the hours your people worked during the Christmas rush to accommodate Becky's need to prepare for exams.) Her comment really disappoints and hurts you.

What would you say now?

A. "Becky, you are not being fair. Do you know how tricky it was to juggle schedules last Christmas?" (GO TO 487A)

B. "I'm surprised and disappointed to hear you say that my rescheduling didn't help. Maybe if you told me more about your situation, we could find a solution." (GO TO 489A)

C. "Just because it didn't work out before doesn't mean that it can't work out this time. Do you have any suggestions we might put to use?" (GO TO 508B)

Decision Point 492B

You decided not to specify ground rules for your meeting with Phyllis and Virgil. This is unadvisable. Without ground rules, the meeting has a greater potential to deteriorate into a "free-for-all" or one that favors the party who shouts the loudest or is the most persuasive.

Re-evaluate your last decision. Circle the #492B you just wrote in your flow diagram. Then move back to the first uncircled step above this one in your flow diagram.

Decision Point 492C

You decided to give your boss a 20-minute briefing, during which you would lay out the issue in some detail, outline the options, and make a recommendation for approval.

This was not a good plan. Your boss is experiencing data overload. In interacting with her, you should be guided by the KISS principle (Keep It Simple, Stupid!).

Re-evaluate your last decision. Circle the #492C you just wrote in your flow diagram. Then move to the first uncircled step above this one in your flow diagram.

Decision Point 493A

How would you define your own role in the negotiations at the beginning of the meeting?

A. You will hear both sides and then announce your settlement. (GO TO 501C)
B. You will help the two parties reach a settlement by facilitating the exploration of alternatives. (GO TO 500A)
C. You prefer to mediate the conflict, but if the meeting ends in a stalemate, you will impose a solution that may not please one or both of the parties. (GO TO 484A)
D. You refuse to settle this situation for them. You will work with them to identify alternative settlements, but the ultimate decision must be theirs. (GO TO 513A)

Decision Point 493B

The two of you agree on a time, and the meeting proceeds. Later, at an agreed-on time, you appear at her office. Her secretary tells you she is in conference and cannot be disturbed. You tell her you are expected, but she tells you she knows nothing of your scheduled meeting. Apparently your boss forgot the appointment. You caught her at a bad time when you tried to set up the appointment just before the staff meeting.

Re-evaluate your last decision. Circle the #493B you just wrote in your flow diagram. Then move to the first uncircled step above this one in your flow diagram.

Decision Point 493C

Virgil very reluctantly agrees to try to do better. The next week he is able to get his report filed by Monday at 2 p.m. (two hours late). The following week goes better with Virgil actually submitting his report by 11. However, that week a major quality problem develops due to carelessness in setting up an extrusion machine. Virgil informs you that if he hadn't had to work on the report on Monday, the problem would not have occurred. The problem cost the plant $6,000. You may have avoided this expense if you had handled the conflict differently. You were doing fine until you decided to side against Virgil. Actually there is a resolution to this conflict situation that is satisfactory to both parties and to you.

Re-evaluate your last decision. Circle the #493C you just wrote in your flow diagram. Then move back to the first uncircled step above this one in your flow diagram.

Decision Point 494A

Marion's secretary tells you that she is most receptive in the morning. Hence, you decide to meet with her then. How would you approach her?

A. Plan for a five-minute briefing, during which you will lay out an abbreviated description of the issue, outline at most three options, and make a recommendation for approval. (GO TO 488A)

B. Plan for a 20-minute briefing, during which you will lay out the issue in some detail, outline the options, and make a recommendation for approval. (GO TO 492C)

C. Plan for a 30-minute meeting, but let your boss control how it unfolds. (GO TO 517A)

D. Plan for a five-minute briefing, during which you will lay out an abbreviated description of the issue, outline at most three options, but withhold your recommendation unless asked. (GO TO 522B)

Decision Point 494B

She tells you that she has already prepared such a list and hands it to you. You are impressed with her preparation. The list is impressive, including a series of episodes that go back one full year. Apparently Virgil has not only been repeatedly late with his reports, but also has objected openly to her schedules. In one instance he even argued with her in front of several members of his crew. What would you say after reviewing her list?

A. Tell her that settling this issue is her responsibility. Let her know that you consider it important for her development as a new employee to try to work out these problems first before coming to you. Point out to her that one of the considerations in determining the promotability of staff people is that they work well with line personnel. (GO TO 486B)

B. Call Virgil into your office now to meet his accuser. (GO TO 523C)

C. Acknowledge that her position in this conflict is an important one, but tell her that she is going to have to work with Virgil for a long time, so it is important that the three of you approach this situation with that in mind. (GO TO 513C)

D. Inform her that you will instruct Virgil to be more cooperative. (GO TO 495C)

Decision Point 495A

You decided to pressure the parties to come up with alternatives by threatening to settle the conflict yourself. This was incorrect. As a general rule, managers should not announce their intention to resort to arbitration. Doing so only hardens the position of those who seem not to be benefiting from mediation. Saying nothing about arbitration does not preclude a manager from resorting to it in cases of a deadlock.

Re-evaluate your last decision. Circle the #495A you just wrote in your flow diagram. Then move back to the first uncircled step above this one in your flow diagram.

Decision Point 495B

The Divisional Merchandise Manager "hits the ceiling" when you mention the change. She immediately phones your boss, who joins your meeting. After the meeting, your boss gives you a tongue-lashing the likes of which you have never gotten before.

As well meaning as your action was, it had serious consequences. You violated the most important rule of subordinate-boss relations--*No Surprises!*

Re-evaluate your last decision. Circle the #495B you just wrote in your flow diagram. Then move to the first uncircled step above this one in your flow diagram.

Decision Point 495C

You order Virgil to comply with Phyllis's need for timely information. Virgil reluctantly agrees to try to do better. The next week, he is able to get his report filed by Monday at 2 p.m. (two hours late). The following week goes better with Virgil actually submitting his report by 11. However, that week a major quality problem develops due to carelessness in setting up an extrusion machine. Virgil informs you that if he hadn't had to work on the report on Monday, the problem would not have occurred. The problem cost the plant $6,000. You may have avoided this expense if you had handled the conflict differently.

You decided to side with Phyllis before even hearing Virgil's side of the story. As a result Virgil was not really committed to your solution, and he may have even created the quality problem as a way of indicating his dissatisfaction. Your approach to this conflict is known as "arbitration" and is actually quite common in practice. However, it is seldom effective in bringing about satisfactory long-term resolutions to conflicts.

Re-evaluate your last decision. Circle the #495C you just wrote in your flow diagram. Then move back to the first uncircled step above this one in your flow diagram.

Decision Point 496A

You decided to ask Phyllis and Virgil which alternatives they like the most. Predictably, Phyllis likes those that require Virgil to comply with her information needs, and Virgil likes those that require Phyllis to give him longer cycle times. You are now in a position where you want to try to break down the positions in this conflict. The only way to do this is to investigate the interests that underlie each party's position. Otherwise you will be caught in this stalemate.

Re-evaluate your last decision. Circle the #496A you just wrote in your flow diagram. Then move back to the first uncircled step above this one in your flow diagram.

Decision Point 496B

She responds, "Yes, I have a tutor, but she is no help either." She is growing increasingly frustrated with the conversation.

How would you react to this?

- A. "Why don't you wait until you get your exam back before you worry about it. Who knows, maybe you did fine." (GO TO 521A)

- B. "Are you telling me that you want to cut back on your hours?" (GO TO 492A)

- C. "I'm sure you'll work it out. Things will get better, you'll see. You're a smart person." (GO TO 519B)

- D. "Sounds like a frustrating situation. Can you think of anything I might do to help?" (GO TO 505B)

Decision Point 496C

You decided to brainstorm alternatives at this point. This is actually a bit premature. There are two important things that you don't know at this point. One, you are unsure about just what is motivating Virgil and Phyllis to take the stands they have taken. And two, you are unclear why they cannot comply with one another's requests. After determining one or both of these things, you will be in a much better position to brainstorm the alternatives.

Re-evaluate your last decision. Circle the #496C you just wrote in your flow diagram. Then move back to the first uncircled step above this one in your flow diagram.

Decision Point 497A

You attempt to discredit the arguments of the marketing research people. This has little effect. The report Jean has is an impressive document, and your argument falls on deaf ears.

Re-evaluate your last decision. Circle the #497A you just wrote in your flow diagram. Then move to the first uncircled step above this one in your flow diagram.

Decision Point 497B

You decided to meet with Virgil to explore the interests that lie behind his desire to delay submitting his production reports. Before you even get to that question, Virgil tells you: "The beginning of each week is real hectic. My crew needs me then to help set up and troubleshoot. Those reports take me at least two hours to complete, and I don't have the time. Lately we've been having so much trouble with the "Weber" (an extrusion machine) that I have to help Ivan fine-tune it. You remember the defective brushes that came out of that 'baby' three months ago? If you want to risk another disaster like that, I'll be happy to get my reports in on time. But don't tell me to take two hours on a Monday and then come down on my case if we have quality problems!"

At that point, you consider options like doing a major overhaul on the machine in question, having someone else help Ivan with the Monday adjustments, and encouraging Virgil to get a head start on the production reports so it doesn't take him two hours on Mondays to complete them. However, there are credible reasons that make each of these options unworkable.

How would you respond?

A. "As I understand it, then, your only concern is with quality. That is the only thing that keeps you from getting your reports in on time." (GO TO 487B)

B. "Beside the possibilities of quality problems, what other negative things might happen if you were forced to get your reports in on time." (GO TO 511B)

C. "I'll be honest with you, Virgil, I think your position here is pretty flimsy. I believe that you are overreacting to the possibility that Ivan can't do the work himself." (GO TO 525A)

D. "Put yourself in Phyllis's shoes. What would you do if you were her?" (GO TO 508A)

Decision Point 498A

Your seating arrangement works out well. You open the meeting by considering two new alternatives that occurred to you during the private meetings.

Alternative 1: Ivan should complete the paperwork for Virgil on Monday while Virgil works on the Weber machine.

Alternative 2: Phyllis should contact the headquarters staff responsible for determining weekly quotas with the intention of getting them to factor into their equations the likelihood of quality problems on the brush machines.

The discussion of these alternatives goes well. Virgil indicates that he doesn't want to give up his authority to complete the reports to Ivan. Since you now know Virgil's need to seem "in control," you suggest that perhaps Ivan could assemble the numbers and Virgil could review them and approve the report. This seems to satisfy Virgil to some extent.

The discussion then turns to Alternative 2. Initially Phyllis expresses pessimism about the likelihood that this will result in any change. You point out to her that you think that even if no change is made, she will be seen by the staff as someone who takes efficiency seriously and wants to make the mathematical formulations even better. This disguised appeal to her interests is sufficiently persuasive that she agrees to try.

The meeting ends with firm commitments to try the new approaches to see how they work. The next week Virgil's report is on time. The following week Phyllis is invited to headquarters to meet with the staff about the toothbrush line problem. She returns elated that not only does the staff decide to extend the planning cycle to two weeks for that line, but she had the opportunity to meet with several highly placed executives that she hadn't met before.

Congratulations! You have dealt effectively with a very touchy conflict between two of your subordinates.

Decision Point 498B

Your logic is unpersuasive. She holds to the line that the marketing research data indicate that the assortment should reflect a higher level of fashion.

What would you say now?

A. Indicate that if she does not cooperate and replace the line with one more suited to your customer pool, you will have to hold her responsible for any decline in volume. (GO TO 516B)

B. Ask her if her boss told her to build more fashion into her lines. (GO TO 520A)

Decision Point 499A

Your assertiveness has no effect. Now what would you do?

A. Remind her that her boss is likely to be more pleased with volume figures than with the consistency of product across the entire chain. Translate your expected volume for a fashion-versus-quality assortment into volume figures to reinforce your point. (GO TO 515A)
B. Discredit the arguments of the marketing research people by asserting that they are not sufficiently close to local conditions. (GO TO 497A)
C. Find out how difficult it would be for her to replace the merchandise that you have received with an assortment more tailored to your store's needs. Offer to help her with the additional effort required to make that happen. (GO TO 490A)

Decision Point 499B

You chose the best seating format for the brainstorming procedure. The meeting goes well. Although you have to enforce the "no criticism rule" on several occasions, the three of you come up with the following six alternatives (ruling out the obviously inappropriate ones):

1. Virgil could ask Ivan to complete the production reports for him while Virgil tends the machine.
2. Phyllis could complete Virgil's reports for him.
3. Phyllis could contact the headquarters office to see if they could factor the quality problems of the dental brush line into their calculations of weekly quotas.
4. You could complete Virgil's production report for him.
5. You could try and persuade the headquarters staff of the necessity of biweekly quotas for the dental brush line.
6. You could look into the possibility of getting Virgil a computer terminal, so he could finish his production reports more efficiently.

Having finished with brainstorming, what would you do now?

A. Call a two-hour recess with the idea that you will get together with each party privately during that time to try to ascertain what concerns each has that underlies his or her position on this issue. (GO TO 505A)
B. Ask Phyllis and Virgil to indicate which alternative they favor. (GO TO 496A)
C. Propose that the best options are 5 and 6 above. Agree to work in those directions. (GO TO 518C)

Decision Point 500A

You introduce the meeting by stating the ground rules and defining your role. The meeting begins with both parties making initial statements. Phyllis's voice cracks during her presentation, but Virgil seems a bit more controlled. It is clear that both are nervous. Disappointingly, no new information is revealed during the initial presentations except that the conflict appears much more emotional than you had first thought.

The part of the meeting where each party summarizes the positions of the other is very rocky. Neither side is satisfied with the other's summary of his or her position at first, and it takes a great deal of your time and patience to finally get that part of the meeting completed.

At that point both Phyllis and Virgil turn to you. What would you say?

A. "Let's take a 20-minute break at this point. During the break I ask only that you don't discuss this meeting with anyone. If you have a chance, think about what we might come up with to solve this thing." (GO TO 518A)

B. "Okay, we understand where we all stand on this problem. Let's begin to explore alternative ways of solving it. Do either of you have any suggestions?" (GO TO 504C)

C. "At this point, I'd like to ask each of you to state what you want the other to do as simply and clearly as you can." (GO TO 509C)

D. "Well, it seems that we have two alternatives on the floor. One, proposed by Virgil, is that Phyllis refashions production schedules in order to cut back on setup time. The other, proposed by Phyllis, is for Virgil to turn in his production reports to her office by Monday at noon. At this point I'd like to ask each of you what impediments you are experiencing to keep you from doing what the other wants. Let's start with you, Virgil. Why can't you get your reports in on time?" (GO TO 512A)

Decision Point 500B

Candace follows your instructions to the letter, but it takes her 11 hours instead of the seven hours you had estimated. By telling her precisely how to complete the assignment instead of leaving that up to her (within limits), you robbed her of some motivation. In giving assignments, it is far better to be directive on ends than means.

Re-evaluate your last decision. Circle the #500B you just wrote in your flow diagram. Then move to the first uncircled step above this one in your flow diagram.

Decision Point 501A

You decided to call Phyllis into your meeting with Virgil to hammer out a solution. This is a bit premature. Before inviting Phyllis to join you, it would have been better if you had "primed" Virgil's perspective a bit. Namely, research indicates that if one tries to get conflicting parties to approach conflicts from the viewpoint of a long-range relationship, they tend to approach the conflict more cooperatively.

Re-evaluate your last decision. Circle the #501A you just wrote in your flow diagram. Then move back to the first uncircled step above this one in your flow diagram.

Decision Point 501B

Candace decides not to use the readout method, and this really delays her completion of the assignment. However, the method she did use enabled her to discover a mistake in pricing that, once corrected, saved the company $6,000. The delay cost you $40 in overtime, so on net, Candace did very well.

The Monday following the Easter Sale, a load of summer dresses arrives from the warehouse. You and Candace do an initial inspection and look over the manifests. Both of you conclude that the assortment represents a level of fashion that is far too avant-garde for your clientele. It appears that Jean Volk (the buyer for dresses) really screwed up. You decide to confront Jean with your observations and try to get her to send you a different assortment.

How would you address this issue with Jean?

A. Send Jean a memorandum detailing your concerns. Send a carbon copy to her boss. (GO TO 507B)

B. Meet with Jean to discuss the matter. (GO TO 511A)

Decision Point 501C

You decided to opt for an approach to resolving this conflict that resembles that of a judge. This is an appealing posture, but in this situation, mediation is called for. Generally, it is preferable if the conflicting parties come up with their own settlement. Consequently, you want to try to help them first to see if that is possible. You don't have to give up the option of ultimately "playing judge," but you don't want to preempt other possibilities by announcing your intentions too soon.

Re-evaluate your last decision. Circle the #501C you just wrote in your flow diagram. Then move back to the first uncircled step above this one in your flow diagram.

Decision Point 502A

You decided to tell Virgil that his position is weaker than Phyllis's. This was incorrect. If you want open negotiations, you do not want to make one party feel that his or her chances are poor. When a manager does this, the conflicting parties often take some additional risks to try to sway him or her. This endangers the negotiations rather than helping them. It is far preferable to have the parties to a negotiation feel that they are equal in influence than to have one feel that he or she has the upper hand.

Re-evaluate your last decision. Circle the #502A you just wrote in your flow diagram. Then move back to the first uncircled step above this one in your flow diagram.

Decision Point 502B

The apologetic tone of your message emphasizes the negative features of the assignment. Thus, Candace lacks motivation for the assignment and fails to meet your deadline. In communicating assignments, try to avoid phrases like "I hate to ask you to do this" and "would you mind."

Re-evaluate your last decision. Circle the #502B you just wrote in your flow diagram. Then move to the first uncircled step above this one in your flow diagram.

Decision Point 502C

Virgil responds, "Well, that's your opinion, but I'll tell you that Ivan just doesn't have the ability or the confidence to handle setups on his machine himself, and there is no one else around who can work with him. It's a risk, but if you want to take it, fine; just order me to get my reports done, and I'll do it!"

What would you say now?

A. "As I understand it, your only concern is with quality. That is the only thing that keeps you from getting your reports in on time." (GO TO 523A)

B. "Beside the possibilities of quality problems, what other negative things might happen if you were forced to get your reports in on time." (GO TO 521B)

C. Tell Virgil you are willing to take the risk. Order him to get his reports in on time. (GO TO 493C)

D. "Put yourself in Phyllis's shoes. What would you do if you were her?" (GO TO 506A)

Decision Point 503A

You now need to communicate this assignment. You decide to open your statement to Candace with the following lines: "Our vendor for the Easter Sale can't provide the product. Thus, we need to supply the sale from our existing merchandise. It's really important that you create a comparable assortment to serve as our sale items from our existing stock."
What would you say next?

A. "The only constraint you have is to avoid marking down any item more than 30 percent. Get back to me tomorrow by 5 p.m. to let me know what assortments you have chosen. Do you have any questions?" (GO TO 491B)

B. "This is a difficult problem, but I think if you work hard, you can solve it. Ask the financial people to give you a readout on all the lines involved. This will be your guide in deciding what items to mark down. Stay away from products that involve a markdown of more than 30 percent. I need the list by 5 p.m. tomorrow." (GO TO 518B)

C. "Some things in this assignment are important to me. First, there's no reason for you to make the same mistakes I have. Ask the financial people to prepare you a list of all the product lines involved. This will give you a first cut on what items to mark down. Second, check with me first before you mark down any item more than 30 percent." (GO TO 500B)

D. "I'll need the list by 5 p.m. tomorrow so I can get the salespeople started on the markdowns. Keep items out of your assortment that exceed a markdown of 30 percent. When I had to do this last autumn, I began by asking the financial people to give me a readout on all the lines involved. This was my guide in deciding what items to mark down. You may want to do this job the same way, but it's really up to you." (GO TO 501B)

Decision Point 503B

Jean finally agrees to replace the assortment. You follow up by helping her with the paperwork and by feeding the grapevine via your boss to hers. The new line arrives and it is an excellent one. Your summer sales volume figures hit an all-time high.
Congratulations! You have just completed the Communication Interactive Case.

Decision Point 504A

Your choice of a seating arrangement is not appropriate. You want to create an atmosphere that shows that the problem is the focus of attention, not you.

Re-evaluate your last decision. Circle the #504A you just wrote in your flow diagram. Then move back to the first uncircled step above this one in your flow diagram.

Decision Point 504B

Precisely how would you approach her on this subject?

A. Plan for a five-minute briefing, during which you will lay out an abbreviated description of the issue, outline at most three options, and make a recommendation for approval. (GO TO 488A)

B. Plan for a 20-minute briefing, during which you will lay out the issue in some detail, outline the options, and make a recommendation for approval. (GO TO 492C)

C. Plan for a 30-minute meeting, but let your boss control how it unfolds. (GO TO 517A)

D. Plan for a five-minute briefing, during which you will lay out an abbreviated description of the issue, outline at most three options, but withhold your recommendation unless asked. (GO TO 522B)

Decision Point 504C

Neither Virgil nor Phyllis says anything. You coax them further, but they still say nothing. What would you do now?

A. Ask them to use brainstorming with you as a means of getting some alternatives "on the floor." (GO TO 496C)
B. Tell them that if they can't suggest alternatives, it will force you to make a decision siding with one or the other. (GO TO 495A)
C. Say, "Well, it seems that we have two alternatives on the floor. One, proposed by Virgil, is that Phyllis refashions production schedules in order to cut back on setup time. The other, proposed by Phyllis, is for Virgil to turn in his production reports to her office by Monday at noon. At this point I'd like to ask each of you what impediments you are experiencing to keep you from doing what the other wants. Let's start with you, Virgil. Why can't you get your reports in on time?" (GO TO 512A)

Decision Point 505A

During the recess, you meet first with Virgil. You ask him what concerns underlie his position. He asks you what you mean. You indicate that behind each position in a conflict are interests that motivate these positions. You ask him what reasons he has for his position. Again he balks, "I've already told you that short production runs make my machines touchy. I can't be expected to do paperwork if that risks higher reject rates." What would you say now?

- A. "As I understand it, then, your only concern is with quality. That is the only thing that keeps you from getting your reports in on time." (GO TO 523A)

- B. "Beside the possibilities of quality problems, what other negative things might happen if you were forced to get your reports in on time." (GO TO 521B)

- C. "I'll be honest with you, Virgil. I think your position here is pretty flimsy. I believe that you are overreacting to the possibility that Ivan can't do the work himself." (GO TO 502C)

- D. "Put yourself in Phyllis's shoes. What would you do if you were her?" (GO TO 506A)

Decision Point 505B

She responds, "I don't know. I can't just cut back on my hours. That would mean having to move out of the dorm and back home. I hate to say this, but the last time I asked for your help in a situation like this, things didn't work out at all." (Four months ago you went to a lot of trouble rescheduling the hours your people worked during the Christmas rush to accommodate Becky's need to prepare for exams.) Her comment really disappoints and hurts you. What would you say now?

- A. "Becky, you are not being fair. Do you know how tricky it was to juggle schedules last Christmas?" (GO TO 487A)

- B. "I'm surprised and disappointed to hear you say that my rescheduling didn't help. Maybe if you told me more about your situation, we could find a solution." (GO TO 489A)

- C. "Just because it didn't work out before doesn't mean that it can't work out this time. Do you have any suggestions we might put to use?" (GO TO 508B)

Decision Point 506A

Virgil responds that he guesses he would be pretty sore about not receiving the reports on time. You counter that you think she is concerned about the efficiency of the plant, and you don't think her motive is to be a troublemaker.

Now what would you say?

- A. "As I understand it, then, your only concern is with quality. That is the only thing that keeps you from getting your reports in on time." (GO TO 523A)

- B. "Beside the possibilities of quality problems, what other negative things might happen if you were forced to get your reports in on time." (GO TO 521B)

- C. "I'll be honest with you, Virgil, I think your position here is pretty flimsy. I believe that you are overreacting to the possibility that Ivan can't do the work himself." (GO TO 502C)

Decision Point 506B

You decided to write your boss a thorough memo. This was incorrect. Your boss suffers from a common malady--data overload. Your detailed report is likely to add to this overload, and you can count on her missing the forest for the trees. One rather crude way of classifying the communication styles of bosses is that some are readers and some are listeners. Marion is a listener (a poor one at that), but she dislikes paperwork. Therefore, think again about how to approach her orally and in an abbreviated way.

Re-evaluate your last decision. Circle the #506B you just wrote in your flow diagram. Then move to the first uncircled step above this one in your flow diagram.

Decision Point 506C

Your choice of a seating arrangement is not appropriate. While it is correct in terms of the three of you facing the flip chart, it is probably better for you to stand next to the chart instead of sitting between the conflicting parties. You want to create the impression that there is nothing "between" the parties, that both of them are "together" in solving the problem.

Re-evaluate your last decision. Circle the #506C you just wrote in your flow diagram. Then move back to the first uncircled step above this one in your flow diagram.

Decision Point 507A

You call Phyllis to clarify her memo. She comes to your office and tells you her relationship with Virgil has deteriorated steadily since she joined your staff. She describes him as an "obstructionist" and uses the words "uncooperative" and "unprofessional." She tells you that she has no problems with the other six line foremen.
How would you respond?

A. Challenge her use of labels and ask her to prepare a specific list of situations with Virgil that she wants changed. (GO TO 494B)

B. Agree that Virgil can be a problem, but tell her that you intend to hear his side of the story before taking action. (GO TO 519C)

C. Tell her that settling this issue is her responsibility. Let her know that you consider it important for her development as a new employee to try to work out these problems before coming to you. Point out to her that one of the considerations in determining the promotability of staff people is that they work harmoniously with line personnel. (GO TO 486B)

D. Call Virgil into your office now to meet his accuser. (GO TO 523C)

Decision Point 507B

This pressure tactic fails miserably. Jean is very resentful of your intervention with her boss. She has no motivation to assist you with a new assortment, and by the end of the year you realize your sales in the dress line are at an all-time low.
Re-evaluate your last decision. Circle the #507B you just wrote in your flow diagram. Then move to the first uncircled step above this one in your flow diagram.

Decision Point 507C

You decided to call Virgil into your office at this juncture in order to hear his side of the conflict. This invitation is a bit premature. All you have to "go on" is the memo from Phyllis. Since this document does not detail specific areas of concern, it is too early to involve Virgil in this issue. Doing so runs the risk that if Phyllis's accusations are not warranted, the relationship between Virgil and Phyllis will be permanently harmed.
Re-evaluate your last decision. Circle the #507C you just wrote in your flow diagram. Then move back to the first uncircled step above this one in your flow diagram.

Decision Point 508A

Virgil responds that he guesses he would be pretty sore about not receiving the reports on time. You counter that you think Phyllis is concerned about the efficiency of the plant, and you don't think her motive is to be a troublemaker.

Now what would you say?

A. "As I understand it, then, your only concern is with quality. That is the only thing that keeps you from getting your reports in on time." (GO TO 487B)

B. "Beside the possibilities of quality problems, what other negative things might happen if you were forced to get your reports in on time." (GO TO 511B)

C. "I'll be honest with you, Virgil, I think your position here is pretty flimsy. I believe that you are overreacting to the possibility that Ivan can't do the work himself." (GO TO 525A)

Decision Point 508B

Becky notices that your body language (communicating disappointment and hurt) is incongruent with your words. Accordingly, the discussion becomes strained and ends without resolution. Two days later, upon arriving at work, you find a note from Becky on your desk. It reads: "I got my Statistics test back, and it was a D-. I've talked to my Dad, and he's given me a loan so I won't have to work anymore. Although I'd like to work for you this summer, I can't give you hours until then. I hope you understand."

You call her, but she has her mind made up. You have lost a valued employee needlessly.

Re-evaluate your last decision. Circle the #508B you just wrote in your flow diagram. Then move to the first uncircled step above this one in your flow diagram.

Decision Point 508C

You decided to ask Phyllis and Virgil to prepare position papers to refer to in their meeting with you. This is unadvisable. If anything, preparing such documents will simply harden their positions on the issue.

Re-evaluate your last decision. Circle the #508C you just wrote in your flow diagram. Then move back to the first uncircled step above this one in your flow diagram.

Decision Point 509A

You meet with Virgil to try and formulate an action plan with him. He reluctantly agrees to try to do better. The next week he is able to get his report filed by Monday at 2 p.m. (two hours late). The following week goes better, with Virgil actually submitting his report by 11. However, that week a major quality problem develops due to carelessness in setting up an extrusion machine. Virgil informs you that if he hadn't had to work on the report on Monday, the problem would not have occurred. The problem cost the plant $6,000.

You may have avoided this expense if you had handled the conflict differently. You decided to side with Phyllis before even hearing Virgil's side of the story. As a result, Virgil was not really committed to your solution and may have even created the quality problem as a way of indicating his dissatisfaction.

Your approach to this conflict is known as "arbitration" and is actually quite common in practice. However, it is seldom effective in bringing about satisfactory long-term resolutions to conflicts.

Re-evaluate your last decision. Circle the #509A you just wrote in your flow diagram. Then move back to the first uncircled step above this one in your flow diagram.

Decision Point 509B

She thanks you for your offer and promises to think about it. Three days later you contact her again, and she announces that she has discussed the matter with others and that a replacement for the summer assortment is out of the question. Apparently you were not forthcoming enough to encourage her to comply with your request.

Re-evaluate your last decision. Circle the #509B you just wrote in your flow diagram. Then move to the first uncircled step above this one in your flow diagram.

Decision Point 509C

You asked them to state what they want the other party to do for a second time. This is unnecessary. It is not only redundant, but it serves to harden positions. Flexibility in the positions of the parties is something that you should be particularly concerned about right now.

Re-evaluate your last decision. Circle the #509C you just wrote in your flow diagram. Then move back to the first uncircled step above this one in your flow diagram.

Decision Point 510A

Becky looks at you angrily and storms off. Two days later upon arriving at work you see the following note on your desk: "I got my Statistics test back, and it was a D-. I've talked to my Dad, and he's given me a loan so I won't have to work anymore. Although I'd like to work for you this summer, I can't give you hours until then. I hope you understand."

You call her, but she has her mind made up. You have lost a valued employee needlessly.

Re-evaluate your last decision. Circle the #510A you just wrote in your flow diagram. Then move to the first uncircled step above this one in your flow diagram.

Decision Point 510B

He states, "All I ever get from Phyllis is pressure. She doesn't understand that my machines are very touchy. Every time we set one up, we have to watch it like a hawk to be sure it stays plumb. Her schedules don't account for these things, and I've told her that again and again. She just doesn't understand machinery."

You press him for specifics, and he offers the same general excuse for each situation on Phyllis' list: her schedules call for a great deal of difficult machine setups, and since her weekly quotas repeat runs completed the week before, Virgil thinks larger runs are possible.

How would you respond now?

A. Call Phyllis into the meeting at this juncture to hammer out a solution. (GO TO 501A)

B. Tell Virgil that his position sounds reasonable but emphasize how important it is that the two of them work more cooperatively in the future. Schedule a meeting between Virgil and Phyllis as soon as possible. (GO TO 519A)

C. Tell Virgil that he has a weak case. Side with Phyllis, and tell him to get his reports to her on time. (GO TO 495C)

D. Describe your experience as a line manager working with staff people with the intention of sympathizing with Virgil's position. End by indicating that your experience is that line managers should accept working with staffers as an unavoidable part of their jobs. Tell him that you are going to schedule a meeting between the two of them as soon as possible. (GO TO 516C)

Decision Point 511A

You ask Jean to come over to the mall. The two of you exchange pleasantries, and she opens the issue by asking you how you like the summer line. You admit to her that you think it is entirely too daring and not well suited to your customer base. She tells you that the Manager of Marketing Research advised her to put more fashion into her line. How would you respond?

A. Present a logical argument that she should replace the line with one more suited to your customer pool. (GO TO 498B)

B. Indicate that if she does not cooperate and replace the line with one more suited to your customer pool, you will have to hold her responsible for any decline in volume. (GO TO 516B)

C. Try to discover diplomatically if her boss told her to build more fashion into her lines. (GO TO 520A)

Decision Point 511B

Virgil responds, "Okay, I understand what you are getting at. Listen, if you side with Phyllis on this issue, my crew is really going to think that I have no influence whatever in this organization. I can't afford to lose their respect, believe me. There is nothing worse than a foreman whose crew thinks he has 'lost control.'"

"Furthermore," he continues, "paperwork is a real pain in the neck for me. When I come in on Monday morning, I want to get my hands dirty; I don't want to pansy around shuffling papers!"

In effect, Virgil has just told you that he has two interests beside the risk of quality problems: (1) he wants to appear in control with his crew, and (2) he doesn't like doing paperwork on Mondays. As your private meeting with Virgil ends, what would you say?

A. "While I agree with you that seeming in control is important to every manager, I don't buy your personal preferences for not doing paperwork on Mondays. Doing paperwork is part of your job, and if that's what your job is, you should do it. I don't think there is any room for personal preferences in these negotiations. When we get back together I hope you will keep that in mind." (GO TO 517B)

B. "This meeting has been real helpful, Virgil. When we get back together, let's focus on alternatives that reflect all your interests. For example, think about finding an alternative that will not result in your losing the respect of your crew." (GO TO 514A)

Decision Point 512A

Virgil says, "The beginning of each week is real hectic. My crew needs me then for setup help and troubleshooting. Those reports take me at least two hours to complete, and I don't have the time. Lately we've been having so much trouble with the "Weber" (an extrusion machine) that I have to help Ivan fine-tune it. You remember the defective brushes that came out of that 'baby' three months ago? If you want to risk another disaster like that, I'll be happy to get my reports in on time. But don't tell me to take two hours on a Monday and then come down on my case if we have quality problems!"

At that point you consider options like doing a major overhaul on the machine in question, having someone else help Ivan with the Monday adjustments, and encouraging Virgil to get a head start on the production reports so it doesn't take him two hours on Mondays to complete them. However, there are credible reasons that make each of these options unworkable.

You then turn to Phyllis for her statement. She says, "Well, the quotas we get from headquarters are weekly quotas. I've tried to get them to give us more advance time, but they won't do it. They know that smaller runs increase costs, but the savings in inventory costs outweigh these. It's a well-thought-out mathematical solution they give us, and it is correct. I had an elaborate briefing on the formula during my training."

At this point you try to determine if headquarters could give biweekly schedules for the brushes produced by Virgil's crew (i.e., dental brushes), since it does seem to be a special case. Phyllis tells you that she has tried to convince headquarters of that with no success. Unfortunately, you don't consider your ability to convince headquarters any better than hers.

Secretly you are beginning to believe that there is no way to settle this matter without siding with one side or the other.

What would you do now?

A. Call a two-hour recess with the idea that you will get together with each party privately during that time to try to ascertain what concerns each has that underlie his or her position on this issue. (GO TO 505A)

B. Ask the two parties to estimate the financial consequence of complying with Phyllis' position. Phyllis would estimate the financial impact of procurement and inventory problems likely to occur if Virgil continues to submit his reports late. Virgil would estimate the financial impact of quality problems likely to occur if he does his report on Monday as she wants. These calculations will enable you to determine whose position would result in the lowest expected loss for the plant. (GO TO 515B)

C. Ask the parties to brainstorm other options with you. (GO TO 491C)

Decision Point 513A

You decided to tell Phyllis and Virgil that the responsibility for handling this conflict is theirs. You indicated that while you will help them identify alternatives, they are the ones who must decide on a solution. This statement is inadvisable since it restricts your options. At this stage you don't want to preclude the possibility of determining the settlement should the negotiations deadlock.

Re-evaluate your last decision. Circle the #513A you just wrote in your flow diagram. Then move back to the first uncircled step above this one in your flow diagram.

Decision Point 513B

When you follow up, she tells you she can't remember the specifics of your note. She also seems a bit perturbed. Under these circumstances, you decide that this is not the right time to discuss this matter. Apparently you got off on the wrong foot.

Re-evaluate your last decision. Circle the #513B you just wrote in your flow diagram. Then move to the first uncircled step above this one in your flow diagram.

Decision Point 513C

Phyllis asks you how you intend to approach this matter. What would you say?

A. "I'm going to talk to Virgil to get his side of the story, then I will make my decision." (GO TO 501C)

B. "I am going to show Virgil your list and work out an action plan with him that hopefully will get him to be more cooperative." (GO TO 509A)

C. "I will interview Virgil to get his side of the story, then the three of us will get together to come up with a satisfactory solution." (GO TO 484C)

D. Tell her that settling this issue is her responsibility. Let her know that you consider it important for her development as a new employee to try to work out these problems before coming to you. Point out to her that one of the considerations in determining the promotability of staff people is that they work harmoniously with line personnel. (GO TO 486B)

E. "I'm not sure yet. Let me talk to Virgil first to see what his side of the story is." (GO TO 522A)

Decision Point 514A

Your meeting with Virgil ends on a positive note, and you go on to meet privately with Phyllis. At the beginning of your encounter, she says:

"Well, the quotas we get from headquarters are weekly quotas. I've tried to get them to give us more advance time, but they won't do it. They know that smaller runs increase costs but the savings in inventory costs outweigh these. It's a well-thought-out mathematical solution they give us, and it is correct. I had an elaborate briefing on the formula during my training."

At this point you try to determine if headquarters could give biweekly schedules for the dental brushes produced by Virgil's crew, since it does seem to be a special case. Phyllis tells you that she has tried to convince headquarters of that with no success. Unfortunately, you don't consider your ability to convince headquarters any better than hers.

You then probe into Phyllis's interests that underlie her position on this issue. After several attempts to clarify your question, she tells you that she has two interests besides the economic ones:

(1) Getting Virgil's reports late means that her reports to headquarters will be late, and she is afraid that will make her look bad there.

(2) Getting Virgil's reports late means that she has to work late hours, and she has concerns about her safety when she leaves the plant late at night.

You end your meeting with Phyllis in much the same way you ended your meeting with Virgil. When your meeting reconvenes, you want to explore new options.

In creating the proper atmosphere, how would you position the parties to this conflict physically in your office?

A. Sit at the head of the table, with Virgil and Phyllis on either side of you facing each other. (GO TO 504A)

B. Sit between Phyllis and Virgil, all facing a flip chart on which you will jot down alternatives for consideration. (GO TO 506C)

C. Stand at the flip chart and position Phyllis and Vigil in chairs next to one another facing the flip chart. (GO TO 498A)

Decision Point 515A

She seems persuaded by your arguments but tells you that replacing the merchandise will come to the attention of her boss and may cause her problems. In addition, it would involve a great amount of paperwork that she personally doesn't have the time or the resources to do.

What would you say?

A. Offer to help her with the paperwork and agree to talk with your boss about getting the message to her boss that she is being extremely helpful and alert to local conditions. (GO TO 523B)

B. Be sympathetic but offer no help. After all, the mistake was hers. (GO TO 517C)

C. Offer to help her with the paperwork. (GO TO 509B)

Decision Point 515B

You all work together in generating the financial estimates. After about 30 minutes of questioning and calculating, you come up with the following figures:

Estimated Loss Due to Procurement/Inventory Problems of Virgil's Position = $4,157/year
Estimated Loss Due to Quality Problems of Phyllis's Position = $11,319/year

Both parties seem to be giving you honest estimates, so you are sure that they are reasonably accurate.

How would you proceed at this point?

A. Settle the dispute by announcing that you are going to have to side with Virgil for purely economic reasons. Explore with Phyllis ways that she might be able to work on reducing the costs of getting Virgil's reports late. (GO TO 491A)

B. Explore Virgil's willingness to prepare his reports over each weekend at an additional salary adjustment of up to $4,157. (GO TO 483A)

C. Tell both parties that these calculations have clarified the negotiations considerably, and that it is now time for all of you to work hard to identify alternative solutions that are less costly than these two. Suggest that it is probably best to take a recess at that point. Plan to meet individually with the two parties during the recess to explore the interests that are behind their positions. (GO TO 505A)

Decision Point 516A

You decided to ask other foremen whether they have difficulty getting their reports in on time. As a result, Virgil learns through the grapevine that you are about to side with Phyllis in his conflict. Accordingly, he begins to try to persuade other foreman that they really should help him "win his battle" with Phyllis. As your questioning continues, more and more foreman begin to criticize Phyllis' work.

Your action has caused the conflict to escalate to other employees. As a general rule one should be very careful in "asking around" while one is working to solve an employee conflict. Oftentimes a large number of people know about the conflict and know that you are involved in settling it. Others may also have interests in how you solve it. For these reasons managers should have a low profile when it comes to information gathering during the conflict-management process.

Re-evaluate your last decision. Circle the #516A you just wrote in your flow diagram. Then move back to the first uncircled step above this one in your flow diagram.

Decision Point 516B

She accepts that challenge and remains firm that you should stock the assortment she has assembled. Apparently your message had no effect.

Re-evaluate your last decision. Circle the #516B you just wrote in your flow diagram. Then move to the first uncircled step above this one in your flow diagram.

Decision Point 516C

You schedule a meeting between Phyllis and Virgil. What ground rules would you set for the beginning of the meeting?

A. Each person must first state his or her position on the issue, starting with Phyllis. After each party has presented his or her position, the other must summarize this position in his or her own words until the first is satisfied that he or she is understood. (GO TO 493A)

B. Before the meeting, each person must prepare a position paper in writing including specific requests of changes in the other's behavior. At the outset of the meeting, each party presents his or her position paper, giving a copy to the other so there is little possibility for misunderstanding. (GO TO 508C)

C. No specific ground rules. Play it by ear. (GO TO 492B)

Decision Point 517A

You decided to let your boss dictate how the meeting unfolded. This proved to be a problem. Distracted and perturbed by your apparent lack of preparation, your boss fails to grasp the issues or trade-offs. Finally, at the end of the meeting, she does not give you a decision but tells you she will think about it and get back to you.

Two weeks later you ask her if she has made up her mind, and she confesses that she doesn't remember what decision she had to make. You're right back where you started.

Re-evaluate your last decision. Circle the #517A you just wrote in your flow diagram. Then move to the first uncircled step above this one in your flow diagram.

Decision Point 517B

You have decided to tell Virgil that his case is pretty weak. This is likely to make him more pessimistic about the outcome. This is particularly dangerous since, if you now hesitate in making a final decision, Virgil will be prone to take some serious risks in getting you to modify your position. This could result in severe escalation of the conflict.

In general, unless you are ready to settle a conflict yourself in a way that would be unpopular with one of the parties, it is unadvisable to make either side pessimistic about their chances.

An additional problem with your statement to Virgil is that you negatively evaluated the interests that are behind his position. This was inappropriate because your probing aimed at doing just that. When probing into interests that lie behind a position, it is important to be neutral about them for the time being so that you will be able to probe on another occasion without fear of only hearing what someone thinks you want to hear.

Re-evaluate your last decision. Circle the #517B you just wrote in your flow diagram. Then move to the first uncircled step above this one in your flow diagram.

Decision Point 517C

She advises you that she will think about your request to replace the summer assortment. Three days later you contact her again, and she announces that she has discussed the matter with others and that a replacement is out of the question. Apparently you were not forthcoming enough to encourage her to comply with your request.

Re-evaluate your last decision. Circle the #517C you just wrote in your flow diagram. Then move to the first uncircled step above this one in your flow diagram.

Decision Point 518A

You decided to take a brief recess at this point in the negotiations. What would you do during this period?

A. Meet with Virgil and Phyllis individually and privately in order to ascertain what interests they have that underlie their positions. (GO TO 497B)

B. Meet with Virgil to let him know that you think his case is weaker than Phyllis's and that if he wants to avoid having you side with her, he had better approach the next part of the negotiations in a more conciliatory fashion. (GO TO 502A)

Decision Point 518B

Candace follows your instructions to the letter, but it takes her 11 hours instead of the seven hours you had estimated. There were two problems with the way you gave the assignment. First, by telling her to "drop everything," you were insensitive to the fact that she may have had other pressing things to do. Second, by telling her precisely how to complete the assignment instead of leaving that up to her (within limits), you robbed her of some motivation. In giving assignments, it is far better to be directive on ends than means.

Re-evaluate your last decision. Circle the #518B you just wrote in your flow diagram. Then move to the first uncircled step above this one in your flow diagram.

Decision Point 518C

You have worked hard to specify the alternatives available to the three of you. You decided to totally take responsibility in a very personal way for the outcome of this conflict. Unfortunately, this sets a dangerous precedent. If you think about it, Virgil and Phyllis have been rewarded by taking strong and rather unyielding positions here. From this experience they have learned that if they ever have conflicts with colleagues in the future, all they have to do is come to you, be assertive and inflexible, and you will exert effort yourself in solving it. Actually, there is a resolution to this incident that involves far less effort on your part and more work on the part of the parties involved. In order to discover it, however, you will have to look behind the positions of Phyllis and Virgil to their motivations.

Re-evaluate your last decision. Circle the #518C you just wrote in your flow diagram. Then move back to the first uncircled step above this one in your flow diagram.

Decision Point 519A

You schedule a meeting between Phyllis and Virgil. What ground rules would you set for the beginning of the meeting?

A. Each person must first state his or her position on the issue, starting with Phyllis. After each party has presented his or her position, the other must summarize this position in his or her own words until the first is satisfied that he or she is understood. (GO TO 493A)

B. Before the meeting, each person must prepare a position paper in writing including specific requests of changes in the other's behavior. At the outset of the meeting, each party presents his or her position paper, giving a copy to the other so there is little possibility for misunderstanding. (GO TO 508C)

C. No specific ground rules. Play it by ear. (GO TO 492B)

Decision Point 519B

Becky seems a bit relieved by your reassurance. Two days later you arrive at work to find the following note on your desk: "I got my Statistics test back, and it was a D-. I've talked to my Dad, and he's given me a loan so I won't have to work anymore. Although I'd like to work for you this summer, I can't give you hours until then. I hope you understand."
You call her, but she has her mind made up. You have lost a valued employee needlessly.

Re-evaluate your last decision. Circle the #519B you just wrote in your flow diagram. Then move to the first uncircled step above this one in your flow diagram.

Decision Point 519C

You decided to tell Phyllis that Virgil can be a problem, but that you want to hear his side of the story before taking action. As reasonable as your statement seems, it is actually incorrect. The problem is that Phyllis has engaged in behavior-labeling of a sort that, if not confronted on the spot, leads to an escalation of the conflict. Effective third parties confront such statements and make clear that labels like "obstructionist," "uncooperative," and "unprofessional" are not helpful but counterproductive to conflict resolution.

Re-evaluate your last decision. Circle the #519C you just wrote in your flow diagram. Then move back to the first uncircled step above this one in your flow diagram.

Decision Point 520A

She says that her boss hasn't spoken to her about this, but that the marketing research people have been urging her to make her line more fashion conscious. She then shows you a 20-page report completed a year ago that indicates that in fact, in women's ready-to-wear, Gamage-Nash is seen as the outlet for upscale, fashion conscious consumers. Moreover, it shows that your store lags behind all but one other store (Gamage-Nash in Pueblo, Colorado) in the volume for fashion goods. You counter that there are two other retailers in the Academy Mall that deal with women's fashion goods and that your store, like the one in Pueblo, is *the* high-quality store in the mall.

She seems unpersuaded by that logic. What would you say next?

A. Tell her that the new summer assortment is really all wrong for your store and insist that she replaces it. (GO TO 499A)

B. Remind her that her boss is likely to be more pleased with volume figures than with the consistency of product across the entire chain. Translate your expected volume for a fashion-versus-quality assortment into volume figures to reinforce your point. (GO TO 515A)

C. Discredit the arguments of the market research people by asserting that they are not sufficiently close to local conditions. (GO TO 497A)

D. Find out how difficult it would be for her to replace the merchandise that you have received with an assortment more tailored to your store's needs. Offer to help her with the additional effort required to make that happen. (GO TO 490A)

Decision Point 520B

You have decided to tell Virgil that his case is pretty weak. This is likely to make him more pessimistic about the outcome. This is particularly dangerous since, if you now hesitate in making a final decision, Virgil will be prone to take some serious risks in getting you to modify your position. This could result in severe escalation of the conflict.

In general, unless you are ready to settle a conflict yourself in a way that would be unpopular with one of the parties, it is unadvisable to make either side pessimistic about their chances.

Re-evaluate your last decision. Circle the #520B you just wrote in your flow diagram. Then move back to the first uncircled step above this one in your flow diagram.

Decision Point 521A

Becky responds, "I don't have to wait. I know. If I passed the exam, it will be a miracle. Besides, I know in my heart that I am not getting it." At that point, she breaks down and sobs.

How would you react?

A. "Becky, things are not as bad as you think, you'll see. In the meantime, if you want me to rearrange your hours, let me know." (GO TO 492A)

B. "Sounds like you are really frustrated. That's really understandable. You don't have to tell me right now, but if there is anything I can do to help you through this difficult time, please let me know." (GO TO 505B)

C. "Becky, try to get hold of yourself. This situation is frustrating, but believe me, in a month or two, you'll look back on this time and laugh." (GO TO 510A)

Decision Point 521B

Virgil responds, "Okay, I understand what you are getting at. Listen, if you side with Phyllis on this issue, my crew is really going to think that I have no influence whatever in this organization. I can't afford to lose their respect, believe me. There is nothing worse than a foreman whose crew thinks he has 'lost control.'"

"Furthermore," he continues, "paperwork is a real pain in the neck for me. When I come in on Monday morning, I want to get my hands dirty; I don't want to pansy around shuffling papers!" In effect, Virgil has just told you that he has two interests beside the risk of quality problems:

(1) he wants to appear in control with his crew; and
(2) he doesn't like doing paperwork on Mondays.

As your private meeting with Virgil ends, what would you say?

A. "While I agree with you that seeming in control is important to every manager, I don't buy your personal preferences for not doing paperwork on Mondays. Doing paperwork is part of your job, and if that's what your job is, you should do it. I don't think there is any room for personal preferences in these negotiations. When we get back together I hope you will keep that in mind." (GO TO 517B)

B. "This meeting has been real helpful, Virgil. When we get back together, let's focus on alternatives that reflect all your interests. For example, think about finding an alternative that will not result in your losing the respect of your crew." (GO TO 490B)

Decision Point 522A

Phyllis leaves your office, and you ask Virgil to come in. After exchanging pleasantries, you open the discussion of his conflict with Phyllis and invite him to comment. He responds: "I guess I am in the doghouse again, huh? Well, okay, I'll try harder to work with 'Miss Smarty-pants.'" What would you say?

A. "Yes you are in the doghouse. From what Phyllis tells me, you have been pretty uncooperative." (GO TO 520B)

B. "Let's soft-pedal the name-calling, Virgil. I want your side of the story. Here's a list of situations that Phyllis has prepared. Now then, describe these situations as you see them." (GO TO 485A)

C. "You're not in the doghouse, Virgil. You are a vital member of this organization. I'm trying to get to the bottom of what is going on between the two of you. Name-calling is not going to get us anywhere." (GO TO 510B)

Decision Point 522B

Marion asks you for your recommendation. You ask for an increase of square footage for furs. She quickly approves your recommendation contingent on her discussing the matter with the Divisional Merchandise Manager, Dresses and Cosmetics. Four days later Marion calls you and gives you the go-ahead. You rearrange your section to increase the space for furs.

The following Tuesday afternoon you are approached by Becky Stark, who seems obviously distraught. You ask her what the problem is, and she says, "I'm in a terrible fix. I think I just flunked my Statistics midterm. I don't know, I just can't seem to get math. I've talked to the professor, but he's no help. I just don't know what to do." What would you say?

A. "Well, have you considered getting a tutor?" (GO TO 496B)

B. "Why don't you wait until you get your exam back before you worry about it. Who knows, maybe you did fine." (GO TO 521A)

C. "Are you telling me that you want to cut back on your hours?" (GO TO 492A)

D. "I'm sure you'll work it out. Things will get better, you'll see. You're a smart person." (GO TO 519B)

E. "Sounds like a frustrating situation. Can you think of anything I might do to help?" (GO TO 505B)

Decision Point 523A

Virgil responds, "Okay, I understand what you are getting at. Listen, if you side with Phyllis on this issue, my crew is really going to think that I have no influence whatever in this organization. I can't afford to lose their respect, believe me. There is nothing worse than a foreman whose crew thinks he has 'lost control.'"

"Furthermore," he continues, "paperwork is a real pain in the neck for me. When I come in on Monday morning, I want to get my hands dirty; I don't want to pansy around shuffling papers!" In effect, Virgil has just told you that he has two interests beside the risk of quality problems: (1) he wants to appear in control with his crew; and (2) he doesn't like doing paperwork on Mondays.

As your private meeting with Virgil ends, what would you say?

A. "While I agree with you that seeming in control is important to every manager, I don't buy your personal preferences for not doing paperwork on Mondays. Doing paperwork is part of your job, and if that's what your job is, you should do it. I don't think there is any room for personal preferences in these negotiations. When we get back together I hope you will keep that in mind." (GO TO 517B)

B. "This meeting has been real helpful, Virgil. When we get back together, let's focus on alternatives that reflect all your interests. For example, think about finding an alternative that will not result in your losing the respect of your crew." (GO TO 490B)

Decision Point 523B

Jean finally agrees to replace the assortment. You follow up by helping her with the paperwork and by feeding the grapevine via your boss to hers. The new line arrives and it is an excellent one. Your summer sales volume figures hit an all-time high. **Congratulations!** You have just completed the Communication Interaction Case.

Decision Point 523C

You decided to call Virgil into your meeting with Phyllis. This is premature. You should really not conduct a confrontational meeting until you have had a chance to interview both of the parties. Your decision would have been acceptable in an emergency situation, but there is no indication that this is truly an emergency.

Re-evaluate your last decision. Circle the #523C you just wrote in your flow diagram. Then move back to the first uncircled step above this one in your flow diagram.

Decision Point 524A

John reacts with the following: "But that's not really fair. The redistricting plan is unfair, and you know it!"
At this point how would you respond?

A. Try to persuade John that the redistricting plan is fair. Be prepared to compare his performance with Susan Brown's (such comparisons are not improper since performance records are open within the company). (GO TO 582A)

B. Tell John that you do not like his attitude, and that you cannot give his future employers a good recommendation unless he improves his performance next quarter. (GO TO 574B)

C. Ask John what changes in redistricting that he would suggest to correct the inequity that he is experiencing. (GO TO 538A)

D. Tell John you will be sorry to see him go, but you understand that if he still thinks the redistricting is inequitable after your last discussion with him, perhaps this is the best thing for him to do. (GO TO 570A)

E. Ask John what things he likes about his present territory with the idea of trying to remind him of the positive things about his job instead of the negative things he seems to be emphasizing in his own mind. (GO TO 528A)

Decision Point 524B

John agrees to try harder if you promise to look into the fairness of his territory. You agree to get back to him at the end of the following quarter.
In the meantime, what would you do?

A. Get John to commit himself to calling on a specific number of M.D.s during the next quarter. (GO TO 566A)

B. Tell John that you are very pleased that he has agreed to improve, and encourage him to do the best he can. (GO TO 543C)

C. Negotiate a level of performance with John that you would consider an adequate sign John is doing all he can with the territory he has been given. (GO TO 549A)

Decision Point 525A

Virgil responds, "Well, that's your opinion, but I'll tell you that Ivan just doesn't have the ability or the confidence to handle setups on his machine himself, and there is no one else around who can work with him. It's a risk, but if you want to take it, fine. Just order me to get my reports done, and I'll do it!"

What would you say now?

A. "As I understand it, then, your only concern is with quality. That is the only thing that keeps you from getting your reports in on time." (GO TO 487B)

B. "Beside the possibilities of quality problems, what other negative things might happen if you were forced to get your reports in on time?" (GO TO 511B)

C. Tell Virgil you are willing to take the risk. Order him to get his reports in on time. (GO TO 493C)

D. "Put yourself in Phyllis's shoes. What would you do if you were her?" (GO TO 508A)

Decision Point 525B

You accompany Lisa on several calls and notice several errors that she is making. First, she is not particularly friendly to receptionists and other people who could get her in to see the doctor. Second, she is too quick to leave company literature without seeing the obstetrician personally. And third, she uses powerless and overly polite language in her detailing speeches.

You give her feedback on these observations and watch her practice techniques that you give her on subsequent calls. Confident that she has benefited from your counseling, you return to your other responsibilities. In a month, you contact her again and ask for a progress report. Since it is optimistic, you decide to wait for the next quarter results. They are excellent. Her sales volume has improved to 440 units and her inventory levels to 57 days!

You correctly deduced that Lisa had a problem with abilities and skills. To recapitulate, when you originally talked with Lisa, you learned that she believed that her efforts would lead to outcomes she valued. Thus, effort was not the problem. This left "Abilities and Skills" and "Understanding of the Job" as key factors. By accompanying her on her sales calls, you were able to discover that she lacked specific skills associated with making effective sales calls to obstetricians.

GO TO 579A to move on to your next motivational problem, John Crosby.

Decision Point 526A

You ask to accompany Jim on a sales call. He agrees and the two of you leave early the next morning. Observing him, you conclude that Jim knows the products well and is effective in detailing them. One call to a pharmaceutical wholesaler results in a hefty order. Clearly Jim's motivational problem has nothing to do with his sales abilities or job understanding.

What would you do now?

A. Ask Jim how the death of his father has changed his outlook on his work. (GO TO 553B)

B. Let him know you think his performance is really seriously low, and you would like to know exactly what he plans to do about it. (GO TO 570B)

C. Find out whether he realizes that his sales are probably suffering from the low inventory levels being held by wholesalers in his territory. (GO TO 590A)

D. Ask Jim if he needs some time off now that his personal crisis has passed. (GO TO 572A)

E. Suggest that Jim may want to attend a sales seminar sponsored by the company next month. Coincidentally, it is being conducted in the city where Jim lives. (GO TO 567B)

F. Ask Jim why he was only able to contact 73 percent of the doctors in his territory. (GO TO 596A)

G. Do nothing. It is clear to you that Jim's performance problem is caused by a factor outside of your control. (GO TO 586A)

Decision Point 526B

With the action plan complete, you now have to decide how to implement it without regular contact with Wilson Thomas.

What would you do?

A. Keep in touch with him by phone asking for weekly progress reports. (GO TO 582B)

B. Schedule a return visit in one month in order to go with him on some sales calls again. (GO TO 578B)

Decision Point 527A

Your diagnosis is that your Warehouse Group is Moderately Immature. That is correct. Several facts that support this diagnosis appear below:

Maturity Factor	Facts That Suggest Maturity	Facts That Suggest Immaturity
Desire to attain high but attainable goals		Resistant to carry full load until Al is replaced
Willingness and ability to accept responsibility	Reasonably obedient	No one volunteered to take the lead job; motivated by compensation alone
Relevant education and/or experience	Task rather routine relative to skills; procedures in place	High turnover

Your must prepare for the Fourth of July Clearance Sale, one of the store's biggest sales of the summer. A circus tent is erected in the large parking lot in front of the store, and all the sale merchandise is moved outside. You and Al Thorn have planned for this sale for some time. You have scheduled no deliveries for this week so you have the manpower to move all the furniture.

Several issues remain to be decided before the sale begins. First, you have to figure out how to schedule the necessary overtime in order to get everything done. You have worked out all the tasks that have to be done and worked out a schedule of how many hours of overtime each day will be necessary.

How would you schedule the overtime among the warehouse workers?

A. Give the workers what you have come up with and ask them to decide on their own which people will work which hours. (GO TO 588B)
B. Make the assignments on the basis of seniority, i.e., those with the most seniority get the most desirable hours. (GO TO 567A)
C. Call the entire group together, show them what you have come up with, and help them to decide on the allocation of overtime hours as a group. (GO TO 576B)
D. Ask each member of the group to give you a list of his or her overtime hour preferences. Integrate these the best you can into your final schedule of who works which overtime hours. (GO TO 580A)

Decision Point 528A

This is an excellent motivational strategy, but not in this situation. Emphasizing the positive aspects of a job is an effective approach, but only as one part of a long-range motivational strategy. In this situation, you face a short-term, emergency situation. Persuasiveness of this sort is unlikely to be enough to create a set of perceptions which would result in better performance.

Re-evaluate your last decision. Circle the #528A you just wrote in your flow diagram. Then move back to the first uncircled number above this one in your flow diagram.

Decision Point 528B

"I thought I would do much better. My husband and I were counting on me making 400 units so we could make our first house payment."

"I really don't know what it is. I visited every obstetrician's office in my territory at least once. I wasn't really prepared for how difficult it is to get to see doctors. It's tough even getting in the door. And when you do, the most you have is five minutes. And that's a very distracted five minutes, I'll tell you. As for my relations with wholesalers, I called on each one twice during the quarter. Even though their supply is only 50 days right now, that's up from 43 when I started."

You were not aware of this improvement in inventory levels, which is fairly substantial; therefore, you congratulate her on her improvement.

Given this information, how would you motivate Lisa?

A. Transfer her to a different territory within your district known to be an easier region for sales. (GO TO 556A)
B. Tell her not to be discouraged since building a relationship with the doctors is often a time consuming process, and it may take a while to reach her 400-unit quota. (GO TO 572B)
C. Ask to accompany her on several sales calls with obstetricians. (GO TO 525B)
D. Ask her to attend a seminar on salesmanship offered by an industry association to develop her skills. (GO TO 590B)
E. Ask her how much her house payment is, and then calculate what her sales volume would have to be for her to earn a satisfactory commission. (GO TO 555B)
F. Indicate that unless her sales volume improves, you may be forced to take disciplinary action. (GO TO 583A)

Decision Point 529A

You decide to pose the issue of tardiness to the group by asking them to think about things that might solve the problem. You require that they submit to you a written report on how they plan to solve the problem, and tell them that if they do not meet the standards in their report, disciplinary action will be taken. The group hands you a written report three days later. It contains a number of suggestions that are totally unacceptable. For example, the report recommends that you excuse tardy events when they were not intended. You now face the specter of going back to the group and rejecting portions of their recommendations.

Your leadership approach was the reason your decision failed. The group is Very Immature, but your approach was indicative of a strong people orientation (concern for fairness in tardiness penalties). You should have been much more task oriented.

Re-evaluate your last decision. Circle the #529A you just wrote in your flow diagram. Then move to the first uncircled step above this one in your flow diagram.

Decision Point 529B

Jim says, "I really don't know. I'd miss some parts of the job like seeing some of the doctor friends I have now, and I'd really miss working with you. But I certainly don't need the job financially anymore. My dad left us a real nice inheritance, so I don't have to work to eat anymore."

How would you respond?

A. Tell Jim that you will be sorry to see him go, but that you have to have 400 units per quarter from a sales rep in his region, and you cannot afford to keep him while he decides what to do. (GO TO 574A)

B. Ask Jim if he needs some time off to get himself together now that his personal crisis has passed. (GO TO 572A)

C. Indicate to Jim that you don't want to stand in his way if he doesn't want to work anymore, but that there may be some way that you could work something out with him. (GO TO 559A)

D. Tell Jim that you will be personally disappointed if he gives up on his job and that you wish he would reconsider. Remind him of what he would be giving up in terms of the nonfinancial rewards the job gives him. (GO TO 566B)

Decision Point 530A

Jim says, "I just am not sure. I've told you my priorities have changed. I want to spend more time with my family. I know the amount of work necessary to make my quota, and that's about all I am prepared to do."
What would you say now?

A. Tell Jim it sounds like his job with Omega isn't important enough for him to work to keep it. (GO TO 529B)

B. Indicate that unless he is willing to try for higher level of sales, you'll have to ask for his resignation. (GO TO 574A)

Decision Point 530B

You call a meeting of the salespeople and help them come up with a solution to the priority policy problem. The group reacts to your query with laughter. One salesperson asks you if you are really serious. Three others walk out of the meeting in disgust, telling you they had come to the store from home for this meeting and that they have better things to do. With several people having left, you find yourself trying to lead a discussion with only a part of the group present.

In effect, your action was inappropriate because it was far too directive for a very mature group. In general, your posture should have been consistent with a low-task orientation and a low-people orientation. We have referred to this as a Delegation approach.

Re-evaluate your last decision. Circle the #530B you just wrote in your flow diagram. Then move to the first uncircled step above this one in your flow diagram.

Decision Point 530C

She thanks you for your kind offer, but she admits to not being able to determine the problem. She seems very frustrated.
At this point what would you do?

A. Ask her if her frustration stems from the low amount on her commission check. (GO TO 537A)

B. Indicate that her problem may be that she's not calling on pharmaceutical wholesalers. (GO TO 576C)

C. Ask her if there is anything that has happened in her job that she was unprepared for. (GO TO 561B)

Decision Point 531A

You concluded that your group of Furniture Salespeople and Decorators is Moderately Mature. This is incorrect. This group is Very Mature. Several facts support this diagnosis:

Maturity Factor	Facts That Suggest Maturity	Facts That Suggest Immaturity
Desire to attain high but attainable goals	Recently set a new sales record	
Willingness and ability to accept responsibility	Work with very little supervision; will do anything necessary to satisfy a customer	
Relevant education and/or experience	Very experienced and able group	

Two days after your boss leaves on vacation, you get word from your Warehouse group that several of your salespeople have been violating the policy of giving priority to orders. The policy reads that any salesperson can request priority on only five orders per month. The logic behind the policy is that the warehouse and delivery people can only accommodate that number on a truly priority basis. Excesses of this kind mean that promises made to customers cannot be fulfilled.

How would you handle this situation?

A. Remind the group of the policy, but take no further action. (GO TO 581A)

B. Find out who the policy violators are and tell them that they may file no more priority orders that month. (GO TO 536A)

C. Call a meeting of the salespeople and help them come up with a solution to the problem. (GO TO 530B)

Decision Point 532A

You carefully review his performance record since you became his manager and detail what you've done to help him with his work. Then you ask him for a renewed commitment to do something about his "marginal" performance.

His response is markedly defensive. He blames anything and everything besides himself for his low performance. For example, he asserts that many obstetricians are more interested in the gifts and favors given to them by competing firms than the attributes of the products. He even claims that competing firms have targeted his territory as a place in which they are making most of their sales and advertising expenditures (this is impossible to verify). He then delivers a description of his sales approach that you've heard before:

"I have always believed strongly that a professional sales approach is not a pressure approach. I come on slow, building my credibility and expressing interest in the physician's individual problems with malpractice, uninformed patients, and unqualified hospital staffers. You can't be product-driven in this business; you have to be doctor-driven. What you might gain in the short run, you lose in the long haul."

While you don't disagree in principle, you are concerned that Thomas's soft-sell approach is too indirect for wholesalers. What now?

A. Accompany him on a series of sales calls. (GO TO 547A)

B. Confront the differences between his stated approach and the sort of approach you know works well for some of your highest performing reps. (GO TO 589A)

C. Tell him that you think he is being defensive. (GO TO 548B)

D. Tell him that this is it--that you are at the end of your rope with him. Establish your willingness to help in any way you can, but either he comes up to standard next quarter or he's through with Omega. (GO TO 545A)

E. Tell him his sales approach may be correct, but he can't make it work unless he improves his effort. Ask him to explain why he only was able to contact 77 percent of the doctors in his region and why his inventory figures are so low. (GO TO 564A)

F. Assert that you don't disagree with his personal sales technique, but you think he needs to be hard-hitting when the occasion calls for it. Schedule him for a training program known to emphasize a contingency approach to selling. Warn him that this is his last chance. (GO TO 593B)

G. Check to see if his job is really important to him. (GO TO 583B)

Decision Point 533A

Your plan works very well. Your people are pleased that you have defended their interests by setting up the roped-off corridor to the tent and by forcing salespeople not to encourage disruptive customer behavior. This overshadowed the concern that existing procedures about off-loading merchandise created inconveniences.

Your action was consistent with the type of leadership style that fits a Moderately Immature group. Specifically, by defending your group you were demonstrating a people orientation. And by insisting on compliance with existing procedures you showed a task orientation. It is precisely this high-people orientation and high-task orientation that is appropriate to Moderately Immature groups.

On the following (Friday) morning, two additional issues arise. First, one of your warehouse workers (a very popular member of the group) shows up wearing running shoes rather than the steel-toed shoes that are required by prevailing work rules. His excuse is that his shoe laces broke and he couldn't tie his shoes. Second, the issue of break time comes up. Employees complain that since you forced them to "off-load" merchandise by the invoice number, they think it is only fair to have longer breaks after they have loaded all the low number merchandise (the numbering system is roughly related to weight, meaning that they have to carry heavy objects in the same time period).

What would you do?

A. Grant them longer break periods after they have had to move heavy objects, *and* require the worker with the nonregulation shoes to go home and get the proper shoes. (GO TO 558A)

B. Tell your group that they should comply with existing break times, *and* require the worker with the nonregulation shoes to go home and get the proper shoes. (GO TO 595B)

C. Grant them longer break periods after they have had to move heavy objects, *and* tell the worker with the nonregulation shoes that he can work today without regulation shoes but he must comply tomorrow. (GO TO 593A)

D. Tell your group that they should comply with existing break times, *and* tell the worker with the nonregulation shoes that he can work today without regulation shoes but he must comply tomorrow. (GO TO 571A)

Decision Point 534A

Jim Clemmons has worked for Omega for three and a half years, and never before has his performance been so low. You are unsure what is causing this situation. His performance figures are listed on page 19.

Your meeting with Jim takes place at his home while you are on a business trip. (This is common, as most reps work out of an office in their homes; moreover, you have a friendly relationship with Jim). After a pleasant dinner, the two of you move into his office in a small bungalow behind the family residence. You ask him if he's seen the sales data. He responds: "Yes, I have, and I'm embarrassed by them. You may not know this, but my Dad passed away five months ago. He'd been ill for some time, but I guess I just let things slip. I guess I'll have to put all that behind me now and build up those figures." Out of courtesy, you spend some time talking about Jim's father. Clearly Jim took the loss of his father very hard.

What would you say after the conversation turns again to his performance?

A. Ask Jim how the death of his father has changed his outlook on his work. (GO TO 553B)

B. Let him know you think his performance is really seriously low, and you would like to know exactly what he plans to do about it. (GO TO 570B)

C. Find out whether he knows that his sales are probably suffering from the low inventory levels being held by wholesalers in his region. (GO TO 590A)

D. Ask Jim if he needs some time off to get himself together now that his personal crisis has passed. (GO TO 572A)

E. Suggest that Jim may want to attend a sales seminar sponsored by the company next month (By coincidence, it is being conducted in the city where Jim lives). (GO TO 567B)

F. Ask to accompany Jim on a series of sales calls. (GO TO 526A)

G. Ask Jim why he was only able to contact 73 percent of the doctors in his area. (GO TO 596A)

H. Do nothing. It is clear that Jim's performance problem is caused by a factor or factors outside your control. (GO TO 586A)

Decision Point 535A

She exclaims, "Very disappointed! My husband and I were counting on me making 400 units to make our first house payment."
How would you motivate Lisa?

A. Transfer her to a different territory within your district known to be an easier region for sales. (GO TO 556A)

B. Tell her not to be discouraged since building credibility with obstetricians is often a time consuming process, and it may take a while to reach her 400-unit quota. (GO TO 572B)

C. Ask to accompany her on several sales calls with obstetricians. (GO TO 525B)

D. Ask her to attend a seminar on salesmanship offered by an industry association to hone her skills further. (GO TO 590B)

E. Ask her how much her house payment is, and then calculate what her sales volume would have to be for her to earn a satisfactory commission. (GO TO 555B)

F. Indicate that unless her sales volume improves, you may be forced to take disciplinary action. (GO TO 583A)

Decision Point 535B

You tell security people to rope off a corridor from the warehouse to the tent and tell your salespeople to stay away from the tent to discourage interference with the warehouse people and allow your people to deviate from existing procedures regarding the movement of merchandise. These two actions result in less positive results than you expect. Notably, several of your group members curse a salesperson who seems to be in their way but is actually assisting them in moving a customer away from the roped-off area. The salesperson then complains to your boss, and the resulting "flap" causes you to reprimand the people in the warehouse group who were involved.

Your leadership approach is the cause of this situation. Although your group is Moderately Immature, your strong people-oriented style reflects a higher level of maturity than they presently possess. They still need a modicum of task orientation to be effective.

Re-evaluate your last decision. Circle the #535B your just wrote in your flow diagram. Then move to the first uncircled step about this one in your flow diagram.

Decision Point 536A

You decide to find out who the policy violators are and tell them that they may file no more priority orders that month. You do so, and these salespeople tell you that they were not aware that they had gone over their limit. That done, you feel good that you handled the matter successfully. However, when your boss returns from vacation, he criticizes your approach on the grounds that several of "his" best salespeople complained that you treated them like common employees.

In effect, your action was inappropriate because it was far too directive for a Very Mature group. In general, your posture should have been consistent with a low-task orientation and a low-people orientation. We have referred to this as a Delegation approach.

Re-evaluate your last decision. Circle the #536A you just wrote in your flow diagram. Then move to the first uncircled step above this one in your flow diagram.

Decision Point 536B

It is clear to you that Buff's goodwill could be very valuable in helping his replacement establish good relations with the doctors and wholesalers in his territory. Also, it seems to you that Buff's primary concern is in not getting immediately cut off from company benefits. You make him a proposal that would have him work with the new representative for six weeks in exchange for a continuation of his employee benefits for six months. He makes a counter proposal, and you negotiate an agreement whereby he will make calls with the new representative for three weeks and be on call to help his replacement for another three weeks. In return, you will pay him two weeks salary and continue his benefits for six months. Both personnel and your supervisor agree to his plan, and you put it in operation.

This seems like an effective solution in that Buff's replacement is likely to benefit from the goodwill that clients accord Buff. In addition, you have removed a poor performing employee with a minimum of disruption to the rest of the group. The problem presented by Buff was a difficult one. Spaulding was performing poorly because he had great incentives on nonperformance. By identifying and verifying those incentives, you were able to use those circumstances to allow Buff to make a positive contribution at the same time that you terminated him.

In the six months this case covers, you have faced a variety of motivational problems. By applying the motivation theory to each individual, you have been able to diagnose and make recommendations which lead to effective solutions.

Congratulations! You have successfully completed the Motivation Interactive Case.

Decision Point 537A

She exclaims, "Very disappointed! My husband and I were counting on me making 400 units to make our first house payment."
What would you say now?

A. Indicate that physician calls are important but that it is equally important for her to build up wholesale inventory levels in her region. (GO TO 541A)

B. Offer to help her any way you can to build her sales volume. (GO TO 557B)

Decision Point 537B

"As a matter of fact, I've been giving it some thought. I view life very differently now. My priorities are my life first, my family second, and my job third. For example, I find myself more involved in my son's activities. He's been in soccer for eight years, but I never got involved. Now I'm an assistant coach. My wife's been trying to get involved in my work. She goes with me on most of the out-of-town calls I make, and as a nurse herself, she understands Omega's products. The biggest problem that I have is making calls on rural doctors. I don't like being away from home for more than two days, and that really makes certain physicians out of reach."

"If I resigned, I'd miss some parts of the job like seeing some of the doctors I know well, and I'd really miss working with you. But I certainly don't need the job anymore. My dad left us a real nice inheritance, so I don't have to work to eat anymore."
How would you respond?

A. Tell him that you will be sorry to see him go, but that you have to have 400 units per quarter from a sales rep in his region, and you cannot afford to keep him while he decides what to do. (GO TO 574A)

B. Ask Jim if he needs some time to get himself together now that his personal crisis has passed. (GO TO 572A)

C. Indicate to Jim that you don't want to stand in his way if he doesn't want to work anymore, but you aren't sure there isn't some way that you could work something out with him. (GO TO 559A)

D. Tell him that you will be personally disappointed if he gives up on his job and that you wish he would reconsider. Remind him of what he would be giving up in terms of the nonfinancial rewards the job gives him. (GO TO 566B)

Decision Point 538A

This is not advisable. Any redistricting would simply create problems with other reps. In addition, a deviation from the scheme sanctioned by the company and endorsed by others in the industry requires more than one person's lack of satisfaction with it.

Re-evaluate your last decision. Circle the #538A you just wrote in your flow diagram. Then move back to the first uncircled number above this one in your flow diagram.

Decision Point 538B

William Spaulding has been a difficult person for you to understand ever since you joined the company. His recent sales performance figures are on page 19.

"Buff," as he is called by his friends, has been with the company for eight years, and his performance has been nothing short of terrible for the last two years. What makes Spaulding's performance so hard to understand is that in so many ways, he appears a natural for this business. He has a fine educational background, is very personable, and possesses a marvelous, relaxed sense of humor. And then there is his golf. A former PGA professional, Buff is an avid golfer, a hobby he uses to entertain his clients on their days off. Buff is something of a "character" at the company. He always shows up at company functions in brightly colored golf clothes, tanned and well groomed. He asks questions articulately. What with his fashionable clothes and large home (on a golf course), you have often wondered how he maintains his lifestyle in the face of such low commissions. His persuasive, slick, sophisticated personality has bought him a great deal of time from you. In fact, you feel rather taken advantage of. He has promised improved performance on many occasions, but somehow he has never delivered. You are not proud that you have let him get away with such "subpar" performance.

How would you approach your conversation with him?

A. Ask around the company discreetly to find out more about Buff's reputation as a salesman and how he is able to maintain his life-style when his earnings are so low. (GO TO 568B)

B. Tell him that if he does not turn his performance around, you are prepared to take disciplinary action like never before. (GO TO 592A)

C. Ask to accompany him on several sales calls. (GO TO 557A)

Decision Point 539A

When Buff arrives, you tell him that his plan to put off making a decision for six months is unacceptable. Also, you tell him that it appears to you that he has already decided to go with a real estate career and that under the circumstances, what he can provide Omega is not worth six months salary.

Buff responds by saying that he likes doing real estate deals and that he has been successful in them. He goes on to say that he is indeed thinking about forming a corporation and selling real estate full time, but he is not sure that he wants to give up the security--particularly such things as a steady paycheck and good insurance--which Omega can provide. As Buff continues to talk, it seems clearer to you that his goal is to develop his own business but that he doesn't want to leave until he has arranged some details, such as replacing the company car and getting insurance.

What would you do now?

A. Discharge Buff and begin making plans for his replacement. (GO TO 545B)

B. Try to negotiate a deal with Buff in which you would keep him on in a limited capacity. (GO TO 536B)

Decision Point 539B

Wilson is reluctant to put his commitments down on paper. You press him for specifics, and after making a few, it becomes clear to him that you want something quite detailed; that is, you want him to submit a weekly schedule of planned activities on the Thursday following each week.

At that point he says: "You know, I felt you and I got to know each other this week. I began to develop an appreciation of your point of view, and I find myself respecting you more than I ever did. However, you're treating me like a five-year-old. I thought you were beginning to respect some of my sales practices, but what you're asking me to do is humiliating!"

How would you respond?

A. Review the positive feedback you have given him, and indicate that he has earned your respect on these aspects. Indicate that you don't intend humiliation, only building respect based on results. (GO TO 592B)

B. Tell him that you would do the same for any employee who was not performing up to expectations. Let him know that he has to earn your respect. (GO TO 543A)

C. Back off on your expectations a bit since you don't want to damage Wilson's self-respect. (GO TO 551B)

Decision Point 540A

You analyze the situation carefully yourself and figure out the best way to allocate the necessary tasks. The results, however, are disappointing. A number of transfers require a great deal of coordination among your people, and the ill-feelings that accompanied your task allocations stand in the way of the necessary cooperation. You need to assign overtime, and for the first time your group is very resistant to working late. You find yourself having to work one night until 3 a.m. to compensate.

Your approach was essentially direction. This is ill suited to the maturity level of your group. As a Moderately Mature group, you should have used participation.

Re-evaluate your last decision. Circle the #540A you just wrote in your flow diagram. Then move to the first uncircled step above this one in your flow diagram.

Decision Point 540B

When Buff arrives, you lay out the evidence of his violation of policy and tell him that he could either agree to end real estate dealings with his Omega clients and improve his performance or resign. He seems taken aback by your abruptness and for the first time in your memory is at a bit of a loss for words. As you press him, he becomes defensive, first denying that his real estate interests are in any way related to his Omega responsibilities, later almost bragging about how he has signed up most of the doctors in his area to one or another of his partnerships. The meeting ends with Buff announcing that he isn't going to give up his real estate practice and if it was an "issue" with you, you could have his resignation.

The outcomes of Buff's resignation are mixed. Although you have eliminated a poor performer and someone who was in direct violation of company policy, the timing and nature of his departure cause difficulties. First, you do not have anyone to replace Buff on such short notice and the district is not covered by two months. Second, you hear from reps in other districts that doctors are saying that Omega has really been unfair to Buff. You suspect that these stories are coming from Buff and the doctors in his real estate deals, but they are affecting Omega's reputation and the reps' morale, nonetheless.

In this case, firing Buff was certainly justified; however, you might have been able to avoid such a direct confrontation until your replacement plans were better laid if you had taken a different approach in your meeting with Buff.

Re-evaluate your last decision. Circle the #540B you just wrote in your flow diagram. Then move back to the first uncircled number above this one in your flow diagram.

Decision Point 541A

She responds as follows: "But I called on each wholesaler in my region twice during the quarter. And even though the average supply is only at 50 days right now, that's up from 43 when I started."

You were not aware of this improvement in inventory levels, which is fairly substantial; therefore, you congratulate her on her improvement.

Given all this information, how would you motivate Lisa?

A. Transfer her to a different territory within your district known to be an easier region for sales. (GO TO 556A)

B. Tell her not to be discouraged since building credibility with obstetricians is often a time consuming process, and it may take a while to reach her 400-unit quota. (GO TO 572B)

C. Ask to accompany her on several sales calls with obstetricians. (GO TO 525B)

D. Ask her to attend a seminar on salesmanship offered by an industry association to further hone her skills. (GO TO 590B)

E. Ask her how much her house payment is, and then calculate what her sales volume would have to be for her to earn a satisfactory commission. (GO TO 555B)

F. Indicate that unless her sales volume improves, you may be forced to take disciplinary action. (GO TO 583A)

Decision Point 541B

You spell out the issues for your supervisor and summarize the issues and risks as you see them. Your supervisor agrees with your analysis and says that he thinks that Buff has to go and that he will do whatever possible to back your decision. In short, your supervisor has said that he understands the situation and will support you in what you do--but he doesn't have much specific advice about how you should handle Buff and the potential problems his resignation might create.

At this point what would you do?

A. Call Buff in and attempt to find out why he wants six months to make his plans about resigning. (GO TO 539A)

B. Discharge Buff and begin making plans for his replacement. (GO TO 564B)

Decision Point 542A

You concluded that your Office Staff is Very Mature. This is incorrect. The group is Moderately Mature. Several facts that support this conclusion:

Maturity Factor	Facts That Suggest Maturity	Facts That Suggest Immaturity
Desire to attain high but attainable goals	Willing to work overtime on short notice	
Willingness and ability to accept responsibility	Accommodate changes introduced without inputs	Somewhat dependent (tendency to ask for unnecessary permission/approval)
Relevant education and/or experience	Secretarial & bookkeeping skills good	Data processing skills weak; documentation poor

This morning you received word that, in anticipation of your Fall Clearance Sale, a number of recliners and dining room sets will be transferred from the Dade County store. This will greatly add to the paperwork of your office staff, and you need to plan how to handle it.

How would you proceed?

A. Call the group together, give them a briefing of the tasks necessary to handle the transfers, and guide a group problem-solving session. (GO TO 556B)
B. Do nothing. The group will be able to handle the problems without your help. (GO TO 562A)
C. Analyze the situation carefully yourself, and figure out the best way to allocate the necessary tasks. (GO TO 540A)
D. At a weekly staff meeting, gather information from your staff as to how you should decide to divide up the extra responsibilities. (GO TO 547B)

Decision Point 542B

Jim's performance during the next quarter continues to be poor. His commitment to do better was not sufficient as a motivator.

Re-evaluate your last decision. Circle the #542B you just wrote in your flow diagram. Then move back to the first uncircled number above this one in your flow diagram.

Decision Point 543A

Wilson's statement that you are treating him like a five-year-old is an attempt to salvage his self-respect. The past week has been hard on him, and now that you are insisting that he not only digest your criticism but also act on it, his ego has become very fragile. Had your statement been more balanced and personal, it would have provided him with more motivation for turning his behavior around.

Re-evaluate your last decision. Circle the #543A you just wrote in your flow diagram. Then move back to the first uncircled number above this one in your flow diagram.

Decision Point 543B

Jim is notably nervous in responding, "I'm disturbed that I've let you down, believe me. I don't want to disappoint you, but I'm not sure what to suggest. I'll try harder if you like, but I'm hesitant to promise much more than 400 units for the time being."
How would you respond?

A. Ask Jim if he needs some time off to get himself together now that his personal crisis has passed. (GO TO 572A)

B. Probe whether he really wants to continue as an Omega sales rep. (GO TO 529B)

C. Tell Jim that you do not consider 400 units good enough. Ask him why he cannot commit to do even better. (GO TO 530A)

D. Do nothing. It is clear to you that Jim's performance problem is caused by a factor outside of your control. (GO TO 586A)

Decision Point 543C

You encourage John to do better, but his performance during the next quarter continues to be poor. Your conversation with John was fine except that you didn't nail down a specific performance commitment from him. In general, it is more effective to establish specific performance goals than goals that are vague such as, "Do the best you can."

Re-evaluate your last decision. Circle the #543C you just wrote in your flow diagram. Then move back to the first uncircled number above this one in your flow diagram.

Decision Point 544A

You concluded that your group of Home Furnishings Clerks is Moderately Immature. This is incorrect. The group is actually Very Immature. Several facts support this diagnosis:

Maturity Factor	Facts That Suggest Maturity	Facts That Suggest Immaturity
Desire to attain high but attainable goals		Complacent; won't co-operate with salespeople they don't like
Willingness and ability to accept responsibility		Little initiative; "not my job"
Relevant education and/or experience		Untrained; high turnover

The situation that captures your attention is tardiness. Your store's policy allows three "excused" tardy episodes per year (the policy in Caraway's store in Orlando allows four such episodes because the local work force demands it). Over the last four months there has been a higher incidence of unexcused tardiness episodes than ever before. In fact, when you consult your log, you notice that there has been more tardiness this month than in any month on record. You meet with this group every Tuesday at 3:00 p.m. in order to accommodate all your people.

How would you address the tardiness issue during this week's meeting?

A. Pose the issue of tardiness to the group. Ask them to think about things that might solve the problem. Require a written report on how they plan to solve the problem. Tell them that if they do not meet the standards in their report, disciplinary action will be taken. (GO TO 529A)

B. Ask them if they think the policy at their branch (Miami) should be brought in line with the Orlando branch. (GO TO 597A)

C. Insist that the members of the group adhere to the policy on tardiness. (GO TO 577B)

Decision Point 545A

He responds: "Well, if you have your mind made up that you're going to can me, then there's nothing I can do about it."

You assure him that your mind is not made up, but you are going to have to see significant improvements in his performance. He asks you what he has to do. You respond by negotiating a standard of performance (400 units, 95 percent of doctors contacted, and wholesale inventory level of 45 days).

Halfway through the following quarter, Wilson phones you to tell you that he knows his inventory figures are not going to meet your agreed-to goal. He tells you that Omega's competitors are offering an attractive incentive plan to their reps and that he is finding it difficult to make progress.

How would you respond?

A. Tell him that you don't consider competitors' perks an acceptable excuse. Let him know that you're expecting him to live up to the terms of your agreement. (GO TO 585A)

B. Accompany him on a series of sales calls. (GO TO 547A)

C. Schedule him for a training program that involves modern sales techniques. Warn him that this is his last chance. (GO TO 593B)

D. Check to see if his job is really important to him. (GO TO 583B)

Decision Point 545B

In analyzing this situation, you realized that there was no alternative for Buff but discharge. His performance had been low, he consistently violated a major company policy, and you had little likelihood of changing his behavior. After discharging Buff, a new set of problems develops for you. Buff's replacement seems to have a hard time making contact with doctors, and wholesalers' inventories drop to a lower level than Buff's. Two large wholesalers tell you that they were thinking about dropping your obstetric line because "Doctors just aren't prescribing it." Your colleagues in other districts mention that there is a rumor going around among doctors that Omega was "out to get" Buff and that you summarily fired him rather than let him resign. Since Buff continues to see his old Omega clients--because of the real estate deals--you know these rumors won't die easily.

You were clearly justified in discharging Buff; however, you might like to select another way of doing so.

Re-evaluate your last decision. Circle the #545B you just wrote in your flow diagram. Then move back to the first uncircled number above this one in your flow diagram.

Decision Point 546A

You assign taking inventory to three of your clerks. Immediately they object, claiming that the "chore" should be shared equally. You respond that this year the store especially needs a correct count, and you have chosen them because they are the best at it. This allays their concern for the time being, and they begin their counts.

Two weeks later when the entire audit is completed, you feel confident that it is the most accurate ever. Your decision to allocate the inventory responsibility with an eye on the task rather than being oriented to your group's concerns was the best given that the group is Very Immature.

Your attention now turns to your Accounting and Office Staff. Recall that this group is composed of nine clerks, bookkeepers, secretaries, credit specialists, and a switchboard operator/receptionist. Since your office is within the office complex, you are probably more familiar with the people in this group than any other. It is a good group. A number of changes have been introduced by the home office without consulting you or your staff. Among these is a new computerized credit analysis system that created significant problems for them. Although the documentation for the system was poor by any estimate and your people lack data processing skills, your three credit analysts pulled together to demystify most of the system's elements. They are still learning, but are doing well under the circumstances. It has made some of them more tentative than before. They often bother you with questions that they should be able to answer themselves, but the situation is improving.

All your staff members have good office skills. In fact, they are better than they think. Too often they ask you for permission or approval to handle situations they should be able to deal with themselves. On the other hand, they are very loyal to you. Just last week an emergency came up that required all but one of your people to work overtime. Even though it came up on very short notice, they were willing to reschedule their personal lives and put in the extra hours.

All things considered, how would you assess the maturity of this group?

A. Very Immature. (GO TO 565A)

B. Moderately Immature. (GO TO 591A)

C. Moderately Mature. (GO TO 548A)

D. Very Mature. (GO TO 542A)

Decision Point 547A

You accompany Wilson on an entire week of his sales calls. Your observations are as follows: (1) Wilson does not budget his time well. He takes a large number of breaks, and he does not push himself during the day. (2) He has an excellent reputation with older obstetricians, but the younger ones are impatient with his slow, plodding approach. (3) He has a good reputation with one of the two wholesalers in his region. The other is a very large wholesaler whose very young buyer seems to consider Wilson an old jerk.

Through the course of the week, you give Wilson repeated verbal feedback on your observations and follow this up with a written report at the end of the week. At the beginning of the week, he is quite defensive about your feedback, but by week's end you notice that he is asking you for advice and encouragement. However, when late Friday afternoon arrives, you note that Wilson is getting somewhat anxious about what you're going to do.

What would you do?

A. Ask him to prepare a series of effort and performance commitments in light of the feedback you've given him. (GO TO 539B)

B. Tell him that you expect him to work on the feedback you've given him. Be firm that you expect him to report next quarterly sales above 400 units or that you'll be forced to terminate him. (GO TO 561A)

Decision Point 547B

At a weekly staff meeting, you gather information from your staff as to how you should divide up the extra responsibilities. They give you their rather conflicting recommendations, and you have a difficult time making the assignments. Yet you are the manager and the one paid to make such decisions.

The results, however, are disappointing. A number of transfers require a great deal of coordination among your people, and the ill-feelings that accompanied your task allocations stand in the way of the necessary cooperation. You need to assign overtime, and for the first time your group is very resistant to working late. You find yourself having to work one night until 3 a.m. to compensate.

Your approach was essentially consultation. This is ill suited to the maturity level of your group. As a Moderately Mature group, you should have used participation.

Re-evaluate your last decision. Circle the #547B you just wrote in your flow diagram. Then move to the first uncircled step above this one in your flow diagram.

Decision Point 548A

You concluded that your group of Accounting and Office people is Moderately Mature. This is correct. Several facts support this diagnosis:

Maturity Factor	Facts That Suggest Maturity	Facts That Suggest Immaturity
Desire to attain high but attainable goals	Willing to work overtime on short notice	
Willingness and ability to accept responsibility	Accommodates changes introduced without inputs	Somewhat dependent (tendency to ask for unnecessary permission/approval)
Relevant education and/or experience	Secretarial & bookkeeping skills good	Data processing skills weak; documentation poor

This morning you received word that, in anticipation of your Fall Clearance Sale, a number of recliners and dining room sets will be transferred from the Dade County store. This will greatly add to the paperwork of your office staff, and you need to plan how to handle it.

How would you proceed?

A. Call group members together, give them a briefing of the tasks necessary to handle the transfers, and guide a group problem-solving session. (GO TO 556B)

B. Do nothing. The group will be able to handle the problems without your help. (GO TO 562A)

C. Analyze the situation carefully yourself and figure out the best way to allocate the necessary tasks. (GO TO 540A)

D. At a weekly staff meeting, gather information from your staff as to how you should decide to divide up the extra responsibilities. (GO TO 547B)

Decision Point 548B

You tell him he's being defensive. With that he totally clams up. Re-evaluate your last decision. Circle the #548B that you just wrote in your flow diagram. Then move back to the first uncircled number above this one in your flow diagram.

Decision Point 549A

John Crosby's performance during the next quarter improves. He calls on 86 percent of the physicians in his territory, and his sales increase to 410 units, ten greater than standard.

He calls you after the quarterly performance report appears, and reminds you of your commitment to do something about the size of his territory. Since you do not want to go through a redistricting, you consult with your boss and others in the organization and find out that John could work part time with the company's market research group conducting "focus groups" of physicians in his territory. Available budgetary funds enable you to sweeten his "draw" (the salary he earns independent of his commission) for the extra responsibilities. This arrangement is a "one-shot deal," and you make that clear to John. He jumps at the offer, and his sales performance continues to be good (but not spectacular) while he works with the market research group.

Upon hearing of this situation, Susan Brown complains to you that she should have been given this special assignment; that is, she is now experiencing a perception of inequity. Luckily, however, you were careful to determine that the characteristics of the physicians in Crosby's district made them better candidates for focus groups than the physicians in other districts. Accordingly, you are able to convince Susan Brown that Crosby's special assignment was not given at her expense.

When you promised John that you would look into his assertion of inequity, you took a very serious chance. Had you done nothing, he would have felt you had gone back on your commitment. As it was, you risked creating inequity elsewhere among your reps.

Congratulations! By bringing Crosby's perceived inequity back into line with realities, you successfully dealt with a volatile situation. You found that you had to identify a specific reference person to convince Crosby that his equity calculations were exaggerated. Additionally, you found you had to address Crosby's eroded belief that arose because of the inequity perception that his efforts would no longer matter.

GO TO 534A to begin your analysis of the case of Jim Clemmons, the next of your employees in need of motivation.

Decision Point 549B

You decide to do very little about the housekeeping problem. This is correct. This is a rather minor infraction considering that the group has recently set a new sales record. Of all the options you were offered, this was the only approach that was appropriate to a Very Mature work group.

Congratulations! You have successfully completed the Leadership Interactive Case.

Decision Point 550A

You diagnosed the Warehouse Group as a Very Mature group. Actually, the group is Moderately Immature. Consider the following:

Maturity Factor	Facts That Suggest Maturity	Facts That Suggest Immaturity
Desire to attain high but attainable goals		Resistant to carry full load until Al is replaced
Willingness and ability to accept responsibility	Reasonably obedient	No one volunteered to take the lead job; motivated by compensation alone
Relevant education and/or experience	Task rather routine relative to skills; procedures in place	High turnover

Your must prepare for the Fourth of July Clearance Sale, one of the store's biggest sales of the summer. A circus tent is erected in the large parking lot in front of the store, and all the sale merchandise is moved outside. You and Al Thorn have planned for this sale for some time. You have scheduled no deliveries for this week so you have the manpower to move all the furniture.

Several issues remain to be decided before the sale begins. First, you have to figure out how to schedule the necessary overtime in order to get everything done. You have worked out all the tasks that have to be done and worked out a schedule of how many hours of overtime each day will be necessary.

How would you schedule the overtime among the warehouse workers?

A. Give the workers what you have come up with and ask them to decide on their own which people will work which hours. (GO TO 588B)
B. Make the assignments on the basis of seniority, i.e., those with the most seniority get the most desirable hours. (GO TO 567A)
C. Call group members together, show them what you have come up with, and help them to decide on the allocation of overtime hours as a group. (GO TO 576B)
D. Ask each member of the group to give you a list of his or her overtime hour preferences. Integrate these the best you can into your final schedule of who works which overtime hours. (GO TO 580A)

Decision Point 551A

It is two days later and you are reading over the material Buff has given you. Looking at it, you are amazed at the extent of Buff's operation. He has involved most of his Omega clients in deals and many of their friends as well. Many of the doctors have invested with Buff for years.

The plan Buff provides for separating his real estate operations from his sales calls is unacceptable to you. In it he asks for a six-month "grace period" to "investigate" ways of reducing the overlap between his real estate deals and his sales calls. At the end of that six-month period, he says he will provide you with either a detailed plan for eliminating the "apparent conflict of interest" or his resignation. As you read over Buff's proposal, you become convinced that what he really wants to do is to set up his own real estate business but stay on your payroll for another six months while he does it.

You realize that the situation you are in presents you with a number of problems. First, Buff is clearly in violation of company policies and you can't tolerate that. Second, Buff has very good relations with the doctors in his territory (both through his pleasant personality and his real estate dealings), and you don't want to create ill will on the part of the doctors toward Omega. Third, the plan that Buff has presented you was not responsive to your request, and you strongly suspect that his entire purpose was to try to buy some time before leaving. Fourth, a potential replacement for Buff is just finishing training, but you think that it would be difficult to throw that person into Buff's district without more training and help than you can provide.

What actions would you now take?

A. Lay out the entire situation for your superior and ask him for advice in dealing with Buff. (GO TO 541B)

B. Call Buff and attempt to find out why he wants six months to make his plans about resigning. (GO TO 539A)

C. Discharge Buff and begin making plans for his replacement. (GO TO 545B)

Decision Point 551B

Just because you have bruised Thomas's ego a bit is not reason to lower your expectations.

Re-evaluate your last decision. Circle the #551B you just wrote in your flow diagram. Then move back to the first uncircled number above this one in your flow diagram.

Decision Point 552A

You concluded that your group of Home Furnishings Clerks is Very Mature. This is incorrect. The group is actually Very Immature. Several facts support this diagnosis:

Maturity Factor	Facts That Suggest Maturity	Facts That Suggest Immaturity
Desire to attain high but attainable goals		Complacent; won't co-operate with salespeople they don't like
Willingness and ability to accept responsibility		Little initiative; "not my job"
Relevant education and/or experience		Untrained; high turnover

The situation that captures your attention is tardiness. Your store's policy allows three "excused" tardy episodes per year (the policy in Caraway's store in Orlando allows four such episodes because the local work force demands it). Over the last four months there has been a higher incidence of unexcused tardiness episodes than ever before. In fact, when you consult your log, you notice that there has been more tardiness this month than in any month on record. You meet with this group every Tuesday at 3:00 p.m. in order to accommodate all your people.

How would you address the tardiness issue during this week's meeting?

A. Pose the issue of tardiness to the group. Ask them to think about things that might solve the problem. Require a written report on how they plan to solve the problem. Tell them that if they do not meet the standards in their report, disciplinary action will be taken. (GO TO 529A)

B. Ask them if they think the policy at their branch (Miami) should be brought in line with the Orlando branch. (GO TO 597A)

C. Insist that the members of the group adhere to the policy on tardiness. (GO TO 577B)

Decision Point 553A

You meet with your boss, give him a summary of Spaulding's performance, and tell him that you have heard a rumor about him conducting personal business with his Omega clients. He informs you that there is not much you can do on the basis of rumors, but that you should do something about Buff's substandard performance.

What would you now do?

A. Ask around the company discreetly to find out more about Buff's reputation as a salesman and how he is able to maintain his life-style when his earnings are so low. (GO TO 555A)

B. Confront Buff with your hunch about his real estate deals, and ask if this is the cause of his poor performance. (GO TO 562C)

C. Do nothing, since it seems your feedback on his sales efforts has led him to try harder. (GO TO 577A)

Decision Point 553B

Jim's lower lip begins to quiver as he says, "I view life very differently now. My priorities are my life first, my family second, and my job third. For example, I find myself more involved in my son's activities. He's been in soccer for eight years, but I never got involved. Now I'm an assistant coach. My wife's been trying to get involved in my work. She goes with me on most of my trips, and as a nurse herself, she understands Omega's products. The biggest problem I have is making calls on rural physicians. I don't like to be away from home for more than two days, and that really makes certain doctors in my territory out of reach." At this point, what would you say?

A. Acknowledge his comment but let him know that you think his performance is really low and that you would like to know exactly what he plans to do to improve it. (GO TO 543B)

B. Ask Jim if he needs some time off to get himself together now that his personal crisis has passed. (GO TO 572A)

C. Suggest that Jim may want to attend a sales seminar sponsored by the company next month. By coincidence, it is being conducted in the city where he lives. (GO TO 567B)

D. Probe whether he really wants to continue as an Omega sales rep. (GO TO 529B)

Decision Point 554A

You diagnosed the Warehouse Group as Very Immature. Actually, the group is Moderately Immature. Consider the following:

Maturity Factor	Facts That Suggest Maturity	Facts That Suggest Immaturity
Desire to attain high but attainable goals		Resistant to carry full load until Al is replaced
Willingness and ability to accept responsibility	Reasonably obedient	No one volunteered to take the lead job; motivated by compensation alone
Relevant education and/or experience	Task rather routine relative to skills; procedures in place	High turnover

You must first prepare for the Fourth of July Clearance Sale, one of the biggest sales of the summer. A circus tent is erected in the large parking lot in front of the store, and all the sale merchandise is moved outside. You and Al Thorn have planned for this sale for some time. You have scheduled no deliveries for this week so you have the manpower to move all the furniture. Several issues remain to be decided before the sale begins. First, you have to figure out how to schedule the necessary overtime in order to get everything done. You have worked out all the tasks that have to be done and worked out a schedule of how many hours of overtime each day will be necessary. How would you schedule the overtime among the warehouse workers?

A. Give the workers what you have come up with and ask them to decide on their own which people will work which hours. (GO TO 588B)
B. Make the assignments on the basis of seniority, i.e., those with the most seniority get the most desirable hours. (GO TO 567A)
C. Call the group members together, show them what you have come up with, and help them to decide on the allocation of overtime hours as a group. (GO TO 576B)
D. Ask each member of the group to give you a list of his or her overtime hour preferences. Integrate these the best you can into your final schedule of who works which overtime hours. (GO TO 580A)

Decision Point 555A

Before meeting with Spaulding, you decide to gather information discreetly about his reputation and the conflict between his low earnings and abundant life-style. As a result, one staff person tells you that a doctor friend of his has shown him a flyer advertising a real estate partnership put together by Buff. The staff person says that it seems that all of Buff's Omega clients are receiving these and many are investing. You now feel that you have the "iron-clad" proof necessary to confront Buff. You know you must act.

What would you do now?

A. Consult with your superior about how to handle the situation. (GO TO 588A)

B. Call Buff in and ask him if the rumors you have heard are true. (GO TO 559B)

C. Call Buff in, lay out the evidence you have and tell him he must eliminate his outside deals and improve his performance. (GO TO 540B)

Decision Point 555B

You and Lisa calculate that she requires a volume of 420 units to make the house payment. With that as a salient goal, Lisa enters the next quarter with renewed vigor. However, at the end of the quarter, her volume had dipped to 340 units (from 360). Discouraged and very frustrated, Lisa resigns.

Your analysis of Lisa's motivation revealed several things. Clearly Lisa has a strong belief that her efforts will pay off in terms of performance since she has a history of succeeding in nearly everything she has attempted. You can also be certain that Lisa believes that performance will be rewarded at Omega, since she is on an incentive pay system that relates her income directly to two indices of performance, volume and inventory. As for Lisa's particular preference for the her work outcomes, you know Lisa values the monetary outcomes of her job since she has indicated that she needs her commission check to make her first house payment. Given these factors, it is not surprising that Lisa's efforts are high (she called on 100 percent of her M.D.s, and each wholesaler twice). However, her performance is still low. In light of this assessment, think about what additional factor may account for her low performance.

Your approach did little more than reinforce what was already a strong belief that performance results in important outcomes. Thus, it was actually a rather redundant action that only added to Lisa's frustration level when she didn't improve. Re-evaluate your last decision. Circle the #555B you just wrote in your flow diagram. Then move back to the first uncircled number above this one in your flow diagram.

Decision Point 556A

Lisa opposes the option of being transferred since it would separate her from her husband, who is in medical school. Moreover, this option is very unpopular with some of your other sales reps, notably John Crosby.

Your analysis of Lisa's motivational circumstances revealed several important pieces of information. First, it is clear that Lisa does believe that her efforts will produce positive results since she has a history of succeeding in nearly everything she has ever attempted. In addition, given the reward system she certainly must believe that her monetary outcomes are in direct proportion to her performance. Monetary outcomes are important to her because she is counting on her commission check to make her first house payment.

Given these factors, it is not surprising that Lisa's efforts are high (she called on 100 percent of M.D.s and each wholesaler twice). However, her performance particularly regarding her obstetrician calls is not up to expectations. In light of this assessment, think through what additional factors may account for her low performance.

Re-evaluate your last decision. Circle the #556A you just wrote in your flow diagram. Then move back to the first uncircled number above this one in your flow diagram.

Decision Point 556B

The meeting gets off to a slow start. With patience, though, all goes well. A number of suggestions come up that you would not have thought of. By the end of the meeting, the group itself has decided who will do what and in what order. Your decision to use participation was perfect. That is precisely the correct approach to use with a Moderately Mature group.

Two weeks later another matter comes up. At the end of the week, the people in the office hold a birthday party in the office for the receptionist. Although you did not attend because you had to be out of the office, you learn upon returning that the party had been very loud, and one furniture salesperson complained that one of her best customers had to wait three or four minutes before getting any service at the window during the party.

Next week another member of your Office Staff has a birthday, and you know that your staff is planning a big celebration. What would you do?

A. Cancel the party on the grounds that the group had not acted responsibly with their last party. (GO TO 596B)
B. Tell them of the complaints of the salespeople and let them handle the situation as they see fit. (GO TO 585B)
C. Offer to let the group use your office for the party (thus reducing the noise level) on the condition that the staff (including you) take turns covering the window during the party. (GO TO 575A)

Decision Point 557A

You accompany Spaulding on several calls and you are very surprised by the results. He demonstrates a fine knowledge of the company's products, and his approach is very effective throughout all the calls. Both wholesalers and doctors seem very responsive to his efforts.

After this dazzling performance, you let him know that he did an outstanding job and ask him to explain why his performance is so low when he clearly has such aptitude for the job. He asserts that he simply has been too casual about his performance but that now he understands that he had better improve.

As you are driving back to your office, you recall something that took place in one wholesaler's office. While Buff was making a count, the wholesaler asked if you were in on any of Buff's "little deals." When you responded with an uncertain look, the wholesaler said, "You know, condos." The conversation ended there as Buff and others came into the room; however, upon reflection, the wholesaler seemed to imply that Buff was putting together real estate deals with the customers he calls on. If true, this is a direct violation of company policy. There is no clear procedure for dealing with such infringements without "iron-clad" proof.

What would you do now?

A. Ask around the company discreetly to find out more about Buff's reputation as a salesman and how he is able to maintain his life-style when his earnings are so low. (GO TO 555A)

B. Confront Buff with your hunch about his real estate deals and ask if this is the cause of his poor performance. (GO TO 562C)

C. Consult with your supervisor about how to deal with this situation. (GO TO 553A)

D. Do nothing, since it seems your feedback on his sales efforts has led him to try harder. (GO TO 577A)

Decision Point 557B

Your conversation with Lisa is not yielding the type of information that you need to complete a motivational analysis. Re-evaluate your last decision, and consider how to get information that would be helpful in identifying the correct approach to motivating Lisa.

Re-evaluate your last decision. Circle the #557B you just wrote in your flow diagram. Then move back to the first uncircled number above this one in your flow diagram.

Decision Point 558A

By Friday at 3:00 p.m. all the merchandise is moved to the tent, and you find yourself giving the rest of the day off to your warehouse group because they had more than met your expectations. Clearly you got more work out of the warehouse group than Al Thorn ever did. You tell your spouse this at dinner that night in your favorite restaurant (paid for by Paul Thielman, who was delighted with the results of the sale and attributed it in part to your "coming through" with the warehouse group under "adverse circumstances").

The reason your action worked out well was that it was appropriate to a Moderately Immature Group. By combining your concern for procedures (the shoes regulation) with your concern for compassion (the break schedules), you balanced a concern for task with a concern for people. This is precisely the combination (task orientation + people orientation) that works well with Moderately Immature work groups.

The sale over, you relax a bit. Three weeks pass without event and all of a sudden the situation with your Home Furnishings Group begins to capture your attention. Recall that the Home Furnishings Group is made up of six relatively inexperienced and low-paid female employees who sell towels, sheets, and other relatively inexpensive decorative items. The employees in this group are almost all over 50 and provide their family's second source of income.

Of all your groups, this is your most troublesome. Over time you have found its members complacent, unwilling to take initiative, and resistant to change. They are cliquish, uninformed about how to be good retail salespeople, and indifferent to the interests of Caraway's. You know that they intentionally withhold cooperation from decorators and furniture salespeople whom they do not like or find "too pushy." Every effort you have made to lead them in the past has been greeted with some variation on the theme "It's not my job."

Your first decision is to diagnose the maturity of the Home Furnishings Group. Which category do you think it falls into?

A. Very Immature. (GO TO 594A)

B. Moderately Immature. (GO TO 544A)

C. Moderately Mature. (GO TO 584A)

D. Very Mature. (GO TO 552A)

Decision Point 559A

The two of you begin to talk about alternatives, and it appears that if you are in agreement, he and his wife might be willing to share the territory as "co-reps." This would enable Jim to be with his son for more time while covering for the rural portions of the territory. You and Jim invite Jim's wife, Kathy, into the bungalow, and she is enthusiastic about the plan to share Jim's job.

You follow up with a call to the Director of Employee Relations (at home) to be sure that this arrangement is possible. It is, and Jim's wife is scheduled for company training. This settled, you stress the necessity of making the standard 400 units per quarter. Both Jim and Kathy agree to coordinate their work to meet that figure.

The next quarter's performance figures are better than your wildest dreams Jim and Kathy produce 525 units! Your questioning revealed that Jim's motivational problem was the value he had for the outcomes offered by the job. Because of a personal tragedy, Jim began to question the rewards (financial and otherwise) that he was getting from his work. You determined that by problem solving with Jim, you could turn Jim's altered lifestyle into an advantage.

Congratulations! GO TO 586B to begin to deal with your next motivational challenge, Wilson Thomas.

Decision Point 559B

When you call Buff in, you begin the conversation with some pleasantries. After a few minutes, you tell him that you have heard rumors about his using his job primarily to develop his real estate interests. Buff responds by talking about the problems of teamwork in any company. As he continues, you get the strong impression that he is "ducking" the issue you are trying to raise. You finally interrupt him and tell him that you have two reliable reports of his dealings and that you are asking him straight out if he is involving his Omega clients in his real estate deals. Buff seems a bit surprised by your directness, but he admits to you that the allegations are true. When you ask Buff to give you the details of his deals, he lays out a story of real estate partnerships much broader than you thought possible. He has involved many doctors and wholesalers in a variety of partnerships. He says that his income from these deals is about the same as his salary. He also says that although some of these deals are risky, the potential payoff is great. You both know that he is in clear violation of company policy and that you must face it. What would you do?

A. Tell Buff that you have no choice but to discharge him. (GO TO 564B)
B. Tell Buff that he has a choice. He can either resign or end his real estate dealings. If he doesn't resign, you expect him to deliver a plan within 48 hours for ending his real estate involvements. (GO TO 551A)

Decision Point 560A

You diagnosed the Warehouse Group as Moderately Mature. Actually, they are Moderately Immature. Consider the following:

Maturity Factor	Facts That Suggest Maturity	Facts That Suggest Immaturity
Desire to attain high but attainable goals		Resistant to carry full load until Al is replaced
Willingness and ability to accept responsibility	Reasonably obedient	No one volunteered to take the lead job; motivated by compensation alone
Relevant education and/or experience	Task rather routine relative to skills; procedures in place	High turnover

Your must prepare for the Fourth of July Clearance Sale, the biggest sales of the summer. A circus tent is erected in the large parking lot in front of the store, and all the sale merchandise is moved outside. You and Al Thorn have planned for this sale for some time. You have scheduled no deliveries for this week so you have the manpower to move all the furniture.

Several issues remain to be decided before the sale begins. First, you have to figure out how to schedule the necessary overtime in order to get everything done. You have worked out all the tasks that have to be done and worked out a schedule of how many hours of overtime each day will be necessary.
How would you schedule the overtime among the warehouse workers?

A. Give the workers what you have come up with and ask them to decide on their own which people will work which hours. (GO TO 588B)
B. Make the assignments on the basis of seniority, i.e., those with the most seniority get the most desirable hours. (GO TO 567A)
C. Call the group members together, show them what you have come up with, and help them to decide on the allocation of overtime hours as a group. (GO TO 576B)
D. Ask each member of the group to give you a list of his or her overtime hour preferences. Integrate these the best you can into your final schedule of who works which overtime hours. (GO TO 580A)

Decision Point 561A

You decide not to have him participate in the development of an action plan. Instead you are firm that he should come up to an acceptable performance level. Generally it is preferable to use participation in the development of an action plan. You could have demanded the same performance level as part of that participative process.

Re-evaluate your last decision. Circle the #561A you just wrote in your flow diagram. Then move back to the first uncircled number above this one in your flow diagram.

Decision Point 561B

She responds that she wasn't prepared for the difficulty she's faced getting in to see doctors: "I'll tell you. It's tough even getting in the door. And when you do, the most you have is five minutes. And that's a very distracted five minutes, I'll tell you!"

How would you respond?

A. Ask her if she was disappointed with her commission check. (GO TO 537A)

B. Indicate that physician calls are important, but that is equally important for her to build up wholesale inventory levels in her region. (GO TO 576C)

C. Offer to help her in any way you can to build her sales volume. (GO TO 557B)

Decision Point 561C

You meet with your supervisor, give him a summary of Spaulding's performance, and tell him that you have heard a rumor about Spaulding's conducting personal business with his Omega clients. He informs you that there is not much you can do on the basis of rumors, but that you should do something about Buff's substandard performance.

What would you do?

A. Confront Buff with the rumor about his real estate deals and ask him if this is the cause of his poor performance. (GO TO 562C)

B. Ask to accompany him on several sales calls, but don't mention the rumor you have heard. (GO TO 589B)

Decision Point 562A

You decide to do nothing, believing that the group will be able to handle the problems without your help. The members meet during lunch that day to hammer out assignments and plan how they will deal with the problems. They return from their meeting deadlocked over several issues. Clearly they were not prepared to deal with the situation themselves.

Your approach was essentially delegation. This is ill suited to the maturity level of your group. As a Moderately Mature group, you should have used participation.

Re-evaluate your last decision. Circle the #562A you just wrote in your flow diagram. Then move to the first uncircled step above this one in your flow diagram.

Decision Point 562B

You decide to assign the inventory tasks to every member of the group on a rotational basis. When you announce your plans to the members, they seem to accept them very well. The results of the inventory, though, are unsatisfactory. A number of errors appear that are traceable to the fact that, with so many people involved, some lacked a sense of detail.

Your leadership approach was the reason your decision failed. The group is Very Immature, but your approach reflected a strong people orientation (concern for fairness in assignments). You should have been much more task oriented.

Re-evaluate your last decision. Circle the #562B you just wrote in your flow diagram. Then move to the first uncircled step above this one in your flow diagram.

Decision Point 562C

When you talk to Buff, you lay out his record of performance and tell him that it is not at an acceptable level. As you begin to discuss possible remedies for this low performance, you mention that there is a rumor floating around that he may be involved in some real estate deals which are taking him away from his work. As soon as you say this, he asks what you are talking about and challenges you to document your charges. Buff's approach puts you on the defensive and effectively ends the discussion about his low performance. In fact, by the time he leaves, he has so thoroughly manipulated the situation that you almost feel guilty for confronting him.

Re-evaluate your last decision. Circle the #562C you just wrote in your flow diagram. Then move back to the first uncircled number above this one in your flow diagram.

Decision Point 563A

Jim tells you that he will sell 425 units next quarter. However, halfway through the next quarter he phones to tell you that he won't be able to meet that goal. When you express disappointment, he tells you he has decided to resign. Establishing precise performance targets is usually an effective motivational technique. However, in this instance, it does not work. Jim is suffering from a great deal of inner conflict which you haven't dealt with.

Re-evaluate your last decision. Circle the #563A you just wrote in your flow diagram. Then move back to the first uncircled number above this one in your flow diagram.

Decision Point 563B

You express concern that John is not giving his territory a chance. With that, John responds: "Why should I? You've dealt me a low hand. Even if I did call on 100 percent of my doctors, I couldn't make my quota."

At this point you challenge his observation, but he insists there is no use. What would you do now?

A. Try to persuade John that the redistricting plan is equitable. Be prepared to compare his performance with Susan Brown's (such comparisons are not a problem since performance records are open within the company). (GO TO 582A)

B. Tell John that you do not like his attitude and that you will not give his new employers a good recommendation unless he improves his performance next quarter. (GO TO 574B)

C. Ask John what changes in redistricting he would suggest to correct the inequity he is experiencing. (GO TO 538A)

D. Mention to John that there may be some way to respond to his concerns, but you won't even talk about that until he demonstrates greater efforts to improve his sales (GO TO 524A)

E. Tell John you will be sorry to see him go but you understand that if he still thinks the redistricting is inequitable after your last comments, perhaps it is best that he leave the company. (GO TO 570A)

F. Ask John what things he likes about his present territory with the idea of trying to make the positive features he mentions more salient (obvious) compared with the negatives he seems to be emphasizing in his own mind. (GO TO 528A)

Decision Point 564A

When you ask Wilson to explain his low-effort figures, he is a bit taken aback by your question, but he recovers quickly.

"I always worked hard for this company. Five days a week, eight hours a day, I assure you. Do you want to look at my date-book? My territory is real spread out as you know, so I can't be expected to make 100 percent of my calls each quarter. As for my wholesale figures, I know they're low, but I called each one at least once during the quarter. I've been trying to tell you that our competitors are pulling out all the stops to take over in my territory. It's hard to beat them off with what you have given me."

How would you respond?

A. Review what you've done in the past to try and turn his performance around, and ask him to commit to do something about his "marginal performance." (GO TO 532A)

B. Accompany him on a series of sales calls. (GO TO 547A)

C. Schedule him for a training program that involves modern sales techniques. Warn him that this is his last chance. (GO TO 593B)

D. Check to see if his job is really important to him. (GO TO 583B)

E. Tell him that this is it and that you are at the end of your rope with him. Establish your willingness to help in any way you can, but either he comes up to standard next quarter or he's through with the company. (GO TO 545A)

Decision Point 564B

Since Buff has violated company policy, you decide to terminate him. This has some negative repercussions for the district. First, you receive a substantial number of complaints from doctors and wholesalers in his district. Second, and more important, the new sales rep who replaces Buff has a difficult time establishing relationships with area doctors. Although terminating Buff may be appropriate given his poor performance, the close relationships that Buff developed had the potential to disrupt Omega's customer relationships. Under these circumstances it may be better to either work further with Buff or develop a plan for reducing the negative impact of his departure.

Re-evaluate your last decision. Circle the #564B you just wrote in your flow diagram. Then move back to the first uncircled number above this one in your flow diagram.

Decision Point 565A

You concluded that your Office Staff is Very Immature. This is incorrect. The group is Moderately Mature. Several facts support this conclusion:

Maturity Factor	Facts That Suggest Maturity	Facts That Suggest Immaturity
Desire to attain high but attainable goals	Willing to work overtime on short notice	
Willingness and ability to accept responsibility	Accommodates changes introduced without inputs	Somewhat dependent (tendency to ask for unnecessary permission/approval)
Relevant education and/or experience	Secretarial & bookkeeping skills good	Data processing skills weak; documentation poor

This morning you received word that in anticipation of your Fall Clearance Sale a number of recliners and dining room sets will be transferred from the Dade County store. This will greatly add to the paperwork of your Office Staff, and you need to plan how to handle it.

How would you proceed?

A. Call group members together, give them a briefing of the tasks necessary to handle the transfers, and guide a group problem-solving session. (GO TO 556B)

B. Do nothing. The group will be able to handle the problems without your help. (GO TO 562A)

C. Analyze the situation carefully yourself and figure out the best way to allocate the necessary tasks. (GO TO 540A)

D. At a weekly staff meeting, gather information from your staff as to how you should divide up the extra responsibilities. (GO TO 547B)

Decision Point 566A

You and John agree that he should try to call on 90 percent of the obstetricians in his territory next quarter. You follow this up with a phone call half way through the next quarter to remind him of his commitment and to get feedback.

When the quarter is over, the record indicates that John called 90 percent of his physicians (exactly). However, his performance dropped from 330 to 315. When you call him on this performance deficiency, John asserts: "I told you the territory divisions were inequitable. Look, I called on 90 percent of the obstetricians as we agreed, but I still produced only 315 units!"

This places you in an impossible situation. By increasing his effort but not his performance, he calls the entire redistricting plan into question. However, it is likely that John's calls on M.D.s were not intended to develop sales. In general, it is not prudent to establish effort goals without associated performance goals.

Re-evaluate your last decision. Circle the #566A you just wrote in your flow diagram. Then move back to the first uncircled number above this one in your flow diagram.

Decision Point 566B

Jim is persuaded by this statement. He says: "You know, I really would miss those trips with my wife. In fact, do you think the two of us could share my job?"

This is an interesting idea. It would enable Jim to be with his son for more time and at the same time provide coverage for the rural portions of the territory. You and Jim invite his wife, Kathy, into the discussion. She is enthusiastic about the idea.

You follow up with a call to the Director of Employee Relations (at home) to be sure that this arrangement is possible. It is, and Jim's wife becomes scheduled for company training. This settled, you stress the necessity of making the standard 400 units per quarter. Both Jim and Kathy agree to coordinate their work to meet that figure.

One quarter later the resulting sales figures are better than your wildest dreams. Jim and his wife produce 525 units! Your questioning revealed that Jim's motivational problem was the value he placed on the outcomes offered by Omega. Because of a personal tragedy, Jim began to question the rewards (financial and otherwise) that he was getting from his job. You determined that, by problem-solving with Jim, you could turn his altered life-style into an advantage. **Nice going!** GO TO 586B to move on to your next motivational challenge.

Decision Point 567A

You decide to make the assignments on the basis of seniority, i.e., those with the most seniority get the most desirable hours. This seems to be a satisfactory arrangement at first, but it fails in the end. Your less senior people are actually the ones with the most problems integrating their personal lives with the overtime schedule. One quits outright and one tells you that she is unable to accommodate the schedule you have worked out.

Your approach to leading this group was incorrect. As a Moderately Immature group, it required a consultative approach rather than a directive one.

Re-evaluate your last decision. Circle the #567A you just wrote in your flow diagram. Then move to the first uncircled step about this one in your flow diagram.

Decision Point 567B

Jim jumps at the chance to attend the seminar. He especially likes the convenience of being able to attend it without leaving home. Upon completion of the seminar, Jim returns to work. However, his performance continues marginal. Though his wholesale inventory levels improve slightly, his calls on doctors continue very poor (67 percent). Clearly, Jim's performance did not benefit from the training.

Re-evaluate your last decision. Circle the #567B you just wrote in your flow diagram. Then move back to the first uncircled number above this one in your flow diagram.

Decision Point 567C

You tell your people to ignore the distractions caused by customers and salespeople and insist that existing procedures regarding the movement of merchandise should be followed. This does not work out very well. In order to avoid a customer, one of your people strains her back and has to be taken to the hospital for X rays. Some of the other members of the group begin to complain that you are a lot more "hard-nosed" than Al Thorn. Several of your people arrive late for work the next morning.

Your leadership approach is probably behind these developments. You are trying to lead a Moderately Immature group. This requires a balance between task orientation and people orientation. It also calls for a participative approach to decision making. In comparison, your approach was entirely too task oriented.

Re-evaluate your last decision. Circle the #567C you just wrote in your flow diagram. Then move to the first uncircled step about this one in your flow diagram.

Decision Point 568A

You call a meeting of the group members and ask them to attend to their house-keeping responsibilities. You give specific examples as a guide to action. Immediately, several of your group members offer suggestions to their colleagues about how they work housekeeping into their daily routine. You are pleased with the outcome. It appears that the group itself can work out the problem, so you back off.

When your boss returns from vacation, he calls you into his office and tells you that he received several complaints from the group that you had acted like a "schoolmaster" in lecturing the group about the housekeeping problem. He expresses disappointment in you for using this approach.

In effect, your action was inappropriate because it was far too directive for a Very Mature group. In general, your posture should have been consistent with a low-task orientation and a low-people orientation. We have referred to this as a Delegation approach.

Re-evaluate your last decision. Circle the #568A you just wrote in your flow diagram. Then move to the first uncircled step above this one in your flow diagram.

Decision Point 568B

Before meeting with Spaulding, you decide to gather information discreetly about his reputation and the conflict between his low earnings and opulent life-style. As a result, you hear a rumor from a staff person that Buff has been putting together real estate deals with many of the doctors he calls on. If these rumors are true, this is a direct violation of company policy. There is no clear procedure for dealing with such infringements, unless there is "iron-clad" proof.

What would you do now?

A. Confront Buff with the rumor about his real estate deals and ask him if this is cause of his poor performance. (GO TO 562C)

B. Consult with your superior about how to deal with this situation. (GO TO 561C)

C. Ask to accompany him on several sales calls but not mention the rumor you have heard. (GO TO 589B)

Decision Point 569A

You concluded that your group of Furniture Salespeople and Decorators is Very Mature. This is correct. Several facts support this diagnosis:

Maturity Factor	Facts That Suggest Maturity	Facts That Suggest Immaturity
Desire to attain high but attainable goals	Recently set a new sales record	
Willingness and ability to accept responsibility	Work with very little supervision; will do anything necessary to satisfy a customer	
Relevant education and/or experience	Very experienced and able group	

Two days after your boss leaves on vacation, you get word from your Warehouse Group that several of your salespeople have been violating the policy of giving priority to orders. The policy reads that any salesperson can request priority on only five orders per month. The logic behind the policy is that the warehouse and delivery people can only accommodate that number on a truly priority basis. Excesses of this kind mean that promises made to customers cannot be fulfilled.

How would you handle this situation?

A. Remind the group of the policy but take no further action. (GO TO 581A)

B. Find out who the policy violators are and tell them that they may file no more priority orders that month. (GO TO 536A)

C. Call a meeting of the salespeople and help them come up with a solution to the problem. (GO TO 530B)

Decision Point 570A

John seems taken aback by your statement, but he thanks you for your support. You ask him how you can help him with him job search. The remainder of the meeting seems relaxed as you problem-solve various approaches John is taking to get another job. As the meeting ends, you again promise your support but indicate forcefully that the company cannot afford to keep him in his territory while he conducts his job search unless he "acts in good faith" by continuing to complete his work. You ask for his resignation effective in 30 days. In three weeks, he calls you and tells you of his new job. He also informs you that he has called 50 percent of the M.D.s in his territory (in this three-week period!).

Some people would assert that a manager should fight hard before "letting go" of an employee. In this instance, however, John Crosby was at best an average employee. In addition, he suffered from a motivational problem that was difficult for you to do anything about beyond the attempts you have already made. Luck would have it that it was relatively easy to replace him, and since John left with good feelings and a level of exit performance that was excellent, everything worked out for the best.

John suffered from a perception that his payment was inequitable. This was compounded by a belief (attributable to the perceived inequity) that effort didn't really matter. This was a difficult situation to reverse. You could have salvaged John but only at the expense of careful work and increased vigilance, and you apparently considered that not worth the effort. GO TO 534A to move along to your next employee to motivate, James Clemmons.

Decision Point 570B

Jim is notably nervous in responding, "I'm disturbed that I've let you down, believe me. I don't want to disappoint you, but I'm not sure what to suggest. I'll try harder, I promise." What would you say now?

A. Nothing. Clemmons has committed himself to do better. (GO TO 542B)

B. Find out whether he realizes that his sales are probably suffering from the low inventory level being held by wholesalers in his region. (GO TO 590A)

C. Ask Jim if he needs some time off to get himself together now that his personal crisis has passed. (GO TO 572A)

D. Tell him you appreciate his willingness to try harder. Ask Jim how the death of his father has changed his outlook on his work. (GO TO 553B)

E. Press Jim for a specific performance commitment. (GO TO 563A)

Decision Point 571A

You tell your group members that they should comply with existing break times, and you tell the worker with the nonregulation shoes that he can work today without regulation shoes but he must comply tomorrow.

By Friday at 3:00 p.m. all the merchandise is moved to the tent, and you find yourself giving the rest of the day off to your Warehouse Group because it had more than met your expectations. Clearly you got more work out of the Warehouse Group than Al Thorn ever did. You tell your spouse this at dinner that night in your favorite restaurant (paid for by Paul Thielman, who was delighted with the results of the sale and attributed it in part to your "coming through" with the Warehouse Group under "adverse circumstances").

The reason your action worked well was that it was appropriate to a Moderately Immature group. By combining your concern for procedures (the break schedules) with your concern for compassion (the shoe incident), you balanced a concern for task with a concern for people. This is precisely the combination (task orientation + people orientation) that works well with Moderately Immature work groups.

The sale over, you relax a bit. Three weeks pass without event and all of a sudden the situation with your Home Furnishings Group begins to capture your attention. Recall that Home Furnishings Group is made up of six relatively inexperienced and low-paid female employees who sell towels, sheets, and other relatively inexpensive decorative items. The employees in this group are almost all over 50 and provide their family's second source of income.

Of all your groups, this is your most troublesome. Over time you have found the members complacent, unwilling to take initiative, and resistant to change. They are cliquish, uninformed about how to be good retail salespeople, and indifferent to the interests of Caraway's. You know that they intentionally withhold cooperation with decorators and furniture salespeople whom they do not like or find "too pushy." Every effort you have made to lead them in the past has been greeted with some variation on the theme "It's not my job."

Your first decision is to diagnose the maturity of the Home Furnishings Group. Which category do you think it falls into?

A. Very Immature. (GO TO 594A)

B. Moderately Immature. (GO TO 544A)

C. Moderately Mature. (GO TO 584A)

D. Very Mature. (GO TO 552A)

Decision Point 572A

Jim responds as follows: "Maybe that would be a good idea. A month off would be real helpful." You work out the details and Jim starts his leave of absence immediately. When he returns to work, however, his performance continues to be poor. Apparently the time off did not enable Jim to become more motivated himself.

Re-evaluate your last decision. Circle the #572A you just wrote in your flow diagram. Then move back to the first uncircled number above this one in your flow diagram.

Decision Point 572B

Your decision to encourage Lisa results in sales the next quarter similar to the last one. More frustrated than before, Lisa's efforts begin to wane, and she leaves the company.

When you talked to her, Lisa was at a critical point in her career. You were correct in encouraging her, because often sales of this kind lag a bit behind sales efforts and sales calls have a cumulative effect. However, she needed something more than pure encouragement.

Your analysis of Lisa's motivation revealed several important things. It is clear that Lisa has a strong belief that her efforts will pay off in terms of performance since she has a history of succeeding in nearly everything she has attempted. In addition, you can be certain that Lisa believes that performance will be rewarded at Omega, since she is on an incentive pay system that relates her income directly to two indices of performance, volume and inventory. As for Lisa's particular preference for her work outcomes, we can be sure that Lisa values the monetary outcomes of her job since she has indicated that she needs her commission check to make her first house payment. Given these factors, it is not surprising that Lisa's efforts are high (she called on 100 percent of her M.D.s, and each wholesaler twice). However, her performance is not up to expectations. In light of this assessment, think about what additional factor may account for her low performance.

By encouraging Lisa, you may have caused her belief that effort does result in performance to weaken in the following quarter. Perhaps she concluded that a particular obstetrician call makes little real difference in determining sales volume (the "drop in the bucket" idea). Pure encouragement may have reduced the sense of urgency that she showed in your conversation with her.

Re-evaluate your last decision. Circle the #572B you just wrote in your flow diagram. Then move back to the first uncircled number above this one in your flow diagram.

Decision Point 573A

You concluded that your group of Furniture Salespeople and Decorators is Moderately Immature. Actually this group is Very Mature. Several facts support this diagnosis:

Maturity Factor	Facts That Suggest Maturity	Facts That Suggest Immaturity
Desire to attain high but attainable goals	Recently set a new sales record	
Willingness and ability to accept responsibility	Work with very little supervision; will do anything necessary to satisfy a customer	
Relevant education and/or experience	Very experienced and able group	

Two days after your boss leaves on vacation, you get word from your Warehouse Group that several of your salespeople have been violating the policy of giving priority to orders. The policy reads that any salesperson can request priority on only five orders per month. The logic behind the policy is that the warehouse and delivery people can only accommodate that number on a truly priority basis. Excesses of this kind mean that promises made to customers cannot be fulfilled.

How would you handle this situation?

A. Remind the group of the policy but take no further action. (GO TO 581A)

B. Find out who the policy violators are and tell them that they may file no more priority orders that month. (GO TO 536A)

C. Call a meeting of the salespeople and help them come up with a solution to the problem. (GO TO 530B)

Decision Point 574A

Jim says he understands your position completely, and he tells you that you will have his resignation.

Jim Clemmons provided you with an extremely difficult motivational problem. As a person experiencing much inner conflict, Jim was reluctant to commit to much more than average performance, and that was not good enough for you. Fundamentally, Clemmons' motivational problem is that he doesn't value the outcomes of his work very much. The rewards offered by his job are not a sufficient inducement to do more than average work. Moreover, he is obtaining valued outcomes (being with his family) for not working. Thus, his problem is compounded by positive incentives for not performing.

About the only motivational strategy that works in such situations (assuming you cannot really lower the positive incentives on non-effort) is to (1) find out the outcomes he does value and increase them or (2) change the nature of the job to conform to his present level of motivation. In contrast, your action was to insist on performance without responding specifically to what he wants from work.

Re-evaluate your last decision. Circle the #574A you just wrote in your flow diagram. Then move back to the first uncircled number above this one in your flow diagram.

Decision Point 574B

He responds that he does not like your attitude either, and he walks out of the meeting. In light of this, you phone the Personnel Department to discuss your disciplinary options. Accordingly, you send John a written warning on his low performance in conjunction with company procedures, since you cannot fire him without a written warning.

Three weeks into the next quarter, you call John to check on his performance. He doesn't return your call. You call two of the wholesalers in his territory, and they indicate that they have not seen him. You send him a registered letter indicating that if he doesn't phone you, he's fired. You don't hear from him, and you fire him.

The stern posture you took resulted in John leaving under adverse circumstances. Given that he was, at best, an average performer, he was not the worst person to leave, especially since he apparently was suffering from a perceived inequity problem that is difficult to resolve. However, his exit would have been much less costly had you been less threatening and more conciliatory. In addition, your options in this case included a strategy that would have turned John's performance around.

Re-evaluate your last decision. Circle the #574B you just wrote in your flow diagram. Then move back to the first uncircled number above this one in your flow diagram.

Decision Point 575A

This arrangement works well. The noise level of the party is contained, and the window is covered. No salespeople complain. Your decision to use a people-oriented approach was correct. This fits your Moderately Mature group.

A month later, Paul Thielman, your boss, goes on vacation and you become Acting Store Manager. This makes it necessary for you to exercise direct leadership with a group you typically don't get involved with, the Furniture Salespeople and Decorators. Recall that the members of this group sell the "big ticket" items in the store. They are all paid on commission and most had substantial sales experience before they were hired. Many of these people have been with Caraway's for more than 10 years. Most earn upwards of $50,000 per year. The decorators are a subset of this group. They work directly in customers' homes giving advice about colors and decors. Like the Furniture Salespeople, the Decorators are paid on a commission basis, but they have little physical presence in the store since they come in only once or twice a week.

Your salespeople are among the best in the entire Caraway line. Two of them are used as "model salespeople" by the headquarter's training staff. Both are members of the "President's Club" (meaning that they earn over $100,000 per year in commissions). The group at your store is known for doing anything and everything they can to keep a customer satisfied. This includes working directly with warehouse people to make certain that deliveries are scheduled to meet customer requirements, working with credit people to insure that they get credit if they are deserving, and working with decorators on color schemes for customers who need advice with accessories that will complement sofas and chairs.

While there are occasional complaints about one salesperson "stealing" a customer from another, you are generally persuaded that these instances are rare by industry standards.

Considering that you will now have to provide leadership for this group while your boss is away, you should estimate the level of maturity of the group.

A. Very Immature. (GO TO 587A)

B. Moderately Immature. (GO TO 573A)

C. Moderately Mature. (GO TO 531A)

D. Very Mature. (GO TO 569A)

Decision Point 576A

If the list of commitments you are asking from Wilson is substantial, asking him to "go it totally alone" may be overwhelming. It is important to keep the list of commitments attainable, and of all Wilson's objectives, improving his relationship with this wholesaler is perhaps unattainable. Moreover, by taking over this task, you may be able to improve Omega's reputation with this firm, and use this experience as a training tool for Wilson.

Of course, managers can't do their subordinates' work for them on a regular basis. However, this situation calls for that! Later you will have to be careful in making Wilson responsible for this task again.

Re-evaluate your last decision. Circle the #576A you just wrote in your flow diagram. Then move back to the first uncircled number above this one in your flow diagram.

Decision Point 576B

You decide to call the group members together, show them what you have come up with, and help them to decide on the allocation of overtime hours as a group. This results in a great deal of resentment on the part of your group. Many of them have family constraints that are not reflected in your plan. Two of them refuse to work the hours that you have scheduled, and another quits outright.

Your approach to leading this group was incorrect. As a Moderately Immature group, it required a consultative approach rather than a directive one.

Re-evaluate your last decision. Circle the #576B you just wrote in your flow diagram. Then move to the first uncircled step about this one in your flow diagram.

Decision Point 576C

She responds as follows: "But I called on each wholesaler twice during the quarter. And even though the average supply is only fifty days right now, that's up from forty-three when I started."

You were not aware of this improvement, which is fairly substantial. Therefore, you congratulate her for this accomplishment.

What would you say now?

A. Offer to help her in anyway you can to build her sales volume. (GO TO 557B)

B. Try to ascertain if she is satisfied with her present level of sales. (GO TO 535A)

Decision Point 577A

It is four weeks later, and Buff's performance figures are lower than ever. Waiting for Spaulding to improve is not the answer.

Re-evaluate your last decision. Circle the #577A you just wrote in your flow diagram. Then move back to the first uncircled number above this one in your flow diagram.

Decision Point 577B

You chose to be firm on the tardiness policy. You back up your words with tough actions. In the course of the following two months, you have to terminate one chronically tardy clerk and give one other a written warning (the last disciplinary step before termination). The results of your action are generally positive. The clerks show a marked improvement in coming to work and returning from breaks on time.

Your actions were effective because they were appropriate to the maturity level of this group. As a Low Maturity group, the Home Furnishings Clerks needed direction and control. In other words, they require a leader who doesn't have a people orientation but has a high task orientation. Moreover, direction is far superior to delegation, consultation, or participation for a group like this one.

This week your Home Furnishings Clerks must complete an inventory count. This is the least-liked task of the clerks' job. It requires highly meticulous and thorough work, and if it is not done accurately, the risks of costly over- and understock events in the future are tremendous. Some members of the group are much better at taking inventory than others, but group sentiments are high that this assignment should be shared by everyone since it is so tedious and takes people away from the more desired sales activities.

How would you make this assignment?

A. Consult with group members about how they would like to divide up the task and consider this when making assignments. (GO TO 598A)

B. Assign those clerks to the inventory task who are best at it. (GO TO 546A)

C. Assign the inventory tasks to every member of the group on a rotational basis. (GO TO 562B)

Decision Point 578A

You tell your people to ignore the distractions caused by customers and salespeople and insist that existing procedures regarding the movement of merchandise should be followed. This decision results in very serious problems. A customer is injured by one of your people moving a wardrobe. Two of your senior warehousemen come to work late on Friday morning, an apparent response to your indifference to their welfare. You find, too, that your initial estimates of the number of overtime hours were seriously underestimated.

Your leadership approach is the cause of this situation. Your group is Moderately Immature, so your lack of a people-oriented style is a problem.

Re-evaluate your last decision. Circle the #578A you just wrote in your flow diagram. Then move to the first uncircled step about this one in your flow diagram.

Decision Point 578B

You return in one month and notice some but not spectacular progress on Wilson's part. His sales calls are up, but you again have to coach him on managing his time. You note that he's altered his sales approach with the younger doctors, and you help him further refine his techniques.

The fact that you have taken over responsibility for the major wholesaler pays off. Druggist stock-outs are less frequent, and Wilson begins to see more results from his efforts. He accompanies you when you call on this troublesome wholesaler, and this serves as a model for him to copy.

In spite of these improvements, Thomas continues to be rather defensive about your criticism and he continually asks for approval in subtle ways.

With two months remaining in the quarter, you again schedule another visit to his region. This time you only stay two days, but again there is some progress. You begin to ease up a bit on the number of specific commitments you ask him to make.

At the end of the quarter, the performance figures come out and Thomas meets his quota: Sales = 400 units; M.D.s contacted = 93 percent; wholesale inventory level = 44 days.

Although Thomas will require more effort to reduce his need for your help and feedback, you have accomplished a difficult motivational assignment. Wilson Thomas is a classic plateaued performer who has developed poor work habits that he defends with excuses and closed-mindedness. In this situation, training will not suffice. He needs practice, firmness, encouragement, and frequent feedback. Your actions worked well.

Congratulations! When you are ready, GO TO 538B for your last motivation problem, William Spaulding.

Decision Point 579A

The next employee targeted for motivation is John Crosby. His performance record is shown on page 19. John has worked for Omega for six years. For five of those years, his performance record was average. Six months ago, to accommodate the addition of Lisa Dolan to your staff, you had to redistrict territories. This displaced four of your sales reps including John. The redistricting was done with the use of a computerized mapping formula developed by Omega's operations staff. The formula establishes equitable territories, and birth rate is one of many factors in the program. It is an award-winning model, and one that has been used throughout the industry. When the redistricting was announced, the three other sales reps affected accepted it, but not Crosby. He asserted that the birth rate in his new territory was too low. You explained that his new territory's birth rate was actually understated because it includes a large obstetric hospital (associated with a medical school) that does not report births in an ordinary way. This did not satisfy John. Susan Brown's territory was also affected (she was also given a territory with a large hospital), yet her last quarter sales were excellent. You decide to talk with John about his low figures. You ask for his side of the story.

He responds: "My greatest fears have come to pass. You gave me too small a district. I can't be expected to come up to my 400 unit quota in that territory. It will probably come as no surprise to you that I'm actively looking for another job right now." How would you respond?

A. Indicate that you are concerned that he has not given his new territory a chance. Point out that he only contacted 61 percent of the M.D.s in his region. (GO TO 563B)
B. Try to persuade John that the redistricting plan is equitable. Be prepared to compare his performance with Susan Brown's (such comparisons are normal; performance records are open within the company). (GO TO 582A)
C. Tell John that you do not like his attitude, and that you cannot give his future employer a good recommendation unless he improves his performance next quarter. (GO TO 574B)
D. Ask John what changes in redistricting he would suggest to correct the inequity he is experiencing. (GO TO 538A)
E. Mention to John that there may be some way to respond to his concerns, but you won't even talk about that until he demonstrates greater efforts to improve his sales efforts. (GO TO 524A)
F. Tell John that you will be sorry to see him go but you understand that if he still thinks the redistricting is inequitable after your last discussion with him, then perhaps this is the best thing for him to do. (GO TO 570A)
G. Ask John what things he likes about his present territory, with the idea of reminding him of the positive features of his job compared with the negative things he seems to be emphasizing in his own mind. (GO TO 528A)

Decision Point 580A

Once your receive each worker's statement of preferences, it is fairly easy to integrate these into the final overtime schedule. When you show your workers the schedule, everyone seems reasonably pleased. One worker complains that his preferences should have been given more weight since his wife is pregnant, but the other workers agree to "cover" for him if she goes into labor during the week of the sale. You correctly decided to use a consultation approach to assigning overtime. Moderately Immature groups do best with this.

On Wednesday before the sale week begins (it begins on Saturday, Al Thorn's last day), your people begin moving merchandise out into the parking lot. In spite of an unpredicted rain shower, all the merchandise you had hoped would be moved has been when you do your survey on Thursday morning.

However, two issues come up at your regular morning meeting the next morning that are of some concern. First, several of your people complain that there were far too many people in their way when they were moving the furniture. The erection of the tent and all the commotion of furniture being moved was a beacon to passers-by. A small crowd gathered, and furniture salespeople rushed from the showroom to serve them. The results posed both a safety hazard and a distraction to your warehouse people. For example, as two of your people were moving a heavy sofa bed to the tent, a customer tried to read the sale tag attached to it and asked a salesman running along with him whether the fabric was soil-resistant.

The second issue that was raised concerned several of your people's complaints that the standard procedures for moving merchandise out of the storeroom caused them serious inconvenience. Under the procedures, if merchandise is to be moved, it is supposed to be moved in order of invoice coding. This enables a more correct accounting of inventories. After listening to these two concerns during the Thursday morning meeting, how would you respond?

A. Tell security people to rope off a corridor from the warehouse to the tent, tell your salespeople to stay away from the tent to discourage interference with the warehouse people, *and* insist that existing procedures regarding the movement of merchandise should be followed. (GO TO 533A)
B. Tell your people to ignore the distractions caused by customers and salespeople, *and* insist that existing procedures regarding the movement of merchandise should be followed. (GO TO 578A)
C. Tell security people to rope off a corridor from the warehouse to the tent, tell your salespeople to stay away from the tent to discourage interference with the warehouse people, *and* allow your people to deviate from existing procedures regarding the movement of merchandise. (GO TO 535B)
D. Tell your people to ignore the distractions caused by customers and salespeople *and* insist that existing procedures regarding the movement of merchandise should be followed. (GO TO 567C)

Decision Point 581A

You remind your group of the policy but take no further action. This works out well. When you check back in a couple of days with the warehouse people, you learn that there has been no further violation of the policy.

Your action was correct because it fit a Very Mature group. The gentle reminder essentially delegated action to the work force.

A week later one other problem comes up. Upon touring the showroom, you notice that it looks rather sloppy. An examination of some of the fabric samples shows that they are incomplete and out of order. This would seem to indicate that salespeople have not been careful in contacting customers who have taken samples home, and have hastily returned them to the binders without arranging them in order. This is part of their jobs, and you feel they are shirking their responsibilities.

How would you react?

A. Post a low-key note on the bulletin board reminding the salespeople and decorators of their housekeeping responsibilities. (GO TO 549B)

B. Call a special meeting of the group and ask them to attend to their housekeeping responsibilities. Prepare to give specific examples as a guide to action. (GO TO 568A)

C. Gather data from the group in terms of how you might proceed from this point. (GO TO 585C)

Decision Point 581B

A member of the Operations Research Group explains the redistricting formula to John's satisfaction, and he indicates that he will try harder next quarter. What would you do?

A. Get John to commit himself to calling on specific number of M.D.s during the next quarter. (GO TO 566A)

B. Tell John that you are very pleased that he has agreed to improve. Encourage him to do the best he can. (GO TO 543C)

C. Negotiate a level of performance with John that you would consider an acceptable improvement for the next quarter. (GO TO 588C)

Decision Point 582A

You try to convince John that his perception that the redistribution plan is inequitable is false. He disagrees at first, but when you describe Susan Brown's performance, he modifies his position slightly. At the same time, he persists that the redistricting is unfair. John pulls out his quarterly sales report (the same one as in your initial description of the situation). He states, "Look at Brown's standard-over-birth-rate--10.92. Now look at mine--13.39--the highest in your region. Do you still say the territories are fair?"

At this point what would you do?

A. Tell John that you do not like his attitude, and that you cannot give his future employers a good recommendation unless he improves his performance next quarter. (GO TO 574B)

B. Ask John what changes in redistricting he would suggest to redress the inequity he is experiencing. (GO TO 538A)

C. Indicate to John that you will look into the territorial question, but that you can't guarantee anything. Insist that he bring his effort up as a sign of good faith. (GO TO 524B)

D. Tell John that you will be sorry to see him go but you understand that if he still thinks the redistricting is inequitable after your comments to him, perhaps this is the best thing for him to do. (GO TO 570A)

E. Ask John what things he likes about his present territory with the idea of trying to make the positive features he mentions more salient (obvious) compared with the negatives he seems to be emphasizing in his own mind. (GO TO 528A)

F. Persist with your argument. Call in a member of the Operations Research Group that developed the redistricting formula to explain it to John. (GO TO 581B)

Decision Point 582B

Wilson Thomas's phone calls are sporadic, and you are concerned that he is not living up to his commitments. What action would you take?

A. You've done enough. If he does not live up to his commitment, terminate him. (GO TO 585A)
B. Go on even more sales calls with him in order to refine his action plan and give him feedback. (GO TO 578B)

Decision Point 583A

Your analysis of Lisa's motivational circumstances revealed some important information. First, you may conclude that Lisa has a strong belief that her efforts would pay off in terms of performance because throughout her life she succeeded in everything she attempted. In addition, it is probable that she also believes that monetary outcomes are linked to performance since much of her earnings are directly related to sales volume and inventory levels. Clearly, monetary outcomes are important to her because she is counting on her commission check to make her first house payment. It is not surprising that Lisa's efforts are high (she called on 100 percent of her M.D.s and each wholesaler twice). However, her performance, particularly regarding her obstetrician calls, is not yet satisfactory. In light of this assessment, think through what additional factors may account for her low performance. Your approach did little more than remind her of what was already a strong belief that performance is linked to outcomes. Therefore, it was actually a rather redundant action, and it added little except frustration when Lisa's performance did not improve.

Re-evaluate your last decision. Circle the #583A you just wrote in your flow diagram. Then move back to the first uncircled number above this one in your flow diagram.

Decision Point 583B

He responds: "What do you think? My wife and I are looking forward to retirement in four years. We've got a place down in Orlando." Now what?

A. Tell him he is dangerously close to being terminated unless he turns his performance around. Be precise about just what level of performance is necessary to keep you from taking this action. (GO TO 545A)

B. Ask him if he has considered an early retirement. (GO TO 595A)

C. Review what you've done in the past to try and turn his performance around, and ask him for a renewed commitment to do something about his "marginal" performance. (GO TO 532A)

D. Accompany him on a series of sales calls. (GO TO 547A)

E. Schedule him for a training program that involves modern sales techniques. Warn him that this is his last chance. (GO TO 593B)

F. Tell him that this is it; that you are at the end of your rope with him. Establish your willingness to help in any way you can, but either he comes up to standard next quarter, or he's through with Omega. (GO TO 545A)

Decision Point 584A

You concluded that your group of Home Furnishings Clerks is Moderately Mature. This is incorrect. The group is actually Very Immature. Several facts support this diagnosis:

Maturity Factor	Facts That Suggest Maturity	Facts That Suggest Immaturity
Desire to attain high but attainable goals		Complacent; won't co-operate with salespeople they don't like
Willingness and ability to accept responsibility		Little initiative; "not my job"
Relevant education and/or experience		Untrained; high turnover

The situation that captures your attention is tardiness. Your store's policy allows three "excused" tardy episodes per year (the policy in Caraway's store in Orlando allows four such episodes because that work force requires it). Over the last four months there has been a higher incidence of unexcused tardiness episodes than ever before. In fact, when you consult your log, you notice that there has been more tardiness this month than in any month on record. You meet with this group every Tuesday at 3:00 p.m. in order to accommodate all your people. How would you address the tardiness issue during this week's meeting?

A. Pose the issue of tardiness to the group. Ask them to think about things that might solve the problem. Require a written report on how they plan to solve the problem. Tell them that if they do not meet the standards in their report, disciplinary action will be taken. (GO TO 529A)

B. Ask them if they think the policy at their branch (Miami) should be brought in line with the Orlando branch. (GO TO 597A)

C. Insist that the members of the group adhere to the policy on tardiness. (GO TO 577B)

Decision Point 585A

He agrees to try again, but his quarterly figures continue poor (320 units; 83 percent of doctors contacted; 41 days inventory). You follow through on your promise and terminate him.

Wilson Thomas offered perhaps the most challenging motivational assignment any manager ever faces--the plateaued performer. There is no one remedy in cases like these, but there is one in this situation. While you might argue that Wilson Thomas is not worth salvaging as an employee, re-evaluate your last decision. Circle the #585A you just wrote in your flow diagram. Then move back to the first uncircled number above this one in your flow diagram.

Decision Point 585B

You tell your office staff members of the complaints of the salespeople and let them handle the situation as they see fit. This seems to work out well at first. Your group decides to cover the window on a rotational basis during the party. However, the party once again is loud and raucous, and this time your boss tells you that you may have no more parties in the office.

Your approach to this situation assumed a level of maturity higher than your group had yet attained. As a Moderately Mature group, they needed an approach that used participation rather than delegation.

Re-evaluate your last decision. Circle the #585B you just wrote in your flow diagram. Then move to the first uncircled step above this one in your flow diagram.

Decision Point 585C

You decide to gather data from the group in terms of how you might proceed from this point. You talk with three of the most senior salespeople and one decorator. They tell you that housekeeping is "no big thing," and that they don't think the showroom is any more sloppy than usual. When you diplomatically ask several customers who are purchasing merchandise, you learn that they have noticed that the salespeople's desks are messy and that it took time for salespeople to find fabric samples that had been mistakenly put back into the wrong fabric binders.

You can think of two options:

A. Post a low-key note on the bulletin board reminding the salespeople and decorators of their housekeeping responsibilities. (GO TO 549B)

B. Call a special meeting of the group and ask them to attend to their housekeeping responsibilities. Prepare to give specific examples as a guide to action. (GO TO 568A)

Decision Point 586A

Jim's performance the next quarter continues to be poor. Inaction on your part was apparently predicated on the assumption that there was nothing you could do. However, such pessimism is premature.

Re-evaluate your last decision. Circle the #586A you just wrote in your flow diagram. Then move back to the first uncircled number above this one in your flow diagram.

Decision Point 586B

Wilson Thomas has worked for Omega for 21 years, but since you arrived, his performance has been quite poor. Wilson's present sales figures are on page 19.

His poor performance has been exasperating for you. For the past three years, you have "tried everything" to turn his performance around. You have sent him to company training and refresher courses. You tried skill building. However, Wilson seems to consider his old-fashioned, laid-back, soft-sell approach better than any approach he's been taught. You've tried warning him, and at one point issued him two written warnings on his performance. You stopped short of firing him only because he came up to standard nine months ago. Too often Wilson's defense is that factors outside his control are against him. He is an expert at denying personal responsibility, and will latch onto any convenient excuse to hold onto his present practices and overinflated self-image. This time, however, you are determined to give him only one more chance. How would you approach your conversation with him?

A. Review what you've done in the past to try and turn his performance around, and ask him for a renewed commitment to do something about his "marginal" performance. (GO TO 532A)

B. Accompany him on a series of sales calls. (GO TO 547A)

C. Schedule him for a training program that involves modern techniques. Warn him that this is his last chance. (GO TO 593B)

D. Check to see if his job is really important to him. (GO TO 583B)

E. Ask him to explain his poor figures (77 percent M.D.s contacted; 38 days inventory). (GO TO 564A)

F. Tell him this is it; you are at the end of your rope with him. Establish your willingness to help in any way you can, but either he comes up to standard next quarter or he's through with Omega. (GO TO 545A)

Decision Point 587A

You concluded that your group of Furniture Salespeople and Decorators is Very Immature. This is incorrect. This group is Very Mature. Several facts support this diagnosis:

Maturity Factor	Facts That Suggest Maturity	Facts That Suggest Immaturity
Desire to attain high but attainable goals	Recently set a new sales record	
Willingness and ability to accept responsibility	Work with very little supervision; will do anything necessary to satisfy a customer	
Relevant education and/or experience	Very experienced and able group	

Two days after your boss leaves on vacation, you get word from your Warehouse Group that several of your salespeople have been violating the policy of giving priority to orders. The policy reads that any salesperson can request priority on only five orders per month. The logic behind the policy is that the warehouse and delivery people can only accommodate that number on a truly priority basis. Excesses of this kind mean that promises made to customers cannot be fulfilled.

How would you handle this situation?

A. Remind the group of the policy but take no further action. (GO TO 581A)

B. Find out who the policy violators are and tell them that they may file no more priority orders that month. (GO TO 536A)

C. Call a meeting of the salespeople and help them come up with a solution to the problem. (GO TO 530B)

Decision Point 588A

You lay out the evidence that you have collected. Your supervisor agrees that you do have "iron-clad" proof that Spaulding has been using his Omega job to foster his real estate business. He says that you need to deal with Spaulding's actions but that you will want to make sure that your actions don't create more difficulties with customers than necessary. Now what?

A. Call Buff in and ask him if the rumors that you have heard are true. (GO TO 559B)

B. Call Buff in, lay out the evidence you have, and tell him that he must eliminate his outside deals and improve his performance. (GO TO 540B)

Decision Point 588B

Your choice was to give the workers the overtime schedule you have come up with and ask them to decide on their own which people will work which hours. The inputs you receive are full of conflicts. Every person but one wants to work late on Thursday night but refuses a Friday evening assignment. You decide to proceed with the scheduling on an equity basis, but when you announce your schedule and tell the team of your logic, there is a great deal of resentment. One of your people even tells you that he will not work his assigned schedule even if you threaten to fire him.

Your leadership approach was not calibrated to the Moderate Immaturity of the group. This group required more task orientation (direction) than you gave them.

Re-evaluate your last decision. Circle the #588B you just wrote in your flow diagram. Then move to the first uncircled step about this one in your flow diagram.

Decision Point 588C

John Crosby's performance during the next quarter turns around positively. He calls on 86 percent of the physicians in his territory, and his performance improves to 410 units, ten greater than the standard.

Congratulations! By bringing his perceived inequity back into line with realities, you successfully dealt with a volatile situation. You found you had to identify a specific reference person to convince Crosby that his equity calculations were faulty. Additionally, you found you had to address his problem of not believing that his efforts would pay off.

GO TO 534A to begin your analysis of the motivational needs of Jim Clemmons, the next employee in a sub-par performance situation.

Decision Point 589A

You choose to debate Wilson Thomas on the type of sales approach that is most effective in selling pharmaceuticals. He reacts defensively to your comments, and comes very close to calling you a liar on several occasions.

Wilson Thomas is a very anxious and defensive person. He wants to salvage some self-respect, and your approach doesn't enable him to do that.

You are walking a tightrope with this individual. You deserve to be firm, but you also have to be somewhat acknowledging. In general, it is much easier to walk this tightrope by talking about specific behavior in specific situations than engaging in abstract debates. Re-evaluate your last decision. Circle the #589A you just wrote in your flow diagram. Then move back to the first uncircled number above this one in your flow diagram.

Decision Point 589B

You accompany Spaulding on several calls, and you are very surprised by the results. He demonstrates a fine knowledge of the company's products, and his demeanor is very effective throughout the call. Both wholesalers and doctors seem very responsive to his efforts.

After this dazzling performance, you tell him that he did an outstanding job and ask him to explain why his performance is so low when he clearly has so much aptitude for his work. He tells you that he simply has been too casual about his work but he now understands that he had better improve.

About two weeks later, you receive a call from one of the doctors you visited with Buff. He tells you that Buff is a terrific sales rep and asks you to be understanding with him. You wonder whether Spaulding has asked him to call you. A few days later one of your sales reps calls you to relay some interesting information. It seems that one of this rep's obstetrician clients knows another doctor who asked whether you are "out to get" Buff Spaulding. Further, this client indicated that Spaulding and this other doctor have several real estate deals together and that the doctor is concerned that Buff may not be able to make a mortgage payment on some property if he loses his job. You now feel that you have the "iron clad proof" necessary to confront Buff. You know that you must act. What would you now do?

A. Consult with your boss about how to handle the situation. (GO TO 588A)

B. Call Buff in and ask him if the rumors you had heard are true. (GO TO 559B)

C. Call Buff in, lay out the evidence you have and tell him that he must eliminate his outside deals and improve his performance or resign. (GO TO 540B)

Decision Point 590A

Jim tells you that he is aware that the wholesale inventory levels are very low. He says that he realizes that he will have to make many more calls on wholesalers if he stays on with Omega.
How would you respond?

A. Ask Jim if he needs some time off now that his personal crisis has passed. (GO TO 572A)

B. Ask Jim if he is considering resigning. (GO TO 537B)

C. Ask him why he was able to contact only 73 percent of the doctors in his territory last quarter. (GO TO 596A)

D. Ask Jim how the death of his father has changed his outlook on his work. (GO TO 553B)

Decision Point 590B

Lisa attends the program, and her next quarter's sales are only modestly better. Apparently this training effort was not the answer to her performance problem.

Your analysis of Lisa's motivation revealed several important things. It is clear that Lisa has a strong belief that her efforts will pay off in terms of performance since she has a history of succeeding in nearly everything she has attempted. In addition, you can be certain that Lisa believes that performance will be rewarded at Omega, since she is on an incentive pay system that relates her income directly to two indices of performance, volume and inventory. As for Lisa's particular preference for the her work outcomes, we can be sure that Lisa values the monetary outcomes of her job since she has indicated that she needs her commission check to make her first house payment. Given these factors, it is not surprising that Lisa's efforts are high (she called on 100 percent of her M.D.s, and each wholesaler twice). However, her performance is not up to expectations. In light of this assessment, think about what additional factor may account for her low performance.

Your decision to give Lisa additional training was consistent with an appraisal that she needed abilities and skills not developed in the formal training program she completed with the company. However, you know little about just what Lisa's specific training needs are at this point.

Re-evaluate your last decision. Circle the #590B you just wrote in your flow diagram. Then move back to the first uncircled number above this one in your flow diagram.

Decision Point 591A

You concluded that your Office Staff is Moderately Immature. This is incorrect. The group is Moderately Mature. Several facts support this conclusion:

Maturity Factor	Facts That Suggest Maturity	Facts That Suggest Immaturity
Desire to attain high but attainable goals	Willing to work overtime on short notice	
Willingness and ability to accept responsibility	Accommodates changes introduced without inputs	Somewhat dependent (tendency to ask for unnecessary permission/approval)
Relevant education and/or experience	Secretarial & bookkeeping skills good	Data processing skills weak; documentation poor

This morning you received word that in anticipation of your Fall Clearance Sale a number of recliners and dining room sets will be transferred from the Dade County store. This will greatly add to the paperwork of your office staff, and you need to plan how to handle it.

How would you proceed?

A. Call the group members together, give them a briefing of the tasks necessary to handle the transfers, and guide a group problem-solving session. (GO TO 556B)

B. Do nothing. The group will be able to handle the problems without your help. (GO TO 562A)

C. Analyze the situation carefully yourself and figure out the best way to allocate the necessary tasks. (GO TO 540A)

D. At a weekly staff meeting, gather information from your staff as to how you should divide up the extra responsibilities. (GO TO 547B)

Decision Point 592A

Your meeting with Spaulding goes better than you anticipated. He apologizes for his performance, and quickly (perhaps too quickly) agrees to a set of performance objectives that you consider reasonable. You also inform Spaulding that you will monitor his performance closely.

A few weeks later, you check Buff's log and the records from his region. Nothing seems to have changed regarding his performance. Later that day you receive a call from an obstetrician in Buff's territory. He tells you that Buff is a terrific sales rep, and asks you to be understanding with him. You wonder whether Spaulding asked him to contact you. After some independent checking you find out that this doctor is one of Spaulding's frequent golf partners. Three days later you hear from another client, this time a wholesaler, who tells you that Spaulding is one of the best reps who calls on him and that he has just decided to place a huge order that would bring his stock of Omega drugs up to 75 days. You are surprised by this call and mention it to one of your colleagues. He says that he has heard that this wholesaler "owes" Spaulding and is repaying a favor. He also told you that he doubts if the alleged order would ever be booked. He seems to be correct, as two weeks have passed and the order has not been received.

What would you now do?

A. Since his performance has not improved, begin the process of terminating Spaulding. (GO TO 564B)

B. Ask to accompany Spaulding on several of his sales calls. (GO TO 557A)

C. Ask around the company discreetly to find out more about Buff's reputation as a salesman and how he is able to maintain his life-style when his earnings are so low. (GO TO 568B)

Decision Point 592B

He shrugs his shoulders and completes a rather detailed set of commitments. He balks, though, when it comes to implementing your suggestion regarding interacting with the large wholesaler with which he's had difficulty.

In light of the fact that Thomas is considered an "old jerk" and already has made a substantial series of commitments, would you assume responsibility for interacting with this wholesaler yourself for one quarter?

A. Yes. (GO TO 526B)

B. No. (GO TO 576A)

Decision Point 593A

You decide to grant members of your group longer breaks after they have had to move heavy objects and tell the worker with the nonregulation shoes that he can work today without his regulation shoes but that he must comply tomorrow.

This very people-oriented approach doesn't work well with your Moderately Immature group. Your team takes advantage of the longer breaks, and the fellow with the nonregulation shoes shows up a second day without them once again. You now face the prospect of having to tighten up after your first, rather permissive leadership approach.

Re-evaluate your last decision. Circle the #593A you just wrote in your flow diagram. Then move to the first uncircled step above this one in your flow diagram.

Decision Point 593B

You schedule Wilson Thomas for a training program that involves sales skill building. You also warn him that this is his last chance. He attends the program, but much to your chagrin, you receive the following letter from him:
"I have completed the program you scheduled me to take, and I want you to know that it was a total waste of time. Nothing covered was new, and I fail to see why a professional approach is now out of date. The trainers of the program couldn't answer that to my satisfaction."

How would you respond?

A. Review what you've done in the past to try and turn his performance around, and ask him for a renewed commitment to do something about his "marginal" performance. (GO TO 532A)
B. Accompany him on a series of sales calls. (GO TO 547A)
C. Tell him that you think he's being defensive. (GO TO 548B)
D. Tell him that this is it; you are at the end of your rope with him. Establish your willingness to help in any way you can, but either he comes up to standard next quarter or he's through with Omega. (GO TO 545A)
E. Tell him his sales approach may be correct but he can't make it work unless he improves his effort. Remind him that he only contacted 77 percent of the doctors in his territory and that his inventory figure (38 days) is very low. (GO TO 564A)
F. Confront the differences between his stated sales approach and the sort of approach you know works well for the highest performing reps in your region. (GO TO 589A)
G. Check to see if his job is really important to him. (GO TO 583B)

Decision Point 594A

You concluded that your group of Home Furnishings Clerks is Very Immature. This is correct. Several facts support this diagnosis:

Maturity Factor	Facts That Suggest Maturity	Facts That Suggest Immaturity
Desire to attain high but attainable goals		Complacent; won't co-operate with salespeople they don't like
Willingness and ability to accept responsibility		Little initiative; "not my job"
Relevant education and/or experience		Untrained; high turnover

The situation that captures your attention is tardiness. Your store's policy allows three "excused" tardy episodes per year (the policy in Caraway's store in Orlando allows four such episodes but has a much smaller potential work force). Over the last four months there has been a higher incidence of unexcused tardiness episodes than ever before. In fact, when you consult your log, you notice that there has been more tardiness this month than in any month on record. You meet with this group every Tuesday at 3:00 p.m. in order to accommodate all your people.

How would you address the tardiness issue during this week's meeting?

A. Pose the issue of tardiness to the group. Ask them to think about things that might solve the problem. Require a written report on how they plan to solve the problem. Tell them that if they do not meet the standards in their report, disciplinary action will be taken. (GO TO 529A)

B. Ask them if they think the policy at their branch (Miami) should be brought in line with the Orlando branch. (GO TO 597A)

C. Insist that the members of the group adhere to the policy on tardiness. (GO TO 577B)

Decision Point 595A

Thomas indicates that he might be interested in early retirement if a satisfactory financial arrangement could be reached. You call the Director of Employee Relations and get a figure. You share that information with Wilson, and he refuses it outright. You warn him that it might be better to take the offer and remove the threat, but he is firm.

What would you do now?

A. Tell him he is dangerously close to being terminated unless he turns his performance around. Be precise about just what level of performance is necessary to keep you from taking this action. (GO TO 545A)

B. Review what you've done in the past to try and turn his performance around, and ask him for a renewed commitment to do something about his "marginal performance." (GO TO 532A)

C. Accompany him on a series of sales calls. (GO TO 547A)

D. Schedule him for a training program that involves modern sales techniques. Warn him that this is his last chance. (GO TO 593B)

E. Ask him to explain his poor figures--77 percent of doctors contacted, 38 days inventory. (GO TO 564A)

Decision Point 595B

You tell your group members that they should comply with existing break times, and you require the worker with the nonregulation shoes to go home and get the proper shoes.

This action does not work well. Your group is irritated by your rather "hard-nosed" approach. Moreover, you have trouble enforcing break times after the group has just moved heavy objects. You alter the break time schedule accordingly, but it doesn't work, and the furniture is not moved as quickly as you had planned. You need to schedule even more overtime than you originally planned.

The reason your approach failed was that it was not calibrated to a Moderately Mature group. It should have represented a high concern for task and a high concern for people. Yet both of your decisions opted for task concerns.

Re-evaluate your last decision. Circle the #595B you just wrote in your flow diagram. Then move to the first uncircled step above this one in your flow diagram.

Decision Point 596A

Jim tells you that he is embarrassed by that figure. He says that he knows he'll have to raise that figure for your sake.
How would you respond?

A. Ask Jim how the death of his father has changed his outlook on his work. (GO TO 553B)

B. Let him know that you think his performance is really seriously low, and you would like to know exactly what he plans to do about it. (GO TO 570B)

C. Find out whether he realizes that his sales are probably suffering from the low inventory levels presently being held by wholesalers in his territory. (GO TO 590A)

D. Ask Jim whether he needs some time off now that his personal crisis has passed. (GO TO 572A)

E. Suggest that Jim may want to attend a sales seminar sponsored by the company. Coincidentally, it is being conducted in the city where Jim lives. (GO TO 567B)

F. Ask to accompany Jim on a sales call. (GO TO 526A)

Decision Point 596B

You decide to cancel the party on the grounds that group members had not acted responsibly with their last party. As a result, morale plummets. They had been planning the party for some time, and your edict forces them to plan it for the noon hour, when they can leave the office. They do so, and when they return 90 minutes late from the event, you are now faced with the necessity to discipline them.

Your action was inconsistent with the maturity level of your group. As a Moderately Mature group, they needed an approach that favored a concern for people rather than a concern for task. Your approach was too task oriented. Consequently, it was viewed as harsh and arbitrary.

Re-evaluate your last decision. Circle the #596B you just wrote in your flow diagram. Then move to the first uncircled step above this one in your flow diagram.

Decision Point 597A

You decide to ask your Home Furnishings Clerks if they think the policy at their branch (Miami) should be brought in line with the Orlando branch (a more permissive policy exists at Orlando). Every member of your group agrees, and you talk with your boss (Paul Thielman) about the change. He firmly opposes such a move, and when you tell them you have failed to convince him, the group's morale sinks measurably.

Your leadership approach was the reason your decision failed. The group is Very Immature, but your approach was indicative of a strong people orientation (concern for fairness in policies). You should have been much more task oriented.

Re-evaluate your last decision. Circle the #597A you just wrote in your flow diagram. Then move to the first uncircled step above this one in your flow diagram.

Decision Point 597B

You tell your two Leads to deal with the situation themselves. You hear nothing more about the matter until you hear through the grapevine that Hopkins and Post seriously exaggerated the situation as a way to test how you would react in this sort of situation. Knowing that you "passed the test," you decide to let the matter drop.

Your next appointment is with LeRoy Jackson. He is the Lead who took your old position with Unit 2. The two of you have a delightful conversation. He was one of the people you used to play cards with at lunch before your promotion.

At the end of your conversation, LeRoy tells you that some of the people in your old unit have been asking why you aren't playing cards with them at lunch any more.

What would you say?

A. "Well, now that I am a supervisor, I don't think it is appropriate for me to do that any more." (GO TO 372B)

B. "I'll be there tomorrow. I wouldn't want the old card game to go on without me." (GO TO 417B)

C. "I'll come around at lunch from time to time, don't worry." (GO TO 374A)

D. "I'll tell you what. I have to spread my lunch time evenly among all the units now. Tell the group that should mean that they'll have to suffer my presence about once a month." (GO TO 392B)

Decision Point 598A

You decide to consult with your group members about how they would like to divide up the task and consider this when making assignments. You receive some very helpful inputs from your group, and you conclude that you should assign every person but one to the inventory task (the person exempted has had no experience with the inventory coding scheme). After you make the assignments accordingly, though, you discover that a number of your clerks are not well suited to the task at all. Lacking the concentration to detail required by the task, a number of them make very serious errors that cause you to insist on a total recount. This results in a serious decline of morale.

Your leadership approach was the reason your decision failed. The group is Very Immature, but your approach was indicative of a strong people orientation (concern for fairness in assignments). You should have been much more task oriented.

Re-evaluate your last decision. Circle the #598A you just wrote in your flow diagram. Then move to the first uncircled step above this one in your flow diagram.